WHO DEFENDS ROME?

Who Defends ROME?

The Forty-five Days,
July 25–September 8, 1943

MELTON S. DAVIS

ll

London
GEORGE ALLEN & UNWIN LTD
RUSKIN HOUSE   MUSEUM STREET

First published in Great Britain in 1972

Grateful acknowledgment is made to the following for their assistance in providing photographs for this book: Associazione Nazionale Partigiani d'Itali, Corpo Volontari della Liberta, Ministero Difesa-Marina, Alessandro Perrone, Centro Documentazione Rizzoli, Ufficio Stampa del Comune di Roma, Ufficio Storico dello Stato Maggiore del Esercito, Ezio Vitali.

ISBN 0 04 945012 3

To Ferda, who though not a Roman has
most of their virtues and few
of their faults

Foreword

Here are no banners flying bravely in whatever breeze there might have been, few of the commonly accepted virtues, a minimum of courageous men. Instead, an abundance of treachery, double-dealings, lies and betrayals, compounded by blunders, indecision and misjudgment; influenced by fear of the unknown, the known, the future and in some cases the past.

The cupidity of commanders, the conspiracies of those in power reluctant to relinquish high positions, reveals men whose foresight is applied only to their careers, whose country's interests are callously sacrificed to their own concern, a concern not with posterity but with the moment.

This is not a pretty picture, but rather a roll call of human frailties: Italian leaders playing a double game (with some justification), anti-Fascists hesitant and disorganized, the monarchy vacillating, generals confused and fumbling, the Vatican cautious, Hitler and the Germans vindictive, the Allies divided in their aims but united in bluffing a beaten nation, and the people of Rome deluded, inert, most of them suspended in trance-like positions from which they would be roused to movement only by the ultimate betrayal.

Rome, open city, open only to those who bring death, destruction, disillusion and despair—suicides, ambushes, meetings in the night, decisions made on the basis of whispered words.

Here is no rush of patriots to hastily constructed barricades—instead, a sporadic, uncertain movement to abandoned positions. And yet here are men who, stirred by something most of them can not define, go to their deaths—men from every class, holding varying political beliefs.

These are the Forty-five Days, that strange interregnum between the fall of fascism and the fight for freedom, as witnessed and felt by individual human beings—the high and the mighty, the obscure, the pitiful, the vengeful and the fearful.

Subjects Interviewed

All dialogue and descriptive scenes in this book are based on my interviews with protagonists or witnesses and the writings and testimony of historians, observers and others who were involved in various ways. Nothing has been invented nor has anything been added. Events, places and characters have been, within these limits, placed by me in the framework of the story as I see it.

Below is a partial list of the people who were questioned on the Forty-five Days. They come from every social, economic and political level. Occasionally it has been difficult to obtain information from persons obscurely bound by self-imposed secrecy or from those overly cautious of their personal or class interests. Some informants had to be disregarded because their versions were in evident contradiction to documented facts or because they tended to amplify their particular roles in events. Still others volunteered excellent information but preferred to remain anonymous because use of their names might open old scars.

The authors and journalists whose books or articles are listed in the bibliography were interviewed as far as their personal experiences were concerned.

Romano Antonelli—psychiatrist
Michelangelo Antonioni—film-maker
Adriano Barocco—film critic and writer
Alfonso Benedetti—official, national Partisan organization
Giacomo Benedetti—mechanic
Rosario Bentivegna—doctor
Corrado Bianchini—doctor
Adriano Bolzoni—writer
Carla Capponi—former deputy
Giorgio Caputo—writer
Tomaso Carini—government official
Attilio Casati—building superintendent

Lucia Casati—housewife
Giulio Castelli—journalist
Karin Cavicchioli—broadcaster
Felice Chilanti—journalist-writer
Salvatore Ciriacono—radio technician
Federico Comandini—lawyer
Giorgio Conti—publicist
Renzo D'Avanzo—industrialist
Enzo De Bernart—publicist
Dino De Laurentiis—producer
Ettore Della Riccia—journalist
Enzo De Vitali—clerk
Piero Dorazio—painter
Robert Gordon Edwards—executive
Sigismondo Fago-Golfarelli—government official
Paolino Fedrigo—plumber
Federico Fellini—film-maker
Ennio Flaiano—screenwriter, playwright
Arnoldo Foá—actor
Mario Foligni—insurance agent
Laura Formiggini—writer
Guerrino Franzini—official, local Partisan organization
Mario Gallotti—lawyer
Vittorio Gassman—actor
Robert A. Graham, S.J.—editor
Donatella Valori Haertter—painter
Mario Jemma—typewriter repairman
Sandy Koffler—editor
Giose Lippolis—poetess
Luigi Marchesi—army officer
Mario Masenza—jeweler
Giulietta Masina—actress
Marcello Mastroianni—actor
Carlo Mazzarella—actor
Eraldo Meloni—studio watchman
Ugo Moretti—writer

Vittorio Ortali—medical director
Giorgio Nelson Page—publisher
Angelo Paoletti—gardener
Angelo Pellegrini—masseur
Alessandro Perrone—publisher
Luigi Persichetti—surgeon
Patrick Persichetti—actor
Antonio Pietrangeli—film-maker
Frances Persichetti Reilly—theatre director
Giovanni Roberti—lawyer
Claudio Rocchi—trade union official
Luciano Sacchetti—dental surgeon
Benedetto Santarelli—Foreign Office official
Antonio Santovito—garage owner
Elio Savelloni—photo editor
Gino Savoni—government employee
Emilio Schuberth—fashion designer
Toti Scialoia—painter
Rodolfo Siviero—Foreign Office official
Mario Soldati—writer
Alberto Sordi—actor
Lillo Spadini—journalist
Mimmo Spadini—sculptor
Franco Stipa—surgeon
Vincenzo Talarico—journalist
Daniele Tognazzi—doctor
Renzo Trionfera—editor
Luigi Ventura—civil servant
Ezio Vitali—photographer
Leonardo Vitetti—Foreign Office official
Alfredo Zambelli—auto mechanic
Arturo Zanardelli—building superintendent
Ruggero Zangrandi—writer
Lelio Zorzin—doctor

Table of Contents

Illustrations

If a man does not keep pace with his companions, it is because he hears a different drummer. Let him step to the music which he hears, however measured or far away.

—Thoreau

Book One:

THE WEAVING OF WEBS

*The fathers have eaten sour
grapes, and the children's
teeth are set on edge.*

Ezekiel xviii.2

Prologue

In Rome that summer there was no sense of what Mussolini later called "a great drama to be performed." If there were, the Romans, those inveterate actors, were not participating. Their faces were rigid, the curtain was down; for once the actor inside every Italian was off-stage. Instead, ordinary life went on in the monotonous, depressing routine that had become habitual.

The heat wave had upset the city's already bomb-damaged water supply, and Romans lined up before those small fountains that were operating like oases in a desert. Swifts skittered by to sit for a moment on a column in the Forum, then darted off as if scorched by the hot stone. Throughout the city they flew in frantic spurts, chattering over the trees, crisscrossing, soaring upwards, to wheel and then swoop down in banked formation looking for all the world like dive bombers. Only six days earlier the war, for the first time, had physically touched Rome and Allied bombers had devastated the populous sections of Prenestino and Tiburtino around the ancient Aurelian walls. Rome with its dead, its wounded, its homeless, still smelled of smoke and sorrow.

Although the gaudy trappings of fascism had for a time convinced modern Romans that their country was once again an empire, they no longer believed in the mirage of glory. With the myth of Rome's inviolability destroyed, they wanted more than ever to see an end to the war, even if it also meant an end to fascism's paternalistic and grandiose projects.

To many, fascism had seemed neither ferocious nor cruel; it was—or at least it appeared—solicitous, accommodating, thoughtful. It watched over children with the *Balilla* organization and summer

5

camps; made up for low salaries with cut-rate movie tickets, train trips and holidays; drained swamps, planted forests, built bridges, highways, hospitals and blocks of offices—mainly governmental, of course, and all contracted to friends of the regime.

Fascism, following Mussolini's dictum that it was "a method not an end," had been a way of life rather than a political movement. People had become accustomed to having their family life regulated and to being told how to dress, how to greet one's friends, and what everyday vocabulary to use. From that it had been only a step to accepting the dictatorship-imposed limits of conscience, the complete control, by a few, of politics, economics, literature, art, with feelings soothed over by slogans and torchlight parades.

The cult of the dictator, the mass rallies, the immense piazzas filled with cheering crowds—moved possibly by love, definitely by the presence of *Il Duce*—was part of their past, as was the shouting of *"Vincere! Vincere! Vinceremo!"* "Win! Win! We shall win!"

At his call, they had invaded the Balkans, joined in Germany's attacks on France and Russia, and gone to North Africa to conquer it as they had Somalia, Libya and Ethiopia. In 1943, there were almost three-quarters of a million Italian soldiers outside the country. But after three years of war, the tide had turned; colonies, prestige, men and matériel were going down the drain. Italians saw Germany, though master of Europe, being forced to give up great parts of Russia. Stalingrad had been retaken by the Soviets, and their summer offensive was pushing the Nazis back to where they had been during the autumn of 1941. In the process, the Italian expeditionary corps in Russia had been wiped out. However, Hitler had rescued Mussolini from his misguided Balkan adventures and the *Wehrmacht* supported Italian troops in occupied Yugoslavia, Albania and Greece, as well as in France, that unhappy country half occupied by the Nazis and half run by Marshal Henri Petain's puppet government. But the English, having survived the retreat from Dunkirk, the blitz, and the Battle of Britain, had beaten back Nazi-Italian troops in North Africa. The United States had entered the war on December 8, 1941, and the Allies—after thirty-five months of battle—had cleared Africa of Axis troops. On July 10, 1943, the Allies, now fighting in the name of the United Nations, had landed in Sicily and brought the war to Italy's backyard.

Italians felt it was the beginning of the end. If Albania and Greece and defeat in North Africa had not convinced them earlier, hopes of victory now seemed dim indeed. In the South, the Americans and the

English were nearing the toe of the boot, while in the North, more German troops hovered just over the border. Italians were in the middle with their mistakes and vanished illusions.

But they still remained under the hypnotic spell cast by the master spellbinder who had evoked their secret dreams, promised them fulfillment, and given them hardship and ashes instead. Although no longer mesmerized by magic visions, these Romans who were so teeming and noisy in their open-air markets and crowded streets, quarreling in queues, jostling in streetcars, appeared politically to be automatons, no more than raised hands.

Which was not quite true. The secret was that after twenty years of dictatorship—admittedly tempered by disorder—and four years of war—till then fought far from Italy—the people of Rome had developed a kind of self-defense, meeting adversity with apathy till it had become part of their souls. All they could do was hide their misery in ironic smiles, forestalling the loss of more illusions by not having any.

In any event, the relentless sun left no room for illusions. The fountains trickled without echoes, the piazzas were static and drowsy, and the whole city smelled of old stone and dried emotions. The stagnant air suffocated the Romans, lulling them into lethargy until only negative qualities remained—inertia, indecision, inaction. Like their city, they looked exposed and bare, fixed by a colossal x-ray. During that period of intense heat, all the worst came out— boils, acids, boredoms, hatreds—while below the surface simmered a myriad of plots, intrigues and cabals.

The night brought little counsel and less sleep, and those who slept dreamt fitfully, turning and twisting as if seeking a way out of the labyrinth into which Mussolini had led them.

Chapter 1

THE CRITICS

The Idealists

One of the few in Rome who still thought for himself on July 24, 1943, was a tall, thin young man who woke early, stepped over to a window and looked out on one of the world's most beautiful squares, Piazza Navona. Raffaele Persichetti could see the heat beginning to rise from the semi-circular cobblestones, and the statuary of Bernini's "Four Rivers" fountain seemed to him to be straining to come out of its stone prison to escape the sun. His eyes traveled over the old brown and ochre houses becoming burnt orange and moved past the Church of Saint Agnes with the sun turning its dome to pale gold and gilding the bronze doors. What would happen to his beloved Rome? Outside he could see two old men sitting on a stone bench, shoulders hunched, disconsolately watching the birds. That was Italy, he thought. The birds were free, the men prisoners, not even rebelling against their fate.

Inside, Raffaele's room was spartan, almost bare of furniture but filled with books and scraps of paper on which he sometimes jotted down, as he did now, some of his thoughts. They were a strange mixture; art, history, freedom, tyranny, the search of a young man for himself, at twenty-eight torn between thinking and doing, between austerity and love of life, between ideals and the harsh realities he saw all around him. His writing, brilliant and fertile, fully expressed neither his self-doubts nor his preoccupation with the paradox of identity; it was more concerned with the motives of decision. He knew that Mussolini had said, "Philosophers solve ten problems on paper but are incapable of solving even one in real life," and he recognized this weakness in himself.

As he wrote, he looked at the crucifix on his wall—the Persichettis were traditionally and profoundly Catholic, and confirmed anti-Fascists as well. His grandfather, Augusto, concerned with social problems, had been a president of Italian Catholic Youth. His father, a general practitioner like his father before him, was a liberal Catholic who had belonged to the outlawed Popular party founded by the dedicated priest Don Luigi Sturzo.

Although Raffaele had been a member of Fascist University Youth, he had begun to have qualms about fascism during the Spanish Civil War. His inner questioning was at least partially resolved when he joined the clandestine Action party along with many young intellectuals who could not tolerate either Mussolini or his doctrines. Only that day, Raffaele had returned from secret missions for the party in Milan and Genoa.

He lived with his family at one end of Piazza Navona on a street called "Five Moons." With his lean figure, burning eyes and dedicated look, he resembled a slightly flawed picture of a nineteenth-century romantic. And though his room was monastic, Raffaele was not. Three years earlier he had had a son by an attractive Irishwoman. He continued to see them although he was at the same time going out with a girl named Jeanne Volkoff, the daughter of a Bulgarian general. With her red hair and large green eyes, Jeanne had the carriage and tension of a young tigress. Despite her Nazi sympathies, she was very much in love with young Persichetti, while he remained somewhat detached, taken up by thoughts of the situation in which Italy found itself.

While turning phrases over in his mind, he dressed. One of seven children, five boys and two girls, Raffaele was the third son. From choice more than necessity he wore the cast-off clothing of his two older brothers, Augusto, an architect, and Luigi, a doctor. Luigi had married a year earlier, had just had his first son, and lived in another part of Rome. He remained closest to Raffaele and worried about his missions for the Action party.

Raffaele, because of his 6'2" height, looked like an imposing scarecrow. Although his clothes hung loosely or had too evidently been lengthened, an inner fire and vision made him stand out, an idealist abroad in a world of tawdry values.

A devoted student of humanist philosopher Benedetto Croce, Raffaele had in 1937 obtained a degree in literature with honors at Rome University and a Master's in the history of art in 1939. As a reserve officer, he had trained recruits and in the fall of the year had begun teaching at Visconti High School.

For some time the political situation had been weighing on Rome's schools. Visconti, although its student body was filled with children of the well-to-do and of aristocrats, was anti-Fascist, following the lead of most of the teachers. Its rival was Virgilio High School, which had mainly lower middle class students and was definitely Fascist.

In May 1940, some of Virgilio's Fascist bullies came over to force Visconti students to join them in a pro-Fascist demonstration. The police, forbidden by law to go into schools, were powerless. When the Virgilians started roughing up a teacher named Giorgi who was also a priest, Persichetti, to the admiration of his astonished and still uncertain pupils, went to Giorgi's defense. He was beaten up, but returned to teach several days later with a bandaged head, to be greeted with enthusiasm by teachers and students alike.

Fluent in French, Spanish and German, he was not an ordinary teacher. Enthusiastic about his subject, the history of art, he had a constant flow of ideas and continually introduced new teaching methods. In the middle of a lesson on eighteenth-century art, he would examine the literary aspect of the same epoch, take up music and then return to art. Or he would talk of the importance of light, how it sometimes fell "like moonbeams rolling down steps." His gestures were large and his phrases graceful, if a touch grandiloquent.

In 1941, he was called up. Although he was against war and against fascism, he reluctantly served as a second lieutenant of the grenadiers in Greece. In the army he was a tireless marcher, an agile gymnast, an able swimmer and an excellent marksman. The men of his platoon idolized him just as his students had, and his superiors called him "a benevolent but firm commander."

"He takes care of his men," said Captain Campagna, one of his superiors, "as well as his matériel. A strong character, determined, enthusiastic and gifted with considerable charm."

Later that year Raffaele was wounded and returned to Rome. Again he took up teaching, convinced more than ever of the need to fight against fascism.

To this end he became an active and trusted member of the Action party, not as aggressively antimonarchist as some of its members, more anti-Fascist than most. He was so active that in the first part of 1943 his father was warned by the authorities that Raffaele was on the list of suspects and under surveillance for anti-Fascist activities. In the spring, a nurse, a member of a Jewish family named Pacifico, told Raffaele that the police were waiting for an excuse to arrest him.

Because of these warnings Raffaele's father worried about his son. An affectionate but strict man, normally honest and uncompromising, he became cautious and refused to let his children discuss politics. If they did, he quickly put a pillow on the telephone, convinced that in some occult manner it was, though not in use, somehow functioning as a microphone.

Raffaele hurriedly finished dressing; it was time to go to work on the Action party's clandestine paper, *L'Italia Libera*, for which he wrote. Today was important; a meeting of the Fascist Grand Council had been called by the dictator for the first time in four and a half years. The *Duce* had not wanted to call the hierarchs together even now, but his hand had been forced by one man.

The Conspirators

Not far from Renaissance Rome, where the Persichettis lived, Dino Grandi, president of the Fascist Chamber of Federations and Corporations, awoke in his apartment in the Montecitorio Palace, once Italy's Chamber of Deputies.

Unlike Raffaele, he dressed carefully, debonair as befitting a former ambassador, minister and Fascist luminary for over twenty years. By the time Raffaele had left his house, Dino Grandi was combing his black hair and trimming his spade-like beard. Although his pointed face and beard gave him a diabolic appearance, he too was a practicing Catholic. He, however, had managed to reconcile his religious beliefs with fascism.

Despite his suave, well-mannered exterior, Grandi was mercilessly tough and could, if necessary, show a complete disregard for the Marquis of Queensberry rules. Although he had been next to the summit, he had never quite reached it. The next forty-eight hours would tell if the summit would come within his grasp.

If it is true that tyranny is harder on those near the top, Dino Grandi, count of Mordano since 1937, had had a difficult time. When fascism began, he and Benito Mussolini had been rivals for its leadership; but then Grandi had been forced to yield to Mussolini. Minister of foreign affairs until 1932, he had been removed by the dictator, who did not want Grandi to have access to the king; every Thursday the monarch received the cabinet, and ministers maneuvered to be received alone. Grandi served as ambassador to the Court of St. James's until Mussolini withdrew him, saying sarcastically that the count had been over-Anglicized.

Grandi may have been secretly opposed to fighting Britain, but he had congratulated the *Duce* on Italy's entrance into the war, had unhesitatingly described British democracy as decrepit and decadent, and even prophesied a Fascist revolution there.

But Grandi's private thoughts did not match his public adulation of Mussolini. He once wrote the *Duce* that he was fascinated by the last meeting he had had with him in Rome and could not allow himself to stay away from Italy because from afar he would not be able "to work near the *Duce*, warmed by his faith, invigorated by his energy, galvanized by his genius." On another occasion he wrote to him, "You know how limitless and unconditional my loyalty to you is."

Even that spring, when Mussolini spoke to the people of Rome from the balcony of the Palazzo Venezia on May 5, Grandi had told him, "What a speech; it expressed the spirit of the eve of the Fascist revolution. We all felt as though we were reborn."

But on the morning of Saturday, July 24, 1943, all of Dino Grandi's considerable energies were directed towards breaking the dictator's grip on the country. Things were coming to a head, all the hectic meetings Grandi had held the last few days were now bearing fruit.

He had worked hard to bring about this assembly of the Grand Council. Only there, might he force Mussolini to admit that with the war virtually lost his reign would have to end. But to visitors, Grandi represented his move as a terrible chance that he was taking. The *Duce* would never forgive him and might call in the Fascist militia; Grandi and the others who had promised to support him could all be arrested. But Grandi, at least, was determined to gamble that behind the façade, the regime was so weakened that countermoves were improbable. The stakes were high, and Grandi was convinced there was backing in high places for what he was about to attempt.

Of the many plotters that July, Dino Grandi was seemingly *primus inter pares*. He was a hard man, and although he usually kept his own counsel, his piercing eyes appeared to see through others.

He told no one of his meetings with the king and the king's men or of their virtual assurances that all he had to do was push through his motion and the monarchy would see to the rest.

Even so, the forty-seven-year-old Grandi acted as if that day might be his last on earth; he left his apartment, walked a short block to Piazza Colonna, and, instead of going to Palazzo Chigi where he had been foreign minister, went across the piazza to the small church of San Bartolomeo. There he confessed and received Holy Communion. Then, as if he were intent on building a legend, he returned to his office, where he wrote his will and two letters, one to his wife, one to his children. Because of the heat, he put on a sports shirt. Still dapper, even in this garb, he received other members of the Grand Council whose acceptance he wanted for his motion to restore power to the king.

He had the backing of six of the twenty-eight members of the Grand Council when Tullio Cianetti, minister of corporations, appeared at his office. Grandi showed him the motion. "An innocent piece of bravura," said Cianetti and gave his assent.

Two of the more rebellious Fascist leaders, who had been for neutrality and against the war, had given their support earlier. They were Giuseppe Bottai, the "best mind" of fascism, a Roman who was a professor of law, an excellent writer, a witty if malicious speaker, a ferocious *frondeur* by nature, the youngest man in the Grand Council, and Luigi Federzoni, formerly Speaker of the Senate, a f.i.nd of Grandi's and a devout royalist who lived on a street named for the House of Savoy. Federzoni was the only hierarch who did not owe his position to the Fascist revolution of 1922. He had founded his own party, which Mussolini had persuaded him to merge with the Fascists. All through the double decade of the regime he had maintained a detached position, accepting however, as had Grandi, a cabinet position after the assassination of thirty-nine-year-old Socialist deputy Giacomo Matteotti in 1924.

The bushy-browed, grey-haired Federzoni had met with Grandi in Bologna earlier in July to draft the motion, and both had returned on the twentieth. Now he worked with Grandi on polishing the text to be presented to the Grand Council that evening.

All three—Grandi, Bottai and Federzoni—although publicly devoted to "the infallible genius of the *Duce*," privately accused him of one mistake after another: of approving the Pact of Steel with Germany, furnishing Italian armed forces with inadequate armaments and obsolete weapons, entering the war unprepared, and directing campaigns badly. As members of the Grand Council, supposedly fascism's ruling body, they felt particularly miffed. This organ, including some cabinet and party members *ex officio* and others appointed by Mussolini, was set up by him contrary to the constitution. It was supposed to meet on the twelfth of every month, but it had last been convened in December 1939, following Adolf Hitler's invasion of Poland, to ratify Mussolini's declaration of nonbelligerence and had not met again, not even for the successive declarations of war against France, England, Greece, Russia and the United States.

That Grandi had never spoken out against these moves was not surprising. A skillful opportunist, he had for years, in return for important posts, concealed his opposition with fervent expressions of loyalty to *Il Duce* and to fascism. His motion contained no hint of blame due fascism, nothing about its responsibilities and, most important, not one word about fascism's abdicating political direction of the country.

Which was why most of the members of the council to whom Grandi showed the motion felt reassured. Even so, as he spoke with other members of the council, he explained his motion in different terms to each, occasionally describing it as only a routine gesture. To some, he emphasized that his motion would above all give back to the king that which was his right, for the war was going badly and the king should resume command of the armed forces. The fact that this could mean the end of Mussolini was only hinted to others. Grandi let most understand that this would be the only way in which they could retain their positions and privileges. Some, like Giuseppe Bastianini, under secretary for foreign affairs, gave their approval only because they were convinced that nothing would happen: "Mussolini will make one of his special speeches and everyone will go home content and tranquilized."

Others, shown the text in between constant revisions, were led to believe that the motion called only for internal changes enabling Italy to continue the war in a more organized fashion. This was what appealed to Roberto Farinacci, a former Fascist party secretary who displayed his pro-German sympathies so publicly that he was known as "the Gauleiter." Farinacci had reservations about the king's assuming command of the armed forces. "Why not the Germans?" he asked Grandi, who then proceeded to stress the motion's bland points.

Grandi reserved no such sugar-coating for Mussolini. He had called on him two days earlier and told him brutally that he intended to ask for an end to dictatorship, for the restoration of parliamentary government and for the return of statutory powers to the king. His meeting with the *Duce* (which was scheduled for twenty minutes but lasted an hour and a quarter, incidentally keeping German Field Marshal Albert Kesselring waiting in the hall) was one of the strangest conversations in history. In essence, Grandi was telling the dictator that he was out to depose him, obviously in the hope that Mussolini would retire voluntarily, thus allowing the king to ask someone like Grandi to form a government. But Mussolini listened courteously to the man who, at least according to appearances, was the prime conspirator against him. For his part, he was thinking of using Grandi and the council meeting for his own purposes, possibly to ask for greater powers, more police repression, martial law and the unquestioned subordination to the Reich which Hitler was demanding as the price for more aid.

At one point, after listening without interruption to a long harangue from Grandi, Mussolini said quietly, "You would be right if the war were lost. It seems lost, but it isn't. I can't tell you about some important military secrets, but Germany and Italy will win this war. We'll speak about all the rest at the Grand Council. But remember"—and here Mussolini's voice hardened—"I won't cede my powers to anyone!"

Yet that was what Grandi wanted. For years he had submitted to the force of events, but now his plot was a passport to a new regime even if its leaders were Fascists who would be labeled turncoats. He knew that in the United States and England there was support for a Grandi government. Earlier in the year, Cardinal Spellman had said of him after a visit to the Vatican, "We have our Italian Darlan," and Churchill had conceded that "a government under someone like Grandi would be in a position to negotiate a separate peace."

Besides, the king had told Grandi that he should take the initiative the monarch needed and thus provide a constitutional pretext for Mussolini's overthrow; the rest had been implicit. That Wednesday, the king asked Grandi to the royal palace, but Grandi, having received notice that the Grand Council meeting was to be held on

Saturday, had refused. Matters were too delicate, and a visit to the palace would compromise both Grandi and the king.

By Saturday morning it was obvious that news of the anti-Mussolini move was getting around. The cynical Filippo Anfuso, Italian minister to Hungary, who was just outside the inner circle, heard of the plot and wanted to get in on it. He came to see Grandi, who had little time for him. Anfuso, after all, was not a member of the Grand Council.

Another caller was Alfredo De Marsico, a balding man with a luxurious moustache, who promptly sat down at a desk to go over Grandi's motion from a legal point of view. De Marsico had been professor of penal procedure at the University of Naples and had replaced Grandi as minister of justice earlier that year. He thought the Grand Council would be the occasion for going over problems raised by the Anglo-American invasion of Sicily. For instance, he felt that Mussolini no longer led the war but followed its course. If he gave up command of the armed forces, the next problem, that of getting out of the war, would be approached with dignity. De Marsico saw the council as a way of achieving this goal, without either discarding fascism or diminishing Mussolini's personal prestige.

The definitive resolution was mainly De Marsico's work, even though the ideas were Grandi's and the embellishments those of Federzoni and Bottai. Only that morning Bottai had added an introduction saluting Italy's heroic soldiers and the proud people of Sicily, and the night before he had added still another phrase giving the king constitutional powers as well as military command. "We can't," he had said grandiloquently, "return to the king a sword that's now blunted and dull unless we also give him back the sceptre of political power."

Still another of Grandi's visitors that morning, Zenone Benini, minister of public works, favored shortening a long codicil. De Marsico worked over the revised text until it was satisfactory.

After Benini had signified his approval and left, Grandi received Dino Alfieri, Italian ambassador to Germany, who had been called back to Rome to attend that night's meeting. Alfieri read the resolution, and when he requested some explanations he was told, "You don't have to have any worries or misgivings, it's only a memorandum. When we discuss it we shall, of course, treat the *Duce* with the usual respect and deference." Alfieri hesitantly consented, and Grandi, with an indelible pencil, added his name to the others.

Then Bottai, who had been meeting with Grandi almost constantly, came in. Although he was a vigorous thinker with an independent character, he had once followed Mussolini with affection. Years earlier, seeing the dictator ill and depressed, he had written in his diary: "You wanted to take his hands in yours and comfort him." Now he was almost hostile, and doubt gnawed at him about what would happen. Only the night before he had called to his office Giovanni Balella, a friend of long standing, who, as president of the Italian Confederation of Industry, was automatically a member of the Grand Council.

Without mentioning Grandi's resolution, Bottai had said, "Some very grave things may happen tomorrow at the Grand Council meeting. You're not a politician and there's no reason for you to run risks."

Balella, not as worried as Bottai, had thanked him for his concern, but had added that he saw no reason for not attending.

The next day, when Bottai perceived Grandi's cool determination to see things through, his own confidence returned. Around noon, they counted adherents; between them, they had fifteen, a clear majority. With the pressure lessened, Bottai, who had called Mussolini a self-taught person with a very bad teacher and a very bad pupil, started attacking the *Duce*. The others present joined in, and ran through the possibilities of outvoting the dictator, discussing how and when Grandi's motion should be presented, wondering if Mussolini would stand on parliamentary order.

Ettore Muti, former secretary of the Fascist party, a major in the air force and holder of the Gold Medal, Italy's highest military award, for his military achievements in Spain, swaggered around Grandi's apartment. A handsome young man, impulsive, generous, impudent, rude and yet sensitive, he believed that the socialist ideals of fascism had been betrayed by Mussolini. He impatiently listened to the others as they discussed ways and means of getting rid of the dictator. He had to be put aside, they agreed, but in a lawful manner. Muti walked up and down, ridiculing the others while adopting the patronizing air of a man of action towards wordmongers. Then he stopped and stood with his feet wide apart.

"You make me laugh," he said, "with your parliamentary rules. If you like I'll solve your problems quickly enough. I'll kill the *Duce* myself, tonight."

But Dino Grandi, concerned with giving the king a legal, consti-

Pope Pius XII at San Lorenzo after the bombing of Rome on July 19, 1943

Badoglio in 1937, surrounded by other Italian Fascist hierarchs

Mussolini standing between Hitler and Count Galeazzo Ciano

King Vittorio Emanuele III with Fascist Party Secretary Carlo Scorza on his right and Marshal De Bono on his left at the Quirinal Palace just before the coup d'état

tutional excuse to act, continued his efforts, certain that after that night he himself would be called by the king to form, if not lead, a new government.

The Disillusioned

Count Galeazzo Ciano was a man Grandi regarded as the very antithesis of himself in everything, in "mode of living, political ideas, diplomatic methods, functions within the party, [and in his views of] the ideals of fascism." They saw each other rarely and between them there was neither confidence nor friendship. They found common ground only insofar as getting rid of Mussolini was concerned, and then for different reasons.

On July 24, 1943, Count Ciano left his top floor apartment in the residential section of Parioli, the most modern part of Rome, where generals, admirals and Fascist hierarchs moved into apartments as they were completed. Before its huge front door, a *portiere*, functioning as janitor, building superintendent and doorman, saluted the count, while along Via Angelo Secchi, other *portieri*, many of them busy gathering snippets of information and gossip to pass on to the Fascist secret police, stood before other squarish buildings, waited for the postman so that they could examine the mail, and measured their bows according to rank as tenants left or visitors arrived.

When Ciano had been foreign minister, he had shown an extraordinary capacity for absorbing facts, a prodigious memory, and an ability to grasp the significance of events. At the time of Hitler's menacing moves towards the seaport of Danzig, he had telephoned Mussolini.

"He says he wants a corridor," Ciano had reported, "but he's going to take the whole apartment."

An intelligent executor of orders, he was perfectly suited to Mussolini, who objected if his subordinates displayed too much initiative. Although Ciano thought of himself as a consummate politician and was, in fact, not without political intuition, he was vain and superficial, and his considerable charm was tempered by profound weakness of character.

Ciano's basic insecurity stemmed from his character, not from his background. After all, he had an assured position as the son of a wealthy Livorno family. His father, an admiral, had been a legend-

B

ary hero of World War I, a member of the Grand Council, and a cabinet minister for ten years, even standing by Mussolini after the murder of anti-Fascist Matteotti, saying he refused to quit a possibly sinking ship. It was at that time that Mussolini had named him his successor in the case of his death.

The elder Ciano thought that the place for Galeazzo was the foreign service, and in 1932 the young count went to work at Palazzo Chigi, the seat of the Foreign Office and the name by which the ministry was popularly known. He fitted right in; his manners and clothes became those of other young diplomats. Aided considerably by the fact that he had married Edda, Mussolini's favorite daughter, he rose quickly, becoming foreign minister in 1937. When his father died in 1939, he took his place as Mussolini's heir-apparent, and his father's influence on him was replaced by that of Mussolini.

But because he was a late-comer to fascism, Ciano still felt a slight sense of guilt towards people like Grandi. He knew little of fascism's ideology, since it had never been a factor in the Ciano household. Later, he had been abroad as a diplomat, and although he didn't like what he spoke of as "playing at soldiers," he had piloted a plane in the Ethiopian war at Mussolini's behest, winning two Silver Medals for valor. Despite his lack of clear orientation in politics, he was fiercely patriotic. But, traditionalist and conservative, he could never have been a revolutionary moved by faith in an idea.

Nor was he too good as a conspirator. He might have been better as a leader of overt opposition or even as a courageous subversive, but now he saw himself as a clandestine semi-hero. Only a few evenings before the Grand Council was to meet, he and his wife received aristocratic friends as usual. He had greeted Filippo Anfuso, taken him aside, and whispered in his ear, "Everything is in readiness. I can't tell you anything about it but you understand." This was enough of a hint for the other man to get in touch with Grandi.

Ciano moved mainly by intuition, a characteristic which frequently betrayed him. His culture was limited. The Ciano apartment had few paintings, because Ciano was always looking for a bargain, and although he knew the value of money, he admittedly did not know the value of art. Nor did he have many books. He was not the kind of man to buy books if he was not going to read them. The few he did own had been recommended by his more literary friends. However, there were plenty of magazines, above all American ones, which had been purchased by his wife.

In 1930 Galeazzo had married Edda Mussolini with Dino Grandi as one of the witnesses. They got along as well as two such different people could. Edda, though tall and slim, bore a striking resemblance to her father because of her hard face and round penetrating eyes. She was called a "wild filly" because of her brusqueness, her restlessness, and her unpredictable bursts of anger. However, she still followed the latest styles: padded shoulders, wedge heels, plastic handbags, upswept hairdo and violent red lipstick.

It was natural that the Cianos would be invited everywhere, and Galeazzo never tired on the dance floor, though in his office he complained of having to read any memorandum over a page long. At social gatherings he would dedicate himself exclusively to the attractive women present, ignoring ambassadors and their wives. Edda did the same with the young men who surrounded her. Even though Ciano was in love with his wife, he delighted in taking mistresses. He thought of himself as irresistible, and women did nothing to convince him to the contrary. His past loves were known as "Galeazzo's widows."

Unlike the austere Grandi, Ciano frequented fashionable salons and bathed in the flattering attention reserved for the powerful. His favorite was the Piazza Sant'Apostoli palace of Princess Isabella Colonna, where he spent so much time that when he was foreign minister it was referred to as "the branch office of the Palazzo Chigi."

Like his father, he had a happy disposition. Only rarely did he give way to anger, and when he did, it passed quickly. But he did not like to be alone. He enjoyed life, eating and the company of the "smart set," which was why he passed so much time at the Rome Golf Club, with its mineral water swimming pool and its golf course along the Appia Antica. Ciano was a poor golfer, and he tore around the course mainly in the hope of keeping his weight down. He made up for it at lunch, where no ration card was necessary, as the golf club enjoyed extraterritorial rights as far as food was concerned.

Despite an expanding paunch, he maintained a youthful appearance. Of medium height and stocky build, he was nevertheless darkly good looking, his hair combed straight back and full of brilliantine.

Although his title had, like Grandi's, been awarded under fascism, Ciano reveled in the company of the princes, dukes and barons who frequented the club. With them he would discuss politics, men, women, episodes, gossip and forecasts. He expressed pungent criticism with a disconcerting frankness which occasionally embarrassed his listeners, never hesitating to pass on state secrets or to relate the latest developments with Tuscan irony and Roman cynicism.

Few diplomats liked him. With his boyish face, he appeared to many as a high school student dressed up like a diplomat. At thirty-three, Ciano had been named foreign minister, only ten years after having entered government service as a lowly vice-consul. English writer Harold Nicolson, who met him on a trip to London, described him as "a picture of a young man painted by an older one."

During a visit to Rome, Joseph Kennedy, American ambassador to England, said he had never in his life met ". . . such a pompous, vain fool. He dedicated most of his time to talking to young women and couldn't talk seriously to anyone for fear of losing sight of two or three girls he was chasing. I left with the conviction that we would have obtained more by sending a dozen good-looking girls here rather than a group of diplomats."

For years Ciano carried out Mussolini's orders, even when he was diametrically opposed to them. He limited his contrariety to entries in his diary, the existence of which was known throughout the little world of Fascist dignitaries. Much of his criticism of Mussolini concealed admiration, and occasionally he would entrust to his diary the idolatry in which he held the man. "The *Duce* praised me several times today," he once wrote. "It's overwhelming, I wasn't even capable of thanking him."

Ciano frequently imitated Mussolini's expressions and mannerisms, such as his forehead-wrinkling, his jutting chin, and his outthrust lower lip. He tried to affect the dictator's staccato speech, full of emphatic phrases emitted in bursts; but his high nasal voice, in contrast to the *Duce*'s which was several tones lower, made his unconscious mimicry ring false. He never really understood Mussolini who, like every man conscious of responsibility, went through various phases, pro and con, before making a decision. Instead, Ciano gave each of these phases the same importance as the definite moment of decision.

After reproaching him on several occasions for his disordered life, Mussolini had had enough of his son-in-law's frivolities and his too open disapproval of the war. One day in February 1943, in the phrase he used for dismissals, the dictator had asked, "And now what will you do?" Ciano had opted for the post of ambassador to the Holy See, where he could continue to be a spectator and actor, albeit at a minor level. To secure the post, he immediately sent an aide, Raffaele Guariglia, to the Vatican secretary of state to secure a *nihil obstat* to his appointment. He acted none too soon. The next day, Mussolini called to tell him he had changed his mind, but Ciano had moved too quickly. When he told Mussolini, the dictator hung up the phone without a word.

Once Ciano left the foreign ministry, he started to change. Where formerly he had expressed his opinions openly, now he began to plot and scheme behind the scenes. He made contacts with anti-Fascists, dissident Fascists and generals known to be anti-Mussolini but not necessarily anti-Fascist. A friend described him as "a politically sick man hanging on to various strings of numerous plots," and longtime intimate Filippo Anfuso said that he was "up to his neck" in so many anti-Fascist, anti-royalist, anti-German plots that Anfuso could not figure out "who was in what conspiracy."

For several days now, as the time for a showdown with the dictator approached, Ciano had taken to his bed with an illness that was partially real—he was subject to attacks of tonsillitis—and partially feigned, in order to avoid a summons from Mussolini which could prove embarrassing.

As he dressed on Saturday morning, July 24, Ciano received Giuseppe Bottai. In his diary, Ciano had made fun of Bottai. "He cavils uselessly at everything," he wrote. Yet the stocky count agreed when Bottai said, "Even the war is illegal since the Grand Council wasn't consulted," and then joined in heaping calumny on the *Duce*.

Two days earlier, after he had officially recovered from his illness he had gone to Bottai's house and met Grandi there. After reading the text of Grandi's motion, he said, "I'll go along with it, although in my opinion the Grand Council isn't the place to put forth such an ultimatum."

There was no love lost between Ciano and Grandi. Ciano suspected that Grandi had his eye on Mussolini's place, but nevertheless respected both the man and his complex character. Grandi, in turn, felt that at the showdown Ciano would back his father-in-law.

"You don't have to support my motion," he told him. "Just repeat in the Grand Council what you said about Italy's remaining non-belligerent."

"If my father had been living," Ciano answered, "he would have been with you. I don't want to shirk my duty."

While Grandi was moved by a feeling that what he was doing was for the best of the country, Ciano was convinced that what he was about to do was for the good of the dictator.

At noon on Saturday, Ciano went to his former domain, Palazzo Chigi, and responded gravely to the doorman and ushers who saluted him obsequiously. They had their jobs to protect and Ciano, besides being a former *"padrone,"* was still the son-in-law of the dictator.

Quickly disposing of pending papers, Ciano left to call on Giuseppe Bastianini who had, after succeeding Grandi as ambassador to London, taken Ciano's place at the foreign ministry. Bastianini was only under secretary for foreign affairs, Mussolini having retained the title of minister. Though Bastianini was only a few years older than Ciano, his temperament and character were quite different. When Bastianini had replaced Ciano, he had argued with Mussolini about foreign policy and on one occasion, told Ciano his troubles. Ciano had laughed. "You're still at the period when it was possible to talk to Mussolini. Now he doesn't listen to anyone and always wants to be right. Happily, his ideas change like the wind."

Bastianini had come to share Ciano's point of view and had already signified his support for the Grandi resolution. That morning, however, he was silent and preoccupied. With him was Dino Alfieri, who was also worried. Ambassador to Nazi Germany, he had succeeded Ciano as minister of popular culture—that is, propaganda—when Ciano left the post for the foreign ministry. Alfieri knew nothing of the intrigues and the others filled him in. Ciano displayed more enthusiasm for Grandi's motion than he had two days before with Grandi and Bottai. He went so far as to confide to Alfieri that his wife Edda was also in favor of it.

"You did well to come," he told Alfieri. "We are all agreed that we have to save Italy and get out from under your Germans."

Alfieri protested, reminding Ciano that the Germans were rather *his;* it was Ciano, after all, who had signed the Pact of Steel with Hitler.

"I'm fooling," Ciano said quickly. "I know very well you've done what you could, but he, stubborn fellow, doesn't want to understand. Today in the Grand Council we won't mince words and he'll have to understand." Then he had taken Alfieri along to Dino Grandi's.

In July 1943, Ciano was no longer the exuberant, youthful heir-apparent to Mussolini. The dark circles under his eyes were beginning to be permanent, his robust physique was degenerating into fat, his features thickening, and his cheeks more jowly than ever. Although he was only forty, he had already passed the apogee of his career. His wife considered him the most imprudent of her children, grown up too quickly, incapable of having clear ideas about life, and perhaps still fundamentally irresponsible for his thoughts and actions.

Although Ciano had long since moved from his position of enthusiastic follower of fascism to that of outspoken critic, now he railed more strongly than ever against Mussolini, as if he were a misguided ruler, rather than a disliked father-in-law.

"I'm the only one to stand up to him," he still delighted in saying. But where once he had called Mussolini "the old one," now he was describing him as "the tyrant."

"One day," he told journalist Orio Vergani, "we will have the courage to put our cards on the table and tell Mussolini the word no one has said to him since we were kids at the time of Matteotti: 'Basta, enough!' "

But now that Ciano had finally decided to take a stand, and to formalize his opposition, he had the feeling that he had somehow missed the bus. His irony had deteriorated into sarcastic self-sufficiency, and his sensitivity had been transformed into susceptibility. Still cordial with intimates, he became increasingly distant and haughty with people he didn't like. His dreams were cracking, his illusions dimming. He now saw life as a game, alternating between strokes of fortune and pieces of bad luck. He realized that he had become the most disliked man in Italy.

"I know all the jokes about me, about my private life, my wealth, my frivolity," he told Vergani. "I know that in the movie houses they laugh and whistle when I appear in newsreels, but I hope that one day it will be known that I tried to keep Italy out of the war and that I did my best to finish it."

He was not without hope for the future. In one of his brief stops in his office on July 24, Ciano spoke to his *chef de cabinet,* the young Marquis Blasco Lanza d'Ajeta. They discussed the Grand Council meeting and Ciano revealed that there was indeed hidden support for the plotters. He spoke vaguely of the king, and of Marshal Pietro Badoglio, the former head of Italy's armed forces now in semi-retirement.

"*Certo,*" he told d'Ajeta, "Mussolini will have me arrested tonight but tomorrow Badoglio will let me out."

The Rank and File

Much less optimistic about the future was Gino Savoni, a Roman, one of the multitudes who worked in the government ministries which dotted downtown Rome. Mussolini, determined to turn the provincial city into a showcase capital superior to corrupt Paris and London, had increased its population from 700,000 to 1,500,000. Many of the newcomers were chronic unemployables from Southern Italy, high school and university graduates with general educations but no technical skill. Because they were fit for not much else, they were given paper-shuffling jobs and meaningless titles in the inflated bureaucracy.

At Gino's level, no one knew anything of plots and intrigues, of soaring ambitions brought to earth, and of the deadly games, with people as pawns, played by the high and the mighty. Gino knew only that he was unhappy. He was not only thoroughly disgusted with the regime in general, but with his office manager in particular. Gino called him a miniature Mussolini, although the office manager was taller than the 5'6" dictator.

Gino was in the office as usual on Saturday, a full working day despite Mussolini's promises of a Fascist weekend from Saturday at noon until Monday. He seethed inwardly as the office manager—one of the many petty tyrants fascism had fostered—strutted between the desks giving orders.

Of course, Gino too was a member of the party: state employees were virtually compelled to be. The party card meant bread. You had to be a member of the party to show your paintings, to get a passport, or to be a prison guard. Gino wore the party emblem in his button-hole at work, then took it off when he returned home.

His financial position was good; he was in Group B, getting 791 lire a month, a considerable step up from Group C, where he had received only 600 lire, or somewhat less than 100 dollars. His rent was controlled, he had managed to get clothes without coupons, and he was single. That wasn't always an advantage. Mussolini hated bachelors; he had even put a tax on them.

Gino used a bicycle for his personal transport; care was essential because tires were scarce. The fact that everything was rationed and that the regime, particularly the office manager, played favorites annoyed him more and more.

That day Gino knew nothing of the Grand Council meeting, and if he had he would not have given it much thought. They were all puppets, he thought, and that went for his office manager too.

Chapter 2

THE ANTAGONISTS

The Dictator Charisma

In the early morning hours of Saturday, July 24, Mussolini suffered one of his gastric attacks. Rather than tell his wife, he telephoned his mistress, who was alarmed at his recital of ills. "What will happen if you're not feeling fit this day of all days?" she asked.

"I shall be strong," answered the dictator, affecting self-confidence, "and dominate the situation as usual."

But his health was not what it had been when he had invited the press to open-air demonstrations of chest-beating masculinity. Now, exercise was forbidden to him, he was restricted to a bland diet of rice and milk, and he rarely appeared in public.

He had delivered his last speech exactly two and a half months earlier, on May 5, the anniversary of the conquest of Addis Ababa. He spoke from the balcony at Palazzo Venezia, flanked by the symbols of fascism—an axe and lictor's rods. The piazza was packed, people flowed into the adjoining streets, and Mussolini, in the black uniform of commander in chief of the Fascist Militia, smiled, grimaced, shouted and saluted, with the crowd responding on cue as they had in the days of his political and military successes. In a deep sonorous voice, he had told them, "Have no fear for ultimate victory, your sacrifices will certainly be rewarded. This is true as God is just and Italy is immortal."

He might have added a word about his own imperishability but it would have been too much at variance with his appearance—cavernous cheeks, scrawny neck and sunken eyes. He also had to use glasses to read, although he attempted to mitigate this by wearing dark lenses and prohibiting the publication of any photos showing spectacles either on his face or in his hand. But, for several months he had passed from moments of passivity to times when he looked almost like his former self, full of dynamism and energy.

Now, however, as he was being driven to the Palazzo Venezia in his big black Alfa Romeo, he could not suppress the twinges of his stomach. His daughter Edda had told Count Ciano, "His stomach burns, he is irritable and depressed," and the family feared the reopening of an old ulcer which they thought he had.

Ciano himself was convinced that his father-in-law was no longer completely healthy. At the beginning of the year Mussolini had suffered a long and serious relapse, and although he referred to it as his "little ulcer" the word was around in public that its real origin was syphilitic.

It was not. Mussolini had no ulcer, but his constant subjection to Hitler had seriously aggravated a long-standing stomach complaint.

At Kleissheim near Salzburg, where he had met Hitler in April, he had spent two days in his room doubled up with gastric pains, and had been unable even to obtain the return of survivors of Italian divisions decimated in Russia. He had tried in vain to persuade Hitler of the value of a separate peace with Stalin and a new European order as an answer to the demand for unconditional surrender launched by Churchill and Roosevelt at Casablanca in January. If the Fuehrer would come to terms with Russia, his armies there could be withdrawn to the West to help the Italians against the threat of Anglo-American forces in the Mediterranean.

The Italians were convinced, of course, that many more American divisions had passed through the Straits of Gibraltar than had actually done so. Italian intelligence had not realized that an American division required more ships than a European division because it had more equipment.

Still, even a true evaluation of the forces menacing the peninsula made it clear that Mussolini had bitten off more than Italy could chew. He still hoped the Nazis would save him. His General Staff had asked him to demand large reinforcements from the Germans, and if they refused, to tell them that Italy had therefore no choice but to get out of the war. This was an alternative that Mussolini could not bring himself to accept. He had permitted a number of peace moves by Italy towards the Anglo-Americans, but they had been hesitant, feeble gestures, not one of which had been followed through.

The alliance between Hitler and Mussolini had really collapsed five days earlier at their thirteenth—and last—meeting, called by Hitler. Mussolini had done his best to get out of the trip. He had told intimates that he was tired of being rung for like a servant. The encounter, loaded as it was with generals, ambassadors, diplomats, experts, functionaries and translators, was unwieldy. The two groups arrived at Treviso, near Venice, by air and climbed aboard an asthmatic and smoky train which brought them to Feltre in something over an hour. After that came an hour's trip by automobile to the eighteenth-century Villa Gaggia. Nothing could have been less conducive to a successful meeting; the participants arrived nervous, tired and covered with dust. The villa itself, at the foot of the Dolomites, had seemed to Mussolini "like a crossword puzzle frozen into a house." It was gloomy and ambiguous, full of old Venetian furniture casting strange, ghostly shadows—hardly the place for clear and resolute discussions.

In fact, there were no discussions. Hitler held forth alone, from 11:20 A.M. to 1:30 P.M. reviewing the situation in Sicily, in Europe and throughout the world, pausing only to consult the maps and papers he held in his lap. Mussolini listened silently, seated on the edge of a big armchair, his legs crossed. He made no secret of being in pain, as he rocked back and forth emitting frequent sighs.

Mussolini did not speak until around noon when, after a hesitant knock on the door, his secretary came in and handed him a message. He read it, passed it to Hitler, and said dramatically in German, "At this moment the enemy is carrying out a heavy air attack on Rome."

The Italian delegation excitedly discussed the event but Mussolini no longer seemed to be listening. Hitler took no notice whatever, and after a moment's pause continued his flow of words. Mussolini, distressed by the news, remained seated, apathetically ignoring the nods and urging gestures of his generals and ambassadors as Hitler went on with what was really no more than an elementary lesson in strategy. The Italian dictator followed the Fuehrer's tirade so badly that he later asked Paul Schmidt, the official German interpreter, if he could read his notes. When the meeting broke up for lunch he said, "It upsets me to be away from Rome at a time like this. What will the people think?"

The Italian representatives at Feltre were upset for yet another reason. Their demands for more troops had been met by the German counterproposal to put the Italian army under German command. As they came down the stairs with Mussolini, they stopped the dictator to ask him once again to press Hitler for more equipment and raw materials or to try to disengage Italy from the alliance. "The only way to get anything out of Hitler is to stand up to him," he was told.

Mussolini listened silently and then erupted, his voice trembling with emotion. "Do you think I haven't been tortured by the same thoughts as you?" he shouted.

The others were taken aback at the violence of his expression. They stood silently as he admitted that he had examined the possibility of splitting with Germany. But he had also considered the consequences. "I am in an agony of spirit," he said forcefully, as if giving way to inner torments. "But if we detach ourselves from Germany, what then? One day at a certain hour we broadcast a message to the enemy. What would happen? They would demand, quite justly, our outright capitulation and that would mean the instant annulment of the regime. But can we give up so easily twenty years' work and abandon the realization of all our hopes, accept the recognition of military and political defeat, the disappearance of Italy from the world scene? And what about Hitler, what do you think Hitler would do? Do you really think that he would leave us freedom of action?"

The *Duce* was more profoundly moved than they had ever seen him, but when someone made a remark about the war not being popular in Italy, he lashed out furiously.

"Oh for God's sake let's not have any platitudes," he snapped. "No war has been or will be popular. Wars only become popular when they end in victory."

Then the two dictators had lunch together. Only Hitler ate, however, while Mussolini hardly moved his fork to his mouth. Whenever Mussolini summoned up sufficient courage to ask about more men and arms, he would retreat into silence again as the Fuehrer spoke glowingly of his famous secret weapon which would shortly resolve the war on all fronts.

When Mussolini returned to Rome, his plane was unable to land at its usual airport, now pockmarked with bomb craters. Driving in, he saw panic-stricken people leaving the capital in cars, on bicycles, in wagons and on foot. The sight depressed him so much that when he reached Villa Torlonia he went right to his room. His mood was not enhanced by his audience with the king, three days later, on July 22.

"It's a tense situation," King Vittorio Emanuele, frowning and nervous, told him. "It can't go on like this much longer. The Holy City doesn't mean anything any more. Now Sicily is gone. The discipline of the troops has broken down."

All Mussolini could do was admit Hitler's refusal to help and make it clear that he had decided to withdraw from the alliance by September in accordance with a plan prepared the previous evening.

Seated at his desk on the morning of the twenty-fourth, Mussolini thought of the coming meeting of the Grand Council. He did not see it as posing a threat to him. For one thing, he had convinced himself that the king had actually promised to support and protect him. For another, Mussolini did not really think much of his cohorts, even though he had secured titles of nobility for many of them while refusing one for himself. At the meeting that resulted in the decision to call the Grand Council, a score of members—but neither Grandi nor Ciano—had come to Palazzo Venezia. The *Duce* had looked at them obliquely, one by one, ready to defend himself but trying to divine their intentions at the same time. His smile, which he had intended as a frank laugh of welcome, had been a nervous one, hovering between pretended serenity and defiance.

Later, he castigated those present. "What do they want? What authority do they have? Only that of orators which lasts as long as their speeches."

"You can be sure," he told the head of his police, "that I won't find anyone opposing me or causing disturbances. Don't you know these members of the Grand Council? They have poor intelligence, very poor, hesitant faith and even less courage. They are people who live because of a light coming from a flood-lamp; if you turn off the source, they'll fall into the darkness from which they came."

Now the dictator called his confidential secretary, Nicolo De Cesare, from the next room and instructed him to telephone the commander of the Fascist Militia. He wanted no musketeers, his personal guard, that night. Nor did he want extra police or troops to be stationed inside or outside Palazzo Venezia. The commander, General Enzo Galbiati, was incredulous.

"Is it possible?" Galbiati asked De Cesare. "This is the first time that's happened since the Grand Council has been meeting. They're always present. I think it necessary that they appear tonight especially."

De Cesare told him not to insist. "It's useless to try to put on any pressure. In any case, there'll be the special section of the militia on guard on the ground floor. But the *Duce* wants to give the meeting a very restricted character."

There were several reasons for this. If the importance of the meeting were diminished, Mussolini would be in a better position to direct its discussions and limit its subjects. Besides, Mussolini was working out a surprise to spring on the members. In any event, he was sure the Grand Council would be made to serve his purposes. And, with no results to show from the Feltre meeting, this meeting of the Grand Council would provide an opportunity to pass on to its members the responsibility for remaining in the war.

At that time Mussolini was prime minister, minister of war, minister of the navy, minister of air, first marshal of the empire, supreme commander of the forces in the field, minister for foreign affairs, minister of the interior and president of the Grand Council.

He had always managed to come out on top. For twenty years, since October 28, 1922, he had imposed his will. There was no reason why July 24, 1943, should be any different. There were still those who respected him, who feared or hated him. He would bend them to his will once more.

The Radical Left

One person, who hated Mussolini and was determined not to bend to his will, watched his office from the top floor of an apartment house four hundred yards away. This was twenty-year-old Carla Capponi, who had been born in Rome and raised at Piazza Foro Traiano, almost directly across from Palazzo Venezia. She was an attractive, fair-skinned girl, whose titian hair framed a lovely oval face with expressive green eyes. Just out of school, Carla now worked in a chemical laboratory, although she still identified with the students and shared their problems. The older generation, she thought, had been pacified by fascism. It was up to youth to do something. In her hatred for fascism she had become interested in Marxism, although she had not yet joined the minuscule Communist party. Carla burned with the desire to do something, to translate into action the credo she was learning. She would have liked to assassinate the dictator as he stood opposite her on his narrow balcony, but he had not appeared there in months, since May, even entering and leaving by a back entrance. In addition, her house was continually watched, as were all vantage points around the building that served as his office.

Now, on the morning of July 24, 1943, Carla looked over a clump of trees, across Trajan's Forum, at the rust-brown palazzo built with stones taken from the Colosseum. The fifteenth-century building had housed popes, ambassadors, a king and now Mussolini. It did not look as if the *Duce* would come out, and besides—she glanced down —the plainclothesmen were still at her door.

Carla turned to look at the piazza itself. No one was allowed to pass there on a bicycle, or to stop, even to sun themselves or to admire the view, nor could they loiter on the steps of the nearby church. Some small hotels and the Faraglia Caffè had been closed because they faced on the piazza.

It was not quite deserted, for dark-suited men were grouped here and there, the plainclothesmen who silently followed the dictator wherever he went. Writer Paolo Monelli described them as patient lovers waiting for their girlfriends at the *Duce*'s many rendezvous, paddlers when he swam in the sea, novice skiers when he came down the slopes at Terminillo, robust patients in hospitals when he was ill, anonymous soldiers as he watched maneuvers, top-hatted dignitaries while he officiated at public ceremonies.

Carla sighed at the irony of the situation. From her window, a well-aimed shot could put an end to the hated dictatorship. No one could take Mussolini's place. There would be chaos and a perfect opening for the Communists. They would set Italy free and Rome would be itself again—the despised Germans gone, a better life in view.

Her father, a mining engineer who was anti-Fascist, kept his children seated at the movies when the Fascist hymn, "Giovinezza," was played. He was so convinced that fascism would not last that he had not allowed Carla to attend school until she was ten.

Once Carla and her sister explored a cupboard which was closed to them, and therefore the object of their keenest curiosity. Inside they found a pamphlet on the Matteotti assassination and some Socialist booklets. The knowledge of the crime was like a revelation for Carla. She and her sister immediately made handwritten copies to give out at school, but Signora Capponi discovered them and convinced the children of the risk to which they would be putting their father. This led to a family political discussion in which, for the first time, the children were told of the political events surrounding the coming of fascism. After that, Carla had watched the pompous Fascist ceremonies in Piazza Venezia with increasing fury.

Now, however, she began feeling the heat beating down on Rome. She thought briefly of going to the beach at Ostia, Rome's popular seaside resort, even though swimming was forbidden there because of the danger of mines. A week before she had been stopped there by a guard, but after she had spoken to him with all the persuasive energy in her voice, he had let her sneak by for a swim. Nevertheless, she did not like Ostia. Mussolini had favored it, had launched it as a beach resort, a puritan one where women's slacks were banned as well as men's sports shirts. Besides, it was full of German troops on coastal guard.

With a sigh, Carla decided to study her political textbooks. At the time she was enthralled by *Das Kapital*. Like other anti-Fascist students she had attended Visconti High School and been a pupil of Raffaele Persichetti, a center of attraction for young people who could not swallow fascism. Another was Giaime Pintor, one of the most knowledgeable of the young intellectuals. An authority on the German theatre and on French and Italian literature, he had translated Rilke and written essays which were models of lucidity.

Carla borrowed "forbidden books," as did other students, from Persichetti, from Pintor, and from the Amendola brothers, whose father had been fatally beaten by Fascist thugs. Little by little, a group of young people formed around a teacher or older student "who had read the books," and then discussed them—everything from Karl Marx to Croce, Hegel to Hemingway, Kant to Kafka, and Gide to Thomas Mann.

Carla knew, however, that without any organization behind them, young people were powerless. Some fitted into clandestine parties, as Persichetti had done with the Action party. But as his pupils left Visconti, they followed varying political paths. Carla had joined the Communists, but there were many young Catholic leftists, from traditionally Catholic families and surroundings similar to Persichetti's, who joined Catholic organizations such as *La Scaletta* at the Visconti High School, or Catholic Action which, since the Lateran treaties, had been tolerated by the regime. Other groups of Catholic young people gathered in private homes and distributed anti-Fascist leaflets by stuffing them inside mail boxes.

The most active group was the Movement of Christian Communists, one of whose founders was Franco Rodano, a pupil of Persichetti. The leaders, conscientious Catholics, had as their objective the Christian practice of Marxism, that is, the freeing of Marxism from its materialistic approach and the preserving of its historical materialistic philosophy as a technique in politics. They printed a newspaper called *The Clenched Fist* in a clandestine printing shop in a private house and established contacts with similar Catholic formations in Milan and Turin. Their main tie in Rome was with the older anti-Fascist parties, particularly the Communists. The two groups exchanged information and plans through girlfriends, wives and sisters.

Using these attractive go-betweens, they agreed to organize a joint demonstration for Easter 1943 in order to take advantage of the traditional papal blessing in Piazza San Pietro. On Easter morning, four hundred of them mixed with the crowds in front of St. Peter's, ready to raise their voices in unison at the peak of the ceremony to invoke peace and express their anti-Fascist feelings. The police, however, had been informed of the project, and since it might have been untimely to arrest so many demonstrators in a public place, it was arranged that the pope, in an extraordinary break with custom, would not appear on the balcony to deliver his annual public blessing. This in itself produced an uproar among Romans and disclosed, even if indirectly, the success of the young people's plan. A few weeks later the organizers were all arrested.

Although it became difficult to take effective action against fascism, ways were found. One anti-Fascist youth phoned the police. "I'm a loyal member of GUF (Fascist University Youth)," he said, "and some students here at the university must have gone mad. They're distributing subversive leaflets and are on their way to Piazza Venezia to demonstrate against Mussolini."

In reality this group, composed of GUF's most Fascist members, was out to demonstrate solidarity *with* fascism, not opposition to it, but the police, who were unaware of this, started manhandling the students before any explanations could be offered. At that time these were usually staged scenes: everyone knew, after all, that the police were only there to make a good impression. They too were Fascists.

The black-shirted students, thinking the police had received the usual instructions, threw themselves against them to make things look more convincing. This time, however, the police had received different instructions and the GUF leaders were beaten and a large number arrested. The next day the university was closed and some thirty students (the most noted Fascists) were expelled.

Other efforts by Rome's youth to show their dislike for dictatorship followed. On April 21, 1943, a number of students ostentatiously appeared at the University of Rome for a compulsory celebration of a Fascist holiday without wearing the prescribed black shirts. A fight broke out with a Fascist youth, who took a beating until the police arrived. The demonstrators were said to have been inspired by Raffaele Persichetti, but the police were unable to prove anything.

On May 1, Labor Day, some of the same students, emboldened by the reaction to their earlier move, stationed themselves at the University entrance and distributed leaflets saying, "Out with fascism!" "Down with the war!" Within minutes these phrases had gone throughout the university and even into the nearby quarter of San Lorenzo. Any die-hards who protested were thrown into the fountains that dotted the campus. The police, furious, attributed the action to "foreign elements" and closed down the university for ten days.

Partially as a result of the success of these protests, an anti-Fascist group, MUL (Movement of University Liberals) was formed by Italo Calvino and Eugenio Scalfari; it was designed to compete with the "liberal" socialists surrounding Guido Calogero for the allegiance of youngsters who had been in the Fascist party and now wanted new ties. By then, however, hundreds were in prison or had been confined in isolated villages or islands. By the summer of 1943 most young anti-Fascists had either been arrested or had fled Italy.

Still, Carla Capponi was determined to make her gesture against fascism, although it certainly did not look as if any opportunity would present itself on July 24.

The Diplomats

That morning, as Count Leonardo Vitetti prepared to leave his room in the Hotel Excelsior on Rome's Via Veneto, he was aware of just how important July 24 was. He knew that the Grand Council was meeting, and for weeks, in his position as minister plenipotentiary of Italy's Foreign Office, he had been told of the various plots to dethrone Mussolini. He had listened to the military who wanted to arrest everyone; to the circles around the monarch, who, following the king's lead, wanted a moderate transition; and to his colleagues in the Foreign Office who were fed up with Mussolini's tantrums, with the intrigues of the dictator's mistress to secure favored positions for members of her clique, and with the use made by her family of diplomatic pouches to enrich themselves.

In his position at the ministry, Vitetti had met all the top Fascists. Were they acting from courage born of despair or, after twenty years of megalomaniacal rule, had they felt ruin imminent and were now trying to avoid it with a jump into the dark? Vitetti discounted their daring; he was well aware of the conniving that had gone on, the weaving of a thin cloth between the royal house and the no-longer faithful followers of Mussolini.

The short, active Vitetti was a wealthy man with extensive land holdings. The papal title he held dated back to 1775. He had come from Calabria, in the South, and had found his place in government where he had forged a close friendship with Galeazzo Ciano. As Vitetti was about to enter his car for the drive to Palazzo Chigi, he was stopped by Zenone Benini, Mussolini's minister of public works and another close friend of Ciano.

"What do you think, Leonardo?" asked Benini. "Who will take Mussolini's place and run the country? A quadrumvirate of Grandi, Bottai, Federzoni and Ciano?"

Vitetti pointed above them to the entrance façade, where four sculptured giants appeared to be supporting the building.

"They look as if they're all that's supporting it," he said slowly, "but if it falls, they'll fall with it."

The King

Another mainstay of the regime who could conceivably fall with it was Vittorio Emanuele III, king of Italy; emperor of Ethiopia; king of Sardinia, Cyprus, Armenia and Jerusalem; prince vicar of the Holy Roman Empire; holder of the crown of Albania; and prince, duke or marquis of several dozen smaller places. That day, as he received emissaries at the Villa Savoia—the modest mansion which served as the royal residence of the House of Savoy—he looked as though he could hardly support his titles, much less the duties which went with them. In fact, he was burdened with few regal chores; Mussolini had relieved him of almost all of them.

A hesitant and cautious monarch, he had been a virtually silent partner to both Mussolini and fascism for more than twenty years. He had accepted all of Mussolini's actions, no matter how radical, undemocratic or illegal they had been—such as changing the emblem of Italy to the Fascist symbol, approving racist legislation, adopting the Fascist salute, putting the crowns of Ethiopia and Albania on his head and declaring war on seven countries. Only in 1943, with the Axis virtually beaten and ruin inevitable, had he decided that the country needed a change, but long acquiescence had atrophied his initiative. How and when to act were questions he just began to examine that summer. He despised politicians. He never believed they would do anything, and usually they did not. So whom could he trust, what means could be used, and which persons? Dissident Fascists, yes; liberal Fascists, maybe; but not anti-Fascists—too many of them wanted to see an end to the monarchy as well as to fascism.

"It has to be done carefully," thought the king. "Who knows what it may set off."

Although personally courageous he had an obsessive fear of threats to his dynasty, which to a certain extent was understandable. His father, Umberto I, had been assassinated by an anarchist from Paterson, New Jersey at Monza, on July 29, 1900. At the time, Vittorio Emanuele had been thirty-one years old.

The king was also hampered by his ill-favored physical appearance. Only about five feet tall, his legs were ridiculously small in proportion to his size. His face was equally unprepossessing; he had whitish, rheumy eyes, a beak nose and a prognathous jaw. Royal attachés were instructed to warn visitors to keep their glances from the king's legs; and the king himself rarely looked callers in the eye in order to avoid seeing there an instinctive expression of shock.

Still, he was extremely conscious of his role as king and highly sensitive concerning constitutional prerogatives. When, after the assassination of Matteotti in 1924, he had been offered evidence incriminating Mussolini, he had put his hands over his eyes, then over his ears, saying, "I'm blind and deaf. My eyes and ears are the Chamber and the Senate." He had told anti-Fascists that he would need a vote of the Chamber of Deputies in order to get rid of Mussolini. In June 1943, when he was urged by Grandi to oust the dictator, he had been only slightly less meticulous. "I am a constitutional king," he had said. "Give me a vote of the Chamber or at least of the Grand Council. I need an indication from an organ of the state, definitive, indisputable."

Grandi had protested that this was virtually impossible; the Senate, the Chamber and the Grand Council could be convoked only by the head of government, Mussolini himself.

All the king would say was, "Do what you can to set the machinery in motion. I will intervene but I must be the one to choose the moment and that has not yet arrived. We still have time. I know I can count on you. Have faith in your king."

This had been enough for Grandi, and he had begun working out his plot. It seemed a clear signal—as clear, in any event, as Vittorio Emanuele ever gave—for a go-ahead which would naturally favor whoever obtained the vital "indication."

But the king had his own plans. Even though he had named Grandi a knight of the Supreme Order of the Collar of the Most Holy Annunziata—which, in the parlance of royal protocol, made the wearer a cousin of the king—he considered Grandi ". . . a man lacking in solidity; I don't like him too much. He is not a sure element and with Mussolini he's two-faced." Then, thinking he had said too much, the king added, "Of course these are personal impressions and I could even be wrong." And although Grandi was convinced that the king had given him the award on his own initiative despite Mussolini's opposition, the truth was just the opposite.

Few of the people who came to see the taciturn king knew where they stood once the audience had ended. Frequently the king would ask them to keep the conversation secret, even though nothing had been said. Almost everyone left disgusted because the little monarch had listened, or had appeared to be listening, and then had failed to betray his feelings by gesture or word, not even regarding the least provocative of proposals. Petitioners were never sure if his habitual frown was intended for them or for what they were saying.

On June 13, 1943, he had received Galeazzo Ciano in the latter's position as ambassador to the Holy See. Ciano told him that the Vatican secretary of state, Cardinal Luigi Maglione, had personally indicated that if the sovereign did not move to depose Mussolini before the expected invasion of Sicily, the Allies might recognize a government formed abroad by Count Carlo Sforza, former Italian foreign minister then teaching at the University of California.

"Have you told any of this to Mussolini?" the king asked.

When Ciano said no, the king instructed him not to speak of it to the *Duce.*

"The situation is grave," he admitted. "I have the impression that many people are asking themselves where it will all lead."

"What is even graver," Ciano had replied, "is that many are asking it of Your Majesty." But when Ciano added that it would be necessary to replace Mussolini, to aid the Allied landings, to seek an armistice, the king remained silent. Later Ciano said to a friend, "He's more of a Hamlet than Hamlet."

What Ciano did not know was that the king promptly related the incident to Mussolini, who called in his son-in-law and accused him of plotting against him.

This was not the first time the king had acted behind the foreign minister's back. In his twice-weekly meetings with the dictator, when the two went over the general situation and discussed particular problems, the king frequently told Mussolini the latest gossip about his son-in-law, citing Ciano's outspoken anti-German feelings which, the king said, could be dangerous for Italy.

What would Hitler do, wondered Vittorio Emanuele, if the king removed Mussolini? Would he get rid of the monarchy in turn? Therefore, although he wanted to end the alliance, he wanted to do so only with the Germans' consent. He had told this to his son, Crown Prince Umberto, prince of Piedmont, saying that the overthrow of Mussolini did not pose an internal problem but rather that of avoiding German reaction. He rarely spoke to his son about affairs of state, believing him, at almost forty years of age, still immature. When Umberto later complained about this, he said, "My dear Beppo, I wanted to keep you out of all this mess."

The king may have known his son's limitations better than others. According to Edda Ciano, the crown prince had the mentality of a Piedmontese colonel of the old school; if he was not speaking of regiments and maneuvers, he was exchanging off-color stories.

The king, a timorous man, admired Mussolini's undoubted courage, his forthright use of power, his ingenuity at ruling. Whenever the *Duce* brought off a particularly outstanding coup, the king was the first to congratulate him.

Their relationship was facilitated by Mussolini's scrupulous regard for protocol in dealing with the monarch. When Hitler came to Rome in 1938, the king took the Fuehrer to the Quirinal Palace through main streets in a royal car while Mussolini came through the secondary streets of Testaccio, the slaughterhouse district. During the welcoming ceremonies, the king was in the front row of the official tribune next to Hitler, who kept turning around to Mussolini in the second row and calling him to come up alongside him.

Although Mussolini respected the king's position, he really despised the little man. Once, following a stormy meeting in which the king had argued against taking Albania, Mussolini told Ciano, "If Hitler had to deal with such an idiotic king he would have never succeeded in taking over Austria and Czechoslovakia."

The *Duce*'s private comments had been no less scathing. Proud of his broad, peasant frame, he derided the king's inability to do the goose step, which Mussolini had renamed the *"passo romano."*

"He doesn't like it," Mussolini told Ciano, "for the same reason he doesn't like riding a horse, because he can't mount without a ladder." Later he said, "It's required all my patience to pull this tiresome monarch along. But I'm biding my time, the king is past seventy and I'm hoping nature will come to my aid."

On still another occasion he asked, "Why doesn't the stupid little sardine stick to his coin collecting? That's all he understands."

Yet the king, awed by Mussolini's robust physique, was extremely subject to his charm. Even when things were taking a turn for the worse, their relationship, which was closer than anyone realized, remained unchanged. As recently as June 18, the king, observing that Mussolini "still has a very great mind," had agreed that no one else in Italy was so well qualified to resolve the situation in which Italy found itself.

Almost exactly one month later, however, on Monday, July 19 —supposedly the same day on which Rome was burned by Nero in the year 64—the king decided that it was time to turn out Rome's modern dictator before he too caused Rome to burn. That morning, while Hitler held forth in Feltre, the monarch had watched through a telescope from Villa Savoia as successive waves of Allied bombers dropped bombs on Rome's eastern suburbs. The news was brought to him as railway stations and marshaling yards were hit, as sections of Tiburtino and San Lorenzo were devastated, and as Porta Maggiore, the University of Rome, and Littorio and Ciampino airports were seriously damaged. At 3 P.M., when he paid visits to most of these areas, he found ruin and disorder, and no one in authority to organize first aid or salvage operations. Soldiers at Ciampino had run away as far as Velletri, and when the king demanded an explanation he was told that the escape was part of a "thinning out" operation.

The king was shocked, not so much by the scene of destruction or by the victims still strewn about the streets, but by the reaction of the people which his aide described as ". . . silent and hostile. We pass among tears and frozen silence." The crowd was indeed hostile, but it was not silent, for the people hurled imprecations and jeers until the little monarch headed for his black limousine.

It was then that the king made up his mind, quickly convincing himself that now there was no danger of German occupation and that Mussolini had suddenly changed for the worse. Later he cited an old Neapolitan adage to the effect that the *Duce* was no longer using his head, but another part of his body, for his thinking.

On Tuesday morning at 10:30 the king held a staff meeting to discuss the bombing. "The regime is no longer functioning," he said at one point, "we must change at all costs." He modified this, however, by adding that the change would be difficult due to the disastrous military situation and the presence of Germans in Italy.

On Wednesday, the king received a letter from Grandi telling him that the country was heading for destruction and dishonor and urging him to take action. The monarch's only reaction was to say that he would speak frankly with the *Duce* at their next meeting.

On Thursday the twenty-second, after he had received Mussolini, the king told his military aide: "I tried to make the *Duce* understand that it is only he, personally, battered by enemy propaganda and by the criticism of public opinion, who impedes a general, internal reorganization and a clear evaluation of our military situation. He didn't understand, or didn't want to. It was like talking to the wind. . . ."

Now it was Saturday, and the king had finally given his orders. He left it up to one man to gather all the strings and see to it that the various plots which had received tacit approval worked out to the benefit of the shaky monarch.

Chapter 3

THE SCENE–SHIFTERS

The Monarchists

The duke of Acquarone was an experienced huntsman, and he knew how to set his traps well. As the man closest to the king, he was frequently entrusted with delicate missions. Now the bald, dandified duke had been handed the most important task of his career. In 1938, when Pietro D'Acquarone had been named minister of the royal household, he had said that he wanted to bring "some fresh air into the place," but on July 24, 1943, he was preparing nothing less than a typhoon.

He seemed eminently suited for the job. He came from an aristocratic Genoese family and, as a cavalry officer in World War I, he had won three medals for valor. After a spell as military instructor for Crown Prince Umberto, in 1934, he became Italy's youngest senator. By virtue of an advantageous marriage, he was in a position to make a good deal of money as head of his father-in-law's company, a firm which collected excise duties. He was also gifted with a certain financial acumen which had served him in advising the king on the debt-ridden royal holdings and even in increasing the Savoy patrimony. As a result, at fifty-three, a Fascist for eighteen years, he knew all the people who could be useful: army officers with whom he had served, industrialists who had earlier backed Mussolini but who now saw their property threatened by war, diplomats and state officials who frequently reported, through him, to the king, and everyone who had ever wanted something from the crown.

He dealt with these people in his own manner, saying much with few words and little with many; conveying ideas with craft and guile, with a glance, a smile; getting things accomplished without compromising the king; assuming responsibility for decisions the monarch found too distasteful to make himself; developing skill at interpreting the monarch's silence.

It was almost inevitable that this astute and industrious intermediary would become indispensable to the little king. Out of gratitude, the monarch made him a duke. According to the head of OVRA, the Fascist secret police, Acquarone regarded himself as invested with all the powers the king did not use. As Vittorio Emanuele was not too active a ruler, this left the duke a large area in which to maneuver, and although Mussolini had taken over many functions for himself, there were still enough for Acquarone. He always acted in the name of the king, whom he alluded to as *Il Padrone*, the boss, without mentioning him directly. Those who disliked Acquarone said that he had "a curious Balkan mentality" and that he saw himself as the power behind the throne. This was not quite correct. For Acquarone, the king always came first, and he saw himself as interpreting the king's wishes, even when the king had not expressed any.

The duke had interpreted the king's attitude towards the overthrow of Mussolini as implying the passing, "little by little, from the Fascist regime to another." This interpretation was based on a phrase Vittorio Emanuele had uttered on July 5, when he had thought that even if Mussolini were replaced it would not be possible to destroy fascism. The only possibility was a gradual change "eliminating those aspects of fascism which had proven to be damaging for the country." In line with this, the morning of Saturday, July 24, found Acquarone busy contacting dissident members of the Grand Council in order to make sure that everything was going as he planned, which was not exactly in line with the course foreseen by Grandi, Ciano and their co-plotters.

Earlier, Acquarone had selected those whose maneuverings he thought would help the monarchy. Naturally, Grandi had been among the first with whom he had spoken.

"*Il Padrone*," he had told Grandi, "is ready to move. It's important to get rid of Mussolini, but how? A Senate vote might be the thing but we couldn't control enough votes with certainty. The same is true of the Chamber—seven hundred members! So a vote by another body is necessary. Then you . . ." leaving an imposing future to be imagined by Grandi.

But while Count Dino Grandi—full of hope both for his future and Italy's—solicited votes in an air of dangerous conspiracy, the duke of Acquarone was busy with a separate but parallel plot. To be sure of its success, however, Acquarone needed the help of the military and above all of the man who held the reins of power in the armed forces while Italy was at war.

The Supreme Command

General of the Army Vittorio Ambrosio, chief of the Italian Armed Forces General Staff, the *Comando Supremo* in 1943, was a military man who was said to remain so even in his pajamas. At sixty-four, however, he had only an undistinguished record as a regular army officer.

When named to his post in February, he was characterized as the best of a bad lot, which did not say much for Italy's generals. Things had not changed greatly since 1915, when Prime Minister Giovanni Giolitti had said that he had faith in Italy's soldiers but not in its generals. By 1943 there were over eight hundred generals, and quite a few of them were making money on the side by parceling out contracts for military supplies. Many drove big cars, had luxurious villas, and enjoyed substantial bank accounts thanks to their under-the-table collaboration.

It was no wonder then that when they saw Mussolini they sympathized with him, flattered him, and obeyed his orders no matter how useless they thought those orders were. But Ambrosio was different. A disciple of simplicity, clarity, order, he tended to make judgments on the basis of facts, disregarding feelings. Which was why, when assuming his post, he had said he would "save the salvable." Still, because he was excessively military-minded, other factors escaped his attention. Although Ciano had told him, "We're going to lose the war," Ambrosio could not bring himself to agree that the mighty *Wehrmacht* could be stopped, until he saw it done in the Russian campaign.

As in any dictatorship, army officers were involved in plotting. The plotting had even included the man Ambrosio was to replace as chief of the Supreme Command, Marshal Count Ugo Cavallero, a pot-bellied businessman who, besides being a senator and former under secretary of war, had been an executive of the Pirelli rubber factory and the Ansaldo shipyards.

Ciano had called him a phenomenon of servility saying, "He'd bow to public toilets if it would help him get ahead." When Ciano heard that Cavallero had persuaded the captured Albanian government to give him 2,500 acres of land, the foreign minister had commented, "Even if some people disagree on his ability as a strategist, no one disputes his reputation as a grafter."

So Cavallero too had his little plot, in this case backed by the industrialists who saw Mussolini's rule as bringing them to ruin. When Cavallero had told Ambrosio, then his army chief, of his plan to depose Mussolini, the younger general had asked for a week's notice before moving into action. Cavallero, removing his pince-nez and turning his beady eyes on Ambrosio, had told him that he would not have more than an hour once the plotters decided to move. But Cavallero's plot was thwarted when he was ousted and replaced by Ambrosio.

For months Ambrosio had been in favor of eliminating Mussolini. Hardly a democrat, the general saw Italy's liberation from fascism not as a revolutionary gesture but as a device necessary to get Italy from a bad situation. From the time of his appointment to the top military post he had brought the monarch detailed reports which showed that Italy was on the verge of collapse. "There's no other way out," he kept telling the king, "but to replace Mussolini."

On July 5, Ambrosio had even spoken about the advantage of a military dictatorship headed by one of Italy's marshals, Badoglio, who had been fired to make way for Cavallero. As usual, the king showed no enthusiasm.

In their weekly audiences Ambrosio had withheld nothing, talking freely of his plans, his preparations, his hopes. The king, as usual, let his caller talk, listening attentively, nodding once in a while but doing little more than that. Occasionally when he dismissed Ambrosio, he would say, "Thank you. You are loyal, you are telling me the whole truth."

On some visits, Ambrosio left reports for the king, which the monarch would put in his pocket only to return them without a word of comment the next time he saw Ambrosio. These meetings left Ambrosio perplexed. "He didn't say anything to me. He listened, he didn't contradict me and that was all."

When people came to see Ambrosio in hope of hearing something, he would say, "Go see the king, try and find out what *he* has in mind."

Acquarone also left Ambrosio puzzled, even though the king's counsellor had served under him. "He's like an eel, he slips out of your hand." But then more recently Acquarone had said, "One fine day, we'll kick him [Mussolini] out the door without notice." Ambrosio was not to worry; at the right moment he would be told to go ahead.

As time passed Ambrosio became impatient. While waiting, he saw just about everyone who ever thought of conspiring: marshals of the regime, Fascists in office and out, anti-Fascists, exponents of high finances, and members of the royal house including Crown Prince Umberto's wife, the Belgian-born Princess Maria José.

As head of the Supreme Command, however, he refused to join their amateurish and self-seeking plotting. Among others, he had seen Grandi, and he was convinced that the goateed hierarch "hopes to take Mussolini's place."

This kind of attitude was repugnant to Ambrosio, who besides being loyal to the king had no thought of self-aggrandizement. For the king's taste, Ambrosio was a bit too honest. "I have the impression," the monarch had told his military aide after seeing the general on July 5, "that Ambrosio is a man of his word, reliable, forthright, someone who calls a spade a spade. But that's not always the wisest thing to do. He is too open, he reveals too much of himself and of his plans, and he has too many contacts with elements outside the military."

This was particularly true of Ambrosio's friendship with Ciano to whom, after all, he owed his post. Ciano had urged Mussolini to name Ambrosio, who had been army chief of staff for a year, to the nation's top military job. Ciano and the general were allied in their hatred of the Germans and in their belief that Mussolini's dependence on them was leading Italy to disaster.

Ciano felt that the Germans had betrayed Italy and besides, at the golf club, it was fashionable to make fun of them as overly serious, badly dressed men accompanied by heavy, unattractive women. Ambrosio was opposed to the Germans for purely military reasons.

On April 16, after Mussolini had failed to secure aid at Kleissheim, he told the king, "We didn't get anything from them and we'll never get anything any more."

Still, he had continued to act as if obtaining more arms from Germany was his most important goal, with a separate peace a subordinate aim. Nor was Ambrosio pro-Allied, being an advocate of strenuous resistance to the Anglo-Americans. He did, however, think that Italy's military possibilities were not being fully exploited. "If we only could have more arms," he thought, "we could stand up to the invaders."

At the Feltre meeting between Mussolini and Hitler, Ambrosio had asked General Field Marshal Wilhelm Keitel, chief of the German High Command, for reinforcements: munitions, cannons, tanks, planes, antiaircraft weapons. Keitel had said he could not send anything, "not even a single division." Stung by this remark, Ambrosio had simmered while Hitler told the Italians how to fight the war. When the delegations had lunch apart from the two dictators, Ambrosio had said to Bastianini, "Is that all there is to the meeting? Did we come here only to hear ourselves put on the alert? After all that we told Mussolini, you and I, he kept silent like a schoolboy who didn't know his lessons. You know what we'll do after lunch, we'll get hold of him, take him to a quiet place, sit him down and talk to him. The meeting's finished but he can still profit from the trip to Treviso to speak to Hitler."

When the pair had cornered Mussolini, Ambrosio addressed the dictator through clenched teeth.

"You've brought the country to ruin. Now you've got to get it out. You must speak clearly, explain the situation to the Germans, who only want to use Italy to take the brunt of the attack; they don't care if we go over the precipice."

Mussolini: "You think I'm trying to save my skin?"

Ambrosio: "It's not only your skin that is concerned, it's Italy."

Mussolini: "I'll think about it."

When they met again at the Treviso airport, Ambrosio immediately looked for Hitler, noticed that he was unchanged, his face arid and wooden, without expression. Obviously Mussolini had not talked to him. "Didn't you say anything to him?" Ambrosio asked the *Duce*.

"We'll speak about it later," Mussolini answered, turning his back.

This was too much for Ambrosio. The next day in Rome, the still-furious Ambrosio offered his resignation. Mussolini refused; he felt that Ambrosio was the only one around him that could be trusted. He liked to say that Ambrosio told him the truth, while his predecessor never had. As army chief of staff, Ambrosio had tried to tell him the truth all through 1942, but the dictator had always refused to see him alone. It was only after Ciano had suggested that Mussolini name Ambrosio that the dictator agreed to receive him. When he did, on January 30, 1943, Ambrosio was so full of facts and figures that Mussolini decided to take Ciano's advice. Besides, for some time he had not been happy with Marshal Cavallero, who was too openly pro-German. He wanted someone to stand up to his powerful ally.

"Cavallero is finished," Mussolini had said to Ambrosio, "what do you intend doing?"

"I'm going to stick my toes in with the Germans," Ambrosio answered.

"Very good," approved the dictator. "I'll help you."

It was only after Ambrosio had been chief of General Staff for a while that he began to see the situation in its whole terrible reality. He had known the military position—the defeats in Russia, the constant guerrilla warfare in the Balkans, the losses in Africa, the scarcity of arms. Now he learned the truth about Italy's lack of the food, fuel and basic materials needed to fight a long war, how it had too few merchant ships and no aircraft carriers. He saw that its beautifully handmade planes, although impressive at the dictator's military parades, were too few for battle. He became more aware of the army's tanks, which were slow, ineffectual and so lightly armored as to be easily put out of commission by machine-gun fire. The navy lacked radar which it did not even know existed.

Ambrosio, not a good man with words, found it difficult to put his ideas across and felt bound by his duty as an officer. But as a military man he had been impressed by the bombing of Rome the day of the Feltre meeting. From his subordinates he had learned that more than five hundred Flying Fortresses and Liberators had dropped thousand-pound bombs, destroying, among other things, much of the rolling-stock in Rome's marshaling yards. On his return, he reported to the king and found that the king too had been impressed by the bombing.

"Mussolini will have to go," the monarch had said.

Then, two days later, Ambrosio was told that the king, after long months of indecision, had agreed to set the plot in motion. As usual, he had not been too specific, vaguely fixing the date of July 26.

Ambrosio protested; it would normally take at least a month's preparation to have things go smoothly; still, he would do what he could to get everything ready.

Now, on the morning of July 24, 1943, Ambrosio sat at his desk in the Raphael-designed Palazzo Vidoni and thought over the part the military was to play. The news of the convening of the Grand Council had hit the plotters like a stroke of lightning, threatening to upset all their plans. Acquarone understood that after the Grand Council meeting Mussolini would be in a weakened position and at the mercy of the Fascist chieftains who, if they voted against him, might then prepare a plot to take over his powers. The king feared that they might even revolt against *him* in order to form a government without Mussolini, invoking the Grand Council's constitutional power to nominate successors to the head of the government. Given his respect for form and protocol, the little king would be put in a serious predicament.

Acquarone had to move fast. He told Ambrosio that it was necessary to turn the tables, take advantage of the council meeting, and profit from the occasion. Everything had to be speeded up, the last accords clarified, the last counsels heard.

There was plenty to do and time was short. Ambrosio, however, did not trouble himself with details no more than the king did. He too had his Acquarone, someone who was in many ways the power behind the throne, who interpreted his thoughts, who urged him to action, who did everything but present him with *faits accomplis*.

The Police

On the morning of July 24, Brigadier General Giuseppe Castellano arrived at his office early. As special aide to Ambrosio, he was in a way the free-swinging alter ego of the more formal chief of General Staff. But while Ambrosio was primarily concerned with the conduct of the war, Castellano was the intriguer behind the scenes, arranging meetings for his chief and seeing people on his own. His bright eyes darted everywhere, ready to seek out whoever could be useful in advancing Ambrosio's aims. Castellano was careful, however, never to move on his own, but only to prepare everything, waiting for his chief's approval before making any final moves. Still, if Ambrosio held the key to the military plot, it was Castellano's hand that turned it in the lock.

Dino Grandi, Count of Mordano

Badoglio with Crown Prince Umberto

General Enzo Galbiati, Chief of staff of the black shirt militia, greeting troops returning from the Russian front. (Right) Count Ciano, on the left, with General Giacomo Carboni

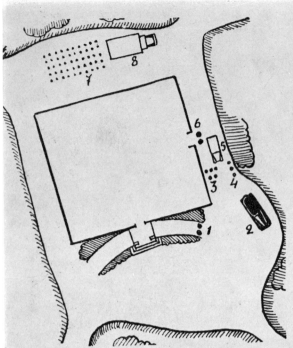

Plan for Mussolini's arrest at Villa Savoia. The ambulance was hidden behind the villa. Between the two hedges were carabinieri armed with machine guns

Villa Savoia. Mussolini and his secretary were arrested as they came down the front steps

To do so he paid little heed to rank and grade, using the authority and prestige of Ambrosio's office to bypass the usual channels. The man most frequently bypassed was the officer Ambrosio had named to replace himself as army chief of staff, Mario Roatta, one of Italy's most intelligent generals and an able linguist due to service as a military attaché. Roatta was discreet but ambitious, brilliant but boring. That he was known as pro-German would help Ambrosio with their ally. For the same reason, Ambrosio told him nothing of his plans. Castellano, however, was told everything, for Ambrosio trusted him more than the king did Acquarone.

The youngest general in the Italian Army, Castellano was full of ideas. He had the quick wit of the Sicilian in high places and, like many, in civilian clothes he resembled a bank clerk. Since he was completely at home with intrigue, he was the ideal man to handle the military end of the conspiracy.

As Castellano sat in his office at Palazzo Vidoni, black hair slicked over a large bald spot, wearing his reading glasses, he examined the situation as of that day. The plotting had undergone an annoying number of cancellations, renewals and changes.

It had begun with Castellano's peppering Ambrosio with ideas for disposing of Mussolini. "There's only one way out," he had said. "Mussolini must be gotten rid of. Either assassinate him or isolate him from the Germans."

Finally, on April 12, 1943, Ambrosio, returning from the Kleissheim meeting between Hitler and Mussolini, had told Castellano of the poor show Mussolini had put on, hardly opening his mouth and not daring to stand up to Hitler.

"All right," Ambrosio had said to the young general, "put your plan on paper and we'll see."

Castellano had quickly summoned a lieutenant colonel and set him in front of a typewriter. First he outlined what had to be done in order to forestall a reaction on the part of the Fascists who represented, in Castellano's opinion, the greatest danger to the plot. Then he listed the moves necessary to capture Mussolini and his closest collaborators. Finally, he put down what the army could do to insure a minimal reaction from the Germans, pointing out that there were few German troops in Italy.

Ambrosio was noncommittal, but he did take the project to Acquarone, who in turn showed it to the king. The king, still timorous, said nothing. Acquarone was hopeful, which was not enough.

"Any further moves," the duke warned Ambrosio, "would be

C

premature . . . the least discussion with any other military authority or with the police would be much too dangerous at this time."

At the right moment Ambrosio would be given the order of execution. Ambrosio had handed the plan back to Castellano, telling him to halt his preparations, but the swarthy Sicilian had trotted the plan over to Ciano, convinced that it might persuade Ciano to talk about what was happening in Fascist circles. Certain that it would not be in Ciano's interest to betray him, he had said, "With this I put myself completely in your hands."

Ciano read it, gave it gingerly to his *chef de cabinet* d'Ajeta and said, "This is dynamite. You take it. I haven't seen it."

After the Allies attacked Sicily, Italy's difficulties became alarmingly evident and all the various groups plotting behind the scenes stepped up their activity. At least three of the plots—Fascist, anti-Fascist and military—went ahead, none with overt approval but each feeling itself assured of royal support. Of the three, thanks to Castellano, the "plot of the generals" was the most precisely conceived. While some of the plotters had told the king of the need to act, Castellano, through Ambrosio, was the first to have offered a specific plan. Still the king had hesitated, shifted positions, delayed and said nothing. The generals, who were trying to save his crown and rescue Italy from the ruin that a lost war would represent, remained in the dark as to his intentions. They could only wait for Vittorio Emanuele to make up his vacillating mind. But the monarch continued to waver, letting each of the plotting groups believe it was on the right track.

On July 14, 1943, Ambrosio had told Castellano to dust off his project, taking new developments into account and studying all possible variations. The old plan had become outdated and in the meantime Fascists and Germans, now on the defensive, had become more suspicious. In the previous three months, Mussolini's bodyguard, the Presidential Police, had been reinforced; the Fascist party's new secretary had reactivated the *Arditi*, the Fascist bully-boy commandos, and transformed the *fasci*, or ward organizations, into veritable arsenals; the German-equipped armored division, Littorio, had been moved thirty miles north of Rome; a militia legion had been posted in the capital's outskirts; and a German Panzer division was fifty miles away, near Viterbo.

Castellano's original plan had called for moving several Italian divisions into Rome, but this had been ruled out for fear of arousing suspicion. It would have entailed bringing too many officers into

the plot, and he and Ambrosio were already convinced a spy network was operating right under their noses.

In bringing his plan up to date, Castellano personally made on-
the-spot investigations of Villa Torlonia (Mussolini's residence),
Palazzo Venezia and the Quirinal, the largest royal palace in Europe.
Every time Castellano went to Palazzo Venezia with documents for
Mussolini he studied the dictator's office and adjoining rooms, fixing
their layout in his mind. When that seemed insufficient, he told Major
Luigi Marchesi, an Ambrosio aide who brought Mussolini the daily
war bulletins, to make more detailed observations. Marchesi became
a friend of Navarra, the powerful head usher and, on the pretext of
being interested in architecture and works of art, examined other
rooms on the second floor of the building.

Palazzo Venezia's ground floor presented a complication. A robust bodyguard stood at the entrance hall on the small San Marco
square. In the interior courtyard was a company of the *Duce*'s musketeers as well as a unit of the Presidential Police.

An attempt to kidnap Mussolini at the Palazzo Venezia would
mean real fighting, since the palace was impossible to take by surprise. There were, in addition, too many secret exits. This left the
Quirinal, which was somewhat isolated; but that struck Castellano
as an advantage. Mussolini usually went there with a small guard
and the idea would be to arrest him at the Quirinal Palace at the close
of one of his biweekly audiences with the sovereign.

But this was sheer daring. Arrest the man who had ruled the
country for twenty years? Still, when Leonardo Vitetti at the Foreign
Office heard of Castellano's plan he thought that the proposal's very
audacity was the best way to get action. "If you go to the king and
say, 'I'm going to arrest the head of your government,' and the king
doesn't arrest you for it, that means he consents." Vitetti thought
that Castellano was going too far too fast. Months earlier the youthful general had told Vitetti, "Everything is set."

"But," Vitetti had asked, "what about the other Fascists in the
government?"

"We'll arrest them all," Castellano had said dogmatically.

Then came the complication of the Grand Council meeting. When
Castellano was told of it, he was sure that Dino Grandi had heard of
the monarchic-military plan to depose Mussolini and was attempting
to exploit it for his own benefit. Castellano advocated putting the
whole council under arrest that very night, and was only dissuaded
when Ambrosio told him the king would never consent. Besides,

Grandi's motion had meaning only if the king moved, and the king would not move without the military.

Late in the afternoon of Tuesday, July 20, the conspiracy began to get under way; every precaution was taken to insure secrecy. Castellano went to see Acquarone, who told him, "*Il Padrone* has decided to accept your plan; all the details must be put in order and be ready to operate within six days."

The most important consideration, in Castellano's view, was complete cooperation from the police. Since law enforcement in Italy was divided among several forces, this meant that the strategic posts had to be occupied by those enjoying the full confidence of the plotters. These were the heads of the *Polizia*, the civil police, and the *Carabinieri*, a military organization which also served as an internal police force. Although these were the two main law-enforcement agencies in Italy, their jurisdictional limits had never been clearly defined. The *Carabinieri*, being a military organization, was responsible to the Ministry of War. The police, through the *Questuri* and prefects, were controlled from Rome. Thus, at least two men had to be brought in: the commander of the *Carabinieri* and the chief of police.

Before July 19, the *Carabinieri* had been commanded by General Azzolino Hazon, whose loyalty to the king made him acceptable. In fact, when Mussolini had ordered Hazon to have Acquarone watched, Hazon had promptly informed the king's counsellor. But on that day, at the beginning of the Allied raid, Hazon was struck by a piece of shrapnel while on his way to the bombed area and killed immediately. Hazon was so much part of the plot that when Ambrosio was told at Feltre of his death he almost had a fit at the thought that the dead general's papers might reveal something compromising.

With Hazon gone, it was necessary to find an equally amenable commander for the *Carabinieri*. Castellano recalled General Angelo Cerica, who was thought to be not too favorable to the regime. To avoid the danger of Mussolini's making one of his rash decisions and naming somebody else, a minor plot was staged. At Castellano's urging, Ambrosio went to Mussolini and proposed naming Cerica.

Everyone else had taken it for granted that Hazon's successor would be Giuseppe Pieche, deputy commanding general of the *Carabinieri*, who outranked Cerica. Suddenly, Pieche discovered that there was high level plotting going on against him. "Someone was telling Mussolini I was anti-Fascist while others were telling the king I was pro-Fascist."

The generals were moving too fast for him. The commission on military advancement was convened and Cerica was given the highest classification.

Cerica was worthy of the other plotters. On the morning of July 22, he had met with Roberto Farinacci, the most pro-German of the Fascist leaders. After their talk, held at the Grand Hotel, Farinacci persuaded the secretary of the Fascist party to support Cerica for the post.

Another assist came from the Ministry of War, of which Mussolini technically held the portfolio. Mussolini had installed his own man, General Antonio Squero, loyal to the dictator and to the Germans. On the same day that Ciano had suggested Ambrosio as chief of staff, he had put forward the name of another man to replace Squero, Antonio Sorice, a reticent but intelligent general, considered an exceptional administrator even though he owed his appointment to the effectiveness of the private intelligence service he had built up as *chef de cabinet* of the ministry. Thanks to his personal network, Sorice knew Ambrosio's plans to the last comma, although he had not been told anything. He, too, hastened to support Cerica for the post.

Buttressed by all this support, Ambrosio told Mussolini that the classification was not binding and that, if he liked, he could choose one of the other candidates. Mussolini, without the slightest suspicion of what was happening, agreed to Cerica.

As soon as Ambrosio had received Mussolini's consent, Castellano called Cerica to Palazzo Vidoni. "I'm speaking to you in the name of the Chief of the General Staff. At noon today you'll be named Commanding General of the *Carabinieri*. General Ambrosio wants to know if you still think as you did several months ago when you asked me to tell him that you were ready to carry out any orders."

Cerica, who had received an award for bravery in World War I, did not hesitate. Later, when Ambrosio began to outline the real import of the plot and Cerica's part in it, he had asked, "Is what I'll be asked to do legal or illegal?" Once he was assured that the order came directly from the king, he posed no further questions.

With the *Carabinieri* taken care of, Castellano turned his attention to the police. Fat, jovial Carmine Senise, an extremely competent law officer, had been named chief of police in 1940. The Fascists were against him because he had always refused to become a member of the party. The Germans did not like him because he had not returned the visit SS Chief Heinrich Himmler had made to Rome when Senise was appointed, and because he had pointedly avoided attending Heydrich's funeral following his assassination. Moreover, Senise had protested the German attempts to get Italians to step up their anti-Jewish campaign. On the excuse that Senise had failed to put down strikes in northern Italian factories, Mussolini kicked him out in April, 1943, even though, aware of his exceptional ability, he had always trusted him. Senise had never betrayed the dictator in the strict sense of the word, although, convinced that the war would be lost, he had kept in contact with Acquarone.

During Senise's farewell visit, the king in a rare moment of foresight had said, "We'll have another occasion to see each other." Afterwards, Acquarone had taken Senise aside, had whispered, "The king asks you to maintain your contacts with the police," and had given Senise one of his all-conveying winks.

Castellano had been just as eager to keep track of the police official.

"Let me know where you'll be," the general had told Senise. "We could need you from one moment to the next."

Sure enough, on July 21, Acquarone summoned Senise to the palace. The duke leaned forward, and in a confidential tone told him that the king "wanted to free Italy from the Fascist regime."

Senise observed that the decision was late. Germans were all over the place, and if the army could not hold them the Nazis might well put Mussolini back in power.

"Wouldn't it be better," he proposed, "to wait for the Anglo-Americans and then leave to *Il Duce* the obligation of getting out of the alliance?"

Acquarone protested that they could no longer count on Mussolini's "moral" help nor could they be sure of the Allies. The best thing would be a new government of experts and civil servants with Senise as minister of the interior.

Senise refused the job but said he had no objection to returning to his old post. Acquarone replied that it was a matter of indifference to the king whether Senise was chief of police or minister, as long as he would arrest Mussolini.

Senise objected on the grounds that he was still on the retired list and could only be recalled to service by a new government. He suggested that the arrest be carried out by the head of the *Carabinieri*.

Castellano had already thought of this. On the morning of July 23, he went to see the newly installed General Cerica at *Carabinieri* headquarters. In a corner of the office, he saw a man hiding his face in a handkerchief. It did not take much to recognize him as Senise. When told that Castellano was virtually leading the plotters, the former chief of police hastily explained that he had not been informed of this and was trying to avoid being recognized.

The next day, on the morning of the twenty-fourth, Castellano, this time accompanied by Senise, returned to Cerica's office to make up a list of Fascists to be arrested after Mussolini. The list was then submitted, through Acquarone, to the king, who added some more names for reasons of his own.

Now that Castellano had the *Carabinieri* and police all prepared, a third element had to be taken care of—the army. While the head of the *Carabinieri* would be busy carrying out the plot, and the chief of police busy watching for possible internal trouble caused by Fascists, who would defend Rome from external attack? The man chosen had to be completely reliable, imaginative, intelligent; not too distrusted by the Fascists, yet loyal to the king. Above all, he had to be anti-German. The Nazis might choose to stage another march on Rome once news of the coup became known. There was only one man qualified for the all-important job.

The Secret Service

Early on the morning of July 14, Major General Giacomo Carboni was summoned to the office of the chief of General Staff at the Supreme Command. Flamboyant but brilliant, Carboni had, like Castellano, once been the youngest general in the Italian army. The debonair Carboni could easily have doubled for Errol Flynn with his thin precise moustache, his highly polished boots, and his hat worn rakishly to one side. He was also a witty conversationalist who moved the corners of his mouth like an actor. He had the habit of assuming poses, almost as if he were playing a role.

Now suddenly he was to take a prominent part in Italy's future. Months before it had been decided that his earlier experience as head of Military Intelligence Service would be invaluable to the plotters; he had been in on the planning ever since the plot to depose Mussolini had begun to take shape. While remaining in the background with as much discretion as he was capable of mustering, he offered suggestions and pointed out pitfalls. From time to time he came out of his anonymity. Called to an audience with the king in June, he impressed the monarch with his devil-may-care appearance and self-assured handling of facts.

Without formality, Ambrosio informed Carboni that he would be in command of the key mobile defense of Rome. His orders, explained Ambrosio, were being given verbally so as to bypass Carboni's nominal superiors—Lieutenant General Mario Roatta, chief of staff of the army, and Lieutenant General Alberto Barbieri, who as commander of the capital's Territorial Army Corps headed the internal defense of Rome and was higher in grade than Carboni. Several months earlier, Barbieri had been judged both insufficiently resolute and insufficiently discreet for the events to come, and Carboni had been called in from the field. To justify his presence in Rome, Carboni was named commander of a motorized corps as yet only partially set up.

Carboni was not at all awed by his responsibility. High-strung and dynamic, he thought it right and fitting that he should be entrusted with defending Rome. Still, there were few men in the army who had attracted so many contrasting judgments. At the Ministry of War, Sorice thought Carboni energetic and strong willed. Others described him as brazenly impudent, a braggart, capable of twisting the truth to serve his own ends. He also had a reputation for quarreling with his superiors; one general's evaluation report read: "First-class intelligence but little will to work."

The son of an Alabama-born mother and a Sardinian father, Carboni had at first seemed to fit perfectly into army routine and to accept soldierly discipline. However, it did not take long for it to become evident that, notwithstanding his father's example as an army officer and his own military bearing, he was his own man, with independent opinions which he never hesitated to express.

Despite his nonconformity, Carboni had elegant manners, which served him well with women. He once boasted that Mussolini had told him that "it seems that you roll on carpets of women." The two had met twenty years earlier in a *salle d'armes*, where both had gone to fence; Mussolini had been at a social disadvantage because when he changed clothes, his underwear was noticeably patched.

Carboni was then only a second lieutenant and shortly thereafter he entered the Secret Service. His first mission, entrusted to him by Marshal Cavallero, involved espionage against the Arabs. He performed so brilliantly that from then on he bore the label of "secret agent." When any seemingly insoluble espionage situation arose, Carboni was called in; frequently, he received promotions as rewards.

He had, therefore, many occasions on which to see Mussolini; it was the dictator himself who, in 1939, put Carboni at the head of SIM, Italy's Military Intelligence Service. From 1934, while the young general had been military attaché in Paris, Roatta had been running SIM and had built it into a powerful organism, far surpassing its nominal rival, OVRA (Organization for the Vigilance and Repression of Anti-Fascism), the political secret service concerned with internal defense of the regime.

If anything, Roatta had been over-efficient. From the time he had taken over, SIM elements had committed a whole series of crimes, including the assassination of the anti-Fascist Roselli brothers near Paris in June 1937. SIM had also played a part in the assassination in Marseilles of King Alexander of Yugoslavia and French Foreign Minister Louis Barthou; it had seen that Ethiopians were supplied with faulty gas masks; it had sunk Spanish Republican ships by loading explosives in the holds; and it had introduced bacteria in food destined for Spain in order to spread epidemics.

During the war SIM had over 300 officers, 1,200 noncommissioned officers and specialists, and directed the activities of more than 9,000 secret agents spread abroad. Seven sections performed various functions: the first was charged with securing military information in foreign countries; the second sorted and filed information; the third handled counter-espionage; the fourth administration; the fifth decoding; the sixth telephone, cable and radio interception; and the seventh translated secret coded messages: all with a cold efficiency which made SIM one of the most formidable secret services in the world.

Obviously, anyone operating SIM was in a position of tremendous power and influence. Carboni found that the military archives alone contained operational plans and statistics, correspondence between Mussolini and the Supreme Command, verbatim reports of top brass meetings, personal files on high-ranking officers, correspondence between Mussolini, the king, Hitler, and German and Italian commanders, and documents verifying sabotage by military and diplomatic personalities in favor of the enemy.

Even richer were the thirty-six series of confidential archives: personal files on ministers, under secretaries, and others in positions of responsibility, dossiers regarding politicians and party leaders, confidential correspondence between Mussolini and government heads abroad, dossiers on the activities of industrialists and financiers, files on "persons of every social standing who have turned against the government for personal reasons, especially anti-Fascist refugees and prisoners," information on the activities of Freemasons, information about assassination attempts and political plots, correspondence regarding the Grand Council, its meetings and its membership, information regarding the management of financial institutions, the finances of newspapers and journalists, details on members of the royal family, on Mussolini's family and on people "of both sexes who have had intimate relations with the Head of the Government and his relatives," correspondence concerning relations with the Vatican, and reports on the Matteotti case.

Armed with all this, Carboni had made no secret of his feelings about the Germans, whom he disliked with a fervor worthy of the most ardent anti-Fascist. Roatta warned him, "I can't approve of your policy because it's against war. We generals must always be favorable to war. Germany is armed for us too."

Despite this admonition, Carboni did his best to dissuade Mussolini from entering the war on the side of Germany. In 1940, after a trip there, he sent in a pessimistic report in which he referred to Germany as "a country violently under the wind of folly, being led on a desperate course towards self-destruction."

Several days later, Mussolini called him in.

"I've read your report," he said. "It's that of a man who detests the Germans but who doesn't know them. I don't agree with any of your conclusions."

Obviously, Carboni could not remain in his sensitive position; in 1940 he was relieved from his position of power and appointed commandant of Italy's West Point, the military academy near Modena. There, as the war began, he remained aloof from the increasing ties Italy forged with Germany, but in his speeches to the cadets he pointed out the dangers of alliances which were contrary to Italy's traditions.

In 1942 he was given command of the Friuli Assault Division stationed at Livorno. Here he started seeing Ciano, whom he had met often as head of SIM. Ciano, then foreign minister, found in Carboni a kindred soul for whom he had unlimited admiration. Introducing him to Serrano Súner, Franco's foreign minister, Ciano said in a joking but emphatic tone, "If one day you hear Italy has been saved from Germany and from fascism, know that you'll owe much to this general."

The two men grew even closer, and together they maneuvered behind the scenes to boost army officers they considered anti-German. It was Carboni who introduced Castellano to Ciano and who later worked with him to get Ambrosio named chief of General Staff. In October 1942, Carboni was put in command of the Italian VII Army Corps on the island of Corsica, but in March 1943 he was recalled to Rome.

In the capital he continued his opposition to the regime and to the alliance with the Germans. But Carboni was a strange man. As the plot began to take shape he settled in a small villa fifteen miles from Rome. As befitted his image of a movie star general, he took his horses with him and pretended to be disinterested in the war and to be resting from the strain of his service abroad. His villa, however, was two hundred yards from the residence of Field Marshal Kesselring, commander in chief of German forces in Italy, and less than four hundred yards from that of the head of OVRA.

Nor was Carboni a great admirer of Ambrosio. He did not consider him ideal for the post, possibly because he saw himself as better fitted. Still, thought Carboni, Ambrosio was the least bad of the available top generals, if only because he was anti-German. As Carboni left Ambrosio's office, however, he concentrated on the matter at hand, his just-awarded assignment to defend Rome.

The broad lines having been laid down by Ambrosio, Carboni moved on to Castellano's office. Castellano called in Major General Junio Ruggiero, commander of the Grenadiers of Sardinia Division, and in Carboni's presence, ordered him to bring as many men as he could into Rome. Ruggiero, a monarchist, said he could put together only two battalions and to scrape together other units he would have to take them away from the coastal defenses, a move that would alert everybody. For the moment, Castellano said, two battalions would be enough; they were to be in Rome the next day, one outside the king's residence and the other near the Viminale, seat of the Ministry of the Interior.

After that, Castellano and Carboni saw the *Carabinieri* head, General Cerica, who said he did not have enough men to stand up to the Germans. The two young generals decided that Carboni's groups would assume that responsibility, and General Barbieri's men (to be informed only at the last minute) would be charged with guarding military depots.

Chapter 4

THE SPECTATORS

The Lotus-Eaters

It was one o'clock, lunchtime for Romans, and those who could afford it ate in restaurants. One of these was Roman-born Mario Masenza who, due to restrictions, was permitted to sell only non-precious jewels in his swank shop on Corso Umberto. As a result, he worked only from eleven to one and then had lunch, usually at a restaurant nearby. Restaurants had meals at a fixed price, ten lire, and ration cards were supposed to be presented. But Mario, a steady customer, could have full meals without them, including steaks, which were artfully hidden under piles of vegetables. Real coffee was available in a slightly different disguise. All he had to say was, *"Il solito—the usual,"* and the waiter would shout the order, *"Il solito per il dottore."*

Mario had not been comforted to learn from government propaganda that coffee was bad for one's health, like butter, oil, sugar and other commodities in short supply. For consolation, Italians were told that the British were destroying themselves by eating too much! As for the French, they had not been able to stand up to the enemy because they were corrupt people with too few children and too many loose women.

Since the war the cost of living had gone up 65 per cent. Pasta had climbed from three lire to nine a kilo, and eggs from five to ninety-six lire a dozen. A steelworker, however, still earned under five lire an hour, and a common laborer, three. Although Mussolini had ordered every bit of earth on the peninsula cultivated, truck gardens were fitfully tended.

Like most Italians, Mario somehow maneuvered between high prices and privation. Most people he knew dipped into their personal savings, indulged in contraband activities, or were helped through family connections. Italy was still 50 per cent rural, its urban population made up of people like Mario who still had relatives and friends in the country. On Sundays, Mario would go out of Rome and round up all the food he could. On Saturday, July 24, he made plans with friends for a food searching expedition the following day.

As a professional man, Raffaele Persichetti's father was in a slightly better position, although the table the Persichettis set included only substantial, simple dishes. Since Dr. Persichetti insisted that his sons join the family for all meals, that Saturday noon, as usual, Raffaele came home to eat. The table had always been the gathering place for the family; there the brothers quarreled when they were small and argued when they grew up. Raffaele did not eat much on July 24. He had heard more about the meeting of the Grand Council and had the idea that it could be important for Italy, even mean drastic changes.

At the same time, Count Ciano had returned to his apartment and was entertaining a luncheon guest, a close friend since school days named Zenone Benini. They ate, and when the white-gloved servant had left the room, their talk turned to the Grand Council.

"Everybody's afraid," said Ciano, "and it could mean that we'll all finish behind bars. But you'll see that in the end *he* will be finished and we can straighten things out somehow."

Then the pair took up the question Benini had posed to Vitetti that morning. Ciano waved airily: "Bottai will likely be Minister of the Interior, Grandi, Foreign Minister. Then we'll all change posts. You'll see."

Ciano laughed, as if to give himself courage, and then he became serious. "Yes, there's the war. But we can take care of that when the moment comes, and if we make peace and get the Germans out of Italy we can avoid occupation by the Americans."

He laughed again, possibly because he saw his dreams coming true and possibly because he felt a bit guilty at the thought of their realization at the expense of the man he had once adored.

Benini noted that Ciano was rather agitated as he donned the prescribed uniform for the Grand Council and that his assurances that everything would come out all right seemed to be addressed to himself as much as to Benini.

The Mistresses

At Palazzo Venezia the day before, the faithful Claretta Petacci, the last of his many mistresses, had been waiting for the *Duce*. He had avoided her for weeks, partly because of his health, partly because of the press of affairs, and partly because their relationship alternated between excitement and weariness. On May 1, in fact, the dictator had given orders to forbid her entry to Palazzo Venezia. A week later he had revoked the order; the couple had been reconciled, and then, after a stormy meeting, they had parted. On June 3, 1943, on her return from Rimini, he wrote Clara a letter which was made public twenty-five years later:

> Clara, for three days my gastritis, let's call it that to understand each other, has been raging. I'm sick, very sick. So much that today at two I called your number, thinking to find your father. A woman answered that he wasn't there and added that you had said you'd be back at six. While waiting I've been rolling myself over all the available chairs. From what's happening I think that, even though you detest me, you love me, while I, even though loving you, don't detest you. I apologize for the strange handwriting but I've been suffering for five hours and I do nothing but drink sugared water. Welcome back. Love. Answer me. Ben.

It was a rare letter for the dictator, who had said, "If you must write to a man, cut off one of your hands; if you must write to a woman, cut off both."

They had met in 1933, when he was a married man of fifty and she a young girl of twenty-one engaged to be married. Three years later he had made her his mistress, her marriage to an air force officer having lasted only four months.

In 1943, at thirty-one, Claretta was an undoubted beauty; she had curly black hair, liquid green eyes, a cupid's bow mouth, a long-legged, firm figure, and a Roman woman's full bust and small waist. Her daytime dress was that of the times: wedge-heeled shoes, wide skirts tight at the waist and falling just below the knee, a shoulder bag, and furs, even when they were out of place.

Though she was a cousin of Raffaele Persichetti—Claretta's mother was a Persichetti—she did not have a political thought in her head. She did retain an ironic sense of humor. When, on the occasion of Hitler's birthday, Mussolini asked her advice on a present for the German dictator, she suggested, "A pair of suspenders; his pants are always slipping down." Her main obsession was jealousy. If Mussolini phoned her after a state dinner, her first question to him was likely to be: "How many women were there?"

Her family exploited the liaison for all it was worth. Her sister, who called herself Miriam di San Servolo (possibly unaware that this was the name of an insane asylum in Venice), had pretensions to being an actress. When one of her flimsy films was shown at the Mussolini-subsidized Venice film festival, however, the producers were so fearful of its reception that it was shown solely to the press.

Her brother trafficked in import-export licenses and her father, a doctor, became an instant medical authority and wrote a column for *Il Messaggero*. Her mother, as befitted a parent of one daughter who was an actress and another who was involved in a real-life story that outshone any film scenario, appointed herself the quasi-official censor of Italian movies.

The Petaccis saw themselves as resembling the large and illustrious families of the Renaissance, whose powers accrued from the private donations of public favors. Even Bottai once said that "since the only way to get on in Italy is to know the Petaccis, I have decided to accredit an ambassador to their court."

They were courted by all kinds of people, among them Ugo Montagna, a Sicilian, self-named Marquis of San Bartolomeo, who sent them bouquets of flowers and baskets of fruit until he paved the way to selling the Petaccis a stock of Persian rugs. Chance had it that the sale was consummated on July 24. The origin of the rugs was somewhat suspicious to say the least, but the police, who knew quite well where the rugs came from, would not have dreamt of moving in on the Petaccis as receivers of stolen goods.

Never was a secret love affair so widely known, at least in certain circles. The SSR, the *Servizio Speciale Riservato*, tapped the telephones of important personalities; transcripts of their conversations would then be seen by the dictator, his cabinet, minor officials, generals, prefects, and even by anti-Fascist elements, the Vatican, newspaper offices, legations and embassies. Officially, the *Duce* was excluded from controls; but frequently, contrary to orders, the personnel would take down the texts of his calls so that Claretta's intimate conversations with Ben—as she called him—were seen by almost everyone in the inner circles.

Mussolini lavished regal gifts on Claretta—automobiles, jewels, furs and grand pianos—all at state expense. Her love for music caused Mussolini in the middle of the war to conduct a personal search for two Bechstein grand pianos. Claretta also once pretended to be a painter. When Mussolini told her that one of the capital's best art galleries would show her works, she hurriedly hired a hack painter, a cousin, to turn out landscapes, anonymous portraits and, to please Mussolini's plebian taste, a huge seascape. On opening night, everybody in Rome appeared, and the entire selection was sold —mainly to Mussolini, at state expense.

When Mussolini sent Claretta some poetry, she disdainfully replied that she preferred his prose; sometime later a truck pulled up to the villa with a monumental edition of Mussolini's speeches and writings.

At first, the Cianos did not mind Claretta. "Better one woman than many and she seems to be the best of a bad lot," Edda had said. But her husband later changed his mind when he, a known Don Juan, was reproved for criticizing Mussolini.

"It's not too bad if you have a flock of mistresses," Ciano defended himself. "It's grave and scandalous to have only one."

Both the king and Bottai were convinced Mussolini's continuing affair with Claretta was responsible for his ill health, but it was more his intense public life that aged him prematurely. As Claretta occasionally pointed out, cabinet ministers, high officials and generals all had young mistresses too, and Claretta was furious at their hypocrisy. "They hate me," she told her lawyer, Gino Sotis, "because *Il Duce* loves me . . . because I am the most faithful human being he has in the world."

In spite of her fidelity, Mussolini never deified her. For him, a woman was an object, "a pleasant parenthesis" in a man's life. Before his wife, donna Rachele, joined him in Rome in 1929 he had, for seven years, lived the life of a bachelor. Over the years he had had a series of mistresses, including Ida Dasler, whom he married when she bore him a son, Benito Albino. A girl from Trento, she owned an "Oriental Studio of Physical Beauty." Ida had once been visiting Mussolini in a military hospital when Rachele found her there and with considerable energy tried to strangle her. Rachele had probably discovered that Benito was a bigamist who had married her a month after he had been wed to Ida in a civil ceremony.

Nevertheless, Mussolini liked to tell his loves, as he did the Moslem anarchist Leda Rafanelli: "I'm free as the air. If you find that I have a family you can send me away."

Claretta, however, was a possessive mistress who visited her lover at Palazzo Venezia almost daily. To dissuade him from going with other women, she gave him a book on venereal diseases and their dangers. Then in 1943, she saw him less, and when she did, Mussolini was frequently depressed, easily irritated and often angry.

Just as most dictators despise the people they rule and thereby attract them even more, Mussolini hated women and usually muttered curses as he made love to them. He thought nothing of making love to his female admirers between affairs of state; with most of his clothes still on, he would take them quickly, frequently on the floor of his office.

Even so, Claretta adored Mussolini with undying devotion. On Friday, July 23, she had entered a side door and taken Mussolini's private elevator to his apartment. In a small wardrobe she had undressed and put on a nightgown and negligee from among the ones that Mussolini had chosen for her. Then she had dutifully waited for the appearance of her lover. As she lay on the divan-bed in the sitting room, with its colored glass windows and the gilded signs of the Zodiac on the blue ceiling, she played some of her favorite records until the dictator made his appearance.

Claretta loved, suffered and feared Mussolini; to her he was both father and lover. It was something of the same sort of erotic ecstasy that the dictator inspired, in accordance with Hitler's idea that the masses were feminine and wanted to be seduced. The Italian writer Carlo Emilio Gadda likened Mussolini to "an enormous phallus that seduces, deflowers, persuades, cheats," and added that he kept the country in grotesque subjection, "forcing families into an absurd prolificacy so as to breed cannon-fodder" and that, in a kind of mass rape by a mad Eros, "he evoked venereal sobs and ovarial cries" at his public appearances, which were in turn described as "priapic exhibitions."

Again on the afternoon of Saturday, July 24, Mussolini went to his private apartment. But this time Claretta was not there. Forty-five minutes later he had another gastric attack, just two hours before the Grand Council was to convene.

The Press

In Rome that day, the press made no mention of the Grand Council meeting. Instead, headlines shouted that Palermo had fallen to Anglo-American forces, and articles carried dispatches concerning efforts by the English to make peace between the Jews and the Arabs.

Several papers said that it was time, now that five days had elapsed since the unprecedented bombing of Rome, that water, light and transport be restored to normal, and they protested against the state of air raid shelters. It was reported that the Central Dairy had suspended pasteurization of its products, but the populace was told that as long as the milk were boiled there would be no hygienic dangers.

If one believed what the newspapers printed, the Italian people under fascism had become puritanical geniuses who avoided every frivolity. Writer Giovanni Guareschi said that, according to their stories, no wife betrayed her husband, no husband made love with his wife's girlfriends, and no one committed suicide. In any event, any article containing such news was limited to an arbitrary thirty-two lines. Divorces, scandals, adulteries, murders and suicides happened only in America.

Ironically, Giorgio Nelson Page, descendant of a signer of the Declaration of Independence and nephew of a former U.S. ambassador to Italy, was the official responsible for Italian propaganda broadcasts. A former correspondent of the *Chicago Tribune*, he had given up American citizenship in 1933 and, thanks to his friendship with Ciano, had entered the Ministry of Popular Culture.

On Saturday, July 24, Page sat in his office on Via Veneto wondering what was going to happen at the Grand Council meeting that day. A few days earlier an Italian journalist had asked him if he would be willing to take over in the event of a right-wing coup d'état or a cabinet reshuffle, but everyone with whom Page had spoken had told him the meeting would produce no drastic changes.

Besides, although he had been a top official of the ministry since its creation by Ciano in 1934, he saw himself only as a functionary carrying out orders. He refused to become the titular head of propaganda just as he had earlier refused to broadcast personally to the United States; instead, he limited himself to editing radio propaganda and supervising radio and radio-telegraphic monitoring. His department also supervised the news programs of the Italian radio, which was even less informative than the press, with the result that, even though it was forbidden, many listened to Allied radio broadcasts hoping to hear of Allied victories. These broadcasts were badly jammed, however, and most Romans had to rely on EIAR, the national radio. War bulletins, with their emphatic style and euphemisms, were listened to with boredom or not at all.

Much more popular was a kind of soap opera called "Cico and Pallina." This was the work of a young man, Federico Fellini, who had drawn an Italian version of Flash Gordon after Mussolini banned American comic strips. He had also written screenplays for director Roberto Rossellini and revue sketches for actor Aldo Fabrizi.

For months he had avoided the draft when he was writing and drawing for the weekly, "Marc' Aurelio." One day a group of black-shirted officials strode in and confiscated the current edition. Fellini had been sabotaging instructions (to draw Anthony Eden as a homosexual, England sinking into the ground under Italo-German bombs —"I just couldn't do it") and was ordered to appear for his medical. Fellini presented himself at the Celio, Rome's military hospital, and in ten minutes found himself passed. No sooner was he out the door than he tore the papers he was given into shreds. "I couldn't bear them near me," he explained to his friends who, afraid he was heading for more trouble, secured other documents for him and arranged for another physical in Bologna. Here he ran up and down the stairs pretending he had mistaken the floor until his hands were trembling and his breath coming in short gasps. By then the examiners were at the "F's" and he heard "Federico Fellini" in what seemed to him to be the voice of the Last Judgment. But just at that time the wail of sirens was heard and shortly afterwards bombs started falling. The hospital was severely damaged, its records destroyed and Fellini, with a flesh wound in his shoulder, ran through the deserted city till he reached the countryside, there to throw himself on the grass to catch his breath and feel himself bursting with joy.

Fellini later met Giulietta Masina, the girl who played Pallina, and courted her through the lines he wrote for the soap opera. The pro-

gram was heard through 1943 on the radio between reports of bombings and defeats made to sound like victories.

The Jews

A newspaperman who could neither write nor express his feelings publicly was Ettore della Riccia. Although Roman-born, he was
well outside the mainstream of Italian life. For Ettore was a Jew. On
Saturday, July 24, he walked down Corso Umberto, thinking about
where his religion had brought him.

He had managed to survive the Fascist racial laws, but survival
had meant being ostracized and humiliated. Jews were subject to a
long list of restrictions: their children could attend only segregated
schools; they could not have gentile servants; they were not allowed
to have telephones under their own names; and they were forbidden
to hold official positions, or to be teachers, bankers, lawyers or journalists. Ettore, who once had been a reporter on the newspaper *Giornale d'Italia*, now worked in the office. He might not even have managed that had it not been for an influential cousin.

He knew what the Germans were doing in other parts of Europe
and of their plans for the "final solution." In the list drawn up by
Himmler's deputy, Reinhard Heydrich, and Karl Adolf Eichmann,
chief of the Gestapo's Jewish Office, 58,000 were listed to be extermi-
nated in Italy. Ettore did not particularly blame Mussolini for this.
Indeed, the dictator seemed to have no particular feelings on the matter. As late as October 1941 he had told writer Yvon de Begnac, "I
have had affectionate relationships with many Jews—there were Jews
among the founders of fascism and Jews have sustained it. Jews have
never represented any danger to Italy . . . they have been loyal and
have supported the regime, serving its interests as well as their own."

Mussolini had pursued his own kind of anti-Semitism for years.
When his favorite child Edda fell in love with a Jewish suitor in 1929,
he opposed the match, mainly because he was the leader of Catholic
Italy and the signer of the Concordat with the Vatican. He insisted
that his opposition was due to the fact that most mixed marriages
ended in failure, but he heaved sighs of relief when Edda later chose
Galeazzo Ciano.

Until the alliance with Germany, Mussolini's anti-Semitism had
been based on superstition more than on anything else. Still, when he
heard that the Venice public library had a book by an eighteenth-

century Jewish writer, Moishe Mussolin, he ordered the book destroyed.

In 1932, he had referred to anti-Semitism as "a German vice," and in the middle thirties he facilitated the exodus of Jews from Germany so that many could embark from Trieste for Palestine or the United States. But then he had not yet met Hitler. It was after he was definitely under the German's sway that Mussolini told Ciano that America was in the hands of Negroes and Jews, that Jews did not want children because they were afraid of pain, and that the world, outside of the Axis nations, would be destroyed by Jewish corruption.

Mussolini also viewed anti-Semitism as a means of transforming Italians into tough-minded, implacable, hateful masters, thus enabling him to move the Italian bourgeoisie to take more materialistic attitudes.

In 1938, following Hitler's visit to Rome, Mussolini put through the Fascist racial laws, modeled on the Nazi pattern, and a surprising number of Italians suddenly developed racial antipathies. A magazine, *La Difesa della Razza*, Defense of the Race, joined the Italian press in accusing Italian Jews and "international Jewry" of all kinds of crimes. Following the example of the German publication *Der Stürmer*, Jews were represented with hooked noses and claw-like hands; they were portrayed as big-bellied and sinister, trembling and moaning, or in the form of cankers or squids.

To a Fascist historian who protested, Mussolini denied any theoretical adherence to anti-Semitism: "I am carrying it out entirely for political reasons."

Still, many distinguished Jews had been fired from top positions in the government, army and navy; confiscation of Jewish property was far from unknown; and Jews could participate in the life of the state only in the ratio of their percentage of the population.

Although Jews numbered only one in every thousand, they had been prominent in every walk of life. Many of the. country's outstanding professional men were Jews, as were highly respected painters, poets and writers. Among these latter were Carlo Treves, Renato Morpurgo, Leone Ginzburg, Alberto Moravia and Dino Segre, better known as Pitigrilli.

Earlier, Mussolini had himself placed Jewish journalists on the staffs of the newspapers and magazines he controlled; he gave direction of *Gerarchia* to Margherita Sarfatti, an attractive intellectual who had also been his mistress. Even after the racial laws were passed,

Mussolini helped Jewish friends who were in trouble. Enrico Rocca, a Fascist since 1921 and a follower of d'Annunzio, was a serious student of German literature and a highly regarded theatrical and literary critic who for years had written for the Fascist paper *Il Lavoro Fascista*. With the institution of the racial laws he began to sign his work with his initials only. The paper's editor wanted to dismiss him, but Rocca wrote a letter to Mussolini, who promptly informed the editor that Rocca was to remain. A compromise was eventually worked out under which Rocca's articles were to be signed with a pen name.

Though Mussolini was not overly zealous about the enforcement of the racial legislation, he did make a few gestures. He changed his dentist, Dr. Piperno, and his librarian, Professor Foa, and warned a few officials to get rid of Jews in their offices.

But Fascist officials still pursued the phantom. One, Alfredo Cucco, an oculist who was vice-secretary of the party, sent out a circular to provincial secretaries on June 15, 1943, warning that "the anti-Semitic battle is today more than ever the order of the day for the nation in war," and invited them to "keep in mind that the source of propaganda against Italy, from outside as well as inside of the country, is Jewish."

Individual Italians did their best to soften the effects of the laws against Jews. After all, the place of Jews in Italy had in modern times been no more, no less, than that of any Italian citizen. For Italians to say "Jew" was like saying "Neapolitan" or "Tuscan." Even so, the result for Jews was hardship, both material and moral. Many, like Ettore della Riccia, had to give up their professions, while others, professors and students, were relegated to segregated schools and still others had to face separation from their families. Thousands left Italy for the United States, South America, Palestine or those parts of Europe still untainted by the Nazi brush of intolerance. Particularly hard was the position of foreign Jews, who had come from Germany and Austria in search of refuge, and who were forced instead to continue their wanderings.

Ettore della Riccia was in love with an English girl who was Catholic; he was a Jew and an Italian, and since any marriage involving those of the non-Aryan race—a description never really defined by the authorities—was forbidden, he could not marry a foreigner, especially a Catholic. So, they lived together. Several months earlier, they had gone to see a priest on Lungotevere Prati to find out if there were some way they could get around the regulations. Ettore knew that much of the racial legislation was enforced in a haphazard, uncertain way. Possibly there was a way out.

"Not right now," said the priest, "but fascism will pass. The Church will remain and one day we shall be able to thumb our noses at fascism."

The Church

In 1943, the Church was not thumbing its nose at anyone. Pressure was being brought by both the Axis and the Allies on matters ranging from appointments of bishops to the content of Vatican radio newscasts. Fears of more drastic action, particularly on the part of the Germans, were acute. Cardinal Maglione, Vatican secretary of state, was quoted in a 1969 Vatican white paper as having heard "rumors that Germany allegedly asked Italy either to remove the Pope from Rome and Europe or isolate him in the Vatican." As a result, Pius XII considered delegating wide powers to bishops outside Italy in the event the Nazis captured him or sealed him off from the outside world.

To some it seemed that the papal throne was already vacant. Pius XII, however, still made his appearance at the window of his apartment in the baroque Apostolic Palace accompanied by the good-natured Cardinal Maglione, while ever-present Assistant Secretary of State Monsignor Montini (later Pope Paul VI), austere in black, was one step behind the white-clad pontiff. The trio had tried to keep Italy out of the war, and once it started, they saw to it that the occupant of the Throne of Peter took no precise stand. Despite the efforts of some Italians, the Vatican steadfastly refused to act as an intermediary. The reason given to Count Vitetti was that the Germans could not be antagonized too much.

The German ambassador to the Holy See, Baron Ernst von Weizsaecker, reported to Berlin that "the official Vatican newspaper, the *Osservatore Romano*, consistently abstains from publishing even the smallest item of news on the military situation to such an extent that they won't even mention the fighting taking place in Sicily." He noted, however, that the Church hierarchy was almost entirely Italian and was certainly reacting to what was going on.

Nazi agents from half a dozen organizations spied on the Vatican, tapping telephones, monitoring radio transmissions, intercepting cables, and paying informers for gossip, hearsay and imagined tidbits.

Weizsaecker complained to the German Foreign Office in 1943, "In place of this river of unreliable information, we need authentic news. . . ." As far as Berlin was concerned, even Weizsaecker was suspect; in 1943, Martin Bormann sent a man to Rome to keep an eye on both the ambassador *and* the pope.

Not that there was much to garner from the pontiff. Roman-born Pius XII, at sixty-seven, was noted for keeping his own counsel, even to the extent of eating all his meals alone. Tall and sparse, with aquiline nose, thin lips and almost feverish eyes, he looked like a dedicated mystic. Yet he was one of the most politically-minded popes, even though it had been his predecessor, Pius XI, who had not hesitated, while powerful nations remained silent, to protest against Hitler's racist excesses. Pius XII, however, was not, as Cardinal Tardini wrote, "born with the temperament of a fighter."

When the Vatican had protested against the shooting of 250 Polish priests in 1942, Hitler threatened a second massacre and Pius XII, responding to pressure from high prelates, halted his protests. In the same year, the Papal Nuncio to Germany went to a German Foreign Office official to "say a good word," unofficially of course, for seventeen Jewish professors arrested in Lvov, Poland. It was, however, too little and too late. The professors and their families (thirty-eight people in all) had already been brutally executed.

The Holy See did help about 1,500 Jews to emigrate by giving them the necessary visas (Brazil had put at its disposal three thousand visas for Jews converted to Catholicism). In addition, the Church gave aid to thousands of the needy, Jews and non-Jews.

Catholic writers, including Jesuit Father Robert Leiber, Pius's private secretary, wrote that the Holy See's cautious line was due to wariness of the "damage which would have followed [taking a stand against the persecution of the Jews], for the Church, for Catholics in Rome and wherever Hitler's power extended. Instead of running such a risk . . . Pius's fundamental principle was this, 'save lives,' that is help Jews concretely, without taking a stand that would exasperate and provoke the Nazis."

The former Eugenio Pacelli had occupied the throne of St. Peter since March 2, 1939, just before the start of World War II; he thus assumed leadership of the Church after it had already forged ties, even if reluctantly, with fascism. As top adviser to Pius XI, Pacelli had been involved in several deals made with Mussolini, who was hailed by his superior as "the man Divine Providence has sent to Italy."

For his part, Mussolini, while editor of *Lotta di Classe,* had called priests "professional liars" and had said, "Christ is dead and his teachings moribund." Two of his books written about that time, *John Huss* and *The Cardinal's Mistress,* were fiercely anti-clerical. Later, he softened his attacks. In November 1922, a few days after the constitution of his government, Mussolini, speaking before parliament, had said, "God help me to complete my difficult task victoriously." It was the first time a head of government in Italy had invoked God publicly in parliament. In 1923 Mussolini went further by having his children baptized; in 1925 he married their mother, Rachele, with religious rites. This sanctimonious procedure was clouded somewhat by the fact that he was already married to Ida Dasler, as previously mentioned, by whom he had had a son, who had also been baptized. And, Mussolini still followed the pagan custom of touching his testicles to ward off the "evil eye" that any ill-wishers might be casting at him.

Meanwhile, the pope's link with Palazzo Venezia, Jesuit Father Pietro Tacchi-Venturi, who had been with the dictator since 1929 and was known to Romans as his confessor, was advising Mussolini of the pope's desire for peace without proposing any concrete moves or offering the Vatican's good offices.

As the fighting moved closer to Italy, the pope's desire to see an end to the war was even less in evidence. Instead, the Vatican's concern appeared to be concentrated on avoiding "grave danger to Vatican City."

The two representatives of the Allies in the Vatican were warned that Allied bombardment of Rome might provoke a popular uprising against diplomats residing in Vatican City which, said Cardinal Maglione, was already regarded by large segments of Rome's population as a nest of spies.

Harold Tittmann, assistant to Roosevelt's personal representative to the pope, Myron Taylor, cabled Washington:

> I replied that I felt confident that if in the opinion of Allies war could be shortened and thousands of lives saved by bombing Rome they would not be deterred therefrom out of consideration for safety of a few diplomats.

Then Pius pursued a different tack, telling Roosevelt of his concern for the Italian people. Roosevelt answered that "the government of Italy for a period of twenty years has glorified the use of force and has used it ruthlessly against the Greeks, the Ethiopians, the Albanians—to mention only a few of the victims of Fascist aggression. The people of Italy have been made the instrument of this pagan policy."

This led to a lull, until Pius replied to Roosevelt's July 10 message announcing the invasion of Sicily. Stressing the Vatican's neutral status, the pontiff took the position that he was "above any armed conflict between nations," then warned that the Italian capital "cannot be attacked without inflicting an incomparable loss on the patrimony of Religion and Civilization."

After the bombing of Rome, the Church tried still another tack by having the Spanish Episcopacy protest. A possible follow-up by the Holy Father himself was likely forestalled by Secretary of State Hull's reply to the Spanish bishops: "The responsibility clearly rests with Italy and it may be pointed out that the Axis exhibited no compunction over a period of years about the destruction carried out wantonly by its forces, of Christian shrines in a number of countries. It is not recalled, incidentally, that the Spanish Episcopacy ever protested against the unchristian acts that have characterized Axis warfare."

When the pope employed the device of a letter to the cardinal vicar of Rome to bewail the bombing, Tittmann, on July 23, told Cardinal Maglione that it was regrettable that the pope "did not raise his voice clearly in some such manner as this when civilians and cultural monuments of other countries were being bombed by Germans in early stages of the war."

Tittmann agreed with the cardinal, however, that it was impossible to bomb military objectives in Rome without damaging Vatican property and cultural monuments at the same time. "But," he said, "I think the answer to this is that military objectives should be removed from the city which can not serve the God of Peace and the God of War at the same time."

In his further conversations that day with Vatican officials, including Monsignor Montini, Tittmann was told that the pope had been "desperately hoping that Rome would not be bombed during the war since it would have meant so much to his prestige afterwards if it could be said that city had been spared out of respect for the Holy Father."

But it is likely that Pius was less concerned about his prestige than about larger matters. His greatest fears were of change, the disruption of the status quo, and the uncertainties to which this might subject the Church. For the Church was being threatened by more than dictators. The world was beginning to question the Church's qualifications to make moral judgment on right and wrong, confidence had been shaken when cracks of uncertainty had appeared in the tremendous edifice, and a secular vision of society was emerging which would increasingly shake confidence in the Church's infallibility.

But the people of Rome, who had not yet felt the impact of man's increasing knowledge and manipulation of his physical world, still viewed the white-clad figure as a symbol of hope and refuge. When, after the bombing of July 19, 1943, Pius, in his capacity as bishop of Rome went to visit the stricken areas with Monsignor Montini, he was greeted with reverent respect by people who went down on their knees and pleaded that he stop the war and bless their dead.

Mussolini, on the other hand, did not dare show his face when he returned from Feltre that day. The king ventured to the bombed areas and was received with insults and scorn. The silent women who were still scraping the ground in search of their children stopped for a brief moment and stood up cursing.

Pius remained reluctant to use his power even though the Vatican had, earlier in the year, given its implicit approval to moves aimed at replacing Mussolini. Around the middle of May, Cardinal Maglione had intimated to Marquis d'Ajeta, Ciano's aide, that the Vatican, unofficially of course, considered the situation in Italy dramatic, and that the intervention of the king, of the army and of the people of good will, was urgently needed for the salvation of the nation.

Chapter 5

IN THE WINGS

The Anti-Fascists

On Saturday afternoon around the time that Mussolini was preparing himself for the Grand Council, Ivanoe Bonomi was hearing confirmation of the impending meeting. As a former premier, the acknowledged leader of Italy's anti-Fascists had been allowed to remain in exile in the center of Rome. Arrested during the 1924 elections which Matteotti had denounced, he had spent the next nineteen years studying, writing, waiting. On April 27, 1943, spurred by Allied landings, isolated anti-Fascists in Rome had formed, under his leadership, a loose coalition called the Rome Committee of Parties for Freedom.

The meeting place was Bonomi's house at 4 Piazza della Libertà, where Bonomi received opponents of the regime with the full knowledge of the police, who tolerated the plotting without attributing much importance to it.

At seventy, with a white goatee and horn-rimmed glasses set small in his long oval face, Bonomi was the soul of integrity. He saw his mission as reconciling the various groups, rather than leading them in an active fight against the enemy.

Many were pre-Fascist politicians considered by Mussolini as too harmless to jail. By 1943, after all, fully 95 per cent of the active anti-Fascists were in prison, confinement or exile. Still there were young people like Raffaele Persichetti, Carla Capponi and others who were burning for more direct action. The Communists restrained their hotheads and called for a more realistic approach. The Action party tried to live up to its name although it contained intellectuals, writers and men of culture like Sergio Fenoaltea, Piero Calamandrei, Feruccio Parri, philosopher Guido Calogero, economist Ugo La Malfa and younger idealists like Raffaele Persichetti. The party had too many leaders and too few soldiers. Even so, its radicalism, anticlericalism and antimonarchic feelings never failed to worry Bonomi.

He got along better with Liberals like former cabinet ministers Alessandro Casati and Marcello Soleri, and younger men like Nicolo Carandini, Leone Cattani and Enzo Storari who wanted a return to parliamentary government as it existed before fascism.

Bonomi's own party, Labor Democracy, consisted of older men. Although minuscule, it regarded itself as the standard-bearer of Italy's historic Left. However, Bonomi's belief in democracy was confined to the abstract; in fact he was all for rule by an elite. He had written in his carefully kept diary: "We cannot look to mass movements nor to strikes for the power to overthrow Mussolini."

The Catholic Democrats, led by Alcide De Gasperi, who had left the safety of the Vatican to reorganize the old Popular party, retained its Catholic flavor.

The Rome Committee's meetings were full of talk; plans were always on the verge of completion, action was always just ahead. Bonomi was afraid the Actionists would push the monarchy into alliance with dissident Fascists, and that the Anglo-Americans might then deal with both the monarchy *and* the dissident Fascists. He thought the transition from fascism to democracy should be realized in harmony with the crown, and, like almost all the plotters, he believed that he and his group had the tacit support of Vittorio Emanuele.

He was received by the king without any real encouragement but with just enough warmth to allow him to think that anti-Fascists would have a role to play in the overthrowing of Mussolini and the forming of post-fascism governments.

In reality, however, Bonomi had little justification for his views. His meetings with the king were, in his own words, disappointing. On June 2, he had written in his diary: "He passes over every proposition. He doesn't discuss it or confute it: he contemplates it with the eye of the skeptic . . . and finds a way to comment ironically on Roosevelt, president of a plutocratic republic and now allied with Communist Russia." Bonomi confided to his diary that the king "seemed old, tired, discouraged. He kept complaining about his health."

A few days later, Marcello Soleri, a former Liberal cabinet minister, was given a tidbit of information by Acquarone: Mussolini would be arrested and replaced in the first days of June 1943. But the date passed and the king was still hesitant. On the eighth, in fact, Soleri was received by the king, who let him talk for more than half an hour without either interrupting or offering an opinion. "The king," Soleri told Bonomi, "is spiritually against the Anglo-Americans and is still breathing the atmosphere of the Axis."

In his own way Bonomi was as irresolute as the king and almost as fearful. Although loyal to his ideals, he could not adapt to reality and was continually surprised by events. In his diary for July 24, Bonomi wrote:

> Today at 5 P.M., a well-known anti-Fascist, Domenico Maiocco, from Piedmont, a close friend of Quadrumvir de Vecchi [a founder of fascism], came to see me. He confirmed that the Grand Council was about to meet and that the deliberations would be of exceptional importance. De Vecchi had told him that in the morning Grandi and Federzoni had persuaded him to sign a motion returning rule to the king, asking him at the same time to use this to get rid of Mussolini. De Vecchi was sure of victory, Mussolini would be out and those who presented the motion would form the new government. But de Vecchi wanted to know if I would join them. I thought it was like something out of a novel.

The Marshals

While Bonomi was seeing his informative friend, Marshal Pietro Badoglio was playing bridge with some of his cronies in the sumptuous villa he had been given by the city of Rome. As he dealt the cards, Badoglio gave no hint to his friends that at noon he had been visited by an imposing delegation consisting of the duke of Acquarone and Generals Ambrosio and Castellano. They had told him that the king wanted to oust Mussolini and that he had Badoglio in mind as future head of the government. Badoglio was shown a draft copy of the proclamation he was to read over the radio once the plot had come off. The marshal found no fault with it, particularly when he was told that it had been written by a friend, eighty-three-year-old Vittorio Emanuele Orlando, a former prime minister who had once brought a halt to an investigation into Badoglio's dereliction of duty.

With his bald head and round face, Badoglio appeared to be a superannuated baby despite his seventy-two years. Beneath this ingenuous exterior he concealed the natural astuteness of a peasant from Piedmont. As the intrigues thickened between the royal palace, Badoglio's villa, the offices of ministers, the hotels of Via Veneto, and the villas and offices of ruling Fascists, Badoglio dealt out cards, bid, was doubled, made his hand.

A virtual hero to the Italian people mainly because of his successes in Ethiopia, Badoglio was typical of the country's military leaders. Italy had never been known for its generals: outside of Garibaldi—not a professional soldier—and Napoleon—brought up in France even if born of Italian parents—none were outstanding. They did not do too badly in local wars mainly because, if the country had bad generals, it also had good soldiers.

Italy's worst defeat, Caporetto, came about at least partially because of Badoglio. It was the third year of World War I and his army corps, the XXVII, was the first to retreat before the Austrians. Generals who were on the spot said Badoglio, in command of artillery, had not been at his post, and his failure to use the corps' eight hundred cannon caused the loss of several divisions and the collapse of the entire front.

But it was a measure of Badoglio's ability off the battlefield that he was not censured, that an investigative commission had its work halted by Orlando, prime minister at the time, when he learned that it was about to confirm Badoglio's irresponsibility, and that thirteen pages "extremely critical of Badoglio" were taken out of the commission's report and subsequently disappeared for fifty-one years, until they were mentioned in an army report in 1967.

Despite the charges, Badoglio was made deputy chief of staff of the Italian Armed Forces. If he had failed as a tactician, he now showed his worth as a strategist. He was so successful that he was promoted to general of the army and was generally credited with stopping the Austro-Hungarian offensive on the Piave and forcing the signing of an armistice. In 1922 he became ambassador to Brazil. When in 1924 the *Duce*, urged by Cavallero, communicated to the king his decision to name Badoglio chief of General Staff, the king told him, *"Signor Presidente,* think it over. I have known Badoglio longer and better than you. It would be well to leave him in Brazil and then retire him. He's a strange and difficult fish."

But Mussolini had replied, "His telegram during the Matteotti crisis involved him so much with fascism that I don't think we can have any more doubts about him."

Badoglio's first notable success as chief of General Staff came in Libya, where he had fresh concrete poured down the throats of captured rebels. Leading Italian forces in the brutal subjugation of Ethiopia, he did not hesitate to use poison gas, even mustard gas, despite the Geneva Convention. He was still losing the war in 1936, however, when SIM intercepted the emperor's phone calls and tipped Badoglio off to the plans and positions of the Negus' army.

As soon as Badoglio entered Addis Ababa, he had himself named viceroy and took everything not nailed down in the imperial palace. He is said to have sold part; with the rest he furnished his villa in Rome, using the imperial throne of the Negus as a couch for his poodle. At the end of the Ethiopian war, he asked for and obtained the hereditary title of duke of Addis Ababa, although the king had earlier given him the title of marquis of Sabotino, also at his own request. He also arranged to be paid his viceregal salary for life in addition to his pay as chief of General Staff, which he had received on top of his emoluments as governor of Libya.

Besides the villa in Rome, he had another in his native Piedmont which was the result of public subscription. So as not to spend any of his various stipends, Badoglio charged the equivalent of half a dollar for each visit. Still another home was built for him by industrialists on his father's vineyard. He also received a check for five million lire from the Fascist party in return for which he outdid Fascist toadies in his fulsome praise of Mussolini.

Because of all this he was characterized as hypocritical and treacherous. One critic, Nino d'Aroma, wrote: "Never in the history of our country have we seen a more calculating man, one so greedy for honors and soft jobs, completely lacking in intelligence and courage, yet named to the nation's highest posts, even in our most desperate circumstances."

After he had told Mussolini that the armed forces could be ready "at any moment and in any necessity," the development of the war showed him guilty of a shocking lack of preparation. On June 8, 1940, General Carboni suggested that his resignation as chief of General Staff might halt Italy's declaration of war. Badoglio answered, "I really don't think there's anything to do. And then, who knows but that Mussolini is right; we can be sure the Germans are very strong and they *could* obtain a quick victory." It was obvious that Badoglio hoped to hide his own unpreparedness with German superiority. Finally Mussolini had had enough and, after the Greek debacle, forced Badoglio to resign, although Badoglio later attempted to paint this dismissal as punishment for having stood up to the dictator.

Roberto Farinacci, Badoglio's most incisive critic, called him "traitor number one. His telegram to Mussolini, his Fascist speeches, his petition for titles, his protests of loyalty were false, all false. Only Mussolini could believe him. This man took everything he could from the regime, squeezed it like a lemon, but, while squeezing it, he was already thinking about how to throw it away. From the moment he retired to private life he was the pole of all the discontented generals, ministers, ex-ministers, important personalities, industrialists and even some hierarchs I could name. Even the Royal House."

Farinacci could have added the anti-Fascists who, attracted by Badoglio's opposition to Mussolini, went to him with their plans and hopes.

Now, in 1943, although the generals knew that the war was virtually lost, they were more concerned with the ferocious rivalry which existed between them. This was particularly acute among the four active marshals of Italy among whom the king had thought to find a new head of government. A fifth, eighty-year-old Emilio De Bono, had led the March on Rome but now confined himself to sitting on the Grand Council.

Ugo Cavallero, Badoglio's successor as chief of General Staff, was president of the giant Ansaldo Steelworks, and well known for his Fascist sentiments and bonds with the Germans. He had been made a marshal by Mussolini while in Africa so that he would be equal in rank to Erwin Rommel, who was promoted to field marshal by Hitler. Rodolfo Graziani, Badoglio's deputy in Africa, who became a marshal after Ethiopia, was also a noted pro-German.

The oldest marshal, Enrico Caviglia, definitely anti-Fascist, enjoyed as much prestige as Badoglio and was more respected for his integrity. But he had been far from active command for too long and had lost contact with the army's top officers. He hated the "conspiratorial" marshals—Cavallero, whom he judged dishonest, and Badoglio, whom he characterized as "a dog of straw ready to go where the mouthful is biggest"—and thus preferred to keep himself above the mess.

D

The king had long hesitated between Caviglia and Badoglio, but he regarded Caviglia as too oriented towards the Anglo-Americans, too anti-Fascist, and as likely to bring about a revival of Freemasonry. Badoglio, on the other hand, had been known to the king for thirty years, was also from Piedmont, and, despite the charges against him, had always maintained a following among the masses. As chief of General Staff during the first part of World War II, he had left behind him personal coteries in the army and enjoyed a certain popularity among lower officers and subalterns. Due to his long career, he had impressive connections. There was Acquarone who had been his ordinance officer and later kept him informed of the king's plans. There was Ambrosio, considered by many to be Badoglio's man, his confidant, who filled him in on the generals' plotting.

The Church approved of Badoglio; in January 1943, emissaries had been sent to him by Vatican Secretary of State Cardinal Maglione to find out if he would cooperate in getting rid of Mussolini.

Besides, he was a valid representative of the men around the monarchy and, with his avidity for wealth, an extreme conservative. No one could be more qualified to maintain the status quo. The king wanted a man who could get rid of the bad features of fascism without abrupt shocks, as well as save it from its reactionary core, the monopolists, the plutocrats, the exploiters. The new government would have to detach itself from the German allies without reaction on the part of the Nazis. In addition, a close control would have to be kept on the anti-Fascists. What the king really wanted was a return to pre-Fascist days with respect for authority embodied in the king and, above all, "healthy social conservatism."

When notified that day of his coming appointment, Badoglio was not overly surprised. He had had an audience with the king on July 20, when the monarch had mentioned the possibility to him and asked him if he would accept. He answered affirmatively, adding that he had been assured of the cooperation of Bonomi and other anti-Fascist politicians. The king said, "That would be a government of ghosts." To which Badoglio had replied, "Then you and I, too, Your Majesty, are ghosts."

Although the king was vague as usual, he insisted that he did not want a government of anti-Fascists. For one thing, if he undertook negotiations for peace it would look as if he were following their lead. For another, an anti-Fascist government would mean action taken against Fascists with whom the king had been allied for twenty years.

On Saturday, Badoglio was told that the plot was ready to go into operation. The old marshal was not fazed at all. That afternoon, in fact, he invited his friends to return the following afternoon for the usual game. He would worry about the burden of responsibility later.

The Party Hacks

When Mussolini, having brought his gastric attack under control, returned to his office, the weight of his self-assumed burden began again to fall heavily upon him. For too long, although he had always described his dictatorship in terms of headlines, he had occupied himself with some of his regime's most minute details. He ran the four ministries of which he was titular head so thoroughly that when he was out of town they virtually stopped functioning. Now, suddenly, it all began to close in on him. His personal attendant at Palazzo Venezia, Chief Usher Quinto Navarra, did his best to buoy up the dictator's sagging ego, but to no avail. As Navarra later said, "It was easy to see he was fed up with it all—he had stopped sticking colored flags in his war map."

This dispiritedness was undoubtedly the reason the dictator ignored the warnings of plots that came to him from almost all sides. It had begun at lunch at Villa Torlonia, where he had tried to pass as much time as possible. His wife, known to Romans as donna Rachele, uncomfortable in the big house, kept doing domestic chores, even feeding the chickens as she had done on their farm in Carpena. Intuitively suspicious of those close to her husband, she again repeated her warnings. Four days earlier she had told him of a list she had been given and said it was "time to do something about Ciano, Grandi, Badoglio and the rest." But he had told her he was more worried about American tanks than Italian intrigues.

At the door of the villa on Saturday, she warned him again: "Have them all arrested before the meeting begins." But he said nothing, kissed her, and walked to his car. After he had gone she wrote in her diary: "He honestly believes that everything will work out for the best."

In his office he did his best to control his stomach pains; in the past, Navarra had seen him roll on the floor groaning in pain. From the papers on his desk he took up one he had written earlier. It was a list of the armed forces ministries he held. Next to each he had written the names of generals and admirals. Although he might not yet have made up his mind, he had clearly thought of pacifying opposition in the council by giving up his posts to the men he had listed. According to the small piece of paper, even Ambrosio was out, to be replaced by Roatta. This maneuver was to be used only as a last resort, and now Mussolini looked at it again and then put it in the blue folder which had been given him by his secretary. On its cover, in firm forceful script, he wrote: "July 24, Grand Council."

As he sat there thinking over what he would say at the meeting, he must have been reminded of the position he had been in during the Matteotti crisis in 1924. Then his office was a mile up Corso Umberto at Palazzo Chigi, and outside, people were ostentatiously throwing away their party buttons, the *cimicette*, little bedbugs.

Supposedly he had told the murderers, "You haven't killed Matteotti, you've killed fascism." But they had not; it was still alive even if it had begun to resemble a hollow shell. Officially, there were over four million Fascists in Italy in 1943, but only seven hundred thousand or so were card-carrying members. The party secretary was Carlo Scorza, a fifty-one-year-old Calabrian who had been charged with the murder of Liberal leader Giovanni Amendola in 1925. A hard man, his bullet-like head virtually bald, Scorza was a journalist without scruples and a former Fascist Youth leader. He kept busy attacking defeatism and pumping up optimism despite defeats and the resultant dissatisfaction.

On July 24, Scorza came to Mussolini in the guise of a faithful servitor. He had seen Grandi three days earlier, had said he was with him, and had volunteered to present Grandi's resolution at the Grand Council. Instead, however, he had shown his copy to Mussolini. Now, as Scorza spoke again of the conspiracies against Mussolini, the dictator was skeptical and annoyed.

"Does this seem to you the moment to speak of such foolishness? Don't make up detective stories," he snapped.

Then Scorza told him of an intercepted telephone conversation between the duke of Acquarone and Badoglio that day concerning "making a parcel out of the *Duce*."

"I don't like cowards," Mussolini answered.

A former party secretary, Roberto Farinacci, had also warned Mussolini. Violent and discredited, without friends in high places, Farinacci was the man who had forced the resignation of Badoglio after Italy's defeats in Greece. Considered to have completely sold out to the Germans, he wanted to entrust them with the direction of the war with the armed forces back under Marshal Cavallero, another devoted follower of the Third Reich.

After meetings with various groups of plotters, he had told Mussolini details involving Acquarone, Ambrosio and Badoglio. The dictator, however, did not take him seriously.

Farinacci also quoted Cavallero as warning of plots, and passed on the marshal's note: "Be more and more careful. Grandi and Company are conspiring to defenestrate Mussolini, but their game will be in vain anyway as the royal house, together with Acquarone, is carrying the fight and will deceive them all."

"Calm down," Mussolini replied. "As far as the king is concerned, I am perfectly covered."

He was still head of the Fascist party with its militants, its armed forces, its adherents. They would stand by their *Duce*. But just as many Italians were beginning to understand the real essence of fascism, very few Fascists were really ready to resist an attack on the regime or even on its leader. The various groups of conspirators, though, thought much as Mussolini did, that the Fascists would stand by the *Duce*, and they worked out their plots accordingly.

The Germans

The Germans in Rome were surprisingly unaware of plans and plots. For nineteen months the German commander in chief of Forces South (Mediterranean) had been Field Marshal Albert Konrad Kesselring. When he chose, Kesselring exercised a good deal of charm which concealed the ruthlessness of a trained German field officer. A soldier to his fingertips, he had been in the *Wehrmacht* for thirty-four of his fifty-eight years. In World War I he had been a captain of artillery. From then on, he had risen almost as rapidly as Hitler; he helped Reich Marshal Hermann Goering build up the *Luftwaffe* and used it against Britain and Rotterdam.

On July 24, Kesselring was in his small private office in a villa near Frascati, high above Rome, mapping his next military moves. Politically he seemed to believe he had no worries. The day before, the German ambassador to Italy, Baron Hans Georg von Mackensen, had told him that he had positive information that there was no danger from the Grand Council meeting and that Mussolini was still master of the situation. Mackensen himself had sent the Fuehrer a telegram saying that Mussolini and fascism were stronger than ever and that Mussolini would very likely use the pro-German Farinacci to overcome the crisis.

Besides, Kesselring himself had gone to see Mussolini several days earlier and waited in the room being prepared for the Grand Council meeting while the dictator saw Grandi. When Kesselring had finally been admitted into the impressive office a half hour later, Mussolini had beamed at him. "Do you know Grandi?" he had asked. "He's just left me. We had a heart-to-heart talk, our views are identical. He is loyally devoted to me."

Although Kesselring had limited forces at his disposal, he managed to make the most of them. In July 1943, four divisions were still fighting in Sicily; two armored divisions (the 16th and 26th) were in southern Italy, another was in Sardinia, and only the 3rd Panzergrenadieren Division was in central Italy, incompletely equipped and short of tanks. Some parachutist regiments were in the same area but the 3rd Panzergrenadieren represented the only immediate striking force at the disposal of the Germans for internal action near Rome.

In maneuvering these forces, Kesselring was aided by his chief of staff, General Siegfried Westphal, ingenious, full of ideas, and the youngest general in the German army. Headquarters of Ober Befehl Sud (Superior Command South) were near Frascati, seventeen miles from Rome.

Because Italy was a military ally, a certain number of liaison functions were carried out by officials at the German embassy. At the time this was Villa Wolkonsky, located in a five-acre park in the southern part of Rome. That July the swimming pool was seeing a lot of use. One of the first in Rome, it was built in 1939 by Hitler as a gift to the then German ambassador, Field Marshal August von Mackensen.

In 1943, August von Mackensen's son, Hans Georg, as ambassador, tended to trade on his father's reputation. The conflict of personalities within the embassy was so constant that the thin-lipped Mackensen usually left day-to-day details to his aides.

His principal assistant was Eitel Friedrich Moellhausen, at thirty the youngest chief of a diplomatic mission in Europe, with the rank of consul. Tall, slim, ascetic, he was known as the Byzantine Christ, although he liked to dance in semi-darkened rooms, his chest bared, his eyes half-closed, gyrating in voluptuous gestures.

His *bête noire* was SS Standartenfuehrer Eugen Dollmann, who had given him the appellation. Although Dollmann's only real affection was for his mother, female aristocrats of Rome doted on him and on his brilliant, if superficial, conversation delivered in perfect Italian. He had lived in Italy almost from the advent of nazism. No one really knew what his job was at the beginning of his mission, although he reported directly to Heinrich Himmler, chief of the dreaded SS. He quickly became the official interpreter between Hitler and Mussolini and the friend and confidant of members of both regimes. Though he was only a colonel, he occupied a more important position than that of many three-starred generals, providing a striking contrast to the men around Hitler, many of whom suffered from an inferiority complex because of their ignorance of worldly things. As a result, he occupied an unusual but unofficial position as a sort of cultural counselor, a kind of bard of the system, and, as such, was right next to the top of the regime. It shocked American art critic Bernard Berenson who said of him, "How can a man of such excellent culture, sensitivity and judgment be Himmler's lieutenant?"

Despite the Semitic cast of his nose, Dollmann was definitely a Nazi. He showed a marked inclination for uniforms, and when he put one on it became like a second skin. Dressed in black with the hooked cross on his sleeve, and driving around in a sleek Mercedes, he was a familiar figure in Fascist Rome. Meticulously dressed and beautifully mannered, he was a favorite of the Fuehrer and his mistress, Eva Braun.

The Gestapo was represented by thirty-six-year-old SS Obersturmbannfuehrer (Lieutenant Colonel) Herbert Kappler, security head in Rome. Kappler, who had small, piercing eyes set in a taut, bony face, was an introvert; he had a difficult wife whom he was trying to divorce. His hobbies were roses, photography, dogs, and the blond son he had adopted from the *Lebensborn,* the ill-famed SS institution which mated Germans of pure Aryan blood to breed "experimental" children. Because he was much more realistic than any of his colleagues, he had a better grasp of the political situation than they did. Speaking in his habitual monotone, he had once said, "Politics is not my field, but if I were asked I would say that neofascism has to disappear so that we can hold onto the last vestige of German prestige in Italy. This requires the elimination of Mussolini, and if I were charged with that task, I would know how to carry it out."

Although Infantry General Enno von Rintelen, German military attaché and liaison officer to the Supreme Command, was subordinate to Kesselring for command functions, he reported directly to OKW, the German High Command, as well. He had come to Italy in 1939 after having been trained in espionage and security. He liked Italy and Rome so much that he had learned the language and had had his parents join him while he devoted himself to the collection of Etruscan vases.

Hitler, meanwhile, was more concerned about the Italians than were his men in Rome. From his point of view the Italians were not sufficiently interested in the war. Two months earlier he had been told by Baron Konstantin von Neurath, a former foreign minister, that Rome had a peace-time appearance, with "the streets presenting a picture as if nothing had happened in the last two years." Lieutenant General Walter Warlimont, an able, farsighted Rhinelander who was present when Neurath made the remark, protested that this had been true only when Neurath was there.

But the diplomat insisted that German soldiers were hardly visible: "Germans are only in uniform at headquarters and the railroad station." It was his impression that Kesselring had adopted this posture because of Vatican pressure and the attitude of the people in Rome to the Germans.

When Neurath told Hitler that these same people supported a flourishing black market, the Fuehrer was indignant. "How can you get rid of this [the black market] in a country where the leaders of the armed forces and of the state . . . the whole country is nothing but a mass of corruption?"

On July 24, despite Mackensen's telegram from Rome and a report from Prince Philip of Hesse, the Germans' confidential liaison officer to the Italian court, Hitler was worried about the rumor that Mussolini would have to give up personal command of the armed forces.

"At any moment," he had said two months earlier, "there may be a crisis there on the lines that we've been discussing. One has to be on the watch like a spider in its web. Thank God I've always had a pretty good nose for this kind of thing so that I can generally smell things out before they happen."

He had already received from Colonel General Alfred Jodl, chief of the High Command Operations Staff, his "Survey of the situation should Italy withdraw from the war." He had instructed Field Marshal Rommel to make all preparations, in collaboration with OKW, to take over as commander in chief in Italy, in place of Kesselring, the moment an Italian collapse took place. In Hitler's opinion, Kesselring saw everything through rose-colored glasses. "We must be careful," he said, "that in his optimism he doesn't fail to see the moment when optimism must be discarded and severity takes its place."

Hitler briefed Rommel personally, as he did Colonel General Alexander Loehr, the commander in chief in the Balkans. Because he was determined to keep matters secret from the Italians, Hitler forbade any written instructions, merely using the code names ALARICH for German protective measures in Italy and KONSTANTIN for the Balkans.

Hitler was convinced that the men around Mussolini wer pro-English spies. "Every memorandum I sent the *Duce* was immediately transmitted to England," he once recalled. "So I only put in things I definitely wanted the English to see. It was the quickest way to get through to England."

After Rommel had been briefed, however, Hitler postponed the announcement of his appointment. One reason was the protestations of Ambassador Mackensen in Rome, supported by Air Chief Goering, who thought he knew the situation better than Hitler. Much of Mackensen's information came from Fascist hierarchs who, following an ancient Italian custom, told the Germans what they wanted to hear.

The Allies

At times the Allies—the United States and Great Britain—appeared to be getting their information about Italy from completely contradictory sources. This, added to their varying attitudes and contrasting forms of government, resulted in points of view concerning that country that were so dissimilar as to threaten the conduct of the war.

That Saturday, their differences were coming to a head. General Dwight D. Eisenhower, commander in chief of Allied forces in the Mediterranean, sat in his office in Algiers and wondered at the spate of messages which had flown between Washington, London and his headquarters in the past few days.

Exactly one year earlier, on July 24, 1942, the decision had been made to mount an invasion of North Africa, and two days later Eisenhower had been named to lead it. Now, after the Sicily landings, the operation could be considered more than a complete success. As Eisenhower read the various cables, Colonel James Gavin's paratroopers were taking Trapani and the trucks which had transported them turned back to shuttle the 504th Parachute Infantry to its objective on the north coast. By noon on July 24, the 504th was in Alcamo; by 5:30 P.M., just as the Grand Council convened in Rome, they were in Castellamare. Meanwhile, the Canadians took the key town of Nissoria.

At this rate, the conquest of Sicily was well under way. The step after this was the Allies' next problem, and here the Americans and the British found themselves seriously at odds.

The Americans undoubtedly had a conservative and deliberate approach; the Joint Chiefs of Staff wanted to stage only limited operations in the Mediterranean, while conserving most of their resources for the invasion of northern France, seeing this latter course as the quickest, most efficient way to break through to German power.

General George C. Marshall, U.S. Army chief of staff, had told Eisenhower that this was "the decisive effort" to win the war; future considerations would be taken care of when they came up. Why occupy Italy? It was not a vital area, and occupation would involve a huge shipping derangement. Occupation would only help the Germans—saving them rolling stock, coal and other materials they were supplying Italy—while the Allies would be forced to maintain the Italian economy. Italy could be brought to her knees without invading the mainland, said the Americans; the conquest of Sicily and stepped-up aerial bombardment would do it.

The British, on the other hand, wanted to throw nearly all available resources into Mediterranean operations and to force Italy out of the war; in the words of British Prime Minister Winston Churchill, "weakening the enemy at every point of his over-extended circumferences before striking at the most vulnerable . . . the soft underbelly." For Churchill, this meant controlling the Mediterranean, the "Sea of Destiny." The German Afrika Korps lost on land because, like Napoleon, Hitler did not control the sea. Churchill wanted the Mediterranean to be held "at all costs," and, once it had been secured, an attack made on the Axis right flank through the weakly held Balkans. He had already written South African Field Marshal Jan Smuts on July 16: "Not only must we take Rome and march as far north as possible in Italy, but our right hand must give succour to the Balkan patriots."

Before the invasion of Sicily, Churchill had also wanted to bring Turkey into the war as a base for Allied air-sea operations in the Balkans, but the Americans had again insisted on priority for the invasion of northern France from England. The switching of emphasis away from the Mediterranean, as Harold Macmillan, Churchill's representative in North Africa, later wrote, meant sowing "the seeds of the partition of Europe," leading to "the tragic divisions which were to dominate all political and strategic thinking for a generation." But the Americans, in their determination to remain uncommitted in Eastern Europe, had already turned thumbs down on the quaintly named Operation Armpit, the British plan to advance northeast to Trieste and Austria, which if carried out might have saved the independence of some of the East European countries later ruled from Moscow. Rumania and Bulgaria were already trying to use Rome's good offices to get out from under Hitler's domination.

With the Balkan gambit doomed, Sir Charles Portal, British air chief, maintained that a full scale attack on German industry, particularly on factories producing fighter planes, could only be effective with the help of Italian airfields. In addition, possession of Italian airfields would help the Allies to protect their shipping in the Mediterranean. To make their point, the British chiefs of staff sent a memo to the Combined Chiefs of Staff—American and British—saying that the Sicilian campaign was proof that Italy could be eliminated from the war and that Italian defeat was "the best if not the essential preliminary to the earliest possible defeat of Germany."

The Americans remained unmoved. The State Department followed the line of Secretary of State Cordell Hull, who had said that Italy was "of doubtful interest strategically," and the U.S. Joint Chiefs of Staff refused to believe that the conquest of Italy would threaten Germany or that bombing Germany from Italian airfields would advance the war effort. Harold Macmillan thought the Americans saw the war as an athletic contest instead of as a continuation of policy—except in their terror of British imperialism. The arguments had persisted for so long that Americans had become distrustful of British strategic intentions, calling them "over-optimistic" and "typically vague."

In fact, in their *idée fixe* that the British were trying to use the Mediterranean campaign as an alternative to a cross-Channel invasion, the Americans at the TRIDENT conference in Washington that May had insisted on troop and ship movements out of the Mediterranean and had seen to it that the Pacific and Burma were given priority over the Mediterranean for the last half of 1943.

This movement of naval and land forces and amphibious equipment was also based on other political factors. The emphasis on a cross-Channel invasion was to keep the promises made to Stalin. At the time, both England and America were bidding for Russia's support, even going so far as to deal occasionally with the Soviet Union unilaterally. Stalin, for his part, was doing his best to keep the Allies as far away from Eastern Europe as possible. He already had his eye on Greece and would have preferred to leave Italy to the Axis for the time being rather than have the Anglo-Americans there. So, along with the Americans, he pushed the project of Channel invasion. The date had been initially set for 1942, then reset for 1943, and then postponed again, with apologies and reassurances to the Russians.

The Pacific priority was due to the insistent demands of General Douglas MacArthur's friends in Washington that aid be increased to that area. With elections coming up in 1944 and MacArthur a potential candidate, President Franklin D. Roosevelt felt compelled to soften criticism. If the American people were going to express their opinion on how the war was being conducted, strictly military considerations would have to take second place.

Eisenhower was caught in the middle. "Ike," wrote his navy aide, Lieutenant Commander Harry Butcher in his diary, "is confronted with a difficult situation. If he fails to exploit what now appears to be a rapidly approaching victory over Italy, history will say that he 'missed the boat,' yet our own government seems to want to slam on the brake just when the going gets good."

With success in Sicily, an attack on Italy from the south had become attractive. On Sunday, July 18, Eisenhower cabled his recommendation to the Combined Chiefs of Staff that, as soon as Messina was taken, his forces should cross the straits and carry the war to the mainland. He also proposed that an attack on the toe and heel of Italy be accompanied by a landing in the Bay of Salerno, almost two hundred miles up the coast, in order to cut off Calabria and seize the port of Naples.

All the next day, on Monday the nineteenth, the Americans and the British debated the issue in Washington. Though General Marshall had always been opposed to Britain's concentric strategy, he had said that if the Sicilian campaign ended quickly enough to allow for further operations without prejudicing the build-up of the cross-Channel operation, an attack should be made on Italy at Salerno.

On Tuesday, the twentieth, to London's surprise, both he and Admiral Ernest J. King, United States chief of naval operations, went along with Eisenhower's proposal.

Churchill was delighted. "Why crawl up the leg like a harvest bug from the ankle upwards?" he asked. "Let us rather strike at the knee." In addition, he made it known that he would be content with nothing short of the capture of Rome. Earlier, in Algiers, he had talked of Rome as the most productive Allied objective in the theatre. "The capture of Rome with or without the elimination of Italy from the war," he concluded, "would be a very great achievement for our Mediterranean forces."

Churchill was a leader who tended to give the impression of omniscience, but his desire for the invasion of Italy was based as much on chauvinism as on foresight, and his military justification cloaked, at least in part, political and personal motives. Sir Alan Brooke, British chief of the Imperial General Staff, had even written in his diary that Churchill was "inclined at times to put up strategic proposals which in his heart he knew were unsound purely to spite the Americans. . . . There lay . . . at the back of his mind the desire to form a purely British theatre when the laurels would be all ours."

In addition, there was the prospect of revenge on Mussolini, once much admired by Churchill. The Italian dictator's actions in the Mediterranean after 1935 had dealt British prestige a severe blow, and losses imposed on the once impregnable British fleet by the Italian navy had left the English thirsting for revenge.

The British chiefs of staff, swept along by Churchill's optimism, believed that American consent on the twentieth for the Salerno operations known as AVALANCHE meant a really full scale invasion. They even assumed that extra shipping, aircraft carriers and escorts would be available, and that a direct attack on Naples would be possible. When, two days later, they noted that the Axis dictators had not gotten anywhere at their Feltre meeting, the British issued a temporary standstill instruction to all aircraft and ships which had been under previous orders to leave the Mediterranean.

However, this was a grave misreading of American intentions. Washington insisted that the original movement orders be carried out and that no reinforcements be sent to Eisenhower, who would have to get by on what he had. That was not all—four of Eisenhower's heavy bomber groups (B-24 Liberators), four American and three British divisions, and the bulk of the landing craft were to be gradually withdrawn to Britain, there to remain idle until the Channel operation scheduled for May 1944.

On that day, July 24, 1943, Brooke wrote in his diary: "A very disappointing wire from American Chiefs of Staff. Marshall absolutely fails to realize that strategic treasures lie at our feet in the Mediterranean and hankers after cross-Channel operations. He admits that our object must be to eliminate Italy and yet is always afraid of facing the consequences of doing so. . . ."

What the British did not fully realize was that an even higher authority, Henry Stimson, the seventy-three-year-old secretary of war, was the main opponent of invasion of Italy. He stuck stubbornly to his belief that a Western Front was the only way to end World War II. To Stimson, the invasion of Sicily was an unfortunate diversion. The only effect of such entanglements, as he called them, would be to withhold resources from the Channel operation and give the British more excuses to abandon their commitment to invade France the following spring. And so, still unpersuaded by British arguments, Stimson prepared to depart for Allied headquarters in Algiers.

In Algiers, Harold Macmillan served as the voice of Winston Churchill. As British minister of state, his duties were rather indeterminate. His American counterpart was the State Department's Robert Murphy who viewed Americans in the Mediterranean as "a reluctant tail to the British kite." He also saw this relationship with the British as damaging ties with the French. The British, plumping for the Mediterranean campaign to extend into Europe, tried to establish a strong central French authority. The Americans did not agree, partly because they kept looking at the Mediterranean expedition as a temporary one and partly because of Roosevelt's views about the future of France and the presence of Charles de Gaulle.

A little over a month earlier, the president had written to Churchill:

> I am fed up with De Gaulle and the secret personal and political machinations in the last few days indicates that there is no possibility of our working with De Gaulle. I agree with you that he likes neither the British nor the Americans, he has more recently been interested far more in political machinations than he has in the prosecution of the war and these machinations have been carried on without our knowledge and to the detriment of our military interest. One result of this scheming on the part of De Gaulle has been that Eisenhower has had to give half his time to a purely local political situation which De Gaulle has accentuated. The war is so urgent and our military operations so serious and fraught with danger that we cannot have them menaced any longer by De Gaulle.

On July 24, despite Soviet Foreign Minister Vyacheslav Molotov's urging, De Gaulle's government was still not recognized as such by what the French leader termed the Anglo-Saxons. In fact, the

Americans complained that day about being unable to get the French to adopt and enforce adequate economic warfare controls. De Gaulle, for his part, was irked because he had not been included in the North African landings and was not being fully consulted on plans for Italy.

There was a good reason for this. With the invasion of Sicily having proceeded so quickly, it was necessary to agree on surrender terms. The British had drawn up a draft to which the United States Joint Chiefs objected, since, among other things, it failed to include unconditional surrender. The differences between British and American views were so wide that the subject was referred to a newly created Combined Civil Affairs Committee. From the time this committee took up the problem on July 10, the Anglo-American war policy machinery was stalled. How could they complicate matters further by having the cantankerous De Gaulle put in his two *sous* worth?

The United States was having enough trouble with its closest ally. Britain had set the policy regarding Italy's future rule. As expressed by Churchill, the British position was: "One man and one man alone [is] responsible for Italy's being in the war." Later, however, he indicated a willingness to deal with almost anyone who could command the people of Italy. Although Churchill's policy implied the destruction of fascism, it failed to identify the Fascists. Obviously, in any drawing of lines, the king and his son would have to be included, but the British surely did not want to see the monarchy discarded. As a consequence, for awhile, the Americans soft pedaled condemnation of the House of Savoy in broadcasts to Italy and attacked Mussolini rather than fascism until, according to American author Norman Kogan, "Italian anti-Fascists in America thought the Allied goals were to restore Fascism without Mussolini."

Churchill was not the only one to allow political and personal considerations to influence policy. The United States contained large numbers of Italian voters likely to be alienated if overly severe measures were meted out to the homeland; and since the territorial position of Italy meant nothing to American global policy, official attitudes, as expressed in propaganda broadcasts, changed. The House of Savoy was no longer exempt from condemnation, the king was caricatured, and anti-Fascists were again singled out for favorable mention.

These divergent policies had almost collided on the question of bombing Rome. Although the Allies seemed to agree in public, the

Americans were inclined to avoid bombing the Eternal City, while the English kept asking that military objects in and near the capital be bombed when necessary. Thus, the July 19 raid was in accordance with British wishes to bring about an Italian surrender as quickly as possible.

Five days later, however, the State Department had no idea of what peace terms to dictate should such an eventuality come to pass. It was not that the possibility had not been discussed, but the British had proposed a long and detailed list of conditions to which the Americans, given their political exigencies, could not agree. On July 24, the British were still waiting for an answer from Washington.

The Hierarchs

Unity of purpose was far from an outstanding characteristic of the hierarchs who constituted the Fascist regime. Each spent the afternoon of the twenty-fourth in the way most suited to his personality. Dino Grandi passed two hours after lunch in heavy discussion with Ciano and Bottai, hammering out the final version of his motion. Then he had it typed on two foolscap sheets of the Chamber by Angela Tarantini, a secretary there. At the bottom of the text he wrote the date, July 24, 1943, without adding the year of the Fascist era. He signed as "President of the Chamber," intentionally omitting "of Federations and Corporations."

Finally he wrote the king what, shorn of its rhetoric, could only be seen as his signal that he was about to provide the monarch with the constitutional pretext needed to overthrow Mussolini. "Sire," he wrote, "it is my duty to bring to the knowledge of Your Majesty the enclosed motion that, at this moment, comforted by the support of some friends, I am submitting to the Grand Council at Palazzo Venezia. This will be the extreme attempt aiming at determining the restoration of statutory guarantees and prerogatives to the Crown. Not only as 'President of the Chamber,' but also as soldier, may I plead with Your Majesty in such serious and decisive hours for the future of the nation and of the monarchy, not to abandon the country. Only the king can still save the nation. Devotedly, Dino Grandi."

After enclosing a copy of the resolution with his letter, he called Mario Zamboni who, besides being a national councillor and a lieutenant colonel at the Supreme Command, was also a friend of Acquarone. Receiving Zamboni in his private apartment at 4:00 P.M.,

Grandi said with a forced smile, "Give this to the duke of Acquarone as soon as you can, but in person. It's my political testament."

Then Grandi put the finishing touches to his will and dressed in the comic opera costume called for by the occasion—a *sahariana*, the three-quarter-length black bush-shirt which council members, at Mussolini's orders, were required to wear along with breeches, boots and Sam Browne belt.

It was 4:45 P.M. Grandi went to a desk, took two small hand grenades from a drawer, and put them in his briefcase along with two copies of the resolution. Driven by Zamboni, he went once more to church, to the little baroque Chapel of Sudario in back of Palazzo Vidoni, seat of the Supreme Command.

At a few minutes before five he emerged, and Zamboni drove him to the main entrance of Palazzo Venezia, dropped him off, and drove several blocks farther to the office of the duke of Acquarone, where he delivered Grandi's letter.

That afternoon, Bottai wrote in his diary: "I await what will happen this day with emotion. At a crossroads. Duty has placed us at this crossroads, between the country and the party, between Italy and the regime, between the king and the *Duce* . . . it's a game without alternatives from which will emerge renunciation, sacrifice, devotion to the country."

Then, after looking once more at his books, paintings and plants, and wondering again if he were doing the right thing, he put on his costume and left for Palazzo Venezia.

Built like a medieval castle with battlements and a low tower, Palazzo Venezia was warm brown in the afternoon sun. By five o'clock on that hot and heavy summer's day the twenty-eight council members, all but two in black uniform, had arrived. After depositing them, their cars had been driven to the rear of the palace to be parked in Via degli Astalli. On Mussolini's orders, none were to be left in the piazza, so that there would be no discernible sign that a meeting was being held. For the same reason, no Fascist pennon flew from the famous balcony.

Only the ubiquitous and obvious plainclothesmen remained in the piazza. As Mussolini had instructed, there were none of the *Duce*'s musketeers who had served as honor guard at previous meetings, but an armed battalion of the Fascist militia was drawn up in the inner courtyard.

They were headed by General Enzo Galbiati, an aggressive, military-looking man who was also there as a member of the council. Scores of bored and sleepy secret service men did their best to remain unobserved. The rooms of Palazzo Venezia also concealed an additional unit of the militia and a good many of the dictator's personal police known as the "Presidential."

When acting Minister of the Interior Umberto Albini came to Palazzo Venezia for the meeting, he saw, or rather sensed, this formidable array and hastened to have some non-Fascist police called in. All in all, five security forces were represented, along with as many chiefs: Albini, Galbiati, Chief of Police Renzo Chierici, and Presidential Police heads Giuseppe Stracca and Vincenzo Agnesina. All but the first two, who were there to attend the council, stayed behind the door of the Pappagallo Room ready to intervene and, incidentally, to listen to the proceedings so that, despite the imposed secrecy, major developments could be relayed to interested parties in Rome.

In another adjoining room were some of the indefinable characters who formed an integral part of the furniture of the palace during the Grand Council meetings—a dozen or so secretaries and assistants who had come, out of affection or patriotic anxiety, in the wake of their respective ministers and chiefs.

In the inner courtyard Grandi looked at the troops and said, "This is the end." Bottai replied, "It's your fault for having talked to him."

Grandi, worried that those who had promised him support might desert in the face of force, began to think that Bottai was right. He wondered if he had not underestimated Mussolini and counted too heavily on the king. Then, with a look on his face that echoed Dante's "All hope abandon ye who enter here," he walked into the building.

Upstairs, the top dignitaries of fascism were assembled in the Pappagallo Room, awaiting Mussolini. They were one room removed from the dictator's office, the Sala del Mappamondo, which had the same kind of heavy wrought iron chandelier hanging from an ornamented and frescoed ceiling. The windowed wall had heavy curtains, and nineteenth-century paintings in gilt frames hung on walls upholstered in dark blue velvet.

Large tables, placed together to form a squarish horseshoe, virtually covered the colored marble floor. On a dais was the crimson velvet-covered desk, decorated with golden laurel leaves and fasces, that was to be occupied by Mussolini. On each side were blue velvet chairs, twenty-eight of them in all, for the members of the council.

For over twenty years these worthies had held their intelligence, imagination and ambition in check, deferring to *Il Duce* and never espousing open opposition. After all, that would have meant the end of their reflected glory, their virtually unquestioned power, their feeling of belonging to the elite. It would have meant the giving up of elaborate uniforms, big cars, luxurious homes, young mistresses.

Yet when the hierarchs had first arrived—some from Rome, most from the provinces—they had been far from well-to-do. Nor had they been very expert in politics; the very confusion of their ideas had led them to fascism. But one thing they almost all shared was an eagerness for action coupled with a hunger for positions of command. At first they had been ill at ease, had furnished their homes with excessive haste and bad taste, gone to expensive and inept tailors, dined in black market restaurants. Over the years, however, they had gradually become used to privilege.

And now, suddenly, due to the way the war was going, they could no longer enjoy their prerogatives. Their positions, along with that of their leader, were being threatened.

In addition, the hierarchs had lost their militancy. Along with power, showy titles and easily accrued wealth had come flabbiness. The excitement, the spur of their youth when they had been bound together in *fasci,* was gone and now they wanted an end to adventure, to battles and to wars. *Their* fighting was over; the liberal and left-wing opposition had been dominated, beaten and at times murdered. Now the hierarchs wanted peace.

It was all too clear that Mussolini's attempts to revive the old spirit had failed. He had appointed Carlo Scorza secretary of the Fascist party for just that purpose, hoping for a resurgence of militancy among the faithful. The resurgence had not materialized, and the Grand Council meeting proved it. So the hierarchs waited, torn by conflicting feelings—loyalty, chauvinism, self-interest and fear.

Carlo Scorza entered Palazzo Venezia through Piazza San Marco at a little before five. The courtyard was empty except for two or three groups of chauffeurs standing around. As Scorza walked into the Pappagallo Room he greeted those already there; he nodded to Grandi, Bottai and Ciano, who were talking together, and received their cold nods in return. He noticed the two men not in black, Galbiati in the uniform of chief of staff of the militia and Emilio De Bono in that of marshal of the army. An usher walked up and down before a door. The door opened, and a message was whispered to the usher, who turned and told Scorza that the *Duce* wanted him.

Seated at his desk, Mussolini, attired in the Sardinian wool uniform of commander of the Fascist militia, asked, "Is everyone here?"

"I haven't called the roll but I think so," replied Scorza.

"Anything new?" asked Mussolini.

"Grandi's been having people to his office all day to sign his motion. I don't know how many," answered Scorza.

"It's of no importance," the *Duce* said. He asked Scorza for the motion the secretary had drafted, glanced at it, and put it in his leather briefcase, along with his speech and various papers marked in colored pencil.

"It's after five," he said to Scorza. "As I told you this morning, watch everyone, but most of all keep calm. Take notes and we'll complete them tomorrow morning." A smile whisked across his face. "I still have an iron memory."

The door between the two rooms opened and Chief Usher Navarra announced the *Duce*'s impending entrance. For several minutes more, the waiting continued. Now it became almost unbearable, turning curiosity into embarrassment and tension. Many of those present expected some tempestuous incident, perhaps even a *coup de force*.

Seeing Federzoni, Grandi pulled him into a corner, took the two hand grenades out from under his ample *sahariana* with a bit of bluster, and marveled at the fact that Federzoni was not similarly armed. Federzoni tried to tell him that if it came to an armed showdown they would not have a chance, but Grandi paid no attention, even when Federzoni admitted that he too had gone to confession and taken communion before coming to the meeting.

At fourteen minutes past five, Mussolini, preceded by Navarra (carrying the briefcase) and accompanied by Scorza, made his entrance. Without looking at anyone, he went straight to his imposing chair, his face frowning but calm, exuding confidence even if a bit drawn and pale. As Party Secretary Scorza called out "Salute the *Duce!*" a unanimous "*A noi!*", the World War I battle cry of the *Arditi* assault force, rolled out, and all raised their arms in the Fascist salute. Mussolini sat down, wincing a bit from the pain in his stomach, and instructed Scorza to call the roll, all the while taking papers from his briefcase.

This bureaucratic and almost scholastic procedure surprised the hierarchs; the tense, expectant atmosphere, at least in the eyes of elder members of the council, should have justified the omission of formality. In fact, they answered the roll in an annoyed and indifferent manner: the newer members, on hearing their names, reacted by timidly standing; still others, who neither understood anything of the situation nor realized its drama, stood mechanically and, giving the Fascist salute, said loudly, "Present!"

With the roll finished, the tension rose once again. Mussolini started to speak.

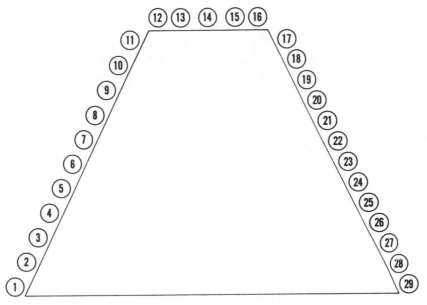

The seating arrangement of the meeting of the Grand Council on July 25, 1943. From left to right: 1. Gottardi, 2. Frattari, 3. Rossoni, 4. Albini, 5. Farinacci, 6. Ciano, 7. Galbiati, 8. Polverelli, 9. Pareschi, 10. Acerbo, 11. Grandi, 12. De Vecchi, 13. De Bono, 14. Mussolini, 15. Scorza, 16. Suardo, 17. De Marsico, 18. Biggini, 19. Federzoni, 20. Cianetti, 21. Bastianini, 22. Tringali, 23. Bottai, 24. De Stefani, 25. Alfieri, 26. Buffarini, 27. Marinelli, 28. Balella, 29. Bignardi

Chapter 6

THE CURTAIN RISES

The Unseen Audience

As the dictator spoke, life outside slowed down. Movement came virtually to a halt while the meeting went on—six, seven, eight o'clock—devouring the pause between the day's activity and darkness.

Now it was evening, with the slow diminishing of sunlight closing the day like a long sigh. Radios were switched on. All across the city the people of Rome listened through crackling static to forbidden broadcasts. During the day it was difficult to hear clearly, because the BBC broadcasts in Italian were usually jammed. Many had learned, however, that if you put your hand against the speaker the interference lessened, and one could hear the opening notes of Beethoven's Fifth, a soft mysterious knock, and "Colonel Stevens" saying *"Buona sera."* At eight o'clock the Italian radio broadcast a popular speaker, Mario Appelius, who usually cursed the English. Candidus, a German, was more moderate; he gave the Nazi view of the news, stressing hopes for victory.

At nine o'clock lights were being doused, and thick curtains were pulled to shroud restaurants and bars; through the blacked-out streets, the few pedestrians and fewer cars moved in dream-like silence. Then ten, eleven, and the city seemed ready to sink in a miasmic trance, suspended till dawn as if a spectral troop had swooped over Rome, whispering, "Sleep, sleep, leave Rome to us." Piazza Venezia seemed to be a painting by Giorgio de Chirico; only in its center was the air lighter and the darkness less compact. The sentries remained at their posts, unmoving; the big front door remained impenetrable. At the side of the piazza, the Vittorio Emanuele II monument stood out, white, ghostly.

Throughout the city troops were confined to quarters. The news of the meeting still had not appeared in any newspaper.

As he had countless times before, an air raid warden reprimanded someone who had a light showing. When the violator jokingly responded with a Fascist salute, the warden tiredly shouted, "I said *luce* [light], not *Duce!*"

The black-out had never been very popular among Romans, and the whole city knew the lines attributed to Pasquino, the armless statue:

> *Duce, Duce.*
> We almost feel dead.
> Days without bread.
> Nights without light.
> Rome in the dark after ten.
> With no one knowing how or where or when,
> Will make you see, thanks to obscurity,
> What will come to dawn
> Nine months from now
> How many children will be born.

There was another kind of activity at the Supreme Command, at the Vatican Secretariat of State, at the royal palace, and in newspaper offices, where word began to filter through of the secret meeting.

A group of anti-Fascists were gathered at the Viale Parioli home of Oreste Lizzadri, a Socialist. There they waited for news, wondering what they could do to speed events to a satisfactory conclusion. Only at ten that night did they have the first word: "Grandi has viciously attacked Mussolini and been followed by Bottai and Ciano." At eleven they heard that so many curious people had flocked to Piazza Venezia that Fascist militia were called out to disperse them. At midnight they were told that "Mussolini counterattacked menacingly but without too much conviction," and by one in the morn-

ing, the small groups that had been broken up in Piazza Venezia had
re-formed.

Those close to the protagonists were strangely anxious that evening; they knew of the meeting but not what it might bring. One of
these was Mario Zamboni who, after leaving Grandi at Palazzo
Venezia, drove to Acquarone's office. The anteroom was empty.
Zamboni handed the envelope to the duke, who opened it and said,
"I'll take it to the king immediately." There was a pause, and then
he added, "I have to admit that I was wrong to have doubted
Grandi's decision." As Zamboni started to leave, Acquarone gave
him a password to use on the phone to indicate the moment had arrived for Acquarone to meet with Grandi. Zamboni went to Grandi's
office at the Palazzo Montecitorio, called Acquarone from time to
time, and finally asked if he did not want to postpone the meeting
till the next day. "No," was the reply. "If necessary, I'll wait all
night."

Count Vitetti passed the night two blocks from Palazzo Venezia
—in the salon of Princess Colonna's palace—along with other friends
of Ciano, including Zenone Benini and Blasco d'Ajeta.

Still another group stayed up all night at the Excelsior Hotel on
Via Veneto. It included newspapermen and war profiteers, meeting
on common ground. From time to time, as the Grand Council meeting showed no signs of ending, they walked to the telephone in the
lobby and then returned to their friends, muttering, "It's still on.
Nothing new."

Most Italians remained unaware, uninformed. For them it was a
night just like any other. But now the overture was finished, and the
play was about to start. For the curtain was up, the players in battle
array. The weaving of webs was over, and the sharpened knives
were in their scabbards. The plots had matured, the way for action
been cleared. Who would hold the seat of power, who would rule
Rome?

The Grand Council

As Mussolini looked around at the men with whom he had been
ruling Rome, at these pillars of fascism, many of whom had been at
his side for twenty years, his thoughts were not defeatist nor were
they particularly tender towards his comrades. On his right sat the
only two survivors of the quadrumvirate who had led the March on
Rome in 1922, eighty-year-old Marshal De Bono and the insignificant

Cesare Maria de Vecchi, count of Val Cismon, a lawyer noted for his monarchist feelings. Next to de Vecchi was Dino Grandi, and on Mussolini's other side sat Scorza as secretary of the Fascist party and Count Giacomo Suardo, president of the Senate. All the rest were placed along the sides in somewhat hierarchical order, Ciano in the middle on the right side, next to Farinacci; Bottai and Alfieri occupied similar positions on the left side.

For a few moments there was silence, interrupted briefly by Mussolini's rustling papers. Then, without preliminaries, he spoke, his voice calm and distant, intent on playing down the importance of the meeting. "The story of this convocation is known. I accepted the request for it from some comrades who were asked by the Party Secretary to make propaganda speeches. They thought it their duty to give me personally their point of view on the present situation of the country. . . ."

The members stirred uneasily. They had been warned that the discussion was to be confidential; there was not even an official stenographer there to take down the minutes.

As Mussolini went on speaking, Federzoni thought he looked tired. An experienced orator himself, he noted that the dictator was not making his points, that he was uncertain of his facts, and that the speech itself was disorderly and incoherent. Even Scorza, who was busily scribbling phrases so that he could go over the speeches the next day with Mussolini, was struck by the weakness of the dictator's arguments, the rambling manner of his speech and his omission of points he had told Scorza he would make.

By now Mussolini was well into the subject that lay in the back of everyone's mind. "The military situation," he said, "after the intervention of the United States, has reached a point once thought impossible, the invasion of our national soil. The war has entered an extremely critical phase since the Americans appeared in the Mediterranean with their overwhelming superiority of arms and men. In a situation like this all those against the regime, official and unofficial, open or hidden, are united in opposition. . . ."

Then Mussolini gave his version of how the war had come about and described the attitude of Italians towards other wars, such as World War I when Italy had had 535,000 deserters. His tone was cold, self-assured, and a trifle arrogant. "No war is popular when it starts," he said. "It becomes popular if it ends in victory. War is always a party war, a war of the party which desires it; it is always one man's war—the war of the man who declared it." Raising his eyes from his speech, he looked around him. "And at this moment," he declared, "I am the most despised and hated man in Italy. . . . But the moment has come to tighten the reins and assume responsibility, although I have never asked for military responsibility nor exercised it."

This was a move unworthy of the old Mussolini. He had, after all, led his country for all this time, for better or worse, controlling even the smallest of details, vaunting himself as a skillful strategist, audacious and clever at taking advantage of weaknesses. But now, rather than admit that he was too weak to confront Allied strength, he was attempting to pass the blame to others.

He produced a secret exchange of correspondence with Marshal Badoglio in which Badoglio, while chief of General Staff at the beginning of the war, had urged Mussolini to take over the reins of the armed forces from the king. "Once and for all, let it be said that I never asked for command of the armed forces given me by the king on June 10. The initiative was that of Marshal Badoglio who in a letter dated May 3, 1940, proposed transferring the responsibility from the king to myself.

"I must say that I have never technically directed operations," he went on, "leaving full responsibilities to the separate commands." He said that he had, however, exercised his responsibility on one occasion, a minor battle which ended in victory.

Having attacked the Supreme Command for Italy's defeats, he bemoaned the lack of spirit of sacrifice on the part of Italian soldiers. "Only Stalin and the Mikado," he said querulously, "can give orders to fight to the last man." Referring to the happy greetings that many Sicilian villagers gave American soldiers, particularly those of Italian origin, he spoke disparagingly of Sicilians "who had welcomed the Anglo-Saxons as saviors." In contrast, he lauded Germany and the Germans' military attitude. He accused Rommel, however, of not heeding his counsel at El Alamein.

Many of the hierarchs noted that the customary colorful phrases were lacking from Mussolini's speech, that the mockery in his voice had given way to willful confusion, and that he was resorting to a conscious falsification of the facts. Is this the man, they asked themselves, who is defending Rome, fascism and our interests?

Giacomo Acerbo, baron dell' Aterno, a professor of economics and minister of finance, listened to the man who had fascinated him since the beginning of fascism.

"His report went on, weak, disordered, contradictory," Acerbo wrote afterwards, "and we heard it like a voice out of tune in time, like a thought estranged by the impetuous tragedy of the nation. . . . It seemed to wander in an unreal world and not be he who was speaking, but another man pronouncing a concise reprimand against himself, Mussolini . . ."

As for Mussolini, he sensed cold hostility in the air, and because of it, he claimed later, he delivered his speech without enthusiasm. He felt he was watching his own trial, spectator and defendant at the same time, and his energy suddenly left him.

He went on to list the vicissitudes of the war suffered by Italy, until he came to the Anglo-American landing in Africa, on which, with a rare note of prescience, he commented, "A fact, this, of historical value with consequences which—as far as it concerns Americans in our sea—will extend much beyond this war."

Mussolini blamed Germany for failing to occupy all of France and for thus provoking the Anglo-American landing in North Africa. England, he said, was fighting not fascism, but Italy, because England wanted to assure itself another century of uncontested European mastery. "Britain," he said, "wants to occupy Italy and stay here. For the rest we are tied to alliances, *pacta sunt servanda*, 'pacts are to be maintained.' "

By now he had been talking for almost two hours, but he had not really touched upon any of the vital reasons for the convening of the Grand Council. Rather, his speech represented a defense of the moves which had brought Italy to its present state. He had made little impression on the council members, and it was clear that he had hoped to limit the meeting to a discussion of the military aspects of the situation.

Still Mussolini remained calm, almost indifferent. Pausing a moment to put his papers back in his briefcase, he rested his hands on it and said, "I think the Grand Council must ask itself, is it to be war or peace, surrender or fight to the finish, resistance or capitulation. I think this is what the nation is awaiting from the Grand Council at this moment."

He leaned back and crossed his arms, almost as if in challenge. By then it was seven o'clock, but the sun was still strong as it entered through the blue curtains covering the two big windows. The heat, like the atmosphere, was oppressive. A long, embarrassing silence ensued.

It was finally broken by Mussolini's calling on the council's oldest member, white-bearded Marshal De Bono, who, as a general, had deserted the army to participate in the March on Rome. Even the most hardened Fascist felt it strange to hear him defend the army against the "accusation of treason." De Bono, who maintained that the trouble was political, not military, continued despite interruptions by various members who cried, "And the men and materials? Do they exist?" Eventually he was interrupted by Mussolini who insisted on the accuracy of the figures he had given earlier concerning desertions, quantities of weapons available, etc. De Bono passed over this. "Above all, it was your responsibility," he said. "You chose the military leaders. Who, for example, made Carboni a general? Certainly no one of us who occupy the highest ranks would entrust him with an army corps."

De Bono's speech had also been interrupted by Farinacci, who had warned against provoking the Germans. Now, without asking authorization, Farinacci took the floor to fire arrows in every direction, at Mussolini, at the Italian people, at other hierarchs and at the Supreme Command. He said that Mussolini had trusted in those who had betrayed him, and he proposed that Ambrosio, as chief of the Supreme Command, be called before the Grand Council to "repeat here what he had previously said, that if the Germans left Italy, we would be defeated in fifteen days." This led to a long confused debate until finally Mussolini said, "Such a move would be superfluous. I can supply all the information necessary."

It was then the turn of Cesare de Vecchi, the other quadrumvir, a landowner from Piedmont who did not get along particularly well with Mussolini. He, like De Bono, defended the army, although he said it was full of cliques, contained anti-Fascists, and was lacking in both technical and professional capabilities. "Remember that until a few days ago you were intriguing to get yourself a military command," Mussolini snapped at him. There was an appreciative laugh, which grew when Mussolini added that, because of de Vecchi's scarce capabilities, he had only been allowed to command a small coastal strip.

Soon Bottai rose to speak in a cutting, cold, almost metallic voice. Rigid, controlled, looking straight in front of him, he emphasized the wealth of enemy matériel and the paucity of Italian equipment. "Although I am in accord with Farinacci about convoking Ambrosio, being a man of politics I don't want to go into the technical aspects of the military situation where I have no particular competence." But Bottai insisted that the Anglo-Americans would never give up occupying the capital of their adversary, Rome. He reminded listen-

ers, "Hitler gave priority to occupying Paris. Rome means Italy. . . .
I disagree with the opinion of the Supreme Command which excludes
an enemy attack on the mainland of Italy. On the contrary, I am convinced that political criteria will induce them to invade the Italian
mainland so as to occupy Rome . . . the home of fascism. Is Italy
prepared to receive the impact?"

He discussed the state of mind of the country and the gap between Mussolini and his collaborators. Mussolini had assumed responsibility for the entire war effort, and even so, his orders were
not always followed, or were followed only partially and not faithfully.

At this Mussolini wrote down the sarcastic comment: "This
eagerness to lift responsibility from my shoulders is very touching."

"The war has been badly run because the political arm of the
government hasn't held the military in check," Bottai continued. At
this Mussolini wrote: "But if he's been one of the men in political
command for twenty years?"

"Your speech," Bottai concluded, "destroyed our last illusions.
The war has gone badly because, being isolated from us, you haven't
been capable of commanding nor of having yourself obeyed by the
Chiefs of the Armed Forces."

This was the first direct attack against Mussolini and it shocked
the assembly out of its heat-induced lethargy. Scorza, whose duty it
was to call on each speaker, hesitated a moment, waiting for a reaction from Mussolini. But instead, almost as if to bring things to a
head, Mussolini turned toward the third man on his left. Scorza had
no choice but to call on Dino Grandi to speak next.

Many of the hierarchs, already sitting upright after Bottai's
speech, looked at the elegant count of Mordano whom they believed
would now assume the role of prosecutor of the regime. With a
nod to Bottai, Grandi stood up and, after a few remarks, read his
resolution, adding, "I have always found myself appearing to be in
internal opposition and external obedience. This has not been so,"
thus confirming his loyalty to Mussolini. "But tonight I must say that
after hearing the *Duce's* speech to which we have listened with
anguish, I have seen the dream of a generation broken to pieces."

Mussolini bent over a note pad and under the heading, "The
Count of M.," he wrote: "But he prepared his motion before he saw
the dream of a generation break to pieces!"

"In the present, grave situation," Grandi continued, "it is indispensable and urgent to correct old and recent errors so as to facili-

tate the solution of the crisis facing the nation. But above all, *Duce*, everyone must accept his responsibility. Restore to us the old faith you once had towards us. The party no longer has a voice, you haven't let us speak freely, you've chosen people without consulting us, so that you have incompetents in posts of command. Give us back the credo of our youth which led us to follow you in the victorious battles against the old ruling class that had prostrated Italy after a victorious war which cost six hundred thousand dead."

After recapitulating the history of fascism starting with the First World War, Grandi complained that "when, after seven years absence, I returned to the government I became aware of the damage caused by the political and moral decadence of the regime." Mussolini leaned to his left and whispered to Scorza, "But he's always been in the government."

Grandi then condemned totalitarian dictatorship as the major cause of Italy's disaster, admitting that dictatorship was inevitable in the life of a nation but claiming that it should be limited to exceptional moments, giving way as soon as possible to a government more attentive to the aspirations of the nation.

Describing some of the men closest to the dictator as mediocrities who had betrayed Mussolini's real ideas, Grandi singled out Minister of Popular Culture Gaetano Polverelli and his censorship of the press and raked Polverelli over the coals for his censorship of news accounts of events in Sicily: "very likely, to please the Germans." When Polverelli protested, Grandi retorted, "You shut up, you who the night of the landings in Sicily bawled out *Il Messaggero* for a misplaced comma in the headline."

Although Grandi's speech was hardly the vicious condemnation of Mussolini's regime that it was later made out to be, and could hardly be compared with the philippic of Tallien against Robespierre, it did make some telling points. It was, in fact, strong enough and long enough—he spoke for an hour—to confuse many of the members of the Grand Council, including Grandi himself, who later reconstructed highly colored versions of what was actually said. Not until twenty-five years later was it possible to put together most of the speech, balancing what Grandi would have liked to have said and what others thought or hoped he said, against the notes that his ally Federzoni jotted down and those that Scorza, in his privileged position as party secretary, was able to make.

Grandi spoke with vehemence of the deep fracture between the party and the people. "Today no one speaks of fascism's war but of Mussolini's war," he said, and he repeated Mussolini's remark about being the most hated man in Italy. But, claimed Grandi, he and the others present could not consent to a falsification of history; Mussolini had been distracted by the direction of the party, by the various ministries he ran, by foreign affairs, by the complications brought about by the war.

"You, *Duce*," he said, "have pointed out that this war too is unpopular as all wars are, but you must permit me to tell you that the fault is ours, of the regime in general and of the Ministry of Popular Culture in particular which made the war a war of the party, suffocating it under the Fascist label. At the beginning the whole nation was behind it but they waited in vain for a common sacrifice."

At about this time the spasms in Mussolini's stomach increased, and he grasped his stomach with one hand, shielding his eyes from the lamp with the other. Meanwhile some of those present noted that Grandi, far from making a revolutionary speech, was asking for a return to the fundamental principles of fascism. In his mind, Scorza went over the points Grandi had made: heal the fracture between the nation and the regime caused by monopolistic and dictatorial systems, reduce the heavy responsibilities Mussolini had shouldered, extend the responsibility for the conduct of the war in such a way as to lift the party label from it. In other words, Grandi's was not a particularly anti-Mussolinian position. "This is exactly what I want, what we all want," Scorza thought to himself.

Now Grandi began to speak in a sharper, more concise manner of the constitution, of the monarchy and of the king who had been relegated to a secondary role by Mussolini's personality. "It is absolutely wrong that the monarchy, after having accepted everything from the regime, the crown of Ethiopia and that of Albania, should remain aloof from responsibilities now that the war is going badly."

It was evident that this was a dialectical game. To justify his motion, Grandi did not attempt to defend the crown; rather, he did the opposite, defending the regime against the crown. It was an habile move which deceived many of those listening. Grandi, possibly the only hierarch who really knew the political importance the Grand Council's decision could have for the future of the country, then tried to take the onus off his motion by claiming that the restoration of military powers to the king would ease the dictator's burden. "It is now up to the king in this difficult moment to assume the real and effective command of the troops and the supreme direction of the war with its consequent responsibilities." Turning to Mussolini, Grandi said, "We understand your reluctance to go to the king and tell him, now that things are going badly, it's necessary for the monarchy to return to be the fulcrum of the nation and of its unity. My motion is intended to overcome your understandable and human hesitation. But the restoration of military powers to the king under the constitution will lift the Fascist label from the war. It will even give you, *Duce,* more autonomy vis-à-vis our German ally."

This was such a transparent move that Mussolini passed a note to Scorza: "The republican revolutionary," it read, "invokes the monarchy and the constitution."

But Grandi, as if he were aware of Mussolini's reaction, now recalled the early Mussolini, the chief followed faithfully by Grandi, by all Fascists. "The Mussolini of the early days," Grandi said, "has been replaced by the Mussolini of uniforms, of manifestations, of choreographic assemblies in which no one believes. Restore to us, *Duce,* our tired, old, unforgettable black shirts without eagles, galons and decorations. Please believe, *Duce,* that we prefer to see you once more in our midst, you too with the simple black shirt, not with the frets of First Marshal of the Empire which add nothing to the leader who came out of the revolution."

Mussolini exhibited no reaction as Grandi called for the separation of military powers from political ones in order to remove from the regime the outstanding characteristic of dictatorship. Then, recalling the sacrifices of an entire generation, he saluted the ideals of the old fascism calling for the concord of all Italians, according to a Mussolinian formula of 1924: "Let all factions, even our own, perish, as long as the country lives." Turning once more to Mussolini, Grandi closed with these words, "Listen to this cry of anguish which comes from the hearts of your faithful. *Duce,* let us share all responsibilities. With you we will win united or, united, we will fall."

When Grandi had sat down, Mussolini slumped back in his chair. Although he was still in pain, he had heard Grandi very well. The members of the Grand Council turned their eyes to him waiting for his answer. However, he chose to maintain his silence, one hand in his belt and the other attempting to shield his eyes from the reflections of the large lamps. Suddenly he changed positions, leaning over his desk with one hand pressed strongly on his stomach. His face remained impassive; not a single muscle moved to show the pain he was suffering. Only one leg, crossed over the other, swung to reveal his feelings. Instead of making the anticipated reply, he turned in his chair and said in an indifferent voice, "I call upon Polverelli who has asked to speak for personal motives."

The minister of popular culture rose to reply to the accusations launched against him by Grandi. When he had finished, Mussolini flicked his glance at those present and stopped at Ciano, six seats away from Grandi.

Although few of the members thought that Ciano had really been ill, his pale face clearly showed the signs of convalescence. He stood up and began his speech by quoting Mussolini's final remark about maintaining pacts, recalling calmly that the first who had not done so was the German ally. Speaking without notes, he used his surprising memory to recall episodes, quoting precise figures and dates, unpleasant incidents and acts of disloyalty and insolence by Germany. Although he had started in an embarrassed tone, he gained assurance, and though he still showed respect towards his father-in-law, he listed proofs of German duplicity. As he spoke of the frequent violations by Germany of the Pact of Steel with Italy, Mussolini was silent but Federzoni thought he saw repressed anger in his eyes and unspoken imprecations on his lips.

Yet at one point, when Ciano discussed Germany's declaration of war despite Hitler's assurances to Mussolini, the latter said, in a low voice, "Very, very true." Ciano then went into the various times the Germans had acted unilaterally, deceiving Mussolini or leaving him in the dark as to their real intentions. "All the attacks after the one on Poland were communicated to us at the last minute. From that on Belgium to that on France which Mackensen, who was in my company until after midnight, didn't announce until four o'clock in the morning when the German troops were already across the frontier."

Ciano's speech, precise in form, ordered in its exposition, proceeded without dramatic emphasis to explore the political and historical motives behind Ciano's anti-German attitude. "Gentlemen," he concluded, "those are the facts of our relations with our ally, Germany. Let us recall that we can make our decisions with full liberty as far as our ally is concerned, since it is the Germans who betrayed us, starting the war. We will not have to fear any negative judgment by history as far as the correctness of our international relations are concerned if we should decide to separate our decisions

E

from those of our ally. No one can accuse us of being traitors because the incontrovertible truth is this, we will never be the traitors, only the betrayed."

Impressed by the profound silence which greeted his last words, Ciano, a bit pale, sat down. At least one of those present thought that if Mussolini had wanted to plump for peace, he might well have ordered Ciano's speech.

Then Farinacci took the floor to read his motion calling for the creation of a single command, which in essence meant putting the Italian armed forces under Hitler's control. He agreed that the party no longer had the support of the nation, "not because the nation has withdrawn from us but because we have withdrawn from it." He attacked Grandi and Bottai for their criticism of Mussolini and combatted the anti-German thesis of Ciano by saying, "The German presence in Italy is a reality" and that it was time to speak frankly with the Germans "to show ourselves men and not courtiers."

At this point Mussolini, having learned from Scorza that eleven speakers still remained on the agenda, decided to reply to Grandi, particularly on the matter of relations with the king. He spoke briefly, defending his actions and those of the Fascist party which, he said, should not be made the scapegoat for the present situation. In essence, his speech was another summing up, as if he were saying, "This is the way things are, and nothing you think or say will change it."

Defending the propaganda moves of the regime, Mussolini said, "Let us not forget that in that very democratic England the newspapers are full of the smallest gesture and the most insignificant speeches of Signor Churchill while the crown is put in the shade, and that in the still more democratic America, even the restless wife of the president, that is Signora Eleanor [Roosevelt], has her own particular and well-organized press. Relations between the State and the Crown have always been carried out with reciprocal comprehension." The dictator admitted that things had cooled between the regime and the Crown in recent weeks, but he attributed this to the anti-Fascists at court. He referred again to Badoglio's insistence that he, Mussolini, take over the armed forces, maintaining that this represented no diminution of the monarchy. When stomach pains halted his speech, Mussolini attempted to cover up by looking through his papers. Recovering, he attacked Grandi's motion, pointing out that in all these years no member of the Grand Council had ever raised the question. He noted his intention to renounce military powers and repeated that the conduct of the war was the responsibility of the Supreme Command.

After a comment on the Italian defeats in Greece, Mussolini paused and called on De Marsico, the minister of justice, whose long, confused speech ended with the words: "It is my confirmed conviction that the regime must take a new constitutional form. . . . We must restore to the king the right and the responsibility of guiding the nation."

By now the meeting had been going on for six uninterrupted hours. Scorza wrote a note on a piece of paper and passed it to Mussolini. "Given the late hour and the other speakers to be heard," Mussolini announced, "the Secretary of the Party proposes that the meeting be adjourned until tomorrow."

Grandi pushed back his chair and jumped to his feet, taking the members of the council completely by surprise. "Ah, no," he cried in a raucous voice. "Excuse me, *Duce*, when we discussed youth organizations and workers' theatre parties, you kept us here until four in the morning. We can continue to work now that it concerns vital problems for the nation."

Scorza seemed to sense a note of fear in Grandi's voice. But of whom, of what? Why should it be so important for him to have the Grand Council end that day instead of twenty-four hours later? His thoughts were interrupted by Mussolini, who replied indifferently, "All right, we will continue. But then we'll suspend the meeting for half an hour." After Federzoni and Annio Bignardi had spoken, Mussolini rose, and the members lifted their hands in the Fascist salute.

Erect, his step long and decisive, Mussolini seemed to have regained some of his vigor. He walked towards the door, leaving behind him a silence composed of uncertainty and stupor.

The Pappagallo Room was caught up in a cross-current of conversation. In one corner were grouped Grandi, Ciano, Bottai and Albini, and in another, Bastianini, Federzoni and Alberto De Stefani, former minister of finance. One of the die-hard Fascists was certain that he heard Ciano say, "He's like a wounded bear, if we don't defend ourselves, he'll tear us to pieces."

Scorza, confused by the sudden turn of events, followed Mussolini to the door of his office, where the dictator turned to him and said, "Wait, I'll have you called in a little while." Passing near Alfieri, Mussolini said, "Come in with me."

Alfieri, who thought that Mussolini had earlier spoken in a passive, apathetic way, almost as if Grandi's motion were already approved, left the men with whom he was talking and followed.

In his office, Mussolini made Alfieri wait while he went through war dispatches, then asked what was happening in Germany. Rather disconcerted, Alfieri said the Russians were still attacking with success: the German people, in spite of their evident war-weariness, kept going because of their sense of discipline, their fear of the Gestapo, and the influence of unceasing propaganda. But they felt the war was lost. When Alfieri spoke of the German attitude towards events in Italy, Mussolini interrupted brusquely, "In Berlin they know nothing of Italian psychology. If the enemy bombs Rome again, nothing tragic will happen. It has been proved that raids against big cities have an effect on the population only the first or possibly the second time. Then a sort of mystic heroism is formed in the population, making them indifferent and causing them to bear destruction and sorrow with resignation."

Alfieri attempted to refute this, but his words had no effect. "Believe me, you're not well-informed," replied Mussolini. "The situation is not as bad as you think. We still have time."

After dismissing Alfieri, Mussolini went back to reading the dispatches on Sicily, looking up only when Guido Buffarini-Guidi, the fat, former under secretary of the interior, came in.

"Arrest them!" Buffarini exclaimed. "It's a plot. There'll be less than twenty, and outside, Badoglio and another dozen. A hundred men will be enough." Buffarini talked excitedly: "The king doesn't even have to know about Grandi's motion. He'll have to accept the arrests and that's all. You can still save everything . . ."

"Keep quiet," said Mussolini.

Scorza, having noticed the surprising number of police in the hall, was about to ask Albini for an explanation when Mussolini sent for him. He found the dictator seated at his desk, both hands pressed against his stomach. As Scorza approached him, Mussolini straightened up and started tapping the desk with his pencil.

"I watched you during the meeting," he told Scorza, "and I noticed you were a little nervous. You're not used to these long discussions." The dictator went on to give his impressions, saying that the evening had been a useful exploration. Then, leaning back, he passed his hand over his mouth and chin, a habitual gesture. "It's obvious that most of them are oriented towards peace even though none of them had the courage to say it openly. Well, I can use them independently of their resolutions. Monday, I'll speak to the king."

At this moment Apriliti, one of the ushers, brought Mussolini a tray with a glass of milk and a roll. Taking the milk, Mussolini went on: "But even if they've made some kind of clandestine agreement, they're fooling themselves if they think they can count on the king's support. . . . There's a war on which continues to go badly; otherwise this business would have long been finished."

Mussolini expressed his approval of much of what the speakers had said; he objected, however, to Grandi's motion. After reading over Scorza's motion, he told him how to present it and outlined the phrases with which he should accompany it. While Scorza went to appraise the mood of the council members, Mussolini put a call through to Bologna, which had been severely bombed during the night, and ordered the local newspaper to carry Mussolini's praise of the population on the front page.

Soon Scorza returned. He told Mussolini of the increasing number of police and that he thought the atmosphere among the members had changed for the worse. Mussolini beat a devil's tattoo on the table with his fingers. "Let's go," he said.

Forty-five minutes had passed.

During that time some of the hierarchs had left the Pappagallo Room for another room, where drinks and sandwiches had been prepared. Some of them went into the corridors to obtain relief from the suffocating heat or to smoke, which was prohibited during the meeting. But as soon as Mussolini and Scorza had left the room, Grandi had placed two copies of his motion openly on the table. De Bono was the first to sign, then de Vecchi. When Ciano approached, Grandi asked him to think it over before signing, but Ciano repeated that his father would have wanted him to. Everyone used his own pen, and some wrote their titles after their names. Several, clearly moved, blotched their signatures. Among those who signed was the doddering Giovanni Marinelli, one of Mussolini's most faithful followers, who, very hard of hearing, was believed not to have followed the details of the discussion too closely. Twentieth and last to sign was Alfieri.

When Mussolini and Scorza returned, some of the hierarchs were still clustered around Grandi. Others were grouped near a window, and most of the rest had taken their seats. It was a quarter past midnight. Mussolini read some dispatches from Sicily telling of the advance of Anglo-American troops there. Then he called on Bastianini who had asked to speak. After a recapitulation of the German double-dealings, the acting foreign minister talked of the Italian people's discontent. Instead of being united and ready to face any ordeal, they had been divided by poor propaganda methods into small groups that were the object, one by one, of insults, ridicule and humiliation—today youth, tomorrow the middle class, then the industrialists, the intellectuals, the aristocracy, Catholic Action, the Jews and so on. A profound gap existed between the country and the party, to which was added a terrible military unpreparedness.

Mussolini interrupted. "This gap could also have had its origin in the rapid accumulation of wealth by certain people," he said.

Bastianini replied that he surely was not one of those, that there were many causes, and the way to eliminate most of them was to lower the party pennant and raise the national flag. "The country is in danger and all the rest doesn't count."

When Bastianini had finished speaking, Mussolini recognized Dino Alfieri whose attempts to gain the floor he had previously ignored. Alfieri repeated what he had told Mussolini of the increasing lack of belief in military victory among Germans. "From now on we're a dead weight for the Germans and they're not going to let us forget it. For Hitler, Italy is only a bastion against the occupation of Germany. I am convinced that if Germany could find a convenient way out of the war, she would take it, ignoring our interests and sacrifices." As for Italy's chances of victory, it was "necessary to be realistic, every sacrifice had its limits." He concluded by saying, "As ambassador to Germany, it is my duty to tell the Grand Council that it is perfectly useless to let ourselves be deluded as to the possibility of fresh military aid from Germany."

Mussolini quickly replied that Alfieri's statement contradicted the assurances he had received from Hitler at Feltre. Other speakers followed, for the first time daring to criticize the leader, and blaming him, indirectly, for destroying their privileges. A few, somewhat more generous, tried to clarify Mussolini's vague allusions. Among them was acting Minister of the Interior Albini, who gave an alarmist report on the internal situation, citing strikes and other manifestations against the regime. This was news to many of the hierarchs, who for years had not considered the possibility of popular opposition.

Galbiati delivered a violent speech which Grandi, misled by the military rhetoric, construed as a threat against him. Galbiati called on all to be faithful to Mussolini and to follow him until death. "You are for the constitution or for the revolution. Who is not for Mussolini betrays the revolution. I invite the Grand Council to weigh its decision."

Encouraged by Galbiati's words, Mussolini took to the offensive, discussing again the reputed accumulation of wealth by some hierarchs. "Defeatism and hostility to the regime are the privileges of the bourgeoisie. If there are gaps they are between the hierarchs. . . . Grandi's resolution speaks of reestablishing the functions of the state. What functions? The cabinet is only for administration, command belongs to one man only, that's the way it's understood by Churchill, Roosevelt and Stalin. . . . Fascism, revolution, party and Mussolini are inseparable. Who demands the end of dictatorship knows he wants the end of fascism. I will shortly be sixty and I can also close this beautiful adventure of my life. My confidence in the victory of Germany and ourselves is still intact, as it was at the beginning of the war. I cannot reveal to the Grand Council the secret plans of a military nature which have convinced the Fuehrer and myself of final victory. But the day is near when our enemies will be inexorably beaten."

Mussolini paused for a moment. "Gentlemen, attention! Grandi's motion can pose the question of the very existence of the regime. Have you thought that in this case another delicate and personal problem would be raised—my own?"

There was silence in the room, broken only by the slight squeaking of a chair; several members wiped their brows, while others remained still, looking at Mussolini.

"When I tell the king what has happened this night, he will surely say to me, 'Your men have abandoned you, but the king who has always been close to you, remains with you.' I am certain that the king will tell me that, and then what will be your position? Be careful, gentlemen. It is most probable that the king will also say, 'Ah, the gentlemen of the regime, now that they realize they're in up to their necks, they suddenly discover that there is an out for them in the constitution and that besides the constitution there is a king. Very well, I'll accept their intervention, but since I hold them all responsible for the present situation I'll profit from the occasion to liquidate all of them at once.' " After a long pause, Mussolini went on: "Or else this resolution goes beyond its literal significance, and in that case gentlemen, beware! I repeat that it can put the existence of the regime in doubt and also pose a personal problem for all of you. It is necessary to state clearly the goal you really want to reach."

The speech must have shaken the members, and undoubtedly caused some of them to waver in their allegiance to Grandi's motion. Grandi himself, keenly aware of the danger, began to speak in an emotional tone of the affection they all had for Mussolini. "But I ask you, *Duce*, also in the name of the comrades who have signed my motion, not to resort to sentimental blackmail. Your presence, to which we remain attached with devotion and faithfulness as always, is beyond discussion and above the motion which we have presented, which has no hidden significance. . . . Our only aim," said Grandi, after repeating parts of his previous speech, "is to be able to render ourselves more useful to the nation and to you, our chief." Grandi sat down. There was a murmur of approval. Mussolini called on Scorza.

Scorza began to read his motion, which called for the continuation of the war, co-responsibility of the monarchy, cooperation with all segments of the population and reform. He stressed the need to pursue the war without weakness, to concentrate all powers in the party and to remain faithful to the alliance with Germany. Introducing an unexpected religious note, he spoke of Rome, mother of Catholicism, and of the sorrow of the pope at the destruction of sacred places. Then he read the changes that Mussolini said he would make, which included restoring powers to the Chamber of Deputies and the Senate, reshuffling the cabinet, putting new men at the head of the armed forces, re-forming the Supreme Command and the possibility of returning its control to the king.

Halfway through, Mussolini became irritated. "Pass over all of that, it's superfluous," he snapped. Scorza had hardly finished speaking when six of the opposition demanded to speak. Ciano rose to object to the fact that the motion referred to the pope, asserting that the Vatican would not approve. Scorza replied that exactly forty-eight hours earlier, in the presence of the *Duce*, he had been told by an authoritative source (Padre Tacchi-Venturi) that the pope would appreciate this mention.

Minister of Corporations Cianetti said that he had signed Grandi's motion because he had felt the need for reforms; now that he had heard Scorza relate Mussolini's plans, he wanted to withdraw his adhesion to that motion.

Bottai counterattacked: "Are we children or clowns who sign such a serious document and at the first severe glance from our elders withdraw our signatures? Or are we Fascists, soldiers, men well aware of what we're doing?" He then took up the question of dictatorship. "We have already seen what is happening with the system where everything depends upon *Il Duce*. The regime has been deprived of the collaboration of its best elements, it has been isolated from the nation and has reduced a national war to that of the party; we can even say to that of one man . . . who, according to public opinion, wanted it, imposed it and conducted it. It is necessary to recognize frankly that the time of dictatorship is finished, at least in the forms and with the mentality which has guided it until now." With that Bottai sat down to be replaced by Count Suardo who, with tears in his eyes, said that he too withdrew his adhesion to Grandi's resolution. Cianetti still seemed undecided; he proposed a compromise, uniting the resolutions of Grandi and Scorza. Ciano said that he too would approve the fusion.

By now Grandi had begun to assume that the fight was lost. The glances from across the table, from Federzoni, Bottai and De Marsico only served to strengthen this impression.

Bottai asked to speak again; he pointed out the differences between Grandi's motion and those of Scorza and Farinacci, noting that the latter omitted "the call to the king to reassume his duties which in this grave hour is the only way to guarantee the health of the nation and of the regime."

Among those who believed that this was true was Alberto De Stefani, an economics professor who, as Mussolini's minister of finance, had managed the rare feat of balancing the budget. Raising his leonine head, he delivered a speech, obviously prepared before the meeting, which made it clear that he, too, thought Grandi's motion left the way open for the maintenance of fascism. He concluded by saying, "*Duce,* you know that if I thought Grandi's motion meant reducing your authority I would not have signed it. I did so because it offers you a freedom of action which today you lack as head of the armed forces and because, even though no one here has yet said it, the war is lost."

Grandi, speaking for the third time, added that his intention was to have each of the members face up to his responsibility. He claimed that Scorza did not represent the will of the party, and that it was up to the Grand Council to speak. "As for the dilemma presented to us by the head of the government, it resembles a blackmail which the Grand Council, conscious of its responsibilities, cannot accept. There are no traitors among us as some have insinuated, but our loyalty to Mussolini is subordinate to the oath of allegiance which he, like all of us, has given the king."

Then Scorza spoke, addressing himself to Mussolini. "You, *Duce,* were never enough of a dictator. We have many dictatorships, those of the police, of the bureaucracy, of industrialists. You couldn't see all that happened behind the scenes of the great stage. One day you called yourself the Grand Master of the Order of the Umbrella—because all the disasters caused by these intriguers took refuge under it. All this is known to the people, that you're really the most disobeyed man of the century. It's all these dictatorships—to which, directly or indirectly, all of us here present have contributed—which have created the moral climate from which the regime and the people are now suffering."

De Marsico now spoke again to rebut Scorza's motion and support Grandi's. He too thought it would make it easier for Mussolini to get out of the war. Others, like Bottai and Cianetti, thought it meant a return to revolutionary fascism. De Bono thought it was a call for harmony. Grandi's motion obviously held something for each of them.

Last to speak was the tearful Suardo, who asked all to vote for Scorza's motion so that the reforms could be actuated. He admitted, however, that he did not fully comprehend the differences between the motions.

By then it was 2:30 in the morning. The meeting had gone on for nine hours and the members were showing signs of fatigue. Mussolini looked around.

"If no one wants to add anything," he said, "I can declare the discussion closed and call for the vote."

Scorza, thinking the *Duce* would now read his motion, passed it to him. Mussolini looked at it, moved it to his left, and continued, "The motions will be voted for in the order of presentation. Therefore I open the vote on the first, that of Grandi. Call the roll." When Scorza hesitated, Mussolini snapped, "Well then, start."

Scorza picked up a blue pencil with which to mark yes or no opposite each member's name, and took the initiative of calling on himself first, answering with a resounding no. Then he called on Suardo, president of the Senate, who, with tears still in his eyes, abstained. The next four, De Bono, de Vecchi, Grandi and De Marsico all voted yes. From then on, the yes and no votes alternated, with a growing preference for yes. Cianetti, still disturbed, said yes. Polverelli withdrew his support for Grandi's motion and thereby saved his life. Five of those who voted yes were to pay for it with theirs.

The members answered quickly, sometimes without even waiting for Scorza to finish pronouncing their names. The last to be called was Antonino Tringali-Casanova, head of the dreaded Special Tribunal, who said no.

Nineteen votes were cast for Grandi's resolution, eight against. There was one abstention, Suardo's; Farinacci had announced that he intended to vote for his own resolution.

Scorza totaled the votes at the edge of the page and handed it to Mussolini. "Grandi's motion is approved," Mussolini said. "There's no use voting on the others." Then, calmly gathering up his papers, he turned to Grandi and asked: "Who will take this to the king?"

"You will, as head of the government," Grandi answered.

"Gentlemen," said Mussolini, "you have provoked the crisis of the regime. The meeting is over."

He stood up and the others followed suit, standing immobile and silent at their places. When Scorza invoked the salute to the *Duce*, to which only Gaetano Polverelli responded in a loud voice, Mussolini checked it with a gesture. "No, let it go," he said. Then he walked rapidly towards his office.

It was evident that the dictator's magic spell had at last been broken, even if it had not vanished completely. For Federzoni, Mussolini that night was the great actor who had become old, who for the first time during his long triumphant career did not know his lines and blundered. Others, however, noticed that after the single *"A noi"* in response to the ritual salute of the party secretary, the dictator's lips had seemed to wrinkle into a fleeting grin of irony.

The Actors Depart

Behind him Mussolini left a whirlpool of conjecture. Was the regime really finished? And if Mussolini had been defeated, who had won? Possibly more important, what would the dictator do now? After all, he was still *Il Duce*, and his authority as head of the government and commander of the armed forces remained unchanged. A slight feeling of fear touched some of the conspirators. Despite Albini's strategy in calling his men, there were still plenty of police loyal to Mussolini at Palazzo Venezia ready to carry out his commands. Albini took no chances. Making sure that he was the first to leave the room, he strode quickly across the adjoining hall, saying to one of the heads of Mussolini's Presidential Police as he passed, "The session is over. We finally came to an agreement. You can send your men home."

But the questions concerning the dictator's conduct remained. Why had he abandoned his usual aggressive approach and spoken mainly on the defensive? Why had he defended his position so weakly and allowed himself to be outvoted so easily? Alfieri had been surprised by Mussolini's indifference, apathy and passivity. He recalled that the dictator, even after he had been told in his office what Alfieri had thought, had not kept him from repeating it at the Grand Council.

Could it have been that Mussolini, weakened by his gastric pains, had wanted to avoid putting up too much opposition to Grandi and his cohorts? Or was he playing from a weak hand, fighting as well as he could in the face of circumstances?

Federzoni thought that Mussolini believed he could use the vote to blackmail Hitler, either to get more aid or eventually to sue for a separate peace.

Was it possible that Mussolini was secretly craving for a way to get off his high perch? Ever the actor, perhaps he had grabbed at the chance to play the "mighty hero betrayed by his nearest and dearest."

Through the now-opened windows the hierarchs could see the star-filled sky. They came down the stairs in groups talking animatedly despite their fatigue and the late hour. Bottai left in Ciano's car; Alfieri with Bastianini. By the time Grandi and Federzoni left together, the hall and the nearby rooms were already empty and the big square lay deserted under a sliver of moon.

When Ciano reached home he telephoned the palace of Princess Colonna. The lady-in-waiting hurried to Princess Maria José at the Quirinal to report the news. Count Vitetti, d'Ajeta and Minister of Labor Benini went to meet Ciano. He told them that Mussolini might have him arrested: "But you'll see, the king will intervene and the madman will leave without incidents, with all his honors."

To Scorza, following Mussolini to his office, it seemed ironic that a dictatorship, an antidemocratic regime, could be brought to a crisis by such a typically democratic procedure as an open vote. The immense office was lit by only a few bulbs in the large chandelier and by the yellow lamp on Mussolini's desk. The dictator passed his hand vigorously over his chin and mouth several times and tugged at his collar with two fingers. Then, as if speaking to himself, he said, "That motion is really an infamy," and hit his open hand against the folder containing it.

Scorza tried to minimize the importance of the vote; the Grand

Council, he insisted, could only express an advisory opinion which did not bind the initiative of the dictator.

Mussolini nodded. "We'll talk about it later," he finally said.

The usher, Apriliti, came in to tell Mussolini that half a dozen hierarchs wanted to say good-bye before leaving. They remained with him for about ten minutes, saying that they too saw the session as nothing more than an internal clarification. When one mentioned something about arresting the signers, Mussolini glared.

"Arrest them!" he snorted. "It would mean the putting behind bars of the President of the Chamber, the President of the Academy, two ambassadors and a good part of the cabinet!"

After they had left, slightly abashed, Mussolini talked dispiritedly with Scorza and, although he normally disliked being accompanied by anyone, he agreed to ride home with the party secretary. He put his hand on Scorza's shoulder. "You fought well, with conviction and warmth. Thank you."

As they walked out, Mussolini continued, "It's easy for these gentlemen to talk about peace. If it were only me I'd leave, even right away. But don't they understand that Churchill and Roosevelt don't want my departure but the suppression of Italy as a Mediterranean power?"

They arrived at the dictator's elevator. "I might even be able to obtain an acceptable peace," said Mussolini, "but we'll need at least one military victory so we don't present ourselves with only a series of heroic disasters."

It was after three when Mussolini and Scorza got in the car and left for Villa Torlonia. The streets were deserted. The trip was a silent one, broken only by Mussolini's exclaiming, "Even Ciano, Albini and Bastianini."

Scorza was walking up to the house with Mussolini when he saw donna Rachele standing under the portico. He said good-bye and returned to his car on Via Nomentana.

While heating some broth she had prepared, Mussolini's wife asked how the meeting had gone. Mussolini told her a bit about the meeting. "At least you had them arrested?" she snapped.

"No, I'll do it tomorrow," he answered dully. "Tomorrow will be too late," said his wife skeptically.

Mussolini shrugged this off, went to the phone linked with the Supreme Command, and asked for the latest news.

"Nothing new," he was told, but when he repeated this to his wife she snatched the receiver from him and shouted into it. "You're lying," she cried. After a time, her exasperation died down and soon, noticing that it was five o'clock, she urged him to go to bed.

At Fascist party headquarters in Piazza Colonna an anxious group of Fascist officials, including three vice secretaries of the party, had also been up all night. Towards midnight they had been informed by phone from Palazzo Venezia about the pause. Then, at a quarter past three, they had been told that the meeting was over, and shortly thereafter Polverelli had come over to tell them what had happened. Scorza came in a little after four. He was laconic, insisting that the vote was only consultative, but he asked for several books concerning the legality of the Grand Council. Then he telephoned Mussolini, and after apologizing for the lateness of his call, restated his belief that the council's vote was simply advisory and that there remained, therefore, many possibilities for maneuvering.

"I'll ask for an audience with the king tomorrow," Mussolini replied.

In retrospect, many of the hierarchs took the view that the vote was purely a recommendation. Among them was De Stefani, who regarded the meeting as an orderly and constructive exposition of ideas and attitudes. Upon returning to his apartment at the Hotel Plaza, he told his wife, "I would have liked to have had the whole of Italy at this meeting because it would have profited from it."

One man knew what the events of that night had really meant. Dino Grandi met his *chef de cabinet*, Giovanni Talvacchia, outside Palazzo Venezia and walked with him to his office a little before three. Upstairs, Marquis Zamboni heard the guard announce Grandi's arrival with three sharp rings of the doorbell. Zamboni told Grandi that the duke of Acquarone wanted to speak to him immediately, and that he was waiting for him in a car at the rear exit on Via Velichi.

Grandi wanted him to come up, but Acquarone thought that it would be imprudent. They all left in Acquarone's car for Zamboni's house on the fashionable Via Giulia. There, for two hours, Grandi gave Acquarone a detailed story of what had happened and how he saw the future. He maintained that the Fascist party should not be destroyed but its dissolution postponed to serve as an ace in the hole when negotiating with the Anglo-Americans. Grandi had already told this to the king; now he repeated it to Acquarone while giving him the signed copy of his motion. "Maybe by tomorrow morning our troops guarding the Alpine passes will find themselves fighting the Germans since the Germans won't resign themselves to losing Italy. Therefore, we must prevent them from taking over the country. But negotiations for peace should start immediately. Then, if the Anglo-Americans come up from Sicily and find our army and the Italian people already fighting against the common enemy, it would cancel the Casablanca decisions on unconditional surrender. We won't be able to avoid an encounter with Germany but at least this will help us to immobilize the Anglo-Americans and secure better peace terms."

Then Grandi made his suggestions for a new government, telling Acquarone that Fascists who had had positions in the regime should be excluded. He thought that Marshal Caviglia, the only marshal to have nothing to do with fascism, should be prime minister, and that industrialist Alberto Pirelli should be foreign minister since he was favorably known to both the English and Americans. Former anti-Fascist deputies like De Gasperi, and Liberal Ministers like Soleri, would round out the cabinet.

Acquarone, who had already told Badoglio the day before that he was to head the new government, asked, "What about Badoglio?" Grandi was horrified.

"He's an anti-Fascist who has accepted honors, titles and money from the Fascist regime," cried Grandi. "He's been an accomplice of Mussolini and is one of those most responsible for the war's being lost. He's the last person in the world to evoke the faith of the king and of the people, the worst possible choice as head of government."

Acquarone looked at Grandi. "But what will you do now?" he asked.

After repeating his reasons for keeping Mussolini's old lieutenants out of the new government, Grandi offered to leave for Madrid. There he would get in touch with the English and the Americans and explain to them the true significance of the Grand Council meeting. He was sure he could obtain concessions for Italy, something better than unconditional surrender. At any event, he would be at the king's disposal.

The conversation ended at six in the morning, when Grandi returned to his apartment and Acquarone went off to see the king.

Chapter 7

THE BACKSTAGE
MANEUVERS

On the morning of July 25, events began to take on all the aspects of a gigantic chess game: on one side was Vittorio Emanuele, the legitimate king; on the other the usurper, Mussolini. On the king's side were General Ambrosio and Marshal Badoglio; on Mussolini's were Scorza and General Galbiati. The heads of the country's security forces were divided: the chief of police stood ready to defend Mussolini, the commanding general of the *Carabinieri* was ready to attack him. The pawns were the members of the Grand Council: some on the king's side, some on Mussolini's.

But it was Grandi, acting for the king, who had broken through Mussolini's defenses. Now Mussolini was about to be checked and King Vittorio Emanuele—or rather his men—would be free to dispose of the men around the dictator. Having used Grandi, the king was ready to sacrifice him and bring out Badoglio, along with Ambrosio, in order to assure the defense of his kingdom.

The various moves started at 6 A.M. on Sunday, July 25, when the duke of Acquarone presented himself at the royal residence. The duke told the king of his meeting with Grandi, pointing out the need to act urgently and independently of General Castellano's plan. The king agreed, telling Acquarone to take the necessary steps.

Acquarone lost no time in having the decree nominating Badoglio as prime minister drafted; he took it immediately to the king to sign, met with General Ambrosio to coordinate plans for the day, and, at 7:30 A.M., went with him and Castellano to Badoglio to inform him and to have him countersign the decree. From that moment on, Italy had two prime ministers.

By then Mussolini had been up for half an hour. When he emerged from the villa he acted as if it were just another day. Ercole Boratto, his long-trusted personal driver, was amazed to see Mussolini looking calm and carefree, despite the Grand Council meeting of the night before.

Mussolini's carefree appearance would also have amazed the Vatican, which had already been told what had happened by Fascist hierarch De Stefani. At seven thirty that morning he had telephoned his friend, Monsignor Celso Constantini, and said that he wanted to see him, if possible in the company of Monsignor Montini. When he arrived at the Apostolic Palace, Constantini was waiting with Montini by his side. De Stefani told them of the meeting and said, "It's now the duty of the Church to do something so that this crisis doesn't have a damaging effect."

"How do you know that we haven't already begun to take care of Rome's safety?" Montini replied enigmatically, and then hurried to the pope.

As Mussolini's Alfa Romeo sped toward the center, the city appeared quiet, immersed in the usual calm of a hot, sleepy Sunday in Rome. By nine, Mussolini was at his desk at Palazzo Venezia, where he learned that Cianetti had retracted his support of Grandi's motion and was sending a letter confirming this. Cianetti was also resigning as minister of corporations and, as a reserve Alpine artillery captain, asked to be sent to the front.

Mussolini carefully read the military bulletins, the various reports collected by the Secret Service and the account of monitored foreign broadcasts from Giorgio Nelson Page's office, all brought to him along with his morning papers. Not finding the police report, he complained to Chief Usher Navarra and asked that Scorza be summoned.

The party secretary found Mussolini in excellent form; his stomach was better, the rigors of the previous night could be seen only in his eyes, which were redder, somewhat dulled. The dictator had already passed a busy morning; he seemed bent on showing that he was determined to stay in office. He told Scorza that he had been looking for Grandi, but without success.

"Perhaps the count of Mordano is resting from last night's efforts," he commented ironically.

He told Scorza his plan for reforming the Grand Council, reorganizing the party, reshuffling the cabinet. He talked of sending Scorza and some cabinet ministers to see the pope. At the end of their meeting, Mussolini gave Scorza a file.

"Here are the notes I took on the meeting. I'm sure they're almost the same as yours. In any case, check them against each other and make a complete account of the proceedings. I'll see you later this afternoon."

Immediately afterward, Albini, acting secretary of the interior, came in to make his usual daily report. When he had finished, Mussolini raised his eyes and asked in a menacing whisper, "Why did you vote for Grandi's motion? You aren't even a member of the Grand Council; you were there as a guest."

Albini excused himself by saying that his mistaken gesture was proof of the confusion he felt at the meeting and that he remained devoted and faithful to Mussolini.

The dictator disregarded this. "I've been seeing experts on constitutional law," he said, "and they're convinced the vote has no value."

After Albini had left, Mussolini was told that Grandi could not be found. He insisted that the search for him continue. De Cesare saw that more calls were made to the Senate, to Grandi's villa at Frascati, to his newspaper in Bologna, and to his office in Rome.

Grandi was at his office, avoiding the calls. He was preoccupied about another matter. Despite his disavowal of personal ambitions, his activity that morning seemed to indicate that he expected some sign of recompense from a grateful king. When he had left Acquarone a little after dawn he had immediately set to work writing legislative measures that he thought the king should put through as soon as he had disposed of Mussolini. They included the immediate dissolution of the Fascist Chamber of Corporations with the automatic reestablishment of the Chamber of Deputies, the convocation of Parliament and the cancellation of all the special and racial laws passed by the dictatorship. He had sent his measures to Acquarone, but still no word came.

Grandi had overlooked a centuries-old Savoy tradition, betrayal of those who helped the House. Of course, the king had never actually said that Grandi would be elevated to a position of command. Nor had Acquarone, although he had allowed it to be understood. Now Grandi had no choice but to stay huddled in his office, ignoring Mussolini's calls and waiting to see what the House of Savoy had in mind.

One of the hierarchs faithful to Mussolini, Carlo Alberto Biggini, managed to reach Grandi; he told him the dictator wanted to offer him the post of foreign minister in a cabinet reshuffle. Although this hardly jibed with Grandi's fears that Mussolini was out to arrest him, Grandi, fearing to use the possibly tapped telephones, sent his *chef de cabinet* Talvacchia to see Acquarone. Talvacchia returned a half hour later with Acquarone's message advising Grandi not to meet Mussolini and the further word that "His Majesty has appointed Marshal Badoglio head of the government."

Now Grandi was really worried; things were not working out as he had hoped. He tried to be received by the king and requested an audience with the pope, but neither would see him that day.

What Grandi had not been told was that Mussolini's secretary De Cesare had called Acquarone a half hour earlier saying that Mussolini wanted to see the monarch that afternoon. Such a request was unheard of, for the king never allowed changes in the schedule of his audiences. There was a hurried rushing about, phone calls between Acquarone, the king and Major General Paolo Puntoni, the king's military aide. Finally Mussolini was told that he would be received at the royal residence at five o'clock that afternoon. This relieved Acquarone's doubts too, since till then he had not known if Mussolini would still see the king on Monday, as he had been doing for twenty years.

By now Mussolini was his usual dynamic self, and he was embarked on a daring diplomatic plan. At twelve he had Acting Foreign Minister Bastianini come in to discuss Goering's visit, which was scheduled for July 29, Mussolini's sixtieth birthday. The dictator, believing Goering to be more inclined towards a separate peace with Russia than other Nazi chieftains, said he preferred seeing him on the twenty-seventh. The sooner such a peace plan could be gotten under way, the better it would be for Mussolini's position.

Before Mussolini could reproach Bastianini for his vote the previous evening, Navarra came in to say that Japanese ambassador Hidaka was waiting. Mussolini, who was usually precise in his appointments, looked up in surprise and ordered Hidaka shown in. He told Hidaka that he was determined to try to convince Hitler to halt hostilities on the Eastern front and reach agreement with Russia. He asked the ambassador to have Prime Minister Tojo use his influence to support this. When Hidaka was escorted out, Mussolini asked Bastianini to prepare a proposal for Rome to be demilitarized and considered an "open city." Bastianini was to bring this back that afternoon after Mussolini had met with the king.

At one o'clock, Mussolini received Militia General Galbiati, who handed the *Duce* a neatly typed list of suggested drastic measures. Mussolini read it, looked at Galbiati, got up, stared at a portrait of his son Bruno and sat down again. Galbiati was uncomfortable. "I've learned that Grandi can't be found," he said. "That could be a bad sign. Wouldn't it be better, *Duce*, to arrest all nineteen?"

"Let's not even talk about it," replied Mussolini with a wave of his hand.

Galbiati proposed a meeting of Fascist party heads without, of course, those who had voted for Grandi's motion. And, in view of the worsening military situation and the possible Anglo-American occupation of Rome, he suggested a plan for resistance similar to that put into action by De Gaulle. Mussolini rejected the first proposition and said the second might be considered.

Meeting Galbiati later, Mussolini told him of the appointment with the king. The belligerent Galbiati again urged the arrests and advised Mussolini to take some other precautions. The dictator said that they would be unnecessary and that he would be under the protection of the king, but he added that the idea of a De Gaulle-like resistance should be examined carefully and gave Galbiati an appointment for the next day.

As Mussolini and Galbiati drove through the working class area of San Lorenzo, afflicted first by poverty, now by bombing, the people stopped their digging among the collapsed buildings to salute the dictator mechanically. The ruins were still smoldering and Ercole Borrato noticed that the *Duce* looked at them with a kind of piteous despair. More than once he asked Ercole to stop while he looked over the damaged houses. When he got out of the car to walk about, some young people called his name. He raised his arms to them and asked Galbiati to give them some money. Two old, obviously destitute women came up, but by then Galbiati had no more money and Mussolini ordered their names and addresses taken, assuring them he would send money the next day.

When news of Mussolini's advanced appointment with the king

came to the Supreme Command at Palazzo Vidoni, the generals began to revise their planning. Castellano went over the military situation. Right in Rome were Mussolini's bodyguards, the famous Presidential Police, formed of highly selected men headquartered in Palazzo Venezia. Also in Rome was an efficient and well-trained militia legion and thirty miles north of the capital was the militia's Armored Division Littorio, black shirts organized with German matériel and trained by German instructors, all under the command of Galbiati.

German forces in and near the capital were considerably fewer, consisting mainly of a division being formed near Viterbo fifty miles away and assorted small units near Rome. On the other hand, the plotters could really count only on the *Carabinieri*, with the added possibility of bringing in some troops from outside the city.

So it was up to the king's men to neutralize Mussolini's forces. At around half past twelve, Castellano put out a call for General Cerica, the newly named *Carabinieri* commandant who had been making courtesy calls on Fascist dignitaries, including Scorza and Albini. At the Supreme Command, Cerica was told that Mussolini was to be arrested that very day, not at the Quirinal Palace, but at the royal residence.

At that moment, Acquarone entered. He told Cerica that it would be best to have his men occupy radio, telegraph and telephone centers as well as the Interior and War ministries.

"The king has given orders that no one else is to be informed," he warned. "We'll meet here again at four o'clock."

When, just before leaving, Cerica mentioned the Littorio Division with its thirty-six Tiger tanks, Ambrosio answered sharply, "Just take care of the part that applies to you. The military questions are my concern."

On his way out, Cerica met General Carboni on the way in to discuss taking over *his* command. At his headquarters, Cerica ordered the *Carabinieri* commander of Rome, Lieutenant Colonel Giovanni Frignani, to cancel all leaves, although it was Sunday, on the pretext that the eight thousand men stationed in and near Rome would be undergoing inspection by the corps' new commanding officer. Fifty men, however, were chosen from the Pastrengo barracks and told they were to help capture some Allied parachutists who had been sighted. Then Frignani called in Captains Paolo Vigneri, Raffaele Aversa and Carmelo Marzano. The latter, who was in charge of the motor pool, was instructed to supply an ambulance.

This was all done so quickly that Cerica had time to return the visit of Chief of Police Chierici and then to go in dress uniform to militia headquarters to present his compliments to Galbiati. The meeting was cordial, although by then Cerica knew that he was to arrest Galbiati's superior, Mussolini, that same day. Then Cerica went home to change his uniform and eat lunch.

Also eating lunch were three Fascist hierarchs, Buffarini-Guidi, Biggini and Tringali-Casanova, who met at the San Carlo restaurant with SS Lieutenant Colonel Eugen Dollmann, Himmler's representative in Rome. They joked about handcuffs and someone remembered the phrase: "If you go to see a Savoy, don't forget to take a dagger under your shirt." It was obvious that outside of Grandi none of the hierarchs expected any serious actions as a result of the previous night's meeting.

After lunch, Dollmann took Buffarini-Guidi to see Ambassador Mackensen at the German Embassy, where the Italian gave a dramatic rendition of the meeting. However, Buffarini did not think that catastrophe was imminent; Mussolini would now make up a new cabinet. Embassy Counsellor Doertenbach tried to give Mackensen a more realistic report at 2 P.M., but the ambassador, an authoritarian and a stickler for rigid observance of rules, refused to see him, as he did not receive members of his staff before four in the afternoon. Meanwhile Mackensen sat down at his desk to write a report for Ribbentrop describing the situation in Rome as "serious, but not alarming," and adding that Mussolini was still steady in the saddle, *"noch fest im Sattel sitzte."*

While he was writing, word came that Marshal Badoglio wanted to talk to him; Mackensen, annoyed, ordered that Badoglio be told he was not in and had the embassy counsellor sent in his place. By the time the counsellor returned with the news that Badoglio had formed a new government, Mackensen's telegram had already been sent; it reached Ribbentrop in Berlin together with the news of the fall of the Fascist regime.

Leaving the embassy, Dollmann went to see Galbiati at militia headquarters. When he asked about the Littorio Division, Galbiati replied, "The division must continue its training. Unfortunately, the *Duce* wants to send it to the Southern Front."

But the fact was that Galbiati no longer had it under his command. Very few people knew that eleven days earlier, on July 14, Mussolini, as supreme commander of the armed forces, had given orders that the division be transferred from the militia to the army in preparation for its being sent to the vicinity of Salerno. Galbiati was apparently either too proud or too confused to mention it.

The king was having lunch with his queen who, as usual, had not been informed of the plans for the afternoon. Shortly after three o'clock she went upstairs, and the king promptly called General Puntoni to the corner salon. Pacing up and down, he said that he had decided to replace Mussolini with Badoglio.

"After I see 'il Presidente,' he's to be halted outside Villa Savoia and taken in custody to prevent his contacting extremist elements of the party and also avoid any hot-headed anti-Fascist attempts on his person." The king took a few steps more. "Since I don't know how the *Duce* will react, I want you to remain behind the door where we'll talk. If it becomes necessary, intervene. . . ."

At three, having returned to Villa Torlonia, Mussolini toyed with his lunch of broth and stewed fruit while telling donna Rachele of the appointment.

"You shouldn't go to Villa Savoia today," she said. "Don't trust the king, he's like the rest of them, they're all ready to betray you. First arrest those who voted against you, then go to the king."

"Nonsense, there's no danger," Mussolini reassured her. "The people are with me, I saw it at San Lorenzo, and the king knows we have a treaty with Germany which we can't break."

His wife did not share his optimism. When Mussolini fussed a bit because he had to wear civilian clothes for the audience, she said, "They want you in civilian clothes because it will be easier to arrest you." Mussolini smiled indulgently.

At Villa Savoia, the king too was dressing, putting on the uniform of the first marshal of Italy. He seemed to have forgotten all about the *deus ex machina*, Grandi, who at that time was receiving three high Fascists, Count Ciano, Ambassador Filippo Anfuso and Ettore Muti.

It was only then that Grandi learned from Ciano that the *Duce* was to be received by the king within two hours, and that Mussolini had supposedly ordered severe reprisals carried out against the nineteen signers of Grandi's motion. Muti offered to put Grandi up at his house but Grandi refused.

Anfuso, moved, said, "Your Excellency, last night you saved Italy."

Fascist Party Secretary Scorza, having lunch with his brother, received a phone call at two o'clock from Colonel Rocca, Marshal Rodolfo Graziani's aide, who appeared a half hour later.

"Marshal Graziani," revealed the colonel, "is aware of everything that happened at the Grand Council last night and would like to inform *Il Duce* that he is at the disposal of the nation and of the regime."

When, at four o'clock, Scorza finally relayed the message to Mussolini, the dictator was radiant.

"That's very interesting," he said, "really very interesting. I'm going to the king now but I should be finished by six or six thirty. I'll call you afterwards and we'll meet at Palazzo Venezia or here at Villa Torlonia."

In fact, Graziani's offer of support was most opportune; he could be just the man, thought Mussolini, to replace Ambrosio. He would definitely fit into the thoroughly prepared plan the dictator intended to present the king. Benito Mussolini would not have held the reins of government for twenty years if he had not been able to face eventualities when they arose. Now he was ready to let the king have back the Supreme Command; he would make the changes he had planned earlier, excluding, of course, those members of the Grand Council who had voted against him, and possibly ask the king's help in punishing them.

As Mussolini arranged his papers, he slipped among them a telegram form of a special kind which he used as head of the government. On the back was the list of names and appointments he had prepared before the Grand Council. Now it was apparent why he had not wanted Scorza to go into too much detail at that meeting; he had wanted to get these appointments approved by the king first.

In the confusion that occurred that day, these notes were lost and were not retrieved until almost twenty-five years later. Into the briefcase Mussolini also put a copy of the Grand Council statute, Grandi's motion and Cianetti's letter of resignation. Then he handed the briefcase to De Cesare, who had come to accompany him, and prepared to leave.

"Don't go to see the king," donna Rachele told him again. "He's against you."

"It's not true," answered Mussolini. "He's a friend. He's on my side."

Outside of his phone conversation with Scorza, Mussolini neither made nor received any other calls. He could not conceivably have spoken pessimistically, as has been alleged, to his mistress Claretta Petacci. Nothing in Mussolini's demeanor that day showed him to be convinced of defeat. The appointments he made to meet with

Polverelli and Scorza after his audience with the king and his plan
to meet the next day with Galbiati, as well as the material he prepared to take with him to the king, prove that Mussolini could not
possibly have said to Claretta: "It's all over, you had better hide."

But complications were arising on the king's side. One of Mussolini's men, Fascist Chief of Police Chierici, was quickly taken care
of. He was seated in his office in the Viminale when Carmine Senise
entered with the announcement that he was the new chief of police.
Dumbfounded, Chierici called the Supreme Command, where Castellano told him to come at four. There Ambrosio told the bewildered
Chierici that Mussolini was to be arrested within the hour. Ambrosio watched to see how Chierici received the news. If he registered
the slightest reaction, Castellano was in the next room with *carabinieri*, ready to arrest him. Chierici, however, raised no objections,
saying merely that he was ready to return to the army.

At four o'clock, General Cerica turned up at the Supreme Command to keep his appointment with Acquarone. Not finding him,
Cerica became worried. He went to the villa of one head of government, Badoglio, and asked for a written order to arrest the other,
Mussolini, but Badoglio, ever cautious, refused.

Then Cerica hurried to Villa Savoia, where he found Acquarone
and told him that he would not carry out the plan without a precise
order from the king. Further, he said, his men had considerable apprehension about arresting Mussolini outside Villa Savoia, rather
than within the grounds. He had made all the preparations because
Castellano had told him, "You start things moving, I'll see that you
get the confirmation." Now he wanted it.

"From the king in person?" asked Acquarone.

"No, it's enough if you give it to me in the name of the king,"
replied Cerica.

Acquarone went to the front of the villa where the king was
walking with General Puntoni. He bowed and, as Puntoni took a
few steps aside, asked if the arrest could be carried out *inside* the
grounds. The king, very pale, answered, "All right."

De Cesare had arrived at four thirty, but Mussolini had decided
to wait until four forty-five before leaving. Then the Alfa Romeo
driven by Boratto pulled up. The dictator was dressed in a black suit
and fedora. Followed by three cars with officials and plainclothesmen
of the dictator's escort, Boratto drove slowly north until he reached
Via Salaria and the Villa Savoia. The accompanying cars remained

outside the gate while Boratto drove up to the portico. There Boratto noticed with surprise that the king, accompanied by an aide-de-camp, was standing on the steps to meet *il Presidente* and do what Boratto had never seen him do before—walk down the steps to greet his visitor. Boratto watched as they went to the front door of the villa, as De Cesare handed Mussolini his briefcase and settled in an ante-room with the duty officer. Only then did Ercole drive the car to a corner of the house, open a newspaper, and prepare to wait.

He had been reading for no more than a minute or two when a servant who knew him passed by remarking, "Dear Ercole, what rotten times we live in." A moment later, a police officer came over to tell him he was wanted on the phone. They went to the porter's lodge some fifty yards from the villa. As soon as Ercole entered, three armed men appeared, seized him and took his pistol from his pocket. The police officer tried to calm him.

"Don't get alarmed," he said. "Nothing will happen to you."

Outside, about five yards from the villa, an ambulance was hidden, while between two hedges along the side of the house a number of *carabinieri*, armed with Beretta submachine guns, were posted.

Meanwhile the king, followed by Mussolini, walked to the corner study, where Puntoni had hidden himself behind a door. Unfortunately for history, Puntoni could not hear the complete conversation. He did make out that Mussolini was speaking in a low voice about the military situation and about what had happened during the Grand Council session. For a long time only Mussolini's voice could be heard, then the king's, and then Mussolini's, apparently trying to deny the king's affirmations, but whether on the seriousness of the military situation or on the meaning of the Grand Council vote Puntoni could not make out. But the king, obviously moved, insisted: "Things are not going well, Italy's in pieces, the Army's discouraged, soldiers don't want to fight and the vote, the Grand Council vote was dreadful."

Puntoni heard the king say that despite his personal feelings he was forced to ask for Mussolini's resignation. "I like you," the king said, "and I've shown it on other occasions. But this time I must ask you to leave your post so that I can be free to entrust the government to others."

No one knows for certain what Mussolini and the king actually said to each other; their own later versions are largely suspect. However, it is likely that Mussolini said something to the king of Hitler's secret weapons, of ceding military command to the monarch, of reshuffling the government, and possibly even of getting out of the alliance with Hitler. He very likely asked for time, until September, and in fact the king later admitted that Mussolini had asked to form a new government. "We'll see, in six months," the king had replied.

But the real blow to Mussolini came when the king said, "I think the man for the present situation is Marshal Badoglio." The shock was reportedly so great that the dictator sat down. "Then it's all over," he muttered, and according to the king he repeated this several times. The king repeated himself too, saying, "I'm sorry, but the solution couldn't have been otherwise, I'm sorry." Then Puntoni heard nothing more, only the noise of chairs and of steps approaching the door. The meeting had taken twenty minutes.

When De Cesare saw Mussolini emerging with the king, he noted that Mussolini was impassive, while the king was unusually nervous. The monarch made a remark about the heat, to which Mussolini replied, "Yes, it is hot." Mussolini handed his briefcase to his secretary. Then, something highly unusual happened. After shaking hands with Mussolini for a long time, the king put his hand out to De Cesare. In all these years he had never once offered to shake the secretary's hand.

"Where's the car of *il Presidente?*" the king asked a servant.

Mussolini looked about for it too and spied it at the foot of the ramp.

"It doesn't matter," he said, as he walked towards the car with De Cesare on his right and the servant on his left. When they reached the end of the ramp at the corner of the villa, Captain Vigneri approached Mussolini and saluted him.

"*Duce,*" he said, "I have been ordered by the king to protect your person. Please follow me."

Mussolini was both annoyed and surprised. "There's no need," he said, and started to get into his car.

"No, not that one," said Vigneri. "Over here."

The *Duce* looked around him and noted the armed men for the first time. However, he made no protest, possibly because he still did not perceive the real meaning of what was going on, still accepted the idea of protection. He was, however, somewhat surprised. The king had not told him that he was going to be placed under armed escort. The monarch had only said, "I'm sorry . . . we'll see in six months," and then had stood behind the corner to watch as the swarm of *carabinieri* surrounded the ex-dictator.

An ambulance backed up, its rear doors open. As Mussolini

hesitated, still more armed men appeared. Captain Vigneri took him by the elbow, as if to help him in.

"*Duce*," he said. "I have an order to obey."

"In that case, follow me," Mussolini answered and moved again toward his own car. But Vigneri moved too and put himself in front of him.

"No, *Duce,* you must come with me."

Mussolini got into the ambulance next to his secretary, who held the briefcase on his knees. Three officers in plain clothes and three soldiers with submachine guns entered the ambulance and slammed the door. By now there were eight people in the closed vehicle, which was suffocatingly hot because of its long halt in the sun. The car started off—as Mussolini remembered it—"with a jump," went along the graveled road, stopped at the gate, then turned onto the asphalt. Mussolini was silent; every now and then he touched the bridge of his nose with his index finger. The ambulance careened through the streets of Rome at such high speed that Mussolini asked Vigneri to have it slowed down.

"We'll wind up hitting someone," he said, "or smashing up against a wall."

When the ambulance had gone, General Puntoni walked over to the king and heard the duty officer inform him that all had gone well without the need for force. Then Puntoni accompanied the monarch back to his study. While the general was reading a document that the king had given him, the queen came in. Puntoni left.

The queen had learned of the arrest, and she did not like it. "He could have been arrested anywhere else, but not here, on our doorstep," she told the king, more in sorrow than anger. "Here Mussolini was our guest. The rules of royal hospitality have been violated. It is not worthy of a king." But Vittorio Emanuele hardly heard her. He was intent on having Puntoni bring Badoglio to the villa.

That day, after having signed his acceptance of the order to become prime minister, Badoglio had acted much as he always did, except that he had ordered a bottle of Veuve-Cliquot from his large wine cellar put on ice. As he prepared to continue his bridge game with his cronies, he told his family jokingly, "You're all confined to quarters for the day." He had taken off his too-tight uniform and put on civilian clothes. When Acquarone phoned at five thirty to tell him that Puntoni was coming to take him to Villa Savoia he answered, "Very well, just time to put on my uniform and I'll be there immediately."

"No, excellency, come as you are," said Acquarone.

"I am sorry, but I have never presented myself to His Majesty without being correctly dressed," replied Badoglio.

At Villa Savoia, the king told Badoglio what had happened and spoke of the future. Badoglio took from his pocket the piece of paper on which he had written a list of possible cabinet ministers.

"Oh, no," said the king, "none of these gentlemen. They must be non-Fascist rather than anti-Fascist and technicians rather than politicians."

Badoglio protested feebly, then bowed his way out. At the door was a car at which the marshal stared in bewilderment. He had come in an Artena; this was a luxurious Alfa Romeo. His chauffeur smiled broadly. "This is the car of *Il Duce*," he said.

Badoglio made no objection. On arriving home, he told his family off-handedly, "As of now, I am the Head of the Government," and then ordered the champagne opened.

While Badoglio's family was toasting him, the plotters were hard at work. At 4 P.M., General Castellano had entered the office of Major Luigi Marchesi at the Supreme Command.

"Do you have a revolver?" he asked.

Marchesi pulled open his desk drawer and displayed his Walther.

"Put it in your pocket," Castellano ordered, "and follow me."

The two men drove to a building opposite the royal palace where the duke of Acquarone had his office. General Cerica was there. The four men sat and waited until about five thirty, when the telephone rang. General Cerica lifted the receiver, listened for a moment and hung up.

"It's done," he said. "Everything's gone smoothly."

Mussolini was in check but he still had pieces on the board. They had to be taken, and swiftly. Castellano and Marchesi went to the Ministry of the Interior, entered by means of their Supreme Command identity cards, and headed for the office of Acting Minister Albini. Before the usher could announce them, he was pushed aside and the door shoved open. Albini raised his eyes and saw Marchesi, his back to the door, putting a hand in his pocket to indicate that he was armed. Castellano stepped forward.

"Mussolini has just been arrested," he said, "and you must decide immediately if you are going to collaborate with us."

Albini paled, hesitated a fraction of a second, then answered yes. Marchesi stepped away from the door and opened it. In came Chierici and Senise who had been waiting in the anteroom. A telegram was drawn up and sent to prefects throughout the country containing news of the arrest and instructions for the maintenance of order.

Carmine Senise settled into Chierici's office at the Viminale as the new chief of police and started making the moves necessary to insure that support could not be mustered for Mussolini. He immediately sent telegrams to the various chiefs of police, telling of fascism's fall; then, with the help of Police General Fernando Soleti, he saw that telephone switchboards were taken over at Palazzo Venezia, as well as at the various ministries, government offices and post offices; finally, he gave orders to have guards posted at power stations, telegraph offices and at the radio transmitters of EIAR, where the eight o'clock news was postponed.

General Galbiati, in charge of the Fascist Voluntary Militia, was immobilized also. At eight o'clock, he said to his aides, "There's no doubt it's a coup d'etat, but who did it?" When he learned that Mussolini had been arrested, he tried to contact militia commands and found his communications cut. When one of his generals requested permission to intervene, Galbiati said that if he felt heroic he could march by himself. When another asked what he intended to do, Galbiati shrugged his shoulders. "I stand resolutely at my post," he replied.

At ten o'clock, when a motorized detachment of regular army troops surrounded his headquarters and pointed its 75mm guns at his window, Galbiati made an ambiguous gesture. He sent a telegram to Albini saying that the militia was remaining "faithful to its principles in the service of the country." Albini replied that he had passed his message to Badoglio, who wanted to shake his hand "soldier to soldier," but the apprehensive Galbiati announced that he and his staff would pass the night there. At about midnight, he received an official letter informing him that he had been replaced by another general and that the entire Fascist militia had been incorporated into the army. Galbiati still refused to leave, but he was bottled up and powerless to move.

So Mussolini's key men had been replaced by others who now began to move according to the will of the king.

A private celebration was in full swing at Palazzo Vidoni, where the generals and colonels of the Supreme Command toasted each other. When Carboni arrived to assume formal command of his troops, Castellano and Ambrosio told him that Mussolini had been arrested.

A few minutes after Mussolini had left to keep his appointment with the king, Fascist hierarch Buffarini-Guidi had arrived at Villa Torlonia, and donna Rachele had left her usual domestic tasks in order to speak to him. Their conversation was interrupted by the ringing of the telephone. Donna Rachele answered, and Buffarini saw her face whiten.

"It was a friend," she said after she hung up. "*Il Presidente* was arrested a few minutes ago." Then she began to cry.

"He doesn't deserve your tears," cried Irma, a longtime family maid, who proceeded to reveal Mussolini's long relationship with Claretta Petacci. It was something of which donna Rachele, until that moment, had remained completely ignorant.

Meanwhile, Buffarini-Guidi tried to reach someone in authority, but without success. At half past eight, Agnesina, commander of the presidential escort, came to say that his men had been sent back from the Villa Savoia; they had remained till then thinking Mussolini had stayed to dinner with the king. Later, he admitted to donna Rachele that he was away getting a shave when the dictator was arrested. A little after midnight, *carabinieri* came to arrest Buffarini-Guidi.

Scorza, who had been trying without success to contact Musso-lini, was worried. Suddenly, Marshal Graziani's aide returned with a strange message: "The Marshal has been told that around five thirty the head of the king accompanied by two of his top men, all wearing feathers, went into the Savoy Caffè." This meant, explained Colonel Rocca, that Badoglio, accompanied by two generals, all in dress uniform, had gone to the king's residence at five thirty.

Scorza rushed over to party headquarters and began a series of telephone calls. "You can't speak with Palazzo Venezia or Villa Torlonia," a peremptory voice informed him. "All connections have been interrupted."

"Let me speak with the Chief of Police," insisted Scorza.

"Nor with him," was the reply, and the line was cut.

Scorza called in his assistants.

"Something has happened," he told them. "I don't know quite what it is, but I know it's serious. Gather up as many Fascist militants as you can."

It was seven o'clock and the agitated Scorza went to Palazzo Venezia, taking care, however, to have a car containing two men follow at a slight distance. Palazzo Venezia was shut tight, and Scorza decided to go to *Carabinieri* headquarters. There he was immediately admitted to the office of his old friend General Cerica, who looked at him in surprise.

"Don't you know that Mussolini is no longer head of the government and has been replaced by Badoglio?"

"But where," Scorza stammered, "where is *Il Duce* now?"

"He's the guest of the king at Villa Savoia."

As Scorza left the office he was stopped by the man who had supervised Mussolini's arrest, Lieutenant Colonel Frignani.

"I'm sorry, Your Excellency," said Frignani, "but I have orders to arrest you."

When Scorza protested to Cerica, the latter offered to drive Scorza to his home on Via Civinini so that he could change his clothes. As they passed down Via XX Settembre, Scorza could see reinforced patrols in front of the War Ministry. At his home, he changed his clothes and, finding himself momentarily unwatched, went out the back way, jumped into his car and sped off to pass the night in the home of a friend.

The efforts by Scorza's assistants to round up loyal Fascists ended in failure; no more than fifty answered the call to duty. With Scorza out of the way, Ambrosio called the party and dictated the text of a telegram to be sent to Fascist headquarters throughout the country: "Make no moves, be calm and await developments." Rather than assume the responsibility themselves, the assistant secretaries signed it "Scorza."

Farinacci was standing outside the Foreign Office on Corso Umberto, trying to figure out his next move, when a complete stranger walked up to him and said, "Watch out, they're looking for you." Farinacci went home, packed a small bag and went straight to the German Embassy, where he spent the night. The next morning a German military attaché's car took him to an airport controlled by the *Luftwaffe*, and by noon the next day he was in Berlin, the first to use the improvised airlift which transported Fascists to Germany.

All day, Germany had been rife with rumors about Mussolini's visit to the king. At nine thirty that night, Hitler told his generals, "This is real treason. I want the *Duce* to come immediately to Germany. I think we should have the 3rd Panzergrenadieren Division immediately occupy Rome and arrest the whole government, the whole mob . . . Ciano too."

In Rome, Ciano had discovered at six o'clock that his telephone

Piazza Venezia the day of Mussolini's arrest

Crowds in Rome reading Il Messaggero *announcing the downfall of Mussolini*

July 26, 1943, Rome. Crowds with flags of the House of Savoy and carrying pictures of the Queen

July 26. The Via del Plebiscito in downtown Rome

had been disconnected. An hour later he went to see Grandi. As they were talking, Muti arrived with the news that Mussolini and Scorza had been arrested, and Ciano was finally persuaded to spend the night at Filippo Anfuso's house. When he learned that Badoglio had become head of the government, Ciano telephoned Castellano and Carboni, asking each of them to assure the safety of his wife and children.

Militarily, every key point in the city was occupied either by the *Carabinieri* or by troops brought in that day by General Ruggiero. Any forceful reaction on the part of the Fascists was checked before it even began. They were taken by surprise just as the *Duce* had been. Seeing armored cars under the trees of Viale Giulio Cesare and a row of armored trucks full of *carabinieri* in a piazza nearby, the head of the Fascist press office thought he was witnessing routine maneuvers.

Meanwhile, the ambulance bearing Mussolini was driven into the Podgora barracks of the *Carabinieri* in Trastevere, just across the Tiber from Corso Vittorio Emanuele. When the vehicle came to a halt in the interior courtyard, the officers stood at attention, assuming that Mussolini had come to carry out an inspection. Mussolini, somewhat reassured, assumed his usual stance, fists on his hips. The commanding officer, however, finally realized—after he had been taken aside by Captain Vigneri—that appearances had been deceptive and ordered Mussolini taken to a conference room.

De Cesare was sent to Rome's prison, Regina Coeli, where the briefcase was taken from him and locked up, along with his tie, belt and shoelaces. "How strange," he thought at the time, "no one wants to know what's inside." Then, overcome by his emotions, he fainted.

Mussolini was bundled back into the ambulance and taken to the better-guarded *Carabinieri* cadet barracks at Via Legnano. It was seven o'clock. Mussolini refused dinner, and, when asked if he required medical assistance, complained of a pain in his stomach. Taken to a guarded room, he lay down on the cot, switched off the light and tried, in vain, to sleep.

F

Book Two:

THE FORTY-FIVE DAYS

Necessity is the plea for every
infringement of human freedom.
It is the argument of tyrants;
it is the creed of slaves.

—William Pitt

Chapter 8

THE PEOPLE EXULT

The night of July 25, two brothers, Romano and Sigfrido An-tonelli, students, were on the balcony of their family's second floor apartment on Piazza del Gesù, two blocks from Piazza Venezia. The long, slow Sunday was winding to an end—hot, dark in the blackout, quiet, no cars, no buses, deserted streets, buildings barely discernible in the moonless night.

Suddenly, along the street came a man on a bicycle who slowed down in front of the Jesuit presbytery.

"Padre Tacchi-Venturi!" he called out. "And you, you were his confessor!"

A few minutes later another bicycle came by with the man on this one shouting, "Viva Matteotti!" Now, slowly, the whole city seemed to the brothers to stir, to turn and twist restlessly, to come awake bit by bit while a low dull hum like the buzzing of bees grew louder, erupted into shouts, cries, songs which melded together and expanded into a giant roar. The boys heard the sound of shutters being thrown open, then windows, doors, steps running, and saw lights appear in disordered fashion as if on a giant switchboard.

Raffaele Persichetti sat in his living room, listening to a concert of light music on the radio. He had returned to Rome only a few days before from the North, where he had carried out a mission for the Action party, and earlier that evening he had gone to the movies with his girlfriend. Abruptly, the music stopped, and there was a long, long silence. Raffaele's mother started to turn off the set, but Raffaele stopped her.

They waited; usually a record was played when a program was delayed. But a few minutes later came the warbling of the radio bird and *"Attenzione! Attenzione!"* Then, without further preamble, came the voice of broadcaster Giovan Battista Arista: "His Majesty, King and Emperor, has accepted the resignation as Head of the Government, Prime Minister, Secretary of State, presented by His Excellency Cavaliere Benito Mussolini, and has named as Head of the Government, Prime Minister, Secretary of State, His Excellency Cavaliere Marshal of Italy, Pietro Badoglio."

Then the king's proclamation, in which he announced that he was "assuming command of all the Armed Forces," was read, followed by the recorded voice of Badoglio: "Italians, by order of His Majesty the King and Emperor, I am assuming the military government of the country with full powers. The war continues. Italy . . . keeps faith with its word, jealous of its age-long traditions. Whoever . . . attempts to disturb public order will be inexorably punished. *Viva l'Italia! Viva il Re!"*

There was a pause. Raffaele wondered if there would be a clarifying statement, a declaration by Mussolini, something additional. But there was only the unemotional voice of the announcer saying, "End of the broadcast."

Raffaele could hardly believe his ears. Excitedly, he phoned his friends, his comrades in the Action party, and went out into the streets with his brother to celebrate. He hugged an acquaintance and said, "Finally we can say what we think. We can speak. We can breathe."

He and his friends walked along the streets, at first aimlessly, as happy people emerged in their pajamas, half-naked or in T-shirts. The summer night's silence was soon completely shattered by noise.

"To Palazzo Venezia," someone cried, and arm in arm they strode down Corso Vittorio Emanuele, Raffaele's tall gangling figure towering above the others. Singing and shouting they passed in front of the Supreme Command, which showed unusual signs of life. As they went through Piazza del Gesù, the Antonelli brothers, both former students of Raffaele, stood on their balcony unseen by him, watching the scene with wonder.

By then, Carla Capponi had heard what had happened; now she would not have to assassinate Mussolini. At about 11 P.M., while she was walking homeward, she too saw lights going on, shutters, windows and doors opening, and people coming out and yelling, "Fascism has fallen!"

At home, her mother had been listening to the radio; the family from the floor above came down and, for the first time, expressed strong republican feelings. Carla had looked down at Piazza Venezia, now jammed as if for one of Mussolini's speeches. Some Fascist guards came out and started shooting, but they fired only two or three times, then rushed back inside and slammed the doors. Suddenly the whole square was illuminated; here and there someone would climb atop another's shoulders and give a fervent speech which no one understood, but which was accompanied by cheers as enthusiasm and joy permeated the throng. Carla joined in, identifying herself as a Communist. A worker who heard her said that he, too, was a Communist and introduced himself as Guido Rattoppatore. They sang "The Red Flag," but in muffled tones—the habit of years was too strong—and then Guido walked her home and asked to use her apartment for organizational meetings of the party.

Raffaele Persichetti had joined the multitude in Piazza Venezia, singing, shouting and cheering. When a large number of the demonstrators marched off to the nearby Quirinal Palace to hail the king, Raffaele and his friends, all fervent antimonarchists, refused and led another group up Corso Umberto to Piazza Colonna, where orators mounted improvised platforms to condemn the past, to welcome the future, and to cheer Italy, Badoglio and the army. It all seemed like a big show in which everyone was both actor and audience.

Shouting "Viva l'Italia!" and ignoring the sweat on his face, Raffaele joined in the swarm of people heading up Via del Tritone. His shouts were echoed in the streets, deserted a few minutes before but now overrun, and he was joined by other people who flowed towards the center of the city. As he walked, Raffaele met friends, lost them and found them again, embraced people he had never met and watched grown men run up and down pavements like children, yelling to those at open windows. Laughingly he held his fingers to his ears as columns of demonstrators made an ever-increasing din as their cries echoed along the streets. All around him were people hugging each other with joy and telling each other the news with exuberant gestures. The city was as alive as if it were high noon; staid citizens were dancing in the streets and making up improvised parades. It was like a village *festa*, a return to the old Italy, the romantic Italy of Raffaele's dreams.

Three Socialists—Oreste Lizzadri, Tullio Vecchietti and Achille Corona—forced their way into the editorial offices of *Il Lavoro Fascista* on Via IV Novembre and started putting together an edition of the old Socialist organ *Avanti!* Copies were on the street when police came, but Vecchietti, who was found to be carrying a pistol, was held in arrest until that afternoon.

Members of the press, for years reduced to puppeting the words of the regime, were among the most exultant. That day, as bits of news had flown around the city, they had been unable to do anything; it was a Sunday and the presses were stilled. But the odd stories had plagued them all day long. The evening had carried with it rumors, abetted by the unusual appearance of squads with rifles, submachine guns and light artillery in various places around the city.

Yet when radios were turned on, all that could be heard were the normal programs. Small groups had gathered to speculate on what was happening, and although nothing had been printed or broadcast about the Grand Council meeting, by then most people knew that it had taken place and that some kind of decision had been reached as a result. Here and there word cropped up that Mussolini was involved, that he had gone to his country home or to see Hitler, that he was ill, or even that he had died.

Most of the rumors were greeted with skeptical shrugs, and only later did they begin to take on definite form; the Grand Council had voted against Mussolini, his position was in danger.

At the Caffè Aragno, a gathering place for journalists, artists and writers, a Sicilian journalist came running in sometime between 9 and 10 P.M.

"They've arrested him! They've arrested him!" he shouted. The group poured out into the street, shouting, "Mussolini has been arrested! Mussolini has been arrested! Death to Mussolini!"

Someone had the idea of putting out a special edition of *Il Messaggero*, whose offices were just around the corner. As a group walked exultantly up Via del Tritone, they passed a hotel doorman. He did not understand the cries and raised his arm in a smart Fascist salute. By now entire floors were lit up and their reflections brightened the sky. The group kept on shouting, "Citizens, wake up. Mussolini is finished." From some windows came the angry yells of would-be sleepers, from others, shouts of "Long live the king."

At *Il Messaggero*, typesetters, printers and reporters were called or came of their own will. Mario Pannunzio sat down at the typewriter and started to write. A printer removed the "XXI," the year of the Fascist regime, from the newspaper's logo, hurled it to the floor and stamped on it. Every now and then, reporters and printers had to stop work and rush to the doors to keep back crowds who wanted to come in, smash everything and occupy the place in the name of the people. When Pannunzio came back after one of these defenses, his article was gone from his typewriter. He learned later that the paper's drama critic had taken it as a souvenir. Pannunzio started writing again and, with literary lights Mario Soldati and Leo Longanesi screaming suggestions at him, the new article emerged even more violent than the previous one had been.

Various people were making speeches outside, and from time to time came the courageous cry: "Out with the Germans!" An air force general pleaded with the mob to calm down, while young people continued to try to come in to write their own pieces. Everyone shouted while the reporters worked feverishly. Until then they had written either ambiguously or with hypocritical praise of the regime.

The paper's former publisher, Pio Perrone, ousted by fascism, had just brought out his treasured one hundred-year-old cognac when an infantry lieutenant with fifteen grenadiers came in, guns in hand. They were persuaded to leave only to have their places taken by a group of bare-chested workers with tricolor kerchiefs around their necks, triumphantly carrying one of Italy's best known actresses, Paola Borboni, who was famed for having appeared once on the stage with a naked bosom. Everyone embraced and called each other comrade, and the paper was finally put to press as the actress, wearing only a flimsy robe over her pajamas, was carried off to the fountain at Piazza Barberini, where she gave an incoherent but enthusiastic speech.

The issue was signed by Perrone instead of by Alessandro Pavolini, the Fascist-named editor. Pavolini was not there to protest; he had been on his way, but hearing of the fall of Mussolini, had turned around and run back to his home. The paper came out in the form of a leaflet, which was either given away or pasted on walls until Chief of Police Senise read a copy at two in the morning and had it seized.

"My God!" he said. "They're really going to cause trouble."

A less inflammatory edition was then put out.

Meanwhile, the Press Club, considered a foundry of false news, was ransacked: typewriters were thrown out the windows; desks, back issues of newspapers, photographs of Mussolini, bookcases and even telephones were set afire.

A crowd went to Palazzo Braschi, the Rome Federation of the Fascist Party, and took it by assault. Everything inflammable was thrown out the windows and set on fire. In other parts of the city, Fascist posters and portraits of the *Duce* were torn down and made into small bonfires which blazed on the pavements until they gave the impression that again all Rome was burning.

At the Quirinal Palace, floodlights suddenly came on, illuminating the façade, and flags were hoisted on the columns at the sides of the main entrance. Even though the king was not there, crowds remained, shouting and singing until two in the morning.

Most German soldiers in Rome did not know what to expect; some joined the celebrations, thinking that the war was over. In the state-licensed brothels, there were happy celebrations, with everyone drinking and toasting.

Crowds, seemingly unable to restrain themselves, stormed into piazzas. They cried, "Fascism is dead," and pulled Fascist buttonhole badges off jackets screaming, "Away with these bedbugs!" Those with badges finally realized that discretion was the better part of valor and the streets began to be filled with discarded buttons.

Opposite the Ministry of War, Emilio Schuberth stopped working on dress designs and watched the excited people who were passing by. Reflected in his mirrors were photographs of the Mussolini family, his clients, including one of the *Duce* himself with a dedication. When he heard the news on the radio, he hurried to throw the photos away, but later he ventured out in the street, saw the scores of discarded Fascist lapel buttons, and considered making a dress design from them.

Die-hard Fascists felt that the ground had opened under their feet. What had appeared to be a shifting of responsibilities had turned out to be a rear-guard action; and none were more surprised than those members of the Grand Council who had only wanted to take military powers from Mussolini and had never thought of overturning the regime to which they themselves belonged. Without a chief, without orders, unused to personal initiative, they were powerless. The world had changed and they were already strangers in it. Many did not even believe in Mussolini's resignation. Only one thought it necessary to make a gesture. A few minutes after he had heard the news, Senator Manlio Morgagni, the head of the Fascist news agency, shot himself. The note which he left on his desk said, "*Il Duce* has resigned; my life is finished. Long live Mussolini."

A little before one in the morning, word came to the Supreme Command that the black-shirted Littorio Division was marching towards Rome and that two of its "M" (for Mussolini) battalions had already begun fighting at Ponte Galeria, west of the city. Sudden panic overtook the generals; machine guns were set up at the windows, and tanks and guns were placed in the inner courtyard and in the nearby streets. The generals decided to wake up Badoglio, who came sleepily to Palazzo Vidoni. There was still a good deal of tension and only Castellano gave direct orders to the troops. A call was made to General Ruggiero to speed up the movement of grenadiers to Rome and Carboni was ordered to place extra guards around military establishments and depots.

The precautions were not necessary. The Littorio Division was at Campagnano di Roma, thirty miles north of the capital. At 6:30 P.M. they had received orders from their commander to march on Rome, but before they could get moving, the orders were canceled because Galbiati had refused to take the responsibility. The isolated detachments in Rome had their communications cut and never even contemplated moving.

At about that time, Marshal Cavallero was arrested.

"How can this be?" he asked. "Mussolini knows very well that I'm one of his faithful."

"That's exactly why," the officer answered. "Badoglio gave me the order to arrest you."

However, Cavallero had not been on the list made up by Castellano, Cerica and Senise, all of whom, along with Carboni, were then meeting with Badoglio. When word came of the catch, they informed Badoglio of the arrest of his old enemy.

"Send him to Regina Coeli," ordered Badoglio.

"But he's a marshal of Italy," Carboni said. "We can't put him in the city jail. What about a military prison?"

"All right, Fort Boccea," Bodoglio said reluctantly, drinking from a small bottle of beer he kept on the floor at his side. He then told Carboni to question his old rival, adding in dialect, "*Ca i gava 'l sang.*" ("That'll draw his blood.").

Then, as the old marshal sat intermittently napping, the ambitious

Carboni asked to be appointed to the cabinet as minister of popular culture. The old man, his head wobbling from lack of sleep, answered affirmatively.

Meanwhile, throughout the country, the first completely genuine and spontaneous demonstration in years continued. It was so big, so unrestrainable, that anti-Fascists, non-Fascists and even members of the party cheered in the squares and drank toasts in their houses.

New cries began to be heard: *"Viva la pace!"* ("Hurray for peace!") For what other reason, they asked, if not to conclude peace, had the king gotten rid of Mussolini? They overlooked, however, the position to which Badoglio had been appointed; it was not that of a pre-Fascist premier, but head of government, like Mussolini, with all the dictatorial powers granted by Fascist laws in the middle twenties. In the excitement, only a few had heard, after the radio announcement of the resignation, Badoglio's proclamation, and even fewer understood the real meaning of the phrase, "The war continues." Most felt that the war would continue for a week or so and that then the Americans would arrive.

That night, when the king went to bed, he noted the event in his diary with the succinct phrase: "Today I revoked the government of Mussolini."

In his diary, philosopher Benedetto Croce wrote: "The sensation I feel is that of liberation from a sickness which burdened the mind." And Bonomi wrote: "A great event is being celebrated: the restitution of Italy to the Italians."

Raffaele Persichetti, still excited, finally went to bed, resolved to get up early and to make the most of life in the new, reborn Italy.

On Monday morning, July 26, Rome still had a festive air. At 7 A.M., Giorgio Nelson Page, walking down Via Veneto to his office, noticed that no one was wearing a party badge in his buttonhole. He mechanically touched his; it was still there. He took it off, saying to himself that now that the head of government had changed, the party had changed also. He put the badge in his pocket, determined to keep it for a souvenir. Later, he wrote: "I lost it like all my other memories."

Overnight, flags had been hung out of houses, at public buildings, on monuments, and even along the sides of streetcars. At 8 A.M. the streets surged with Romans determined to enjoy the new situation in which they found themselves. The sudden gift of liberty seemed more intoxicating than any wine. People acted as if in a dream, as if a gust of wind had swept away all the memories of the past. One woman on Campo dei Fiori was carrying her child in swaddling clothes saying, "I want him to breathe this free air."

The early risers rushed to buy newspapers, which had headlines covering half the front page. Badoglio's proclamation was reported but not explained. Instead, the papers talked about demonstrations, crowds, flags. However, the habit of years was too strong to throw off entirely, and a few newspapers felt it necessary to include the usual anti-Anglo-American propaganda. The English, it was said, were still preoccupied by the Arabs in Palestine, and there was a highly colored article about the brutal treatment of Italian prisoners by the English; as for the United States, the aircraft industry in Los Angeles was supposedly paralyzed by a transportation strike, and Assistant Secretary of State Adolf Berle was reported as saying that Washington would not recognize Charles de Gaulle's committee as the government of France in exile. Bulgarian bishops protested about the bombing of Rome while in the same country Zionist spies were condemned to death. Considerable space was given to the bombing of Bologna, which had resulted in forty-seven dead.

By nine o'clock demonstrations were being organized, and the city took on the air of enthusiasm that had exploded the night before, although now it was calmer and less extemporaneous. People walked around holding arms, and soldiers and officers were applauded. There were shouts of "Long live the king," and even Communists carried big pictures of the sovereign.

At Piazza Montecitorio, a plaque honoring Costanzo Ciano was torn down and replaced by one with the name of Giacomo Matteotti. It was quickly removed by the police, along with a photo of the late deputy, which had been placed in front of the Matteotti residence on Lungotevere Arnaldo da Brescia.

All over the country people were pulling down Fascist symbols and destroying them. Stone and ceramic *fasci* were torn off buildings and thrown to the ground, while in some public buildings the lictors, the symbols of Roman authority which had been adopted by fascism, were covered with flags or cloths or hurriedly painted over.

Vulgarity also came to the fore. A well-dressed gentleman on Corso Umberto dragged a bust of the dictator to the center of the street, dropped his pants, and smeared the face with his excreta.

Peddlers who had been banned by fascism began to reappear. An old man set up his table with white mice in front of the Chiesa Nuova with a small sign which read: "After ten years of unjust prohibition..."

Other signs, such as *"Libertà"* and *"Viva l'Italia,"* were painted over walls where whitewash covered Mussolini's *"Credere! Obbediere! Combattare!"* ("Believe! Obey! Fight!") A shouting crowd forced their way into Palazzo Venezia and put an Italian flag on the balcony from which Mussolini used to speak. Part of the crowd rummaging around, barely missed discovering some confidential documents which were hastily collected by officials sent over by General Cerica, who suddenly remembered how compromising they might be.

The country's intellectual life started to revive, as painters and sculptors met and talked of what they would create in this new air of freedom. Film director Roberto Rossellini, at the beach home of his wife's parents in nearby Ladispoli, came back to Rome and immediately started planning a movie with actor Aldo Fabrizi and writer Sergio Amidei. It was to be a satire on fascism but finally turned out to be *Rome, Open City.*

The people's dislike for fascism, whether newly discovered or of long standing, began to be vented on individuals. Occasionally crowds recognized an OVRA agent and gave chase. In some places, Fascist militia who had ventured out in uniform were undressed and sent home in their underwear.

A pitched battle took place in downtown Via Depretis, with soldiers, civilians and militia firing at each other. Two civilians had been killed when Chief of Police Senise sent General Soleti of the *polizia* to separate the combatants and move the militia to "another locality." On Viale Romania, Galbiati and his militia officials still refused to leave. Badoglio sent orders to clear the area. When his regular army troops opened fire with small arms, the militia finally gave in.

There was not a single German soldier to be seen that day, and later it was difficult to find a Fascist. Offices of the Fascist party in various parts of the city were looted and set ablaze. Bonfires of papers, questionnaires, party cards and lists of party members were torn up, piled in stacks and put to the torch. Antonio Santovito, a messenger boy for the party office on Via Bartolo da Sassoferrato, watched in amazement as longtime Fascists took great care to throw membership rolls containing their names into the fire. Others remembered where Fascists lived and painted signs on some of their houses announcing that "The easy life is over." The Petacci family, scenting disaster, was among the first to leave the city.

One of Scorza's assistant secretaries, a dentist named Alfredo Cucco, was huddled in his house on Via dei Pontefici 3 when a crowd came looking for him. Some masons working next door defended him saying he was a doctor. The crowd hesitated, then started to move forward again, until one of the workers said, "His wife is going to have a child any minute," at which the mob turned away.

The monarchists were particularly happy and proud of their king. "He saved Italy" appeared in big letters on walls which had earlier accommodated roughly printed posters with somewhat earthier phrases.

The rest of the country celebrated also. Milan's demonstrations lasted all night long. A group of young people went to the so-called den (a reconstructed room where Mussolini had directed the newspaper *Popolo d'Italia* until the March on Rome) and destroyed it. Posters appeared on the walls of La Scala saying "Toscanini, come back," an appeal to conductor Arturo Toscanini who had left Italy in protest against fascism.

Particularly in the North, Communists moved to take advantage of the situation. They had some difficulty in rounding up their leaders who, to avoid arrest, maintained little contact with one another. Some who frequently changed living quarters or slept in secluded places found out only the next morning that they could, at least for the time being, meet and speak freely. Milanese thronged to Piazza del Duomo, where they cheered the inflammatory phrases of left-wing speakers.

As soon as the first moments of enthusiasm had passed, people began thinking about those still in prison. In Turin, thousands of workers went to the Carcere Nuovo, smashed the front door with a truck, and freed about four hundred political prisoners. In Milan, a group left the Duomo and marched on the San Vittore prison, where troops fired on them, broke them up and arrested some of their leaders.

Not far from there, Felice Chilanti, serving a five-year term of confinement because of his political opposition to the regime, was asleep in his cell when his guards suddenly entered with a stretcher loaded with bottles of wine which they all drank together in celebration of Mussolini's fall.

In Rome, a few political prisoners were lucky enough to be released that same day, including Action party leader Sergio Fenoaltea, who later became Italian ambassador to the United States. Crowds gathered and cheered as every now and then a prisoner emerged, his face pale and a little swollen, confused by the light and by his un-expected release. Later that day, Roman painter Sante Monachesi donned a red sash and led an impatient crowd to Regina Coeli. Where he marched up to the head jailer and took his keys from him. "I won't squash you because you'd stink," he said. Then he began to release prisoners, freeing the wrong ones until his mistake was pointed out to him by police who had been called to the scene. By then, however, almost a thousand prisoners charged with common crimes had forced their way out, along with more than four hundred women from the adjoining women's prison, almost none there for political reasons.

Anti-Fascists who were not in prison met to discuss the turn of events. De Gasperi was against cooperating with the king. "The task of getting rid of the corpse of fascism," he said, "belongs to those who gave it life." But his opinion was disregarded, mainly because of the Communists, whose leader, Concetto Marchesi, declared his party's willingness to collaborate with the monarchy.

Meanwhile, anti-Fascists abroad were also learning the news: Social Democrat Giuseppe Saragat, a future president of Italy, at Lyons, where he had taken refuge; Communist leader Palmiro To-gliatti at the Hotel Lux in Moscow, where he was exiled; and Socialist Pietro Nenni on the island of Ponza, where he was confined. In his diary that night, Nenni wrote: "Here's to the dictator who falls, to the adventure that ends, to the rebirth of freedom over dictator-ship."

Exhilarated with liberty, old and new friends invaded Bonomi's house that afternoon, but that night they heard that *Il Mondo* would no longer be published. The liberal paper which had been shut down by the Fascist regime had been put together in a few minutes on Sunday night in its old printing house on Via Mario dei Fiori. Now, however, faced by a government ban, it would have to go under-ground. It was the first portent of things to come.

At the same time, the demonstrations were losing their force. The king and some of his men had been taken aback by the unprece-dented explosion of popular joy, but by noon, police appeared, along with posters urging calm.

People began to experience second thoughts. As a column of peo-ple came down the Via Veneto, a man shouted, "See, I say 'pig of a Mussolini' and no one arrests me." But another shouted, "Say 'pig of a Badoglio' and see how liberty will chop your head off."

Chapter 9

THE ARMIES PREPARE

The Anglo-Americans

The downfall of fascism took the Anglo-American forces by surprise; their intelligence services had given them no warning, and even Churchill admitted that the Allies had had "no definite knowledge of the inner stresses of Italian politics."

Churchill was spending a quiet Sunday afternoon at Chequers, the country residence of English prime ministers. With him was his wife, his two daughters, his private secretary, Sir John Martin, and one of his top advisors, Viscount Cherwell. The chief of the Imperial General Staff, Field Marshal Sir Alan Brooke, arrived with his wife to spend the night.

Before dinner, Churchill led Brooke to a seat in the orchard to discuss future Mediterranean strategy. The two allies were still at odds; there were still no peace terms since the U.S. Department of State had scarcely discussed them. The British were still inclined towards harsh treatment of Italy but wanted to protect the monarchy as an institution, feeling that it would help to secure Italian military cooperation and to maintain order. The American position tended towards a more lenient attitude. The Americans, as Churchill remarked with some annoyance, had an undue liking for logical, clearcut decisions, whereas the British were inclined towards an opportunistic approach to strategy. In Churchill's opinion, the Americans had to be persuaded to accord top importance to Italy, even though Roosevelt insisted on the Normandy assault and American chiefs of staff had secured priority for the Pacific and Burma over the Mediterranean.

Brooke had told Eisenhower that he would like to reconsider the cross-Channel project, perhaps even to eliminate it. It was no wonder that in his diary Brooke wrote of his talk with Churchill: "We are in complete agreement and fully realize the trouble we shall have with the Americans."

After dinner, the news came from Italy, and Churchill rushed off to consult with Foreign Secretary Anthony Eden, returning to discuss Mussolini's fall with Brooke until 1:30 A.M., when the general finally escaped to bed. Brooke saw the deposition of Mussolini as a memorable moment, as a changeover from "the end of the beginning" to "the beginning of the end."

In Tunisia, General Dwight Eisenhower did not receive the news until just before he sat down to breakfast the next morning in his seaside cottage at La Marsa. Although it was only 8 A.M., he immediately called Harold Macmillan, British minister of state, at Allied headquarters. On Sunday night, Macmillan had been in his room reading when an intelligence officer had phoned to tell him of Mussolini's fall. Now he listened as Ike outlined his plans for exploiting the situation.

Eisenhower had come to La Marsa Sunday afternoon in order to be ready for the conference of senior commanders he had called for Monday morning. When the meeting got under way, there was a great deal of speculation, but, as Macmillan said, the commanders "had no very clear picture of what had happened in Rome." In fact, everyone wondered whether Mussolini's ouster had any connection with the July 19 meeting between Hitler and Mussolini at Feltre. Had Hitler insisted that the defense of Italy be placed under German control? And had this insistence provoked Mussolini's overthrow?

Eisenhower said that he wanted to take immediate advantage of the event. He told his subordinates that the new regime in Italy was probably anti-Nazi and that its policies might affect not only the Sicilian campaign but the war in the rest of Europe as well. An immediate message should be broadcast to encourage this government, to offer it an honorable and easy way out—"a white alley"—in return for the immediate use of its airfields and strategic strongpoints in "a real and proper alliance" against the Germans.

Macmillan and U.S. political advisor Robert Murphy were forced to point out that Eisenhower's command lacked the authority to initiate a political maneuver; Washington and London had to be consulted first. Eisenhower commented that before the days of rapid communications, generals on the spot had done what they thought best. Eisenhower felt that he could deal quickly and advantageously with the Italians; if he had to wait for the two capitals to concur, he thought, a valuable opportunity could be lost. Nevertheless, he cabled his proposals to Washington and London.

It was a strange situation. Italy was in turmoil, but the Allies had no peace terms to propose should Italy want to surrender. What the British had been predicting for six months had actually come about. Now some urgent decisions were needed, but the two men at the top circled the issue. On July 26, Churchill cabled Roosevelt that with Mussolini down and out, Hitler would feel very lonely. Besides, "the changes in Italy probably portend peace proposals."

Roosevelt's message crossed Churchill's. "If any overtures come," the president said, "we must be certain of the use of all the Italian territory and transportation against the Germans in the north and against the whole Balkan peninsula." He added, however, that "in no event must our officers in the field fix on any general terms without your approval and mine."

This was exactly what Eisenhower had feared. The draft of his proposed broadcast traveled back and forth. When Radio Algiers finally aired it on July 29, it merely asked that the Italians surrender, offering them peace with honor and repatriation of Italian prisoners. Nothing was said of terms. Ike was authorized only to repeat the principle of unconditional surrender, if and when the Italian government made an inquiry. Churchill thought that the Italian government was most likely to attempt to communicate with the Allies through the Vatican, the Turks or the Swiss.

Eisenhower, however, had not given up. For a short time he eased the bombing of Italy and had this bruited about as an opportunity for the new Italian government to move towards surrender. Even this relatively minor initiative brought an angry protest from London, although the bombing delay was really caused, as Eisenhower said, "by the necessity of transferring air units and the bringing up of supplies."

Meanwhile, the Combined Chiefs of Staff (British and American) authorized Eisenhower to launch AVALANCHE, the amphibious assault on the Salerno-Naples area, at the earliest possible date. The catch, however, was that he was to carry out the operation "with the resources available to him."

The British, in line with their desire to throw as much force into the Mediterranean as they could, sent Eisenhower one aircraft and four escort carriers. The Americans, who still wanted to fight a limited war in that area, refused to budge, and quick, decisive moves were rendered impossible.

Militarily, operations in Sicily were already hampered by these differences of opinion. The British Eighth Army, blocked from the key port of Messina by four German divisions before Mount Etna, had to remain there while General George Patton's Seventh Army, on General Alexander's orders, was relegated to the secondary role of protecting the British flank. Unwilling to accept this state of affairs, Patton took his protest to the top and succeeded finally in obtaining permission to push on to take Palermo and Marsala and return to beat the British into Messina.

The same ambivalence applied to propaganda. Directives to the psychological warfare branch, which ran the UN radio in Algiers under the joint guidance of the American OWI and the British MOI, swung back and forth between the Allies' opposing views. OWI-inspired broadcasts contained references to "the moronic little king" and called Badoglio "a high-ranking Fascist," which was not likely to encourage Italian peace approaches. Harold Macmillan later wrote that ". . . it became increasingly difficult to give instructions to our propaganda team. What line were we to take towards the Italian people—hard, soft, or alternating?"

There were other complications. In London, U.S. Ambassador John Winant cabled Washington concerning Anthony Eden's statement that "General Badoglio, no more than Mussolini, can make the Italians fight," and then reported Eden's suggestion that the Russians be brought into Allied councils in considering Italian peace terms.

Ignoring these political contretemps, Eisenhower ordered General Mark Clark to work immediately on plans for AVALANCHE, which was scheduled for late October. Eisenhower hoped that he could hurry things up a bit and strike before the iron had cooled too much.

The Germans

Power diplomacy had been neglected by the German diplomats in Rome that summer. The languor of *dolce far niente* seemed to have touched them all. How else could it have been that they were so completely uninformed of what was happening and so unprepared to deal with it? On the weekend the Fascist regime fell, the men who should have been watching events were engaged in other pursuits; some had even left sweltering Rome to seek relief at the sea, the lakes and the sulphur baths. Easy-going Colonel Helfferich, head of counter-espionage in Italy, wanted to remain there and therefore tried not to irritate Berlin with unpleasant or pessimistic reports. He spent Sunday with his young wife taking the waters at Bagni di Tivoli.

German Military Attaché General Enno von Rintelen passed Sunday on the lake of Bolsena and took a motorboat to visit the small islands there. He did not learn what had happened until one o'clock the next morning, when he received an icy phone call from General Walter Warlimont at Hitler's headquarters.

The plenipotentiary minister, Prince Otto von Bismarck, nephew of the Iron Chancellor, was dining with friends in a Roman *trattoria* when a junior member of the embassy came up to him and murmured the news in his ear. Bismarck shrugged him off, saying, "*Keine Bierwitze, bitte.*" ("No poor jokes, please.")

By nine o'clock that evening, Ambassador Mackensen had sent a telegram to Berlin, belatedly telling of Mussolini's deposal.

"It doesn't seem to me that this is an illegal action on the part of the king," he later told the agitated hierarch Farinacci, who appeared at the German Embassy and kept talking obsessively of Mussolini's arrest. "All that's happened is that one Head of Government has gone and another has taken his place."

The next day Mackensen, having been reprimanded by Berlin for his mistaken judgment, stormed over to Badoglio to lodge protests and warn of Hitler's reaction. The marshal gave him his promise that the war would continue and assured him that the change of government was an internal matter that portended no change in Axis relations.

OBS, German military headquarters, near Frascati, was no better prepared. When the news came, OBS ordered tanks into the streets of the little town to assume defensive positions. After waiting in vain for military action by Italian Fascists, Kesselring had them withdrawn.

For some time, Kesselring had been in a position similar to Eisenhower's. His request for reinforcements with which to hold Sicily had been denied, because they would have to come from the Eastern front where an entirely different staff was in command. While Kesselring and the Southern front were the direct responsibility of Germany's Armed Forces High Command, Oberkommando der Wehrmacht (OKW), the Eastern front, was run by the Army Command, Oberkommando des Heeres (OKH). Each fought its own war with little interest in the other's problems or needs. The two staffs rarely met to hammer out their differences; Hitler made the decisions. In addition, the German dictator had, since July 13, personally held the responsibility for command decisions in Sicily, which meant that Kesselring, like Eisenhower, could make no political or tactical decisions concerning the island without prior consultation with the Fuehrer.

Even so, Kesselring wanted to see for himself what the political situation was in Rome. That same afternoon, accompanied by Rintelen, he too went to see Badoglio and came away persuaded that Italy would remain a German ally.

In Germany, Hitler was not so sure. He was then in *Wolfsschanze*, the concrete "wolf's lair" in East Prussia, near Rastenburg, which had been his field headquarters for two years. On July 25, when he held his daily *Lagevortrag*, or situation conference, in the *Lagebaracke*, his generals were trying to substitute a long-range strategy for his snap decisions. General Jodl, the superbly trained chief of OKW operations staff, was expanding on the necessity for long-range planning when Hitler, interrupting him, turned to Walter Hewel, the foreign ministry liaison.

"What is the state of things in Rome?"

"Nothing definite yet," answered Hewel, who had only Mackensen's inaccurate telegram to go on. He then proceeded to tell of various untrue, contradictory rumors relayed by Mackensen, including one that Farinacci had persuaded Mussolini to call the Grand Council meeting and another that anti-Fascist Vittorio Emanuele Orlando would be named prime minister as a result of the meeting.

Hitler, a firm believer in one-man rule, was convinced that the Grand Council had done nothing but "jabber" and quickly moved on to other subjects.

That afternoon and evening more reports came in, and by the time the *Abendlage*, the nightly briefing meeting, took place, Hitler was in a fury. Some of his generals, even though hardened by previous displays of raving and ranting, were aghast. General Warlimont, Jodl's deputy, and incidentally married to an American, called it "a shocking and shattering exhibition of confusion and lack of balance."

It was the closest Hitler had ever come to a serious emotional collapse. Why did Mussolini's downfall have such a powerful effect on Hitler? Perhaps the Italian dictator was more to Hitler than just an ally. At his meeting with Mussolini at Feltre, Hitler, against his generals' advice, had given up his plans for a unified command under the Germans. It was almost as if he relied on the *Duce* for reassurance about his own future. If the *Duce* could be removed, so could he.

In his diary, Paul Joseph Goebbels, Hitler's propaganda minister, wrote: "It's simply shocking to think that a revolutionary movement which has been in power for twenty-one years could be liquidated just like that." He worried about what to tell the German people. "Knowledge of these events," he wrote, "might conceivably encourage some subversive elements in Germany to think they could put over the same thing here. . . ." Goebbels was disturbed about other misfortunes as well. Stalin had hailed the failure of the *Wehrmacht*'s summer offensive, action against England had been delayed by the *Luftwaffe*'s defeats in Sicily, a former prime minister of Bulgaria had criticized the German alliance in that satellite's parliament. There was even criticism in Germany itself: "The letters addressed to me . . . keep asking why the Fuehrer doesn't visit the bombed areas, why Goering is nowhere to be seen, and especially why the Fuehrer doesn't talk to the German people and explain the present situation. One worry after another piles up on us and we hardly know how to meet them."

On July 24, Hamburg, the largest port in the Reich, was hit by over seven hundred Allied aircraft, which dropped showers of metallic strips to jam German radar stations and unloaded more than two thousand tons of high explosives and incendiary bombs. On Sunday, July 25, over six hundred Bomber Command aircraft dropped an almost equivalent number of bombs on Essen, causing so much damage to the Krupp works there that when old Gustav Krupp saw the wreckage he literally had a fit.

At nine thirty that night, Hitler announced to his generals, "The *Duce* has resigned." He was in favor of immediate retaliation—Rome was the center of the rottenness, and the solution was to move in and take it over.

"What's his name [Badoglio] said straightaway that the war would be continued," Hitler ranted, "but that doesn't mean a thing. We can play the same game." He spoke of having the 3rd Panzergrenadieren move into Rome to arrest all the Italian leaders. .

When he was told that the division was sixty miles from Rome, Hitler insisted that it could not be more than forty. He wanted German troops brought into Italy over the Alpine passes, divisions taken from the Russian front, Sicily evacuated, and everything put under Rommel's command. Mussolini was to be found and brought to Germany, those who had overthrown him were to be captured, and the *Duce* was to be restored to power.

Jodl tried to slow him down. "We should really wait for more complete reports of what's going on."

"Of course," snapped Hitler. "But on our side we have got to start thinking. Being traitors they'll say they will remain loyal to us, but that's treachery and of course they won't."

"Get the men back," he said pointing to Sicily on the large map. "Have them abandon the equipment. The men are more important. Their matériel doesn't matter. They can blow it up or make it unusable. There are seventy thousand effectives, they should take only small arms with them, that's enough against the Italians."

Jodl pointed out that they could not ferry over more than seventeen thousand a day.

"Well," Hitler replied off-handedly, "they'll have to crowd together."

Jodl mentioned an intelligence report "from a somewhat controversial personality in Switzerland" saying that the Allies were planning an attack on the mainland, towards Rome. "Occupation of Rome is looked upon as most important psychologically."

"That certainly all adds up," said Hitler, who proceeded to ask about the possibility of a parachute division from France making a drop on Rome.

"Jodl," he said, turning to the OKW operations chief, "work out the orders. We must, of course, act from now on as if we thought they [the Italians] were going to continue fighting."

At a further briefing conference at midnight, Hitler elaborated his plans. "Rome must be occupied. No one is to leave Rome and then the 3rd Panzergrenadieren will move in."

Hewel, Foreign Minister Joachim von Ribbentrop's man, had an idea: "Shouldn't we tell them to occupy the exits to the Vatican?"

"It doesn't matter," said Hitler disdainfully. "I'll go into the Vatican anytime. You think it worries me? We'll take it right over . . . the whole diplomatic corps . . . that riff-raff. We'll get the whole bunch of swine out of there. Later we can say we're sorry."

When Hitler held his midday briefing conference the next day, July 26, Rommel had been flown in and Goering and Himmler were also present.

Jodl's only fresh news from Rome was that some people were yelling, "Peace, peace," while others were hunting down Fascists.

"That's good," said Hitler.

Jodl said that one airport near Rome was completely in German hands, but he was unable to tell Hitler when the parachute division would be ready for the drop.

Goering tried to find out what was really going on. "What Italian forces are there in Rome?" he asked. No one answered him.

After a discussion of moving troops over the Alpine passes, the still-confused Goering turned to Hitler. "Can I ask about the parachute division, *mein Fuehrer*?" he asked. "Where do you mean it to land?"

"Everything must be occupied," Hitler wandered. "All the exit roads."

Goering attempted again to clarify the Fuehrer's instructions. "Not all at the same time, then?"

Hitler was hopelessly vague. "Everything else we shall need in the city can be landed at an airfield. I don't know which for the moment. But we must be sure to get away quickly, because we must reckon on the Allies attacking right away."

Goering was again trying to obtain some more precise information when an aide interrupted. "We can't say exactly what the situation will be this afternoon or tomorrow."

"The situation will be just the same," Hitler proclaimed. "Rome will still be Rome. The exit roads must be occupied."

He then went on to the command organization. "Overall com-

mand should go to Rommel. Kesselring hasn't got the reputation. . . .
Himmler's had a very good idea: Italian soldiers can go home . . . we
won't get those who go home; they're no use anyway."

Himmler spoke up. "We could perhaps take them to Germany
later as a labor force."

Hitler waved this away and returned to the occupation of Rome
by the paratroopers. But Goering still was not sure.

"The opposition," he said, "will naturally call on the Allies for
help," and the Allies, he went on, could "always put down parachute
troops the same as we can."

"Of course," admitted Hitler, "but . . ."

Goering hastened to mollify the Fuehrer. "I only thought I'd
raise the point."

"As always happens in such cases," Hitler went on, "they'll be
caught on the wrong foot."

Goering, the "hard man in crises," suddenly remembered his role.
"If Rome surrenders," he said, "there'll be no call to the Allies for
assistance."

"They've done that already," Hitler said, and a few minutes later,
when he read Badoglio's statement to Mackensen, he exploded.
"What a pack of lies! Listen to this! 'Fundamental cooperation!'
What impertinence!"

Hewel made a feeble attempt. "He's trying hard," he said.

Hitler snorted, "If only I could lay my hands on the bastard."

Goering, again going along with the Fuehrer, said, "It's a piece
of play-acting, a puppet show."

"But who can guarantee," Hitler asked, "that he won't smell a
rat straight away? Every airfield is swarming with Italians and when
a lot of parachute troops come down—what then?"

Goering had a fantastic idea; the parachutists dropping on Rome
could be justified to the Italians as being on their way to Sicily but
unable to land closer because of the lack of forward airports.

Hitler accepted this and ordered that Generaloberst Kurt Student
be brought to headquarters immediately to take charge of the operation.

Hitler then went on to talk of KONSTANTIN, his emergency
plan for the Balkans. Goering urged that Italian divisions there be
disarmed, ". . . otherwise, they'll sell their weapons . . . they'll sell
the buttons off their pants for English pounds."

It hardly seemed like a meeting of men who had conquered most
of Europe and still held a good part of it in a iron grasp. Their am-

bivalent attitude toward their Italian ally was matched only by Hitler's vacillation during the next few days.

At first he was adamant. The 2nd Parachute Division was to be transferred from France to Pratica di Mare, a small military airfield between Rome and the sea. Field Marshal Karl von Rundstedt was told to contribute two divisions from his Southern France command to Rommel's Army Group B. Those were to move into northern Italy along with units in Austria including the 44th Division which was to enter through the Brenner Pass. The Russian front was to contribute the II SS Panzer Corps consisting of two divisions, and it too was to go to Italy where it would become part of Rommel's new command.

General Student, seconded by SS commando specialist Otto Skorzeny, was sent to Rome to assume operational control of the 3rd Panzergrenadieren and the 2nd Parachute Division and with them to occupy the capital and the Vatican, arrest the government, and free Mussolini. Meanwhile, Kesselring would be getting the German troops out of Sicily, off Sardinia, and pulling his forces in southern Italy back up to the Pisa-Rimini line to be commanded by Rommel.

It all sounded very precise, the orders crackled with Teutonic efficiency, the mighty military machine started to move with terrifying alacrity. But then the pieces failed to fit; complications, military and human, arose, and in the end, very few of the elaborately conceived plans actually were executed.

Chapter 10

THE ILLUSION OF
FREEDOM

In Rome, Marshal Badoglio avoided Palazzo Venezia and its connotations by installing himself at the less ornate Viminale, the seat of the Ministry of the Interior, control point of Italy's various police forces. It was not the best of omens, but for the moment few Italians paid any attention. Most looked forward to freedom, to a new government and even hopefully to a new life.

Even Mussolini thought he would share in it. The day after his arrest, at one o'clock in the morning, General Ernesto Ferone brought Mussolini a letter in a sealed green envelope. It was addressed to His Excellency Cavaliere Benito Mussolini and bore the signature of Pietro Badoglio.

"The undersigned," Mussolini read, "as head of the government, wishes to inform Your Excellency that what is being done regarding you is solely out of concern for your personal safety, there having been indications from several quarters of a serious conspiracy against your person. I regret that the steps taken were necessary but I wish to inform you that I am ready to give orders to have you accompanied safely with the regard due you, to any place you indicate."

But Badoglio's promise to transfer Mussolini wherever he wished was never kept, just as no conspiracy existed against Mussolini other than the one that had deposed him. Although the former dictator should have been aware of Badoglio's long record of duplicity, he took his assurances at face value.

After asking General Ferone to sit across the table from him, Mussolini proceeded to dictate a reply with as much assuredness as if he were still dictator of Italy.

He thanked Marshal Badoglio "for his concern." He named his home in the North, Rocca della Caminate, as the place he would like to go, and ingratiatingly assured the marshal that "there will be no difficulty on my part and I will cooperate in every way." He expressed his pleasure at the decision "to continue the war with our ally as required by the honor and the interest of the country."

Mussolini concluded his note by expressing his hope for Badoglio's success in the task which he was undertaking at the order of the king—and here *Il Duce* could not resist a final dig—"whose faithful servant I have been for twenty years and still remain."

Badoglio carefully filed away Mussolini's reply which, together with his own hypocritical note, he would use later for his own purposes. His dilemma now was to make the changeover without annoying the Germans and without provoking a severe internal reaction. The marshal wanted to form a government, headed by himself, with some anti-Fascist elements included in it, but he met with concerted opposition. When prefascism cabinet minister Marcello Soleri (who had been considered as a possible vice-premier) was quoted by Badoglio as saying that the government should be placed in the hands of those who had fought fascism for twenty years, Acquarone replied, "Yes, but all the anti-Fascists are republicans." Nor did the king want a government with these parties represented; it would have reflected unflatteringly on his own position over the years.

Besides, although the parties were full of suggestions, their leaders were reluctant to enter a government already saddled with defeat. Of the six anti-Fascist groups, only the Communists declared themselves ready to participate, reflecting an attitude in part due to Communist support already promised to Badoglio, first in 1941 by Fabrizio Onofri and later by party leaders in January 1943.

Acquarone, however, quickly put an end to this speculation. With no anti-Fascist parties in the government, he said, Italy could string the Germans along for a little longer and gain time; otherwise, the Germans might not believe Italy's protestations that the war would continue. Acquarone proposed a government of functionaries like that of Vichy, France, in office only to carry out orders.

That was the solution accepted by the king, a solution which excluded those who had worked for Mussolini's overthrow: Grandi, Ciano, Ambrosio and others, each of whom had thought that he would be chosen. It also eliminated two generals suggested by Ambrosio: Castellano for foreign affairs and Carboni for press and propaganda. Carboni, in fact, had been so sure of being awarded the post, by virtue of Badoglio's sleepy promise, that the day after Mussolini's arrest he had gone to occupy the offices of the newspaper *Italia* in Piazza di Pietra. When he learned of it, Acquarone phoned Badoglio's secretary.

"Valenzano," he said. "What's this story? Carboni a minister? Somebody must be dreaming . . ."

Of the sixteen ministers in the new regime, ten had held high office under Mussolini, three had been Fascist senators, and, of the four generals and an admiral, one was a Fascist senator and one a Fascist functionary.

Badoglio retained the Fascist title of head of the government, prime minister. Raffaele Guariglia, former Fascist ambassador to Turkey, was foreign minister. Fascist Prefect Bruno Fornaciari became minister of the interior, replaced shortly afterwards by Fascist Senator Federico Ricci. Gaetano Azzariti, a former high functionary in the Ministry of Justice, who had also presided over the hated Fascist Racial Tribunal, took over the ministry. Domenico Romano, the new minister of public works, had been chef de cabinet of his Fascist predecessor. Guido Rocco, minister of popular culture, had been director for the foreign press at the same ministry since 1936. Fascist Senator Federico Amoroso was minister of communications. Giovanni Acanfora, the exchange and currency minister, had been Fascist-appointed director-general of the Bank of Italy. The Fascist director of the state printing house, Domenico Bartolini, assumed the post of minister of finance with his face still showing traces of violence inflicted on him by his employees when crowds were Fascist hunting on the twenty-sixth of July.

Even the three who were suggested by Bonomi and named as sops to the anti-Fascists had Fascist backgrounds: Fascist Senator Alessandro Brizi, minister of agriculture; Leopoldo Piccardi, Fascist state councillor, who had been director-general and chef de cabinet of his predecessor at the Ministry of Corporations; and Leonardo Severi, minister of popular education, a man with a foot in each camp, who had held various government posts in the Fascist regime.

The military men had also been identified with the upper strata of fascism: Brigadier General Antonio Sorice, who moved from under secretary to minister of war, had been in various Fascist governments, was for years Mussolini's assistant and was close to the dictator's mistress; Rear Admiral Raffaele De Courten, the navy minister, was known as pro-Nazi; Major General Renato Sandalli, air minister, had distinguished himself in the Ethiopian war; and minister of war production, General Carlo Favagrossa, had been chef de cabinet in the Mussolini regime.

The similarity of this government to previous governments was striking. The ministers had been trained in the traditions of one-man rule. On major decisions they only went through the motions, for the decisions had already been made, usually by Badoglio but frequently by Acquarone. At his first cabinet meeting at the Viminale on July 27, Badoglio did not even mention the war. "It seemed," according to Piccardi, "an ordinary peacetime meeting. There was talk about the substitution of some prefects but not a single minister raised questions about the military situation."

This was odd, as writer Manlio Cancogni pointed out, "since so many of the ministers were generals. But they lacked sufficient authority to open such a discussion."

At the end of the meeting, only Piccardi asked to speak. He said that he realized the delicacy of the moment, but that it was necessary for Marshal Badoglio to understand how important the military problem was to each of them. "To be part of a cabinet like this," Piccardi said, "is more of a sacrifice than an honor."

It turned out to be neither. Badoglio called the cabinet into session on only a few occasions and then ignored it completely.

Mussolini described the cabinet as a "good government" which probably "will continue the directives of the preceding one." It was one of Mussolini's better predictions; as historian Ruggero Zangrandi pointed out later, this interim government, "more than continuing the preceding policies, as impossible as it seemed, succeeded in doing worse."

In the key Ministry of the Interior, the lack of change was astounding. The police were incorporated into the armed forces. The dreaded OVRA, the Organization for the Vigilance and Repression of Anti-fascism, was *not* disbanded, nor were any of its personnel changed. It was still charged with the repression of political revolts, plots and conspiracies against the king and members of the government.

A few men in lesser positions held out hope for a brighter, more liberal future: one of Bonomi's nominees, Education Minister Severi, who was named rector of Rome University; Guido De Ruggiero, a member of the Action party, who had been imprisoned by Mussolini; Piero Calamandrei, another Action party member, who took over the University of Florence; and Concetto Marchesi, an acknowledged Communist, who was made rector of the University of Padua.

Minister of Corporations Piccardi, another Bonomi nominee, faced by threats of a general strike, named leftists to lead the various confederations which still functioned in place of trade unions; including, for industrial workers, Socialist Bruno Buozzi, a former secretary of the metal workers, who had just been released from confinement, and Communist Giovanni Roveda, former labor organizer in Turin; for agricultural workers, Catholic Achille Grandi and Socialist Oreste Lizzadri; and for the professional categories and artists, Guido De Ruggiero. Any other move might have threatened the government, as Italian workers, until then disciplined in the confederations, moved towards open revolt. The naming of these men would, it was hoped, pacify them.

But Piccardi went only so far along the path of democracy. The trusts, the associations, the local and national institutes which fascism had created were left virtually intact, and when Rome's lawyers elected Federico Comandini, an Action party member released from jail on July 26, as head of the Bar Association, Piccardi ignored him and named someone else.

Giorgio Nelson Page was pleased to see that at least one new minister, Guido Rocco at Popular Culture, was honest enough to confess at his inaugural press conference that he felt embarrassed making his first speech in opposition to "a state of things for which he had been for many years a daily huckster."

Badoglio's domestic policy was to extend formal recognition to fundamental freedoms even if in practice they were to be nonexistent. He announced some minor concessions, ironically using the Fascist system of law by decree. The Fascist party and its associated bodies were dissolved, including the Grand Council and the Chamber of Federations and Corporations.

No move was made, however, to replace these by either a reconstituted Chamber of Deputies or by any other democratically elected

July 26. Rome

July 27. In front of the Quirinal Palace

August 6, 1943, at Tarvisio. Field Marshal Wilhelm Keitel and General Vittorio Ambrosio.
Seen from the back, General Elisio Marras

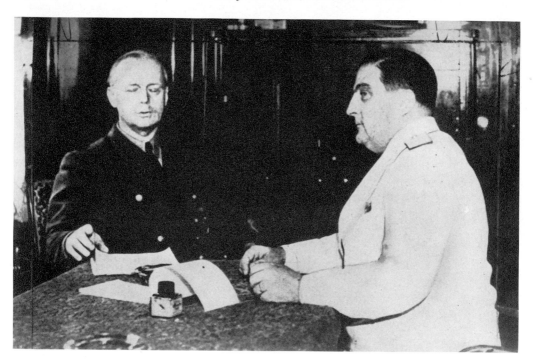

Tarvisio. German Foreign Minister Joachim von Ribbentrop and Italian Foreign Minister
Raffaele Guariglia

organ. While members of the Chamber were dismissed, the Senate
—80 per cent of whose members had been named by Mussolini—
remained untouched; and although Fascist organizations were dissolved, new political parties could not be formed and old ones were
forbidden to function openly. The special tribunal which tried "sub-
versives" in secret was dismissed, but its pending cases and functions
were passed on to military courts. Work permits and school cards
were no longer necessary, but no new publications were allowed to
be started, supposedly due to the paper shortage.

Disciplinary sanctions against students were revoked, but there
were no amnesties, pardons or trial revisions for those who had already been sent to prison. Certain categories of political prisoners
were to be freed and laws penalizing bachelors were repealed; but
the minister of justice, who was supposed to repeal discriminatory
Fascist statutes, omitted—or forgot to include—racial legislation.

Other concessions were made to public pressure for antifascism:
Fascist emblems were removed from banknotes, and the Fascist salute
was abolished. The government changed the names of streets and
piazzas and the Fascist names of ships and divisions were replaced
with noncommittal ones. It was suggested that the sports complex,
Foro Mussolini, be renamed "July Twenty-fifth," but it was renamed
Foro Italico instead.

These steps somehow convinced Italians that the past had been
wiped out and that a new future lay before them.

So, while streetcleaners swept up bricks, paper, pottery fragments, broken glass, Fascist buttons, pieces of Fascist posters and
torn party rolls, the more ardent members of the population again
went out into the streets to express their joy and their hope. They
waved flags and cheered the groups of shirtless youths and shirt-
sleeved workers who held impromptu meetings, convinced that the
end of fascism should be hailed in a kind of continuous celebration.

In Milan, where workers stayed off their jobs for three days,
Communists and leftist intellectuals organized a meeting at Porta
Venezia. Due to the understanding between the Communists and
Badoglio, Communist leaders did not appear; instead, an almost
unknown party member, square-jawed Pietro Ingrao, was a principal
speaker. The meeting was a great success; from the square, the crowd
overflowed into Corso Venezia and Corso Buenos Aires. A worried
police official was held on the shoulders of some of the "comrades"
so he could see just how harmless the meeting was. Every time the

G

official heard one of the speakers pronounce a phrase which sounded dangerous to him, he tried to reach over, only to be, as one participant described it, "borne lovingly away by his bearers."

Then about two hundred soldiers arrived, with their bayonets fixed. A tank began circling the square and the crowds, still joyous, danced around it while big bouquets of flowers were thrown in front of it. When soldiers threatened more forceful measures, two women jumped up on the tank, put flowers on it, and embraced the tank corpsmen.

It was a demonstration of how people wanted peace and freedom from a war they hated. Their cries more and more concerned peace. So did the markings on walls. In Rome they had written on the walls of Trastevere: "We want peace," "Death to the Germans," and "The Germans out of Italy."

The Italian people were tasting the heady delights of freedom for the first time in twenty years. Ordinary citizens received the more or less minor and contradictory concessions granted by Badoglio as if they were harbingers of hope. To the man in the street, it was nothing short of a revolution.

But this reclaimed freedom formed a brief chapter in Italian lives. The new rulers were fearful that these cries would compromise their relations with the Germans or, worse still, indicate that the people were slipping out of their control. Although reforms, minor though they were, had established a façade of legitimacy, they by no means assured Italy of anything resembling democratic government. What Badoglio wanted was a pseudo-democratic framework in which antidemocratic steps could be taken: this he had achieved.

The dreams and hopes which had erupted could not be damped too quickly, but, on the other hand, the mass of Italians still wanted to be told what to believe, how to act, and what to say. It was not only their conditioning over the past twenty years but their uncertainty in the face of this new freedom that led them to look for guideposts. Badoglio did not hesitate to provide them.

Chapter 11

THE REALITY OF
REPRESSION

Dictatorship frequently gives the illusion of freedom; in Italy in 1943, the transition from one type of authoritarian rule to another was accomplished with the ease of prestidigitation.

However, those who had overthrown the previous regime sat uneasily in their provisional chairs, for it was now necessary to see to it that no one would be tempted to topple *them* in turn. Unquestioning obedience was necessary. Criticism was impermissible, for it might be misinterpreted by the Germans, or even by the Italians themselves, and once allowed to exist it could easily spread. If the people were allowed to have freedom, the Germans might march in. Any popular movement had to be repressed.

By the morning of July 26, Badoglio had already moved to protect himself, the king and various government offices from the possibility of reprisal: a considerable portion of northern Rome was put off limits to the population, and the perimeter of the grounds comprising the king's residence was lined with barbed wire curled around wooden barricades. Soldiers armed with submachine guns surrounded the residences of the king and Badoglio and occupied the intervening area. Grenadier units remained on guard day and night. The whole zone, all the way to Piazza Ungheria, assumed the aspect of a battlefield.

Somewhat less elaborate steps were taken to protect ministries, military headquarters and the homes of top army and government personnel. Infected by the atmosphere of fear, many of these men avoided sleeping in their own houses; the minister of war passed his nights in the Colonna Palace, while another top official slept in a small bunker he had secretly erected in his garden.

Late that day, a manifesto was issued, proclaiming martial law for the first time in more than thirty years; a sunset-to-sunrise curfew, unheard of in the history of the reign, was also imposed. Private and public gatherings of more than three people were forbidden; demonstrations, pamphlets and posters were banned; no one could leave his home without an identity card; all public places were closed at curfew; front doors were to be left unlocked; no one could carry arms without permission; private cars were not allowed to circulate; and civil powers were taken over by military authorities so that violators could be judged by military tribunals.

The press was also a target of the new repression. No new papers could be published, existing journals were limited to one edition daily, and preventive censorship was instituted.

Badoglio was indifferent to public opinion; his military background had taught him that force was the final arbiter of any uncertain situation. While the manifesto was being posted on walls throughout the country, a detailed circular was being sent to all military commands. It contained eleven edicts, each one harsher than the last, aimed at maintaining public order.

". . . any act of public disturbance," warned the circular, "no matter how small and of whatever type, is to be considered treason. . . . A little blood shed at the beginning will spare rivers of blood later. Therefore, every movement must be inexorably crushed at the start."

Troops were to "abandon antediluvian systems such as cordons, warning trumpet blasts, intimations or persuasion," and told to carry rifles at firing position on all occasions. They were to "proceed in combat formation, opening fire as soon as within range, with mortars and artillery as well, without warning of any sort, as if against enemy forces. . . . Firing in the air is not permitted. You will aim only to kill, as in battle."

Ringleaders and instigators of disorder were to be put to death immediately, as were individuals who "commit acts of violence or rebellion against armed or police forces or insult them or national institutions. . . ."

Any soldier who offered the slightest gesture of solidarity with demonstrators or who failed to obey orders to fire was to be shot on the spot, while "officers of any rank whatsoever who fail to carry out these orders will be court-martialed within twenty-four hours."

The circular warned commanders against pity hesitation, or indecision and called for the terms of the circular to be carried out "with inflexible rigor."

To make sure that the police would be equally ruthless, police prefects in the various provinces were to take orders from army corps and divisional commanders. All armed forces in the country—including harbor, railway and forest police—were mobilized to carry out the harsh measures. To back them up, five army divisions, including two from France, were sent into Italy's larger cities and thus were no longer available for defense against either Allied or German attack.

The premeditated ferocity astounded experienced military men. Marshal Caviglia said, "Not even the foulest of German corporals would give orders of this kind." General Emilio Canevari commented, "Never in Italy have foreign or enemy troops been given similar orders," adding that Badoglio was pitting his army "against the Italian people as if they were enemy troops."

After having carried out the capture of Mussolini so deftly and bloodlessly, it was paradoxical that the new regime should then resort to martial law, the suspension of civil rights, and to killing and wounding those who had most applauded the coup d'état.

Soon, blood flowed freely in Italy's towns, villages and cities, particularly in the more politically conscious North, where Badoglio's declaration that the war would be continued was met with concrete opposition.

In Turin, feeling was particularly high. Demonstrations were held in factories and on the streets to emphasize demands for peace. Workers went on strike and attempted to persuade others to join them. Civil authorities went to the military commander of the city, General Enrico Adami-Rossi, and proposed that they cooperate, but the general refused, ordering his men to shoot to kill. At one factory, troops fired on the workers, some of whom even cried "Viva Badoglio," and then walked up to those lying on the ground and fired at them again. Eight were killed. The next day all of Turin was on strike, and in the space of a few days a military court sentenced more than four hundred strikers to prison terms.

In Milan, a group of singing youths crossed the Piazza del Duomo, and when the troops sent to halt them refused to fire at them, their commander was immediately removed and *Carabinieri* reinforcements hurried North. That night most of the organizers of the jubilant meeting at Porta Venezia were arrested and kept in prison for forty-five days. At Via Mulino delle Armi and Via Carlo Alberto, gunfire left two dead and more than twenty wounded. By the end of the week, in Milan alone, twenty-six civilians had been killed and almost a hundred wounded.

In Reggio Emilia, at nine thirty on the morning of July 28, black-haired Domenica Secchi, a worker in the Officine Reggiane who was about to become a mother, led a column of workers out of the plant in protest over the continuation of the war. The commander of a battalion ordered his men to fire and nine workers fell dead, including Domenica.

Elsewhere, troops killed scores of unarmed protestors. One of the most serious of these ruthless repressions took place in the southern city of Bari on July 28. Twenty-year-old Graziano Fiori set out for the local prison, along with several hundred youths and workers, to meet his father, the local head of the Action party, who was due to be released along with a number of other political prisoners. On the way they passed a Fascist party headquarters. The officer commanding the unit there misinterpreted the marchers' intentions and ordered his men to fire without warning. The result was twenty-three dead, including Graziano, and sixty wounded. When Graziano's father was released, no one could bring himself to tell him what had happened. Finally he went to the hospital, where he saw Graziano's brains coming out of his head. Nine of the anti-Fascists who had marched, including some who had been wounded, were arrested as "instigators of disorder" and kept in jail for twenty days.

On the same day, a fourteen-year-old boy was killed and nine people were wounded at Sesto Fiorentino, a working-class suburb of Florence. On the next day, in the port of La Spezia, soldiers on the important Viale Villa Savoia killed two workers and injured eleven others.

At the San Marco dockyards in Trieste, military authorities were about to draw lots for the names of two workers to be shot as examples to their fellows, who had engaged in a sit-down strike. The execution was averted at the last minute by the civil authorities.

In Savona, General Salvi, instead of ordering his troops to shoot at a crowd, addressed the assemblage and persuaded the people to disperse. The next day the general was removed from his post.

Troops who fired into crowds of workers were generally lauded by their commanders, particularly one soldier who threw a hand grenade into a group of striking workmen at Turin. When strikers, intimidated by the firing, returned to work, it was considered a victory.

Any infraction, no matter how minor, was severely punished. For participating in an unlawful gathering, one might be sentenced to as much as three years' imprisonment; for being outside after curfew, a year's imprisonment; for refusal to show one's identity card, eighteen months' imprisonment; and for extolling the virtues of the Allies, seven years' imprisonment. For acts of violence against Fascists, a Milanese worker was sentenced to fourteen years in prison, and for distributing pamphlets, Enrico Tarabuci of Bologna received a sentence of eighteen years.

In the days following Mussolini's downfall, twenty-eight people in Turin alone were accused of violating curfew and sentenced to an average of a year's imprisonment.

Twenty years later, Ruggero Zangrandi, then a journalist with a book about fascism to his credit, estimated that in the twenty largest Italian cities during the forty-five days no fewer than thirty-five hundred people were sentenced to prison terms of from six months to eighteen years, while over thirty thousand were detained and later released. But the highest figure Zangrandi could find for Fascists arrested in this period was *eight hundred and fifty!*

The figures are necessarily incomplete. Official records have yet to be made public. However, a research group set up by the National Institute for the History of the Liberation Movement made a detailed study of government archives throughout the country and in 1969 published its findings in a book called *L'Italia dei quarantacinque giorni*. The research group's figures, which came from official sources, tended to confirm those cited by Zangrandi.

At that time, however, the lack of communications helped to maintain the illusion of freedom. Anti-Fascists, deluded into believing that they stood on the brink of a new day, emerged from hiding. Even when confronted by ugly scenes all too reminiscent of fascism —by policies, in fact, whose ruthlessness made the former regime seem almost benevolent—they came out into the light of what they thought was democracy.

The simple truth, however, was that fascism had gone but that democracy had not taken its place.

Chapter 12

THE EXILES RETURN

Somehow the government of Italy convinced its people that freedom had to be sacrificed to "order" and "legality." It was one of the most deft performances of modern times: a despotism of iron, cloaked in the velvet of democracy, was punishing its citizens for any display of their democratic rights. Amazingly, this was all accomplished with the approval of the representatives of the six anti-Fascist parties. The regime succeeded in winning their support to the extent that many volunteered their aid and promised solidarity. Much of the tricky political maneuvering was accomplished by Badoglio. That his government could resort to the measures it did and still retain the myth of democracy was a tribute to his skill.

On the morning after the news of Mussolini's arrest, the Rome Committee of Parties for Freedom had sent Badoglio a motion they had passed asking for an immediate end to the war against the Allies.

Badoglio responded by sending a representative to a meeting of these leaders. The spokesman told the group—ranging from Liberals to Communists—that the government needed time to breathe. The marshal, he said, asked for a truce of five or six days during which they were not to "stir up old anti-Fascist or anti-German hatreds. Hitler is watching everything that's happening."

The next day, Badoglio received Marcello Soleri, one of the group's members. He told Soleri that he wanted to reward the anti-Fascists for their favorable disposition towards the government by naming the most important of them senators. Badoglio showed him a list: it included Orlando, Bonomi, Soleri himself and seven or eight former ministers. This turned out to be one more unkept promise. In other meetings, Badoglio said that any deeper reform would have to be delayed since his was only a provisional government. Besides, Badoglio said, there was the military situation, the presence of the Germans, the difficulty of communications, and the need to keep the Fascists under control. He pleaded for time. "You'll see," he promised, "it will work out."

The anti-Fascists agreed to a truce. Like many liberals before and after, they were only too willing to see both sides, and they did not want to give the government the opportunity to blame them for the continuation of the war by what Badoglio called "the rash opposition and irresponsible impatience of the parties."

Still, the Action party, living up to its name, wanted the committee to call demonstrations and strikes so as to force an immediate armistice with the Allies. The Catholic Democrats and Liberals, however, swayed by Badoglio's siren song, hesitated; the Communists held themselves ready to profit from every opportunity; and the Socialists, whether from caution or fear, confined themselves to speeches.

Anti-Fascists outside of Rome were furious. The truce arrangement did not appeal to the more dynamic leaders, situated mainly in the North. Already on the morning of July 26, at a meeting in Milan's Piazza del Duomo, Communist Giovanni Roveda, going beyond his party's orders, had asked for the setting up of a provisional government formed of anti-Fascist parties, the immediate breaking of the alliance with Germany, and the bringing to justice of Mussolini and other Fascists.

Nevertheless, Badoglio continued to keep his opponents off balance by a concession here, a hardening of a position there, the release of some anti-Fascists on one day, and the jailing of others the next. He was even able to convince left-wing labor leaders to carry out his directives while they were ostensibly looking out for workers' interests.

They should have resigned. Their unanimous and clamorous withdrawal would have forced Badoglio to face public opinion and to assume his own responsibilities. Only the Action party was completely ready to support this; the others were reluctant, and the Communists said they would do so only if there were unanimous agreement on the gesture.

And so, no one resigned; instead, a statement was issued saying that collaboration in the technical field implied neither political collaboration nor approval of political directives and was not to be considered an expression of trust in these directives—a rationalization that satisfied the ego of one or two anti-Fascists, dissatisfied others, and left the situation unchanged.

Still, one development which at first seemed all to the good was the emergence of individual anti-Fascists. Although they had to follow the rules of this strange twilight period, which meant not propagating their beliefs, they could at least be evident. Their ranks were swelled by the return of the exiles, those who had gone abroad, and those who had been in confinement in remote Italian villages, in camps or in prisons.

Those who had come back from abroad immediately, like sad-eyed Communist Giorgio Amendola, son of the murdered Giovanni, were the most fortunate. Socialist Giuseppe Saragat tried to enter on a train from Switzerland and was arrested. Emilio Lussu, an Action party member, tried several times but was turned back to France. Although Ugo La Malfa, Action party leader, arrived in Rome from Switzerland, where he had hidden during the last months of fascism, Communist leader Togliatti was still in Russia, and Republicans Carlo Sforza and Randolfo Pacciardi were still in America.

Anti-Fascists on some of the penal islands were in a paradoxical position. Even when their release was ordered, no means were provided for their return to the mainland.

On the morning of July 28, political prisoners on the island of Ponza stirred restlessly. Mussolini had been brought from the mainland and put in a house at Santa Maria, just outside the island's one little town.

One of the prisoners who rushed to a window to take a look at the fallen dictator was Socialist Pietro Nenni, who had participated in the Spanish War, been captured, and then sent to Italy after the occupation of France. Through a pair of binoculars, Nenni saw Mussolini leaning on a balcony; despite the heat, he was wearing a jacket, and he was wiping his forehead with a handkerchief. It seemed like a trick of fate. "Thirty years ago," Nenni said to himself, "we were imprisoned together, linked in a friendship that seemed sure to outlast time. . . . Today, here we are confined on the same island, I because of his decision and he because of the king's."

On August 3, Nenni's release was ordered. As the fishing vessel took him to the mainland, he looked back to see if Mussolini were there. He was not, and Nenni never saw him again.

Others who had been exiled to isolated parts of the country in what was called *confino*, enforced residence, made their way back to their homes as best they could. But for those in prison, the situation remained uncertain, particularly for the political prisoners who crowded the fourth wing of Rome's Regina Coeli prison.

Whenever possible, Raffaele Persichetti visited friends there. Among those he saw was Ruggero Zangrandi, who had studied and practiced journalism in Rome. Zangrandi had known Vittorio Mussolini, the eldest son of the *Duce*, in high school and had remained friends with him later even though he was cordially disliked by donna Rachele. In 1939 Zangrandi had formed a clandestine party, Partito Socialista Rivoluzionario, for which he was arrested in 1943 and put in the fourth wing, where he was still awaiting trial.

At Regina Coeli on July 26, only prisoners convicted of common crimes had been released or had succeeded in getting out. Political prisoners, however, gathered in the center courtyard and met each other, some for the first time in years. These included Zangrandi, Ernesto Rossi, Mario Alicata and the Puccini brothers, Gianni and Dario.

They promptly formed a committee and agreed that it would not be dignified to run away; they would wait for their rightful liberation. Zangrandi and Ernesto Rossi insisted that they wanted to get out any way they could, but they were overruled.

Zangrandi's father, full of hope, came to the jail but could not even get close to his son's cell. Some relatives of released common prisoners asked him whom he was looking for.

"My son," he answered. "He's a political prisoner."

They said they would free him and started for the fourth wing, but by then police reinforcements had shown up and they were stopped.

The police, who had been sent to Regina Coeli to help the jail guards put down unrest there, shot through the cell windows, and

Zangrandi learned to crouch on the floor to avoid being hit. It was impossible to know how many prisoners were killed, but Zangrandi heard that dozens had been wounded.

Another repression took place on July 28 in the San Vittore prison in Milan. Prisoners seeking release had unhinged the doors of their cells and occupied the buildings. In an attempt to calm them down and disperse the crowd outside the prison, the warden ordered the release of about seventy political prisoners. But then the Seventh Infantry Battalion opened fire from the outside and entered the prison. After several hours of shooting, a committee of prisoners asked for a truce. They were told to surrender their weapons, and when they insisted they had none, the commanding officer of the battalion ordered prisoners led before a firing squad. Several summary executions took place and the revolt was officially over.

In Rome, anti-Fascists were still being put in prison and Zangrandi had the painful pleasure of introducing some of them, like Socialists Mario Zagari and Achille Corona, to other prisoners and telling them how to clean out their communal slop buckets and how to cope with the flat, reddish bedbugs which resembled melon seeds. Each cell had a straw mattress, a pitcher and a small table. Lunch consisted of bread in the form of a figure eight, a few spoonfuls of broth, some fragments of greens and a few solitary beans. For those with a little money, canned sardines could be added; those with relatives and friends able to pay could receive food packages twice a week, although these were usually rummaged through first.

Many of the political prisoners remained in jail because Italy's laws permitted preventive detention, as in fact they do today.

Some anti-Fascists, released from *confino*, were almost immediately put in prison to await a freedom that never came. There they shared cells with violators of martial law, like writers Elio Vittorini and Giansiro Ferrata.

Even those who had been released or returned to Italy were subject to persecution. Emilio Sereni was an intellectual who had been in prison for fifteen years under fascism. Granted amnesty in 1936, he emigrated to France, but when he returned to Italy *after* July 25, he was tried by a military court and sentenced to eighteen years.

Black-bearded, anti-Fascist economist Ernesto Rossi, friend of Nenni and the Fascist-assassinated Roselli brothers, was condemned to twenty years imprisonment in 1930 for setting fire to tax offices. He had spent twelve years reading, translating and writing books.

While in Regina Coeli, awaiting another trial, he was freed on July 30. That same night, however, he was arrested again, this time with friends who had anti-Badoglio pamphlets in their possessions. He was released when he proved that he had not had time to become involved in any political activities.

By means of skillful maneuvering, anti-Fascist representatives were led to believe that all political prisoners were being released. On July 30, newspaper headlines reported that the new government had so decided. In fact, however, no such measure was ever passed.

Most often, the requests for release were passed around between the offices of police chiefs, prosecutors, prison directors and prefectures. Later another stalling measure was adopted: requests for freedom had to be signed by individual prisoners. These requests, too, wandered from office to office; when they did receive approval, they were usually blocked by the minister of war.

When other anti-Fascists—Roveda, Buozzi and Achille Grandi—went to Senise to protest, he was cynical. "Why don't you give me the names of some of your friends in prison and we'll try and let them out," he said. They refused to accept this favoritism and went to see Badoglio. After a three-hour talk, during which the trio threatened both to resign and to institute a general strike, Badoglio yielded.

However, they made the mistake of agreeing that the amnesty would not take place at once and that the families of prisoners would address their pleas for release to police offices. Quite a few prisoners were released, but only after the age-old Italian custom of *raccomandazione*—using pull—had been applied.

Once again, a general amnesty was announced and then denied. Later the government let it be known that political trials held during fascism would be reexamined, a process that would have taken months, if it had ever begun.

Then the government said that many of the anti-Fascists in prison had been guilty of common crimes and could not be released.

When the differentiation between political offenses and anti-military ones was made, the small flow of released prisoners slowed to a trickle. Ernesto Rossi said, "It was enough to have mailed a postcard of ordinary greetings to a friend in Switzerland to be forever suspected of being a spy."

The Communist Catholics—friends of Carla Capponi, who had been arrested a few weeks before July 25—had about four hundred members in prison. When they were not freed along with other political prisoners, they started a hunger strike. None were released, however, until Roveda and the others put pressure on the government.

Il Messaggero later said that it would cease its protests for the release of political prisoners since it knew that the majority had already been freed while arrangements were being made for the others. This was so far from the truth that the next day in many prisons—Fassano, Sulmona and Gaeta—prisoners rebelled and occupied buildings, but were still not able to get out.

The number of anti-Fascists freed still formed but a small percentage of those jailed, and most of the latter were soon to fall into the hands of the Fascists and the Germans.

As the political prisoners who were fortunate enough to be released started to emerge into the world that many of them had not seen for years, Roman members of the Italian nobility opened an office at Piazza della Pilotta to assist them in coping with the exigencies of the post-Fascist era.

But even so, the new arrivals found that they had lost contact during their years of exile and were confused. The Action party, they learned, was supposed to be the continuation of *Giustizia e Libertà* (Justice and Liberty), although the latter had been a Socialist movement and the party was not. The Liberals were divided between those who wanted a small party of the elite and those who wanted to be the elite of a mass party. The Socialists were opposed by other, similar parties and finally merged with them under the unwieldy title of the Italian Socialist Party of Proletarian Unity, which limited itself to the slogan "From the palace revolution to the popular revolution." The Christian Democrats were numerous but allied to the Vatican, while the Communists, few in number, were prone to opportunistic moves such as supporting the monarchy. The Labor Democrats said that theirs was a party of the Left, neither Marxist nor revolutionary, but still opposed to conservatism. Its titular head, Bonomi, was considered half-progressive and half-monarchist and thus half against the regime, half for it. Another of its leaders was Vittorio Emanuele Orlando, the Sicilian lawyer whose formula "the war continues," written for Badoglio, resulted in having the war, which had been declared by Mussolini in the name of fascism, assumed by the nation as a whole.

Thanks to his friendship with Sergio Fenoaltea, Giorgio Nelson Page attended a meeting of the Rome Committee on July 27; he saw

the leaders as surrounded "by an ever increasing number of industrialists, journalists, officials—even General Visconti Prasca who had
marched against Greece—all of them still with corns on their feet
for having worn the overtight boots that went with the uniform of
the Fascist Party." Their arms twitched, he thought, out of constant
fear of unconsciously raising them in the now outlawed Roman
salute.

When Bonomi asked Page what he had done during the tyranny,
he answered that he had been an official of the Ministry of Popular
Culture, and still was. Bonomi, nevertheless, referred to Page as
"one of ours."

At the house where the meeting was being held, people came and
went: each told of his sufferings, his aspirations and his ideals. Page
did not see how these men, who in 1922 had lost power because of
their weakness and incapacity, could hope to do better two decades
later. When he left the house, he wrote that he felt as if he "had left
behind a world of ghosts, ghosts seized by a sudden frenzy, who had
been dancing a tragic, aimless saraband."

Carla Capponi also felt dissatisfied with the inaction of the leaders, and she started using her house for organizational meetings of
the fourth zone of the Communist party. With a friend of the family
and Mario Maggi, a teacher, she maintained contacts with the leaders of the tiny Catholic Communist party. In time the apartment became the depot of arms as well as a distribution point for clandestine
newspapers and propaganda material.

Teachers, in the tradition of Persichetti, did what they could. The
Italian Association of Teachers came into being, and in schools members proselytized new adherents, distributed clandestine publications
and organized meetings.

Raffaele Persichetti himself had not been feeling well. He had
drunk so much the night of the twenty-fifth that he had hema-
turia, blood in his urine. Even so, he continued to drink, particularly
with Ugo Moretti, who had formerly taken out Raffaele's girlfriend
Jeanne. Returning from a mission, Raffaele and Jeanne would meet
with Ugo and another girl, and they would drink and talk, frequently
about politics. Ugo's antifascism was much more visceral than Raffaele's, which was more cerebral and idealistic. Moretti had met Raffaele when he had gone to Visconti after having been expelled from
another school for punching a professor. His political bent had been
formed during the strikes over the Matteotti killing when a cousin,
a railway man living with the Morettis, was beaten almost to death

by a dozen Fascists while his wife had a miscarriage. Somehow the Morettis, along with Ugo, who was then a child, got the couple to a hospital. The cousin never left the hospital alive; from that day on, Ugo hated the Fascists.

Since new publications were prohibited, Raffaele, with Action party friend Tomaso (Tom) Carini and others, took over a trade paper called *Il Commercio Italiano* and tried to turn it into a party organ. However, this was not a success and *L'Italia Libera* remained the hub of action. One of Raffaele's new colleagues was Leone Ginzburg, a Jew who had not hesitated to fight for his anti-Fascist principles. He returned to Rome on August 7, after three years of *confino*, to work on the paper.

Others who had been forced by racial laws into a silence equivalent to exile now made appearances in print. This included those who had written under pseudonyms to stay alive. The short stories of Pitigrilli, who was generally supposed to have compromised with fascism, also reappeared. Enrico Rocca, who had held on to his job at *Il Lavoro Fascista* thanks to his friendship with Mussolini, was named editor of the paper, which then became *Il Lavoro*.

Ettore della Riccia noted that these Jews were returning to journalism even though the racial laws had not been repealed, and on July 27 he went to the *Giornale d'Italia*. He found no one in authority there; Virginio Gayda, who had been editor and semi-official spokesman for fascism since 1926, had been kicked out by anti-Fascist crowds and had sought asylum in the Japanese Embassy.

Several days later Ettore went to see Giovanni Armenise, who, as head of the Bank of Agriculture, was proprietor of the paper.

"I want my old job back as a reporter," Ettore said.

Armenise refused.

"But why not? That's the height of injustice. Fascism is finished, it's all over."

"It's not finished at all, Ettore," replied Armenise. "Take my advice and stay out of things for a while longer."

But Ettore persisted. "I lost my job because of fascism," he cried, "and now fascism is dead."

"Is it?" asked Armenise, his eyebrows arched.

Unabashed, Ettore made plans to continue his efforts to return to journalism. The same day he started his campaign, the man responsible for enforcing the racial laws, Director of Demography and Race Antonio La Pera, was arrested and taken to Regina Coeli. But everything remained the same. Badoglio applied his technique of minor concessions, revoking the ban on Jews' spending their vacations in spas, returning—to those who requested them—radios which had been confiscated and permitting Jews to apply for passports. But the Office of Demography and Race remained in existence and the racial legislation remained on the lawbooks. There was an unwritten understanding that these laws would not be enforced, but they remained like a sword hanging from a tenuous thread over the heads of Jews. Badoglio received members of the Jewish community and assured them that he would take steps to help them, which he never took. Nor did he do anything to dissipate the anti-Semitic propaganda the Fascists had propagated for years.

As a result the Jews' reappearance was no return from exile but rather a surfacing, and they remained in a strange position, suspended between rejection and acceptance.

There was, of course, a certain cachet to being an anti-Fascist now. Intellectuals started to meet once more at their usual hangouts and to deny the progress and improvements which undeniably had come about in twenty years, only because they had taken place under fascism. Others directed their complaints at Badoglio, even though some intellectuals had a reluctant admiration for the old marshal.

Many of those opposed to the regime, long accustomed to a contemplative life, refused to be rushed; not expecting fascism to return, they took their time about organizing to face the new situation.

Chapter 13

WOLVES BECOME SHEEP

It was difficult to discern any nostalgia for Mussolini and his regime among those who had been his most loyal followers and fervent supporters for years. Hardly had the news of the dictator's arrest been confirmed than a flow of hierarchs rushed to the king and to Badoglio to express their congratulations and their solidarity with the ideals of democracy. Others promptly issued statements of fidelity to the king and to democratic institutions; not a single Fascist prefect, wrote Senise in his memoirs, "showed the slightest desire to be retired." Many, as a matter of fact, pressed the king to retain them. One of the most fanatical Fascists, former party secretary Achille Starace, insisted that he had been against Mussolini for a long time.

Men of letters, artists and philosophers described themselves as victims of the Fascist system and asked for jobs, emoluments and stipends. Some newspapermen, undismayed by the fact that they had served fascism lavishly, suddenly became zealous anti-Fascists. One, Tullio Giordana, a member of the party who had been decorated for bravery in Ethiopia, was named editor of *La Gazzetta del Popolo*. "I now take up my pen after twenty years of silence," he wrote, neglecting to say that in the interim he had taken up a rifle for fascism. Others, who had been paid for writing pro-Fascist articles, suddenly equated money with Fascist chains and said that they were now "free."

The spectacle caused philosopher Benedetto Croce to write in his diary of "the revolting display of *volte-face.*"

To paraphrase a sentence of Marshal Caviglia, the Fascists now tried to assume a non-Fascist virginity. The party card had been a necessity; their flattery of Fascist big shots had been only prudent behavior. For them, the job ahead was to please Badoglio, the new boss. Writer Paolo Monelli saw this as an Italian characteristic, "to respect the man rather than the principle."

The country's monstrous bureaucracy continued to function just as it had through hundreds of years of wars, invasions, changes of governments, regimes and rulers. Like other civil servants, Gino Savoni kept going to the office in the days following Mussolini's fall. There he and his colleagues talked and commented, but without heated discussion or argument, as if the whole thing had been inevitable and no further changes were to be expected.

There was a brief work slowdown in some offices, where officials who had been fervent Fascists, fearful of being beaten or insulted, failed to show up. When they did return, it was as if they had forgotten their fascism. Giorgio Nelson Page called it a "rare example of consistency in their work if not in their political convictions."

Many bore smiles of triumph, as if they had been the authors of the coup d'état. "The more they had submitted to the fallen idol," observed Page, "the more puffed up they now appeared." Page noted that top officials hurriedly gave orders to have portraits of the dictator taken from their rooms, and journalist Corrado Alvaro found that the empty spaces were quickly filled with pictures of the king: "a face . . . contracted under a too-large helmet, sly and almost continually trembling, even in the portrait, between his mustache and the lines of his chin."

The sheer effrontery of some of the turncoats was astounding. On July 27, former Fascist party secretary Carlo Scorza wrote to Badoglio implying that it was he, Scorza, who had kept the party from taking any moves against the new regime. "After two days of silent work, I feel I can consider exhausted my task of persuasion and discipline among the Fascists, a task my conscience imposed on me after the change of government." And he concluded, "I will now wait for your decisions concerning the party."

Scorza, who had been shown a copy of Mussolini's letter to Badoglio accepting the *fait accompli*, had thought that if Mussolini could write Badoglio in such terms, the least he could do was to follow suit.

Towards most of the Fascists, Badoglio had an extremely lenient, almost respectful, attitude. Scorza was allowed to stay in Rome undisturbed and was arrested only some time later along with Bottai, Galbiati and Starace. A warrant for Scorza's arrest was issued in August, but Senise saw to it that it was not served. Scorza, in fact, sunning himself on a beach, even received a visit from the local prefect, who paid his respects and joined him in a toast to "the future Fascist resurrection."

No such servility or effrontery was practiced by Dino Grandi, who, after all, was a very wealthy man, the owner of a large newspaper, huge farms and varied businesses. Not until July 29 did the king deign to see the count of Mordano, who promptly protested the direction that the new regime was taking. "The country must be grateful to you," the king said, "as I am grateful to you and your friends for the brave action performed at the Grand Council. The vote facilitated, in a determining way, my action as head of the state."

Grandi remained silent as the king continued, "Now try to take care of yourself as very soon, in a few weeks, I'll be needing you again. Why don't you tell Badoglio your ideas?" Then the king himself called Badoglio to inform him that Grandi was coming to see him. But Grandi knew he was being given his *congè*. The pawn had served its usefulness.

Grandi had earlier balked at the government's banning publication of details of the Grand Council meeting. Naturally enough, he wanted the credit due him for the part he had played. The resolution which the king had first requested, and then used against Mussolini, had been his. When the minister of information refused to publish the communiqué of the Grand Council session which Grandi dictated to him over the phone, Grandi contacted two foreign diplomats, the Spanish ambassador and the Swiss minister, and gave them the text personally, suggesting that they transmit it by coded telegram to the foreign press. It was one of the few times that the censorship set up by the Badoglio government was breached. By the time Grandi saw Badoglio, the Italian newspapers had been forced to report what had happened at the .meeting, even if briefly and without comment. The radio never broadcast a word, and Italians who did not read newspapers remained unaware that the Grand Council had voted against Mussolini.

When he met with Badoglio at noon on the twenty-ninth, Grandi tried to warn the marshal that if he kept on as he had begun, it would be the end of the monarchy and possibly of Italy.

"To have dissolved the Fascist Party at this moment was a great mistake," Grandi told him. "What have you now to bargain with the English? Don't you understand that we, the Fascists, could have been used as spoils of war, something to offer in exchange for concessions?"

"What are you worried about?" answered Badoglio. "You wear the Collar of the Annunziata and no one will arrest you." Grandi forebore to say that Mussolini had worn it also and that one of Badoglio's first acts had been to arrest a fellow marshal of Italy, Cavallero.

That same afternoon, Grandi was received by Pope Pius XII in an audience which lasted for almost two hours. As they were speaking, the air-raid siren wailed through the windows, which opened on Piazza San Pietro. "The Holy Father kneeled," recalls Grandi, "and I knelt with him as we recited the Ave Maria."

Grandi did not know that the list of Fascists to be arrested, which had been prepared by Carboni, Cerica, Senise and Castellano, included not only Ciano, Scorza and others, but Grandi as well.

Grandi never resigned but continued to occupy his apartment at Montecitorio. He did, however, send a letter to Orlando to ask him to lead a national party which would include Liberals, Catholics and moderate Fascists.

Ciano's case was a bit different. He did not get along with Badoglio because, for one thing, he possessed documents proving that the marshal had pulled off some very shady deals in Ethiopia and Greece and that he had even approved the murders of the king of Yugoslavia and French Foreign Minister Barthou in 1934.

Muti warned Ciano to get out of Rome, and one night, when the former foreign minister looked out the window of his apartment on Via Angelo Secchi, he saw below what were obviously plainclothes police. The next day he went to see General Ambrosio.

"You have done a great thing," said the general, "but it means the end of you politically."

"Can I and my family have passports?" asked Ciano.

"I'll ask Badoglio," promised Ambrosio.

That same evening, Acquarone paid Ciano a visit; he told him that the king had been highly astonished at his request and that he had said that the crown would provide guarantees of security to any member of the Order of the Annunziata. Acquarone added that the king wanted Ciano to remain as ambassador to the Vatican. But Ciano realized that this was just another way of refusing him the passports he had requested. Two days later, when he offered his resignation, it was accepted.

To a certain extent the plotters were caught off balance. It was as if, having gathered momentum and rushed headlong against what they took to be a locked door, they found it opening easily and containing nothing behind it. But then, why should the Fascists try to do anything against the Badoglio government? It was distinguishable from the previous regime only by the quality of the men in the ministerial posts. Someone even noted that in the entire government and in all the ministries there was not a single anti-Fascist nor anyone, not even an usher, who had not been enrolled in the Fascist party.

But the king was not satisfied. He sent Badoglio a memorandum warning him that "the elimination of Fascist Party members from public activity must cease. . . . Otherwise, ex-Fascists, suddenly eliminated from public life, might tend to join extremist parties thus adding to future difficulties of the government." The fact was that the king had not really wanted to dissolve the Fascist Party; he had merely wanted the members to stop wearing their badges.

When a few Fascists provoked incidents, they were called into the army, where many held reserve commissions. It was not the wisest of moves because the placing of so many Fascists in the army, where others already were in command positions, meant that they were now able to spread propaganda and lay the groundwork for future dissent, desertion and treason.

After several more small gestures of reprisal, pressure was lifted. Marshal Cavallero was released on July 28 following the intervention of the king. The monarch thought that the pro-German marshal might be useful in the future, perhaps even as a counterbalance to Badoglio, who seemed to be taking too much power.

All sorts of private deals were made—mostly by Acquarone—with other ex-Fascist hierarchs, for it was realized that as many as possible would be needed to defend the monarchy.

Most of the government administrators remained unpurged. The minister of the interior could only come up with the names of three or four prefects who had been compromised by their relations with the old regime. Yet, under the Napoleonic system adapted by Italy, prefects controlled the provinces of the country; they had, naturally, all been Fascists. Fifty were eventually removed from their posts, but only to be transferred to similar positions elsewhere.

Badoglio, who had decided not to disband the black-shirt militia too soon lest it resort to force, now began to coddle it. On August 1, members of the army were ordered not to irritate the members of the militia, which had been declared an integral part of the armed forces: ". . . any offense or expression of contempt aimed at it or its individual members is an offense against the Armed Forces and constitutes a grave crime which will be prosecuted according to law." In an order of the day to the division, Badoglio's former secretary and the new commanding general, Quintino Armellini, lauded "the *Duce* who for twenty years has been in the heart of every Italian."

The Vatican chose this moment to intervene with the Italian government on behalf of persecuted Fascists and the *Duce* and his family, including some twenty relatives of Mussolini, but pointedly omitting any mention of Count and Countess Ciano.

Meanwhile, fewer and fewer Fascists were being arrested. The official responsible, General Cerica, dallied either because of his friendship with these people or because he suspected that personal feuds were at the bottom of some of the calls for arrest. When Claretta Petacci and her family fled Rome on July 27 to hide at Meina on Lake Maggiore, Cerica ordered some of his men to accompany them.

Many of those who wanted to satisfy personal animosities were former Fascists. Several of the top figures in Badoglio's entourage went to Chief of Police Carmine Senise to complain of weakness in carrying out arrests.

"I couldn't," Senise later wrote, "keep myself from telling them, 'We all know each other; until a few days ago you were all disciplined, obedient Fascists. From where do you get this new zeal?' and I made a move as if to order the personal dossiers of the men before me. The effect was amazing, everyone left the room."

There had been proposals that Mussolini be liquidated as if he were a *capo-mafia* or disposed of by drowning or poison like a *condottiere* captured in the Middle Ages. Something of this sort was reportedly urged on the king by an unnamed general who said, "It's a very easy operation which cannot be tied in any way to the monarchy. He would disappear without a trace."

Monarchist writer Giovanni Artieri and journalist Silvio Bertoldi both reported that "one of those who supported the plan most strongly [obviously Badoglio] said: 'The life of a man doesn't count in certain circumstances.' " It was Badoglio, according to Artieri, who told the police official who was to accompany Mussolini to his island prison, "Should the occasion arise, a little shove into the sea could solve everything."

Badoglio claimed to have been indignant at any such idea. On October 18, 1943, he told his officers, "Other people suggested I kill him but I said that I hated to kill the defenseless." Then he added, "It may be that I did wrong."

Paolo Monelli claims that when the possibility was presented to Badoglio as a "radical solution," he at first approved, then changed his mind, saying, "Forget it. I don't want to dirty my hands."

If the subject ever did come up, it is unlikely that Vittorio Emanuele was favorable to the idea, but not for the humanitarian reasons evoked by Badoglio. When Acquarone told the monarch about the ease with which an inconvenient prisoner could be eliminated "with a small dose of poison," the king replied, "No, no, you never know . . . Mussolini could be useful again," and he later used the same phrase in a conversation with his personal physician.

On Tuesday, July 27, at 7 P.M., Mussolini, still wearing his dark suit and homburg, was escorted to a car with drawn blinds. A fat officer sat down next to him; he was Police Superintendent Saverio Polito, who had been appointed head of the military police of the Supreme Command with the rank of brigadier general.

After the car had been on the road for some time, Mussolini realized that they were not headed for his home in Romagna. When he asked Polito about their destination, the police official answered that the authorities were afraid public order would be disturbed if the *Duce* were taken there; instead, he would be put on a small island. "Let's not play jokes," replied Mussolini in a feeble attempt at humor, "I'm not Napoleon."

Then he became more serious: "I've worked for Italy for twenty-one years—I say for twenty-one years. I have a family. I gave one of my sons to my country. I have a right to a bit of quiet." He spoke as if he were an overworked civil servant badly in need of a rest after long service, almost as if he should be receiving a pension for what he had done for his country. Strange as it may seem, twenty-five years later, in 1968, the Italian government ruled that his widow, donna Rachele, was entitled to the pension due civil servants who had worked for the government more than nineteen years and six months.

After a navy corvette had conveyed Mussolini to the island of Ponza, he was lodged in a dreary room on the second floor of a small green house. His dinner that night consisted of a quart of milk and two peaches. From then on he spent most of his days sitting at the window or standing on the little balcony with his arms crossed as if he were about to address an invisible throng. In the evenings he played cards with his guards or read.

One day, while taking a walk under guard, he stopped to speak with a shepherd. "You put us through a lot of trouble," said the shepherd. "Now it's your turn."

Badoglio began to think that Ponza might not be too secure. Hitler could be expected to try to free his old comrade-in-arms, and the British might take it into their heads to capture Italy's former leader. Early on the morning of August 7, Mussolini was put aboard a destroyer and taken to the bleak and lonely island of La Maddalena, an Italian naval base just off the northern tip of Sardinia. Here he was lodged in an isolated two-story house built almost a century earlier.

In charge of the island was Admiral Bruno Brivonesi, whose presence represented yet another trick of fate for Mussolini. When the admiral had been court-martialed for inexplicably losing three warships in a sea encounter with light English units, Mussolini had found the sentence too mild, and the admiral had been relieved of sea duty and put in charge of La Maddalena.

Here the ex-dictator went for walks in the woods near the house, always under guard, and read the twenty-four-volume set of Nietzsche's works, in German, which Hitler had sent him for his sixtieth birthday. No question was ever raised by the Germans concerning the treatment being given him. Somehow even Goebbels was reassured. He wrote in his diary: "As a wearer of the Collar of the Annunziata, the *Duce* retains the privileges of his rank."

In truth these privileges were so meager that donna Rachele, who was escorted by General Polito to the Mussolini home in Romagna, was subjected, despite her age and state of mind, to "unspeakable indignities to which no woman should have to submit."

In the first days of August, Badoglio set in motion "Operation Scandal," with Mussolini's love affairs as a principal target. Soon thereafter the press was directed to discuss the "illicit enrichment" of Fascist notables. This latter move was surprising, since in any list of those who had profited from fascism, Badoglio's name would have had to lead the rest. With the press censored, however, the operation was well controlled and only people selected by the Ministry of Information were named. Understandably, neither Badoglio nor members of his government were ever mentioned.

The revelations of the various scandals were intended not so much to punish the guilty as to divert people's attention from the country's circumstances. The press campaign made pickpockets and sneak thieves appear, by comparison, the bravest and cleanest men in the world, while officials who had been portrayed as models of temperance and rectitude for twenty years were now revealed to have been filthy betrayers of the public trust.

The inquiry was gratuitously delayed long enough to enable most of those named to put their illegal gains in safekeeping. Besides, the rulings had lots of loopholes and the king, who had asked that recrimination be avoided, warned against overly forceful procedures. When the minister of the interior instructed the prefects, still in essence the governors of the provinces, to use their energies mainly "against anti-national elements," everyone understood that this meant members of leftist movements only.

The Fascists started breathing again. Outside of sporadic incidents and some further arrests they were scot-free, at least as much as anyone in Italy at that time.

Chapter 14

THE ONSET OF APATHY

As July melted into August, the great mass of Italians saw their new day disappearing almost before it had dawned. Powerless to influence events, denied civil rights, hemmed in by prohibitions, stripped of self-respect and divested of illusions, they became automatons once again, more concerned with survival than with achieving democracy.

Gastone Novelli, a student, was one of the young Romans who could not stand the general apathy. He thought that the fall of Mussolini had been like a patch on torn pants—an inevitable event, an elementary necessity—not a real act of decision. He felt Italy had passed from one form of nongovernment to another; the status quo seemed to be more important than anything else, and he and his contemporaries were disappointed that none of the leaders stepped forward to say, "No, *basta*, we've had enough," and then do something about it.

Of course Raffaele Persichetti did what he could, carrying out missions, organizing, writing. The younger anti-Fascists might have done more had Badoglio not been so wily and their own leaders so ineffectual. After their first inebriety, many, disillusioned, returned to their passivity. There was surprisingly little bitterness, only a tendency to flow with the tide. Badoglio's guideposts had told them what *not* to do, not what to do. There were no more admonitions to use formal terms of address, the Roman salute, Fascist dress. They were left to their own devices, which were pitifully inadequate after two decades of following Mussolini's dictates.

"It is difficult to be free men," wrote newspaper editor Corrado Alvaro. There were already new idols, for despite the people's newly formed antipathy for Mussolini, they retained their belief in the omnipotence of their rulers.

Newspapers generally followed orders and did their best to establish a climate of normality: the market was firm, they reported; lotteries still went on, and lists of prisoners of war were published as usual. There was not too much editors could do. One who tried to do something was Corrado Alvaro, who had been named to run *Il Popolo di Roma*, a newspaper that had been used by fascism since the Matteotti assassination had marked the end of a free press in Italy. But Alvaro learned that Polverelli, the former Fascist minister of popular culture, kept going to the censorship office every evening to meet with his old officials and that this office had resumed the Fascist system of sending nightly directives to newspapers. The new government had already warned all newspapers that there was to be neither criticism of fascism nor one word about its retirement from the political direction of the country. Editors were admonished to remember the king and to describe him in glowing terms while avoiding any mention of OVRA or of political prisoners. Alvaro rebelled at all this. When he was asked to fill in the censored spaces with other texts, he refused.

He found his countrymen in the grip of a fear that was hardly compatible with democracy. Although the paper wanted to answer readers' letters, it was unable to do so because the return addresses they gave so often turned out to be false. Even letters asking for water in a certain district or better bus service arrived unsigned.

When some employees of *Il Popolo* asked for raises, the demands were put on one sheet of paper and signatures on another. An employee representative refused to leave the sheet devoted to signatures. "You never know," he told Alvaro.

Alvaro thought it curious that "the coup d'état has not resulted in any hatred but created only jealousy and envy." He thought that this might be because it had been finished too suddenly, too simply, without giving people the opportunity to become involved. For the most part, he concluded, the country lacked confidence and feared the worst.

To no one's great surprise, Italians found again in their papers the same high-sounding phrases attacking the Russians, the English and the Americans that Fascist propaganda had been using. The press kept parroting the line that the interests of the country made the continuation of the war necessary. On the night of July 28, 1943, Jewish intellectual Emanuele Artom wrote in his diary: "If we were to win it [the war], an absurd hypothesis, we would fall to Hitler in a week . . ." He then said what he and his friends thought of the Badoglio government:

> The new ministers are all enrolled in the Fascist Party without exception—their photos, published by newspapers, stop at their necks so as to hide the badges in their buttonholes. . . . Not only is the tone of the new temporary regime resolutely monarchical but it speaks of the King-Emperor, and for all Italians the concept of empire recalls that of fascism. . . . For the king to let Mussolini ruin Italy for twenty years, then proclaim himself the country's liberator for having named another prime minister, is too easy. . . .

Artom thought that the only real progress lay in the fact that in trains, on the streets and in shops, people talked more freely, dared to criticize Badoglio more openly than they had Mussolini and repeated without fear the invectives of Radio London and of the clandestine broadcasts against the new government and the "poison gas" marshal.

In spite of all the talk about freedom and democracy, the government suppressed the anti-Fascist Il Mondo and La Riscossa. The Socialist organ Avanti!, after its first postwar edition on July 26, saw the light only four more times during the next forty-five days. Corriere della Sera was reprimanded for its "pro-Communist attitude," and newspapers were reminded that war communiqués were to be printed with headings that did not reflect unfavorably on the situation in Italy or on the alliance with Germany.

Propaganda films were still around. The End of John Bull was being shown as well as the infamous Jew Süss. On the other hand several men of the theatre put forth a proposal that the stage return to its rightful function and that men of artistic talent rather than political ability be chosen to direct and manage theatres.

Except for the symbols of fascism which had disappeared, Rome resumed its usual external aspect. The curfew, originally ordered from 9:30 P.M. to dawn, was shortened on August 1 to 10:30 P.M. to 5:30 A.M. Public services started to function with more regularity, and stores and markets reopened even if merchandise on sale was scarce. The rationing of food remained the same, but everything could be found on the black market, even more plentifully than before. In a short time, the black market expanded widely, due to the lessening of discipline which had been imposed on farmers by the Fascist regime and to the Badoglio government's decision to cut all prices by 20 per cent, which had the effect of pushing even more food into the black market. Housewives were forced to get up at three in the morning to get a kilo of coal and to stand in interminable queues until ten or eleven, after which they started joining other queues to obtain bread. The bread seemed to go from bad to worse; it felt like glue, looked like mud, and tasted like lead. Meals in restaurants became more meager than ever; a cartoon of the time had a waiter saying to a furious customer, "But sir, do you think it nice to spit in the plate from which you've eaten for twenty years?"

Food supplies were beginning to be scarce. On July 28, the newspapers announced that with coupon number 225 of the ration card, three ounces of meat per person would be available.

On August 6, there was a scarcity of milk. Children up to age three were allowed six ounces a day. Bars were forbidden to serve a *cappuccino* unless the milk used was that allowed by the ration card. Later in August, meat was confined only to the sick.

Disillusion set in. One family which had been carried away by enthusiasm—and had lived to regret it—was that of Enzo De Vitali; there were eleven mouths to feed. With no money with which to pay the prohibitive black-market prices, Enzo's wife started to exchange household items for food. The transactions were very complicated since it was forbidden to carry packages around or to take buses and trains to the country without a special permit. Sometimes Enzo's wife would give one or two items away and get nothing in return because (she was told afterward) the person who was supposed to bring her the food had been arrested, and of course she had no way of checking whether this was true or not.

The De Vitali radio went for three liters of oil and two kilos of cheese. A set of twelve Ginori plates went, a couple of pieces at a time, for a sack of flour, much of which was chaff and marble dust. When the exchangeable items were gone, Signora De Vitali started to give away trousseaus; there were four girls in the house, between the ages of sixteen and twenty-five. She hated to do this, because after the war there would be so few men left that even a girl *with* trousseau and dowry would have a hard time finding a husband; but food came first, and so she went on exchanging six towels for twelve eggs, two sheets for half a kilo of beef, and so on.

On July 26, 1943, the De Vitalis were so happy about Mussolini's fall (politically it made no difference to them, but they thought food restrictions would finally be over) that they decided to have a banquet. That night they had a terrific meal which cost them whatever was left of the trousseaus, plus Enzo's silver watch. Within a few days they discovered to their dismay that restrictions would continue, and in fact sharpen; and, since they had nothing left to exchange for food, they had to start eating only within the limits of their ration books in an apartment almost devoid of furniture.

But it made little difference. Most Italians were by now reconciled to seeing their dreams vanish, their hope diminish to a whisper. There was nothing to do but to retreat into their former state of indifference. Their resiliency gone, along with the hope of cutting a *bella figura*, they again believed that there was no solution to their problems. Some consoled themselves with the idea that democracy would not have worked well in Italy and that they would somehow manage to survive, even under Badoglio.

Chapter 15

WAR...

Survival was the key to Pietro Badoglio's policies. He himself had survived for seventy-two years, his career marked by adroit opportunism, an almost complete disregard for moral scruples, and utter disdain for his countrymen, whom he described as "nothing but imbeciles."

Along with the king and Acquarone, he had already decided that the war would continue. In a document made public in 1968, Acquarone admitted that in their plotting "no one had brought up the question of halting the war. . . ." That included the military, none of whom had suggested any other course.

The thought of standing up to the Germans did not enter their minds either. General Francesco Rossi, deputy chief of the Supreme Command, later wrote, "Opposition with force was not even contemplated." And yet such a move, for a less self-interested strategist than Badoglio, would almost seem to have been dictated by the situation. According to General Rossi, an armistice declaration would have been particularly opportune on July 25. "At that time four German divisions were tied up in Sicily and our Navy could have kept them from crossing to the continent. Less than two German armored divisions remained in the South with the 3rd Panzergrenadiers (only 12,000–15,000 men) in the zone of Lake Bolsena. With such a general situation, the task of overcoming the German troops on the mainland [of Italy] would have been easy."

Brigadier General Giacomo Zanussi, Roatta's assistant, thought that such a move could even have been effective later. "Even after the initial mistake of not getting rid of Mussolini and the Germans at the same time," he wrote, "there was much that could have been done. But no moves were taken despite the pleas that everyone made to the Crown and to the government." The truth, as an Italian military court later declared, was that "before July 25th, the Italian High Command had not worked out any military plan to face the situation."

Yet the five Italian divisions charged with maintaining internal order could have been deployed to block the Germans, and with a little initiative, the Italians could have blown up their already mined Alpine tunnels and bridges, which, as Goebbels noted in his diary, would have had the effect of cutting German troops off from their supply source and preventing others from coming in. If force became necessary, Italian soldiers would have battled with much better morale against their traditional enemy, the Germans, than against the Anglo-Americans, particularly, as historian Attilio Tamaro pointed out, "if given a real leader to head them."

Alternatively, Badoglio could have tried to make a deal with the Germans, allowing them to get their troops safely away while Italy withdrew from the war. Finland did this a year later, under an accord permitting the withdrawal of German troops.

But Italy's rulers were determined to go along with the Axis despite Churchill's warning that if the Italians went along with the Germans, the Allies would drag "the red-hot rake of war through the length and breadth of their lovely land."

In any event, the Allies, caught by surprise, could come up with nothing better for the Italians than unconditional surrender. It would have made little difference; Badoglio had made his choice and confirmed it in a speech on October 18, 1943, telling seven hundred assembled Italian officers that he and the king had "done the impossible to continue the war . . . to keep the word that had been given in the name of Italy by that rascal of a Mussolini. . . . You too are soldiers," he said, "and you know the rule of honor."

It was supposedly the same rule of honor which Badoglio evoked

H

later to declare war on Germany. That summer, however, he was an eager pursuer of Germany's favors. Immediately on taking power he sent Hitler a telegram, which the Fuehrer left unanswered. This rankled Badoglio for weeks. He was still determined to come to terms with the Third Reich. When Kesselring and Rintelen had come to see him, he had said, "At seventy-two, my only wish was to spend the last part of my life quietly, but as an old soldier I must now obey my king's orders."

When Kesselring began to murmur something about the rumors concerning Italy's surrender to the Allies, Badoglio drew himself up.

"If the king wanted to capitulate," he said, "he wouldn't have chosen a marshal as head of the government!"

This so impressed his listeners that Kesselring ordered a plane to take Rintelen to Hitler's field headquarters. When Rintelen repeated to the Fuehrer Badoglio's assurances that the war would continue, Hitler glared at him.

"Does he honestly think," he burst out, "that I believe him?"

Rintelen tried to say that Badoglio was a real bulwark against communism and that his sincerity had been impressive. Hitler thought a moment.

"The reason must be," he said, "that Badoglio has failed to achieve separate peace with the Anglo-Americans and now he's looking to us again for our support."

He remained skeptical even when Kesselring himself came up by plane to plead the case for maintaining correct relations with the Badoglio government, at least until more German troops could come peaceably into Italy.

Kesselring was also concerned because he did not like having to pull his troops out of Sicily, withdraw to northern Italy and henceforth take orders from Rommel. He told Hitler that he could hold the south of Italy—possibly even the Etna beachhead in Sicily—if he were allowed to consolidate his forces and to have reinforcements. Kesselring had powerful allies. The German High Command, like its American counterpart, tended to stick to lines previously laid down. In this case, these were a common defense with Italy and avoidance of anything that could give the Italians an excuse to withdraw from the alliance. Grand Admiral Karl Doenitz added that he was against evacuating Sicily; it would, he said, free the Anglo-Americans to make other landings, give them a psychological victory and open the road to the Balkans through southern Italy. He was joined by OKW Operations Chief Jodl, who said, "The Italians in their present situation could be feeling hopeless and therefore want to rely on us once more." Although this was almost exactly what Hitler had said, the Fuehrer was disdainful.

"These are things," he pronounced, "that military men can't understand. Only someone with political intuition can see it clearly."

Then, unpredictably, the Fuehrer reversed himself again. Orders to evacuate Sicily were held up. The carefully worked out plans which he had wanted to put into operation on July 27 were suspended. These included: (1) EICHE, the rescue of Mussolini; (2) STUDENT, capture of the government in Rome (the ministries and the major political, military and court personalities) and the restoration of fascism, and contingent plans if Italy made peace with the Allies; (3) SCHWARZE, occupation of military bases and capture or destruction of the Italian fleet; or 4) ACHSE (formerly ALARICH, undiplomatically named after the king of the Visigoths, the barbarian invader who sacked Rome), which had initially called for securing the Alpine passes, occupying northern Italy and evacuating German troops from the South, but had been expanded to include the disarming of Italian troops and the occupation of all of Italy in case of Italian surrender.

The activation of Operation STUDENT was halted, and General Student was ordered instead just to be ready to seize the Italian government and to liberate Mussolini. He could not have done much more. The first airlift of the Second Parachute Division had arrived only that same day at Pratica di Mare. Only one division could be taken out of Russia where, after the German half-million-man attack on the Kursk salient had failed, the Russians had been, since July 24, pursuing a counter-offensive from Smolensk to the Sea of Azov with superior forces.

Badoglio and the king, who were unaware of all of Hitler's vacillations, were convinced that his bolts of lightning might be loosed at any moment. Yet there were no apparent threats from the Germans, and a broadcast from the Reich said, "The change in the Italian government is to be attributed to Mussolini's bad health," a surprising statement which was printed straight-facedly in *Il Messaggero*.

To forestall the Fuehrer's fury, it was decided to have Lieutenant General Efisio Marras, Italian military attaché to Germany who was then in Rome, see Hitler and propose a meeting. Badoglio gave Marras the exchange of letters between himself and Mussolini to show Hitler how "friendly" the dictator's deposition from power had been.

Marras arrived at Rastenburg in East Prussia on July 30, the day after Kesselring had been there. It was 8 P.M. but still light when Marras, accompanied by Michele Lanza, counsellor at the Italian Embassy in Berlin, walked through the silent, fragrant forest of Goerlitz, past a camouflaged railway car—once the property of French General Maxime Weygand but now reserved for General Field Marshal Wilhelm Keitel, chief of the German Armed Forces High Command, who never left Hitler. As the Italians entered the wooded area, Marras was momentarily reassured. He was the man who had said that Germany would stop the Russians. Soldiers quietly moved through the paved streets under the thick trees; officers in white bathrobes, almost all with the large red General Staff band, were on their way to the nearby lake for a swim, while others were on terraces taking tea.

After crossing a triple blockade of barbed wire, the two Italians came to the *Wolfsschanze*, the Fuehrer's residence; it was made of larch and austerely furnished. The Italians waited in a hall with a large picture window, guarded by two men from the SS. When Marras unfastened his gunbelt with an ostentatiously slow movement and handed it to an orderly, the guards' glares relaxed. Finally Marras was accompanied to Hitler, who stood waiting in the middle of a room, pale and bent. Behind him were Jodl, Major General Rudolf Schmundt and German diplomat Walter Hewel. All three, each with his right hand in a pocket, were obviously holding guns.

Marras stood immobile, afraid even to reach for a handkerchief. Hitler calmly turned to face him.

"I didn't know you were interested in politics," he said.

Marras remained motionless.

"Sudden changes of government," Hitler continued, "are always dangerous. As for Badoglio's soldiers, they're all politicians."

Despite this inauspicious beginning, Hitler seemed willing to accept Badoglio's assurances that the war would continue. Excitedly he told Marras that the Italian people's will for resistance had to be reinforced. Germany, too, was enduring serious bombings, such as those over the Ruhr and on Hamburg. "The day will come," he explained, "maybe three hundred years from now, when we will be able to revenge ourselves. Do not worry about the Americans; one German division can easily handle three or four American divisions."

In a more relaxed tone, he said that he regarded a meeting, particularly one in Italy, as unnecessary at that time. It was obvious that Badoglio had no intention of going to Germany and running the risk of capture there. Since Hitler felt the same way about going to Italy, the two men were destined never to meet. Hitler said, however, that the ministers of foreign affairs and the chiefs of staffs might usefully confer.

Marras and Lanza returned to Berlin with the impression that the Germans considered them enemies. Within a few days, even holders of diplomatic passports were forbidden to leave the country and were forced to remain, virtually prisoners, in Berlin.

In Rome, fear still reigned in high places. General Carboni, *chevalier sans peur* long noted for his belligerency towards the Germans, suddenly developed an unreasoning fear of them. On July 30, accompanied by his aide, Lieutenant Raimondo Lanza di Trabia, he went to see Bonomi and warned him of a German attack on Rome.

On the thirty-first of July, he told the king that the German Third Armored Division at Viterbo alone had more weapons than the four Italian divisions under his command. "I'm afraid," he said, "that the Germans will send their planes in full force as well and we won't be able to do anything about it."

The king was already apprehensive, although he coolly received German Ambassador Mackensen, who came on Hitler's orders to learn Mussolini's whereabouts. Vittorio Emanuele said that he did not know where Mussolini was, but that he would ask Badoglio about it.

Mackensen was bewildered. "Badoglio told me the same thing," he said, "and referred me to Your Majesty."

Then Mackensen expressed the Fuehrer's disappointment at not having been directly informed of the change of government.

"Hitler," replied Vittorio Emanuele, "has always ignored the fact that a king exists in Italy."

Despite his outward display of self-confidence, the monarch, who was convinced that some of the top Fascists who had escaped were organizing an armed revolt with German help, was worried. He told General Puntoni that he did not want to end up like the King of Belgium. On August 2, after he had been further alarmed by Carboni, he told Puntoni to arrange everything for sudden flight. To this end, two destroyers (the queen disliked flying) were ordered to be kept at Civitavecchia, sixty miles up the coast from Rome, to take the sovereigns at a moment's notice to the fortified island of La Maddalena, off Sardinia.

Badoglio, too, was fearful. He would greet Carboni at their morning meetings saying, "Another night passed without the Germans taking me away," even though the Germans had not yet made a single overt move. In fact, when German troops in the Balkans, thinking that ALARICH had been put into effect, started disarming Italians on July 26, the arms were quickly returned and apologies made.

In addition, German soldiers in Italy were being condemned to death for minor thefts and issued precise instructions on how to behave. These included the reminder: "The Italian is jealous of his land and his women. You must respect his private property and habits. . . . Wine and liquor in Italy's hot climate are dangerous. . . . The Fascist regime has fallen due to internal political questions and not for military reasons. Do not be concerned with it and make no judgments on internal Italian questions. . . . Anglo-American propaganda has painted Germans as bullying and maltreating Italians; show by your behavior that German soldiers are open and correct."

Meanwhile German troops began to move into new positions. Although the troop movements resembled a planned invasion, they were in fact nothing more than improvised emergency measures. From the German point of view, steps had to be taken to secure the supply line for troops already in Italy. But the manner in which these steps were carried out, however "correct," hardly befitted a loyal ally. On July 30, the 44th Jaeger Division and the 163rd Mountain Brigade arrived at the Brenner Pass, the great gate to Italy through which earlier Teutonic invaders had descended on the peninsula. Swiftly they passed through the mountains, across the green valleys, past the vineyards and through the picturesque towns of the Tyrol.

Italian troops were taken by surprise and Italian railway men were forced at gunpoint by German officers to move the trains on. Many of the German soldiers had *Viva Mussolini* written on their helmets, and others told local villagers that they had come to overthrow the Italian government. The most menacing were those who advanced in battle formation with automatic weapons at the ready. Soon these troops occupied power stations, bridges, tunnels, railway depots and the key city of Bolzano and started making purchases with Occupation Marks. Several hundred miles to the west, the 76th Infantry Division moved into Italy from southern France, while the 305th began moving towards the Italian border.

The German move, although it was not entirely unexpected by the Italians, raised prospects which were far from pleasant. Although he was willing to continue the war, Badoglio did not want to be eaten up by the Germans. Nor did the king; German occupation of Italy could mean the end of the monarchy. And so, while they smoothly turned aside the German attempts to discover Mussolini's whereabouts, they had the *Comando Supremo* attempt to slow down the unwelcome reinforcements.

Ambrosio called a showdown meeting with Kesselring. The two had never gotten along particularly well. In trying to adapt himself to what he saw as the German attitude, Ambrosio was hard and hostile, while Kesselring, in trying to adapt himself to the Italians, endeavored to be pleasant and conciliating. When they met on July 31, Ambrosio protested the entrance of the two German divisions. It was pointed out that he himself had requested them at Feltre. "It's the manner in which it was done that I don't like," replied Ambrosio haughtily.

Kesselring said that it had been necessary. "This is no longer an Italian theatre of war," he said. "It has become an Axis theatre."

"It always has been," Ambrosio retorted. He went on to complain about German units occupying blockposts on the Italian side of the Brenner and asked that the 305th and the 44th be moved directly to the south against a possible Allied invasion.

Kesselring answered that the defense of the south did not depend on two divisions. He offered to order in another division for that purpose.

Ambrosio: "You're bringing this up only now? In military matters one must be precise. We've always talked about two divisions, now out come others. Let's not talk about other divisions now."

Kesselring: "You must consider the general situation. Just a few days ago General Roatta agreed with me that it would be a good idea to have other forces."

Ambrosio: "I don't care what you said to Roatta. You should have come to me first."

Kesselring: "Your Excellency had told me many times to contact the Army Command directly."

Ambrosio: "That's true, but before bringing the whole German army into Italy you have to talk to me."

Kesselring: "We must adapt decisions to the necessity of the moment. Either the war is to be considered over or more divisions must be brought in."

Ambrosio: "In that case I must ask you to come to me with an overall plan. Not as you've been doing, coming here from time to time talking about a new division. Besides, His Majesty this morning complained to me about paratroopers occupying a Royal estate. And at Viterbo, other paratroopers—there are thousands of them—are making an awful mess. By the way, what are all those paratroopers doing around Viterbo?

Kesselring: "They're supposed to join the 3rd Division."

Ambrosio: "It must be something else. You're not informed. Anyway, they're a big nuisance there."

Further talks proved equally inconclusive. Neither participant brought up the fact that at Feltre the Germans had turned down the Italian request for troops with the excuse that they could not afford to send any. Now, suddenly, they were supplying more divisions than were wanted.

Individual Italian commands did what they could to keep them back. Some German commanders resorted to tricks to get their troops through, such as insisting that there had been agreements with higher-ups for their passage. Only after a lot of checking with the Supreme Command in Rome was it discovered that no such agreements existed, but more often than not, Rome ordered that they be allowed to pass anyway.

In the Tyrol, the Italian XXXV Corps had only one division, just returned from the Russian front. Caught unaware and without orders, the corps commander, General Alessandro Gloria, put up considerable resistance. General Zanussi later wrote: "The Germans didn't dare advance a step until, as usual, Rome intervened and we had to let them pass."

In Piedmont and Liguria, the Italian Fourth Army posted artillery, laid down land mines and tore up rails. The German 305th Division was ordered by Hitler to proceed into Italy on foot, which it did, settling into key posts along the Ligurian coast. Fourth Army commanders received Marshal Von Rundstedt's liaison officer, Colonel Heggenheimer, who requested some facilities; then they saw the 305th taking over ten times more territory than requested until Liguria was saturated with German forces. It was obvious that their officers had precise instructions on how to deal with the Italians. The commander of the Ligurian sector, General Bancale, described their tactics: "They know Italian very well when they come to ask for facilities or data but they seem to forget it when we ask them to do something."

Bit by bit the Germans installed themselves where they wanted to, explaining away any action that had been too energetic as due to some misunderstanding. The Occupation Marks being used in the Tyrol were withdrawn, and the new troops were justified as neces-

sary in order to combat possible Anglo-American landings in the
North. The Italians could only agree that such steps were necessary;
and from then on, by mutual agreement, mixed Italian-German patrols watched over railroads, communications, workshops, road stations and troop quarters in the Alpine passes and the upper Tyrol.

Still other German troops appeared there. After the 44th's initial
breakthrough, the 65th Infantry, the 24th Panzer and the 1st SS
Panzer Division, under the brutal Lieutenant General Josef "Sepp"
Dietrich, followed. The German Army Command, OKH, had been
supposed to contribute two divisions, but its chief of staff, Colonel
General Kurt Zeitzler, who made a point of not telling the High
Command where his units were nor of his plans for moving them,
would only release one.

Although a special section was set up at army headquarters in
Rome to keep track of the Germans and to see to it that adequate
counteraction was taken, its efforts were so secret that it appeared
useless. General Cesare Amé, chief of Italian military intelligence,
noted that not once did he receive a request for information. Finally,
in the first part of August, on his own initiative, he ordered the
gathering of data on the movements and attitudes of German troops.

Meanwhile, the Italians continued to work with the Germans to
hold on to Sicily and to oppose any Allied invasion. But on the fourth
of August, General Roatta sent Ambrosio a memorandum pointing
out that these new German divisions offered no protection to the
South, where the Allied threat lay. Instead, they seemed to be
grouped in positions to take over Italian naval bases, occupy the
North, and seize Rome.

Ambrosio promptly told Roatta that the defense of Rome against
a possible German coup d'état had priority over protecting the coast
against possible Allied landings. Despite these instructions, very
few Italian reinforcements were brought to Rome and the Germans
continued to do almost as they pleased. In a short time the Italian
forces, particularly those around key ports, were found to be scattered across hundreds of miles, while German troops formed solid
blocks around the control centers of the main roads.

It seemed the culmination of a prophesy which had been made
by the personable Admiral Wilhelm Canaris, head of the *Abwehr*,
German Military Secret Service, to his Italian counterpart, General
Cesare Amé, on August 2 in Venice.

"My congratulations on getting rid of Mussolini," Canaris had
said. "We too hope that our July 25th will come. Believe me, let

them [German troops] enter as little as possible, or you'll be in trouble."

But the generals of the *Comando Supremo*, obviously interested in placating the Germans, seemed unable to turn down their requests. As General Zanussi pointed out, even when "they had started by saying no, they ended up invariably saying yes."

In Rome, as was to be expected, the anti-Fascists passed additional resolutions reproaching Badoglio with delays in arranging peace with the Allies. Badoglio's ready answer was that he was trying to deceive the Germans as to his real intentions. The anti-Fascists, of course, had no way of knowing that Hitler was not deceived for a moment and was, in fact, making little effort to mask his real intentions.

When they asked about the additional German troops pouring into Italy, Badoglio put on his strategist's mantle and said that the new German divisions were necessary to protect those already in Italy. Despite this nonsensical explanation, one of the anti-Fascists said later that Badoglio was "always ready to give in to their requests although this was far from collaboration. He was benevolent with individuals but not with their ideas."

The marshal proved his benevolence by turning most of his relations with the anti-Fascists over to his son, and by telling Chief of Police Senise "to open dossiers on the various heads of the anti-Fascist parties and keep them up to date."

If Badoglio's two-faced performance in Rome would have gladdened the hearts of admirers of the thespian art, the acting done by the participants at the Italo-German conference at Tarvisio would have sent them into ecstasies.

Hitler had told Marras that such a meeting might be useful, and so the Axis chiefs of staff and foreign ministers set out for the Italian frontier town where Italy, Austria and Yugoslavia came together. The Fuehrer had given his representatives instructions to engage in no more than a *tour d'horizon*. "Just put on an act of good faith," he had told them. "Avoid any reference to a possible evacuation of Sicily." He also instructed the Germans to appear only as a body, not to undertake any individual negotiations, and to eat or drink only food that had first been tasted by the Italians.

On the morning of August 6, when the German special train arrived at Tarvisio, the Italians were amazed to see between each pair of windows an SS man with a submachine gun at the ready. The train itself was armored, escorted by soldiers in battle dress, and armed with both machine guns and antiaircraft weapons. Italian Foreign Minister Guariglia watched in amazement as German soldiers rushed out and surrounded the train with leveled arms as if afraid of attack.

In marked contrast, the Italian train had in front of it two or three pairs of young *carabinieri* armed only with the characteristic curving sabres which had been used principally against nineteenth-century student demonstrations. Guariglia noted that the "contrast between the two trains and their guards . . . described exactly the different moral and material situation of the two countries."

He neglected to mention, however, that the deceitful tone of the conference was actually set by the Italians, who greeted the Germans with a series of perfectly executed *Fascist* salutes.

Despite the obsequious Italian greeting, the German attitude remained chilly. An unsmiling German Foreign Minister von Ribbentrop emerged first, followed by Field Marshal Keitel, tightly gripping a marshal's baton. The talks started immediately in Guariglia's coach, and Ribbentrop drew first blood when he expressed regrets that Mussolini had been deposed. As Ribbentrop voiced his suspicions of the new government, Guariglia, "a consummate actor" as one of the participants called him, shrewdly assumed the expression of a man half-incredulous, half-offended.

"The first step of His Majesty the King and Marshal Badoglio," said Guariglia, speaking in French with a strong Neapolitan accent, "was to announce that Italy would continue with the war, keeping their word of faith with the ally. This public declaration, formulated by great soldiers like the King and Badoglio, cannot be put in doubt; otherwise the country would feel itself profoundly injured in its sense of honor. To talk frankly, as one should between allies and friends, I repeat and confirm the declaration and the assurances given by the King and by Marshal Badoglio; I repeat them in explicit terms, while I feel that I am hearing the echoes of all those who fell on the battlefields in our common war."

Ribbentrop was taken aback by this flow of partenopean oratory. "I'm happy to hear this," he replied. "The German government has never had any doubts about Italian sincerity."

With a straight face, Guariglia continued. "There have been no negotiations with the Anglo-Americans and there will not be in the future. . . . The new government, being free of burdens [i.e., fascism] will do better than the preceding one to conclude the war victoriously."

As the two men talked, the Germans were trying desperately to find Mussolini, and the Italians were commencing their dealings with the Allies. Ribbentrop remained so thoroughly unpersuaded of Italian sincerity, in fact, that he promptly telephoned Hitler's headquarters. "Danger all along the line," he said, which meant that he was convinced that Badoglio was about to deliver Italy to the Allies.

While the foreign ministers attempted to mislead each other, Ambrosio was meeting with Keitel, his German counterpart, who had once said, "The only Italian army that cannot betray us is the one that does not exist."

When the Italian chief of staff complained about the unwanted influx of troops, the German's eyebrows shot up.

"If the war continues," said Keitel sharply, "Germany's duty is to send troops to defend its friend Italy."

"I am in accord," placated Ambrosio, "but we should have back Italian troops on occupation duty abroad. The Fourth and Second Armies [in France and the Balkans] are needed to defend Italy from Allied attack."

"Since their posts will have to be taken over by German troops," Keitel answered, "I will have to ask the Fuehrer."

Then Ambrosio protested against the manner and rapidity of German troop movement into Italy, complaining that the *Comando Supremo* had the impression that it was no longer master in its own house.

Keitel expressed amazement. "Evidently there must be a misunderstanding," he said, adding almost as an afterthought, "due to the state of Italian communications."

Although he zealously played the part of the loyal ally, Ambrosio again pressed for the movement of these troops to the South, away from the naval bases and from Rome.

Keitel arrogantly answered that he could not accept any questioning of Germany's good faith, and he expressed his indignation that the Italians "were not more grateful for the generous aid given to them by Germany." And to keep Ambrosio in his place he added, "In Italy a regime which lasted twenty years was swept away in a moment. Who can guarantee that the new government might not meet the same fate?"

During lunch in the Italians' restaurant car, the conversation

continued in a more congenial atmosphere. In an amazing conciliatory gesture, Ambrosio, according to the Germans, made a complete
turnabout and asked that their troop strength in Italy be increased
from nine to sixteen divisions—four in Piedmont and Liguria, three
in Emilia, one at the Brenner Pass, two near Rome, two in Calabria
and four in Sicily. The meeting was dotted with statements which
each group did not mean and which the other knew it did not mean,
but Ambrosio's request created the impression that Italy was ready
to go all the way with Germany.

There was even talk of a top-level meeting between the king and
the Fuehrer, but since it was obvious neither would go to the other's
country, the subject was soon dropped. Hitler was still convinced
that the Italians wanted to kidnap him and to deliver him, along with
Mussolini, to the Allies. Towards the end of the meeting, Ribbentrop
communicated the Fuehrer's sympathy and respect for the *Duce*,
saying that he "wishes him well." Then the meeting ended as it had
begun, each side convinced that it had deceived the other.

Eugen Dollmann, who had attended the meeting as Ribbentrop's
interpreter, called it the most deceitful of all conferences: "At the
end I was left with only one doubt: who had lied more, Guariglia or
Ribbentrop!"

As the heavily guarded German armored train began to pull out,
Ribbentrop, without warning, ordered Mackensen to accompany him
to Germany. The German ambassador to Italy turned suddenly pale,
then departed for Germany with only a single suitcase. He never returned, nor did he ever again hold any post in the Third Reich.

Back in Rome, in a meeting at the Quirinale, the Italians told
Badoglio and the king of the extent of German distrust. It was obvi-
us that very few Italian troops could be brought back from abroad
and that the Germans would send no more arms or planes, but only
their own troops. Despite this grim report, the king and Badoglio remained bent on convincing Hitler that Italy would continue on his
side, even though Hitler obviously did not believe it.

This became even more evident when the Germans started ap-
plying an economic squeeze as well. The Italians noted that their
supplies were being increasingly cut off. Giuseppe Gorla, head of
AGIP, the state gasoline agency, wrote in his diary on August 8, "The
mistrust of the Germans regarding us grows every day: coal is sent
by the pound, supplies of diesel oil from Rumania have stopped
since July 25th."

Whereas the Germans had promised to send 1,200,000 tons of coal, they now reduced this figure by two-thirds. Instead of 110,000 tons of oil they sent only 20,000. They did the same with foodstuffs. During the first days of August, the entire supply of Rumanian wheat which had been paid for by Italy was requisitioned by Germany.

Only when all this came to Badoglio's notice did he finally decide to see if he could make peace with the Allies. But first he had to see what the Allies could offer.

Chapter 16

... OR PEACE?

The first tentative contacts with the Allies, in August 1943, were brought about through the realization that the interests of Italy's ruling class, rather than those of the Italian people, were being threatened. The survival of traditional Italian institutions was no longer assured by continuing the alliance with Germany; therefore the only remaining choice was to make overtures to the Western democracies while holding on to Axis ties.

After all, once its suspicions were allayed, Germany could again become a helpful ally. Italy's rulers would have preferred this; for years the two countries had had similar structures, interests and goals. For both, democracy, freedom for the people, even peace were alien concepts.

This was why contacts with the Allies were made hesitantly, even reluctantly, and why peace was among the last subjects brought up. Yet peace feelers from Italy were nothing new. They had been reaching the Allies since 1940, most of them including plans for getting rid of Mussolini. Contacts had been made, emissaries sent and soundings taken, but they had all proven to be either artful dodges or blind alleys; the mediators were frequently obscure and occasionally unauthorized, and they usually presented disproportionate requests which all too often turned out to be demands.

Before July 25, 1943, these peace feelers were mainly advanced by four distinct groups: members of the royal house, dissident Fascists, military officials and anti-Fascists. Most members of the first three groups shared the same incentive, that of having a foot in both camps. During fascism, the king had continued to receive pre-Fascist politicians; Crown Prince Umberto had his clique of monarchist officers who looked down on fascism, while his wife, Princess Maria-José, maintained a salon of anti-Fascist intellectuals. The Belgian-born princess launched her own peace moves and dallied with plots to overthrow Mussolini until wits in Rome called her "the only man in the House of Savoy." In 1942, she tried to reach Churchill through dictator Oliviera Salazar in Portugal. Another royal approach had come from the Duke d'Aosta in Geneva, while Count Ciano broached the subject through the Italian ambassador in Lisbon.

Northern Italian industrialists and financiers, once ardent Fascists, backed some of these peace efforts and initiated others, primarily out of a desire to protect their holdings from Allied bombing, popular revolution and German occupation. Prime movers included Venice's modern doge, Giuseppe Volpi, Aldo Rossini of the Bank of Novara and paper magnate Luigi Borgo.

Even Badoglio had made some moves in this direction. He had established contacts in early 1943 with British intelligence agent John MacCaffery in Switzerland, telling him that he "wanted to assume power and establish a military government in Italy." The actual revolt would be carried out by a friend of Badoglio, General Gustavo Pesenti, whose other dream was to write the music for Dante's *Divine Comedy* using a twelve-note scale. The English turned down the proposal, convinced "that the advantages . . . are not sufficient to outweigh the disadvantages and connected risks. The forces General Pesenti could gather would be of little or no military value."

There were other attempts also, so numerous and so confusing that the Allies could barely distinguish the genuine article when it appeared. The English had the impression that all these feelers were being advanced by a country aware of its defeat, useless either as friend or enemy. Eden had summed it up in the letter he wrote Cordell Hull in January 1943 about Badoglio's peace move: "Our military authorities think that Italy . . . represents only a German burden."

This was one of the rare instances before July 25 when the English informed the Americans of such offers, for the fact was that the English did not really want an Italian surrender; they preferred the spreading out of German forces.

"Therefore," Eden had emphasized in his letter, "the point of view of His Majesty's government is that we should not count on a separate peace but aim at . . . stirring such disorder in Italy as to provoke a German occupation. In the pursuance of such policies we must intensify to the utmost our military attack against Italy."

In line with this policy, Britain's chief of General Staff, Sir Alan Brooke, even after July 25, wanted to draw "German forces from Russia, the Balkans and France in order to face the Italian threat. If we pin Germany in Italy, she cannot find enough force to meet all her commitments."

Speaking to the House of Commons on July 27, Churchill expanded on this theme, saying that the war effort would be impeded by the burden of occupying Italy "mile by mile." He said the Allies might find themselves in the same position as the Germans were in many countries, having to have recourse to firing squads and concentration camps. It would be better, he said, to leave the Italians to "stew in their own juice for a bit and hot up the fire to the utmost to accelerate the process."

But with Mussolini gone, Italy hung onto the illusion that it could bargain effectively even when its potential was at a minimum. Foreign Minister Raffaele Guariglia, who had arrived from Turkey to take up his post on the evening of July 29, dispatched millionaire rubber manufacturer Alberto Pirelli to Switzerland to ask the Swiss to act as intermediaries between the Italians and the Anglo-Americans. The Swiss gently turned him down, since such intervention would have violated their traditional neutrality. Besides, Switzerland, too, was menaced by the Germans and believed it impossible to undertake an initiative which could not be kept secret. If the Germans found out, they would have the pretext they wanted to invade Switzerland.

Although it was evident that the situation became more serious with every passing moment, Badoglio went about establishing contact in a dilatory, tortuously slow manner. Every day after lunch he took a nap and every night he was in bed by nine thirty. His reflexes were slow and he operated in an atmosphere of beatific optimism except for his fear of the Germans. It was obvious that, at least at the start, his approaches to the Allies were a way of stalling for time while he prayed for miracles. There was also the factor that if by chance the Allies did accept, Badoglio did not have the slightest idea what he would do about the Germans.

It was with this foolishly optimistic, blundering approach that Badoglio initiated his first dealings with the Allies. Since, for most Italians, the English remained models of sportsmanship and political savoir-faire, these moves were directed to them rather than to the Americans. Yet journalist Indro Montanelli later pointed out in *Corriere della Sera:* "The Italians would have found more comprehension and sympathy [in the United States] not only because America had suffered less from the Italians but most of all because America had millions of people of Italian origin who were voters."

Badoglio had ignored a third possibility, that of an approach to Russia, which had not yet accepted the Casablanca diktat of an unconditional surrender. Contacts with the British were difficult, in Rome at least. Due to the efficiency of Italy's counterespionage service, the Italians were unable to use the most obvious link, the British diplomatic representative to the Vatican. His code was useless, as Foreign Minister Guariglia had reason to know, for it had been stolen by a footman bribed by SIM while Guariglia was Italian ambassador to the Vatican. By July 1943, it was undoubtedly known also to the Germans.

Italian secret agents had long specialized in stealing other countries' codes without discovery. Colonel Santo Emanuele, head of SIM's Special Section, succeeded in obtaining approximately seventy different codes, and in one year SIM laid its hands on sixteen thousand documents. When the Italians invaded Ethiopia in 1935, they stole an earlier British code from the embassy in Rome. The theft was so cleverly carried out that a Scotland Yard inspector excluded the possibility that the document could have been taken from the embassy and an innocent Foreign Office archivist was fired.

The French code was taken from its embassy at the Palazzo Farnese, photographed, and replaced all in one night, and even the German code was stolen from Villa Wolkonsky. Mussolini found it on his desk one morning in the "Bulletin 1" written for him every day by General Amé, head of SIM.

The American code was stolen from the American military attaché in Rome two months before the United States joined the war, and Harold Tittmann, assistant to the president's personal representative to the pope, was not entrusted with another for fear it might be stolen also.

Badoglio's first two soundings took place in the first part of August, both carried out by men who were woefully unqualified for such a delicate task. Thirty-five-year-old Marquis Blasco Lanza d'Ajeta, who held a modest diplomatic post, initiated the first sounding. His lack of top-level experience and his identification with fascism were passed over in view of his other, rather peripheral qualifications: he spoke English, he was thoroughly monarchist (his father was grand master of ceremonies for the court), he had been Ciano's chef de cabinet at the Italian Embassy to the Vatican, his mother was a Potter-Jones from Cincinnati, and his godmother was the wife of Sumner Welles, U.S. under secretary of state.

Despite his American ties, his assignment was to contact the British in Lisbon. Out of fear of the Germans, he was not furnished with the requisite credentials but merely with a letter of presentation signed by the British minister to the Holy See, D'Arcy Osborne, and addressed to Osborne's cousin, Sir Ronald Campbell, British ambassador to Portugal.

This "old boy" network, although it smacked of dilettantism, might have succeeded if d'Ajeta had been entrusted with a logical proposal. But he was only briefed in vague terms by Guariglia and by General Castellano, who gave him some limited military information. He was then ostentatiously transferred to the Italian Embassy in Lisbon. In his baggage was a portion of the Foreign Office archives which it was thought best to have out of the country. There was so little secrecy in Rome about his trip that it gave rise to the rumor that his real mission was to carry Edda Ciano's jewels to safety.

On August 4, d'Ajeta met for an hour and a half with the British ambassador at his private residence in Lisbon. Sir Ronald, an astute diplomat who later contended with Egypt's King Farouk, was hardly impressed by this young official, who admitted that his aim was not to initiate negotiations but only to clarify the Italian situation for the Allies. However, after saying that he could not comment, the ambassador settled back to listen.

D'Ajeta said that the Italians wanted to make peace with the Allies at first but were obliged to put on a show of continuing the war in order to keep the Germans at bay. He did not add that in putting on this show the Italians were acting exactly as if they really wanted to continue the war.

D'Ajeta then painted a highly colored picture of the situation which, because of the lack of Allied agents in Italy, was provisionally accepted as possible truth. Churchill even forwarded it to Roosevelt with the comment that it certainly seemed to be inside information.

"Fascism in Italy," said d'Ajeta, "is extinct and every vestige has been swept away. But Italy has turned Red overnight and in Turin and Milan, Communist demonstrations have had to be put down by armed force. . . . There are ten thousand Germans inside of Rome, most of them with machine guns. If the Allies bomb Rome again there will be a popular uprising; then the Germans will march in and slaughter everybody. They've actually threatened the use of gas."

It quickly became obvious that d'Ajeta had been given a burden which would have been too heavy for even a more experienced diplomat. After emphasizing the need for secrecy, his first "clarification" was to suggest that military and political accords be reached between the Allies and Italy. His second was to request London and Washington to cease radio attacks against the king and Badoglio on the ground that they were fomenting chaotic extremism. His third was to advise the Allies to lessen their bombing of Italy since this could bring about open revolt and thus pave the way for a German takeover. Fourth, he asked the Allies to mount a landing in the south of France or in the Balkans so as to draw German troops out of the peninsula. D'Ajeta then admitted that Guariglia was going to Tarvisio to reassure Ribbentrop that the Italians intended to continue the war and would not deal with the Allies.

Campbell became coldly correct. Later, in relaying an account of the talk to Churchill, he said, "D'Ajeta never from start to finish made any mention of peace terms and his whole story . . . was no more than a plea that we should save Italy from the Germans as well as from herself and do it as quickly as possible."

In one single short meeting, the Italians managed to suggest that they did not consider peace with the Allies important enough to send someone of stature, that they were capable of lying to the Allies just as they were of lying to the Germans, and that they wanted to initiate talks on equal terms although, by their own admission, they were incapable of maintaining order in their own country. In addition, they asked for nothing less than the second front in Europe which Stalin had been vainly demanding for some time.

The much vaunted secrecy on which d'Ajeta had insisted was nonexistent; American news services had the story the next day and Radio London asked, "Is the Badoglio government trying to be smart?"

Churchill, who was given the substance of d'Ajeta's proposals as he was about to sail for Canada, relayed the report to Roosevelt, "for what it is worth," without recommendation. Its most pronounced effect was to harden the views of those who wanted harsh surrender terms for Italy.

The Communist bugaboo raised by d'Ajeta originated in the Vatican, where it was hoped that the prospect of a leftist uprising would cause the Allies to discontinue their bombing. The Vatican had already warned the American government that undue pressure on Italy might cause the Badoglio government to slide leftward. The warnings were issued through the Apostolic delegation in Washington, which kept bombarding the State Department with official notes to buttress its position. "Under the influence of the bitterness engendered by the dread results of war," one said, "the people fall an easy prey to communism which is ever ready to avail itself of all means afforded by any event of public importance, especially by those of a calamitous nature. Communism is already making noteworthy progress as the result of war."

The note went on to distort completely the meaning of the demonstrations which had taken place after the fall of fascism, citing them as evidence "that the Communists are well organized in Italy and that *they have at their disposal both financial means and arms* [italics in original]. Information reaching the Holy See also shows that Communism is making continual progress also in Germany. These facts are a clear warning of the grave peril that Europe will find itself overrun with Communism immediately on the cessation of hostilities."

American diplomatic representative Tittmann, in a message to Washington dated August 3, raised the question of whether the Vatican "may be playing a game with Badoglio government. In any event," he added, just in case Washington would be in any doubt, "it seems to be fact that this government has had support of Vatican from beginning."

On the same day, the German ambassador to the Vatican, von Weizsaecker, cabled *his* government: "I understand that the Vatican is in possession of a notable amount of documentary material on the recent penetration of Communist propaganda into all strata of the population and even amongst soldiers; this propaganda aims at geting hold of power in Italy."

This material, based on a report of the Italian Ministry of the

Interior, was later revealed to Tittmann who, on the basis of it, cabled Washington that the Communists were well organized, well financed and well armed.

In fact, the exact opposite was true. The party counted members only in the hundreds and new adherents were characterized by one party member as "uncertain and clumsy with no strikes, no other protests in their past activities, no fights, no real participation." When, at the end of August, Mauro Scoccimarro became leader of the Central Committee, he realized that the party could rely only on scattered groups of supporters, mainly in the North. There was no staff; the party did not even have its own printing house. The total number of members at the end of 1943 was no more than a few thousand.

Meanwhile, Badoglio was relying on two advisors, his nephew, Colonel Giuseppe Valenzano, and his son Mario, whom he had had brought back from Tangier where he had been Italian consul general. Mario had not been an outstanding diplomat; it was said that thirty candidates for the Foreign Office had been passed over so that Mario, classified twenty-ninth, could be put on the eligible list. Ciano had noted in his diary, "He's no ace, but his father adores him," and promoted him because "right now I want to be in the marshal's good graces."

Mario recommended that Alberto Berio, a friend of even lower diplomatic rank than d'Ajeta, be sent to Tangier to take Mario's place and make contact with the British. Badoglio, possibly because he could not envision entrusting such a mission to a higher official, agreed.

Even Berio was astounded at having been entrusted with this important job. "Mario told me," he wrote in his book, "that he had gone through the names at the Foreign Office with Guariglia and they had stopped at my name by chance."

Berio, admittedly no expert on military affairs, listened as Guariglia told him about the armored divisions posted around the capital and about Allied landings at various places. He had not even digested this when he was taken to Badoglio. "We need some breathing space," said the marshal. "Tell the Allies to feint the German divisions out of Italy with landings in the Balkans or elsewhere in Europe, outside of Italy."

Berio was told that he was not to reveal any military secrets to the Americans but only "to put things in such a way as to get to meet with Eisenhower," and then to tell him how to win the war.

Without waiting for d'Ajeta's return, Berio was dispatched on what was essentially the same mission, but with authority to discuss the opening of negotiations. Tangier, infested by German agents, was a strange place to begin to discuss dealings with the Allies, but with the help of Marchesa Giuliana Badoglio, Mario's wife, Berio was able to contact British Vice-Consul Watkinson. Consul General Gascoigne was away on vacation.

Berio explained his mission, insisting that, given the presence of strong German contingents in Italy, the Italian government could not conclude official agreements with the Allies. His main points were much the same as d'Ajeta's: reduce bombing so as to help the new Italian government maintain an internal front against Communist attempts to oust the monarchy; force the Germans to reduce the number of their troops in Italy by landing in various other places; and, in contradiction to d'Ajeta's request, *continue* the radio campaign against the Badoglio government in order to divert German suspicions.

These demands from a virtually defeated nation to countries which Italy had fought against for three years and which were now on the threshold of victory must have cracked even the traditional reserve of the British consular official, but Berio misread Watkinson's reaction completely. He wrote in his book that he had seen on Watkinson's face "the dismay of someone finding himself involved in a historic event."

When Watkinson's report reached London on August 4, Churchill was already on his way to Canada and Eden proposed to reply that the Allies insisted on unconditional surrender. Although Churchill wrote, "Don't miss the bus" in the margin in red ink, he cabled Eden the next day that he agreed: "Badoglio admits he's going to doublecross someone. . . . Allowance must be made for the difficulties of his position." When the British prime minister arrived in Canada on August 9, however, he drafted a fuller answer, "Badoglio must state that he is prepared to place himself unreservedly in the hands of the Allied governments," and this was forwarded to President Roosevelt, who approved it.

On August 13, Berio was secretly informed that Gascoigne had returned from his vacation and wanted to see him. The meeting was set for ten thirty that night in a small, lonely street behind the Hotel Rif. When Gascoigne told Berio that he had an important communication to dictate to him, Berio suddenly discovered that he had nothing on which to write. His mission was delayed while he went on foot to the Rif, a hotel noted as the residence of Axis spies. There he searched out the maître d'hotel and asked for pencil and paper. All the maître had was a pencil and a menu pad and with these Berio returned to the rendezvous, where he was told that the Allies would not negotiate but demanded unconditional surrender under honorable conditions.

That night the Italian Consulate in Tangier sent a coded cable to the Foreign Office in Rome: "Concerning pending quarrel [the war] at the international court. Lawyer here [Gascoigne] asked that the Bonaccini family [Italy] should put themselves in the hands of the company [the Allies] which would let them know terms."

The Italian Foreign Office replied that the Bonaccini family was not able to act; it needed comprehension, time and even help.

On August 17, twelve days after his urgent mission had begun, Berio was asked to come to the Chemin des Amoureux, a small road in the country, where he stood in the hot sun until a car came by and took him to an isolated villa. There, Gascoigne, this time equipped with pencil and paper, gave him another message.

"Mr. Berio," it read, "must present a document offering unconditional surrender and asking to know the terms which the Italian government will have to accept."

This was conveyed to Rome, which replied that compliance was impossible: "As you know, the Bonaccini family has its goods under sequestration." In code, Berio was authorized to say that Italy *might* accept unconditional surrender if it could be regarded as an ally in the fight against the Germans.

On August 25, although the Allies were beginning to lose their patience, they repeated their conditions and asked for some proof of Italian sincerity, such as the sabotage of German supply and communication lines. But the Italians' fear of the Germans was too strong. There was no reply from Rome.

Once again, all attempts at secrecy had been unavailing. From the day of Berio's arrival, local papers had published news items concerning an Italian plenipotentiary who had arrived in Tangier to contact the Anglo-Americans.

Meanwhile, the Italians had had a chance for direct contact. On August 5, SIM had picked up a radio communication which said: "Your agent . . . of Malut, captured. This message is from British headquarters at Benghazi to Italian headquarters. We offer you this means of entering into communication with us. Answer if you accept."

General Amé, to whom the message was referred, took it immediately to Ambrosio, who said, "I am agreed and so is the king." Ambrosio wrote a few words on the copy of the telegram and told Amé to take it to Badoglio. Badoglio was agreeable also, saying, according to Amé, "Let's do it." But when the English proposed an exchange of codes by means of a plane due to go to Benghazi, the Italians, fearing interception by the Germans, hastily abandoned the idea without explanation.

Amé then sent an NCO telegraphist with a small transmitter-receiver to Lisbon to assure direct and exclusive communication with SIM and through it with the Supreme Command. But Badoglio, still hoping, despite Tarvisio, for a change of heart on the part of the Germans, preferred the indirect approach with its consequent delays. To this end he was preparing other peace missions. Former Premier Vittorio Emanuele Orlando was asked to serve. He replied that he could not; he did not want to compromise his "political career and future," by such a decisive step. He was only eighty-three!

Then the British, from Greek sources, learned that the Apostolic Nuncio at Berne had made approaches, as had a "certain Signor Bussetti" who, according to Harold Macmillan, "called on our Consul-General in Barcelona, claiming to be the bearer of a formal communication from various political parties of the Left." None of these peace feelers produced any substantial results and, as Macmillan later wrote, "All these somewhat tentative gropings were soon to be replaced by something more solid."

Chapter 17

THE BOMBINGS

In August, the inconstancy of Badoglio's government was matched only by Rome's weather. August was a period of frequent storms, hail, great heat and oppressive humidity. Fear mixed with the evening haze and lay heavy in the morning with the abundant dew. The city tightened around its inhabitants, the walls seemed to crumble in dust, the smell of hot asphalt overcame the odors of oleanders and geraniums, and the all too short hours of freshness following the summer storms emphasized the feeling of imprisonment.

While it was believed that the pope was trying to bring about a peace, the Church was instead urging the Italian government to move its military facilities out of the capital and make Rome an open city and was serving as a mediator between Washington and London on one hand and Rome on the other. Vatican Assistant Secretary of State Montini had started the moves immediately after the July 19 bombing.

But the two Allies disagreed. The English were strongly against it. Churchill feared the effect on British public opinion, was concerned about what the Russians would say, and was convinced that it would be a step towards the abandonment of the principle of unconditional surrender. Badoglio's repeated assurances that the war would continue served further to solidify his convictions. Churchill also thought that Rome would be in Allied hands within a few months and that its facilities would be needed for a further advance.

President Roosevelt was all for it, but his chiefs of staff were strongly opposed. Eisenhower had planned another bombing of Rome for August 4, but when General Marshall sent him the "Eyes Only" message that the Italian government was trying to make Rome an open city, the bombing raid had been canceled. Yet, the bombing might have served to speed up negotiations—the king was particularly susceptible to bombings—and its cancellation led to the impression that Italy was being spared as a concession to Badoglio.

On August 8, Under Secretary of State Sumner Welles stated officially that nothing prevented the Italian government from unilaterally declaring their capital as an open city. But this meant little to the Italians, who wanted recognition of Rome's open city status by the Allies and a subsequent halt to the bombing.

The Catholic Church was involved with Badoglio on other initiatives. Cardinals and bishops never hesitated to put out pastoral letters instructing Italians to obey constituted authority, and, since the Church appeared to many Italians the only beacon of faith in a dark and hostile world, they tended to go along with its wishes.

Badoglio needed all the support he could get, because with the open city question unresolved, the Allies resumed their bombing of the northern industrial cities. Milan, one of Italy's most pro-Allied cities, was particularly hard hit. On August 12, a thousand planes dropped more than two thousand tons of bombs on the city. The historic center was reduced to rubble, famous buildings were ruined, and the royal palace, La Scala and thousands of homes were all badly hit. Public services were brought to a halt and thousands fled to the countryside.

Salvatore Quasimodo, a poet who was later awarded the Nobel Prize for Literature, wrote:

> Search among the dust in vain
> Poor hand, the city is dead.
> Dead: we heard the last rumble. . . .
> Don't touch the dead, so red, so swollen:
> Leave them in the earth of their houses:
> The city is dead, is dead.

It was not, of course, but in those days it seemed as if nothing worse could happen. Genoa too was bombed, and its palaces, theatres and schools largely destroyed. Livorno was so badly damaged that the city was almost completely evacuated.

Bruno Spampanato, former director of *Il Messaggero*, was in Naples between bombings there.

"It was early in the morning," he wrote, "and women were already lining up for bread. The whole city had stayed awake the previous night, women had swollen eyes, some had come out partially dressed, children clinging to their skirts as they queued up pushing each other, screaming and shouting. Suddenly we heard the siren, there was a long spasmodic wavering in the queue but no one ran away. They prayed loudly to the Madonna and the Saints asking for mercy. But no one left. The plane came from the sea; first it was a shining point in the sky, then a silhouette, now it could be seen clearly. . . . The queue vibrated as if it were a single body. The women shivered with terror but no one moved. Then the plane nosed up, climbed and went back out to sea. Hunger had been stronger than fear and then the women again started pushing and insulting each other as they had been doing earlier."

Spampanato also noted that Neapolitans remained in movie houses even during alarms and that in fact a sign outside one said: "Keep your ticket, it's also good after the raid."

Most people were confused. "Fascist Italy was never bombed like this," they said. "Mussolini is no longer here, we've torn up our party cards, we've thrown away our badges, why are we being bombed?"

But workers in the North saw the real causes. On August 9, there were strikes in Turin. In other industrial cities the anti-Fascists formed a permanent vigilance committee and sent a motion to Rome stating that Badoglio had not achieved anything and asking for the total liquidation of fascism, conclusion of an honorable peace, restoration of civil liberties, liberation of political detainees, abolition of racist laws, and numerous additional changes.

The men from the North arrived in the capital saying that if the government did not know how to make peace it might as well have left Mussolini in his place. At their urging, the Rome anti-Fascists gathered on August 11 in the house of lawyer Giuseppe Spataro and denounced the Badoglio regime.

In Rome, civil defense was elementary and improvised, the elaborate plans for adequate shelters having only rarely been realized. People on the streets were supposed to seek refuge from bombs under planks haphazardly leaned against buildings. Antiaircraft defense was in the hands of the territorial militia, which consisted mainly of old or unqualified men, with the blind used as aircraft spotters. Most ministries had underground offices from which affairs of state were supposed to be conducted in case of raids. However, in almost all of them, telephones remained unconnected and lights unattached, and for the most part they were used as summer hideaways from the hot offices above.

Aware of all this, Romans still tried to pursue normal lives. On the morning of August 13, workers had gone to their offices, rising early due to the slow, undependable transport. Housewives were in shops and open-air markets having notches put in their ration cards while others sunned themselves at outdoor cafés. Then at eleven o'clock the air-raid alarm and the first bombs went off simultaneously. People in the streets rushed toward half-closed front doors or huddled under the porticos of ancient palaces, leaving café tables and chairs isolated along the sidewalks.

For an hour and a half, 409 Allied planes from the command of U.S. Major General Doolittle raged over the capital, dropping tons of explosives. Although the target had been railroads and airports, bombs also destroyed houses, churches and the mint. Hundreds died in the southern part of the city, which consisted mainly of poorer districts. The historic church of Santa Croce, one of the "Seven Churches of Rome," was badly damaged, while another, Santa Maria dell'Orto, was completely destroyed. In the midst of the bombing, a train full of repatriates from East Africa, mainly old people, women and children, pulled into the Rome station. The locomotive was hit, the train screeched to a halt, and the passengers ran off. A priest was killed while administering the last rites to the wounded. At half past twelve the all-clear sounded.

Pope Pius, who was talking to Cardinal Maglione in his study when the alarm sounded, personally ordered his car, and, when the raid was over, went to the stricken area, accompanied by Monsignor Montini, giving his blessings, expressing encouragement, praying, and having his white soutane stained with blood.

"Our best antiaircraft battery, the Pope, doesn't function any more," said the king, and through Acquarone he sent Badoglio a sharp note expressing his "disappointment."

That same day Allied bombers attacked Milan, Turin and Genoa as well, a reminder to Badoglio that the Allies were not fooling about their demand for unconditional surrender.

At the pope's order, the Vatican sent notes to London and Washington lamenting the bombing. Instead of speeding up Italian moves towards peace, the bombing served only to compel the Italian minister of foreign affairs to declare the capital an open city on the afternoon of August 14. The next day Radio London said that the Italian declaration, being unilateral, left the Allied command complete freedom of action.

The Italians pointed out that due to the presence in Rome of the Holy See, the sacred and artistic character of the city deserved to be spared. However, this put Rome in an unpleasant position of privilege compared with other Italian cities. It increased the uncertainties of the Italian military about the advisability of fighting around Rome and later allowed the Germans to turn the meaning of open city to their own advantage. For the time being, however, the Allies sent their bombers elsewhere.

In order to feel safer, some Romans moved to the neighborhood of Vatican City or even lodged under the Bernini columns. The next day, while the king visited the bombed areas, huge crowds gathered in St. Peter's for the pope's blessing. In spite of the lack of food and the threat of bombing, scores of refugees kept coming to the capital, especially from the South, drawn to Rome by the hope that proximity to the pope would ensure their safety. But the raid, by putting so many railroad tracks out of commission, had worsened the food situation. Foodstuffs were turning bad in the Casilina station and a new city rule was announced limiting the stay of out-of-towners to five days.

Despite the fact that the Allies had done the bombing, the army was having difficulty with anti-German sentiments. Crown Prince Umberto, commander of Army Group South, issued an order saying, "I have learnt, from various sources, of Italian soldiers who have insulted, scoffed and thrown stones at German troops . . . I have the duty to remind troops that—as is well known—the war continues, as we have given our word, on the side of the ally Germany. . . . It is inconceivable that Italian soldiers should overlook their duty of maintaining comradeship towards the ally who in perfect loyalty fights at our side . . . eventual transgressors must be immediately . . . and severely punished."

Public criticism mounted, and Badoglio strengthened the guard around his villa and that of the king.

The Apostolic delegation in Washington sent a memorandum to the U.S. secretary of state informing him that the Italian government had ordered Rome's defense installations dismantled, that antiaircraft batteries and fighter planes had been forbidden to go into action over the city, that Italian and German commands were leaving Rome, that active troops were being withdrawn, that the railway system of Rome would no longer be used for military purposes, and that steps were being taken to transfer military establishments and ammunitions factories to points outside the city limits.

Despite the announcement of these measures, the Allies, particularly the British, thought that the pronouncements changed nothing, and that the one-sided declaration of the Badoglio government would have no military effect until there was confirmation that all the measures listed had actually been accomplished.

Romans, learning from the newspapers of the declaration, began indicating to the Vatican the continued presence of German commands in the city.

Throughout all this, the Supreme Command remained in the capital. Not wanting to go to the front, it had brought the front to Rome. The Defense Ministry on Via XX Settembre was declared a war zone and those who served there received the same indemnities, promotions and medals as those in battle.

After the open city declaration, however, officers who could no longer appear around Rome in uniform, entered the ministry in civilian clothes—through the rear entrance—remaining as readily identifiable as if they were wearing their campaign ribbons. They were under orders to keep their window blinds drawn even in full daylight, which lent an atmosphere of the clandestine to their paper shuffling.

Radio London denounced the trick and the Allies continued to bomb the rest of Italy in the hope that it would force Rome into serious negotiations for peace.

Chapter 18

THE LAGGARD EMISSARY

In Rome, Italy's rulers remained more worried about the menace of the Germans than the bombings of the Allies. Seeking to defend their interests of caste and class but faced with the rebuffs dealt them by their Axis partner, they set out on a strange, equivocal course, wanting, yet not wanting, to continue the war at the side of the Germans. This led to the ambiguity of trying to keep more German troops from entering Italy and then hurriedly consenting to have them brought in.

This same ambivalence extended to Italy's dealings with the Allies. They wanted peace, or rather they would accept it, but only if their security could be guaranteed. This attitude only antagonized the Allies. Italy's tentative peace feelers made it appear irresponsible, querulous and, in Catholic terms, wanting to receive "absolution without penance."

As for the Italians, the Allied insistence on unconditional surrender left them perplexed. This formula had been aimed at all the Axis partners, but how could Italians submit to a policy based on the idea that certain people, being aggressors by nature, would inevitably attempt world conquest if permitted to bear arms? In Italian eyes it was the ideology of fascism which had an aggressive nature, not the Italian people themselves. And fascism was finished.

Moreover, the desire to bargain was inherent in Mediterranean people. While the Anglo-Americans wanted surrender first and talks afterwards, the Italians wanted to talk first, even though, as Count Vitetti pointed out, they had nothing with which to negotiate.

One man in Rome, General Giuseppe Castellano, was convinced that he personally could provide the solution. "I was sure," he later wrote, "that, if I could get into touch with the Allies, I could obtain better terms than the 'unconditional surrender' on which the English [sic] continued to insist."

"We shouldn't ask for an armistice, we should ask for cooperation," he kept saying at the time. Frustrated in his hopes of being named either minister of war or minister of foreign affairs, he had obtained from Badoglio, as recompense, the promise that eventual negotiations with the Allies would be entrusted to him. Towards the end of July he had told General Zanussi, "By the way, it's understood that when we're to deal with the Anglo-Americans, I'll be doing it; after all, I think I deserve that job."

For days he offered himself as an emissary to either Eisenhower or his representatives "to inform them about Italy's new intentions," and finally, at nine thirty on the morning of August 12, Ambrosio called him into his office. Castellano was to leave that day for Lisbon together with members of the Foreign Office who were going there to meet Italian diplomats repatriated from Chile, which had broken off relations with Italy.

"You must try," Ambrosio said, "to contact the Anglo-Americans, find out what their intentions are, explain our military situation and our needs."

Italian needs, it seemed, included having the Allies carry out two landings, one north of Rome and the other on the Adriatic Sea above the city of Rimini. Nothing was said of the specific rebuffs given d'Ajeta and Berio; in fact, Castellano had never been informed of the full scope of d'Ajeta's mission.

Before leaving, Castellano requested further instruction from Badoglio and Foreign Minister Guariglia. Ambrosio replied that neither had expressed the wish to see him and Badoglio, who had received Berio, did not think it necessary to do the same for Castellano. The young general hurried over to the Foreign Office to settle the de-

I

tails of his departure. By chance, he met Guariglia, who advised extreme prudence.

"Please, General," pleaded Guariglia, "don't let yourself be discovered or the Germans will kill us all. I gave my word to von Ribbentrop that the present and future loyalty of Italy towards Germany would be maintained."

In fact, the Italian fear of German discovery was unnecessary. The Germans were undeceived, even if they were unable to discern exactly what was going on. On August 11, Hitler told his assembled generals, "The Italians are continuing with their negotiations at top speed. . . . Their negotiations are treasonable, they go along with us in order to gain time," a bit of slightly awry clairvoyance which was discounted by his own men although they felt he was on the right track.

Throughout the remainder of the day, Castellano was given documents which identified him as a fictitious Commendator Raimondi, an official of the Ministry of Trade and Currency. Rather than issue him an individual passport, the government instructed the Commendatore (an honorary title given mainly to public officials and businessmen) to travel under a group visa for the Italian delegation. This was as far as the Italian government would go, even though it was sending a man to negotiate the destiny of the nation. Castellano was to leave, therefore, without proper credentials, without precise instructions, without any information about how he was to communicate with Rome, all so that, if necessary, he could be disavowed.

The only other document that Castellano had was still another note from the indefatigable British minister to the Holy See, D'Arcy Osborne, this time addressed to the British ambassador in Madrid saying, "Would you please receive the bearer of this note." The note had virtually no value, because Castellano was headed for Lisbon, with no stop in Madrid on his schedule.

Castellano had been chosen both for his friendship with General Ambrosio and for his supposed knowledge of English. According to General Carboni, Badoglio, thinking that Castellano understood English even if he did not speak it very well, wanted him to pretend not to understand it at all. Hopefully, the Allies would talk freely in front of him and he would therefore be able to learn the secret plans of the Allied command. In reality, according to one of his contemporaries, the Sicilian general understood no English and not too much Italian.

Though he was both ambitious and clever, Castellano was still a lower-echelon member of the military hierarchy, and he was sent, in the words of Paolo Monelli, "in the same spirit with which a radio operator of a sinking ship launches an SOS."

If secrecy had to be maintained, rank had to be respected too, and Castellano was the only Italian to have a compartment to himself in the railroad carriage reserved for his group. He was introduced as Commendator Raimondi to his fellow travelers, one of whom was a tall, young foreign service officer named Franco Montanari whose American mother still lived in Vermont. Montanari was one of Badoglio's many nephews, a Harvard graduate who had been in the ceremonial office of the Foreign Ministry. Due to his knowledge of English, he had been informed by Guariglia of Castellano's mission and advised to help him.

Guariglia had also briefed a functionary named Casardi, just in case something happened to the young general. Castellano had asked to be accompanied by the brilliant ambassador Luca Pietromarchi, but the Foreign Office, ever sensitive about matters of protocol, refused, since Pietromarchi, due to his rank, would have had to be the spokesman and, in addition, Pietromarchi's participation would have transformed the operation from a military mission to a diplomatic one.

The next day was Friday the thirteenth, and the Allied air raids on Rome and other cities slowed up the journey. By the time the train arrived at Genoa, confused railway personnel mistakenly detached the carriage in which Castellano was traveling from the train bound for Modane and Lisbon. The Foreign Office people strenuously objected and local railroad officials finally agreed to couple the carriage to a train which would cross the border at Ventimiglia, continue to Nice and then, after passing through Madrid, arrive at Lisbon. This route was longer than the one originally agreed upon, but it provided Castellano with an unexpected and fortunate layover in Madrid.

At noon on Sunday, August 15, the train finally pulled into a steaming hot Madrid. It was the height of the summer heat, and many Madrileños had left the capital for the seashore. The government itself, in fact, was in San Sebastian. Seeking a little shade, the Italian group went to the Prado museum. There Castellano revealed his identity to Montanari, who, of course, was not surprised.

"I must see the British Ambassador," said the general. "Will you please help me as my interpreter?"

Montanari agreed, as he had been instructed to do in Rome, and together they took a taxi to the British Embassy. That day, Sir Samuel Hoare was the only ambassador in Madrid. He was in the shaded part of the house preparing notes for an impending meeting with Spanish dictator Francisco Franco when he was told that two men wanted to see him. Wary of people who appeared without an appointment, he sent them word to state their business in writing. The butler went back and forth from the front door to the ambassador's suite until he finally appeared with the note from Osborne.

As soon as the visitors were shown in, Sir Samuel realized that one of them was a soldier. "A continental officer in civilian clothes," he later wrote, "can always be recognized." When Castellano introduced himself, Hoare, who had at one time served in Italy, said he knew the country well.

Hoare offered Castellano a glass of sherry, and the general, completely abstemious but afraid of appearing discourteous, drank it. The sherry combined with the extreme heat seemed to muddle Castellano's head. On his first important mission, he disregarded the usual protocol; hastily he explained that if the Italians could know when the Allies planned their Italian landing, Italy would participate in military operations against the Germans. He was in a hurry for an answer, he explained, as the ship which the Italian group was to meet in Lisbon, the SS Cabo de Buena Esperanza, was due there in five days and he would have to return to Rome along with the rest of the mission. He asked if the ambassador could accept an immediate armistice, saying he was ready to give detailed information on the disposition of German forces in Italy and to guarantee that Italian forces would immediately evacuate the Balkans. Italy, however, could make no moves until the Allies landed and gave battle to the Germans.

Sir Samuel wanted clarification. "What," he asked, "would the Italians do with respect to the Allied demand for unconditional surrender?"

"We are not in a position to make any terms," Castellano replied. "We will accept unconditional surrender provided we can join the Allies in fighting the Germans."

Sir Samuel, a bit skeptical, asked if this switching of allegiance from the Germans to the Allies was subject to any particular conditions. Castellano answered that his mission was to discuss the offer at a military level not a political one. However, he was certain that Sir Samuel could agree on the spot to the armistice.

"Speed is of the essence," urged Castellano. "The Germans are rushing reinforcements into Italy."

Although Sir Samuel was convinced this was a genuine peace

offer, he was in no position to accept it; he was not even free to comment on it until he had received instructions from London. He told Castellano this and promised to contact the British government immediately.

Castellano was nonplussed. "I was sure I would find in you," he said in a hurt tone, "a proven friend of Italy who would be able to help my country."

"I appreciate that," answered Sir Samuel, "but I can't discuss the details of an armistice with you."

"In that case," said Castellano, whose opinion of diplomats had never been very high, "I would like to speak with your military attaché."

It was Sir Samuel's turn to be nonplussed. "What I have told you," he said slowly, "also concerns the entire staff of the embassy and besides it would be extremely dangerous to negotiate in Madrid. We are surrounded here by German agents and it's possible your visit has already been signalled to Berlin by the Gestapo."

Sir Samuel advised Castellano to continue on to Lisbon according to plan, while he proposed to London the delegation of a top military man to discuss armistice conditions with Castellano. Sir Samuel told Castellano that Lisbon was full of German spies also and advised him to ask the British ambassador there for the protection of British agents.

True to his word, Sir Samuel sent an account of the meeting to the British Foreign Office, advising them of the Italians' willingness to seek an armistice if the Allies could land on the peninsula and if the Italian Armed Forces could join them in the fight against the Germans.

"Without these two conditions," Hoare telegraphed to London, "the Italian government will not have enough courage and justification to accomplish their about-face and could fall into powerless chaos."

Now the Allies too joined the game of deception and double cross. Knowing that Churchill was already in Quebec awaiting President Roosevelt, Hoare recommended that serious attention be paid to Castellano's proposal if only to obtain from him "precise information about the intentions and arrangements of the Germans."

Chapter 19

THE DOUBLE-TRACK

In the middle of August 1943, any information the Allies could have learned about German intentions from the Italians was bound to be vague and fragmentary, if not downright unreliable; mainly because Germany, not knowing what course to take, was in the process of making and discarding plan after plan. Badoglio's guileful breast-beating about continuing the war and remaining loyal had beclouded their usually ruthless vision and they remained as confused about Italian intentions as the Italians themselves. Hitler assured his generals that the Italians were betraying the Reich, but he had to admit that he did not know exactly what they were up to.

Besides, Hitler was in no rush to push the Italians into an armistice with the Allies; even if the German High Command no longer counted on active Italian cooperation in the war, it hoped that they would not pass over to the other side. The loss of Italy would place the Germans in serious difficulty. They would have to take troops from the Russian front, where Soviet force was building up, and send them to replace Italians in the Balkans and southern France. There would be the problem of the defense of the Dodecanese Islands and Corsica, excellent strategic positions both *for* the Axis and *against* them. And then there were the countries in occupied Europe where ferment was brewing. If Italy were to make a separate peace with the Anglo-Americans, the Germans would have to draw back to the Alps, their troops would lose mobility, their supply lines would be seriously menaced, and their prestige in Europe would be shaken militarily and politically. German policy was to compromise the Italians with Rome's own solemn assurances that the war would continue and to avoid defection at any cost.

Hitler also realized that he could not capture the Italian government and at the same time bring new divisions into Italy peacefully. "More important," as Kesselring wrote, "Italian forces were present around Rome in considerable strength."

In the meantime, the High Command (OKW) went ahead with plans to defend Italy, either without the Italians or in the face of their opposition. Although these measures covered wide areas and came close to involving the use of force, they remained preparatory steps and no major moves were made.

Two Italian gestures, however, in addition to German uncertainty, triggered a new meeting between the wary Axis partners. The day after the meeting at Tarvisio, the Germans discovered that the Italians had brought an Alpine division up from the South to join General Gloria's XXXV Corps at the Brenner Pass and, disregarding previous agreements for joint command of the area, were demanding withdrawal of the German troops. Kesselring expressed his indignation that this would be done while the Germans were moving south to defend Italy. The truth was that the Germans were remaining in the North and the Italians pointed this out, saying they had moved the Alpine division up only so that the German 44th could move southward.

Such thoughtful consideration by the Italians worried the High Command more than outright hostility would have. If the Italians were going to man the northern frontier fortification and block railway lines to Germany, it could mean the end of the Third Reich. Whoever controlled the Brenner Pass and communications running east to Austria and the Balkans and west to France had a stranglehold on Germany. Hitler could not take any chances; somehow he had to get Rommel and his Army Group B into Italy, and he told OKW to meet with the Italians and accomplish this objective.

The second gesture occurred on August 11 when the Italians informed the Germans that they were going to bring their Fourth Army back from southern France and some of their divisions back from the Balkans. OKW wanted to discuss this too, adding that it expected "on this occasion, to clarify the overall strategy and command organization for the defense of Italy and of the southern bastion of *Festung Europa.*"

Rome agreed to the meeting and designated Army Chief of Staff General Mario Roatta as its representative, supported by Lieutenant General Francesco Rossi, the assistant chief of General Staff, and by General Zanussi, Roatta's aide. Roatta, a former military attaché in Berlin, had been named because he was considered pro-German, particularly by the Germans themselves, who had even been willing to accept him as ambassador until Ambrosio rejected the idea, supposedly on the grounds that Roatta was too valuable as army head.

For Hitler, the time had come to force the Italians to show their hand. His representatives were to be High Command Operations Chief Jodl and Field Marshal Rommel in his first appearance as commander-in-chief of German troops in Italy.

The official aim of the meeting was to prepare defensive programs, but the real aim was to continue the game which had begun at the first post-Mussolini meeting. The Germans wanted to intimidate the Italians and to instill in them a fear of what might happen should the southern ally get too far out of line.

On August 15, the participants assembled at Bologna in northern Italy. The preliminaries began with the appearance at the Bologna airport of a completely motorized Waffen-SS battalion to escort the German delegation from the airport to the meeting place, the Badoglio-expropriated villa of former Fascist hierarch Federzoni, which sat on the hill of Casalecchio in the highest part of the city.

To the further surprise of the Italians, the Germans threw a cordon around the villa, including the Italian security detachment within it. Outside the conference room SS men goose-stepped up and down ignoring the Italian ceremonial guard.

When the German representatives finally sat down, they remained armed. With very little deference to formality, Jodl took the floor, turned to Roatta, and said in a challenging tone, "I would like to know if the divisions you want to recall from France are for use against the English in Southern Italy or against Germans at the Brenner Pass."

Roatta rose to the occasion and made a cutting remark which hinted at the Prussian desertion of Napoleon in Saxony in 1813.

"We are not Saxons," he said disparagingly. "Italy doesn't even conceive of the idea of treason and the very hypothesis is offensive."

As far as Roatta was concerned, this was really a meeting between genuine allies. In perfectly good faith he tried to work out with the Germans how best to continue the war. Roatta even interpreted the presence of SS troops as that of an honor guard. At one point he complained that some German divisions acted as if they believed that the Italians sympathized with the Allies: "an attitude which I find to be insulting to Italian honor. Italy has no intention of changing course."

For years afterward, Roatta insisted that he did not know that even while he was talking, Castellano was on his way to propose exactly such a changing of course to the Allies. Even so, despite the obvious sincerity of his declaration, the Germans regarded his insistence on having more of their forces brought south as confirmation that Badoglio wanted them cut off and captured by the Anglo-Americans.

At twelve thirty, Roatta suggested that the meeting be suspended and that everyone have lunch at the Hotel Baglioni in the center of the city. Jodl protested that he had said all that he had to say and wanted to leave immediately. Roatta was shocked. He needed another two hours to set forth his proposals. Military Attaché Rintelen, who had come from Rome for the meeting, suggested that Roatta's invitation be accepted. His proposal produced embarrassed looks between Jodl and Rommel, and they were forced to admit that Hitler had absolutely forbidden them to accept any invitations from the Italians because he suspected that they would be poisoned.

When Rintelen expressed his surprise to Jodl at seeing an entire SS battalion surrounding the villa, Jodl said it had been done on Hitler's orders, to insure their safety. Rintelen said that this was absurd. "Don't you know the stories of the Italian Renaissance?" asked Jodl.

In the afternoon, after agreement was reached concerning some German planes to be brought to Italy and three divisions of the Italian Fourth Army to be permitted to return to Italy, the meeting ended.

Early that afternoon, Jodl telegraphed Keitel at OKW: "Italian intentions are no clearer than before. Our reasons for suspicion are still as valid as ever."

By now, OKW was concerned about other things, particularly its position in Italy's South vis-a-vis the Allies. Without waiting for

Hitler to make up his mind, Jodl ordered the last German troops in Sicily to make a fighting withdrawal to the mainland on August 17. To everyone's surprise, Hitler raised no objection. It was one of the first times that he had, as General Warlimont put it, "bowed to the inevitable."

Kesselring was still insistent on securing both Apulia and the air bases there. On August 18, however, OKW drew his attention to the prospects of an Allied landing in the coastal area of Naples-Salerno. To make sure Kesselring understood, he was given a direct order to move most of his armored units there. Panzer Colonel General Heinrich von Vietinghoff, an experienced tank commander, was sent to relieve Kesselring of tactical control and to head the Tenth Army Headquarters, which for this purpose controlled some seventy-five thousand men.

Simultaneously, the High Command established Rommel and his staff in Italy, on Lake Garda between Verona and Brescia. The result was two senior headquarters in Italy completely at loggerheads, largely because of the respective characters of the commanders. Rommel, a soldier eager to extend German power, had long supported Nazism. Although a brilliant commander of troops in the field, he was nevertheless capable of strategic errors. He retained Hitler's confidence even though, when he had misjudged the situation in North Africa, he had convinced the Fuehrer to go along with him. The Italians disliked him since he had not hesitated to use their transport in the desert, sacrificing Italians to save the remains of his German troops. They insisted that Rommel, who had arrived in North Africa as a colonel, became a field marshal in only two years because every time a higher ranking Italian came to North Africa, Rommel was promoted so as to outrank him.

Kesselring, on the other hand, was not a member of the party, and hated Nazism. Although suave, he had difficulty getting along with Hitler "and his yes men," and was respected by the Italians. OKW had dubbed him an "Italophile," and therefore useful in Italy only as long as he could maintain friendly relations there. He himself wrote:

> For when the time should come to grasp the nettle and talk a different language the man had been chosen, namely Rommel, whose Army Group was already standing to at my rear . . . my continual efforts to dispel Hitler's indiscriminate revulsion only infuriated him. He once said of me, in a long-suffering way, "That fellow Kesselring is too honest for those born traitors down there."

Rommel wanted complete withdrawal from southern Italy and recommended that Kesselring pull his forces out and consolidate them with his own Army Group B in the North, naturally all under his command. But Kesselring maintained that for both political and military reasons it was better to stay near Rome as long as possible. He had little fear of a landing because, somewhat correctly, he attributed a cautious mentality to the Allies.

In Rome on August 16, when the king, already shaken by the second bombing of the capital, received a report of the lack of results achieved at the meeting in Bologna, he called Badoglio, Ambrosio and Roatta to the Quirinal Palace. After Roatta had described the German attitude as cold, suspicious and almost hostile, Vittorio Emanuele placed the blame on Badoglio. The House of Savoy had lived for twenty years in perfect accord with fascism, which had, after all, saved it in 1922, and it remained ready to accept any compromise in order to save its position. The same day, the monarch spoke privately to Badoglio and gave him a written memorandum so that he would remember what the king had said. He admonished Badoglio to separate the responsibility of the government from that of the Crown. He told Badoglio that his was a military government of executives and technicians not a political one, and he was to limit himself accordingly or risk causing the monarchy's ruin. The king wanted political agitation and organization prevented by force, if necessary, in order to "avoid the absurdity of judging and condemning the Crown by implication."

In describing the encounter to General Puntoni, the king said, "I talked to him in such a hard and resentful manner that if he had been at the head of a parliamentary government he would have surely tendered his resignation. . . . But then this is not the time to be talking about resignations nor can we forget that Badoglio is very keen on retaining his position."

To others, the sovereign complained, "Badoglio is on the wrong track," and even admitted, "I'm afraid we made a terrible mistake."

When he spoke to General Antonio Sorice, minister of war, the king said he would have liked to have gotten rid of Badoglio but realized, in view of the tragic situation, that it was better not to create another crisis.

General Sorice had already pointed out to Badoglio the necessity for getting the Second and Fourth armies back to Italy.

"If the Germans refuse," he had advised the marshal, "we should fight."

Badoglio tried to calm him down. "Don't worry," he said. "The English like us and everything will turn out all right without damage and to our advantage."

Fear was still the *leitmotiv*. On August 6, the Italian Supreme Command issued its coded telegram "O" concerning relations with the Germans. In it, commanders were warned not to provoke their ally; any incidents were to be handled with coolness and without verbal excesses, "when possible." The coded telegram went on to say that should the Germans initiate an incident, commanders were to react with any means they deemed fit.

Just to be on the safe side, Ambrosio thought it advisable to send the subordinate commands explicit written instructions, perhaps even containing information about what to do in case of an armistice. Badoglio forbade it, saying that even if it caused the loss of half a million Italian soldiers, Germany "must not be given the least opportunity to know our intentions."

This secrecy extended to the upper echelons as well. After Bologna, General Zanussi, still unaware of Castellano's trip, prepared a memorandum suggesting that a fully authorized representative be sent to London or elsewhere to conclude an armistice and to work out a plan for joint action against Germany.

Although Zanussi had not been told of Castellano's mission, it turned out that the details were known in the most unexpected places. On August 18, General Amé, chief of SIM, was informed that he would no longer head the Italian Military Intelligence Service but was being transferred to command a division in Yugoslavia. To replace him Badoglio named General Carboni, who had originally been replaced by Amé, then his deputy, in 1940.

Carboni lost no time in ordering information about high-ranking officers and political personalities brought to his attention. As he wrote in his memoirs: "In going through them I found a card on which was written: 'All the ushers at Palazzo Vidoni [Supreme Command headquarters] and some women about town frequented by General Castellano are saying that he's left for Spain and Portugal to negotiate an armistice with the Allies.' "

After checking this with the first usher he met, Carboni immediately went to Badoglio, Acquarone and Ambrosio, ostensibly to report the news but obviously to cause trouble for Castellano, whom he blamed for having lost his appointment to Badoglio's cabinet.

Carboni took the occasion to make known his alarm, particularly to Ambrosio, pointing out Castellano's "absolute ignorance of any foreign language" and urging "the need for someone more qualified to check and balance Castellano's mission." As head of SIM, Carboni was in a position of power. Now, having discovered a plan that Badoglio and Ambrosio had wanted to keep secret, he was out to make the most of the situation.

Chapter 20

THE ALLIED DILEMMA

If the situation in Rome could be classified as confused, that of the Allies could only be described as muddled. The intelligence service of each country was usually more efficient at counterespionage than at picking up data. The Italians were not only ignorant of Allied plans, they had no idea of how limited Allied strength in the Mediterranean actually was. On the assumption that Eisenhower had numerous troops at his command, they made all kinds of suggestions for landings. For their part, the Anglo-Americans could not seem to find out what the Italians were doing. The lack of communications within the Allied camp was indicated by the fact that no word of all the Italian peace feelers was communicated to Eisenhower, although some of the military disclosures could have been extremely useful to him.

Max Salvadori, an official of SOE, Special Operations Executive, the British equivalent of the American OSS, wrote: "Although it may seem strange, even absurd, the Allied chiefs were almost totally unaware of the Italian situation. . . . Their intelligence on Italy came for the great part from diplomats, unaware as diplomats usually are, of what was happening outside the very small circles of the snobbish spheres they attended, cut off, with very few exceptions, from any contact with the mass of the population."

There were, of course, sellers of information who approached British and American diplomats in neutral countries, but how were the latter to know if the would-be informers had real revelations or were *agents provocateurs?* Italian agents were particularly skilled at spreading false news and in ferreting out and eliminating enemy spies, which was why, by 1943, the Allies were getting no worthwhile reports out of Italy. The English did have a network for espionage and sabotage in Italy headed by an agent named Giusto, but it was completely run by the Italian secret service! In order to avoid suspicion Giusto, a double agent, had to show some results. He would pass off as sabotage the usual accidents that occasionally took place in factories or on railroads, and then, immediately afterwards, inform the English and take the credit.

The Allies had other reasons to be wary of informers. When Tunisia was occupied in 1943, an Italian refugee there told Allied officers that at the first landing of troops in Sicily, a general uprising would take place. Then, just before the invasion, another Italian assured State Department officials that there were three hundred thousand organized anti-Fascists in Italy ready to revolt. The result was that all information was sifted with excessive caution, and for fear of traps, no contacts were made except for those with the Sicilian Mafia.

Contact was made through Mafia chieftain Lucky Luciano, even though he was then serving a thirty- to fifty-year sentence in New York for "compulsory prostitution." Thanks to his ties with Don Calogero Vizzini, head of the Mafia in Sicily, and Genco Russo, overseer of the vast holdings of Carboni's aide, Prince Raimondo Lanza di Trabia, the landings of the Allies there were so greatly facilitated that troops advanced in the center of the island with a notable margin of security. On the contrary, strong resistance developed in the eastern part of Sicily, which was not controlled by the Mafia.

The contacts served neither the Allied cause nor Italy too well. Taking the island put the Allies in the position of having to come up the peninsula the hard way. As for Italy, the Allied dealings only strengthened the Mafia's hold on the island and "the mayors appointed by the grateful Allies," as English author Norman Lewis wrote, "were *mafiosi* to a man."

The Mafia regained the power lost under the Fascist regime, becoming stronger than ever, and "don Calo" ruled from shortly after the landings until his death, when Genco Russo succeeded him. Luciano had his sentence reduced "in consideration of services rendered the nation," and Vito Genovese, head of the American Mafia, was named unofficial advisor of AMGOT—Allied Military Government—in Italy.

Although the end might have justified the means, the Allies, if they had known the true state of affairs in Italy, could have landed farther north, cut off the German divisions, and avoided bloody battles on the road to Rome. Better still would have been the Eisenhower-preferred plan, submitted at the Casablanca conference, to invade Sardinia and Corsica rather than Sicily. This, as Eisenhower said, would ". . . force a very much greater dispersion of enemy strength in Italy. . . ." In the opinion of British commanders, Sardinia would have provided a better base for quick conquest of the peninsula even if it meant bypassing Rome. Eisenhower said, ". . . if the real purpose of the Allies was to invade Italy for major operations to defeat that country completely, then I thought our proper initial objectives were Sardinia and Corsica."

But Churchill, who was leading the Americans "up the garden path in the Mediterranean," knew that if he expressed such an outright aim, the U.S. Joint Chiefs would turn thumbs down on *any* Mediterranean effort and his hopes of taking Rome would be relegated to limbo.

The plan had also been discarded for fear of "large-scale counteraction by the enemy," an estimate which was later seen to be inaccurate. There was no Mafia in Sardinia, and no one got in touch either with anti-Fascists in Italy or with former Fascist ministers who had resigned or opposed Mussolini, although some of them were privy to vital information.

News of the latest Italian peace offer caught the Allies in the midst of their preparations to meet at Quebec. The Combined Chiefs of Staff were already there and Churchill arrived to be joined later by Roosevelt. The conference, QUADRANT, was to be held almost as if the British and the Americans were opponents, not allies. The American chiefs of staff had carefully prepared the ground; according to the War Department official history, they had "analyzed at length the technique of previous conferences, the debating techniques of the British and even the precise number of planners required to cope on equal terms with the British staffs."

General George C. Marshall, the American army chief of staff, told his aides, "We must go into this argument in the spirit of winning."

Sir Alan Brooke, the British army chief of Imperial General Staff, would have preferred dealing with MacArthur at Quebec, rather than General Marshall.

"When arguing with Marshall," he told his biographer, "I could never get him fully to appreciate the very close connection that existed between the various German fronts. For him they might have been separate wars, a Russian war on the one side, a Mediterranean war on another and a cross-Channel one to be started as soon as possible. . . . I must, however, confess that Winston [Churchill] was no great help in the handling of Marshall, in fact the reverse. Marshall had a holy fear of Winston's Balkan and Dardanelles ventures and was always guarding against these dangers even when they did not exist."

The differences between the two countries lay in their history. The United States had mainly fought on its own continent, but in an overseas war it tended to spread forces thin. British emphasis had usually been on sea-based armies, concentrating striking strength at the fewest points possible.

Just before Quebec, Brooke wrote in his diary: "We are to have a very difficult time of it at this conference. The Americans are determined to carry on with preparations for re-entry into France and for Burma campaign at expense of elimination of Italy. They do not seem to realize the truth of the motto that, 'A bird in the hand is worth two in the bush.' . . . In addition Marshall still feels injured that we turned down his plans for cross-Channel operations last year."

On Monday, August 16, the British had just settled down to a discussion of their plan of action when Winston Churchill sent for them. Receiving his military chiefs while in bed, Churchill told them of a telegram from Anthony Eden giving an account of the interview with General Castellano. Other dramatic news arrived simultaneously. That same day Patton and the Seventh Army had captured Messina and during the night the Germans had begun to stream back to the mainland. The island had been invaded on July 10; thirty-eight days later British General Sir Harold Alexander, Allied commander in chief in Italy, cabled Churchill: "By 10:00 A.M. this morning, the last German soldier was flung out of Sicily and the whole island is now in our hands."

The truth, however, was that the bulk of the German force, forty thousand men, had successfully withdrawn to the mainland across the Straits of Messina without too much difficulty, even taking their weapons and vehicles with them. German orders captured by the Allies said, "The passport to Italy is a gun"; no Italian troops would be evacuated unless they were fighting as coherent units under German command, and all others were to be shoved off the roads if they got in the way. Even so, the Italians evacuated between seventy and seventy-five thousand men, in the process giving up considerable equipment to the Germans, who helpfully transported the Italian matériel across the straits and then kept it.

This successful maneuver by Germans put the Allies in a difficult position and Churchill, while congratulating General Alexander, reminded him of this.

"You are no doubt informed," he cabled, "of General Castellano's approaches to us and the answer we have sent from here. Our greatest danger is that the Germans should enter Rome and set up a Quisling-Fascist government under, say, Farinacci. Scarcely less unpleasant would be the whole of Italy sliding into anarchy. I doubt if the Badoglio government can hold their double-faced position until the present date fixed for AVALANCHE so that anything that can be done to shorten this period without endangering military success will be most helpful."

That day President Roosevelt arrived in Quebec, along with the foreign ministers of Great Britain and the United States, to hear confirmation of the Italian peace feelers. It was now clear that Castellano was asking for more than peace; he wanted to arrange for Italy to dump the Germans and replace them with the Allies. This posed quite a question for Roosevelt, who had stated his intention to "have no truck with fascism in any way." Of the king and Badoglio, Harry Hopkins, Roosevelt's advisor, said, "I certainly don't like the idea of these two former enemies changing sides when they know they are about to be defeated and coming over to us in order to get help to maintain themselves in power."

There was also the possibility that the proposal was a tactic based on the von Clausewitz premise that "negotiation is war carried out by other means with the aim not peace but disadvantaging the enemy." On the other hand, there were those who said that if Badoglio could deliver all of Italy, giving the Allies bases closer to central Europe, it would be foolish not to deal with him.

Eden was against the idea, pointing out that all that would be gained would be unopposed landings and Italian cooperation in running railways, ports, etc.; the Allies could no doubt have this anyway, if unconditional surrender were insisted upon. He thought that Churchill should give Castellano the same answer given Berio.

Overriding all the objections, Churchill and Roosevelt decided to go ahead. But their subordinates had not yet agreed upon the complete armistice terms to present to Italy. The so-called long armistice —including political, economical and financial terms—was still under discussion, and the English and the Americans continued to send drafts back and forth as if playing a leisurely summer game of tennis. Yet something had to be used as a basis.

It was decided to prepare two sets of surrender terms. The first, the so-called short armistice, on which the Allies had managed to agree only ten days earlier, was to be shown to the Italians. Later, they would have to accept the long armistice as well, once its terms were worked out.

While these discussions were going on, Eisenhower was at Allied Forces Headquarters (AFHQ) in Algiers reassessing plans with his staff in the light of the conquest of Sicily. His deputy, General Sir Harold Alexander, had full operational command of the ground forces; he directed the Fifteenth Army group consisting of the Seventh U.S. and Eighth British armies commanded by Generals Patton and Sir Bernard Montgomery, respectively. American Major General Walter Bedell Smith, "Beetle," was Ike's chief of staff. Air Marshal Sir Arthur Tedder was air commander in chief in the Mediterranean; Lieutenant General Carl "Tooey" Spaatz was his deputy. Naval forces, by then 80 per cent British, were under the command of Admiral Sir Andrew Cunningham, who was known by his initials, ABC.

The latter was trying to persuade Eisenhower to make an allied landing on Rome which was "relatively lightly defended." Alexander, too, was all for moving ahead quickly. His thinking was summed up in the conference he gave war correspondents in Cassibile, Allied headquarters in Sicily:

"I think the enemy will reinforce Italy all he can. But can he? What's he got? Can he withdraw forces from Russia? I think not. The Russians know Germany has been badly broken now. The Russians are not going to give up. The end is not going to come next month, but probably some time in the next year. As long as the Russians go on fighting the Germans, we've got him, we've got him, you see. If we can get into Italy, we can make Corsica and Sardinia untenable. We will be in a position to hit France and become a menace to the Balkans."

This made sense; Hitler feared any Allied move into the Balkans, since Axis forces were too scattered there to offer much resistance. On August 10, Roosevelt declared that he did not wish to advance into Italy beyond Rome, let alone into the Balkans. Accordingly, on August 12, Marshall had cabled Eisenhower that his orders remained unchanged despite events in Italy. Harry Butcher wrote in his diary that it was "a pity that we didn't have the landing craft ready to move the Fifth Army on Naples just as the battle of Sicily was ending."

With some of his Liberator bombers returned to England and seven divisions to be moved to England for the cross-Channel invasion, it was difficult for Eisenhower to plan any large-scale landings before September. However, when Eisenhower, after protesting, was allowed to retain eighteen LST's, he set September 9 as the date for AVALANCHE, the landing at Salerno with which the invasion of Italy's mainland would begin.

On August 18, the Combined Chiefs of Staff cabled Eisenhower to send one American and one British staff officer to Lisbon to talk with General Castellano. The meeting was to be confined strictly to military matters lest Allied leaders be charged with "making a deal with Fascists." The active assistance of Italy in fighting the Germans was not visualized, but any aid they gave the Allies would serve to modify armistice terms in their favor. The Italian government was to proclaim the armistice as soon as it was announced by General Eisenhower, and at the same time release all United Nations prisoners in danger of capture by the Germans.

The envoys Eisenhower chose were his chief of staff, Major General Bedell Smith, a tough soldier's soldier who had risen from the ranks, a master of detail but notably short-tempered due to stomach ulcers, and British Brigadier Kenneth W. D. Strong, the tall Scotsman who was head of AFHQ's intelligence section. They were to fly to Gibraltar at two o'clock the same afternoon.

British political advisor Harold Macmillan watched the preparation for the trip with amazement, likening it to "an atmosphere of amateur theatricals." The two officers were to go from Gibraltar to Lisbon in a British civil aircraft. Civilian papers and civilian clothes

THE FORTY-FIVE DAYS 263

had to be provided, for if they arrived openly in Lisbon the international press and the Gestapo would be on to them in no time.

Robert Murphy, Macmillan's American counterpart, thought that General Smith should use his American diplomatic passport. Macmillan objected because on the passport the general's next of kin was given as the adjutant-general of the War Department in Washington, which would surely arouse suspicion. Besides, the Portuguese visa officer at Gibraltar lacked the power to issue a visa for an American passport. As a result, arrangements were made for the governor of Gibraltar to provide Bedell Smith with a British civilian passport. Fortunately both officers had fairly common family names. By juggling their first names and their photographs, passable papers were finally produced.

Civilian clothing gave the two generals a somewhat strange aspect. The hardbitten "Beetle" Smith wore a striking Norfolk jacket bought in Algiers, ill-fitting grey flannel trousers, and an odd hat with a feather in it which Macmillan prevailed on him to remove, insisting that no British traveler "of any class would walk about with this unusual decoration." Strong was somewhat similarly dressed in "improbable" civilian clothes.

They left Algiers at 4 P.M. and spent the night at Gibraltar. The next morning, General Smith showed Strong the four small pistols, one under each armpit and one in each hip pocket, which he was carrying in case of emergency.

In Lisbon, the two men were put up in the apartment of American Charge d'Affaires George F. Kennan. They were given instructions on how to reach the British ambassador's residence by means of a circuitous route while using approved espionage maneuvers to throw the Germans off the scent.

The Sicherheitsdienst (SS Security Service) chief was Baron von Rheinshaben, officially part of the German Red Cross in Portugal but actually head of counterespionage. The nocturnal activities of Lisbon must have slowed his men's reflexes. There were no reports on the new arrivals even though this included two commercial travelers, Smith and Strong, obviously ill at ease in civilian clothes, and an Italian diplomatic delegation which included a certain Commendator Raimondi.

Chapter 21

THE MISSING GENERAL

General Castellano, alias Commendator Raimondi, arrived in Lisbon on the evening of Monday, August 16, unaware of what had been happening in Quebec or Rome and too late to see the British ambassador. The next morning he and Franco Montanari, torn between the need for haste and the desire for caution, made their devious way to the British Embassy. Waiting for them was the ambassador, Sir Ronald Hugh Campbell, cousin of the British minister to the Holy See and the man who had so coldly met a previous Italian envoy, Blasco Lanza d'Ajeta. Much more unbending than Sir Samuel Hoare, he looked over the Italians and immediately voiced his doubts about the validity of their mission.

Admitting that he had no documents or official credentials, Castellano explained the caution of the Italian government in sending him without proper identification. He exhibited his letter of introduction from Ambassador Hoare and suggested that Sir Ronald check with Osborne at the Vatican. Campbell mentioned earlier approaches which had proved futile due to this same lack of authorization. After

Castellano had insisted that the British minister to the Holy See be contacted, cautiously of course, Sir Ronald said that he would get in touch with his government and reach Castellano at his hotel with a message signed "du Bois."

In Rome, Osborne managed to secure assurances from the Italian government that Castellano was in fact its authorized representative, and this information was relayed in code to Lisbon. Finally, on the morning of Thursday the nineteenth, a message was sent to the Italians asking them to present themselves at the ambassador's private residence at 10:30 that night.

Shortly before the appointed time, four men moved through the streets of Lisbon, using back doors and side streets, taking cabs at random, and finally slipping into the ambassador's residence. Castellano and Montanari, who arrived first, were shown to a drawing room. A few minutes later, Smith and Strong were brought in by Campbell and George Kennan and introduced to the Italians. The two Allied generals carefully avoided the usual salutatory phrases and gestures, acknowledging the introductions only by rigidly nodding their heads in unison. They did this so punctiliously that their action seemed to be rehearsed—as in fact it had been.

Despite all the secretive behavior, the curtains were not drawn and the lighted room and its occupants could be seen clearly from the other side of the street. After everyone had found a place on the sofa or in armchairs arranged in a circle, Bedell Smith looked at the Italians.

"I understand," he said, "that you've come to ask the terms for an armistice. I am authorized to communicate the conditions on the basis of which General Eisenhower can agree to the cessation of hostilities."

Putting on a pair of shell-rimmed, Army-issue glasses, he started to read, waiting for the sad-faced Montanari to translate and for Strong, who had some knowledge of Italian, to check to see that the translations were correct. General Castellano nervously listened to the contents of twelve clauses, which included the halting of all aid to the Germans, restitution of Allied prisoners, the transferring of the Italian fleet and air force to places to be designated, and the use of Italian territory for Allied operations. The word unconditional was not actually applied to the surrender terms; its omission was conspicuous.

As at Madrid, Castellano was taken aback; there had been some kind of a misunderstanding about the aim of his visit. He hurriedly explained that he had no authority to negotiate a surrender; his instructions were to clarify the military situation in Italy for the Allies and to offer the cooperation of his country's armed forces in the struggle against the Germans. All this was couched in florid phrases; Castellano said that he had come to discuss "military questions with the aim of jointly carrying out an operational plan that would give the Italians effective help in the crucial moment of separation from the Germans."

The Allied officers could hardly restrain their surprise at such a disconcerting revelation. Smith told Castellano that the conditions of the armistice could only be accepted or rejected, not discussed.

This really cut the ground from under the little Italian. The essence of his mission was to bargain, to match offers with counter-offers, to concede as little as possible, and eventually to reach a compromise. The unbending Anglo-American attitude expressed by Smith gave him no leeway for maneuver. Masking his disappointment and hoping, as he said later, "to fool the Americans and the English," he again emphasized Italy's desire to fight on the side of the Allies.

Smith replied that this was a political question on which he was not authorized to comment. "However," he added, "I must read you a telegram I've just received from Quebec signed by Roosevelt and Churchill."

It said that "the active participation of Italy in the war against Germany would not be taken into account although conditions for the armistice would be more or less modified or attenuated according to the comportment of the Italians and the contribution that Italy might bring to the cause of the United Nations."

Smith handed Castellano an aide memoire based on the so-called Quebec Memorandum which had been titled, "Suggested Action on Italian Peace Feelers." It said that if the Italians were really anxious to speed the Allied landings they should engage immediately in widespread sabotage, particularly against transportation facilities, airports and any public utilities useful to the Germans. The more the Italians impeded the Germans, the more they would be "working their passage" towards better armistice conditions. However, the armistice had to be accepted first; political and economic terms would be delivered later.

The American general was particularly forceful, having realized that the Italians were attempting to jump from one side to the other without surrendering. Although in pain from his ulcer, Smith patiently continued to explain the Allied position, because he was under the erroneous impression, from information he had received, that Castellano was "chief planner for the Italian General Staff." In reality, no such position or office existed; nor was Castellano chief of operations, a post held by another general.

Sparring for time, Castellano queried the clause concerning the handing over and eventual disarming of the fleet.

"I can't put anything in writing," Smith answered, "but as of now I can tell you that the Italian flag will not be lowered on its warships."

Castellano said that his government would be put in an awkward position without information as to where and when an invasion would take place, particularly since the German reaction would compel the government to quit Rome as soon as the armistice was announced. There was the danger, he said, that the king could be seized by the Germans and held hostage. Seven or eight thousand SS or equivalent troops were in Rome, completely in control of the city. When this ploy failed to move General Smith, Castellano feigned naïveté hardly worthy of a general officer.

"What are the Allied plans," he asked, "in respect to Italy?"

Smith cautiously replied that the Allies would attack on the mainland, but he disclosed no place and no date. He did say that Eisenhower would communicate the date and hour to the Italians five or six hours before the actual landing and that the Badoglio government must then officially announce its surrender. This, however, was not what Castellano wanted, and he cheerfully proposed that the Italians be given "possibly two weeks" advance notice, instead of five or six hours.

"As a soldier," observed Smith icily, "General Castellano can understand the reasons which prevent us from giving detailed information about our plans."

Then Castellano assumed the incongruous role of military advisor, telling the Allies where it would be best for them to invade.

"Two landings would be best," he said, "one to the north of Rome on the Tuscan coast near Livorno, one above Rimini on the Adriatic. This would force the Germans to withdraw towards the Alps leaving Rome and central Italy safe."

Although the Sicilian general was only carrying out instructions, these proposals revealed a woeful lack of knowledge on the part of Italy's military leaders. A landing in the North, apart from logistic considerations, was strategically unobtainable. The *libeccio* wind, a strong southwester, made September landings in Tuscany impossible, and the Adriatic coast above Rimini was thoroughly guarded by the Germans. In addition, both sites were beyond the range of Allied fighters and even of some Allied bombers.

Later, Churchill was to tell the House of Commons, "When I hear people talking in an airy way of throwing modern armies ashore here and there as if they were bales of goods to be dumped on a beach and forgotten, I really marvel at the lack of knowledge which still prevails of the conditions of modern war. . . ."

Now Castellano understood the situation and adjusted to it, changing Ambrosio's proposals to suit the circumstances. He explained that his country needed help badly, that the army was short of fuel, guns, ammunition and even boots and that the airports under its control were small and widely scattered.

Until then, Bedell Smith had done all the talking for the Allies. Now Brigadier Strong took over. From time to time he had gone into the next room, where some technicians were, to check military dispositions and aerial communications. Now he moved to the divan and began to shoot questions at Castellano. The Italian general thought that he was being interrogated to find out if he were sincere, but Strong's real motive was to gather, as Eisenhower had advised, as much intelligence as possible in case negotiations fell through. The meeting continued through the night, with the Americans keeping themselves awake with big shots of whisky and ice with very little branch water.

Castellano, who would have preferred a good strong *doppio caffè*, was too intent on achieving his mission to ask for it. Instead, so as to make a good impression, he accepted several glasses of whisky. Being a teetotaller and having learned nothing from his experience in Madrid, he soon began to talk more freely and to reveal more and more military secrets, hoping, he said later, to establish his good faith. On a map, he drew the positions of Italian forces around Rome and described the locations and battle readiness of the other Italian units; he listed the fifteen German divisions in Italy; he told all he knew of the operational criteria of the Germans; and he indicated Frascati, a little hill town outside Rome as their headquarters. This latter information was not entirely accurate, however, as the German Command was in reality located in villas spread out towards Grottaferrata, but the Allied generals later agreed that they had learned a great deal from Castellano.

Their trust in the new Italian regime was shaken, however, by

Castellano's continued reference to Italy's honor while describing the Italian desire to switch partners. It was further diminished when Castellano told the group how Mussolini had been overthrown. According to him, four military leaders, including Badoglio and Ambrosio, had decided that Mussolini was a liability, but to get rid of him, Castellano continued, they had to gain the support of Fascist members of the Grand Council. Dino Grandi was led to believe that once Mussolini had been deposed he would take the dictator's place, but then he was double-crossed. When Smith asked Castellano if he could tell him where Mussolini was, Castellano became secretive. "Hitler too," he replied slyly, "would like to know."

Since Castellano had said that the Italian government was considering not so much an armistice as a change in its policy and since the Allied generals were not empowered to negotiate on such broad terms, it was agreed that Castellano would return to Rome and present the military terms of surrender to the Badoglio government while Smith and Strong returned to Algiers. To expedite matters, Castellano was given a small portable radio transmitter-receiver, set to a specific wavelength, which would serve as the radio channel between the Italians, code-named Monkey, and the United Nations Radio at AFHQ, code-named Drizzle. Once in Rome, Castellano was to give the radio and codes to a captured British agent who would be released from prison. This was SOE's Lieutenant Richard Mallaby, taken earlier at Lake Como and subsequently sent to Regina Coeli prison in Rome pending his trial for espionage. Allied radio operators in Algiers would stand by ready to receive a reply beginning midnight, August 26.

If for any unforeseeable reason the transmitter did not function, the Italians were to send a messenger to the British Legation in Berne. If this also proved impossible, the government was to send a message in Italian to Osborne at the Vatican saying, "The Italian government protests against the delay in the communication of the complete list of names of Italian prisoners captured in Sicily.

Since the exchange of Chilean and Italian diplomats might be delayed until after August 20 and since Castellano could not travel alone lest he attract attention to himself, his expected date of arrival in Rome would be August 25, and possibly even later. Therefore, if by midnight, August 30, no word had been received from Rome, it would be clear that the armistice had not been accepted. On the other hand, if after preliminary acceptance of the armistice, additional negotiations were necessary, Castellano would leave at 7 A.M. on

August 31 from the Guidonia airfield fifteen miles north of Rome to fly with an escort of Allied fighters to Sicily.

By now the meeting had been going on without pause for over nine hours. Kenneth Strong had accumulated all the intelligence he could handle, while General Castellano was convinced that he had cut a good figure. He had, in fact, impressed the Allied negotiators with his "remarkable grasp of detail," having had virtually no recourse to notes.

A verbatim account, secured from a hidden wire recorder, was shown to Castellano, who signed one copy and was given another. The participants stood up. Smith mentioned the bravery of Italian troops at Messina and Castellano thanked him. Then the groups parted, this time shaking hands all around. It was seven thirty in the morning of August 19.

Both sides had done some bluffing. Smith and Strong knew that Italy's surrender was needed to make up for Eisenhower's depleted resources and that any landing on the peninsula stood little chance of success as long as the Italians still fought on the side of the Germans. This had caused Smith to hold out concessions as bait. For his part, Castellano had gone way beyond his instructions, moved by the feeling that he had been sent on a useless mission. No one had instructed him to discuss a surrender, and yet he had let it be understood that a surrender was entirely possible. He had also given more information than he should have in the hope of getting a *quid pro quo* in the form of Allied intelligence.

At noon that day, the two Allied generals departed for Algiers, but Castellano remained even when he was told that the ship's arrival had been delayed at sea. Although it would seem that the Sicilian general could have figured out a quicker way to get back to the Italian capital, he waited for the Italian diplomats to arrive. When Campbell suggested that he take a plane to save time, Castellano refused; commercial flights stopped in Madrid and in France, and Castellano was sure that either the Spanish or the French police would pick him up.

By August 21, he was beginning to get restless, and so, still using cloak and dagger techniques to avoid detection, he went through back streets to the Italian Legation and the office of the counsellor to the embassy, Blasco Lanza d'Ajeta. Together they went to see the Italian minister, Renato Prunas. The minister was both surprised and shocked by Castellano's presence. Several days after Castellano's arrival, the London *Daily Telegraph* had published a dispatch from its Lisbon correspondent saying that an Italian delegation had arrived there to open peace negotiations, led by a Minister De Angelis. The German minister had heard about it and called Prunas. In complete good faith, since he had not been informed of Castellano's trip, Prunas had told the German that it was a false rumor or, more likely, a deliberate lie by the British.

Now came the most difficult part of Castellano's mission, telling Rome what the situation was. On August 22, he hit upon the idea of using the same kind of message that d'Ajeta had sent two weeks earlier when he had cabled that he had been unable to obtain the "wolfram," meaning that his mission had failed. Now Castellano cabled that he had been able to purchase the stock. In order not to arouse suspicion, he also sent a *second* telegram, saying the liberation of sick prisoners would take place in a few days. To Castellano, the import of these messages was crystal clear. "The first indicated," he later explained, "that I had succeeded in making the contact, the second that I would be returning to Rome to report. Their meaning should not have been too difficult to understand because they came from Lisbon and there were no negotiations for wolfram or for sick prisoners."

Days passed, however, without any reply from Rome, and Castellano and Montanari wandered around Madrid, touring museums and purchasing souvenirs. But if Castellano had not been so fearful about security matters, he might have discovered that it was possible to contact Rome direct. For some time SIM had had a special wireless operator on the staff of the Italian ambassador. This semiclandestine operator had a secret radio tuned into military intelligence in Rome and a secret code with which to communicate. Castellano never inquired about the possibility, nor did anyone go out of his way to give him this information.

Finally the SS *Cabo de Buena Esperanza* arrived and preparations were made for departure. Now Castellano had another problem. On meeting the functionaries coming from Chile, he tried to affect the personality of Commendator Raimondi, economic counsellor of the Ministry of Trade and Currency. He was shocked to find that the local commercial attaché, Rinaldo Ossola, was a genuine expert. Overjoyed at meeting what he supposed to be a colleague, Ossola launched a complex technical review of the Chilean economic situation. Castellano, naturally enough, did not have the slightest idea of what Ossola was talking about. Castellano's responses were noticeably short and limited primarily to murmured affirmations. After a bit, the commercial attaché began to realize that this "colleague" did not understand a word he said. Puzzled, Ossola took Montanari aside.

"Is it possible," he asked, "that Raimondi is so ignorant about things concerning his job? He's either an idiot or someone who doesn't come from the Ministry."

"He no doubt is both," replied Montanari, hoping to cover up. "It's quite normal in a ministry set up by the Fascists."

Other, more important problems arose for Castellano. The Italian minister had thought it imprudent to leave the Allied proposals in Castellano's hands. They were kept at the legation in a sealed envelope and then given to the ambassador who had come from Chile. Prunas hinted that they contained figures concerning gold reserves. "Very important papers of Commendator Raimondi," he told the ambassador, "to be given to Raimondi [Castellano] once the train enters Italian territory." The radio was put in the diplomatic pouch.

But Castellano was still worried about the possibility of the train being bombed by the Allies as it passed along the Riviera and on into Italy. At the British Embassy he was assured that an order had been sent to Allied air commands that this train be granted diplomatic privileges. However, this did not satisfy Castellano, and he insisted on waiting until confirmation came that the order had been received by the RAF and USAF.

Finally, on the morning of August 24, Castellano and Montanari left Lisbon on the long, slow trek back to Rome.

Chapter 22

REINFORCING POWER

In the Italian capital, the government, which was still concerned with covering up General Castellano's absence, was going confusedly about its business. The Ministry of Foreign Affairs, unable to figure out the meaning of Castellano's Lisbon telegrams, passed them around among various offices and finally filed them without informing either Foreign Minister Guariglia, Head of Government Badoglio or General Ambrosio and the Supreme Command.

Other things were preoccupying Rome. On August 19, War Bulletin No. 1180 announced the loss of Sicily. Newspapers appeared with the news in black borders and the queen asked that the flag not be hoisted for her birthday. Badoglio and Vittorio Orlando spoke on the radio but the king complained that Orlando's speech devoted more time to condemning fascism and war than to explaining the position of the monarchy in the face of this loss.

Meanwhile the capital was swelling with people from surrounding areas who were terrorized by the bombings and paralyzed by uncertainty. On August 20, Allied planes flew over Rome to drop propaganda leaflets and to set off flares so that they could take photographs. Italian antiaircraft batteries remained silent and neither searchlights nor night-fighters entered into action.

By then, however, popular feeling could be summed up in the popular saying, "*O Francia, o Spagna, purchè se magna,*" "Let France come or let Spain [it's all the same], as long as we eat."

Food was getting scarce. On the day the fall of Sicily was announced, a reader wrote to *Il Messaggero* asking why fresh beans were never to be found in the markets although they were being served in elegant restaurants.

The curfew continued and unidentified shots rang out in the night like church bells tolling the hour, with no official notice being taken of them. On August 20, forty-nine people, including eight women, were fined or sentenced to as much as four years' imprisonment for violating the curfew. Others were arrested for listening to Radio London.

Papers were restricted to only one page and, since censorship continued unabated, there was no change in their attitude towards the war. The Rome press continued to deny that any approaches to the Allies were being made, *Il Popolo di Roma* called peace rumors "a military as well as a political absurdity," and *La Tribuna* maintained that Italy "will defend its honor, its life, its future. The very fact that the enemy, to carry out its plan, can't help destroying Italy shows that the salvation of Italy coincides with the salvation of the world." In *La Gazzetta del Popolo*, Tullio Giordana deprecated the possibility, which he called an absurd one, that Italy might accept unconditional surrender, "betraying the ally that in this moment fights at its side. In that case," continued Giordana, "Italy would lose everything, even prestige . . . as the Italians would be despised from that point on throughout the world."

In the North, people, particularly workers, felt differently. Bombing had been stepped up, and on August 16, when Milan and Turin were hit particularly hard, violent protests against continuation of the war began. Fiat workers in Turin went out on strike the next day and tried to get others to join them. After warning them to disband, troops fired on the strikers, hitting a number of them; although some leaders were arrested, the strikes spread.

This was something unusual. There had been a series of walk-outs in mid-March, beginning in Turin and extending to Milan and Genoa. But since these walk-outs started as wage disputes and only later grew into protests against fascism and the war, an increase in

Ettore Muti speaking to Fascist youth organization, GUF

Pius XII, after the bombing of Rome on August 13, 1943

Letter from Mussolini to his wife and children—Vittorio, Romano and Anna—written during The Forty-Five Days wages in mid-April brought the strikes to an end. Now, however, the protests were predominantly political. Anti-Fascists released from prison provided superior leadership, and the strikes again spread from Turin to Milan and to other areas in the North. Badoglio was worried; the Germans might intervene if the Italians failed to handle the unrest, and now, with their troops in the North, they had the force to do it.

The situation in Turin was particularly bad. On August 19, a general strike broke out all over the city; factories were deserted and transportation was at a standstill. For Jewish intellectual Emanuele Artom the situation was similar to that of Russia in 1917, ". . . useful in showing that Italian public opinion is not that of the government," the beginning of the ascension of communism in Italy. The leftist parties hurried to express their support for a nation-wide general strike.

The king told Badoglio that it was his fault; naming leftists to government posts, he said, had given workers the idea that the government would give in to them all along the line. Alarmed, Badoglio called in Minister of Corporations Leopoldo Piccardi and warned him that intemperance on the part of the workers could ruin everything. It was up to the anti-Fascists to halt the strikes. Badoglio was vague about peace negotiations but he let it be understood that something was under way.

In Turin, General Adami-Rossi had invoked martial law, arrested eighty workers, and occupied the Fiat factories. As soon as Piccardi, along with labor leaders Bruno Buozzi and Giovanni Roveda, arrived from Rome, they rounded up leaders among the workers and held an impromptu meeting at a local police station. It was a dramatic moment. The workers had had enough and were ready to risk everything. They shot questions at Piccardi: "What kind of a game is the government playing? Does it really want peace? If it does, what is it waiting for?"

Piccardi was forced to tell them some of what was going on, and it is to the workers' credit that the secret was well kept although the promises Piccardi made were not. He did manage to get most of the arrested workers freed and to secure wage increases for which the workers had not asked. He also promised them a quick end to the war and assured them of the removal of General Adami-Rossi, the military commander of Turin who had ordered the attack on the workers. Back in Rome, however, Minister of War Sorice opposed this, and Adami-Rossi stayed on.

K

Then Piccardi went to Milan where, at the prefecture, he presided over a meeting of 304 worker delegates and persuaded 294 of them that the general strike should be called off.

But the king was not satisfied. It was becoming increasingly evident that Badoglio was not really solving any of the country's gigantic problems but was, on the contrary, complicating them with incoherent and contradictory policies. On August 15, the king had told Puntoni, "Badoglio is getting me in all kinds of jams. It seems to me that it is his intention, by upsetting everyone, to create a vacuum around the monarchy. There are nothing but complaints about his conduct and most of them are justified."

The king was becoming irritable over other matters as well. Apparently concerned that his son and daughter-in-law might exploit the situation and give more support to peace proposals, he sent Princess Maria-José and her children to the North, omitting, in his haste, to supply her with a passport which, in case of emergency, she would need to enter Switzerland.

Then the king told his intimates that Badoglio would have to go and started sounding out anti-Fascists about the possibility of forming a new government. When Dino Grandi requested permission to leave the country, the king sent him word through Acquarone that he should postpone his departure as he might be needed shortly.

Crown Prince Umberto even suggested to Marshal Graziani that he "remain available because the king might need him soon." When Graziani said that he did not think he could collaborate with Badoglio, Umberto hinted that Badoglio might be out of the government in a matter of days.

Both the king and Acquarone had always been fearful of Badoglio's assuming too much power. When a reshuffling of the government, leaving Badoglio in charge, was suggested, Acquarone said, "Yes, but if it works out all right for Badoglio, who will ever stop him?"

When word of all this got to Badoglio, he immediately took protective measures. Suddenly he seemed to see spies everywhere; he told everyone who came to see him that the Germans planned to assassinate those in power in Rome and that he was living in mortal terror. "I've put fifty mortars around my villa," he told Bonomi.

Bartolini, Badoglio's minister of finance, told a friend, "Badoglio is scared and doesn't even try to hide it."

And, drawing a finger across his throat, Badoglio told many of his visitors, "We'll all end up like this." The old marshal seemed so frightened that the people around him were convinced that he was actually in fear for his life.

The truth was that much of this was play-acting, part of Badoglio's plan to save his political skin. He was much less concerned about his neck than about his position, and now that the king seemed to be preparing to move, Badoglio began to warn of a German coup d'état.

Simultaneously, his security services began to receive reports of a sudden influx of secret agents and of German troops dressed as tourists. SIM, OVRA, the police and the *Carabinieri* were all recipients of bits and pieces of information indicating a mounting threat to Rome and its government.

General Amé, then head of SIM, kept receiving reports of an imminent coup by German SS and paratroopers against the king, the royal family and the government. "This activity," he wrote, "is indicated, still obscurely, as becoming menacing. In the middle of August an exciting bit of information comes from above [Badoglio's office]. Seven thousand Germans are headed towards Rome to arrest the royal family, etc. Verification: none."

Amé had been given precise information about this fifth-column coup; the German plotters were to meet at a specified time at Rome's central railway station to carry out their plans, but when Amé sent men there to check, they reported the presence of only a handful of sleepy Germans, obviously sightseers.

When Badoglio's office passed the coup rumors to other security forces, Chief of Police Senise replied that no unusual movements of Germans had been noted and Guido Leto, the head of OVRA, reported the same thing.

It was then that Amé was removed as head of SIM and replaced by Carboni. Badoglio undoubtedly reasoned that the ambitious young general would be more receptive to a grimly painted picture of plots and conspiracies. Sure enough, in no time at all Carboni began to discuss the existence in Rome of thousands of German SS, ready to initiate a full-scale takeover at any moment.

It remains uncertain whether Carboni fed this news to Badoglio or Badoglio fed it to Carboni, but it was Carboni who told the king that Rome's defenses were inadequate and that the Germans could take the city whenever they liked.

By facing the king with a German plot, Badoglio could make it difficult for the monarch to contemplate a change of government. But Badoglio still needed scapegoats, and what better place to look for them than among the Fascists, where he could at one blow rid himself of possible successors, rivals, adversaries, people he did not like or men who frightened him. He was assisted by the fact that his procrastination had led to some minor activity on the part of the Fascists, who met in small groups to discuss hopefully the possibility of Mussolini's return. This Badoglio now magnified into full-blown political agitation.

But the plot to take over Rome was still insufficiently concrete, particularly as the secret services, apart from Carboni's SIM, kept reporting that nothing substantial was actually happening. And so Badoglio fabricated an elaborate plot against his person, creating an imaginary group of conspirators who, in reality, would never have joined forces: Ciano, Grandi, Bottai, Marshal Cavallero, former Under Secretary of War General Ubaldo Soddu, former Fascist Party secretaries Starace and Muti, and a score of lesser personalities.

Summoning Senise, Badoglio insisted that the conspirators were plotting with the Germans to capture Rome. Using Carboni's manufactured information, he said that a potential fifth column of German civilians in Rome were ready to spring from hiding places in hotels and boarding houses to join forces with the Fascists.

This was what the various peace envoys had been telling the Allies, but Senise said that he did not believe a word of it. It would not be logical for the Germans to employ Fascist accomplices when they had the military force to accomplish a takeover by themselves. Besides, continued Senise, the police, who had been watching the Fascists since July 25, had uncovered no news of any plot. Certain that the whole idea of a conspiracy originated with Carboni, Senise hinted that the young general was a man of excessive imagination who was inclined to stick his nose into affairs that did not concern him.

Badoglio, however, was not about to abandon his carefully constructed plan. He told Senise that he wanted a certain number of arrests carried out by August 28. Unfortunately, there were few Fascists of any importance around to arrest. Alfieri, Bastianini and Albini had gone to Switzerland; Pavolini and Ricci had gone to Germany; Ciano was virtually confined to his home; Acerbo was in the Abruzzi; and others had disappeared from sight. Badoglio insisted and again named the supposed conspirators, undeterred by the fact that some of them were either strongly anti-German or had helped to overthrow Mussolini.

As secretary of the Fascist party, forty-one-year-old Ettore Muti, a man named by Badoglio as a key conspirator, had convinced

Mussolini of the incapacity and faithlessness of Badoglio, who was then chief of General Staff. The marshal never forgot this. He remained terrorized by the man, and after Mussolini's ouster, he found himself unable to refuse Muti's requests for meetings. He justified himself to Carboni by saying that the meetings gave him the chance to control Muti, but the arrogant Muti used the visits as opportunities to tell Badoglio what the German military authorities in Rome were saying about the regime, little of which was flattering.

On August 20, when Badoglio urged Senise to break up the plot allegedly headed by Muti, Senise asked for proof. Badoglio replied that Muti had been secretly meeting German officers and Fascist leaders and had to be put out of the way.

"Muti is still a menace," he said, adding mysteriously, "success is only possible if the operation is carefully prepared. I am sure you have understood me perfectly."

Senise answered that as far as plots were concerned, there was nothing to be worried about. Muti had naturally continued to see the conspirators of the Grand Council, Grandi and Ciano, just as he had continued to see Badoglio, and if he maintained contacts with German military figures like General Manfred von Richthofen, Kesselring's air chief, he did so with the knowledge of Senise and the authorization of Badoglio in order to keep the government informed.

Senise's attitude left Badoglio no choice but to order Carboni to carry out the arrests. Carboni passed the orders to the commander of the *Carabinieri*, General Cerica, who arrested General Soddu at dawn the next day and had him taken to Fort Boccea. Several hours later, due to pressure from someone near the king, Cerica was ordered to free Soddu and return him to his home. Bewildered, Cerica went to see Badoglio, who issued a *new* order, this time to SIM, to arrest Soddu again. As a result, Soddu was arrested at dawn, freed and taken home in time for tea, and then rearrested and taken back to Fort Boccea for dinner, all in one day.

Marshal Cavallero was arrested at the Senate and visited at seven thirty the next morning by Carboni. After insistent questioning, Cavallero dictated a "confession" establishing himself as an anti-Fascist conspirator, even going so far as to claim that it was he who had been the first to plot against Mussolini. Carboni dutifully gave one copy of this compromising "confession" to Badoglio. A second copy went to Minister of War Sorice, and the third was kept by Carboni. One of the copies later fell into the hands of the Germans, with tragic consequences.

The next day, August 21, Badoglio ordered Carboni to arrest Muti "for espionage and plotting against the State." Carboni turned the order over to Cerica, telling him that Muti's arrest could present some problems since Muti spent most nights in his villa at Fregene near an encampment of German paratroopers.

Although Cerica assured Carboni he could handle the matter, Badoglio was going through another crisis of uncertainty. "What," he asked Carboni, "if Muti's arrest should hasten German action against the government? There might be a scandal. Besides, after his arrest where could he be hidden? It's becoming difficult to hide Mussolini. Perhaps it would be better to wait a few days. Besides, Muti always spends his nights with women."

Finally, Badoglio came to the point. "Bear in mind, Carboni," he said ominously, "that if Muti escapes it's the end for all of us."

After four long months of dry weather, Rome was struck by a violent storm on August 23. That night in Fregene the weather was suffocatingly hot. Muti was in bed with his mistress, a beautiful Pole named Edith Ficherowa. At 2 A.M., *Carabiniere* Lieutenant Taddei had Muti's villa surrounded by armed men, then sent someone to knock on the door and request entrance.

Muti, caught completely unaware, opened the door in his pajamas. Seeing three men in civilian clothes carrying submachine guns, he asked who they were. Taddei presented his identification and told Muti that he had orders to arrest him. Followed by Taddei, Muti went to his room to dress and began to put on his air force uniform. Taddei asked him to wear civilian clothes, commenting, "Civilian clothes would be better since your medals won't help you." But Muti, unperturbed, replied, "Remember, Lieutenant, that I am a colonel."

Meanwhile, other *Carabinieri,* searching the house, came up with a toiletry kit in which documents of considerable importance were hidden, apparently letters which, according to Muti's mother, "compromised high personalities in the Army."

Outside the house, on a dirt road, a cortege took form. In front was Muti, at his right a *Carabiniere* sergeant from Rome, and to his left *Carabiniere* Salvatore Frau of the nearby Maccarese station. Then came Lieutenant Taddei accompanied by two of his men; one was a silent, hard-looking man in khaki fatigues; all three carried submachine guns. Ten or fifteen steps further back were a dozen *Carabinieri.*

Suddenly Taddei whistled; his *Carabiniere* sergeant responded with a whistle, fell back, and signaled to the man in fatigues, who immediately raised his gun and started firing at Muti, breaking off only to shoot in the air in all directions as if to feign an attack. The *Carabinieri* immediately threw themselves to the ground; later they said that Taddei had warned them that they might be attacked. While everyone was lying still, Taddei threw two or three hand grenades towards the group in front, but towards the right. Local *Carabiniere* Antonio Contiero thought they had really been attacked, but noticed that Taddei had thrown the hand grenades toward the right while it seemed to him that the shots had come from the left. Then the sergeant who had come from Rome with Taddei shouted in a loud voice, "We were attacked from the right and His Excellency Muti has been hit."

Taddei called for a moment of silence "to honor the corpse of a hero, not a rascal." It was 2:30 A.M.

Retired General Sani, a friend of Badoglio who lived next door to Muti, heard a submachine-gun volley and then an isolated shot like a "coup de grâce." When he rushed to his door he saw Taddei in front of him with a gun in his hand asking if the general could accommodate a corpse.

Newspapers were ordered not to add either details or comments to the brief news item from Stefani, the official wire service, which mentioned Muti's death in six lines. Twenty-four hours later, faced by incredulous public opinion and protests from the armed forces, the government tried to justify the killing with a communiqué that said that Muti had been arrested for mishandling funds belonging to a state institute and that he was killed trying to escape. No Italian, whether Fascist or anti-Fascist, believed a single word of it. It was impossible to try to explain away Muti's killing as that of a gangster killed in a police roundup; Muti, after all, held a gold medal, ten silver medals and four bronze medals, all for bravery.

Finally another version was released to the press. Muti, it claimed, was being arrested for plotting against the government; unknown elements had opened fire on the *Carabinieri*, and one bullet had "unfortunately" hit the "heroic" Muti, killing him. No one believed this version either.

The next morning General Puntoni wrote in his diary of the arrests of several Fascists and the imprisonment of Marshal Cavallero, mentioning that in the process Muti had been killed. "So will be created the myth of 'Muti 'and the Fascists will have their Matteotti," he wrote. The general noted that "a communiqué on the death of Muti has come out which satisfies no one."

However, the event itself satisfied one person, Badoglio, who according to Carboni did not bother to hide his exultation. In an attempt to justify the action, Badoglio sent a telegram to Berlin protesting the collaboration of Germans in his imaginary plot. Ribbentrop replied immediately, challenging the Italian government to give details and to name even one German who was guilty, obliging Italian Foreign Minister Guariglia to reply with a note of obsequious apology. Even the king protested violently and harshly to Badoglio about the incident.

The toiletry kit was turned over to Badoglio and eventually returned, empty, to Muti's family. The family was not allowed to see the body, and at the funeral *Carabinieri* hid behind tombstones in order to photograph anyone who brought flowers.

It was obvious that Badoglio was out to eliminate all opposition and to so strengthen his position that there would be no alternative to his rule.

Chapter 23

HOUNDS AND HARES

Badoglio's ruthless display of force shocked his critics into temporary silence. When the marshal saw how much he had been able to get away with, he loosed his hounds against the Fascist hares. In no time at all they had arrested former Fascist Party Secretary Starace, Vice-Secretary Luigi Freddi, who had been running the Fascist movie industry, Bottai, who had voted against Mussolini, Tringali-Casanova who had voted for him, General Attilio Teruzzi, five generals of the militia (including Galbiati), a journalist, an editor, a senator, a prefect and assorted others.

Claretta Petacci was among them. On August 27, Badoglio used the stolen Persian rugs sold to Claretta by self-styled Marchese Ugo Montagna as an excuse to order her arrest. Although Claretta had not heard from Mussolini after his imprisonment, she remained convinced of his love for her. She had refused to leave for Madrid with her parents and had remained in Italy.

Claretta was put in the Regio Carcere, the royal prison in Novara, and many of Mussolini's letters were taken from her. It was, coincidentally, the third anniversary of a highlight in Claretta's relationship with the dictator, for on August 27, 1940, Claretta had undergone an operation for an extrauterine pregnancy. That night she had written in her diary:

> Remember, Ben? You were in a cold sweat hearing my screams and wild pain. But you were with me and everything seemed sweet to me, everything bearable even the lacerating of my flesh. Your caress, your love, your voice, were my medicine.

Three years later, the hatred which was to cost Claretta her life at the hands of Italians was evident. A hotel owner of Novara refused to bring her food, the press heaped anathema on her, and people in the streets spat when her name was mentioned.

Another of Badoglio's prey, however, got away. Count Ciano had kept asking the Foreign Office for authorization to leave Italy, naming Spain as his destination. The last time Guariglia repeated his request to Badoglio, the marshal refused, saying that Ciano, now accused of "illicit accumulation of wealth during the [Fascist] regime," could not leave because his departure would scandalize public opinion.

Then Ciano heard that Badoglio had ordered Senise to arrest him and take him to the island of Ponza. Senise, out of friendship for Ciano, had stalled. On August 23, Ciano wrote to Badoglio, listing his stock holdings and other wealth and pointing out that most of it came from his father. There was no reply and Ciano, frightened by the killing of Muti, cast about for a way to get out of Italy. His thoughts turned to the Germans, even though a friend, Baron Doernberg, had sent him word not to allow himself to fall into their hands. "If he does," Doernberg had said, "they'll kill him."

Despite this warning, Edda Ciano, using Marchese Emilio Pucci as intermediary, sent word to SS Colonel Dollmann asking for his help in escaping to Spain or Germany. Her plea was passed on to Hitler, who agreed that she and her children, and even Ciano, could come to Germany "so as to save for the future the blood of Mussolini which is in Ciano's children." The Cianos were led to believe that they would then be helped to leave for Spain.

The day most of Badoglio's arrests were being carried out, Ciano and his wife called their servants together, gave them what money they could spare, and went downstairs with their bags, Ciano clutching his precious diary. They climbed over a wall to the next house, at whose entrance they found a large American car which took them to another building. Here the Cianos were put aboard a closed German military truck and taken to Ciampino airport, where SS Chief Herbert Kappler and Otto Skorzeny were waiting. Skorzeny gave Ciano a bottle of brandy and the Cianos boarded a Junker 52, which left immediately. All expenses for the escape were paid by the German secret service with forged English pounds.

In Germany, Ciano was put in a villa on the Lake of Starnberg, near Munich, where he was given everything he wanted, including protection from his former Fascist comrades who referred to him as "the traitor of July 25." However, as the days passed, Ciano realized that the Germans had no intention of allowing him to leave either for Spain or South America. Ciano and his wife then tried to bargain his freedom from Hitler with the diary he had kept, which detailed negotiations with the Germans. But this destroyed his last chance for freedom. It was only a matter of weeks until, thanks to Hitler's pressure, he met his end before a firing squad of Italian Fascists.

Besides reinforcing Badoglio's position, the arrests also served to strengthen the hand of Carboni. Although he should have been getting his Motorized Corps into shape, Carboni really did not have much time to devote to these troops, engaged as he was in Badoglio's intrigues, in his own intrigues, and in the continuing game of cops and robbers he was playing with the formidable Otto Skorzeny.

Although it was well into August, Hauptsturmfuehrer Skorzeny of the Friedenthal Special Formation of the Waffen SS still recalled the night of July 26, when Hitler had received him at the *Wolfsschanze.*

"You, Skorzeny," the Fuehrer had said, "will free my friend Mussolini and spare him a terrible fate; the Italians want to turn him over to the Americans. You and your men will be attached to the *Luftwaffe* under General Student."

Disconcerted and moved, Skorzeny swore to be worthy of the Fuehrer's trust. At the same time, Hitler had ordered Student to seize the seat of power in Rome, but the continuing confusion in the German camp had led to uncertainty about this latter project. As chief of the SS, Himmler wanted it carried out, while the Italophiles in Rome, led by Kesselring, called for moderation. Dollmann, who was really on Kesselring's side, was faced with the orders of his direct superior, Himmler, who as of August 25 was also German minister of interior. The opposition of Kesselring and Dollmann, however, might not have been enough if Herbert Kappler, the representative in Rome of the SS secret service, had not agreed with them; he called the whole idea juvenile, and even went to Germany to try to persuade Hitler to cancel the project.

At about the same time, Lieutenant General Josef "Sepp" Dietrich, who commanded the First SS Panzer Division, came to Rome to meet Kesselring. He found him worried about what Dietrich called "that foolishness Adolf wanted to do in Rome. It's nothing but a colossal bluff—something Adolf dreamed up one of his sleepless nights." He too took off in a plane to persuade Hitler to change his mind. Hitler was a great admirer of the Leibstandarte commander and so taking Rome was temporarily postponed.

Skorzeny, however, continued to dedicate himself, despite Kappler's opposition, to his search. SIM, of course, heard about Skorzeny's activities. Mussolini, after all, would be a fine bargaining piece. Should the Allies get him, Germany's satellites would be tempted to cut down on their support and cooperation. If the Germans got him, on the other hand, his capture would give them an essential morale boost just when they needed it.

But all that German secret agents could uncover were contradictory rumors, most of them planted by SIM. The first clues had pointed to the penal island of Ventotene as the place of Mussolini's internment, but this turned out to be one of SIM's false leads. A German aircraft interception station located on Ponza then reported that the *Duce* was there, but by the time Skorzeny was informed, Mussolini had been moved. Hitler was certain that Mussolini had been taken to La Spezia, but it was learned that the Italians had cordoned off the harbor only as a blind. In Berlin, even astrologers were consulted.

Then on August 17, Skorzeny was told of an intercepted letter—an Italian *carabiniere,* stationed on the Sardinian island of La Maddalena, had written his girlfriend and inadvertently let slip that he was guarding the *Duce.*

The six-foot-seven-inch Skorzeny gathered his men, set up a base at Porto Santo Stefano, and prepared to execute a raid on the island. To avoid any strain on Italo-German relations, he planned to camouflage his men as British commandos. A German U-boat would carry them there and they would execute an Allied-type landing.

But suddenly orders came for OKW to carry out, instead, a parachute drop on an island near Elba where, according to OKW's information, Mussolini was really being held. Skorzeny revised his plans, but soon discovered that OKW's information was just another red herring planted by SIM.

Mussolini, meanwhile, was taking time off from reading Nietzsche to write letters. When he had had to work at Palazzo Venezia and could not see her, he had sent notes to his mistress, Claretta Petacci. Now he wrote only to his wife, his daughter and his sister. Six days after being transferred to La Maddalena he wrote his wife:

> I have received your letter, the second in twenty days and I see that since August 1st you are at Rocca with everybody but Vittorio [Mussolini's son, then in Germany]. I too know nothing about him and I hope he'll soon give us news. As far as De Cesare is concerned I know nothing. I hope that these private matters also will straighten out when the storm calms down. Now I'll tell you about myself. My health is fairly good. My conscience is clear. I have worked for twenty-one years without a vacation, with absolute altruism, with perfect loyalty. You know better than anyone, how I acted for the country.

Two days later he wrote: "The night of July 25 I was asked what residence I chose and assumed that I would be taken there. I chose Rocca. General Polito told me that my arrival at Rocca would stir up hostilities and wasn't then possible."

The evening of August 26, Mussolini saw a German reconnaissance aircraft flying over La Maddalena, coming as low as one hundred and fifty feet. Suddenly the small plane, in its hurry to get away, crashed into the sea. An Italian vessel picked up the survivors, including Skorzeny, who had directed the flight.

Skorzeny, his first hunch confirmed, now flew to Germany, made a personal appeal to Hitler, and finally got OKW's order revoked. Resuming careful preparations, he scheduled the operation for August 29.

At daybreak that morning, a small flotilla of German torpedo boats, ostensibly on a normal cruise, silently and speedily slipped into the harbor of La Maddalena. This was Skorzeny's expedition to "liberate" the *Duce*. He was a day too late. While he and his men had been embarking, *carabiniere* Captain Alberto Faiola had awakened Mussolini and told him to prepare to leave. Within minutes a Red Cross seaplane had touched the water in front of the house, and an hour and a half later, with the former dictator inside, it came down at an Italian experimental seaplane base on Lake Bracciano, not far from the 3rd Panzergrenadieren Division headquarters. Here Mussolini was bundled into an ambulance and, accompanied by a *carabiniere* major and Police Inspector Giuseppe Gueli, was taken to the skiing resort of Gran Sasso, high in the central Italian Apennines east of Rome. Here the former dictator was lodged in a small villa, then taken to the hotel at Campo Imperatore, sixty-five hundred feet above sea level and accessible only by a funicular.

"So," Mussolini exclaimed upon his arrival, "I am in the highest prison in the world."

Although he was not allowed to have any newspapers, he could, for the first time, listen to the radio and hear about the confused political situation in Rome. Things were so confused, in fact, that no precise instructions had been given to the 250 police agents and *carabinieri* assigned to guard him.

So he remained more vulnerable than ever, while Skorzeny, as if sensing this, redoubled his efforts.

Chapter 24

THE NEW NEGOTIATOR

Missions were plentiful in Rome that summer. Besides check-mating Skorzeny, the indefatigable General Carboni was busy on another front. Exploiting the climate of fear, he kept pointing out that there was no word from Castellano. Badoglio began to get rest-less. What could have happened? He, like everyone else, had forgot-ten that Castellano was only due back with the train carrying the diplomats returning from Chile. The inner circles fell easy prey to alarm; who knew whether Castellano had been captured by the Germans, had decided to remain in Portugal, or, anticipating his count-ry, had changed sides.

Searching around for still another emissary to take Castellano's place, Badoglio thought reluctantly of Dino Grandi, count of Mor-dano. Since July 25, the former foreign minister had been asking for permission to travel to Madrid to see his old acquaintance, Sir Sam-uel Hoare, and then to London to see Churchill; but the regime had been wary about entrusting a similar mission to such a high-ranking Fascist, even if he had been ambassador to Great Britain for eight years.

Now aware that the king contemplated replacing him, Badoglio found Grandi's continued presence in Italy threatening. After all, Grandi had proposed to Vittorio Emanuele that Marshal Caviglia, "the only one of the marshals of the First World War not compromised by the Fascist regime," take over the government. The king might even prefer Grandi, who remained a firm monarchist and could polarize the moderate Fascist opposition.

Suddenly, on August 17, Grandi received a passport in the name of Domenico Galli, a lawyer. He promptly went to the foreign minister for final instructions.

"Do what you can," Guariglia told him. "Badoglio who was opposed at first now wants you to leave immediately but this is only to get you out of the way."

That night, after Grandi had packed, Acquarone, acting on the king's orders, tried to persuade him to stay by hinting at Badoglio's dismissal.

But Grandi's old comrade-in-arms, Federzoni, also came to see him. "If your mission," Federzoni said, "could save only one bomb over our poor Italian cities, your duty is to try."

Grandi had heard of Badoglio's treatment of former Fascists, and he realized that he too might be dragged into the so-called Muti-Cavallero plot. Early the next morning, having shaved off his beard, he went to the Guidonia airport to take a scheduled Spanish flight to Seville. His wife and children, who had received passports in the names of relatives of the Italian minister in Lisbon, Renato Prunas, accompanied him. He became the first member of the Grand Council to leave Italy licitly.

In Seville, the count of Mordano was the guest of the Infante Don Alfonso. The next day he telephoned Sir Samuel Hoare in Madrid who, hinting at Castellano's visit, advised him to continue on to Lisbon, where there was to be a meeting that very evening. Also in Lisbon would be a plane, set up by British Intelligence, to take Grandi to Quebec, where Churchill and Roosevelt were meeting.

By August 20, thanks to Carboni's nagging reminders, it was realized in Rome that Castellano had been gone for eight days. Grandi had not been heard from either.

Without waiting for his first doves to return to the stranded ark, Badoglio decided to send forth another, in the person of General Giacomo Zanussi, a monocled, well-educated General Staff officer who was aide to Army Chief of Staff Roatta. Because Zanussi carried out special assignments for Roatta as Castellano did for Ambrosio, his disappearance from Rome would hopefully arouse no more attention on the part of the Germans than Castellano's had.

Ambrosio told Zanussi to try to reach London and to insist on a landing north of Rome. According to Carboni, his last words were, "Do your best and God help you."

Carboni also briefed Zanussi; he told him that Castellano was untrustworthy and urged him to persuade the Anglo-Americans to debark close to Rome, where they could obtain the help of the Italian army.

"Our troops are badly armed but numerous," said Carboni, "with confidence in themselves and with hatred for the Germans. . . . Make the Allies understand the losses they'll suffer if they act impulsively. . . . If they don't help us they'll have to keep fighting for years."

Carboni told Zanussi to contact the Italian minister in Lisbon and use the SIM radio and secret code there to communicate with Rome. At Carboni's suggestion, Zanussi was to take Lieutenant Galvano Lanza di Trabia, brother of Carboni's aide Raimondo, with him as interpreter.

Carboni and Roatta also came up with the idea of sending along an Allied general officer who was then a prisoner of war. He would serve as a kind of living credential instead of a written one. Chosen was Lieutenant General Sir Adrian Carton de Wiart, V.C., who had initially been captured at Tobruk in 1942, had escaped in 1943, and had been recaptured just before reaching the Swiss border. De Wiart was hardly the man to select if the mission were looking for anonymity since he was well over six feet tall, minus an arm and an eye. However, the Italians thought this would convince German spies of the innocence of the Zanussi mission which was bruited about as being concerned with P.O.W.'s.

De Wiart had been imprisoned along with other high-ranking American and British officers in the castle of Vincigliata, near Florence. When he pointed out that he had no civilian clothes for the trip, a tailor arrived to take his measurements, and suits and silk shirts were provided for him, all at Italian government expense.

On the morning of August 24, Zanussi, de Wiart and Lanza debarked from Guidonia airport aboard the Spanish airline on which Grandi had traveled six days earlier. It was to be the airline's last scheduled flight to Seville for some time.

On the second part of the trip, from Seville to Lisbon, Zanussi was seated not far from none other than Count Dino Grandi.

Even the most imaginative novelist would hesitate to place envoys, uninformed about each other, aboard the same plane. And though Zanussi was convinced that his human passport would not be identified, Grandi's wife recognized the English general immediately and told her husband, who then realized that his trip was useless.

In Lisbon, the two groups separated. Grandi's fears that he had come too late were confirmed. When he heard the details of Castellano's mission, he said later, "My heart was wrung with pain and shame. Once more we had lost a chance to behave with courage and dignity."

Grandi's arrival, however, did serve some purpose. Alerted by a Reuters dispatch, Baron von Rheinshaben assigned men to tail Grandi, who was obviously there to contact the English. Even when Grandi went to live in Viana do Castelo, north of Oporto, eager Germans, ducking behind trees and street corners, followed him. This diverted German suspicion from Zanussi and his companions, who then discovered that the Allies could be equally suspicious.

Carton de Wiart hurried to the British Embassy. The ambassador was incredulous. He pointed out that Castellano had left that very morning by train, only a few hours before de Wiart and Zanussi had arrived at the airport. When the astonished Zanussi asked to see him, Sir Ronald replied through a subordinate that he saw nothing to be gained by meeting another Italian general; Castellano already had the armistice terms and further discussion could only complicate the negotiations. He arranged, however, for the Italian general to be hidden in the apartment of a member of the embassy staff until he could figure out what to do about him.

The Allied authorities, who were duly informed, were confused. Who, they wondered, really represented Rome? Zanussi was close to General Roatta, who was considered pro-German. Besides, he had no credentials, unless Carton de Wiart could be called one. At least Castellano had brought a letter of introduction from Osborne. Was Zanussi representing a faction which was cooperating with the Germans? Or had he come in good faith, with Roatta and Ambrosio working independently towards the same end?

Churchill later said, "The purpose of this latest visitor was far from clear. Perhaps Badoglio had feared that Castellano had given too much away and wanted to clarify what he was doing."

Various hypotheses were examined: Zanussi might be a humbug, a mental deficient or even a German agent. For a while, even though Carton de Wiart pleaded his case, the Allies considered hustling him off either to a jail or an insane asylum. Bedell Smith contemplated having Zanussi shot as a spy.

The very next day, at Quebec, the Americans and the English agreed at last on the forty-two clauses of the Full Instrument of Surrender about which they had been squabbling for so long. Known as the long terms, but also as "other," "joint" or "additional" conditions, the instrument contained detailed political, economic and financial provisions which would place virtually every sector of Italian affairs under Allied supervision for an indefinite period. It was to take the place of the short terms in all future negotiations.

Negotiating the form of the final document had been a long, hard battle. For one thing, the United States, although it was willing to accept Badoglio for the purposes of surrender, thought him too compromised to lead the country afterwards. For another, the British had seventy-four thousand men in Italian prison camps and wanted their immediate return.

Roosevelt, annoyed by the bickering, had tried to hurry things along by saying that the short terms should be sufficient. "Why," he had asked Churchill, "tie his [Eisenhower's] hands by an instrument that may be oversufficient or insufficient? Why not let him act to meet situations as they arise?"

But England's top men had wanted to turn the screw on the Italians. Eisenhower's idea of having them not only as collaborators, but possibly even as allies, was unacceptable to the English. Yet many in England had questioned the wisdom of this course; in the Commons, Foreign Minister Anthony Eden was even accused of giving way to personal feelings about Italy. But the British War Cabinet maintained that "attenuation of unconditional surrender would bring no tangible military advantages." And so the British view won out, and the long terms were as harsh as Churchill had wanted.

As soon as Roosevelt had been successfully won over, the document was drawn up; the following day the text was sent simultaneously to Algiers and the Foreign Office in London, along with instructions to substitute it for the short armistice in any future negotiations with Italian envoys.

Now Eden saw a chance to obtain Italy's acceptance of the harsh terms which the Americans so disliked. He ordered the text speedily relayed to Ambassador Campbell in Lisbon with instructions to give them to Zanussi—hastily defined as a legitimate "Italian envoy"—who should take them to Rome so that Castellano could be authorized by the government there to sign them.

On the morning of August 27, Sir Ronald called Zanussi to the embassy, presented him with the long terms, and repeated Eden's instructions, omitting any reference to the short terms. Surprised at the harshness of many of the clauses, Zanussi replied that he would study the document overnight with his interpreter.

Dismay filled Eisenhower's headquarters. In getting the long terms to Lisbon and into the hands of Zanussi, the British had acted with such uncharacteristic speed that Zanussi had the document almost before Eisenhower did. This represented a real danger. The Allies were scheduled to hit Salerno in twelve days, and the operation's chances of success were based increasingly on the premise that the Italians would be helping the Allies, and not fighting them, at the beachhead. Thanks to the information gleaned from Castellano by General Smith, Allied Intelligence had a fuller, and more frightening, picture of enemy strength; the Germans were much more powerful than they had previously assumed.

Eisenhower was also preoccupied with the difficulties of landing. In order to get his troops ashore successfully, he had to bluff the Italians into surrender, but if he suddenly had to yank the short terms and deal with the Italians on the basis of the long terms—which flatly referred to the armistice as an "unconditional surrender" and spoke of "disarming" the Italians—they would probably refuse to sign. As it was, Eisenhower was not at all sure that the Italian King and High Command would accept even the short terms.

Although he was usually willing to leave political decisions to his superiors, Eisenhower felt that he had had enough. He was against the whole idea of the long terms, which he referred to as "a crooked deal," and he resented having to switch terms in the middle of negotiations. In January 1943, when the "unconditional surrender" formula was announced in Casablanca, Ike virtually ignored it, but he now found himself in a situation which could result in the useless deaths of many of his men and a tremendous setback to his plans. Definitely worried, he sent a cable of appeal to the U.S. Joint Chiefs.

British political advisor Harold Macmillan was shocked that members of his government wanted to impose "those brutal terms without any consideration for the military situation," and he protested to his superiors in Quebec and London against the immediate use of the long terms.

The problem of Zanussi remained. Ever since Algiers had received word from London that Zebra (the code name for Zanussi) had been given the long terms, AFHQ had been in a turmoil. What if Zanussi decided to make use of diplomatic channels to radio its contents prematurely to Rome? The already delicate negotiations would receive a body blow. Bedell Smith, hoping to keep Zanussi from sending the new terms to Roatta, proceeded to make arrangements to get the Italian general away from the diplomats and into military hands.

Zanussi was in Lisbon, with the long terms in his briefcase, his aims and authority still in doubt, when he was suddenly told that he was to be flown back to Rome. Carton de Wiart offered to go too.

"I'm a prisoner of war," he said. "I was released to accompany you on a mission to London. Since the mission hasn't taken place and you're returning to Italy, I'll go back with you and take my place at the side of my comrades."

Zanussi declined the offer. Carton de Wiart, he insisted, should consider himself free. The English general was hustled out of sight by his countrymen and later returned to London. Once aboard his plane, Zanussi realized that he was not being taken to Italy. Under the name of Pierre Henri Lamartine, together with Lanza di Trabia, he was flown to Gibraltar, where he landed on the afternoon of Saturday, August 28. Soon he took off again, and that evening he found himself in Algiers, at Allied Forces headquarters.

That night, Commander Harry Butcher, Eisenhower's naval aide, made this entry in his diary: "Beetle came to tell Ike in detail of his conversation with a General Zanessa [sic] who had arrived from Italy apparently oblivious of the previous approach of General Castellano. Was he trying to discover for the Nazis the extent and scope of our negotiations?"

Butcher overlooked the fact that the use of "parallel actions" was an ancient Italian custom, used by them in earlier dealings. Eisenhower, however, had never been informed of the Italians' previous peace feelers. He ordered Bedell Smith to tell Zanussi nothing of the negotiations with Castellano. "Beetle" was to obtain as much information as he could and to keep the Italian under surveillance until confirmation of his identity and mission could be received from Rome.

Not realizing what had happened, Rome sent back word via the secret radio that Castellano was its official emissary. However, when Zanussi repeated Castellano's attempts to give the Americans lessons in strategy, the Allies began to believe that he was in fact a legitimate, if unnecessary, messenger. And finally, while reaffirming Castellano as his representative, Badoglio explained the nature of Zanussi's trip.

However, the incident served mainly to arouse Allied distrust of the Italians and rekindle suspicions of possible treachery. For four days, from August 27 to August 30, Zanussi underwent intense questioning, mainly by Generals Strong and Smith, with Murphy and Macmillan also sitting in. Now thoroughly frightened, Zanussi had a telegram sent to the Italian legation in Lisbon asking that his bag, containing secret documents, be sent to him.

Zanussi revealed secret information concerning the deployment of Italian and German troops, morale in Italy, material conditions and the location of military camps and fuel depots. He later admitted that he had revealed military secrets in order to "give clear proof that we were now with them." Included was his proposal that the Allies invade as far north as possible.

"Why attack from the South?" he asked. "A trip up the road to Rome would be costly and unnecessary. It would mean covering Italy materially from one side to the other. . . . Italy can be conquered by seizing it boldly by the neck and not by advancing inch by inch up its body. The Allies should take advantage of their control of the sea."

His suggestion that the Allies land airborne troops near Rome was better received. Zanussi assured his listeners that there were less than two German divisions in the vicinity and revealed that six Italian divisions, including those under Carboni, had been moved into position to protect the capital. He admitted that the troops had no written orders to this effect, but said they knew what was expected of them. The Italian divisions, he maintained, were well equipped and capable both of holding back the German forces and of cutting off the three German divisions in the South. If the Allies moved boldly and quickly, they could capture Rome and have a substantial portion of the Italian armed forces at their side. But Zanussi's expressed fears for the safety of the king and the government did not quite square with his insistence that Rome could be adequately defended, and the Allied generals continued pumping him for information while at the same time keeping him under "friendly" surveillance.

Chapter 25

THE RETURN OF
THE DOVE

While one Italian emissary was a virtual prisoner in Algiers, another, General Castellano, was sweating on a slow train to Rome, barely bothering to play the part of Commendatore Raimondi. The trip from Lisbon was frightening for him, particularly when the train passed through a long stretch of German-occupied France. When Castellano felt the train jerk to a sudden stop in open country near Lourdes—at the orders of the German police—he was convinced that he had been discovered. But the train was eventually waved on and ultimately passed through Italy without being bombed.

Finally, after three days and nights, Castellano reached Rome on the morning of August 27. Because Ambrosio was absent on leave, Castellano reported to the deputy chief, General Francesco Rossi, and asked to see Badoglio. Rossi managed to set up a noon meeting at the Viminale, with Foreign Minister Guariglia present.

Castellano spoke of his mission in glowing terms, implying that he had managed to have the Allied negotiators do exactly as he wanted. He made light of the armistice terms, explaining that they would be modified as soon as the Italians joined the battle against the Germans. To support this view, he exhibited his copy of the Quebec Memorandum. Guariglia immediately protested that Castellano had not been authorized to offer Italy's military help to anyone. With a touch of pride, Castellano replied that his directives had not been precise and that he had therefore acted as he thought best.

Guariglia, the classic career diplomat, was apparently more interested in form than in content. He continued to object to Castellano's agreements, saying that Castellano had signed the minutes of the Lisbon meeting as if they described the board session of an industrial firm, thereby putting a document in Allied hands that could be used for blackmail or punishment if their conditions were not accepted.

Guariglia charged that although the Allies had said they would treat the Italians more favorably once they got rid of Mussolini and fascism, they still offered the same terms—unconditional surrender. "Armistice," argued Guariglia, was nothing but a euphemism. The Quebec Memorandum consisted only of vague promises that left things more or less the way they were. "What we have to know," he said, "is if and on what aid we can count in case of conflict with the Germans."

Guariglia believed that Castellano had exaggerated Italian strength to the Allies and that they had repaid him in kind. They lacked sufficient forces, he said, to carry off a full-scale landing, and in any event they would land only where their aerial cover would obtain. Furthermore, their prime interests were airfields in the South, such as Foggia, and they would head towards Rome only after seizing them, leaving the Italians to fight the Germans on their own. Italy, therefore, should break with the Germans only after adequate Anglo-American forces had landed, thus avoiding immediate, and probably disastrous, involvement.

Badoglio said nothing, but these arguments undoubtedly influenced him. However, he terminated the meeting, leaving things up in the air.

Castellano immediately hurried to telephone Ambrosio in Turin, asking him to return as soon as possible. The next day, Saturday, August 28, Castellano, accenting Guariglia's opposition, told Ambrosio his troubles.

At eleven o'clock he and Ambrosio met with Badoglio, the foreign minister, and General Carboni. Guariglia proposed that the negotiations be moved into diplomatic channels. Carboni supported Castellano, arguing that a new initiative would only arouse distrust.

No decisions were reached at the meeting, and another meeting was scheduled for the next day. That afternoon Guariglia set to work drawing up a counter-proposal to present to the Allies. Castellano, meanwhile, persuaded Ambrosio that Guariglia's influence on Badoglio could be bypassed by going directly to the king, and a copy of Castellano's report was accordingly given to Acquarone.

On August 29, one day before the deadline set for a reply to the Allies, a meeting was held at the Quirinal Palace, where the king spoke with the participants for a few brief moments. Guariglia proposed that Castellano return to Sicily with the conditions laid out by Guariglia. Castellano objected, arguing that a definite answer had to be given without any further discussion. Again the meeting ended indecisively, but on the way out Ambrosio asked Castellano how they might reply to the Allies in a way that would imply neither an acceptance nor a refusal. When Castellano replied that Guariglia's proposal fitted that description, Ambrosio directed him to send it.

The means to be used was the clandestine radio Castellano had brought from Lisbon in his travel kit. Before the message could be sent, however, Carboni reported an incoming telegram from Zanussi, believed to be in Lisbon, requesting that a plane be sent to the Boccadifalco airfield near Palermo so that certain important documents could be returned to Rome. Though no one could figure out how these papers had gotten to Sicily, the plane was sent as requested.

The real reason for Zanussi's telegram was AFHQ's growing preoccupation. From August 26 onward, four radio operators in Algiers had taken turns listening night and day on the wavelength assigned to Castellano, yet there had been no message from him reestablishing contact with the Allies. The time set for AVALANCHE was approaching and AFHQ was under pressure.

Churchill had already told Eisenhower that he looked forward to having Christmas dinner with him in Rome that year, but Ike was less confident. While invading Sicily, he had given vent to his pessimism, telling his aide that the Germans would breathe a sigh of relief to realize that "we were only going to Sicily. They could destroy the airfields, the ports and let us sweat out the slow approach to their Continental 'fortress.' They could wear us down, absorb our forces..."

Now that he was going onto the continent, the Germans could pursue the same tactics if they chose. Therefore he had to eliminate Italian resistance to his landings in order to meet the Germans on anything approaching an equal basis. The only way to do this was to bring about an Italian surrender as soon as possible. To this end, he agreed that Zanussi's interpreter, Galvano Lanza di Trabia, should return to Rome with the long terms along with a letter from Zanussi to Ambrosio recommending immediate acceptance of the military terms and asking that Castellano be sent to Sicily to sign them.

But as the Italian plane, piloted by the Supreme Command's Major Giovanni Vassallo, approached Sicily, Bedell Smith had second thoughts: wouldn't it be taking too big a chance to have the Italian government see the long terms before an answer came from Washington on their use? Eisenhower and Smith still hoped that they would be abandoned, or at least revised. Besides, the Italians could use their receipt as an excuse for delay, or even for breaking off negotiations. And what if, either through carelessness or design, they fell into German hands? Bedell asked Zanussi for the document he had received in Lisbon, saying it would be delivered to Rome by other means, and Zanussi, who had already read it without realizing that it represented additional terms, passed it over.

Major Vassallo and Lanza di Trabia left immediately for Rome, where everyone was puzzled to see only minor correspondence arriving instead of the important document they had expected. However, accustomed as everyone was to confusion, the incident was not given much attention.

In Sicily, Smith then gave the long terms back to Zanussi. Everything was done to avoid evoking his suspicion concerning the document, and the mix-up was attributed to a misunderstanding. This rather devious maneuver was possible only because of *other* circumstances, strange and grotesque, which led to a series of misunderstandings, half-understandings, false leads, blunders and bluffs.

On that same day, August 29, word came from Washington that Eisenhower's previous instructions were to be modified, and that he was authorized to continue negotiations with the Italians on the basis of the short armistice.

A cable also came from Deputy Prime Minister Clement Attlee, who in Churchill's absence, was head of London's War Cabinet:

> The long terms were the result of months of careful planning: if military exigencies absolutely required it, we could sign the shorter document, but on the clear understanding that this should be regarded as a military convention and that it should be replaced as soon as possible by the comprehensive and complete terms of surrender.

Now dealings with Italy, hitherto monopolized by the British, were placed on a new basis. For the first time, Eisenhower had the armistice negotiations firmly in his own hands. One of the first things he did was ask American and British leaders to delay transmitting the text of the long terms to other United Nations governments. Another step he took was to have a message sent to the Italians through Osborne at the Vatican. "It is of vital importance," read the telegram, "that General Castellano come to Sicily as was agreed in Lisbon."

The message was delivered to Guariglia, who sent it to Badoglio with the observation that Castellano's objections to another trip were no longer relevant since the telegram contained no hint of a demand for a definite yes or no answer.

On August 30, General Puntoni, aide to the king, made this entry in his diary: "The situation is coming to a head. The [Badoglio] government, at the mercy of all the most turbulent currents, is aiming at creating a frightful void around the Crown. The king is being accused of weakness and the same thing is happening that occurred during the last days of fascism."

Puntoni described the arrests ordered by Badoglio and observed that the number of victims was increasing as was the restless mood of the country.

In Germany, meanwhile, Hitler was preparing to send a new representative to Rome, Rudolf Rahn, whose task would be to force Badoglio to put his cards on the table. Mussolini would soon be liberated, thought Hitler, and with the *Duce* returned to power, Italy would get back in step with its ally.

On August 29, Hitler applied further pressure on the Italian government in the person of German Military Attaché von Rintelen, who called on Badoglio in order to express the Fuehrer's doubts about Italian loyalty.

Badoglio assumed an offended air. "I have always kept my word," he said. "If Italy did not want to remain at the side of its ally, would it let its cities be destroyed as is being done?"

The marshal was considerably less resolute, however, on the problem of reaching an armistice with the Allies. Typically, he tried to pass the responsibility on to the king, who, through Acquarone, immediately reminded him of his own responsibilities. "It's the head of the government who decides," said Acquarone, "then the king approves or disapproves."

The king had assumed the role of a constitutional monarch, for in spite of his occasional statements to the contrary he really hated responsibility. For twenty years, after all, he had never had to assume it; Mussolini had relieved him of that burden. But Badoglio and Ambrosio were cautious men and unwilling to make basic decisions.

On August 30, the deadline for the Italian answer, Badoglio called another meeting. Castellano admitted that he could return to Sicily to reopen conversations on the basis outlined by Guariglia. Carboni agreed, adding his approval of Acquarone's sly observation that an armistice could always be revoked later on the excuse that the Italians had changed their minds. They could agree to the Allied conditions with the qualification that the announcement would be given only when Allied forces had landed "with sufficient contingents and in suitable places."

Badoglio asked if any of those present had any objections, but before anyone could answer, he declared the meeting closed.

It was obvious that having waited in vain for the Germans to rescue him from the Allies, Badoglio now wanted the Allies to rescue him from the Germans. But until the Allies were in a position to do so, he did not intend to stick his neck out. German reprisal was sure to be fearful. Besides, if the Germans repulsed the Allies, where would that leave the Italians?

Castellano, however, was feeling better about his mission. "Finally," he said, "I have a piece of paper with precise directives."

These "precise directives"—a note handwritten by Badoglio—called for Castellano to neither accept nor reject an armistice. In reality, they were nothing but reflections of the oft-repeated Italian fear that the country would be exposed to German reprisal unless the Allies landed north of the capital so as to safeguard Rome, the government, the royal family and the Vatican.

Badoglio had taken Guariglia's memorandum, crossed some phrases out, added some others, and then written in pencil eight points for Castellano to follow:

(1) Refer to [Guariglia] memorandum; (2) So as not to be overwhelmed before the English [sic] can make their action felt, we cannot announce the acceptance of the armistice [until] at least fifteen divisions have been debarked, most of them between Civitavecchia and La Spezia; (3) We can put at their disposal the following airfields [incomplete in the text]; (4) The fleet goes to La Maddalena; (5) Find out the date, more or less, so we can prepare ourselves; (6) Protection Vatican; (7) Crown Prince, Queen, government diplomatic corps will remain in Rome; (8) Question of prisoners.

This series of notations was submitted to the king who, always at home with ambiguity, approved them. That afternoon, a telegram was sent from the small room on the top floor of Palazzo Vidoni which housed the secret radio. "The answer is affirmative," it read, "repeat affirmative stop consequently known person will arrive tomorrow morning sept 2 establish hour and locality stop please confirm."

In Algiers, it had been a day of suspense. Having received the telegram, Eisenhower decided it would be best for Bedell Smith, Murphy and Macmillan to go to Sicily and to take Zanussi, named Frattini for the occasion, with them. Thus, the political advisors would be at the side of General Alexander who, as Eisenhower's deputy and senior officer on Italian soil, might be called upon to make critical decisions.

On their arrival, General Alexander told Smith, Macmillan and Murphy that the AVALANCHE landings would be a dangerous gamble because of the inadequate forces available. The Germans already had between sixteen and eighteen divisions in Italy, and the Italians had approximately thirty which might go either way.

AVALANCHE involved an initial landing of between three and four Anglo-American divisions and a buildup, over two and a half months, to a maximum of six; this in addition to Montgomery's two divisions which would land earlier in Calabria and hopefully pull German strength away from AVALANCHE. Unless there was "aggressive assistance from the Italian government and armed forces," AVALANCHE was almost certain to fail, or, if it succeeded, to do so at excessive cost for minimal gains. Such a setback, Alexander and Macmillan agreed, would have serious consequences for the British, many of whom, they admitted, were tired of the war and beginning to believe that the Allies should seek a compromise peace.

Even Churchill was having misgivings about the timetable of the post-landing buildup. He cabled Alexander at Cassibile:

> No effective help can come to enable the Italians in Rome to turn against the Germans, and the dangers of a German Quisling Government being installed, or alternatively sheer anarchy supervening, will be aggravated and prolonged . . . what is to prevent the Germans at the same time from bringing far larger forces against them? They are at present said to have sixteen divisions in the Italian peninsula. I am not myself convinced that these are in fact complete divisions. On the contrary, it would seem likely that they are the

leading elements and headquarters in several cases. But if the liberation of Rome and the gaining of the important political and military
advantages following therefrom are to be delayed for more than
three months from now no one can measure the consequences.

Field Marshal Jan Smuts, whose military judgment Churchill respected, felt the same way; he wrote the prime minister:

> While our Middle East campaign was conducted with conspicuous
> vigour from El Alamein to the end of Tunisia, I sense a slackening
> and tardiness in operations since then . . . there is now another
> strange pause after Sicily at a stage in our affairs when the urgency
> is very great. There is much and constant boasting of our produc-
> tion effort, especially of the colossal American production. And
> after almost two years of war the American fighting forces must be
> enormous. But still, the Russians account for the vast bulk of Ger-
> man Army on land. I have the uncomfortable feeling that the scale
> and speed of our land operations leaves much to be desired.

Smuts felt that the campaign planned by Alexander was
thoroughly ill-advised, and he predicted that the Allies would have to
fight their way "northwards through Italy over difficult mountainous
terrain in a campaign which may take much time before we reach
Northern Italy and the main German defense position. In the Mediterranean we should take Sardinia and Corsica and immediately attack in
North Italy without fighting our way all up the peninsula."

Montgomery, who had objected to the plan because it was based
at least partially on the belief that the Germans would immediately
withdraw to the Po Valley in the North, insisted that it was by no
means certain that the Italians would help the Allies once the armistice was announced.

Faced with these misgivings, the Allies waited at Fairfield Camp,
the Advance Command post of Alexander's Fifteenth Army Group.
This consisted of a series of tents pitched amidst olive and almond
trees on an estate belonging to a Sicilian nobleman named Grande,
not far from the town of Cassibile. It was on the banks of the Cassibile River twenty-three centuries earlier that Athenian General De-
mosthenes and his six thousand men had surrendered. Now it was
hot, dusty, swarming with flies, while generals and diplomats made
worried plans to pull Italy out of the war, bluffing, if necessary. After
all, the stakes were high even if the cards were weak.

Chapter 26

THE BLUFFING

At nine o'clock on the morning of August 31, 1943, General Castellano and Montanari arrived at the airfield of Termini Imerese on the northern coast of Sicily, twenty-five miles east of Palermo. Brigadier Strong met them and escorted them to Cassibile. Waiting there was General Smith and, to Castellano's amazement, Giacomo Zanussi. For a moment, Castellano only stared at Zanussi. "And you! What are *you* doing here?" he finally cried out.

Zanussi answered that Ambrosio had sent him; a reply that must have shaken Castellano.

At that moment, Zanussi had the long terms in his pocket. However, when he tried to tell Castellano this, the latter cut him short, saying that he knew all about it. But Castellano was obviously thinking of the short terms, and Zanussi assumed that Castellano was referring to the long terms. Since there was no love lost between the two, the subject was dropped.

At 11 A.M., as the participants—three Italians and five Allied representatives—were taking their seats for the first of a series of meetings, Zanussi, more curious then resentful, asked Castellano if Badoglio had accepted the armistice.

"Yes and no," answered Castellano. "Wait until you see their faces when they hear what Badoglio has ordered me to tell them."

They were interrupted by Smith, who asked Castellano if he had full powers to negotiate. Castellano was forced to admit that he did not, and when he tried to explain, Smith pretended for the moment to overlook this formality. With admirable sangfroid, Castellano put on his glasses, read off Guariglia's memo and started on Badoglio's points. He had no sooner mentioned the need for fifteen Allied divisions than Smith interrupted.

"If we could establish a beachhead of fifteen divisions," he exploded, "we wouldn't be here now to negotiate an armistice with you."

Then, realizing what he had said, Smith caught himself, passed over the slip, and hastily added that even though the Allies were unable to land fifteen divisions *at the same time*, many, many more units were available. Of course, he admitted, they would be more efficacious with Italian help. "The invasion will succeed," Smith warned, "since we have taken into account not only German resistance but Italian as well."

Absorbed with making his own points, Castellano went on, and the Allied officers present breathed a joint sigh of relief. They knew that Alexander contemplated an assault force of only three to four divisions at Salerno, not counting the two that would land earlier in Calabria. The truth was that the Allies lacked not only the troops in the area but the ships to transport them. And of course Castellano could not be told that the Mediterranean had been relegated to a minor role in Allied plans, with major emphasis having been placed on the invasion of France.

When Castellano kept asking if the Allies would be strong enough to protect Italy from the Germans, Smith encouraged him to believe that the overall Allied forces *could* amount to fifteen divisions.

To further persuade the Italians, the Allied generals put on a little act, purposely allowing a few words to slip which implied that their forces were really much stronger than they actually were.

Smith pushed hard on this theme knowing how badly Italian cooperation was needed. Castellano might have secured better terms if, at that moment, he had threatened to continue to fight. He could have said that, torn between unconditional surrender to the Anglo-

Women using public fountains in front of Colosseum after the August 13 bombing of Rome, which deprived much of the city of water

Pope Pius XII delivering radio message September 1, 1943. To his left, the present pope, Paul VI

Protagonists of the armistice negotiations. From left to right: Brigadier Kenneth Strong, Brigadier General Giuseppe Castellano, Major General Walter Bedell Smith, interpreter Franco Montanari

Bedell Smith signs the armistice for the Allies. From left to right: Smith, Commodore Royer Dick, Major General Lowell Rooks, Captain Deann, Castellano; behind him, Strong, Montanari

Americans and threat of German retaliation, his country preferred to resist.

Unable to learn from Smith just where the landings would take place, Castellano suggested that they occur simultaneously in the North and South and that then, depending on the rapidity with which the Allies established themselves, the Italians would announce the armistice. Smith turned this down flatly. To Castellano's question of how much time the Allies would need to reach Rome, Smith replied that that depended on how much help the Italians would give. When Castellano asked that the fleet be allowed to go to La Maddalena instead of an Allied port, Smith said that this too was unacceptable and that the Italians were obviously trying to change the armistice terms.

Although the American general was under orders from Eisenhower to "show no weakness and no desire to close the negotiations," he knew that to mean anything the Italian surrender had to coincide with the Salerno landing. It was unthinkable now to cancel AVALANCHE and besides, BAYTOWN, Montgomery's invasion of Calabria, was to start within hours. So things had to be speeded up. "Beetle," aware that the Italians were caught between the devil and the deep blue sea, decided to play a hole card.

"Don't worry about the harshness of the armistice terms," he said, "they're really more for public opinion in our country than in yours. If you help us the real terms will be very different from the formal ones. Have faith in us, it's the best way to have it in yourselves. Don't forget the Quebec Memorandum, it gives General Eisenhower full power to modify the conditions of the armistice."

Much of this went over Zanussi's head. Not having seen the short armistice, he was in no position to evaluate the differences between the two texts, and he thought that the others were discussing the long terms.

Castellano, still following Badoglio's points, wanted guarantees for the king and government. Smith replied that the king could come to Palermo, which would then be evacuated by the Allies. Castellano said that the king and government intended to remain in Rome, and that they had to be assured of protection there. Only an Allied landing close to the capital—in addition to the main landing—could provide this, as Italian troops were too badly equipped and too weak to defend Rome by themselves. Besides, if Rome fell to the Germans, the Allies would face a long and costly struggle to regain the capital. It was in their interest to provide help.

Smith, seeing that his chances of getting the armistice signed

L

were diminishing, upped the ante. The Allies, he said, were willing to discuss providing such protection. There was Zanussi's proposal for landing airborne troops around Rome. What else did Castellano think would be necessary?

An entire armored division as well, Castellano suggested hopefully.

Smith thought this over, then said that the airborne division was probable and that he would study the possibility of sending some antiaircraft artillery battalions by sea to the mouth of the Tiber and *possibly* even an entire division sometime later. This was all contingent on the Italians' guarantee that, as he cabled Rome the next day, "the armistice is signed and announced as desired by the Allies; that the Italians will seize and hold the necessary airfields and stop all antiaircraft fire; [and] that the Italian divisions in the Rome area will take effective action against the Germans."

In a moment of optimism, both Castellano and Zanussi said that they were certain that Italy could overcome any German or Fascist opposition, even though a few minutes earlier they had been deploring the lack of Italian strength.

The Italian generals then tried once again to learn the day and place of disembarkment. Smith refused to give specific information, saying only that the main landings would take place soon after the secondary landing, as far north as was compatible with air cover. If the Italians had stopped to think, they could have figured out the place by themselves. Spitfires based on Sicily, even with added ninety-gallon tanks, required two and a half hours' flying time in order to have twenty minutes over the battle area.

As he later admitted, General Smith "deliberately misled Castellano as to the efficiency of Allied forces . . . and the possibility of another debarkation near Rome."

But if Smith was bluffing, so was Castellano, who by no means correctly described the military situation in Rome. In addition, he conveyed an Italian determination to fight against the Germans which was far from realistic.

The Italians were then invited to lunch, and soon the talk turned to Rome. Smith reminded Castellano that there were enough Italian divisions around the city to hold off the Germans. Castellano replied that they lacked armament, and Smith offered to do his best to assure Allied help on this. He went on to say that if Italy passed up this opportunity to agree to the armistice, it would find itself in a very difficult situation. He could give no guarantees about further bombings of Rome, for example, which would take place despite both the open city declaration and Catholic public opinion. If necessary, warned Smith, the city would be destroyed.

The military discussions were suspended while Smith conferred with Alexander and phoned Eisenhower in Tunisia. Meanwhile Murphy and Macmillan came to see the Italians. The political advisors emphasized that this was Italy's last chance, valuable only if seized quickly. If there were no agreement on surrender, the king would receive no further consideration, the Allies would incite anarchy throughout the country, and all of Italy, particularly Rome, would be heavily bombed.

When Smith returned, Castellano again took up Badoglio's idea of a delayed armistice announcement. Told that this was unacceptable, he proposed that the Italians put up token opposition until the Allies were established, and then announce the armistice.

Smith said that public opinion in the United States would raise an outcry at the deaths caused by this resistance. The Italians paid little attention to this explanation, primarily because of the small weight given public opinion in their own country, but Smith, sensing victory, remained adamant. No counter-proposals could be considered.

After some discussion about Allied prisoners in Italy, Castellano said he could not deviate from his instructions, which he again read. He would return to Rome, and if the government accepted, either he or another representative would come back to Sicily.

Bedell Smith told Castellano that the terms were final and reminded him that the deadline had already expired. Nevertheless, he said, the Allies were willing to wait until midnight on Wednesday, September 1, by which time a firm acceptance or refusal had to be given.

The procedure in case of a favorable decision, as Castellano understood it was: (1) Italy would accept conditions and modalities with details of the agreement to be kept secret until later; (2) secondary landings (five or six divisions) with Italian opposition (purely for form and limited); (3) after a short period (one or two weeks?) main landing in force south of Rome without Italian opposition, accompanied by drop of airborne division near Rome and the arrival by sea of a hundred antitank pieces at the mouth of the Tiber; (4) six hours before main landing, announcement of armistice by both parties. Localities of the landings as well as their dates and that of the armistice announcement would be at the discretion of the Allies.

Castellano, Montanari and Zanussi left Cassibile at 4 P.M. in a small American plane and, arriving at Termini Imerese, transferred to their own three-engine Savoia-Marchetti. As it winged its way towards Rome, Zanussi once again attempted to discuss the long terms, but Castellano, who still regarded Zanussi as a rival, refused to listen to him. When Zanussi said that he would try to persuade Carboni to view Castellano's efforts more favorably, Castellano expressed surprise; he was unaware that Carboni disliked him.

Arriving at Centocelle airport at seven that evening, Castellano went directly to Ambrosio's office. It was too late to see Badoglio because the marshal had already gone to bed, but plans were made for Castellano to report to him the next day.

Meanwhile, Bedell Smith, General Alexander, Macmillan, Murphy and other Allied staff officers flew to Tunisia to tell Eisenhower what had happened. According to "Beetle," the Italians would not sign the armistice unless they received assurances that Rome would be protected. The best way to do this, he maintained, would be to drop a substantial part of the American 82nd Airborne Division near the capital and to deliver antitank battalions by sea simultaneously with the landing at Salerno.

General Mark Clark, who would lead the latter landings, protested. He had been asking for the 82nd to drop near the Volturno River, forty miles north of the beachhead, so as to secure his northern flank against German troop movements coming south—an operation called GIANT I.

Smith, backed by Alexander, pointed out that the airborne landing at Rome might induce the Germans, fearful of being cut off, to pull out of southern Italy and leave Rome undefended. Clark remained suspicious of the Italians, and he suggested that Ike listen to the Italian radio to make certain that they announced the armistice before he confirmed it himself.

The next morning, after receiving approval for the Rome drop in a personal message from Churchill and Roosevelt, Eisenhower okayed the project, now named GIANT II. Word was sent via the secret radio to Rome verifying the drop, asking for the names of airfields, and requesting Castellano's return to Sicily. Then the Allied generals and the political advisors flew back to Cassibile to await Castellano's return from Rome.

On the morning of September 1, a meeting was held at the Viminale in Rome; present were Badoglio, Ambrosio, Guariglia, Carboni, Acquarone and Castellano, who refused to let Zanussi attend.

Earlier that morning, Zanussi had gone to army headquarters with the long terms. "I gave them," he wrote later, "to Roatta who was about to go to the Supreme Command, telling him what they were and advising him to give them to Ambrosio. . . . Everything induced me to believe that he did so. I remember, in fact, having had them back the 7th or 8th September without comment."

This meant either that Roatta never informed the Italian chiefs of the long terms on September 1 or, if he did, that the generals handled exceptionally important documents with unheard-of negligence, not even bothering to examine them.

At the Viminale, Castellano described Allied power in grandiose terms. According to his account, thousands of planes, whole armies, enormous amounts of landing equipment, and divisions of trained paratroopers were all ready to be catapulted against the peninsula. He had learned all this, he said proudly, by pretending to have no knowledge of English. In reality, it was Smith's trick that had worked; Castellano had only swallowed the bait.

Now, strangely enough, Guariglia and Carboni switched sides. The foreign minister favored accepting the armistice, saying that it was too late to change the plans set up by the Allies. Carboni, realizing that he would be forced to play a major part in the defense of Rome, suddenly changed his stance. The Allied proposals were only verbal promises, he warned, and perhaps all part of a trick to obtain the military information needed to immobilize the Italians at the moment of the invasion. He said that it was *his* Motorized Corps that would have to fight the Germans, and that they would be unable to do it for any useful length of time since they lacked power, armor and equipment.

Castellano insisted that he was capable of persuading the Allies to postpone their landings so that the Italians could be in a better position to hold off the Germans.

Then Acquarone spoke up. "Well," he said, "the king doesn't want to fall into the hands of the Germans."

Ultimately, however, the majority decided to accept the armistice, and at 5 P.M., after the king had given his approval, the news was radioed to the Allies.

In the meantime, the Allies had sent their telegram number 11, listing conditions for the airborne drop. Since the messages to and from Drizzle and Monkey had crossed and had not yet been decoded, the Allies were also told that Castellano would arrive in Sicily by the next morning.

Despite the decision that had been made, Badoglio gave no orders to Ambrosio, nor did the chief of staff issue any. The rest of the government was left entirely in the dark about what was happening as was virtually the whole of the Supreme Command.

On September 2, at 7:15 A.M., a three-engine S79 belonging to the Italian General Staff took off from Guidonia Airport. In it were Castellano and his interpreter Montanari, Major Luigi Marchesi, Ambrosio's secretary, and Major Vassallo, Ambrosio's personal pilot. Marchesi, who had served under Ambrosio and Castellano in Yugoslavia, was to act both as Castellano's aide and as the carrier of any message sent back to Ambrosio.

To avert suspicion, the plane's destination had been given as Sardinia on the flight plan, and as soon as the plane gained height it headed north. A German fighter hovered in the distance. Once it disappeared, the plane reversed course and headed south over the sea. When the plane landed at Termini Imerese, Castellano looked out. The field was completely deserted. Several minutes later an American officer and two MPs appeared and finally a jeep drove up in a cloud of dust. Out jumped Bedell Smith and Major General John K. Cannon, deputy commander of the Tactical Air Force, who snapped to attention and saluted. The four Italians came down the steps and moments later climbed aboard an American plane which, after a short flight, set down on a military field near Cassibile. From there the group was taken by automobile to Fairfield Camp, where Castellano was promptly asked if he had been delegated to sign the armistice document for Italy.

Castellano feigned surprise. "No one ever spoke of a signature to me," he protested. His mission, he went on, was only to take part in ongoing military discussions.

The Allied generals were furious at what they regarded as another Italian trick. Badoglio, they assumed, had purposely allowed Castellano to leave Italy without authorizing him to sign the armistice, knowing that this would delay Italy's formal acceptance of the Allied surrender terms. Castellano, it seemed, was nothing more than an errand boy.

"He's thrown a monkey wrench into the works," someone commented.

Castellano said that he thought acceptance of the surrender terms had been signified by the telegram and that that was the reason why he had not been authorized to sign; lack of authorization was, he insisted, only a technical oversight.

The Allies were incredulous. Could Castellano actually believe that it was possible for a country to surrender with a telegram? Smith forcefully told Castellano that the telegram was only informative, that documents were required, and that their lack reflected on the good will, the seriousness and the intentions of the Italians.

Castellano and his group were escorted to tents, where they were left to simmer in the hot Sicilian midday sun.

After a while, General Smith appeared. Generals Eisenhower and Alexander were expected for the signing at five o'clock that afternoon. Smith added, however, that the armistice would have to be signed by an Italian representative who had been properly furnished with written authorization.

Although General Smith represented Eisenhower, Alexander was the senior officer. Since Castellano's stand seemed no more than a bluff designed to obtain more attractive surrender terms for the Italians, Smith, Macmillan and Murphy asked Alexander to pay the Italians a formal visit and impress them with the need for action.

General Sir Harold R. L. G. Alexander, deputy commander in chief of Allied Forces, Combined Operations Mediterranean, was every inch a British general. At Dunkirk, he had been the last man to leave, walking the beach and calling, "Any British soldiers left?" Now, worried as he was about the outcome of the approaching landings, he threw himself wholeheartedly into the theatrical comedy they were to play. At Macmillan's suggestion, he put on his full dress uniform, "a well-pressed tunic, beautifully cut breeches, highly polished boots with gold spurs and a gold peaked cap." Then he assembled his aides and set out for the area in which the Italian delegation was confined.

When, at about noon, they arrived at the Italians' tent, Castellano, remembering despite his dark serge suit that he was only a brigadier general, snapped to attention. Montanari translated.

There was no shaking of hands and no exchange of greetings. Alexander executed a sharp military salute. In his left hand he held a riding crop which he kept slapping against his boot. Alexander spoke correctly but coldly. He said that he was happy that Castellano had returned from Rome prepared to sign the armistice. Castellano immediately protested that he could not sign, because he lacked the authorization to do so.

Alexander expressed his amazement. Had the Italians come, he asked, as negotiators or spies? They were to make up their minds immediately. The reason for their return to Rome, as they well knew, had been to obtain the authorization to sign. How could they have returned without it?

Assuming a cold, furious tone of voice, Alexander declared that his patience was at an end and that he strongly doubted the Italians' good faith. "This is an odd way for your government to negotiate," he stormed. "If the armistice isn't signed within twenty-four hours we will be obliged to raze Rome to the ground."

Turning to his aides, he announced that under no circumstances should the Italians be permitted to leave until they had signed the armistice. Then, without another word, he and his cortege strode towards their jeep.

Later that afternoon, General Smith came to the Italians' tent to ask if Castellano wished to radio Rome for permission to sign the armistice. The following telegram, which had been prepared, was approved by Castellano and then sent:

> Superior commander allied forces in no way will discuss questions unless document accepting armistice conditions is signed first stop as military operations landing peninsula will start very soon such signature is very urgent stop superior commander allied forces will accept signature of ferrari [Castellano] if he is authorized by italian government stop please send this urgently give a declaration to minister osborne that I have been authorized.

The Italians nervously paced their tent, awaiting a reply. Suddenly, at a little after 5 P.M., Castellano was escorted to a large tent. As Castellano tells it, standing in the center of it was General Eisenhower, who had come from Tunisia for the signing. Until that moment, Eisenhower had never spoken to an enemy general. He did not offer his hand, but only nodded. Having been informed of Alexander's *Sturm und Drang* approach, Eisenhower adopted a more conciliatory attitude. Mentioning the lack of authorization, he told Castellano how Italy's situation would be changed once it had agreed to military collaboration with the United Nations. Only such collaboration, warned Eisenhower, could save the country.

"You must realize," he said, "that you have been fighting us for three years and that many English and American soldiers have died at your hands."

That evening, the Allies received an unexpected message from Rome, an answer to their telegram of the day before, accepting the airborne operations and listing three airfields—Centocelle, Urbe and Guidonia. It contained no answer to Castellano's request, although this might have been due to a technical delay. Encoding and decoding messages in some cases required several hours. Still, no other word came; finally, at 4 A.M. on September 3, Castellano sent another cable:

> Supreme commander armed forces will operate with agreements already explained by me and with sufficient forces to assure degree of security we wish stop i am personally convinced that operative intentions of the allies are such as to assure the fulfilment of the needs we discussed at conference morning of 2nd of this month.

Of course, "armed" forces should have read "Allied," and the conference had been held on the first, not on the second, but the behavior of the Allies had rattled Castellano. He would have been even more rattled had he known that, to the accompaniment of six hundred guns firing across the Straits of Messina, the British Eighth Army under General Montgomery had just landed on the toe of Italy and, encountering no resistance, had taken Reggio Calabria and a nearby airport. If there were ever a time for the Italians to agree to surrender, this was it. But no reply came from Rome.

Chapter 27

SURRENDER...

On Friday, September 3, the sun rose early in Sicily, arriving punctually and shining with full force on the tent where General Castellano and his companions waited for word from Rome. The Allies began to have doubts; why did Badoglio delay answering a question which had been sent at 4 P.M. the day before? Was a new effort being made in Rome to keep Castellano from signing the armistice?

The hours crept by and the sun rose higher as spirits fell correspondingly lower. Then, early that afternoon, the four Italians were escorted to a tent where a group of Allied officers were assembled, including Bedell Smith and Brigadier General Maxwell D. Taylor, deputy commander of the American 82nd Airborne Division. General Smith was optimistic; a message had been received from Rome and was now being decoded.

When the telegram was delivered, faces fell. It was a message from Badoglio, announcing haughtily that the affirmative answer of September 1 "constituted an implicit acceptance of the armistice conditions."

This was not enough for the Allies. There had been too much sleight of hand, and this message still failed to answer that of September 1; there was no signature authorization, no mention of documents deposited with Osborne. In dead silence the four Italians were taken back to their tent.

Then, just before 5 P.M., young Captain Deann of the British army appeared, a broad smile on his face. "They've accepted!" he said. The Italians relaxed. Obviously Badoglio, aware that the Allies would not back down, had finally capitulated.

"General Castellano," Deann read, "is authorized by the Italian government to sign the acceptance of the armistice conditions."

The document the Allies had demanded was to be delivered that day; another telegram had come in from British Minister Osborne at the Vatican verifying this. Now no time was wasted. Castellano, accompanied only by Montanari, was quickly escorted back to the tent. In the center was a common wooden barracks table, covered with an army blanket, on which were two ashtrays, two bottles of ink, two note pads and a camp telephone. As if by magic, a newsreel cameraman and a photographer appeared.

Standing around the table were the Allied officers: Commodore Royer Dick of the British navy; American Major General Lowell Rooks, Eisenhower's chief of operations; Brigadier Strong; Captain Deann, his adjutant; General Smith; and the commander in chief, General Eisenhower.

As Castellano entered, Eisenhower acknowledged his greeting with a nod. Castellano, still in his double-breasted suit, his black hair slicked down, went around the table and sat down. A light bulb protected by an upside-down tin can hung over his head. Castellano put on his shell-rimmed glasses, looked over the three copies of the armistice Smith had handed him, and saw that they were the terms he knew. From a pocket, he pulled out a fountain pen and signed. Looking over his shoulder were Montanari and General Smith. Then Smith sat down, put on *his* glasses, and signed.

Eisenhower had refused to put his signature on the "crooked deal" and had left it to Smith even though Eisenhower was the only one the Russians had empowered to represent them.

It was 5:15 P.M.

Eisenhower approached Castellano, leaned forward, and, without speaking, stretched out his hand. Castellano took it, smiling. The other officers followed suit. General Rooks brought out a bottle of whisky, glasses were filled, and everyone drank, silently, without toasting. Emerging from the tent, some of the participants reached up and plucked olive branch mementos from a tree overhanging the tent.

General Alexander cabled Churchill that the deed was done, "on the fourth anniversary of the war. . . . Castellano is remaining here and we are starting military talks this evening."

If Castellano had left Rome with the proper credentials, or if Rome had answered Castellano's first cable, preparations would have begun thirty hours earlier, but the devious delay had very likely been a move suggested by Acquarone to avoid definite commitment by the Italians until the very last moment possible.

After the signing of the armistice and some posing for photos, the Italians had returned to their tent. Then Alexander, only slightly more conciliatory than he had been earlier, appeared, shook Castellano's hand, and invited him to dinner.

Dinner began cordially, with Castellano seated at Alexander's right and the table enveloped in an aura of friendliness and good will; in honor of the emissaries, Italian wine was served. Immediately afterwards, however, military discussions began, presided over by General Alexander. Glancing at the Quebec Memorandum, he warned the Italians not to have any illusions. Having fought for so long against the Allies, they could never be treated as an ally. At most, their military collaboration would be limited to sabotage.

Furrows appeared in Castellano's forehead. He turned to Smith and reminded him that he had said the contrary both in Lisbon and in Sicily. The Italians, Castellano said, wanted to fight against the Germans with all their force. Smith moved restlessly in his chair and nodded to the Italian general to wait until General Alexander had left.

Alexander, unaware of the exchange between Castellano and Smith, continued reading from the Quebec Memorandum, dictated a memorandum regarding sabotage as indicated in it, and then finally left. It was 11 P.M. Instead of answering Castellano's protests, Smith gave the Italian general his second shock of the evening, by handing him, for the first time, a folder containing the long terms. Castellano ruffled through it quickly and gave a start.

"What is this?" he exclaimed. "What sort of behavior is this?" He said that he had never seen these terms before and that surely a document of this importance should have been submitted to him. He particularly objected to the covering letter, which made it clear that these stern provisions had automatically come into effect with the signing of the armistice.

He was also shaken by the harsh first clause: "The Italian Land, Sea and Air Forces wherever located, hereby surrender unconditionally." It was a humiliating phrase; Castellano had carefully avoided using it during the negotiations, and now he protested angrily that the Italian government had apparently committed itself to conditions about which it had not been informed.

Smith retorted that this was not true, that the Italian government had been informed of these conditions on August 29, when Zanussi was given an exact copy of the additional clauses.

Castellano continued to remonstrate agitatedly. How could the Italians fight against Germany if the armistice emphasized total disarmament as a preliminary condition?

"The Quebec Memorandum," Smith assured, "cancels many of the conditions, above all, the disarmament of Italian forces."

"But these are still promises," Castellano protested.

In response, Smith wrote out the following note addressed to Badoglio: "The additional clauses have only a relative value insofar as Italy collaborates in the war against the Germans."

This served to calm Castellano; it was signed, after all, by the man who was chief of staff of the Allied command.

By this time the initially festive air of the dinner had been considerably dampened. Now General Rooks took over. Those present included: Major General Matthew B. Ridgway, commander of the 82nd Airborne; Major General Lyman L. Lemnitzer, deputy chief of staff of the Fifteenth Army Group; Generals Cannon, Smith and Taylor; Brigadier General Patrick W. Timberlake, Operations Mediterranean Air Command; and Brigadier Strong. At one point, the amazed Major Marchesi counted fourteen generals.

Castellano, still trying to bargain, wanted at least part of the fleet to go to an Italian port, either to the island of La Maddalena or to Palermo in Sicily. Commodore Dick, Admiral Cunningham's chief of staff, insisted that he had precise orders which could not be changed —the fleet was expected at Malta. Castellano was assured, however, that the ships would not be disarmed and would be able to fly the Italian flag.

General Cannon said that Italian planes should be flown to fields in Sicily or North Africa following detailed instructions which he would put in a memorandum.

Then Generals Ridgway and Taylor began to discuss the 82nd Division's drop on Rome. The first discussions concerned preparations for receiving the paratroopers, the routes incoming planes would take and the location of the airports named by the Italians: Urbe, Centocelle and Guidonia.

Castellano suggested that troop landings take place at the Urbe field, in the northern suburbs of Rome, and at Centocelle, just southeast of the city, and that heavy equipment be dropped at Guidonia, fifteen miles northeast. The safest way in would be from the west-northwest, eight miles north of the Tiber, as the zone south of the river was occupied by German antiaircraft batteries.

General Taylor said that the route proposed by Castellano would be too difficult to follow at night. "Let the Italians mop up German troops south of the river," he said, "and the planes will come in following the Tiber's outline."

The 82nd's commanders pointed out that the C-47 transport planes would come in low and unescorted, and that it was vital that the antiaircraft batteries be in friendly hands. Castellano guaranteed that they would be.

While these details were being hammered out, Major Vassallo was meeting with air officers to discuss the technical preparation: the setting up of radio beams and luminous directional paths, illumination of the runways, and the outlining of fields with colored lights.

Somewhere along the line, Castellano gathered that the Allies had accepted his suggestion that the 82nd come under the command of General Carboni, who was charged with the mobile defense of Rome. Later examination of the minutes of the discussions revealed no mention of this, however, and it is highly unlikely that Ridgway ever would have agreed to it. The trip to Rome would be no milk run. Besides, Ridgway was jumpy. The 82nd had been fired on by *American* troops and ships during the Sicily landings, and hundreds of casualties had resulted. How much more likely would this be with undisciplined, uncoordinated Italian troops who might not realize that the Americans were coming as their saviors?

Late that night Ridgway and Taylor asked Castellano for more information. Was he certain that the antiaircraft would be neutralized?

Castellano, now a little less sure of himself than he had been earlier, admitted that two of the three fields proposed by the Italians were in the middle of extensive flak batteries, most of which were in the hands of the Germans.

The Allied air officers expressed surprise that *Comando Supremo* had proposed them, but Castellano skillfully got around this by substituting the airports of Furbara and Cerveteri, both over thirty miles from the capital and free of Germans, for the first drops. Because they were situated near the coast, Allied planes would be less subject to attack from land-based batteries. In the interim, Centocelle and Urbe could be cleared for later drops.

The Italians would also keep clear a five-mile corridor along each side of the Tiber for twenty miles so that Liberty ships could bring anti-tank self-propelled pieces to the Magliana airfield on the river west of Rome.

Ridgway and Taylor were worried. They had noticed that Bedell Smith had virtually forced concessions from Castellano. When Smith had asked, "Do you guarantee the availability of the airfields around Rome for our paratroopers?" Castellano had answered, "No, no," but Smith had waved this aside saying, "Yes, you can guarantee it! I'm sure it's possible."

General Ridgway was haunted by the feeling that the Italians would be unable to provide the necessary trucks, fuel and other supplies. He seemed to have read on their faces their fear of the Germans. "I knew in my heart," he wrote later, "that they could not, or would not, meet the commitments they were making."

Despite Ridgway's strong disapproval, Smith had continued pushing collaboration plans for the drop. This placed Ridgway in a difficult position; he could not approve of a tactical plan that he was convinced might lead to the sacrificing of his division, yet he could not go over Smith's head to present his opinions to the upper echelon of command.

Ridgway asked to talk to Smith alone. The two American generals sat under an olive tree far from the others and Ridgway poured out his doubts. Finally Smith said, "Well, Matt, if that's your opinion, the only thing you can do is tell General Alexander what you think in person. I'll arrange it for you."

When Ridgway went to see Alexander, however, the British commander almost immediately dismissed him.

"Ridgway," he said, "think no more of it. We will make contact with your division [in Rome] in three days, five at the most."

Alexander was certain that the Germans, faced by the Allied drop and the landing at Salerno, would quickly withdraw to the North, but Ridgway thought it highly unlikely that Allied troops could make their way from Salerno to Rome in a matter of days. More worried than ever, he spoke with Taylor, who agreed with him. The paratroopers would be in real trouble if the Germans decided to fight for Rome and the Italians failed to stand up to them. The only solution would be to have a responsible officer go to Rome and obtain assurances that the Italians really wanted the operation and would supply the promised aid. Ridgway and Taylor proposed this to Smith, who in turn took it to Alexander.

"Too dangerous," said Sir Harold, "too risky."

After thinking about it for a full day, Ridgway returned to Smith and asked to have the matter reconsidered. This time Smith succeeded in convincing Alexander that Taylor and another officer should secretly go to Rome to sound out the real intentions of the Italians.

When the matter went to Eisenhower for approval, Smith volunteered to perform the mission himself. Eisenhower flatly refused, but he did listen to the commanders, who restated their opposition to the drop. They were making headway when Murphy and Macmillan, the Allied political advisors, said that if the operation were canceled it would destroy what little possibility there was of Italian military cooperation and appear to be an act of bad faith on the part of the Allies.

As Murphy tells it, "Ridgway finally growled that he would agree only if the two double-damned political advisors went to the Rome landings in the first plane."

Later, at the staff meeting at Tunis headquarters where plans for the drop were reviewed, Macmillan and Murphy told Eisenhower that, by agreement with Ridgway, they would be in the lead plane. Eisenhower looked at them for a moment.

"Well, all right," he said. "There's nothing in the regulations that says diplomats aren't expendable."

A telegram was sent to the Italians advising them that two public affairs officials would land with the division to help announce the change of sides to the Italian people.

Talks between the Allies and the Italians had continued into the morning of September 4. Meanwhile, the 82nd's planners had worked through the night. In the morning they presented thirty-two closely typed pages called "Giant Two Outline Plan; Program for Giant II." Duly signed by General Taylor, it called for the 82nd Division to "secure the city of Rome and adjoining airfields in cooperation with Italian forces." The command relationship, in contrast to Castellano's impression, was described as follows:

"The airborne troops upon arrival will cooperate with the Italians in the defense of Rome and comply with the recommendations of the Italian High Command without relinquishing their liberty of action or undertaking any operation or making any disposition considered unsound."

The outlined plan was a marvel of meticulous detail; it specified exactly what the Allies would need from the Italians. The 82nd would bring in its own rations for two days, gasoline for one day, medical supplies for the initial period, and all necessary ammunition. The Italians would have to provide 355 trucks, 23,000 rations, 150 field telephones, switchboards, a dozen ambulances, 5,000 wire pickets, 120 tons of gasoline and oil, picks and shovels and 150 miles of barbed wire. The trucks would move the American paratroopers from the airfields into Rome.

That much of this list might be difficult to provide was passed over by Castellano. He agreed to the plan under which the Italians were to secure and protect all five airfields: Italian antiaircraft men were not to fire against any aircraft during the three or four nights of the operation; Italian troops were to block these areas to the Germans as well as provide protection of the fields and drop zones; and, at the same time, guarantee safe passage of naval craft up the Tiber. The two Rome radio stations were to broadcast all night as navigational aids; fields were to be outlined with amber lights, and runways with white lights; all antiaircraft batteries on both sides of the Tiber, and along a secondary route from the sea to the Cerveteri and Furbara fields, were to be either dismantled or silenced.

The Allies were to bomb the German command near Frascati, according to the information given by Castellano, so as to paralyze its reaction to the drop. Smith and Castellano agreed to an exchange of missions before the operation. Castellano would remain with the Allied command as the head of the Italian mission.

The meeting ended just before lunch. Marchesi was taken aside by Captain Deann and given two suitcases, each containing a two-way radio. These—named Romulus and Remus—were to be handed over to SIM, who in turn would give them to trained radio-espionage agents for use in Genoa and Bologna.

SIM was also to receive a memo prepared by Brigadier Strong giving precise information about the signals to be transmitted on the day of the armistice declaration, primarily via the secret radio link and secondarily by the BBC Overseas Service which, between ten and twelve o'clock, would broadcast a half hour of music by Verdi followed by a talk on Nazi activities in Argentina. In addition, the announcements to be made by Eisenhower and Badoglio were to be exchanged beforehand.

All this time, Castellano had been endeavoring to learn the date and place of landings. But the Allies were wary. They were going along with the Italians, although they distrusted them, particularly, as Major Marchesi wrote in 1969, "because of the prevarication about the authorization for the signing of the armistice." In addition, the Italian emissaries had told Allied Intelligence that the Germans had infiltrated high offices in Italy and that their agents were even in some parts of the Supreme Command.

After lunch on September 4, Castellano once again tried to learn from General Smith the date and place of the main landing on the continent.

"I understand your anxiety to know these dates," Smith replied, "but unfortunately I can tell you nothing. It's a military secret." Then, lowering his voice, he added: "I can only say that the landing will take place within two weeks."

For the rest of that afternoon, and well into the night, Castellano and the three Italians remained alone, preparing the various documents Marchesi was to take back to Rome. At three in the morning, Castellano gave Marchesi an unsealed envelope and told him to read carefully the letter it contained so that he could remember the text if it had to be destroyed. Marchesi was to hand it to General Ambrosio personally.

Although a copy of the letter has never been found, Castellano's version, corroborated by Marchesi, seems self-condemnatory enough to be correct.

"Despite every possible effort to succeed," it is said to have read, "I have not been able to get any information on the precise locality of the landing. Regarding the date I can say nothing precise; but from confidential information I presume that the landing will take place between the tenth and fifteenth of September, possibly the twelfth."

Castellano reasoned that Smith had talked to him on September 4. Therefore, he said to himself, "If the landing were to take place within the next seven days, Smith would have said within one week not two . . . and since four plus seven makes eleven, this would be the nearest date, but it could also take place at the maximum date which would be the nineteenth." On the other hand, he had been told at the meeting of August 31 that the period between the secondary and main landing was to be one or two weeks, in any event at least seven days. At least one week, therefore, would elapse between the two landings. But Castellano did not even know when the secondary landing was to take place. In fact, as he was racking his brain, the Allies were already in Calabria, where Montgomery had taken his two divisions across the Straits of Messina the previous day. Castellano says that he wrote Ambrosio specifying the date as "between the tenth and the fifteenth," but presuming that the landing would occur the first day of the second week, "that is the twelfth, since four plus eight makes twelve, and I wrote 'possibly' the twelfth."

At the time, Castellano told no one of the way in which he had made his occult deductions, and it remains a moot question as to whether he wrote "presume" and "possibly" the twelfth, or, as Ruggero Zangrandi later maintained, named the ninth as the precise date, supposedly having learned it from either Smith or Eisenhower.

Smith, of course, knew very well that AVALANCHE had to start on September 9; the plans had been drawn up before July 25, the date forecast by AFHQ on August 9, set on August 16, and confirmed on August 23 in Algiers.

It is unlikely that anyone at a top level of the Allied staff would break security and reveal such all-important information. On June 26, 1946, Bedell Smith told Italian ambassador Pietro Quaroni in Moscow that he would not even have told his own father, much less an Italian general. He also wrote Castellano that no consideration would have induced him to reveal the date; that he would have broken off negotiations rather than do so. Besides, Smith's fierce loyalty to Eisenhower would preclude his going against the commander-in-chief's explicit instructions. The armistice had been signed and it could only be in the Italians' interest to cooperate. Nor is it conceivable that Eisenhower, a man who insisted on assuming personal responsibility for any military failure, would risk his soldiers' lives in response to Italian insistence.

Castellano's abracadabra led to one of the most tragic misunderstandings of modern times. It would have been better if he had avoided this complicated calculation and just reported what Smith had actually said. But Castellano was not that kind of man. The armistice was now his personal project, and he had been pressed so much in Rome to find out the date that he wanted to show how zealous he had been in carrying out his instructions. On the other hand, the documents he gave the young major showed how most of the burden, despite his efforts, weighed on the Italians. These included:

> (1) copy of the armistice signed by Castellano; (2) the additional clauses with, attached, the note from General Smith to Marshall Badoglio; (3) an *aide-memoire* for the navy with instructions for surrendering the fleet; (4) a similar memorandum for the air force; (5) the memorandum for SIM from Allied Intelligence; (6) the operational orders of the 82nd Division, three copies all translated into Italian; (7) General Alexander's note concerning sabotage.

Early on the morning of September 5, Marchesi prepared to return to Rome.

Chapter 28

...BUT WHEN?

The signing of the armistice left Italy just about where it had been before. The country's leaders still wavered between calming the Germans and placating the Allies. Given their state of mind, there was not much else they could do. The king, uncertain as usual, was either uninformed of the most recent moves or unaware of their significance, Badoglio was passive, the lower levels of the government were lethargic, the Fascists were discredited, anti-Fascist leaders issued bombastic statements to conceal their fear, the press was muzzled and supine, the middle class was inert and confused, the masses were distrustful, and patriots like Persichetti wandered in a maze of misleading statements and rumors.

On the morning of September 3, Badoglio called in the heads of the army, navy, and air force and the ministries of war and foreign affairs, warning them of the urgent need for secrecy. "His Majesty," the marshal told them, "has decided to negotiate for an armistice."

Without revealing that the armistice had already been agreed upon, he vaguely ordered appropriate preparations made while, at the same time, refusing to put anything in writing. His fears that news of the armistice would leak out led him to go even further later that day when he officially welcomed German Minister Plenipotentiary Rudolf Rahn.

It was an important moment for Rahn. He had been standing by in Germany ever since the Tarvisio meeting, frequently exhorted by Hitler to find out what was going on in Italy. Half soldier, half functionary, he still had a sense of humor. After Hitler had ordered him to leave for Rome, he had spoken to Ribbentrop.

"Until now," Rahn had said, "I always thought I was following a diplomatic career, now I realize I've chosen my father's."

"And what," asked Ribbentrop," did your father do?"

"He was a receiver in bankruptcy."

On September 1, Rahn had arrived in Rome to replace discredited Ambassador Mackensen, while General Rudolf Toussaint took over from Military Attaché Rintelen, whose sin had been to fly to Hitler to plead Italy's cause. The newcomers were both known as hard-liners and the fact that they were replacing more or less pro-Italian officials was considered a bad sign. In fact, however, the replacements really meant that Hitler had decided to continue normal diplomatic relations with Italy and had *temporarily* shelved his plan to capture the government.

The day of his arrival, Rahn had gone to see Foreign Minister Guariglia. Contrary to what many believed, Rahn had said, the Fuehrer was not a man who acted on impulse, nor was he a theorist. Whether Italy was Fascist or not made no difference to him. Only one thing concerned him—winning the war—and if the Italians intended to keep on fighting, the Fuehrer would give them his complete confidence.

Guariglia fervently assured Rahn that the Badoglio government was "still determined not to capitulate and would continue the war by Germany's side," but Rahn did not pay too much attention to this.

"You are negotiating in Spain or in Portugal," he charged. "I understand. . . . But any unilateral decision by your government will not change the destiny of Italy nor of Europe."

And so it was with suspicion that Rahn, two days later, went with German diplomat Moellhausen to see the head of the Italian government. Badoglio greeted the Germans with calm dignity and assured them that despite the Allied landings in Calabria the population and the army were firmly controlled by the government. Then Badoglio used the technique that he reserved for difficult situations, the flat statement, authoritatively delivered.

"I am," he told Rahn with surprising energy, "one of the three oldest marshals of Europe: Mackensen, Petain and I; and we consider ourselves the representatives and the depositaries of European military honor. It is incomprehensible that the government of the Reich doubts my word. I have given it and we will stand by it. You must trust me."

Rahn proposed reorganizing the chain of command in order to give Germans control of military operations in Italy. Badoglio said that he welcomed Rahn's proposal, but was powerless to interfere in military matters. He would, however, arrange an audience with the king and a meeting with Ambrosio for the next day. As he escorted his visitors to the door, Badoglio looked straight at Rahn. "We shall fight," he said, "and never capitulate."

Rahn was reassured. Coming out of the Viminale, he turned to Moellhausen. "What do you think?"

"He was definitely sincere," answered Moellhausen, "and this should allow you to see things with a certain amount of optimism."

The next day, Saturday, when Rahn went to see General Ambrosio, the latter protested that the Germans had not shown the trust due an ally. Ambrosio insisted that he, like Badoglio, was "motivated by a firm and sincere determination to continue the struggle at the side of Germany," and he asked Rahn to arrange for more frequent exchanges of ideas with German commanders. He excluded Rommel, whom he blamed for the loss of Africa.

Rahn was somewhat pacified, particularly since Baron Rheinshaben in Lisbon, at about the same time the armistice was being signed, had cabled Berlin: "Count Grandi strictly watched. All his contacts are controlled. Nothing to fear."

Badoglio had no intention of approving attacks on the Germans. What he really wanted was German aggression against Italy. Only in that way, he had said late in August, "will the situation have a solution." It is likely that in saying this he was reflecting the thoughts of Vittorio Emanuele III, for whom separation from the Germans would have represented a violation of Italy's honor. Although the king had no desire for armed conflict with the Germans, an attack on their part would enable Italy to turn to the Allies for aid.

Badoglio took no real initiative; he hoped to leave the real decision to the king, who in turn insisted that any such decision was Badoglio's responsibility. Italian officialdom was understandably confused. By now word was around in Rome that something was up and it seemed likely that an armistice was in the offing. Top officials watched each other warily and tried to find out what was happening. Minor officials kept requesting instructions, cables arrived dotted with questions, and telephones rang continually.

Army commanders were equally perplexed. During those first days of September they did everything they could to avoid provoking the Germans. To the queries of one army commander in the field, the *Comando Supremo* answered: "Avoid incidents, take note of all German infringements just as we're making a list of them." When the Germans approached La Spezia, they were halted, but the next day Rome countermanded the order, saying the Germans could pass "since their command has given its word of honor that the troops will not halt in the city."

Strictly speaking, the Germans kept their word. They positioned themselves around the city, poised to seize control of Italy's most important naval base. In Bologna, they occupied the bridges over the Reno River. In Tuscany, they grouped around the key cities of Lucca, Prato and Pistoia.

Some Italian commanders became alarmed. Lieutenant General Mario Caracciolo di Feroleto, commander of the Italian Fifth Army, met with a staff general of the German Second Parachute Division. Caracciolo complained that the Germans had placed themselves literally in front of Italian machine guns and would prevent them from firing if the enemy came.

"Don't worry about the enemy," replied the German, laughing. "I'll look after them."

The Germans were acting on instructions from Germany. Although he had sent Rahn, Hitler remained suspicious. On August 23, in Goering's presence, he had alerted Kesselring to the likelihood that the Italians were getting ready to betray their comrades-in-arms.

The Germans stood ready to meet the two threats to their security: Allied invasion and Italian surrender. On August 30, operation ACHSE had undergone its final revision; in the event of Italy's defection, Italian soldiers were to be disarmed except for those who would fight along with the *Wehrmacht*. Kesselring was to withdraw his units from southern Italy to the Rome area, then take orders from Rommel; the latter was to seize control of the passes, occupy Italy's northern coastal cities, and set up a Fascist government. If Skorzeny could find and free Mussolini, Kesselring was to seize Rome and restore the *Duce* to power. The German navy and *Luftwaffe* were to assume the tasks formerly carried out by the Italians as well as prevent Italian warships from going over to the Allies.

On September 5, OKW warned Kesselring to be ready for any emergency. Kesselring was under nervous strain; he did not like the idea of duplicity and he refused to believe that the king and Badoglio had lied to him. In addition, he feared that aggressive German tactics could push the Italians to overt activity. Nevertheless, local defense units attached to his headquarters near Frascati were strengthened and air raid shelters enlarged, liaison officers attached to Italian staffs were told to keep a close watch on their activities, and the air command was instructed that in the event of Italian surrender it was to lay hands at once on all serviceable aircraft and antiaircraft guns.

Montgomery's Calabrian landing had come too late to disturb Kesselring's strategy. A little earlier it could have cut off his XIV Panzer Corps in Sicily, but by the time the Allies had moved, Kesselring had re-formed these troops and built his forces up to six divisions south of Rome.

"The landing," as Christopher Buckley wrote in his *Road to Rome*, "failed to attract any important German force down into the toe. The bait was a little too obvious for such wily old fish as Kesselring."

Instead, he moved troops towards the Naples–Salerno area, leaving the 29th Panzers and most of the 26th to fight a rear-guard action against the British, destroying bridges, obstructing roads and generally slowing up Montgomery's Eighth Army.

Between September 2 and 4, only one operational order—weak, ambiguous and cautious—was sent to Italian army commanders in the field to prepare them for coming events. This document, classified secret although only relatively anti-German, was drafted by the Special Operations Section of the army which General Roatta had set up in the middle of August.

The circular, in reality an outline order which *required an executive order and further precise instructions and directives to activate it*, was called Memoria 44 OP, OP standing for the maintenance of public order. It has also been called Memory 44, because within days it practically vanished from sight, invisible and irreproducible. No copy was sent to the War Ministry; the original, deposited at *Comando Supremo*, was burnt on September 9, and the only twelve copies made were carried by hand to the various commands where they were read in the presence of the courier, the last page signed, and the rest destroyed by burning. Fear that the Germans might hear of this rather tame communication dictated these steps; yet the document appears to have been more defensive than anything else, dealing only with the need to react to eventual attacks. It made no mention whatever of the armistice. General Castellano regarded it as "absolutely inadequate to the situation that would be created at the moment of the armistice."

It seems to have provided for Italian troops, in case of outright German attack, to protect railways, command posts and communication centers—at the same time holding themselves ready to interrupt German traffic, take over German commands and sabotage their communications. It warned that the steps taken would have to be made to appear as preparations for an Anglo-American attack.

According to one IX Corps general, it said:

> (1) Criminal action is foreseen from the Communists [couriers warned: Communists means Germans] in agreement with the Fascists; (2) We must take protective measures; (3) Act only if provoked or when receiving a message directing that OP 44 put into action. If communication links are interrupted, act on your own initiative.

Subordinate commands received a memorandum which summed up and completed the Memoria as it concerned them. No copies exist because the same instructions for burning were carried out. At La Spezia, troops were to protect the fleet and at Bolzano they were to defend the mountain passes against attack from the German 44th Division. The Italian Fourth Army was to block the passes leading from France.

That OP 44 was not oriented exclusively towards the Germans was proven by the fact that General Antonio Basso, commanding in Sardinia, called Rome September 7, *after its delivery*, and was told, "In case of attempted Allied landing, react together with German forces on the island."

Some commanders in southern Italy, which was being bombed by the Allies, naturally took *them* to be the enemy. Major General Carlo Biglino, commander of the Pasubio Division defending Salerno, had the impression that OP 44 was intended to infuse Italian troops with the most pugnacious spirit possible in case the Anglo-Americans tried to land.

Even Army General Staff headquarters took it to mean that they should fight the Anglo-Americans with the maximum spirit of combativeness. Almost all the commanders received orders to react energetically, followed by other orders counseling prudence. Some took little notice of the order, having seen only a typewritten message

without heading or signature. Many commanders were being transferred or could not be found; Zangrandi maintained that two out of
three of the addressees never received the document.

Despite the slipshod treatment of the order, Ambrosio issued secret Pro-memoria Number 1, which extended OP 44 to the navy and
the air force, and Pro-memoria Number 2, which went to his outlying
commands—Army Group East in the Balkans, the Eleventh Army
in Greece and Italian forces in the Aegean Islands. Even these made
no reference to cooperating with the Allies, and no mention of an
armistice or the possibility of one. In case of German attack, fighter
planes were to fly to Rome, while bombers, assault and reconnaissance planes were to make their way to Sardinia.

Paragraph 3c of Pro-memoria Number 1, referring to British prisoners, advised that, to prevent them from falling into German hands
"white prisoners can be released, keeping, in any event, colored
ones."

Pro-memoria Number 2, drawn up on September 6, instructed
most Italian troops in the Balkans to "withdraw to ports suitable for
evacuation," while in Greece and Crete commanders were to tell the
Germans that they would not fight against them unless the Germans
used violence. All commanders were warned that, before acting,
they were to make sure they were responding to collective action and
not merely to individual episodes of hostility. Thus the main purpose of the memos was to distinguish a collective or general German
attack from isolated local acts so that there would be no reaction to
the latter.

The informative orders issued to the Italian Armed Forces between the signing of the armistice and its announcement displayed
little intent to carry out the "effective action against the Germans"
agreed upon after General Smith's cable of September 1.

On the morning of Sunday, September 5, Major Marchesi landed
in Rome at Centocelle Airport. He called the Supreme Command for
two cars, put Major Vassallo in one of them, and climbed into the
other one along with the two suitcases containing the clandestine
radio sets. He arrived at Palazzo Vidoni at noon and went straight
to Ambrosio to deliver the documents. Ambrosio immediately went
to see Badoglio, to whom he quoted Castellano's date of September
12 for the armistice without, however, actually showing him Castellano's letter. For reasons never satisfactorily explained, neither did
Acquarone or the king see Castellano's letter.

On Monday, Carboni and the individual heads of the armed forces had the 82nd's operations outline in their hands, and high-level meetings, divisions of responsibility and discussions took place. After reading his copy, Air Force Chief, General Renato Sandalli said that he would need a week to prepare the airports for the American drop. Ambrosio, quoting the September 12 date, told him to do it as quickly as possible. These orders, however, applied only to the III Squadron in Rome, commanded by Major General Eraldo Ilari who was responsible for the airports in the area. Other elements of the air force remained uninformed and continued to fly sorties against the Allies.

Much the same thing happened with the navy. That same day, Admiral De Courten issued strict orders to do everything possible to prevent the debarkation of Allied soldiers. That night, in keeping with these instructions, a detachment of twenty-two submarines posted themselves along the probable route of the Allied landing fleet. The navy bulletin for that day announced that an Italian corvette had sunk an Allied submarine. On the morning of September 7, Admiral Sansonetti, deputy chief of Navy Staff, confirmed these orders. That evening, without explanation, De Courten suddenly warned his staff of a possible German attack to which the navy was to react with all its strength.

The heads of both the air force and the navy, receiving Allied instructions to dispose of their forces after the armistice, remained confused. According to General Cannon's instructions, the air force was to direct its planes to fly to airports in Tunisia and Sicily. At the same time, the Comando Supremo had issued orders to concentrate aerial forces in and near Rome in view of the Allied airborne landing, and Pro-memoria 1 had divided them between Rome and Sardinia. The air force, in other words, was told both to keep its planes near Rome and to send them away.

According to Commodore Dick's instructions, the navy was to sail to Malta, but Ambrosio told De Courten that the Allies had been asked to permit the Italian ships to go to La Maddalena. So the navy, too, had conflicting directives.

Roatta, for the army, brought up the difficulty of protecting the three airfields for four days, neutralizing the banks of the Tiber and finding hundreds of trucks, later adding that if his forces could have done all this they could have defended Rome without the help of the Allies.

This latter hypothesis, however, was extremely improbable. Indicative of the army's inability to cope with emergencies was the comment of the head operations of Roatta's Special Section who, when told of the airborne project by Army Operations Chief General Utili, said, "It's mad. They're going to land outside Rome on various nights, send tanks by sea but want us to clear a strip twenty miles on either side of the Tiber even though there's the 2nd German Parachute Division! What a long order; they want trucks, food supplies, water, what a mess!"

However, a chance, at least, to discuss the problems was offered by a telegram sent from Algiers on September 5:

> From the chief allied command to the supreme command no. 29 stop general taylor who will arrive with your steamship the night of the 7th to the 8th of september has full power from the supreme command of the allied forces concerning the operations of the paratroopers.

Around noon on September 6, Carboni ordered Colonel Vincenzo Toschi to "reserve a room at Palazzo Caprara to house a general, commander of an Allied paratroop division who would be arriving." Toschi passed the order on to another colonel while Carboni's aide, Lieutenant Lanza, made arrangements to have food sent in. At 6 P.M. that evening, Toschi learned that the American general was Taylor.

Meanwhile, the other commanders, impressed with the need to protect the big secret, could only ponder the strange missions they were to perform on September 12, when, they were told, the armistice would be announced. That the date was in reality much closer must surely have been clear after the Allied telegrams sent via the secret radio on September 6 were received.

The first asked the Italians to maintain continuous watch "for most important message which will be sent between 0900 hours and 1000 hours GMT [11 A.M. and 12 noon Italian time—Italy was on summer time] *on or after 7th September.*"

The second said that there would be no special program of music as previously established but that, "in addition to all other arrangements for the Great (G) Day," the BBC's Italian program would give two short talks on Nazi activity in Argentina between 11:30 and 12:45 GMT (1:30 and 2:45 P.M.). "This broadcast will indicate the Great (G) Day."

All of this should have made it obvious that the armistice announcement was only hours away, but Ambrosio did not even mention the possibility when he ordered Carboni to have SIM's monitoring service listen for the signals, as well as prepare a microphone in the basement of the War Ministry and a remote line to the radio for the announcement in case Badoglio could not get to the studio.

Carboni, who served both as head of military intelligence and as commander of the mobile defense of Rome, was privy to virtually everything that was going on. Running the two operations was a huge task, but on September 6, Carboni told Ambrosio that he had things well in hand.

This, however, was not the story Carboni was telling to others. He complained that nothing could be done about his Motorized Corps: the black-shirt Centauro Division was still shot through with Fascists; the grenadiers' commander, Brigadier General Gioacchino Solinas, had been a March-on-Rome Fascist; and Carboni had had difficulty with his chief of staff and deputy chief, replacing both of them only a few days earlier.

In addition, Carboni was getting worried about his role in the defense of Rome. When he was given his copy of 82nd's operational plan, he saw that the neutralization of the strip along the Tiber would mean that his troops would have to initiate hostilities against the Germans long before the first American parachutists appeared. Yet Carboni also knew that Italian troops were receiving instructions to do everything they could to avoid fighting first. He went to Roatta and warned him of the dangers inherent in the orders issued for GIANT II.

Roatta had already had his own misgivings even though he had assured Ambrosio the day before that within a week everything would be ready for the Allies' arrival. But on that same day, September 6, he had received word of enormous Allied convoys assembled in the open sea north of Palermo. They would have to move quickly since prolonged immobility would expose them to air attacks. Aerial reconnaissance of North African ports had shown that Allied ships there had been loaded with landing craft, indicating an Allied amphibious operation.

Roatta hurried over to the Supreme Command. He told Ambrosio that the location of the Allied convoys indicated that the Allies would launch their main landing *before* September 12, leaving the Italians with the defense of Rome unprepared.

Although Ambrosio told Roatta that he did not think the Allies would move before the date Castellano had given, he prepared a note containing four proposals for modifying Allied plans. This document has disappeared, but it is generally accepted as having contained a request that the airborne operation take place two days after the main landing rather than simultaneously. It also asked that maximum air support be sent to Rome *immediately* after the armistice announcement. To mollify the navy, the note included yet another plea for the Italian fleet to be allowed to sail to La Maddalena rather than to Malta. And lastly, it proposed a change in the text of Badoglio's armistice announcement.

The document was to be carried to North Africa by the Italian military mission agreed upon in Sicily and scheduled to leave that evening. Carboni later maintained that the mission was also given *another* message, addressed to Castellano, which combined a flat turndown of the air drop—useless since existing conditions would insure its failure—and a thinly veiled threat that if the armistice announcement could not be delayed, the Allies should not expect the Italians to move against the Germans.

This, of course, was much stronger than the generally accepted note and would indicate official sanction of Carboni's position as of September 6. No trace of this has ever been found, however, and Carboni's post-factum reconstruction appears too convoluted and self-justifying to be authentic. The understandable human tendency to color events favorably in retrospect may have played a trick on Carboni's memory; just about everybody but Carboni and his supporters deny it was sent. In any case, its aim was the same as the officially admitted note—to make clear that the Italians had no desire to fight unless the Allies landed in force near Rome.

Chapter 29

SLOW TRAIN TO TURIN

On the night of September 6, 1943, General Ambrosio stepped out of a military vehicle in front of Rome's railway station and went in alone. Dressed in civilian clothes with a big leather bag under his arm, the man responsible for his country's armed forces went to platform number three and boarded a sleeping car on the 10 P.M. train for Turin, supposedly to see his wife. But what of the indications that Allied troops were embarking in Mediterranean ports, the signs that the armistice announcement was imminent, the message that General Taylor was coming to Rome to discuss the airborne landing? Since Ambrosio did not leave until the *night* of September 6, he *must* have seen the telegram dated September 5.

Later it was said that Ambrosio had gone to Turin to burn secret diaries, to pick up a compromising document, or, alternately, to save his furniture. It does not seem logical, however, that Ambrosio left Rome rather than meet the Americans. As an army commander in Yugoslavia, Ambrosio had saved thousands of Jews, and when the Germans had protested, had told them, "You apply your systems in your zone and we'll apply our own in ours." Yet, here he was leaving Rome at a time when the fate of his country was at stake.

It is possible that he attributed little importance either to Taylor's mission or to Taylor himself. Ambrosio was the highest ranking military figure in Italy, on a level with the Germans' Marshal Keitel or with Britain's Sir Alan Brooke; he outranked U.S. General George Marshall. Ambrosio might still have considered himself above meeting with a mere divisional artillery officer.

But even if he were convinced that nothing would take place until the twelfth, he was absenting himself at a most crucial time. Why should he take a slow train to Turin? There were plenty of planes at military airports in or near Rome, and since August 2 specially designated craft at the Italian-controlled Centocelle Airport had been kept at the disposal of the Supreme Command and the royal family. There must have been a reason for Ambrosio's traveling by rail, and it could well be that this particular train stopped at Genoa, forty-two miles from the beach resort of Finale Marina, which was the residence of Marshal Enrico Caviglia, a man Ambrosio respected. Somewhere along the line, Ambrosio would be able to ask the old marshal for advice or even for personal intervention.

Ambrosio's departure from Rome triggered a fearful chain of events. His absence seemed to be the signal for Carboni to embark on a one-man campaign to block the agreed-upon plans to save Rome. He made no effort to hide either his virulent dislike of Castellano or his desire to put Castellano's project in jeopardy. Carboni was undoubtedly also motivated by his own failure, or inability, to prepare and supply his troops. In addition, there was his admitted unwillingness to face battle.

At the time, Carboni's task of supporting the 82nd's drop for four days while maintaining control of five airports, was probably difficult but not impossible. Officially, the young general had always claimed that his troops were prepared. He talked continuously of his frequent nocturnal inspections and of the anti-German feeling he was instilling in his men. Later, his chief of staff confirmed that the Motorized Corps was in a high state of efficiency.

Yet, shortly after Ambrosio left, Carboni went to army headquarters and told General Roatta that his troops could not possibly meet the demands placed on them. Not only would the paratroop drop make no substantial contribution to the defense of Rome, but it would plunge the Italians into certain conflict with the Germans. The operational orders for the airborne division were, in a word, "absurd."

M

Carboni could only supply the trucks needed by taking them from his Ariete and Piave Divisions, thus depriving them of mobility.

Roatta was impressed. He promptly drew up a memorandum emphasizing the danger of announcing the armistice before September 12 and proposing that the main Allied landing take place within striking distance of Rome.

Early the next morning, Carboni was in his Military Intelligence office across the street from the Supreme Command when Major Marchesi brought in the two clandestine radio sets he had been given in Sicily. Carboni greeted Marchesi coldly. Within seconds, Carboni was attacking the means by which the negotiations had been carried out, charging that he had been forced to accept a *fait accompli*, and saying he would openly disavow the agreements made by Castellano.

General Rossi, who had come in, interrupted to say that he did not intend to listen to political discussions.

Carboni told Rossi that he had been to see Badoglio and had given him Roatta's alarmist memorandum emphasizing the weakness of his forces. Rossi knew that most of Carboni's fuel and ammunition shortages had been alleviated, but upon hearing that Carboni had gone to Badoglio, he was inspired to see if anything was really wrong. He hurried to army headquarters at Monterotondo, a village fifteen miles north of Rome, where he found Roatta, General Zanussi and Major Vassallo going over the GIANT II operations outline. Roatta pointed out the difficulties, based on Carboni's complaints to him of the night before, and said that he thought the Allies, rather than defend Rome, were planning to drive north using the city as an operations base. His troops were just not strong enough for this purpose, he insisted, and, though he had told Ambrosio he would have everything ready by the twelfth, this was no longer possible. The Re and Lupi di Toscana divisions could not be expected in the capital until then, and time would be needed to integrate them into the defense of Rome.

General Rossi was shaken. With Ambrosio gone, he was nominally running the Supreme Command. Conscientious but timid, he was afraid to make a basic decision without Ambrosio's approval. Pressured by Roatta and hemmed in by Carboni's maneuvers, however, he agreed to use the special radio for a message to Castellano warning that "a communication of fundamental importance" was being sent to him.

General Carboni has continually maintained that the "communication" cited was the *second* note, flatly turning down GIANT II, which he had given a member of the military mission the night before and which was due to arrive that evening, on September 7. General Rossi, however, has insisted, somewhat less convincingly, that in Ambrosio's absence he refused to send any further message.

Castellano, in any event, recalls receiving the *first* note only. That afternoon he had been busy being transferred from Sicily to Tunisia. A problem had developed in the Italian military mission which had arrived in Bizerte at 3:30 P.M. One of its members, Navy Captain Giuriati, refused to reveal information to the Allies on the ground that he had received no instructions to do so. Castellano told Giuriati that the armistice had been signed and instructed him to comply. Then Castellano was flown to Carthage, where, that evening, he received the telegram from Rome asking to know, at least twenty-four hours in advance, when the king would have to leave Rome in order to obtain Allied air and naval protection.

"I went immediately," Castellano later wrote, "to General Eisenhower who burst out laughing at my request instead of giving an answer." Castellano immediately cabled Rome that it was urgent to prepare the king's departure, adding that "military operations landing peninsula will start very soon."

By then Castellano had received the documents entrusted to the mission and that evening he discussed them with General Eisenhower. Ike refused to modify his plans, but he assured Castellano that there would be all possible air support. He also strengthened the wording of the last phrase of Badoglio's proclamation, so that the Italians would be told to "react to eventual attacks." The Allies, at Brigadier Strong's suggestion, had wanted Badoglio's announcement on tape, but ultimately had to be satisfied with the text.

In Rome, General Rossi had finally learned that a general officer, Taylor, was due that evening and this, added to the complaints of Roatta and Carboni, forced him to take a step that for him would normally have been unthinkable. He telephoned Ambrosio in Turin urging him to return to Rome by plane at once and, when he failed to convince his chief, he ordered Major Marchesi to do his best. Marchesi told Ambrosio that Major Vassallo, Ambrosio's personal pilot, was standing by to fly a plane to Turin to pick him up. Ambrosio replied that a plane was available in Turin and he would either take it, or, more probably, get a train.

A group of anti-Fascists in Milan—among them Giovanni Gronchi, later to be president of Italy; Virgilio Neri, a lawyer; and Count Giannantonio Manci of Trento—realizing that an armistice would be the signal for Germans to pour through the Brenner Pass, worked out a plan for a vast defense system utilizing both soldiers and volunteers. In the capital they presented their plan to Badoglio's son Mario, who insisted that there were sufficient Italian forces at strategic points. When further meetings brought the group up against a brick wall of opposition, they went back to the North.

Rome's anti-Fascist leaders, having learned of the armistice, passed a resolution calling on civilians to prepare to fight alongside soldiers against the Germans, a prospect that disconcerted Marshal Badoglio so much that he threatened the committee members with summary execution if they made the resolution public, upon which Bonomi and the group obligingly suspended its publication.

But Carboni had taken the anti-Fascists at their word and he met with some of them to expound his plan for arming the populace. The general, who according to Zangrandi was not too knowledgeable on political questions, first proposed giving weapons to Alessandro Casati, head of the right-wing Liberals, a far from revolutionary party. Casati declined the offer since he did not know to whom to give them. Carboni got a better reception from Action party members Emilio Lussu and Riccardo Bauer, and from the Communists in the persons of Luigi Longo, Antonello Trombadori and Giuseppe di Vittorio. The Action party representatives, however, were suspicious of the offer; they promised to think it over and never showed up again. This left Carboni with the Communists.

Carboni's idea was to establish assault squads who, a few hours before the armistice announcement, would attack hotels and buildings containing Germans. The signal would be given by the destruction of three hotels, which a squad of army engineers would mine the night before by entering the basements through sewers.

Carboni had secured and set aside 500 World War I rifles, 100 pistols, ammunition for both, and 15,000 hand grenades. To overcome the suspicion of the Communists, Carboni designated his son, Guido, a young army captain, as liaison. Luigi Longo, the Communist leader, was to take charge of the distribution, and the general was to secure further weapons from army depots.

How effective such army–anti-Fascist cooperation might be could have been foreseen by the refusal given other anti-Fascists who asked to distribute propaganda among Rome-based soldiers in view of the coming armistice.

Further efforts by the anti-Fascist committee were blocked by a rather obvious move which could have come from Badoglio or the king or even from both of them. On September 6, Piccardi, a cabinet minister with ties to leftist groups in the committee, asked Bonomi if he were ready to head a political cabinet. Bonomi patriotically answered that he could not refuse to serve his country.

In the midst of this tangle of political maneuvers, most of the country still remained loyal to the king. On September 7, the monarch was visited by a delegation bearing a statement by 280 senators supporting royal policies. This had been drawn up much earlier, but Acquarone had seen to it that it was delivered at this more opportune time. The senators' declaration meant nothing, since they had no way of knowing what the king's policies actually were, but it might have shaken them to know that the king and his closest advisors were already preparing to flee the country. Unknown to the nation at large, Vittorio Emanuele had for some time been sending his possessions to safety in Switzerland. Over forty sealed railroad cars were given safe transit from Rome through the Simplon tunnel to Geneva, and only when one was unsealed by mistake at the border at Domodossola on September 2 were the contents revealed: paintings, sculptures, vases, linens, china and silver.

Further plans were being made for the king's flight. On the morning of September 6, Ambrosio asked Admiral De Courten to make sure that the previously requested vessels were at the port of Civitavecchia, sixty miles north of Rome, in case the king decided to leave with the royal family and part of the government for La Maddalena, off Sardinia. He added that if the situation worsened, the military chiefs would go also. Yet that same afternoon, Ambrosio emphasized to Roatta that if the king and government should leave the capital, the military chiefs would *not* follow, regardless of circumstances.

The king was getting ready for the worst. On the evening of September 6, he turned the crown jewels over to a member of the royal household for safekeeping; these consisted of a crown with seventy-five long pearls and five large diamonds, valued at almost two million dollars, as well as some five thousand diamonds of untold value. As if in exchange, he withdrew large amounts of stock certificates from the safe of his private administrator.

Other leaders were making similar preparations at the same

time. In a space of five weeks, particularly since September 4, Badoglio extracted the equivalent of two and a half million dollars from
the secret account that had belonged to Mussolini and changed most
of it into Swiss francs, while Acquarone sent a number of loaded
trunks to the haven in the North.

The king saw to it that the male members of the House of Savoy
were transferred from their high military posts. Crown Prince Umberto was ordered to Rome; H.R.H. Prince Adalberto, duke of Bergamo, had already been relieved of his command of the Seventh
Army on September 2; while their Royal Highnesses Prince Ferdinando, duke of Genoa, and Prince Aimone, duke of Aosta, serving in
the navy, were later released from their onerous duties and exposed
positions.

At the beginning of September, the monarch sent his daughter-
in-law and her four children, including his grandson, the six-year-old
prince of Naples, to Val d'Aosta, near the Swiss border, which they
later crossed along with other members of the royal family. On September 4, Acquarone's wife and four children followed suit. That
same day Badoglio's wife, daughter and daughter-in-law passed over
Italy's northern border; their flight incurred the wrath of anti-Fascists, who later put up a poster, with a picture of the women in
Switzerland, saying: "The cowardly traitors send their relatives
abroad to safety."

Fear of public disapprobation did not halt the sending of the telegram to Castellano asking for twenty-four hours' warning so that the
king could flee to safety. The reply, that Allied operations were
starting soon, somehow got lost; Zangrandi has implied that in the
absence of Ambrosio, his staff failed to distribute it. However, so
little was being done to carry out Italy's commitments to the Allies
that one more telegram could not have served to speed things up
anyway. It was already obvious that the country's safety was being
subordinated to that of the royal family.

Preparations of a different kind were being made by the Germans. When, on the afternoon of September 7, reconnaissance planes
had reported Allied convoys approaching the southern coast, "destination unknown," Kesselring had alerted his troops. The 16th Panzer
Division, hardy veterans of Stalingrad under Major General Siecken-
ius, had already moved into the Piana del Sele, a twenty-mile stretch
of flatlands south of Salerno, bisected by the Sele River. Here, its
seventeen thousand men were busy setting up their heavy artillery,
constructing reinforced concrete strongpoints, digging foxholes and

camouflaging machine-gun nests. Together with the Italian 222nd Coastal Division they laid mine fields, dug tank traps and helped the Italians place their guns.

That same day, Hitler, who still lacked definite proof, again became convinced of eventual Italian treason. Examining the new developments in the military situation, OKW's Jodl came to the conclusion that Italy was becoming a drain on German resources. The transfer of troops there from the Eastern front after Mussolini's downfall had weakened German forces and the Operation Citadel attack was being turned back by the Russian counteroffensive. The time had come, Jodl told Hitler, "to take the initiative in cutting the cords entangling us in Italy."

The Fuehrer's political and military solution was an ultimatum to Badoglio: either Italy would immediately come under German orders with Badoglio as a virtual *Gauleiter*, or the Germans would seize control of the country and its government. The date set for delivery of the ultimatum was September 9, less than forty-eight hours away.

September 9 also happened to be D-day for the Allied invasion of Salerno. Already on its way was the Fifth Army—169,000 men, 20,000 vehicles, 600 tanks and 1,800 guns—in fifteen convoys loaded in North African and Sicilian ports. The two British divisions, the 46th and 56th, 100,000 strong, had been leaving Bizerte and Tripoli since September 3, while 69,000 men of the American 36th and 45th were putting to sea from Oran and Palermo. General Mark Clark's invasion army lacked the British 1st Airborne Division, originally included but now engaged in the heel of Italy, and the American 82nd Airborne.

The 82nd was preparing its own small seaborne expedition to land at the mouth of the Tiber with an artillery battalion, three antiaircraft batteries, an infantry company and three tank destroyer platoons. Only the day before, Colonel Harry L. Lewis, in charge of dispatching the expedition, had rounded up the various elements and started them moving to the dock area. Not until September 7 did all the landing craft arrive, and then loading was quickly carried out. By evening, Lieutenant Colonel William H. Bertsch, Jr., had taken charge of the troops in Bizerte harbor and prepared to set sail.

In the southeast corner of Sicily, men of the 82nd's 504th Parachute Infantry Regiment with supporting units, under General Ridgway's watchful eye, were making their final preparations for the first drop on Rome.

Chapter 30

CLANDESTINE MISSION

Sometime between 2 and 3 A.M. on the morning of Tuesday, September 7, two American officers had climbed aboard the British PT boat *Duffit* in Palermo—Brigadier General Maxwell Taylor, the 82nd Division's artillery commander and Colonel William Tudor Gardiner of the Troop Carrier Command.

Because General Alexander feared that too early a departure might lead to capture by the Germans and to the leaking of sufficient information about the operation to enable the enemy to take countermeasures, they had not been allowed to leave for Rome until forty-eight hours before the 82nd was to begin its drop on Rome.

Eisenhower had been reluctant to let the two officers go, but he had finally consented. Later, he wrote this of General Taylor: "The risks he ran were greater than I asked any other agent or emissary to undertake during the war—he carried weighty responsibilities, discharged them with unerring judgment, and every minute was in imminent danger of discovery and death."

The two officers were to decide whether GIANT II could actually be carried out. If necessary, they were to radio AFHQ the one word, "Innocuous," which would cancel the operation.

Taylor wore a paratrooper uniform and carried a small Beretta automatic pistol in his pocket. Colonel Gardiner, a tall, massive, fifty-two-year-old who had twice been governor of Maine, wore a dress blouse and carried a regulation Colt .45 pistol. Since Taylor bore his stars and Gardiner bore his eagles (although they both wore plain raincoats, devoid of insignia, over their uniforms), they stood a good chance of being treated as prisoners-of-war if they fell into German hands. They carried 140,000 Italian lire with them, and Gardiner carried a small suitcase containing the receiver and transmitter designed to guide Allied planes to Italian airports on September 8.

While the *Duffit* headed north, another boat, the Italian corvette *Ibis*, sped southward through the calm Tyrrhenian Sea, commanded by Rear Admiral Franco Maugeri, chief of Italy's Naval Intelligence, the man who had taken Mussolini to Ponza. It had left Gaeta, on the Italian mainland, the night before. On board were the ten Italian officers who were to serve as liaison with the Allied forces. Dressed in civilian clothes, their uniforms in their suitcases, they pretended to be political prisoners on their way to a penal island.

Passing the Neapolitan coast, they could see fires burning in Naples. The Allies had just completed their heaviest bombardment of the war, reducing whole sections of the city to ruins. The *Ibis* arrived at the small volcanic island of Ustica, thirty-six miles northwest of Palermo, just after sunrise, and dropped anchor in the cove of Cala Santa Maria. The British PT boat was already there. After the ten Italians had been transferred to the *Duffit*, it left for Sicily. The two Americans boarded the *Ibis* and headed back north.

Around five thirty that afternoon, as the picturesque fortress town of Gaeta came into view, the Americans hastily mussed their hair, loosened their ties, disarranged their clothes, and tried their best to look disconsolate, as they had been advised to do by the English-speaking admiral. They were to act the part of captured aviators; to lend their role more verisimilitude, water was splashed on their clothes.

After landing, the two officers were pushed along a dock, preceded and followed by sailors with rifles at the ready. With them came the small suitcase.

Admiral Maugeri looked around the dock area. Seeing only a navy staff car, he gave orders for the Americans to be put in it. This was done rather roughly while the suitcase was deposited, somewhat more gently, in the trunk. The car then sped off the dock and headed for the nearby city of Formia. Just before the crossroads with the state highway, the driver caught sight of a Red Cross ambulance coming from Rome and both vehicles turned into a side road. The ambulance, driven by Major Augusto Adam of the Italian General Staff, had been dispatched by Major Marchesi to meet the *Ibis* but had not made it in time. Now Admiral Maugeri, the Americans and the suitcase were transferred to the rear of the ambulance, which drove off towards the Appian Way and Rome, eighty-five miles to the north.

The trip was uneventful. The ambulance was stopped several times and quickly waved on as soon as Admiral Maugeri showed his uniform. During the entire voyage, the Americans saw only a handful of German soldiers. After driving through the center of Rome, the ambulance pulled to a stop in front of the four-story Palazzo Caprara, directly opposite the huge Ministry of War. The palace was ordinarily reserved for the use of the Army General Staff but was also the office of General Carboni's Motorized Corps. It was a little before 9 P.M.

Preceded by Admiral Maugeri, the Americans entered the imposing column-lined entrance hall. Waiting to meet them were three Italian officers: Colonel Giorgio Salvi, Carboni's chief of staff; Lieutenant Raimondo Lanza di Trabia, Carboni's aide; and Major Marchesi. Taken to an upper floor, the Americans found themselves in an apartment consisting of two large wood-paneled rooms filled with period furniture. A table was being set with fine linen and silverware.

"A few sandwiches will be enough," protested Taylor.

"Oh, this is not a full meal," he was told. But when the Americans sat down they were served an elaborate repast: consommé, veal cutlets, vegetables, crêpes suzettes and wine, all catered, at Lieutenant Lanza's orders, by the Grand Hotel. The American officers became increasingly worried. It was already past ten and they knew that within twenty-four hours approximately 150 transport planes would carry two thousand American paratroopers to airports around the capital.

"When can we see someone?" Taylor asked.

"Not tonight," answered Colonel Salvi. "It is late. Better take some rest after the long trip. Tomorrow will be enough time for discussions."

As Colonel Salvi continued to pour wine, General Taylor lost his temper.

"That's enough," he said sharply. "We must talk immediately with a responsible commander."

When his demand was met by nothing but blank glances, Taylor went to a corner of the room with Marchesi, whom he had met in Sicily. Speaking in French, the American general asked when he could meet General Ambrosio.

The young major was embarrassed. How could he tell the American that the head of the Supreme Command had been phoned twice that day, by his deputy and by Major Marchesi, and that, after being told that the Allied general was arriving, had still not seen fit to return to Rome? All Marchesi could do was admit that Ambrosio was out of town, say he would be there the next morning and suggest that Taylor see Ambrosio's deputy, General Rossi. Marchesi assured Taylor that orders had been given for the protection of the airfields. This task would fall to the Motorized Corps, he said, and he had asked General Carboni, its commander, to come over.

Taylor insisted on making an immediate reconnaissance of the landing fields. Marchesi replied that such a nocturnal excursion could easily alarm the Germans and would have to be postponed until the next day.

Taylor looked at him in amazement, "But that's when the drop is scheduled," he exploded. "Our men will be landing here tomorrow night!"

Now it was Marchesi's turn to be astonished. According to the agreements, he protested, the operation was to be carried out simultaneously with the declaration of the armistice and the Allies' main debarkation.

"Exactly," said Taylor. "Tomorrow, September 8, is D-day."

Marchesi became seriously worried. "This will create all kinds of trouble in carrying out our plans," he fretted. "The Supreme Command hadn't expected it for four or five days."

Taylor was in the process of pointing out that, at Cassibile, no date had been indicated when General Carboni's arrival was announced.

The seemingly tireless Carboni had been busy that afternoon. Knowing that General Taylor was coming, he had given orders to speed up the distribution of arms to the political parties and then devoted some time to inspecting part of the Motorized Corps. He spent the rest of his day in his Military Intelligence office before having a late dinner at a restaurant. When he had gone home to go to sleep, he had found word that the Americans were waiting for him.

Now Carboni, a lieutenant general, entered the rooms assigned to the Americans. Taylor, a brigadier general, stood at attention and, in French, identified himself and presented Colonel Gardiner.

Then, in a surprising move, Carboni turned to Major Marchesi and abruptly dismissed him, saying that he did not want anyone else to participate in his conversation with the Americans.

Marchesi rushed over to the Supreme Command to urge General Rossi to hurry to Palazzo Caprara to take part in the discussions there, but Rossi, besides being of a retiring nature, was opposed to any armistice with the Allies on the ground that dealing with them while still allied to Germany was tantamount to "treason."

While Rossi hemmed and hawed, Carboni was speaking with Taylor, mainly in French, but occasionally through Lanza. Asked by Taylor to arrange an immediate visit to the airfields, Carboni replied that it was impossible by night and even difficult by day; German troops now dominated the fields, he said, and antiaircraft batteries there were in the hands of the Germans.

Taylor was dumbfounded. He had reason to believe otherwise; Castellano, Zanussi, Vassallo, Allied intelligence reports—all had said just the opposite.

Carboni went even further. He said that the German paratroop division near Rome had recently brought in 12,000 men and that the 3rd Panzergrenadieren had increased its strength to 24,000 men with its two hundred light and heavy tanks, a hundred artillery pieces, mainly 88mm's, with another 12,000 detached troops in the area.

Carboni lamented that his own Motorized Corps had only enough gasoline for a few hours of combat, because the Germans had cut off their supply. If the Italians declared an armistice, the Germans would easily overpower Italian troops and occupy Rome. The arrival of the American paratroopers would only incite the Germans to more drastic action. All this meant that the Italians would not be able to secure the airfields, protect the airborne troops' assembly or provide the requested logistic aid. If the sole solution, an Allied seaborne landing north of Rome, could not be carried out, the only hope of saving Rome would be for the Italians to avoid overt acts against the Germans and await the effect of the Allied attacks in the South. Therefore, argued Carboni, the armistice should be postponed and the 82nd's drop canceled.

The Italian figures on German strength were already known to the Americans, but they were shocked, according to Taylor, by Carboni's "alarming pessimism, certain to affect his conduct and operations in connection with GIANT II."

Carboni also told Taylor that he knew the Allied landings would be at Salerno, too far away to aid the defense of Rome directly. Carboni's source for this revelation may have been a report from an Italian secret agent Ercole Ugo Puglisi, code-named S 21, who, early in August, had cabled Rome from Palermo that Allied landings would take place "in Salerno within the first ten days of September."

Carboni insisted that the airborne operation would be useless since it would take four days to carry out. The Germans would be immediately alerted to Italian and Allied intentions and would attack before the Italians could be in a position to face them.

This plausible eventuality had come up during Allied discussions, but, like Ambrosio, General Alexander had been convinced that the Germans would withdraw. Ridgway, on the other hand, had taken the position that the Germans would stay, although he did not know whether the Italians, in this case, would fight them. Castellano had claimed that the Italian army hated the Germans and was willing to turn on them, but Carboni was now denying this, insisting on the impossibility of facing the Germans alone. Carboni's arguments raised some perplexing questions. The Italians had been willing to fight before in seemingly hopeless situations; why not now? Did Carboni know something that no one else did?

When Taylor suggested that the Italian troops had their part to play during this initial period, Carboni protested that his troops were ill-equipped, that they needed tanks, fuel, ammunition and heavy artillery, and not merely the paratroopers and their light weapons that the Americans were sending.

Later, Carboni admitted to General Roatta that he had exaggerated the situation in order to make his point, and in one of his books, he wrote that he had gone too far: "To be exact I should have said that the antiaircraft organization in the zone was more in German than Italian hands."

It seems fairly clear that Carboni was not merely exaggerating, but lying. In his book *Settembre 1943*, Lieutenant Colonel Mario Torsiello, then head of the Special Operations Section of the army, wrote that the fixed, mobile and antiaircraft defense of all five airports had been entrusted exclusively to Italian units *and remained so until September 14*. This was confirmed by General Siegfried Westphal, Kesselring's chief of staff, who said, "At the time of the armistice announcement, we did not occupy any airports around Rome...."

As for fuel, General Zanussi had told Carboni that the *Comando Supremo* had a large secret fuel dump, and provisions were certain to be made for Carboni to receive gasoline and ammunition. Carboni had remained dubious; his armored vehicles had received no gasoline in July. But Paolo Monelli, in *Roma 1943*, and Antonio Trizzino, in *Settembre Nero*, say flatly that in August the Motorized Corps had received its full fuel allotment and that it was being given an extra consignment of gasoline in connection with the airborne operation. One of Carboni's four divisions, the Piave (10th) Motorized, had already picked up enough for over six hundred miles, and General Raffaele Cadorna, commanding the crack Ariete (135th) Armored Division, had received orders to fill his tanks from deposits at Mezzocammino.

Given the vagaries of the Italian chain of command, however, it remains possible that, as Carboni claimed, he had not been informed of the plans to supply his units with fuel, despite the fact that his chief of staff and divisional commanders all knew it.

It seemed almost as if Carboni *wanted* the Germans to stay. Should they leave, what would become of the intrigues and devious machinations that had become an integral part of his life? A secret desire for the Germans to remain would have been consistent with his headstrong and willful character; he had been against the Germans before such an attitude was fashionable. Now that it was, he opposed the entry of the Americans.

Given Carboni's background as a secret agent, it was understandable if his behavior in a crisis tended toward the clandestine. But arming the Communists against the few Germans in the capital would not solve the problem of Rome's defense. Why did he prefer a few hundred inexperienced civilians to thousands of battle-hardened Americans? Civilian action would surely produce German reprisals also, perhaps even more bloody and ruthless ones, as indeed it did several months later.

It remains possible that Carboni sincerely believed he was helping to save Rome from destruction, and that he misrepresented the facts on the ground that the end justified the means. He has always maintained that he asked for a few days' more time to make further preparations in order to avoid a useless massacre. He could have been right in not wanting to fight the Germans at that time, convinced as he was of defeat. His position, after all, was not far from that of General Ridgway.

Taylor saw that there was nothing to be gained by dealing with Carboni, whose defeatist attitude obviously augured ill for the Americans.

"It's imperative," Taylor announced, "that we see Marshal Badoglio at once."

At first Carboni objected that the marshal would be sleeping, but a few minutes later he agreed to call his residence. One reason for his change of heart may have been the arrival of General Rossi at Palazzo Caprara. Before Rossi could meet with the Americans, Carboni intercepted him in an anteroom.

"Everything has been straightened out," said Carboni. "We're going over to Badoglio now to have him approve a telegram asking postponement."

"Shouldn't I go?" asked General Rossi, who occupied the second most powerful position in the Italian military establishment.

"No, it's not necessary," Carboni reassured. "Everything is settled."

Relieved at not having to assume any new responsibility, Rossi did not bother to insist. As for Carboni, he had already convinced himself that he had persuaded the Americans of the need either to delay or to cancel the entire operation.

It was around midnight when the Americans climbed into a car driven by Carboni and crossed the darkened streets of the capital until, a quarter of an hour later, they arrived at Badoglio's villa.

Lieutenant Colonel Valenzano, the marshal's nephew and secretary, escorted them upstairs and seated them in a study while Carboni went to inform Badoglio. As the Americans waited, they could not help being impressed by the luxury around them. The walls were of white marble, the floors were covered by huge, thick carpets, and there were marble statues and magnificent paintings everywhere.

Nearly a quarter of an hour went by, taken up, Carboni and Badoglio later maintained, by Badoglio's dressing. There is good reason to believe, however, that the marshal had already dressed, and that the quarter hour was instead filled with fast and furious conversation.

Finally Badoglio appeared and shook hands with the Americans. Inwardly, General Taylor recalled being passed in review by the marshal twenty years earlier, while he was still a cadet at West Point.

In very bad French, Badoglio invited his visitors to be seated. Then he sat down behind a large desk and immediately asked Taylor for a delay in the armistice and indefinite postponement of the airborne operation. In order to justify this amazing last-minute *volte-face*, he repeated the German troop-strength figures that Carboni had quoted earlier.

The Americans were convinced that Carboni had used his quarter hour with Badoglio to gain the marshal's support for his views. But so quickly! What could Carboni have said in such a short time to convince the old man?

"We have ammunition for two hours," Badoglio said, repeating Carboni's complaints almost word for word. "The Germans have taken all our fuel from us." He went to a large map of Italy and showed that the Germans had a natural defense line south of Rome.

"Supposing, just for argument's sake," he said, eyeing the Americans fixedly, "that your landings take place at Salerno. You'll come up against many difficulties." He waited for the Americans to react to his mention of Salerno, but they sat quietly, without batting an eye.

Badoglio went on: "The situation has changed since the armistice was signed. Castellano did not know all the facts. Italian troops cannot possibly defend Rome. If the armistice is announced the Germans will immediately occupy the capital and set up a Fascist regime."

Taylor: "Are you more afraid of the Germans than you are of us? If you don't announce the armistice there will be nothing else to do but bomb and destroy Rome ourselves."

Badoglio: "Why would you want to bomb the capital of a country that is trying to help you? Why don't you bomb instead the rail centers and the passes north of Rome through which the Germans are bringing their supplies?"

That day, as a matter of fact, the Allies bombed railroad marshalling yards at Bolzano and the southern exit of the Brenner Pass.

Taylor was astounded at Badoglio's bad faith. The head of Italy's government had transformed the armistice into a meaningless scrap of paper, a mere record of double dealing. Badoglio, however, would have defended his action as realism, not treachery. Integrity and honor, after all, were for those who could afford the luxury of ideals.

When Taylor asked Badoglio if he realized how deeply his government was committed as the result of signed agreements, the old marshal, almost with tears in his eyes, protested his friendship for the Allies. He was asking for a delay, he insisted, nothing more.

"You talk very well," he said to Taylor, "but tomorrow the Germans will be here." He added his customary gesture of drawing his hand across his throat as if cutting it. Then he asked Taylor to return to Allied forces headquarters and to explain the situation in Rome and the Italian point of view.

Taylor declined, saying that he would act as a messenger only if he were so instructed by the Allied command.

Faced with Taylor's refusal, Badoglio decided to draft a message to Eisenhower canceling all his earlier commitments, virtually disavowing Castellano and going back completely on his own word. He wanted to insert a phrase implying Taylor's approval of all this, but Taylor refused as gracefully as he could.

At about two o'clock on the morning of September 8, less than sixteen hours before the first Allied planes were scheduled to take off from Sicilian airfields and head for Rome while Eisenhower announced the armistice to the world, Badoglio completed his message to Eisenhower:

> due to changes in the situation brought about by the disposition and strength of the german forces in the rome area it is no longer possible to accept an immediate armistice as this could provoke the occupation of the capital and the violent assumption of the government by the germans stop operation giant two is no longer possible because of lack of forces to guarantee the airfields stop general taylor is available to return to sicily to present the view of the government and await orders stop badoglio.

General Taylor wrote out a telegram of his own, carefully avoiding any corroboration of Badoglio's statement about the "changes in the situation" and the possibility of German reaction:

> in view of the statement of marshal badoglio as to inability to declare armistice and to guarantee fields giant two is impossible stop reasons given for change are irreplaceable lack of gasoline and munitions and new dispositions stop badoglio requests taylor return to present government views stop taylor and gardiner awaiting instruction stop acknowledge stop taylor.

As the meeting ended, Badoglio retreated into his customary rhetoric, vowing that he intended no trickery and stressing—at embarrassing lengths—his honor as a soldier and an officer. At the door, he admonished the Americans to be careful. "If not," he implored, "the Germans will have my head."

Badoglio and Carboni stood at attention and clicked their heels. The Americans tried, in vain, to imitate them. It was three in the morning. Taylor and Gardiner returned to the Palazzo Caprara while Carboni went off to the Supreme Command to have the telegrams coded for transmission.

Even though it had been an exhausting, frustrating day, the American officers were unable to sleep. If GIANT II could not be halted in time, American soldiers might be forced to fight both the Italians and the Germans. They were virtual prisoners in Rome, surrounded by men who fed them expensive food and equivocal statements. Even if the Italians' position seemed correct from their point of view, the abrupt reversal of loyalties had come as a blow. Then there had been the mysterious absence of Italy's supreme commander, General Ambrosio, Carboni's criticism of the Allied project, and, finally, Badoglio's all-too-hasty renunciation of the armistice.

Worried about the possibility of hidden microphones, for obviously the Italians could no longer be trusted, the Americans spoke to each other in low voices, carefully avoiding mention of either times or locations of planned landings. Time passed and still they could not sleep. By the time the first light of dawn came through the tall windows, the situation appeared even worse to them. They had come to Rome ready to help defend it. Now all they could do was wonder what the new day would bring—to their troops, to the Allied cause, to Italy and to Rome.

Book Three

THE BATTLE FOR ROME

The summer is ended,
and we are not saved.
Jeremiah 9:20

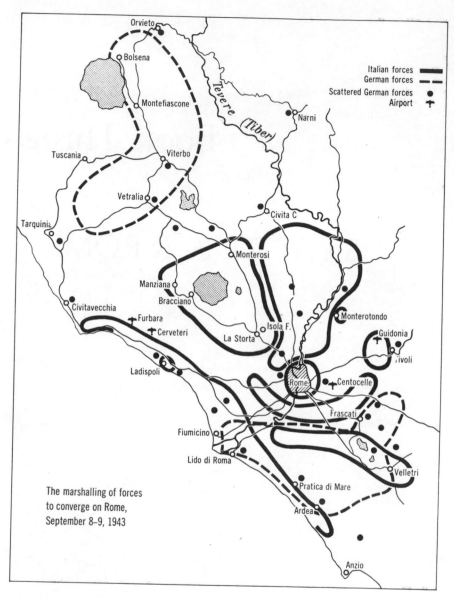

The marshalling of forces
to converge on Rome,
September 8–9, 1943

Position of opposing Italian and German troops, September 8.
Airports at which Americans were to land were Furbara, Cerveteri,
Guidonia, Centocelle. In the early afternoon Italian troops withdrew
to Tivoli as German parachute division attacked Grenadiers.
In the evening there were three Italian divisions at Tivoli, and the
German attack concentrated in the south.

Chapter 31

CAUGHT IN THE MIDDLE

When the sun rose in Rome at six forty-five on the morning of Wednesday, September 8, the outlines of the city, its trees and plants, flowering dahlias and oleanders shone with crystalline clarity. It was to be a fine day, tinged with the melancholy beauty of September. The early morning breeze already had a brisk touch of autumn in it and a few premonitory leaves fell as the calendar poised on the brink of the dark months. Early workers were cycling to their jobs; some women joined lines before fountains, while others, with kerchiefs over their heads, joined the queues which were forming in front of shops and stores.

After a sleepless night, General Taylor and Colonel Gardiner were still worried about the messages prepared early that morning. When General Carboni came in, he explained that since the Italians had no automatic coding system, coding had to be done by hand with painstaking slowness. The two telegrams, therefore, had not actually been sent until 7 A.M. and, due to bad atmospheric conditions, there was no assurance that they had been accurately transmitted or received.

A telegram had come in from Algiers during the night confirming the respective armistice announcements that Eisenhower and Badoglio were to read over the radio, and, an hour later, the Americans were informed that AFHQ had acknowledged receipt of Badoglio's telegram. But Taylor was uneasy about his own telegram. Worried that it had not gone out correctly, he decided to send still another, containing a "summary of situation as stated by Italian authorities" and citing the Italian request for cancellation of the airborne operation.

Taylor did not know that, although Badoglio's message had been received at five thirty that morning, it had not been decoded until eight o'clock, after General Eisenhower had left Algiers for his advanced headquarters on the Bay of Tunis.

In Rome, at nine o'clock that morning, German chargé d'affaires Rahn was having breakfast on the terrace of the German Embassy with Moellhausen, his second-in-command. Rahn said he had had a nightmare in which a man came into his room and tried to strangle him; and as a result, he was beset by a vague sense of irritation and unease.

"Is that how the day will turn out?" Moellhausen asked.

"Try not to talk about disasters," said Rahn.

Italian leaders, however, were euphoric. They had little doubt that Eisenhower would consent to a delay as soon as he received the cables. Still, early that morning, Badoglio had an afterthought. He phoned General Roatta and asked him if he agreed with Carboni. Roatta said that he did not know what Carboni had said and sped across town to see the marshal. When Badoglio told him of the message he had sent to Eisenhower, Roatta suggested sending a high-ranking officer to explain the sudden turnabout to the American general. While Badoglio pondered the suggestion, Roatta went to Palazzo Vidoni, where he told Rossi about his meeting with Badoglio. The two men agreed on a set of instructions to be given to whomever was selected.

It was now nearly ten o'clock. Rossi left to meet Ambrosio, who was returning from Turin on a slow sleeper.

Kesselring, however, remained on the alert. The Anglo-American fleet now appeared to be turning before the Sorrento Peninsula, indicating that the Allies were headed not for Naples but for the Gulf of Salerno. Armed with this information, Kesselring called Italian army headquarters to arrange a meeting to coordinate defense strategy. He had already discussed common naval measures with Admiral De Courten, whose forces had also sighted the Allied ships.

Roatta, who had received word that morning of the approaching convoys, agreed to meet Kesselring's deputy, Westphal, at five thirty that afternoon.

In the meantime, Ambrosio had returned with Marshal Caviglia, who immediately ordered his aide, General Francesco Campanari, to ask for an audience with the king. It was set for the next morning, September 9. It now looked as if this meeting might have been the real reason for Ambrosio's trip.

From General Rossi, Ambrosio learned that Allied convoys seemed to be heading for Salerno, that the armistice announcement was scheduled for that evening, and that Badoglio wanted to send a high-ranking officer to Eisenhower to secure basic changes in Allied plans. When Rossi said that this had become necessary because Carboni had told Badoglio of his lack of fuel and ammunition, Ambrosio was furious.

"How is this possible?" he almost shouted. "Carboni has been heading the Corps for forty days and only now he notices these deficiencies. There's plenty of fuel for him and as much ammunition as he can use except for antitank perforating bullets."

By the time Carboni came to see him, Ambrosio had evidently calmed down. Carboni said, "Everything's been arranged," implying that the armistice announcement would be delayed. Ambrosio apparently never stopped to wonder how an American brigadier general could possibly have promised anything that was contrary to the mission entrusted to him. Italian generals frequently did this, but Ambrosio should have known enough about the American chain of command to realize that Eisenhower would not stand for an arbitrary changing of plans. Instead, Ambrosio was certain that the delay sought by Badoglio was as good as granted, which was far from the case.

When Algiers finished decoding Badoglio's message, there was panic at Allied staff headquarters. At eleven o'clock, Bedell Smith phoned Harold Macmillan to tell him that the Italians now wanted "to call the whole thing off!"

Smith's first reaction was to reply that the 82nd Division would be sent anyway, and that he himself would assume its command. But this was not a decision that Smith could make; only the commander in chief could, and Eisenhower was not available. Less than forty-eight hours earlier, Ike had optimistically cabled the Combined Chiefs of Staff that he had made final adjustments in his planning so as to derive all possible advantage from the Italian surrender. Worried that Washington and London might go ahead on some plan of their own, Smith and Macmillan decided to cable the Combined Chiefs asking if the armistice announcement should still take place as planned. At the same time, they sent an urgent message to Eisenhower's advanced headquarters in Tunisia, hoping that it would reach him before too much time was lost.

In Rome, a little before noon, an emissary from the *Comando Supremo* visited General Taylor at Palazzo Caprara to express Italian concern over Eisenhower's possible reaction to Italy's having reneged on the armistice. When Taylor emphasized the seriousness of the situation, he was again urged to plead the Italians' case with Eisenhower. Finally, Taylor agreed that a senior Italian officer could accompany him and Gardiner when they returned to Allied headquarters, but only if Allied command would approve.

Badoglio had at first thought of sending Roatta, but the German-speaking general was needed to deal with the Germans, particularly at the meeting scheduled for that afternoon. Badoglio finally selected General Rossi.

At eleven forty, General Taylor wrote out still another message:

> In case taylor is ordered to return to sicily authorities at rome desire to send with him the deputy chief of the supreme general staff general rossi to clarify issues stop is this visit authorized

Just to be on the safe side, Taylor asked the Italians to send one more message, using the code words "Situation innocuous," which had been agreed upon before he came to Rome.

Meanwhile, King Vittorio Emanuele was meeting German emissary Rahn at Villa Savoia. The monarch was unusually friendly and talkative, but when Rahn began asking direct questions, he turned them smoothly aside, saying that these questions should be discussed with Badoglio, who enjoyed all his trust. "An old, honorable soldier whose assurances should be believed," said the king.

Then he brought the visit to an end, but only after assuring Rahn that the decision to continue the struggle was his own.

"Tell the Fuehrer," he said as he shook Rahn's hand, "that Italy will never capitulate. It is tied to Germany in life and death."

The king was playing a dangerous game. "At the point where we are," General Puntoni, the king's aide, wrote in his diary that day, "even if we affirm a desire to continue the war with Hitler, he won't believe it and the Americans, indignant at the ambiguity of our attitude, will attack us with the weight of their frightful forces."

Rahn had barely returned to the embassy when air raid sirens sounded and planes appeared overhead. Rushing to a loggia of Villa Wolkonsky to watch the scene, Rahn was worried by the flames and smoke which rose off to the southeast. Kesselring's headquarters were in that direction. Maybe there had been some truth to the nightmare.

It was a little after noon. Hearing the distant drone of planes, Taylor and Gardiner went to a window and tried to identify the aircraft. Had the operation been moved ahead? Could there have been a misunderstanding? They heard the rumbling of distant explosions. After a while an Italian officer came to tell them that the planes they had seen had been American.

When sirens sounded in the capital, some Romans shuddered with fear at the thought that this might be a repetition of the July and August bombings of Rome, but word soon got around that the attack was centered on Frascati, ten miles away.

The raid went on for an hour and ten minutes. The crowded little city was razed to the ground. Members of the Jesuit College at the isolated Villa Mondragone, together with Salesians and Camoldolese from Tusculum, came into town to dig survivors out of the wreckage. There weren't very many. Six thousand persons—mainly women, children and old people—out of Frascati's eleven thousand inhabitants, were killed, and 93 per cent of their houses were destroyed.

In August and during the first week in September, Allied air raids according to Paolo Monelli, had destroyed more of Italy than all its wars, sieges, fires and earthquakes, dating back a thousand years. German headquarters, however, at which this last attack was directed, was hardly touched, even though 135 B-17s had dropped 389 tons of bombs.

Castellano's information concerning the location of German headquarters had not been quite correct. Kesselring's command was *not* in Frascati, but in a series of isolated buildings between Monte Cavo—the German radio center some miles above Frascati—and Grottaferrata. That day, Kesselring was in his office at the Villa Aldobrandini, and he wrote later that the raid barely affected his operations. Some telephone lines were interrupted but, by using the untouched Monte Cavo radio center, the Germans were able to maintain normal contact. Kesselring immediately ordered all his commanders to stand by and had his naval headquarters moved from Rome to the Frascati area.

At *Comando Supremo*, Major Marchesi, hearing of the bombing of Frascati, informed Ambrosio and Roatta that the attack must have been one of the signals agreed upon for the announcement of the armistice. Ambrosio's answer was that he had not received any of the agreed-upon communications, either by secret radio or from Radio London (the BBC). To him, this meant that General Eisenhower had accepted Badoglio's request.

Eisenhower had not yet been contacted when the Liberators were flying over Rome. When he was finally reached at a little past noon, he was infuriated by Badoglio's action. It was not so much the renunciation of the armistice that angered him, as the way it had been done. Ike was also displeased by the cable Smith and Macmillan had sent the Combined Chiefs asking for instructions, and he immediately ordered that this message be canceled or, if that could not be done, that the Combined Chiefs be told that he had already handled the matter himself.

Now he had to make other decisions. The landing was becoming more and more risky. Of course Allied plans could be delayed, but there were pressures from both London and Washington, and enormous difficulties would be involved.

Eisenhower did not trust the Italians. The chances of an information leak to the Germans or even of outright betrayal by the Italians had to be considered.

Since Ike was already in Bizerte to meet with his senior commanders, he placed the problem before them. His decision, to "act as if they did sign," was approved. The deadline for the beginning of the attack on Salerno thus remained firm, but Ike continued to ponder the advisability of the airborne drop.

Allied officers who had been suspicious all along now saw their doubts confirmed. The whole thing had been an Italian stratagem aimed at obtaining information; they had never had any real intention of keeping their agreement. Sir Alan Brooke, chief of the Imperial General Staff, wrote in his diary that a wire had arrived in London "from Eisenhower to the effect that Badoglio was ratting and that he did not consider he could hold the Germans in check; however, he [Eisenhower] had decided to continue with the operations except for the airborne landing outside Rome."

In the meantime, Brigadier Strong, who was in Tunis, went to see

Castellano and showed him a copy of Badoglio's telegram. Shocked, the Italian general wrote out a message urging Badoglio to support the armistice agreement, otherwise the result would be catastrophic. Accompanied by Strong, he then flew to Bizerte, where for a half hour, he was made to stand and wait, completely isolated, in the courtyard of command headquarters. Finally, together with his interpreter Montanari, he was ushered into a large room in the center of which was a long table.

At the table sat Eisenhower, with General Alexander on his right, Admiral Cunningham on his left, and, on both sides, an imposing number of other high-ranking officers. When no one returned Castellano's smart salute, he felt as if he were standing before a court martial.

Eisenhower nodded to the Italians to be seated and then read Badoglio's message. He told Castellano that the Allies could not accept any postponement. If Badoglio did not announce the armistice that evening as had been agreed, the Allies could only conclude that Castellano and the Italian Government had played a suspicious role in the armistice negotiations.

Castellano insisted that neither he nor his government was guilty of bad faith; something of paramount importance, he said, must have developed in Rome. He asked Eisenhower to reserve judgment until such time as Badoglio had replied to Castellano's message. Eisenhower waved this aside and read his own telegram, which was being transmitted:

Part 1. I intend to broadcast the existence of the armistice at the hour originally planned. If you or any part of your armed forces fail to cooperate as previously agreed I will publish to the world the full record of this affair. Today is X day and I expect you to do your part.

Part 2. I do not accept your message of this morning postponing the armistice. Your accredited representative has signed an agreement with me and the sole hope of Italy is bound up in your adherence to that agreement. On your earnest representation the airborne operations are temporarily suspended.

Part 3. You have sufficient troops near Rome to secure the temporary safety of the city but I require full information on which to plan earliest the airborne operation. Send General Taylor to Bizerte at once by aircraft. Notify in advance time of arrival and route of aircraft.

Part 4. Plans have been made on the assumption that you were acting in good faith and we have been prepared to carry out future operations on that basis. Any failure now on your part to carry out the full obligations to the signed agreement will have the most serious consequences for your country. No future action of yours could then restore any confidence whatsoever in your good faith and consequently the dissolution of your government and nation would ensue.

Castellano was dismissed, and promptly returned to Tunis to pass the remainder of the day in anxious worry.

By cable, Eisenhower informed the Combined Chiefs of Staff of the action he had taken:

i have just completed a conference with the principal commanders and have determined not to accept the italian change of attitude stop we intend to proceed in accordance with plan for the announcement of the armistice and with subsequent propaganda and other measures stop marshal badoglio is being informed through our direct link that this instrument entered into by his accredited representative with presumed good faith on both sides is considered valid and binding and that we will not recognize any deviation from our original agreement

By then it was afternoon, and Eisenhower finally sent out orders to cancel GIANT II, hoping that the widespread units would be caught in time. It was problematical. At that moment, the C-47s, loaded with paratroopers, were already warming up their engines and a few were about to take off while others headed for runways. The seaborne expedition had already put out to sea.

At the same time, the amphibious assault troops for AVALANCHE were approaching Italy. They would launch the attack on Salerno at midnight. Fighter planes were going over their orders; a thousand sorties would form an air umbrella over the beaches.

As the hour for the start of GIANT II approached, Taylor and Gardiner, in their wood-paneled confinement in Rome, were worried and restless. There had still been no word. Outside, the city remained silent and seemingly deserted once the echoes of the bombing had died away. The Americans' tension was nearing the breaking point. All day long, they and the Italians kept checking for a warning message on the armistice announcement. It was understandable that there had been no music by Verdi—that had been canceled by the Allies two days earlier. But no talks on Nazi activities were heard over the BBC, despite the fact that SIM had halted its customary jamming of British overseas broadcasts. Only years later was it discovered that, despite General Rooks's orders on September 6 to the radio operators in Algiers and his request to the BBC, the appropriate messages were never transmitted, due to an oversight.

Unfortunately, the oversight contributed to the Italians' belief that the armistice announcement was to be postponed. Ambrosio and Badoglio both believed that the delay was assured.

After lunch, the two American officers decided to take a walk around the city. They did not believe that it was at the mercy of the Germans. If they could come up the coast to Rome, cross the city to the center and ride back and forth to Badoglio in the middle of the night—all without much difficulty—German control of Rome could not be as rigid as it had been made out to be.

The idea of the walk had to be abandoned, however, because the Italians were unable to locate civilian clothes for the huskily-built Colonel Gardiner. Finally the Americans dropped into armchairs, closed their eyes and went to sleep.

At 3 P.M. they were awakened; a telegram had been received ordering them to return to Allied headquarters. There was no mention of any other message nor any intimation that the call-back was really *one* part of the *four* part cable that Eisenhower had sent insisting on the armistice announcement.

General Rossi, aware that no warning signals had been received, believed that the armistice announcement was being held up until he arrived and that he therefore had Eisenhower's permission to make the trip.

The fact was, however, that Taylor's telegram had not yet reached AFHQ. On their own responsibility, Taylor and Gardiner decided to take Rossi and his Italian interpreter, Lieutenant Tagliavia, along with them. As the minutes ticked off, no transport appeared. "Why don't we leave?" Taylor kept asking Carboni.

The Germans were becoming impatient also, and now they began to put pressure on the Italians, who were caught in the middle. That afternoon, Kesselring had asked General Roatta for permission to move the 3rd Panzergrenadieren southward, through Rome, in order to meet the threatened Allied invasion. Roatta, who believed that this was an obvious attempt to move the division closer to the capital, tried to put Kesselring off.

Rintelen kept phoning to insist. At 3:15 P.M., the 16th Panzer Division headquarters had received a message from an air observation post that "a powerful fleet of about a hundred ships" was approaching the coast. Twenty-five minutes later, the code word "Orkan"—hurricane—which meant "battle readiness, landing in view," was issued. German troops began to replace Italians at the more important gun emplacements.

Roatta, aware of all this, finally gave in, at least partially, saying that he would allow advanced elements of the German division to move to a specified line twenty miles north of the capital, but only during the night of the ninth so as to avoid nocturnal incidents between the Panzers and the two Italian divisions, the Ariete and Piave, which stood between the Germans and Rome.

Following orders, Crown Prince Umberto arrived in Rome, leaving Army Group South, consisting of all Italian forces in southern Italy, without a commander. He had not been informed that his post was now vacant, but in any event Umberto had been only a figurehead. With the excuse that his life was precious, he had been kept in the dark about operations. He had not slept much the night before, because he had been told by Marshal Graziani that the armistice had already been signed and that this could be his hour. The crown prince hardly noticed that when his military Alfa sedan entered the main entrance of the royal palace, the big courtyard was unusually full of cars.

Carboni's efforts to arm the Communists were moving ahead. His son, Lieutenant Lanza and Felice Dessí met with Trombadori and Longo at the Grand Hotel. The night before, young Carboni had picked up hidden arms and gone to distribute them, but when he had arrived at his appointment with the Communists, no one had been there to meet him. He had returned the arms to their hiding place and made this appointment for a new meeting at the Grand Hotel.

It was agreed that the Communists would organize squads and have them ready to march against the Germans. It was also decided to blow up several hotels where German army officers were staying. An appointment was made for nine o'clock that night on Via XX Settembre not far from the War Ministry. Carboni's men and the Communists would go to a military museum at Porta Pia to pick up arms. When the Communists came out of the hotel, Trombadori turned to Longo.

"Did you notice the medal that lieutenant wore for fighting in Spain?" he asked. "How can we trust them? They disgust me."

Longo smiled bleakly and said, "Right now our interests coincide."

As the groups were parting, Lanza passed around American cigarettes. Trombadori later wrote that they were the only concrete results of the meeting.

At 4:30 P.M., when Carboni finally came to inform Taylor that they could now leave, the American general looked at his watch and spread out his arms discouragedly. Then he and Gardiner, this time with General Rossi and his interpreter, again climbed into an ambulance, which took them to Ciampino airport. At 5:05 P.M., the four men boarded a trimotored Savoia–Marchetti bomber piloted by Major Vassallo. As far as Taylor knew, no word had been received in Rome and the two-hour trip to Bizerte would bring him there too late. His men, he thought, would be flying towards almost certain death.

Chapter 32

THE COUNCIL OF FEAR

For years, everyone in Italy who was involved has maintained that neither the king, Ambrosio nor Badoglio was informed of the contents of Eisenhower's four-part cable until 5 P.M., in spite of the fact that the third part of it, at least, must have been received in Rome by 3 P.M. since that is how the Italians knew that Taylor and Gardiner had been ordered to return to their base.

Even Carboni claims that he was not aware of the rest of the message when he arranged for the Americans' departure. According to Carboni, he was called to Badoglio's office at the Viminale just as the four officers were getting into the ambulance. Minister of War Sorice was also present.

Badoglio seemed ready to collapse as he showed Carboni a telegram, which he said had just come:

> i see by your behavior you do not wish to comply with agreements stop i have decided to announce the armistice tonight at 6:30 stop follow me stop eisenhower

The Italians were trapped. What Foreign Minister Guariglia had foretold had come to pass: the Allies had all the cards, the records of the negotiations, the signed agreements; there was no longer a chance of persuading the Germans that it had all been a misunderstanding.

A Crown Council was hurriedly convoked and Carboni was ordered to attend. The king was already on his way to the Quirinale and the other leaders responsible for the conduct of the war were being hastily informed. General Roatta, who was preparing to meet the Germans, sent his deputy, Lieutenant General Giuseppe De Stefanis.

Foreign Minister Guariglia had just returned to his office after taking a walk through the Villa Borghese park when he was informed of the meeting. At the royal palace he encountered General Puntoni and asked him what was going on.

Puntoni was not certain. Having spied an unusual accumulation of cars in the palace courtyard, he had asked the first driver he had seen for an explanation. "The war is over," the man had replied. "There's been an armistice."

"Shut up, you fool," Puntoni had shouted indignantly. "I'll have you put in jail!"

Still uninformed, Guariglia hurried towards the salon to the right of the big courtyard. In front of it he met Badoglio, whom he later described as "aged by another twenty years, without energy." When Guariglia asked the marshal what was happening, Badoglio replied, "We're finished." Then, the doors of the salon opened, and Guariglia and Badoglio entered to find the king already seated, along with Ambrosio and Acquarone.

German chargé d'affaires Rahn, who was just as much in the dark as Guariglia, was drinking coffee at the German Embassy with his subordinate Moellhausen and two Italian navy officers when the phone rang. The call was from the Foreign Office on Berlin's Wilhelmstrasse; Ribbentrop himself asked to speak with Rahn. Rahn jumped to his feet, seized the receiver, and listened for two minutes without saying a word. "I can hardly believe it," he said finally. "I saw the king this morning and he confirmed that Italy was continuing the war. . . ."

Rahn was told that Reuters, the English news agency, had announced the capitulation of Italy. Determined to learn whether or not he had been tricked, Rahn called the Italian Foreign Office, which

N

promptly denied the news. The Italian navy officers also told him that Italian capitulation was unlikely. Rahn then called Ribbentrop and reassured him; Ribbentrop, in turn, reassured Hitler at the Berlin Chancellery.

A few minutes later, however, Ribbentrop called again. Other wire services were confirming the news. This time Rahn telephoned Roatta, from whom he received a complete, formal denial. Speaking in German, Roatta called the capitulation story "a bare-faced English propaganda lie which I must reject with indignation." Rahn called back Berlin and again reassured Ribbentrop, who again reassured Hitler.

By then the item had been picked up and broadcast by Cairo, Ankara and assorted national radio networks. The Italian Embassy in Berlin heard it on the French radio and began to burn its secret papers and codes.

The leak, it seemed, had occurred in New York at around 4 P.M., and two minutes later Reuters had had the story confirmed by Allied headquarters in Algiers. The British government, however, prohibited release of the news in Britain, and so BBC foreign broadcasts denied it. American stations were announcing the capitulation, and at 5:45 P.M. the Italian news agency, Stefani, received news of the armistice. Someone suggested issuing a denial, but in the subsequent excitement this was overlooked.

As soon as the German High Command received the news, Chief of Operations Jodl got in touch with OB SUED at Frascati. With Kesselring out, a staff officer phoned the military attaché's office at the German Embassy, which in turn phoned Italian army headquarters at Monterotondo. Here the call was passed to Toussaint who, with Westphal, was talking affably with Roatta about joint defense against the Allies. Toussaint listened for a few moments, slammed down the phone, and asked Roatta for an explanation. Instead of answering him, however, Roatta buzzed for his aide.

"Listen, Zanussi," he said, "the German embassy just telephoned General Toussaint that there has been an armistice between us and the Anglo-Americans. Do you know anything about it?"

With complete sincerity, Zanussi said that he did not. Roatta turned smilingly to his guests. "It's just another trick to divide us," he said coolly. "An outright lie with no basis in fact."

The Germans, thoroughly convinced, continued the conversation, but the moment they left, Roatta called SIM, where Carboni's deputy, General Carlo Fantoni, confirmed the rumor: "The news is exact and official."

Like a good soldier, Roatta called Toussaint. "You have every right not to believe me," he told the German. "But I give you my word of honor that half an hour ago when I said the news was a lie, I did not know it was true."

Toussaint hung up without bothering to reply. Sensing a certain hostility, Roatta packed his belongings, alerted the staff that head-quarters was moving back to Rome and, with Zanussi, prepared to return to the capital. As they left, Roatta turned to Zanussi and said in French, "*Nous sommes foutus. . . .*" (We're done for, damnably so.)

It was an apt prediction, for not long afterwards six companies of German paratroops headed for Monterotondo with orders to capture Roatta dead or alive.

Roatta's deputy, General De Stefanis, reached the royal palace at 6:45 P.M. On the ground floor, in a huge anteroom to the left of the courtyard, he found Navy Minister Admiral De Courten, Air Force Minister General Sandalli, Minister of War General Sorice, General Carboni in his capacity of Chief of Military Intelligence, General Puntoni and Ambrosio's aide, Major Marchesi, who was there be-cause he had been at Cassibile with Castellano at the signing of the armistice. They sat waiting, not aware that a kind of inner council was going on behind the closed doors.

It would have shocked them to know that Badoglio was refusing to choose a course for the government to follow. He merely told the king that he had two alternatives: to disavow Badoglio's pledges, saying that they had been contracted without the king's knowledge, and to announce Badoglio's resignation, or to accept Eisenhower's conditions, regardless of the consequences. The latter alternative would mean complete surrender.

On this note of uncertainty, the doors were thrown open and those outside were invited in. Although they had supposedly been called to help the king arrive at a decision, that was not the real rea-son that they had been summoned. In reality, the king and the mem-bers of his inner council saw this meeting as an opportunity to unload some of their responsibility onto others.

When the dignitaries filed in, they saw the king at the head of a long oval table, with Badoglio and Ambrosio at his right, Guariglia at his left and Acquarone several places down from Guariglia. At a gesture from the monarch, Sandalli sat down next to Guariglia, then Carboni, Sorice and finally De Courten, next to Acquarone. Across from them was Marchesi, next to Ambrosio, who asked for and received authorization from the king for the major's presence.

The king opened the meeting. "As you gentlemen know," he began, "the Anglo-Americans have decided to anticipate the announcement of the armistice by four days. . . ."

The monarch, seeing De Courten whispering to Acquarone, asked him what was wrong.

"As a matter of fact," De Courten protested, "I don't know anything . . ."

Glowering, the king turned to Badoglio. "If you please," he said coldly, "bring these gentlemen up to date."

Badoglio could only nudge Ambrosio, who started speaking.

"A grave misfortune," Ambrosio explained, "is hanging over us. The Anglo-Americans are about to announce the capitulation of Italy, something which should not have taken place until the twelfth. Therefore we must decide what to do."

The faces around the table reflected shock.

"But that's blackmail," protested Air Force Minister Sandalli. "Let's reject the armistice."

Guariglia agreed. "If we don't reject it," he said, "Italy is ruined."

Sorice, who knew nothing, said that the armistice declaration should be delayed, not rejected.

Carboni, who knew everything, seconded this, ferociously criticized Castellano and strongly condemned Allied conduct. The only thing the king could do, he said, was refuse to acknowledge the armistice which was, after all, the result of Castellano's negotiations. If necessary, the monarch could dismiss Badoglio and disown Castellano, claiming that he had not authorized the pledges that they had given in his name. With this as an excuse, he could request a delay of ten days. Then, to pacify the Germans and gain time, the king could provide the Germans with new guarantees of friendship, later telling the Allies that the Italians had only pretended to abrogate their original agreement with the Allies in order to betray the Germans more efficaciously. Then, with Allied help, the Italians could turn on the Germans and finish them off.

Marchesi was silently wondering how Carboni could possibly insist on such an absurd plan of action without anyone's even protesting, when Guariglia voiced his approval of it. Then Sorice said he would approve, and the convoluted proposal seemed on the verge of acceptance. It would save face for the leaders while assuring the generals that their forces would not have to face the Germans alone.

Called out of the room, Marchesi returned several minutes later. Although he had not been asked to speak, he stood up, interrupting Carboni, and announced that Radio Algiers had just broadcast Eisenhower's proclamation of the armistice. Marchesi, who was furious at Carboni for his criticism of Castellano, hoped that these tidings would clear the air so that the situation would be more fully appreciated and the participants spurred to a more logical reaction.

Instead, Carboni spoke again, insisting that this changed nothing at all. It was, he said, and the others agreed, nothing but an Allied trick intended to compromise them vis-à-vis the Germans.

Marchesi scribbled a few notes on a piece of paper and calmly waited until Carboni finished speaking. It was at this point, for the first time in Italian history, that a major took the floor before an assembly of the nation's highest ranking commanders and cabinet ministers and discomfited a lieutenant general.

Standing erect, Marchesi waved a piece of paper which he said was the last telegram sent by Eisenhower, a message about which most of those present knew nothing. He read the complete text, and when he came to the point where Eisenhower threatened to "publish to the world the whole record of this affair," the faces around the conference table paled.

After he had finished reading, Marchesi gave a grim preview of the consequences that would arise from the Italian government's failure to keep its word. If any of those present feared that Rome might be bombed by the Germans, there was even greater reason to fear that the Allies would do it first, and he described the powerful bombing formations that the Allies had ready to fly over Rome. An avalanche of bombs would fall on the capital, much more terrible than anything the Germans could do. If the surrender documents were made public—and he pointed out that the signing had been photographed and filmed—Italy would lose not only all hope of a continued alliance with Germany, but any possibility of support from the Allies as well. To talk of treason, as General Carboni had just done, was preposterous. Strictly speaking, the Allies were acting within the terms of the agreements. It had been a mistake not to give credence to Taylor's warnings and worse still to have deceived themselves about the possibility of a delay. Now it was necessary to act immediately.

As Marchesi spoke, he realized that he was keeping his fists on the table. The faces before him blurred into indistinct images, except for Carboni's, whose eyes burned into him from across the table.

When Marchesi finally finished speaking, there was a long silence. Guariglia rose to say that he had not approved the manner in which the military negotiations had been conducted but that it would now be absurd to disavow them. Support for Carboni's plan vanished. In the course of a few minutes, Italy's leaders had switched allegiances three times. At the beginning of the Crown Council, the Italians had been on the side of the Germans although secretly tied to the Allies by the armistice; after some discussion, they had decided to maintain the alliance with the Germans and to continue, for the moment, the war against the Allies; and finally, a few minutes later, after Marchesi had read Eisenhower's telegram, the new allies had become the Anglo-Americans.

The king, who had remained silent, asked if there were any objections. Carboni tried to breathe life back into his proposal but the king interrupted him with a gesture. "There is no doubt now," said the king in a low voice, "as to what must be done."

The king rose, and his counselors filed out, except for Marshal Badoglio, who remained with the monarch. After a few minutes Badoglio emerged and told Ambrosio that the king had authorized him to announce the armistice. From where could he broadcast it?

Ambrosio turned to Carboni, who had been directed to set up a remote line, but the embarrassed Carboni had to admit that this had not been done.

Marchesi said that the only thing to do was to go directly to the radio, EIAR. Badoglio asked Marchesi to accompany him.

As the car carrying Badoglio and Marchesi crossed over the Tiber on the way to the radio station, there was complete silence.

Things had been hectic in the Allied camp as well. GIANT II had to be stopped, and quickly. Since time was running short and coded messages might take too long, General Lyman Lemnitzer was authorized to fly from North Africa to Sicily to cancel the Operation.

The time of takeoff was getting closer and closer, and in various airfields throughout Sicily the boarding of parachutists had already taken place. By 5 P.M., 62 of the 150 aircraft to be used were circling in the sky while the others, standing in close order, prepared to join them. On the ground, General Ridgway waited near a radio for

Eisenhower's 6:30 P.M. broadcast. Once this went on the air, the planes would head for Rome.

Minutes later, General Lemnitzer landed at Licita, and shortly afterwards a pair of jeeps arrived amidst clouds of dust at the principal field, where U.S. war correspondent Richard Tregaskis was observing the loading. He watched mystified as four men with stars on their collars got out: General Ridgway, General Lemnitzer, General Cannon and a general of the Troop Carrier Command. The paratroopers watched in wonderment too as the group adjourned to a first-aid tent. A few minutes later, a major and a lieutenant, in suntans and wearing air corps insignia, came up to a captain of the 82nd. There was a whispered conversation, and then the announcement: "There's been a reprieve of twenty-four hours!"

The 82nd's seaborne task force had been reached a bit earlier, in time to divert the flotilla to the Gulf of Salerno, where it made rendezvous with the AVALANCHE convoys. That was the end of GIANT II.

Although Ridgway later wrote that he thanked God for not having had to take the chance of sending his men on what could have been a fatal mission, Robert Murphy felt that the airborne commanders had been against the expedition from the start, more "for standard military reasons than because no one trusted the Italians." He thought that the judgment of the airborne commanders should not have been followed and that the Rome landing should have taken place.

German generals thought that the Allies had allowed a fantastic opportunity to slip through their fingers. General Westphal later admitted that the German antiaircraft guns were fixed batteries which lacked the means to move rapidly; a drop that did not fly over the capital would have been out of their range of action. American paratroopers could have landed where and when they pleased, on almost any airport around Rome.

"As a soldier," Westphal said, "I would have been happy to find myself in a situation as favorable as that presented to the Allies."

In Algiers, technicians of the psychological warfare branch prepared to broadcast the record of Eisenhower's announcement. As six thirty neared, the starting of the turntable was followed almost immediately by agitated hand-waving and head-shaking. The record

had been put on at the wrong speed! After hurried, silent consulta-
tions, the record was put on again, and once more there was great
agitation; the record was skipping the grooves! Some of the men
inaudibly mouthed the word "sabotage." Finally, on the third try, the
record went out over the airwaves.

> This is General Dwight D. Eisenhower, Commander-in-Chief of the
> Allied forces. The Italian Government has surrendered its armed
> forces unconditionally. I have granted a military armistice, the
> terms of which have been approved by the Governments of the
> United Kingdom, the United States, and the Union of Soviet Social-
> ist Republics. The Italian Government has bound itself by these
> terms without reservations. . . . All Italians who now act to help
> eject the German aggressor from Italian soil will have the assistance
> and support of the United Nations.

A short summary of the negotiations followed, and then officials
sat back to wait for Badoglio's broadcast. The atmosphere was thick
with tension. Allied troops were almost to Salerno; when they landed,
would they have to fight the Italians as well as the Germans?
Finally, when no announcement from Badoglio came, Eisenhower
authorized the broadcasting in English of the announcement the
Italian leader had been supposed to make.

By this time, German chargé d'affaires Rahn had received still
another phone call in Rome from Ribbentrop. After promising the
foreign minister that he would take immediate steps to clarify the
situation, Rahn ordered a car and left for Palazzo Chigi. There, at a
few minutes past seven, he was shown into the office of Italian Foreign Minister Guariglia.

"Your visit is very opportune," the pale and embarrassed Guariglia told Rahn, "because I have something very important to tell you.
I have the honor to inform you that the Italian government has signed
an armistice with the Allies."

"But this is treason!" Rahn exploded.

"I object to the word 'treason,' " Guariglia protested. "The Italian people have done all in this war that was humanly possible and
no one can insult them."

"I am not accusing the Italian people," Rahn replied, "but those
who brought about the country's surrender, and I tell you that this
will weigh for a long time on the history of Italy."

Then, without waiting for a reply, Rahn stalked out of the room.

At the German Embassy, he called Kesselring, who said that he could guarantee protection for German diplomats only if the entire embassy staff came to Frascati. Rahn decided that they would all leave Rome as soon as possible for haven with Rommel's forces in northern Italy.

Meanwhile, Taylor, Gardiner and Rossi arrived at El Aouina, the airport for Bizerte. An American sergeant greeted Taylor:

"Have you heard the news? The Eyeties have given up. Eisenhower announced it on the radio."

When Taylor saw Brigadier Strong he confirmed that he had been told nothing in Rome that Allied Intelligence had not already known. As Strong later wrote: "The truth of the matter was that the Italian authorities were divided on the Allied proposal and the less courageous were using the presence of the German troops and the immobility of the Italian units as an excuse for cancelling the air landing in Rome."

Taylor then gave Strong back all but twenty lire of the money the Americans had taken with them, a gesture which confirmed Taylor in Strong's regard as "a very careful and scrupulous man."

In Salambó, General Castellano met General Rossi and immediately asked why he had come.

"To obtain the postponement of the armistice announcement," Rossi explained, only to be informed that he had arrived too late.

Then the two Italians were taken to meet Eisenhower. Rossi, tired and confused, protested that the Allies had gone ahead because they distrusted the Italians.

Eisenhower: "But we were enemies until two hours ago. How could we trust you?"

Rossi: "I am aware of your lack of trust, but it led to great damage. . . . The fleet has been told to go to Malta but I can't assure that it will since part of it has been cooperating closely with the Germans. If we had had more time we could have sent it to Sardinia and prepared it to accept the transfer to Malta."

Eisenhower: "You think the fleet will not come to Allied ports? This is of the greatest importance. Weren't orders given for it to do so?"

Rossi: "The orders were given, but their execution is doubtful. That's why we wanted to delay the armistice. We had some troop movements in mind which would have put us in a better position against German forces. That's another reason why we were asking for a delay. We kept our coastal forces small and dispersed because of the agreements with you and now we won't be able to do much against the Germans."

Eisenhower: "I trust your soldiers more than you do. If some mistake has been made we must now accept the situation as it is and cooperate the best possible way in our mutual interest."

Simultaneously, political advisors Murphy and Macmillan were trying to patch things up also. They met with De Gaulle, who congratulated them on the fact that the war between their countries and Italy had ended; France, he said, was still at war with Italy since it had neither been a party to the armistice nor had it been informed of the negotiations which led to the armistice.

At the Rome radio, Badoglio was seated in the studio reserved for notables. It had been decided not to broadcast his speech till seven forty-five, just prior to the regular news period. In the meantime, the evening program featured military marches and songs. Finally announcer Giovan Battista Arista introduced Badoglio. As the old marshal spoke, his words were recorded:

> The Italian government has requested an armistice of General Eisenhower, Commander-in-Chief of the Allied Forces. On the basis of the conditions of armistice, beginning today, 8 September, 1945 hours, every act of hostility on our part should cease towards the Anglo-American forces. The Italian Armed Forces should, however, react with maximum decision to offensives which come from any other quarter whatsoever.

The Italian army abroad was confused. They had heard foreign broadcasts reporting rumors of an armistice, but when their commanders had phoned Rome, the news had been denied. In Albania, General Renzo Dalmazzo, commander of the Italian Ninth Army, heard a broadcast from Turkey at 6 P.M., phoned Rome, and was told that the broadcast was "an infamous calumny." Dalmazzo ordered the Albanian radio to deny the armistice as enemy propaganda. At seven forty-five a denial was duly broadcast, but immediately afterward the same radio, connected with Rome, transmitted Badoglio's proclamation.

The announcement of the Italian armistice found Hitler just returned from Zaporozhe in the Ukraine. He had flown there that day to try to bolster the weakening German front. Then, because he had had "a strange feeling of unrest," he had flown back to the *Wolfsschanze* the same evening. The news he had both expected and feared awaited him. He immediately ordered Kesselring to put Operation ACHSE into action.

In the little town of Sant'Angelo de' Lombardi in the mountains north of Salerno, the German Tenth Army commander, General Vietinghoff, heard a London broadcast of the surrender, which was soon afterward confirmed by Kesselring. Vietinghoff immediately ordered the 16th Panzer Division to take possession of all coastal defenses manned by Italians and to insure that road and rail traffic was in the hands of the Germans. Strongpoints along the mine-sown shore bristled with mortars, field pieces, antiaircraft guns and howitzers. Between the strongpoints were observation squads with radio transmitters prepared to give instructions to gun crews. Batteries of mobile artillery were posted both in the hills and on the Salerno–Battipaglia road, while the nearby Montecorvino airfield began filling up with Stuka divebombers. Vietinghoff ordered the bulk of the 26th Panzer Division to break contact with Montgomery's forces in Calabria and hurry north.

American and English assault troops, sailing to battle that calm, clear evening, had a joyous shock when they learned that hostilities between the United Nations and Italy had ended. The news, as Churchill wrote, "relaxed their tension and had an unfortunate psychological effect," for the fighting spirit of the troops was definitely weakened. They cheered, sang, cracked jokes and drank what remained of their liquor ration. Launches from the larger vessels gave the news to smaller craft. There were rebel yells and Indian war whoops as an American ranger shouted that on the beach to greet them would be "the mayor of Salerno in his cocked hat with bottles of vino!"

Commanders tried to tell their men that the coming battle would be even tougher now that the Italians were out of the Germans' way. But the edge had been taken off their fighting trim and they remained convinced that their task would now be easier.

Chapter 33

THE ORDER OF BATTLE

On Wednesday the eighth, Rome basked in the soft freshness of a September evening. A little after eight o'clock, Romano Antonelli emerged from the Quirenetta movie theatre. Immediately he sensed excitement in the air, heard people talk about *l'armistizio* and saw soldier-packed trucks going up and down Corso Umberto. After a quick celebratory drink with friends at the fashionable Quirino Bar, he rushed home to tell his family.

Other Romans, listening to the record of Badoglio's announcement broadcast every fifteen minutes, learned that their country was no longer at war with the Allies. Deflated were all the belligerent songs, burst were all the dreams of empire; after three and a quarter years of war which had seen Greece resisting, Ethiopia returned to Haile Selassie and Libya lost in spite of Rommel, Italy had been forced to ask for an armistice.

Badoglio's declaration was only the second he had made to the Italian people, the first having been his announcement that the war would continue. Again the people were left without guidance; all

Badoglio had done was acknowledge Italy's defeat, which everyone knew had been inevitable for some time. Nor did the broadcast contain definite instructions for the armed forces, although the army, with its sixty-odd divisions—over 1,700,000 men—was still an effective force.

More than anyone else, soldiers wanted the war to end; to many, armistice meant throwing away their rifles and taking the military stars off their uniforms. Some officers, particularly in or near cities, found their men walking out of barracks, deaf and hostile to all appeals and threats. "We're going home, the war's over," they cried happily. Others slid out of windows, borrowed civilian jackets, and stole away. People stumbled over rifles abandoned in the middle of the streets and little boys bargained with each other for their finds. The going rate was ten bullets for one hand grenade.

In Via del Babuino someone said that Hitler had committed suicide, and passersby watched as two German soldiers tore off their collar insignias and danced on them. "Hitler kaputt," they shouted. "The war is over."

Carla Capponi, returning home from her office, became furious when she heard some people maintaining that the alliance with the Germans should be respected. When she reached the giant Vittorio Emanuele monument, she wrote on the side in chalk, "Out with the Germans!"

In the working-class district of Trastevere, signs appeared on the walls saying, "We want bread and peace."

In the smaller centers, bells were tolled and workers came in from the fields to gather in the piazzas. Even German soldiers joined in the festivities and drank toasts: "Now we will be going home." In places where there were no Germans, a sigh of relief went up from crowds around loudspeakers, and bonfires were lit while villagers danced around them.

In Orte, a rail center, some townspeople asked permission to toll the bells. Refused permission but still jubilant, they went out to celebrate in the streets.

At Monterotondo, half an hour from Rome, parish priests set their bells pealing in celebration until Roatta's headquarters, which was in the process of moving to Rome, sent soldiers to the churches to still the bells. Grumbling at this military intervention, the priests reluctantly silenced the joyous pealing.

Roman officialdom remained confused. The evening papers had already come out with denials of the armistice rumors.

The Italian Ministry of Press and Propaganda issued orders for the next day's papers: "Dailies will not publish special editions, only Marshal Badoglio's message without comment." But then a contradictory directive was sent out saying that comments might be made on Badoglio's message as long as they were written "in a sober and austere manner citing how the request for armistice had been a State necessity and marks an hour of mourning for the country . . . take maximum caution not to publish anything that might displease our ally, Germany." A half hour later, still another order was issued: "In the comments on Marshal Badoglio's message, add words of homage to the king."

Marshal Caviglia was having dinner in the home of his friend Count Miani when he learned of the armistice.

"I imagine," he wrote in his diary, "that provisions for escape were ready . . . perhaps [Badoglio] has already made off . . . but the king and the Supreme Command will remain at their posts."

In Rome, martial law was still in effect and by 10 P.M. the streetcars had started their last run. By ten thirty, curfew time, the streets were normally deserted.

Looking out from his apartment across the street, fashion designer Emilio Schuberth was amazed to see armored vehicles, troops with machine guns, and mortars assembled around the Ministry of Defense. Many of the usually darkened windows of the ministry were lit, and cars kept coming and going.

The royal family had eaten at the Quirinal Palace and then come to the War Ministry with suitcases and trunks. The king wore his uniform as commander in chief of all Italian armed forces, while the queen wore an ankle-length black gown and a small round hat. They settled into the minister's private apartment while a pair of six-foot cuirassiers stood guard with their sabres drawn. The king prepared to go to sleep on the camp bed he had succeeded in having brought from the royal residence. Sleeping on this hard, squeaking cot was a habit he had acquired during World War I. But he was unable to sleep, and he and the queen sat up talking. To a large extent their destiny was in the hands of Marshal Badoglio.

The marshal had already arrived and settled into a small apartment, where he had a frugal meal of broth, boiled meat, and fruit. After asking about his broadcast ("How was my voice? It was calm and steady, wasn't it?"), he sent a hasty telegram to Hitler explaining why Italy had asked for an armistice. Then he told his son and nephew that he was going to sleep.

Badoglio did not think that surrender to the Allies made simultaneous surrender to the Germans inevitable. Although his negotiators had insisted that Italy wanted to fight against the Germans alongside the Allies, his declaration made no mention of this. He obviously hoped that the Germans would leave the country, as if by magic, under the threat of the Allied arrival.

The lack of hard news encouraged a feeling of optimism in the ministry. Relying on his limited experience as an air officer, Mario Badoglio said of the Germans, "They're terrorized . . . they won't attack," and echoing his father, "Everything will go very well."

"If they leave without fighting," added Carboni, "it means they're really in bad shape."

But just in case, units of the Sassari Division were occupying the first two floors of the ministry, machine guns pointed out the windows. Later, more troops were added, taken from the forces protecting the capital.

As head of the army, General Roatta issued orders to troops defending Rome to man the roadblocks around the city. Following Ambrosio's lead, he directed that any Germans leaving were to be allowed to pass, but that any moving towards Rome were to be halted. Italian troops were to "react energetically against any attempt to penetrate by force and act against any hostile actions whatsoever."

Roatta hoped that the Germans would withdraw to the North, and even when reports came in that they had killed some Italian sentinels, he ordered no attacks. Italian forces around Rome remained on the defensive, facing an enemy whose intentions were as yet unclear.

Field Marshal Kesselring sat in his office at Frascati planning his next moves. With him were Richthofen, Rintelen, Westphal and Toussaint, the latter two just returned from seeing Roatta. Kesselring told them that he was specially concerned about the next few days. It was not the armistice that worried him; for some time he had been deploying his troops with that eventuality in view. He was, he said, more preoccupied with military consequences than with political repercussions.

His first move was to give instructions for ACHSE to be set in motion, although he delayed ordering the withdrawal of troops to the North. Then, with his commanders, he examined the position of the forces at his command. They were spread throughout central and southern Italy, eight divisions organized in two commands.

Kesselring had asked for more troops, but the High Command had said that the situation in the East precluded any reduction of forces there. Rommel's Army Group B was in northern Italy with nine divisions. One or two of these comparatively idle units could make all the difference, but Rommel had persuaded Hitler that central and southern Italy should be evacuated. The result was that Army Group B was to remain in the North, and Kesselring's forces, as he wrote later, "were written off at the Fuehrer's headquarters."

For the time being, the Tenth Army could fend for itself. Vieting-hoff had been given tactical control. If the Allies invaded, he was to repel their landings while Kesselring guaranteed withdrawal routes north, particularly problematical at Rome.

At the XI Fliegerkorps office of General Student, Colonel Doll-mann found pessimism pervading the air: "Everyone was expecting Badoglio to issue a proclamation to the population and asssume command of the armed forces. . . . Student, his face dark, examining maps on his desk, said that everything was lost if American parachutists landed that night."

All or part of the Allied invasion fleet might continue northward to land near the capital, possibly reinforced by parachutists who would seize the nearby airports. The Allies, after all, had complete command of the sea, and could therefore make landings almost anywhere on either of the Italian coasts. They also had overwhelming air supremacy, and there were large Italian forces in the vicinity of Rome. If the Allies should come to Rome, either by sea or air, Kesselring's troops would be cut off. It would be impossible, as General Westphal said later, to fight off Montgomery's army in Calabria, repel the invasion force wherever it landed and also deal with the Italian army formations in their midst and rear if they were reinforced with Americans.

Therefore, the means of withdrawal to the North had to be examined. Logic dictated that Vietinghoff's forces retreat to Rome, where Student's troops would join them in the withdrawal. Rome was Kesselring's problem. All lines of communication and supply between the North and South went through the capital. If Kesselring stayed, he would have to protect these lines, which could be cut by the Italian troops defending Rome.

These forces were aligned much as they had been since August 1, their projected regroupment as yet unexecuted. This meant that the Italians had well over eight divisions, more or less wisely deployed, more or less well armed, more or less intelligently commanded, but in any event a force of at least fifty-five thousand men equipped with some two hundred tanks and armored vehicles, possessing artillery superior to that of the Germans, and backed by a more effective air force. Troop morale was good and the advantage appeared to belong to the Italians.

Many military men involved were convinced that the Italians in the area enjoyed a clear numerical superiority over the Germans, but not until 1964, when General Castellano checked German general staff records in Friburg, was it revealed that German troops in the area numbered only 26,855 men, about half the number available to the Italians.

Westphal, interviewed on tape by Castellano at Bad Godesberg, confirmed this: "Considering all the units, including air crews and the various services, I calculate that around Rome on September 8 there were about thirty thousand Germans."

At 10 P.M., the German radio broadcast news of the armistice, accompanying it with an avalanche of insults and threats. Although Hitler might have wanted revenge for what he regarded as a betrayal, Kesselring thought of his outnumbered troops. If the Italians and the Allies had planned well, he could lose scores of thousands of men who were trapped between Rome and the South. Before accepting this possibility, however, he decided that the surest course would be to test the Italians' defenses. There was still the alternative plan of eventual retreat to the North, but he had to keep some troops around the capital in case of an Allied landing there, and he had to maintain a clear route for German units in the South which might be forced to withdraw to the North.

The German commander knew that Italian troops around Rome were in an outdated alignment, almost as much to maintain public order as to fight a former ally. The coastal divisions had been left along the sea, preparing for a nonexistent threat. Kesselring decided to see how the Italians would react. No big movements, just a small thrust here and there, all carried out with as little display of force as possible.

General Westphal has maintained that it was difficult for the Germans to regard yesterday's ally as today's enemy; the Germans and the Italians had fought together, after all, for over three years. "It was not easy, under those conditions, to make up one's mind to assume the initiative."

Ultimately, however, these scruples were overcome and commanders were given their instructions. The coast was to be cleared. The Allies might be planning a seaborne attack and the shore near Rome would be an inviting target. General Barenthen was told to disarm the sparsely distributed Italian patrols, peaceably, if possible. Along with that would come the elimination of the Piacenza Division, whose units were interspersed with Barenthen's troops. Meanwhile, a column would take over the giant Italian army fuel deposit at Mezzocammino on the Ostiense road between the sea and Rome. With 16,000 tons of gasoline, it was the main source of supply for the divisions defending Rome.

There was also an affront to the Third Reich to be assuaged; paratroopers were ordered to leave at daybreak for Monterotondo in order to seize Roatta and the army staff there.

Commands were transmitted to advance elements; soldiers mounted armored cars, motorcycles and trucks, orders were barked, motors were started, and the troops of the Third Reich set out for Rome.

Chapter 34

THE DISTANT DRUMS

The eighteen roads that lead to Rome seem almost designed to facilitate the military movements of a resourceful enemy. The great consular arteries converge on the capital from all points of the compass, yet Rome had never been conquered by an enemy coming from the South and not since 1527 had a German army been able to take the capital.

On the night of September 8, 1943, the Italians had their divisions posted anywhere from five to twenty-five miles from the center of the city. This spreading of men in so-called internal and external lines, although it made defensive maneuvers more difficult, did serve to form solid circles around the city. To the south, however, the Italian forces lacked depth.

It was the Piacenza (103rd) Motorized Division, fifteen to twenty miles from Rome, that the Germans struck first. Components of the division were far from prepared. Captain Enrico Reisoli-Mathieu had received a phone alert that afternoon. But no reason had been given and he learned the reason for it only at 8 P.M. when he heard a broadcast of the armistice. He and other officers phoned XVII Corps headquarters for guidance. General Zanghieri, its commander, told his men not to worry; he was convinced that an accord existed between the *Comando Supremo* and the Germans, arranging for the latter's withdrawal.

That same afternoon, Colonel Formato, operations chief of the XVII Corps, had received a telegram ordering an alert on the grounds that "a huge Allied convoy has been sighted." For him, as for others, this confirmed that Italy's enemy was the one coming from the sea. There were even commands (for example, in Sardinia) in which the news that an Allied convoy had been sighted led to Italian generals' taking joint steps for defense *with Germans.* It was not until that night that subsequent orders made it clear that the Anglo-Americans were no longer the enemy.

By this time, the Germans had started their almost haphazard probing near Rome. The initial probes met little resistance from the Piacenza: strongpoints at Lanuvio and Albano were easily overrun; a few resisted, especially at Risaro and Ardea.

While this was going on, General Barenthen sent one column of parachutists up the Via Laurentina towards Rome, while another moved against Italian coastal batteries. Here, too, the Italians were the victims of confusion. At Latina, Major General Eduardo Minaja, commanding the 221st Coastal Division, had received an alert telling him to halt troops attempting to penetrate his lines. Subsidiary units receiving the orders were confused; what troops, they asked. Only then did XVII Corps headquarters reply, the Germans. But when small detachments of German troops approached, waving white flags and saying that they wanted to pass to the North, the Italians let them by. Once beyond the strongpoints, the Germans turned, attacked from the rear and took over the batteries.

At first it seemed as though no Italian wanted to stand and fight. At Ostia, Colonel D'Auria, after having ordered his men to resist, at the first appearance of a German officer turned everything over to him. Lieutenant Colonel Bianchedi, commander of the seaplane station and radio transmitter at Ostia, not only ordered his 750 men to leave their posts and give up their arms, but took 25 submachine guns out of customs and delivered them to the Germans.

With the Piacenza being scattered and German patrols knocking over coastal units, the 2nd Parachutists continued their march on the southern approaches of Rome. The Italian fuel depot at Mezzocammino had been taken earlier, and now these troops marched up the Via Portuense.

The Germans moved past Acilia and along the tree-lined Via Ostiense. They also moved up the Via della Magliana on the edge of the vast valley of the Tiber and past the Magliana Castle, once the hunting lodge of Pope Leo X.

Taking advantage of Italian confusion and lack of directives, the Germans tried to arrange local truces. Appealing to the honor of Italian officers as former comrades, they argued, "We should prevent the shedding of blood. . . ."

They told Italian soldiers that the war was over and that they could go home if they liked. Since this was one possible interpretation of Badoglio's proclamation, some threw away their weapons and abandoned their posts.

The column on Via Laurentina approached the garrison town of Cecchignola while, around 9:30 P.M., advance patrols moved into the hills of E. 42, the grandiose complex which Mussolini had planned to open in 1942 as a world's fair. Within minutes, the Germans had overcome a stronghold at the Grenadiers of Sardinia (21st) Infantry Division and captured a battalion commander.

North of Rome, General Graeser had started to move his 3rd Panzergrenadieren towards the capital, using as an excuse the agreement made the day before with Roatta. At the level of Lake Bracciano, the Germans encountered units of the Ariete Division and asked to be allowed to pass.

General Cadorna, commander of the Ariete, was perplexed. At 8 P.M., he had received the alert sent by Carboni to all divisions of the Motorized Corps except the Centauro (131st) Armored, which Carboni distrusted as still Fascist. Then, at 10 P.M., Cadorna had received a new order which Carboni, following Ambrosio's information, had sent: "Any German units who advance peaceably can be allowed to pass."

Cadorna phoned Carboni to tell him that Germans were asking to pass through the Ariete.

"If there are only a few, let them," Carboni answered.

Cadorna, who was rather irritated, exclaimed that this was absurd, "If we let them pass in dribs and drabs, later we'll find them all behind us." He told his chief of staff to disregard the order. The Germans, refused passage, retired.

Still farther north, soldiers were hailing Badoglio's announcement as the end of the war and, lacking any other orders, were disbanding. The commander of the Fifth Army, Lieutenant General Mario Caracciolo di Feroleto, receiving a telegram announcing the armistice, became furious. "It's a false alarm," he shouted. "I'll have the officer who brought this shot."

When the news was confirmed, Caracciolo thought that the armistice must have been reached in agreement with the Germans, but he could not check with the German liaison officer, because he had been granted leave in order to get married. Just after 10 P.M., his own liaison officer with the Germans, Major Pettoello, arrived disheveled. The Germans had taken him prisoner upon learning of the armistice announcement, but he had managed to escape. Then Caracciolo realized that there was no agreement between the Badoglio government and the Third Reich, and he started to ask Rome for orders.

At Italy's northwest frontier, Brigadier General Alessandro Trabucchi, chief of staff of the Fourth Army, learned of the armistice while dining with his German colleague Colonel Heggenheimer. He not only assured his guest that he thought the news untrue, but he did not alert his commands. When he discovered that "German units, from the largest to the smallest, had received precise and detailed instructions" and were starting to disarm Italian soldiers, he too started trying to reach Rome. When he finally succeeded in getting General Utili, army operations chief, on the phone, he expressed his surprise that army command had not been informed of the armistice.

"I learned about it just as you did," Utili assured him. "On the radio."

Meanwhile, diverse rumors spread through Rome. Some claimed that the Germans were already in Rome. Others said that they weren't, that the English had landed at Ostia and would arrive within hours.

Kesselring, who was surprised at the lack of Italian resistance, was still prepared to retreat to the North if the Allies reached Rome. Besides, what if Badoglio were planning to attack his rear? German communication lines were weak and tenuous. Kesselring's men had been moving against Italian strongholds, but their movements had been more soundings than skirmishes.

At around 10 P.M., groups of German parachutists came up to

advance posts of the Grenadier 1st Regiment near La Magliana, six miles from Rome. Their attitude was friendly; they were returning to Germany, they said, but they lacked weapons. Why didn't the Italians give them theirs instead of turning them over to the Anglo-Americans? When the Grenadiers refused, the parachutists left.

At around 11 P.M., other parachutists, in small groups and apparently disarmed, came up to mortar sections of the Grenadiers about a mile from the Magliana bridge. They wanted, they said, to give the Italians cigarettes and other articles that they would otherwise have to abandon. About a dozen soldiers who trusted the Germans went with them and were never seen again.

To other Italians still on guard, the Germans offered cigarettes and jam; when the Italians extended their hands to receive them, the Germans suddenly pulled out their guns and fired.

By the time the German parachutists had finally been driven off, they had killed about thirty Italian soldiers and captured half a dozen trench mortars.

Not long afterward, Carboni learned that his son Guido had taken three truckloads of arms to the meeting places established by the Communists but had found no one waiting to receive them. Carboni began to suspect the Communists of trying to trick his son. He jumped into Guido's car and set out to check the meeting places.

After making new arrangements for distributing the arms, Carboni returned to his office at Palazzo Caprara. His aide, Lieutenant Lanza, who had made a visit to the German Embassy, reported that the Germans were busy packing their bags, burning secret documents in the garden and making deals with Italians for their cars and bank deposits. In fact, said Lanza, they were so nervous that Military Attaché Rintelen had asked to be protected while leaving Rome. He had asked whether Carboni would issue him a permit so he and his family could leave by plane. The embassy counselor, Baron von Clemm, wanted similar protection and had asked to be received by Carboni as soon as possible.

At this point, Carboni was called to the War Ministry by Ambrosio, who also wanted to know what the Germans were doing. So far, Ambrosio had heard only of small incidents along the coast; on the whole, his impression was that the Germans were tending to withdraw—at least from southern Italy—without attacking.

Carboni told Ambrosio what he had learned from Lanza. What Carboni did *not* say was that the Germans in Rome who were not attached to the embassy, such as SS head Herbert Kappler, had left for Kesselring's headquarters in Frascati. When it was observed that *four* automobiles were sufficient to carry them all, the myth of the giant fifth column in Rome was exploded. Embassy personnel were leaving to take the special diplomatic train that Guariglia had arranged.

Carboni went on to say that since he had not heard from Roatta —who was still transferring the army command from Monterotondo —he had, on his own initiative, alerted the Motorized Corps to the possibility of German attack.

According to Carboni, Ambrosio became very worried. "We must be very careful," he is reported to have said. "It must never be intimated that we were the first to attack. . . . Let the Germans pass if they present themselves without firing."

Later, Ambrosio denied that he had said anything of the kind. He claimed that he had told Carboni to go to his command and take the defense of the capital in hand.

Carboni wandered around the War Ministry. When he tried to see Badoglio, Mario told him that his father was asleep and could not be disturbed.

The king, however, was still awake and sent for Carboni, who was brought to the mezzanine apartment by General Puntoni. The monarch was in a small salon, hunched up on a sofa. Beside him, in an upright armchair, was the queen, her arm around her husband's shoulders. Was it true that the Germans were withdrawing, asked the king.

Carboni replied that the answer was yes, at least as far as the embassy personnel were concerned. The outlook appeared optimistic.

The king was only partially reassured. "Carboni," he asked, "if the Germans attack Rome, will our troops fight?"

"I am certain of my own troops," answered Carboni with assurance. "In fact, if the Germans retire towards the north, Sire, I am ready to pursue them."

As Carboni kissed the queen's hand, the king grasped him by the elbow. "Carboni, we are in your hands," he said.

When word came of the German thrusts, Carboni became less belligerent. The 2nd Parachute Division had moved against Italian defensive positions south of the city. There was fighting at Magliana and Cecchignola, elements of the Piacenza Division had surrendered at Marargone, and other units were yielding under German pressure.

To the north, the German 3rd Panzergrenadieren was moving in three columns along the consular roads of the Cassia, the Aurelia and the Flaminia.

The navy command in Gaeta had been attacked by a unit of the Hermann Goering Panzer Division. Two corvettes that were in the roadstead were captured; the port was occupied, officers taken, and soldiers freed. Calls came into Rome asking for instructions.

Although Ambrosio brushed aside the news as "scattered and uncertain," he issued his order number 24202 to all Italian armed forces. It repeated pro-memoria number 2 and ordered troops not to "take the initiative in hostile acts against the Germans." It was an order which might have had some logic on July 25 but which could only serve to compound the confusion that already existed on September 8.

Back at Palazzo Caprara, Carboni saw Baron von Clemm and gave him and Rintelen the passes they would need in order to leave the capital. Carboni later tried to justify his benevolence as an attempt to secure information, and Ambrosio maintained that he was following Badoglio's instructions; but the Italian armed forces were paying for their commanders' illogical, contradictory actions.

General Ezio Rosi, commander in chief of Army Group East, comprising twelve divisions, was in Albania when he received Ambrosio's 24202. He noted that it ordered troops moved towards the sea and enjoined commanders to "give German commands notice of movements." Naturally enough, Rosi thought that this meant he was supposed to negotiate with the Germans, but when he did, he and his staff were captured.

On the night of September 8, Italian sailors manning eight German submarines in the Baltic port of Gdynia received a cable from the Navy Ministry in Rome: "Destroy the submarines and ask the Germans for free reentry into Italy." It was almost as if the Navy Ministry expected the Germans to congratulate the Italians and send them home to celebrate.

Other orders were delayed until the very last minute. Since the night of September 6, the navy had had twenty-two submarines posted along the route of the probable Allied approach to the Italian coast. Only at nine o'clock on the night of September 8 were they sent orders to limit themselves to exploration. Some submarines, not receiving the order, went out and attacked Allied convoys. Four of them failed to return.

The air force had been preparing to act with the *Luftwaffe* against the Allied landing in the South. Only at 7:30 P.M. on the night of September 8 were Italian planes called back by radio. Four failed to receive the order in time and fought against the Allies. None returned.

In the Salerno area, General Ferrante Gonzaga del Vodice, Commander of the 222nd Coastal Division stationed between Battipaglia and Eboli, had been meeting with his officers when the armistice was announced on the radio. Immediately he sent a message to the commander of the German 16th Panzer Division saying that collaboration had ceased but that he would discuss an agreement for the withdrawal of German troops to the North. The German response was to dispatch planes to bomb the Italians.

The general promptly ordered his men to retreat into caves which had already been prepared as headquarters in the nearby hills. There he was found by an armed party of Germans under Major von Alvensleben. The Italian general was told that his division must either join forces with the Germans or lay down its arms.

"What do you intend doing?" the German major asked.

"My duty," replied Gonzaga. "Cooperate with you so as to prevent incidents among our soldiers."

This answer did not satisfy the Germans. When the major demanded Gonzaga's personal weapons, the general turned to the interior of the cave and shouted, "To arms!" He had taken only a few steps when the Germans started firing. He was hit by two bullets, in the throat and head, and died immediately. The other Italian officers and soldiers were captured.

Following agreement with *Comando Supremo*, General Arisio's entire Seventh Army had been under German General Vietinghoff since August 23 and Arisio himself had read OP 44 to his generals, substituting Communists for Germans. Later, on its way south, the 15th Panzergrenadieren virtually destroyed the Italian Pasubio (9th) Infantry Division, while other divisions along the coast were either torn to pieces by German troops, disarmed, imprisoned or allowed to go home.

That night, unaware of the disintegration of Italian forces, the Allied invasion fleet moved towards its goal. Forty miles off the coast, convoy commanders, sighting Capri, passed orders to change course. They had been sailing north, hoping to delude the Germans, but now they headed into the Gulf of Salerno. The ships' outlines faded in the gathering darkness; soon they were blacked out and only blue lights were visible. The decks were crowded with tanks, trench mortars, armored cars, howitzers and machine guns. As the ships slowly made their way into the gulf, German planes began a series of attacks, but inflicted little damage. Soon the vivid half-moon diminished and the ships were enclosed in darkness.

The beacon submarine H.M.S. *Shakespeare*, which had been in the zone for the past week, raised its periscope and then surfaced. A green light was put on the conning tower to serve as a guide for the incoming craft. At 10 P.M. the beacon lights of inshore reference vessels were sighted. These marked the assault transport area and the convoys gradually moved towards their allotted stations some twelve to twenty miles offshore.

At one minute past midnight, orders rang out, whistles sounded, boats and nets were lowered, and soldiers began to scramble down rope ladders and into landing craft. The first group of landing craft was swung overboard and dropped onto the calm waters.

Behind the long crescent of sand which extended below Salerno, the enemy lay waiting. In the foothills, backed by a jagged mountain, German infantrymen huddled in their foxholes, observers scanned the sea, tank units moved to tactical positions, planes revved up their motors, artillery regiments checked their pieces.

The initial Allied boat waves headed for the rendezvous area three to five miles off the beach. Behind them came more landing craft and amphibious trucks carrying heavy weapons, antitank pieces, crews and ammunition. A few hundred yards off shore, small scout boats slid slowly and methodically through the thickly mined waters. It was 2 A.M.

By now General Roatta had settled himself in an unused office across from the War Ministry; in it was a huge portrait of Mussolini wearing a militia uniform. With folded arms and an imperious look, it stared at Roatta throughout the night.

Contradictory news was arriving; it seemed that many of the Germans did not intend leaving Rome. The XVII Corps reported that more coastal batteries had been lost, taken by surprise.

Roatta still hoped that these were minor moves which would not lead to any attacks in force. He continued to issue defensive orders—

"To acts of force react with acts of force,"—which under the circumstances might be invitations to a massacre. Leaders at the War Ministry also waited, hoping nothing would happen. They had double-crossed the Germans, but maybe now the Germans would be good fellows and go home.

Kesselring could not afford the luxury of effortless waiting. He ordered the pressure stepped up, and his forces moved swiftly toward their first real confrontations.

In the South, General Barenthen had cleared out the initial soft spots, and now he moved vigorously to new ones. At La Magliana, a little after midnight, his men attacked again, but by now the Grenadiers had formed a defensive line. Even so, many of the Italians were firing in earnest for the first time; inexperienced young soldiers and officers, up against trained troops, were easily hit. The Germans seemed to know the exact positions of Italian forces. Officers in motorcycle sidecars accompanied by self-propelled artillery appeared and demanded: "Either a declaration of loyalty to Germany or give up your arms."

At one point, the Germans asked for *pourparlers*, insisting that they only wanted to cross the Magliana bridge to go north. A Grenadier captain, encouraged by Germans shouting *"Kamerati!"* from their trenches, led a squad out to meet them, but as soon as the Italians were in the open, the Germans set off flares to blind them and mowed them down with machine guns.

From that time on, the German action developed with increasing rapidity, although their activity that night remained limited.

Roatta was at his desk at Palazzo Baracchini when Carboni rushed in to say that the Germans were attacking the Grenadiers and that armored cars and artillery were proceeding up the Ostiense towards Rome. Most of the coast had been taken over. The Piacenza had been largely disarmed, partly by persuasion and partly by force, and General Carlo Rossi and his staff had been captured in private homes.

Roatta went to see Ambrosio. In view of the militant attitude of the Germans, he said, wouldn't it be a good idea to warn them that unless their belligerent acts ceased, the Italians would be forced to retaliate? Ambrosio agreed and sent a message to Kesselring's headquarters at 2:10 A.M.: "The 2nd Parachute Division has assumed a hostile attitude towards us. I wish to call your attention to the fact that this can force us to answer in a similar manner although it is our intention to maintain peaceful relations with you."

Just then, Air Chief Sandalli received a call from Lieutenant General Eraldo Ilari, commander of the III Air Squadron, who said that he was on the line to Ciampino airfield, ten miles from Rome, where the Germans were trying to disarm Italian airmen. "Our men are resisting," he said.

Sandalli asked if the Germans had committed acts of violence. Ilari said no, but after a few seconds Sandalli heard a crackling of submachine gunfire over the phone and the line with Ciampino was cut.

More calls from the field poured into the *Comando Supremo*. Milan reported a German attack and asked for instructions. General Cerica, head of the *Carabinieri*, reported that Germans were marching on Tarquinia, north of Rome.

Should OP 44 and its measures for offensive action against the Germans be put into effect? Roatta refused to take the responsibility and sent General Utili across the street to the War Ministry to ask if Ambrosio would order it applied.

Ambrosio said that he could not take such action without first consulting Badoglio, who had forbidden OP 44 to be made operative. Although the marshal was asleep only a few yards away, Ambrosio said that he could not be found. The instructions stood; no initiative was to be taken against the Germans. OP 44 remained a dead letter.

But the pressure from the South was becoming heavier. The Grenadiers were being forced back towards Magliana, and so notified Rome. Worried, Roatta ordered the Ariete to send its Montebello Lancers Armored Regiment and a semipropelled artillery group south to the Grenadiers. Antiaircraft and field artillery units on the right bank of the Tiber were to support the Grenadiers along the Via Ostiense. Roatta told Colonel Giorgio Salvi, Carboni's chief of staff, to issue the orders immediately, without Carboni, who by then was trying to catch a little sleep.

At 3 A.M., word arrived of Germans at Tor Sapienza, five miles from Rome on the Via Prenestina. Although this news was as yet unconfirmed, it disturbed Roatta. A little before 4 A.M., Roatta called Carboni to his office and asked his opinion.

"In the present situation," Carboni replied, "our resistance can't last more than twenty-four hours."

Then he and Roatta examined the situation. The 220th Coastal Division no longer existed, and the Piacenza was in shreds. General Cerica had told Carboni that the 15th Panzergrenadieren Division had been sighted marching north along the Via Appia, seventy miles from the capital. Thus there was concentric action against Rome from at least three of the cardinal points, with the Germans menacing in the North, attacking in the South, and moving in the West.

Now Roatta allowed himself to believe that the capital was about to be surrounded, even though, given the numerous roads, this would represent an almost impossible achievement for two enemy divisions.

When Roatta returned to the War Ministry to tell Ambrosio the latest news, he found him in War Minister Sorice's office. Ambrosio listened, then ordered Roatta to assume the defense of Rome personally. Roatta repeated Carboni's opinion that Rome could not be defended for long, but Ambrosio, while not denying this, said that he was convinced that neither the king nor the government would leave the capital.

In the North, the 3rd Panzergrenadieren Division had made no further moves against the Ariete, but its commander, General Graeser had sent a column southwestward towards the port of Civitavecchia. The Germans' intent was to oppose an eventual Allied landing on the coast, but the result was to render invalid the royal family's plans to leave from Civitavecchia for Sardinia.

Without checking all the reports, Ambrosio finally decided to awaken Badoglio. General Puntoni went to see the king; someone else roused the crown prince. It was 4 A.M.

There was no sign of an American landing near Rome, and as far as the *Comando Supremo* knew, the Allied ships were still at sea, but their aid could yet save the day. Hoping to mitigate American resentment, Badoglio sent Eisenhower an artful radio message: "Missed reception signal agreed wireless and delayed arrival your number 45 . . . proclamation would have occurred as requested even without your pressure being sufficient for us to pledge given stop excessive haste has however found our preparations incomplete and caused delay. . . ."

The Allies were having their own troubles. At Salerno, assault boats had set out for the flat, sandy shore at the same time that the *Luftwaffe* had started bombing and strafing. Under a curtain of fire from Allied ships, troops left their boats and hit the beaches. First ashore, at 3:10 A.M., were three American Ranger battalions. Then at H-hour, 3:30 A.M., British army commandos came ashore to their right.

The sea was still crowded with flat-prowed craft carrying more troops, armored cars, antiaircraft batteries, cranes and metal runways.

Stukas divebombed the ships; some of them were hit and soldiers threw their equipment into the sea and swam to the beach. Other vessels either had to change course or withdraw.

Many of the troops in the initial waves met no resistance at first, but then encountered well-defended positions which could only be taken by hand-to-hand combat. As they cut their way through barbed-wire fences, German machine guns opened fire, bombs and mines exploded, German guns threw shells against the still-approaching landing craft, and planes passed overhead firing rockets until the beach became an illuminated hell. Further assault waves landed on the beach while the Germans laid artillery barrages into them from batteries in the hills, then followed up with counterattacks led by tank formations.

General Mark Clark had counted on catching the Germans by surprise, but it was the Allies who were surprised. The unforeseen dispersion of Italian divisions meant that the Allies were deprived of their needed aid and the Germans freed for maneuvers. The euphoria following the armistice announcement, the lack of experienced soldiers available for the landing, the shortage of landing craft, the tactical errors in planning, all these combined with Clark's insistence on withholding preliminary naval bombardment, put his men in a perilous position. The Allied troops were in danger of being forced back into the sea.

As though sensing that no help would arrive, Italy's leaders in Rome prepared to save their skins. It was obvious that the Germans were not leaving, and if Italian troops attacked them, reprisal would be certain. Until then, having been told not to provoke the Germans, they had been restrained. Now it would be better to move the troops defending Rome out of the Germans' way.

This had probably all been decided by the time General Roatta, on his way back to his office, saw Crown Prince Umberto and stopped to speak to him. Almost immediately Badoglio, Ambrosio, Sorice and General Puntoni came in. At Ambrosio's request, Roatta expanded on his belief that the Germans were about to surround Rome. There was no sign of the Allies and, all things considered, it seemed to him that the best course was not to expose the king and government to the possibility of capture.

"Gentlemen," said Roatta, "if the Germans get hold of us, they'll shoot us all. Why should we let ourselves get shot?"

There was one road free, Roatta added, the Tiburtina.

Badoglio, having learned from the crown prince that his father was not asleep, went to the king and found him listening to General Puntoni, who was repeating Roatta's information to him. Badoglio did not have to do much talking to convince the monarch. After a few minutes he returned and said that the king had decided. Then Badoglio said that he, the royal family, Acquarone, Ambrosio, the chiefs of staff and the military ministers would leave Rome—by the Via Tiburtina—and meet later that day at Pescara, 170 miles away, on the Adriatic coast.

Troops defending Rome would cease resistance, withdraw to the east and reassemble near the ancient city of Tivoli, twenty-four miles east of Rome.

When Sorice asked who would run the government, Badoglio told him to have Minister of the Interior Umberto Ricci set up a caretaker cabinet. No other government ministers, outside of military ones, were informed; in any event, most of them, moved by fear, were sleeping away from their homes. Perhaps Badoglio thought that the Germans would allow the rest of the government to carry on; other than Foreign Minister Guariglia, no one had known of the negotiations and therefore bore no responsibility for them. But when Ricci was found, he refused the job on the grounds that he had not been informed about the armistice.

As yet, no real battles with the Germans had broken out. The northern front was quiet, and in the South the Germans had not been able to break through the Grenadiers' defense to any appreciable degree. Some soldiers, weapons and positions had been lost, but Rome's defenses had yet to be really tested.

Ambrosio called Admiral De Courten and told him that he was to join the others at Pescara and to route ships there instead of to Civitavecchia as previously planned. The air force was instructed to concentrate as many planes as possible at the Pescara airport.

Then Ambrosio issued an order naming Brigadier General Vittorio Palma the responsible head of the *Comando Supremo* in Rome, but no one could locate him. General Silvio Rossi later testified, "No orders were left for General Palma."

As Badoglio, preparing to join the king, headed towards an elevator, Ambrosio managed to catch up with him.

"Perhaps you too, marshal, want to leave some orders?"

"Yes, of course," Badoglio murmured. For a moment he remained wrapped in thought. Then he said, "No, nothing," took the elevator downstairs, and got into his car.

Castellano shakes hands with General Dwight Eisenhower after signing

Frascati after the September 8, 1943, bombing, which killed 6,000 people after the armistice had been signed

Fighting at Porta San Paolo on September 10, 1943

Porta San Paolo, September 10, 1943. Raffaele Persichetti, the tall figure at right in civilian clothes, reporting for duty

Chapter 35

THE FLIGHT

At 5:10 A.M., Vittorio Emanuele III stood before his grey-green Fiat 2800. "Have all orders been issued?" he asked. Badoglio nodded. "I am an old man," added the king. "What can they do to me?"

Then the chauffeur-driven limousine, bearing the king's standard as first marshal of Italy, left the courtyard. Seated inside were the queen, General Puntoni and Lieutenant Colonel de Buzzaccarini, aide-de-camp on duty. Next came the queen's car, another chauffeur-driven Fiat 2800, carrying Badoglio, his nephew Colonel Valenzano and the duke of Acquarone, who had asked for a lift at the last moment. Two Fiat 1100s with the royal family's luggage, the king's valet and the queen's maid came next, followed by two Fiat 1500s—one belonging to General Puntoni, driven by his orderly, and one belonging to Crown Prince Umberto's aide, General Gamerra, with another orderly at the wheel. Last came Umberto's Alfa Romeo, driven by a sergeant, with the crown prince, General Gamerra and two aides seated inside.

The two destroyers Ambrosio had previously ordered were left

O

waiting at Civitavecchia, as were the motor launches which were standing by at Fiumicino to carry the royal party to them. Admiral Luigi Sansonetti, navy deputy chief of staff, ordered the cruiser *Scipione* and the corvettes *Scimitarra* and *Baionetta* to leave their respective ports on the Adriatic and head at full speed for Pescara, where they were to "take a high personage aboard."

There remained a glimmer of hope that the Allies would sweep northward from Salerno and take Rome. War Minister Sorice even decided to stay in Rome. "Remain hidden for a few days," he told the others, "then come back."

A little later, General Sandalli was in the War Ministry looking for Ambrosio. "I was certain," he later said, "that the order not to attack the Germans first was a tactical and strategic error. In the position of material inferiority in which we found ourselves, we were leaving to the adversary the possibility of choosing when and where to hit us."

Suddenly, in the hall, he came face to face with Ambrosio.

"What!" exclaimed Ambrosio. "How come you're still here? The king has left, Badoglio and the government. The chiefs of staff are to leave as well, immediately. We meet at Pescara."

When Ambrosio went down the stairs to the ground floor, Sandalli sought clarification from Sorice.

"Has war with Germany been declared?" he asked.

"No, but there have been some encounters," replied Sorice.

"Serious?" asked Sandalli.

"No, not especially," answered Sorice.

"Then why is everyone going to Pescara?"

"It's on the only road not controlled by the Germans."

The logic of this escaped Sandalli, but he promptly ordered his deputy to take over and prepared to leave for Pescara.

Major Marchesi, called from a cot at *Comando Supremo*, was told by General Ambrosio to burn compromising papers, gather the nucleus of an operations office and be out of Rome by 7 A.M. He left for Centocelle airport with five or six officers, three noncoms, British Lieutenant Mallaby and an Italian wireless operator who carried the clandestine radio link with Eisenhower's headquarters. Their plane, piloted by Major Vassallo, took off in the midst of a grey haze, followed by the other craft based at the field, all bound for Pescara.

Carboni was awakened and summoned to Roatta's office, where Roatta was writing something on a sheet of notebook paper. The army chief looked up, took off his pince-nez, and said, "Carboni, you'll have to concentrate all troops defending Rome at Tivoli. The king has already left."

Zanussi, who had come into the office, started to object. Roatta pointed out that Carboni had said prolonged resistance was impossible. "The retreat can be carried out. Isn't that so, Carboni?"

The young general stretched out his arms in a vague gesture. "Aren't you going to give me a proper order?"

"Not in an emergency like this. Here," Roatta said, handing Carboni his scribbled notes. "It's a drumhead order. Have it filled out properly."

Carboni started to protest that he could not carry out the instructions as his troops were already engaged with the Germans, but Roatta insisted that they be disengaged promptly.

As far as can be made out today, the original hand-written order read as follows:

5:15 A.M.—9 September 1943
To the Command of Motorized Army Corps.
By order of the Supreme Command:
The situation is such to exclude the defense of the capital.
Consequently only police forces will remain in Rome for the maintenance of order.
The Motorized Corps is to withdraw immediately to Tivoli and, beyond it, take up positions facing east.
Retreat in groups, in order.
All troops at present in Rome will pass to the orders of General Carboni.

Chief of Staff of the Army

When Carboni took the scribbled note to his office, Colonel Salvi pointed out the difficulties in carrying out such an operation. "There's nothing else to do," Carboni answered, "even His Majesty is there."

After protesting further against the inopportune order, Salvi broke it down into numbered paragraphs, had it typed by a major, and took it to Roatta's office. The army chief was absent. His deputy, General De Stefanis, checked the text, revised it further, had it retyped, and then signed it.

Now it read:

1.   . . . any prolonged resistance [against German troops marching on Rome] will expose the city and its inhabitants to grave and useless losses.
2.   Therefore, troops engaged in the defense of Rome (internal and

external), which you will take under orders, will be withdrawn to Tivoli and the nearby zone . . .

3. . . . assume positions to the east, straddling Tivoli . . .

4. Orient yourself to continue the movement eventually to the east . . .

5. *Carabinieri* and police to remain in Rome . . .

6. Transfer your command to Tivoli where we will contact you.

> Signed for the Chief of Staff of the Army
> General De Stefanis

General Carboni has always maintained that these copies were false, that after the introduction it really read: "Therefore the troops of the mobile defense (Ariete and Piave Divisions) will retreat to Tivoli taking up positions on the high ground adjacent there, to face east. . . . Orient yourself to continue the movement eventually to the east. . . . Transfer your command to Tivoli [*Carabinieri* barracks] where you will contact us. The Grenadiers Division will remain at the defense of Rome but will no longer be at the orders of the Motorized Corps."

While the two first versions differed only in form, Carboni's contained substantial modifications. The striking differences lay in Carboni's responsibility for the defense of Rome, in the troops that were to be under his command, and in who was to contact whom at Tivoli. The additional phrase at the end, excluding the Grenadiers, obviously meant that Carboni would be free to leave the capital and therefore would *not* be responsible for the capital's defense.

However, subordinate commands, including the Grenadiers, received orders which conformed more nearly to the two first versions than to Carboni's, and in 1949 the military tribunal of Rome confirmed this, saying that "the assumption of General Carboni, absolutely isolated in contrast with all those involved, does not appear reliable." So, to all intents and purposes, the responsibility for the defense of Rome passed at 5:15 A.M. from the chief of staff of the army to General Carboni.

For years, people have wondered why this movement of troops to Tivoli was ordered. Was it in the hope that Italian troops, having left the city to the Germans, would be able to regroup, return to the capital, and reconquer it, a virtual impossibility unless the Allies showed up in force? Or was it to have these troops continue to retreat to the East, to the mountainous region of Abruzzi? If so, why? How were they to be supplied?

The more Carboni thought over the order, the more confused he became. Even if the transfer could be effected, why were the troops being moved to Tivoli? Just to protect the king? Would royal headquarters be set up there?

Carboni returned to Roatta's office for clarification, but Roatta accompanied by Zanussi had already gone to the War Ministry. There he saw Ambrosio, who was about to leave. It was 5:45 A.M. Roatta dashed back to his office for a moment, then climbed into Ambrosio's car. Only after they were a half hour out of Rome did Ambrosio tell him that they were bound for Pescara.

The generals' convoy was accompanied by two armored cars. In the first was Zanussi; in the last, two of Zanussi's officers. As the column pulled away, most of the soldiers in front of the ministry stared at it stonily, not saluting, keeping their hands in their pockets.

By now the king's cortege had passed through the Porta San Lorenzo and entered Via Tiburtina. Because of the still uncertain light—the sun was about to rise—the cars proceeded with only their parking lights on. In the royal car, no one spoke. In the crown prince's Alfa Romeo, Umberto hid his head in his hands. "My God, what a figure we're cutting," he said.

The column was stopped several times, twice at German checkpoints, but waved on after de Buzzaccarini said, "General officers."

A little past Tivoli, the queen's car broke down. The water pump had burst. General Puntoni's small car was halted, and its occupants and the luggage were left on the side of the road with the assurance that another car would be along soon (it never did arrive). Badoglio moved into the crown prince's car while one of the officers joined Acquarone and Valenzano in the 1500.

When Prince Umberto saw Badoglio shaking, supposedly with cold, he took off his army greatcoat and gave it to him. Badoglio put it on, but after a moment Umberto saw him furtively roll up the sleeves to hide the insignia of rank. "If the Germans catch me, who knows to which of these trees they'll hang me," Badoglio said, nodding at the poplars which lined the road.

Other cars were leaving Rome as if competing in a rally. The generals were more concerned with getting out of the capital than with issuing instructions. Precautions were taken to burn any piece of paper which might prove embarrassing, including the only copies of OP 44 and Castellano's letter to Ambrosio from Cassibile.

General De Stefanis left at seven ten with another army general. An hour later, General Utili finished sorting documents to be burned or taken along and prepared to leave. When someone inquired about his departure, he answered, "I'm not such an idiot as to stay." Earlier, he had been more precise. Referring to the generals, he had said, "There's nothing to do with these gentlemen, they'll let all of Italy, Rome, the Army, the population, go to the dogs. You can't change their mentality." At eight fifteen, he too left Rome, taking with him three lieutenant colonels and other officers of his command.

Carboni moved even before seeing what Salvi was doing with the troop transferral orders. Hurrying to his SIM offices, he ordered some documents destroyed, then went home and changed into civilian clothes. From there he telephoned General Solinas, who was commander of the Grenadier Division, despite the fact that Carboni later maintained that the division no longer was his. Ignoring the fact that Solinas' men were already fighting, Carboni told him to act on his own initiative if necessary.

Returning to SIM, Carboni emptied the safe, filling a small suitcase with over a thousand pounds sterling, around $130,000 in lire and all the jewels he could lay his hands on.

Then with his son, Captain Guido Carboni, Lieutenant Lanza and his aide, Captain Gola, he climbed into one of the SIM cars with diplomatic plates that the intelligence organization kept hidden for emergencies. Driving out on the Tiburtina, the car came to Bagni di Tivoli, the ancient thermal baths were Caesar and Augustus had taken the sulphurous waters. This was the headquarters of one of Carboni's divisions, the Centauro. Although it was commanded by fifty-six-year-old Major General Count Carlo Calvi di Bergolo, the king's son-in-law and the only member of the royal house who had not been relieved of his command, Carboni made no effort to see him. Instead, he traveled eight miles farther, to the hill town of Tivoli.

Carboni has always maintained that he set out to find Roatta at the latter's orders. However, testimony of most of those involved indicates that these had not been Roatta's instructions. Carboni was to go to Tivoli to take command of the troops that would be assembling there. That he went before he had seen to the transfer of his troops was a definite breach of military conduct. Carboni explains this by saying that he went to inspect the zone, but for the commander of an army corps to leave in order to do something which could easily have been accomplished by a staff officer was unthinkable. Besides, as head of SIM, Carboni was also responsible for the internal defense of the capital.

Reaching Tivoli at about 8 A.M., Carboni stopped at the *Carabinieri* barracks but found no indication that the column had halted. Further inquiries failed to uncover any news of the generals, although he was told that Admiral De Courten had been seen driving through Tivoli at around 7:30 A.M. The admiral had left Rome at 6:30 A.M. and had caught up with the king's cortege several hours later.

General Sandalli, driving his own car, had headed for the Guidonia airfield to take a plane. However, just before Bagni di Tivoli, he came across a column of German troops. Thinking that the airport, which was nearby, might be occupied, he continued on. He passed Carboni and Lanza, but did not speak to them. Twenty miles later, Sandalli caught up with the king and Badoglio.

The generals had not been traced by Carboni because they had taken, for reasons best known to Ambrosio, a roundabout route. Leaving Rome by Via Nomentana, they had traveled northeast to the little town of Mentana, fifteen miles from the capital. Here where Garibaldi had been defeated in 1867 when he had tried to seize Rome, the generals' column turned east; at the hill town of Palombara, they came down through the Sabine hills to rejoin the Tiburtina, past Tivoli.

By now thoroughly confused, Carboni followed the Tiburtina until he arrived at Arsoli, fifteen miles beyond Tivoli, where he heard that several cars had passed. He sent Lieutenant Lanza ahead to see if he could trace the elusive group. At a railroad crossing, Lanza caught up with Roatta and asked him if he had any orders. The army chief said that Carboni was to carry on and that he had no other orders to give.

Returning to Arsoli, Lanza transmitted Roatta's vague message. Seeing that Carboni was puzzled as to what his next step should be, the young lieutenant mentioned that a friend of his, movie producer Carlo Ponti, was in the process of making a movie in the local castle of the Massimos. The picture, *Arrow in the Side*, starred Vittorio Gassman and the extremely attractive Mariella Loti, Lanza's girlfriend. According to Lanza, there were large cellars in the castle which could provide excellent shelter.

Carboni agreed, and they promptly set out for the castle.

Just before they reached the castle, they met Carlo Ponti. Lanza asked the producer if he could put them up. Ponti said that he did not think that Arsoli was the place, but that he could offer them hospitality. Ponti was introduced to Carboni, who asked if he might make a phone call. Ponti accompanied Carboni to the *Carabinieri* barracks, where the general made two calls, identifying himself as Colonel Della Martina. First he called the *Carabinieri* at Tivoli, to see if any troops had arrived. The second call was to a number in Rome which Ponti recognized as that of movie actress Clara Calamai.

Ponti later testified: "From the attitude and the requests made to me, I had the conviction that General Carboni wanted to hide. My friend [Gianfranco] Casnedi who was present had the same impression; so much so that speaking with some friends and in the presence of General Carboni's driver, he said that if all generals behaved like that, Italy was finished."

Despite Ponti's attempts to dissuade him, Carboni, accompanied by Lanza, entered the castle and went to the apartment occupied by Mariella Loti. Lanza greeted his girlfriend with the words, "You must save us."

The actress replied that she could not accept the responsibility of causing danger and embarrassment to her friends. According to Mariella Loti, General Carboni took no part in the conversation. She asked them to leave, as their presence was putting the lives of her colleagues in jeopardy.

Here the story becomes rather confused. Carboni has maintained different things at different times; he has even said that he went to the castle only to see if the king could be sheltered there. He has also testified, "When I arrived at the castle, still looking for Roatta, I was surprised to see it invaded by movie-makers. I wanted to leave immediately but it was becoming a problem to contact Rome. Therefore, urged by the pressure of Mariella Loti, fiancée of Lieutenant Lanza di Trabia, and because of the insistence of the latter, I decided to spend the night at the castle."

According to Generals Calvi di Bergolo and Oscar Gritti, the real reason for Carboni's trip to Tivoli was his desire to leave with the fleeing generals. Unable to catch up with them, he decided to find shelter for himself. For one reason or another, possibly because his reception was not as warm as he would have liked, he decided to leave but not to return to Rome.

Chapter 36

WHO DEFENDS ROME?

On the morning of September 9, Emilio Schuberth was up early. Looking out the window, he saw that the street below was full of military vehicles. Only a handful of soldiers were on the scene, lounging around in a far from military manner. When he went out for his morning walk, he found the normally crowded Via Nazionale, where he went to buy newspapers, empty.

Back in his apartment, Schuberth's phone, which usually rang incessantly, was silent. Maybe, he thought, people were afraid of what they might hear from one another. Yet, as he opened his newspapers, he read only calming news. In the center of the front page, Schuberth saw war bulletin number 1201, signed by Ambrosio. The Italo-German air force had damaged five enemy ships totaling twenty-eight thousand tons at the port of Bizerte and shot down ten Allied planes during the bombing of southern Italy. "On the Calabrian front," it went on, "Italian and German units in local fighting are delaying the advance of British troops." There was no word of the bombing the day before which had taken six thousand lives at Frascati.

Above the war bulletin, Schuberth was perplexed to discover black headlines announcing the armistice and saying that hostilities between the Italians and the Anglo-Americans had ended. *Il Messaggero* called Badoglio "the great soldier who with firmness and courage had assumed the responsibility of the government," then continued on in a similarly laudatory vein.

Schuberth turned on his radio, but it provided even less information than the newspapers had. Journalist Gianni Cagianelli later described the radio as "a wall: everything that happened was ignored, submerged by a wave of songs that filled the few hours of broadcasting."

Four doors away from Schuberth, at Motorized Corps headquarters at Palazzo Caprara, a remarkable scene was taking place. Its chief of staff, Colonel Salvi, had just learned that Carboni had left Rome, and faced with the onerous duty of transmitting the incredible orders for retreat to divisional commanders, he had panicked. He had prepared the detailed instructions, but instead of issuing them he tried to get the original order revoked.

At seven thirty he went to General Utili and asked for guidance. Carboni was dead, lamented Salvi in the throes of hysteria. Who, he asked, could he get to sign the orders to the divisional commanders? Utili, busy preparing for his own departure, was not much help. He suggested that Salvi get the senior general in the corps to do it. This would be General Calvi di Bergolo, but the king's son-in-law replied that he would not sign the orders unless he received a written statement from Salvi giving Carboni's whereabouts and incorporating the request that General Calvi assume responsibility for the defense of Rome.

By this time, Salvi had gone virtually to pieces. Alone in his office, he burst into tears and wrung his hands. He had not even known that Roatta had left, and he learned about it from an officer who reported having seen Roatta in the Abruzzi. "We're abandoned by everybody," Salvi cried. When General Solinas of the Grenadiers came in for precise instructions, Salvi told him, "The cowards! They've all escaped and left me alone." To others he shouted that Carboni had gone off with the king and Badoglio.

Finally Salvi issued the instructions for the retreat, but by then the divisional commanders were confused, disturbed, pessimistic and distrustful.

When General Tabellini of the Piave received a copy, it seemed so absurd that he believed it must have been garbled in transmission. He sent his chief of staff to Palazzo Caprara for clarification and refused to accept his confirmation although he was told that similar instructions had been given to the Ariete. Even after a motorcyclist arrived with a written order, Tabellini, unable to accept the idea of taking a whole division away from Rome, delayed execution. He did, however, see that the Piave was prepared for movement.

At 9 A.M., Tabellini received word from a forward post at Ponte del Grillo, off Via Salaria on the banks of the Tiber, that German paratroopers had landed in force near there and at Monterotondo. Fifty Junker 52s had dropped some eight hundred paratroopers with the intention of moving on Monterotondo and capturing Roatta and his army staff.

The paratroopers, who had just come from Norway, had been launched in what was regarded as a successful operation—only eighteen had missed their drop zone and drowned in the Tiber. Though temporarily isolated, the Italian troops were fighting back, helped by civilians. The men of Monterotondo opened fire from behind trees, from windows, from doorways, from dining rooms and from terraces and balconies. Most of them were experienced hunters, and they inflicted heavy losses on the Germans; by the end of the day there were three hundred Germans dead. This slowed down the paratroops, but their leader, Major Gericke, placed women and children who had been taken prisoner at the front of his troops and started advancing toward the Orsini Castle at the highest point of the town. Slowly, relentlessly, the Germans moved ahead, house by house.

Now Tabellini ordered his 58th Infantry Battalion, reinforced by artillery, to move immediately to Monterotondo, while another battalion was sent to free the stronghold at Ponte del Grillo. At the Monterotondo railway station, two units of the Re Division hurriedly formed and marched to the town, where they joined the battle. When units of the Piave and *Carabinieri* showed up, they held their own throughout the day; with civilian aid, they even succeeded in destroying a German unit at Mentana.

To the north, in the early hours of the morning, the Ariete had been in line between Via Cassia and Via Claudia when German motorcyclists of the 3rd Panzergrenadieren approached an advance unit at Lake Monterosi, thirty miles north of Rome. They asked passage to go south and were refused. At dawn, a German armored column drove up and a German colonel gave the Italians exactly fifteen minutes in which to let his armored cars pass.

Twenty-three-year-old Second Lieutenant Ettore Rosso, commanding a platoon of the 134th Engineers Battalion on the bridge at the entrance to the town of Monterosi, used the time to connect a minefield to a single detonator. After sending the rest of his men away, he hid behind a barricade with four volunteers. The Germans advanced, and Rosso let them come forward. When they were up to the barricade, Rosso plunged the detonator. The explosion blew up the bridge, along with Lieutenant Rosso, his four men and thirteen Germans, including the colonel commanding the column.

It was at about that time that the Ariete was told to retreat, but General Cadorna refused to comply. "I am fighting," he said. "I refuse to disengage."

His forward units at Manziana and Bracciano were also being attacked. How could he turn his men around? Cadorna was furious; he had asked for air support and none had come.

The man left in command of the air force, deputy chief of staff Brigadier General Giuseppe Santoro, had only returned the night before with the air force command, which had been transferred from Palestrina. When he had received the request to send planes against German columns, he had passed the order to the III Air Squadron— which had more than 120 fighters and bombers in central Italy—saying that the actions were to be preceded by air reconnaissance. The planes took off but were unable to contact Italian commands for the identification of armed units. Santoro chose to wait for new orders from the army, which never arrived.

The absence of Sandalli, the only air official familiar with the armistice clauses, meant that Santoro, who was to execute them, was at a loss as to how to behave. His rather vague instructions, now superseded by events, left him no choice but to send the planes left at Rome to Pescara, even though they were also being awaited at Allied airports.

The navy was in the same position. According to Commodore Dick's memorandum the fleet was to go to Malta but Ambrosio had assured the navy command that it could go to La Maddalena.

The result was that from that time on there was no record of military collaboration between the Italian army and its air force or navy, although individual airmen, making personal decisions, flew sorties against the Germans.

The army, however, continued to hold its own; it suffered some losses and enjoyed some gains. Towards midnight on September 8, a detachment of colonial police under Major Giovanni Licari had reached a stronghold on the Magliana road held by the 13th Artillery Regiment of the Grenadiers. A German parachute officer had appeared, assuring Licari that he had no intention of firing on the Italians; he and his men wanted to reach Rome, he said, because they were being chased by the English, who had landed at Ostia. While they were talking, the German troops attacked, killing thirteen men and capturing seventeen.

The Italians had withdrawn, but at dawn on September 9, Licari's men, along with the Grenadiers, a unit of *Carabinieri* cadets, and some of the semipropelled guns of the Montebello Lancers, had reconquered the stronghold.

A short while later, a Grenadiers battalion, led by Major D'Ambrosio and supported by armored units of the Montebello Lancers, regained the captured strongpoint of E. 42.

Then things worsened. The village of La Magliana was lost when the Germans, waving a white flag, tricked their way in and killed the company commander. German forces moved towards the Magliana Bridge, on the way capturing Lieutenant Colonel Giuseppe Ammassari, commander of a mortar battalion. Using him as a shield, they made him advance towards the bridge while behind him they pointed their guns at the Italians and a loudspeaker blared: "Don't shoot, your commander is in front of us!"

At the sight of their officer, the Italians hesitated. When the loudspeaker was silent for a moment, Ammassari stopped in his tracks. "Fire!" he shouted. "Don't worry about me. Fire!"

The soldiers obeyed, and Ammassari miraculously escaped; the Italian resistance continued.

The situation south of the capital remained essentially unchanged. All the main roads leading to Rome were still in the hands of the Italians and the fighting was in their favor. The Germans were still practicing more or less peaceful infiltration and were attacking only sporadically. They were also having difficulties with the remnants of the Piacenza, mainly because Italian civilians fought alongside soldiers.

Meanwhile, army and corps commanders were calling *Comando Supremo*—from Naples, from Padua, from Milan, from Bolzano—asking if they were to fight against the Germans.

The night before, a green and red rocket had soared into the sky over the Upper Tyrol, the signal for German troops to seize control of Italy's northern frontier. In the valleys of the Dolomites, German artillery started firing at Italian strongholds. The occasion had been planned well in advance with the complicity of pro-German Tyroleans, who had hidden armored cars, ammunition depots and German soldiers in their houses, stables and haystacks.

Northern Italian anti-Fascists had warned Rome but nothing had been done. By morning, the German 44th Division had taken over General Gloria's XXXV Corps headquarters at Bolzano, while a column occupied Bologna later the same day.

Other distress calls came in from Yugoslavia and from Greece, with unit and garrison commanders making continuous and frantic requests for clarification and instructions: "The German commander demands the disarmament of my troops," they would ask. "What shall I do?"

When officers in Rome did reply, they seemed more concerned with concealing the fact that the Supreme Command did not exist than with transmitting orders: "We have no orders," they would insist. "You will receive orders. . . . We can tell you nothing. . . . There's no one here."

A few generals were still around, but their number was being rapidly depleted. General Aliberti left at 9:30 A.M., along with two dozen officers of his staff. Others who had not been given orders also left to catch up with their fleeing chiefs.

General Vittorio Ruggiero, commander of the garrison of Milan managed to catch General Odone in Rome. "What am I to do?" asked the general from Milan.

"Ruggiero," replied Odone, "you decide. Everyone here has left."

General Caracciolo, Fifth Army commander, was able to contact an officer of the Supreme Command, Colonel Torsiello, who advised him: "Do not attack, but if you are attacked, fight back."

In other words, put OP 44 into execution. Since the Germans had initiated hostilities in various places, Caracciolo immediately ordered counterattacks made, in the hope of reducing the pressure on Rome. Unable to reach many of his subordinate commands, he himself went to the railway station of Tarquinia, where three battalions of the Lupi Division had arrived only to find no orders waiting for them. Caracciolo left his artillery commander, General Tosatto, in charge of the men, but when he returned to his headquarters at Orte, he found that squads of the 3rd Panzergrenadieren had disarmed his drivers at gunpoint and taken their cars.

After asking in vain for their release, he took a rifle and, ordering his aides to do the same, opened fire. Caracciolo described the scene:

> The Germans took cover in a house opposite and returned fire. I ordered groups of *Carabinieri* and Grenadiers to join in. The firing increased. A civilian presented himself to me, shaking, red in the face: "General, give me a rifle. I have five children but I'm prepared to risk my skin to fight the Germans." A German officer and some men were injured, and in the end they gave up and retreated. In our possession were trophies of war; one of their motorcycles, a machine gun and other matériel. The German lieutenant later died in the hospital at Orte.

Now requests for orders, for reinforcements, were flooding into his command post. Even garrisons in Lazio, the province of Rome, asked him for help. Realizing no guidance could be had from Rome, Caracciolo assumed responsibility for these troops on his own initiative.

He was handicapped, as were all Italian field commanders, by the fact that superior orders had been drafted, delayed, altered, distributed, countermanded, repeated, annulled and sometimes eventually disregarded. Each command was left to its own devices, and decisions were made more difficult by the fact that the armistice had come just when many major commands were being moved, generals transferred, and troops assembled, shifted and reorganized. The XIX Army Corps near Naples was caught while moving into "a better strategic position to meet the Salerno landing," and it, like most of the Seventh Army, was dismantled by the Germans. When army headquarters at Potenza was seized, the garrison commander, Deputy Chief of Staff Colonel Giovanni Paccin, was so distraught at seeing his troops overpowered that he killed himself.

Foggia, too, was taken, and its commander, General Giovanni Caperdoni, tried to commit suicide, but the bullet he aimed at his temple, instead of killing him, left him blind. The Germans moved hurriedly, trying to secure bases for support so as to keep communications free and to accumulate as many motor vehicles as they possibly could.

At Salerno, Vietinghoff was proceeding on his own. By daylight, realizing that the major Allied forces had come to Salerno and that no other major assault was likely, he decided not to withdraw to Rome but to repel the invasion. Unable to establish contact with Kesselring, he ordered the rest of General Hube's XIV Panzer Corps (the Hermann Goering and 15th Panzer Divisions) to Salerno. However, General Hube was on leave, and the acting commander, who was also unable to contact Kesselring, felt too insecure to execute Vietinghoff's order. At noon Kesselring was reached; he approved Vietinghoff's order and the XIV Panzer Corps started moving.

Meanwhile, the 16th Panzers, with little more than one hundred tanks and thirty-six assault guns, and lacking both combat experience and fuel, were still managing to fight off the Allies.

Near Rome, the Italians were holding their own, but under strange circumstances. The huge base of Cecchignola, between E. 42 and the sea, was a veritable city. The announcement of the armistice had found it with a new commander, who immediately called together the men at his disposal: about one hundred reserve officers—almost all Romans—about fifty noncommissioned officers and a few dozen soldiers. Weapons were distributed even though there were only a few muskets and hand grenades and no cannon. German 88s began firing from Ostia and continued through the night. Then, in the morning, German patrols and snipers appeared.

Inside Cecchignola, volunteers formed squads to repel the attacks. The first squad to go out was successful in reoccupying a fortified position that the Germans had taken. In the action, twenty-one-year-old Roman artilleryman Paolo Spinelli was killed, and in a similar action, a few minutes later, another twenty-year-old artilleryman died. The Germans continued to advance; more Italians lost their lives in the ensuing hand-to-hand combat.

The officers met to decide what to do. Telephone lines outside had been cut; the base, they decided, would have to surrender. Before taking such drastic decision, they sent a soldier out to see what the situation was. To everyone's surprise, he returned to report that the Germans, impressed by the resistance of the base, had passed around it and moved on towards Rome. To avoid detection by the Germans, the Italians waited for nightfall and then crept through fields until they reached the Grenadiers headquarters at the gates of Rome.

Most of Rome moved in a nervous atmosphere of uncertainty. People were worried: "Will the armistice defend us from the Germans?" It was noted that Badoglio's villa was closed and no longer guarded by soldiers and armored cars.

Early that morning, the Communists, led by Luigi Longo, had finally received weapons from General Carboni, but the armistice had caused the cancellation of the big insurrectional plan. At 8 A.M., the

Communist Party Central Committee met in the Via Ovidio studio of writer Fabrizio Onofri and agreed that the anti-Fascist committee should be transformed into a committee for national liberation.

Giorgio Amendola had gone from there to the Ministry of Corporations on Via Veneto and found it virtually abandoned. "I opened the door of the minister's office," he told Manlio Cancogni, "and I saw, seated at the desk, a man holding his head in his hands. It was Piccardi. This is the image I retain of the armistice."

Minister Piccardi, who had learned of the armistice during the night, had been awakened at 5:30 A.M. by Pietro Baratono, under secretary to the cabinet.

"You know what they've done?" Baratono had said, half-jokingly. "They've left."

At nine o'clock, Piccardi went to the Viminale where what he described as "a strange and grotesque council of ministers" took place. This was under the reluctant presidency of Senator Ricci, minister of the interior, who early that morning had been handed the file left for him by Badoglio. It contained a copy of the armistice and nothing else—no explanation, no instructions.

Other members of the government knew even less. Some had found out about the armistice by reading their newspapers, while others had heard about it on the radio and still others had been told about it by people in their offices.

The ministers reached no conclusion. Accompanied by Amendola, Piccardi went to the meeting of the anti-Fascist committee at Via Adda and told his friends that he was no longer a member of the Badoglio ministry but a citizen at the disposition of the committee.

Approving the Communists' proposal, the committee changed its name to that of National Liberation, elected Bonomi president, called on Italians "to reconquer for Italy the place it deserves in the community of free nations," and sent still another delegation to the Viminale for information and reassurance.

The delegation consisted of Bonomi and his chief aide, Meuccio Ruini. They met with Minister of the Interior Ricci in the presence of Under Secretary Baratono, Chief of Police Senise and an unidentified general. Bonomi said that he had been told that the government was leaving Rome and asked if it were true. Ricci was indignant; the members of the government, he said, would remain, but even as he talked he was taking papers from his desk, tearing them up, and throwing them in the wastepaper basket.

Bonomi and Ruini asked about the possibility of resisting a German invasion. Ricci's answer was that in case of a German attack "it will be necessary not to exasperate the invaders."

Now into the breach came Marshal Enrico Caviglia, that day a private citizen, and long out of the fray. Still not knowing what had happened but suspecting the worst, he had gone that morning to keep his appointment at the Quirinal Palace; no one had been there, not even guards. He had then gone to the War Ministry, where he had been unable to locate a responsible official. By chance he met Lieutenant General Vittorio Sogno, a corps commander stationed in Albania who had come to Rome in civilian clothes to obtain orders. Sogno said that he had looked for General Barbieri, commander of the Territorial Command of Rome, but that he was not to be found. Carboni too had disappeared, Sogno said, although he had been placed in command of the forces around Rome.

Then Caviglia went to Palazzo Caprara, where he met Colonel Salvi. Salvi, his eyes swollen from the tears he had shed, told Caviglia that he did not know where Carboni had gone. Caviglia moved on to Palazzo Barrachini, army staff headquarters. There he saw only some noncoms, a few soldiers on guard and, as he later wrote in his diary: ". . . an oil painting of Mussolini in uniform, a very mediocre work."

It was obvious that there was no one in command and Caviglia decided to act on his own responsibility, capitalizing on his prestige as marshal of Italy. His first move was to appoint Sogno, the only general in sight, provisional head of the army. Caviglia told War Minister Sorice that, as the highest ranking military man present, he was taking over, and he installed himself in Sorice's office. Then he called for all members of the government still in Rome to report to him.

Civilian members of the cabinet, informed that the king and Badoglio had left, were dumbfounded. Fearing the worst, Propaganda Minister Carlo Galli immediately called in a notary public and had him make an official record of Galli's complete ignorance of the armistice negotiations.

In an attempt to reconcile the conflicting rumors that were circulating around the city, the Action party set up an information center in the home of Tom Carini, a twenty-seven year old noted for his organizing ability. He had come from Milan where his job, like that of Raffaele Persichetti, had been to organize youth groups.

Now in Rome, in his parents' apartment at 24 Via Cicerone, he had a score of young men equipped with bicycles who carried messages between anti-Fascist leaders and went to outlying districts to find out what was really happening militarily.

That day, Carini was busy trying to track down arms which could be given to civilians who wanted to fight. At the same time efforts were being made to publish the party paper, *L'Italia Libera*.

Little by little members of the party, anxious to do something, gravitated to the Carini apartment. One of the first was Raffaele Persichetti, who came with another young professor. At 9 A.M., Raffaele had gone to the home of Catholic leader Mario Cingolani to discuss his forthcoming trip to the North, and after that he had met with friends, including Ugo Moretti, at a printing shop on Via Flaminia where they were putting out their small clandestine paper under the name *Il Comercio Italiano*. Raffaele had returned home to prepare notes for a speech he was going to give the next day, and then, feeling that the time had passed for words alone, he had gone to Carini's.

Soon the apartment held about sixty members of the party, mainly young men who wanted to persuade their leaders to form fighting groups to battle the Germans. To do so, they had to assemble manpower and get weapons.

As one of them, Vittorio Gabrieli, wrote: "We telephoned uninterruptedly. Nearly all our friends left home and came. We had some revolvers, a few bullets and grenades. . . . Persichetti arrived with a strange light in his eyes, questioning and almost supplicating; he wanders nervously around the room, he barely listens to the radio, he seems distracted, he asks for a rifle."

Unable to get news on the radio, Carini sent emissaries on foot and by bicycle to the Ostiense, the Aurelia and the Cassia. All was quiet on the Aurelia; the Grenadiers were still holding out at the Magliana Bridge.

A call came in from the university that students had found some weapons there. Some of the youngsters left to get them. They picked them up, but minutes later they were confiscated by the police. There was word that arms were being distributed by Vincenzo "Cencio" Baldazzi, an Action party member, in the Trionfale district. One of the boys got on his bike and headed there. He returned covered with sweat and frowning. The rifles had already been distributed and immediately afterward the police had gone from house to house to take them back.

That day, Raffaele had spent many hours arguing with himself. He was confronted by the liberal dilemma of whether—and how—to put his theories into execution. He was not, after all, a man of action. He was a humanitarian, not a revolutionary.

For six weeks many anti-Fascists had been saying that Badoglio and the king had been looking out only for their own interests. Should Raffaele and his companions now turn around and exhort the people to fight for these same interests? Should they fight the Germans only to have the Allies take their place—only to exchange one master for another?

Caught in the age-old crisis of the intellectual as the events around him hurtled towards a climax, Raffaele felt frustrated and helpless. Suddenly, after saying that he would call Carini later, Raffaele walked out alone into the darkening night. He knew he could not keep pace with his companions; he already heard the music of a far-away drummer.

Chapter 37

THE WITHDRAWAL

The decampment of Italy's leaders, while still only a rumor in Rome, was even less than that abroad. In North Africa, Allied headquarters, with no idea that Italy's leaders had fled, broadcast an appeal for Italians to collaborate in expelling "the oppressors." Ironically, the Italians were also asked to obey their military chiefs, who were no longer giving instructions.

Goebbels, meanwhile, referring to Hitler's September 9 decision to retreat from Russia's Dnieper River, told a hastily convoked meeting of high officers in Berlin, "The Italians have abandoned us at the worst possible moment. If we could have had, on the Eastern Front, the divisions we sent to Italy after the fall of Mussolini, the present crisis there would never have taken place."

About Italy, Goebbels was more hopeful, writing in his diary: "Since the fall of Mussolini we have expected and waited for this moment. We won't have to make substantial changes in our plans. We will start with what the Fuehrer wanted to do immediately after Mussolini's fall."

His optimism, however, was not shared by German commanders

near Rome. Kesselring could hardly believe that there had been no agreement between the Italians and the Allies for a landing near the capital. He therefore continued to move cautiously, with few men and little equipment. An all-out fight with the Italians could seriously delay the re-forming of his divisions, and he could not afford to overlook the possibility of a civilian uprising. General Student was particularly worried about the resistance that his paratroopers had encountered at Monterotondo. And where was Marshal Badoglio? Even if the rumors were true about his escaping with the royal family, the old soldier must have left a concrete plan of action behind for his subordinates to follow.

General Westphal, Kesselring's chief of staff, was more fearful of the possibility of an Allied air drop: "Having understood that the main Allied attack was at Salerno," he has said, "for days after we watched the air space around Rome. . . . it seemed impossible that the Allied command wouldn't take advantage. . . ."

Westphal was so uncertain of the Germans' chances should the Allies come to Rome, that he asked Kesselring to authorize him to negotiate an immediate surrender of Italian forces. Kesselring was skeptical, but that afternoon Colonel Dollmann said that he was convinced that General Calvi di Bergolo might be receptive.

"No one," Dollmann said later, "believed rumors of the flight of the king and the government. But all the members of the royal family had been taken from their posts except Calvi di Bergolo. There must be a reason for that. Calvi must have been omitted for some special reason."

Kesselring decided to let Westphal go ahead.

By now Carboni's commanders were beginning to withdraw their troops, as originally ordered, to Tivoli.

General Cadorna of the Ariete, having seen a small part of his division overcome the Germans at Monterosi and on the other side of Lake Bracciano at Manziana, finally agreed to withdraw the bulk of his troops from their position north of Rome. He was comforted by the assurance that newly arrived units of the Re Division would move up to hold his lines. He sent his reserves first—a tank regiment, an infantry battalion, a company of Bersaglieri and the 225th Artillery—then, bit by bit, his line troops. They moved down the Via Cassia to Rome, going through Viale Parioli to the Tiburtina where German and Italian units peacefully passed each other on the march, going in opposite directions. Never had Tolstoy's observation, that war was against all the rules of human conduct, been truer.

As elements of the Ariete arrived at Tivoli, they came under the provisional command of General Calvi di Bergolo, who, in Carboni's absence, had moved his headquarters up from Bagni. But the once-great division arrived with only half of its effectives, the rest having fallen out of ranks along the road and headed home.

Calvi was just beginning to take things in hand when General Carboni reappeared. He was found at 2 P.M. at the *Carabinieri* barracks in Tivoli, where he was having lunch in civilian clothes. Both Calvi and his deputy, General Oscar Gritti, after listening to Carboni's explanations, became convinced that Carboni had wanted to catch up with the fleeing generals but, unable to find them, had returned.

Told of Salvi's hysterical reaction to his absence, Carboni appointed Colonel Giuseppe Cordero di Montezemolo—who had acted as interpreter between Mussolini and Hitler at Feltre—as his new chief of staff.

Now all the bad news—as well as the calls for orders, help and guidance—was being routed to Tivoli. Montezemolo told Carboni that Lieutenant General Gastone Gambara, commanding the XI Corps in Fiume, had phoned to ask if OP 44 should be carried out.

"What!" Carboni exclaimed. "Gambara hasn't received the order to apply OP 44?"

"From the calls that have been coming in," Montezemolo said, "it is obvious that there are others who haven't received it."

"That's incredible," Carboni said. "Anyway, don't tell Gambara we're out of contact with the Supreme Command. Going on Badoglio's proclamation and actions, it's evident that OP 44 has to be applied."

Even those commanders who had put OP 44 into effect found themselves in trouble. General Caracciolo saw his troops being dispersed, killed or captured. He saw supposedly trustworthy officers overcome by panic and consumed by the desire to get away from the Germans.

The centers from which he had hoped to launch an attack on the 3rd Panzergrenadieren's rear fell, one after the other: Orvieto, where the general fought alongside his soldiers, Chiusi, Viterbo and Tarquinia. But his men were still at the Futa Pass before Florence, and still fighting at Livorno and Pisa.

To the south of Rome, things were more hopeful. Radio messages came into Grenadier headquarters saying that German intentions would soon be clarified, although to the troops on the line, German intentions already seemed quite clear. This was particularly true around the bitterly contested Magliana Bridge. At about 4 P.M. commanders in the area received orders to pull their men back over the bridge towards Rome. They were told that an agreement had been reached between Italian and German authorities allowing Germans south of the Tiber to cross over the river and withdraw to the North without passing through the city.

The Grenadiers grumbled. They were more than holding their own even though they were restricted by the defensive instructions they had received. They were also furious at being forbidden to attack German lines and free the prisoners and mortars that had been captured.

While their commanders were discussing the strange orders, news arrived that the other divisions of the Motorized Corps were withdrawing towards the Tivoli hills. This seemed to indicate that there was in fact some kind of an agreement, and the Grenadiers and supporting units left their blockposts and started back over the bridge.

No one could figure out where the orders had come from. Only later was it learned that the Germans had gotten hold of the cipher used for giving orders and were using it to send orders both by phone and radio in the names of nonexistent Italian commanders. Other units received instructions not to fight if they came up against the Germans, and officers were told to present themselves in civilian clothes at distant headquarters.

Suddenly, inexplicably, an order came for the Italians to *retake* the bridge. The troops were only too willing, but they had lost their strategically located defensive posts, and the conflicting orders, the ferocity of the enemy attack and the treachery had severely sapped their morale. To add to their troubles, the Germans, instead of withdrawing to the North, had begun pressing towards Rome.

It was at about this time that Carboni phoned the commander of the Grenadiers. As reported by Carboni, the conversation went as follows:

"How are things going, Solinas?"

"Very badly, Your Excellency. There's terrible confusion here."

"What orders have you received?"

"None, besides the alert from you."

"But who's in command in Rome?"

"I don't know. There are Sorice and Caviglia who haven't given me any orders. . . . We're short on munitions and the situation is becoming critical."

Carboni ordered Solinas to stand fast, something the Grenadier commander had been doing to the best of his ability since the night before.

With Carboni's appearance at Tivoli, General Calvi di Bergolo had moved back to Centauro Division headquarters. At 5 P.M., Captain Hans Schacht appeared there. He brought a verbal message from General Student, expressing his personal esteem for Calvi and requesting that his German troops be treated as friends. It was unclear whether this was a demand for surrender, an offer to surrender, or merely a request to let German forces pass undisturbed. After some discussion, however, it became increasingly apparent that the Centauro was being asked to give up its arms.

Calvi went to Carboni who, according to the king's son-in-law, ". . . agreed that the proposal was acceptable as long as it was extended to the entire Motorized Corps. Following Carboni's orders, with a note dictated by him, Lieutenant Colonel Leandro Giaccone [Calvi's chief of staff] and other officers left for Frascati to negotiate the surrender with Marshal Kesselring."

Carboni later maintained that he approved negotiations only in order to delay Kesselring's sending his divisions to Salerno, but this account fails to explain why Carboni tried to dissolve the Motorized Corps shortly thereafter. By now exhausted, both physically and mentally, the young general went to sleep.

Although it had more alert leadership than the army, the navy was not faring much better. On the morning of September 8, Admiral De Courten, navy chief of staff, had told Kesselring—in a tearful discourse full of references to De Courten's German ancestry—that the fleet was preparing to join the Germans in attacking Allied convoys. In reality, he had ordered it to surrender to the Allies.

Before dawn on September 9, three battleships—the *Roma*, the *Vittorio Veneto* and the *Italia*—accompanied by three cruisers and eight destroyers, left the northern Italian port of La Spezia. At 6:30 A.M., they were joined off the northern tip of Corsica by other ships from Genoa. The combined forces constituted a really formidable battle fleet: three battleships, six cruisers, ten destroyers and smaller craft. Fleet commander Vice Admiral Carlo Bergamini, an ardent royalist who was commander of Italy's naval assault forces, was on his flagship, the 35,000-ton *Roma*, the most powerful unit the Italian navy had ever possessed.

Bergamini had not wanted to take his ships to an Allied port; he would have preferred to sink them, but De Courten had told him that Italy would receive preferential treatment if the armistice clauses were executed, that the king had approved the armistice, and that the royal family might be going to La Maddalena. Bergamini agreed to compromise and take his ships there. Before leaving port, he spoke to his commanders:

> Tell your men that the interests of the country demand that we meet the victor with our flags flying; the men can hold their heads high. This is not what we had hoped for; what we must do now, we must do without hesitation because what counts in the life of a people are not dreams and hopes . . . but duty carried out to the end despite the cost. To shirk this duty would mean a halt to our lives and to that of an entire nation, depriving it of a rebirth. . . . Tell this to your men and they will follow you obediently as they followed you in actions involving danger.

At 1 P.M., when the flotilla had traveled the length of Corsica and was approaching Sardinia, Bergamini received word that the Germans had occupied the La Maddalena base. He ordered the fleet to reverse course and head east for the open sea.

A little after 3 P.M., planes of unknown nationality appeared in the sky and began dropping bombs. While the ships zig-zagged, the bombers were driven off by antiaircraft barrages.

Convinced that the fleet had been attacked by the Allies, Bergamini radioed this news to Rome. Naval headquarters immediately protested to the Allies, who insisted that the planes were not theirs.

What had happened was that the commander of German naval forces in Italy, Admiral Meendsen-Bohlken, had informed Berlin of the ships' departure and Marshal Goering had then ordered General Sperrle, commander of the III Fleet Air Arm in France, to search out and attack the Italian fleet. Sperrle transmitted the order to General Fink, commander of the 2nd Luftwaffe Division, who had given the mission to the Third Group of the 100th Squadron, which was stationed at Istres, near Marseilles.

At 3:52 P.M., from a height of 1900 feet, the fifteen twin-engine Do-217 K3s began a second attack. Two rocket bombs fell on the *Roma*, one hitting its powder magazine. There was an explosion, and a huge cloud of white and black smoke reached towards the sky. The

Roma listed, capsized, and split into two stumps, which tilted verti-
cally and were swallowed by the sea, dragging with them Bergamini
and 1,352 of his men.

While two detroyers were lost to German shore batteries, three
other destroyers and a cruiser picked up survivors and made for
Spain, where they were interned. The rest finally reached Malta.

Admiral Da Zara, commander of the Taranto squadron in the
Adriatic, had been surprised by the armistice announcement on September 8. His orders had originally been to fight the Allies, and until
that time he had intended to give battle to the British convoy—consisting of two battleships, five cruisers, six destroyers and a mine-
layer—and then sail in the direction of Taranto. Now he told the
components of his squadron to head for Malta. When one of his commanders, Vice Admiral Giovanni Galati, refused to obey the new
orders from Rome, he was arrested.

Da Zara also ordered the just-arrived Italian battleship *Giulio
Cesare* to Malta, but its crew rebelled and tried to convince their
commander to sink the ship instead. By the afternoon of September
9, the British fleet was off Taranto and the crew of the *Giulio Cesare*,
seeing that they might as well be in Malta, were persuaded to leave
port and head there. As the *Giulio Cesare*—accompanied by another
battleship, two cruisers and a destroyer—left the harbor, it passed
the British flotilla, which, at 6 P.M., started debarking sixty-seven
hundred men of the British 1st Airborne Division.

The fleeing king and generals were more fortunate than the Italian
armed forces. As they made their way through the Abruzzi Mountains, they passed not far from Campo Imperatore, where Mussolini
was being kept prisoner. The royal caravan halted at a crossroads ten
miles from Pescara. To the right, two miles distant, was Chieti, a
thriving city that had existed before Rome.

To the amazement of workers in the nearby fields, seven or eight
cars lined up on the side of the road and dignitaries emerged. There
was a great consulting of maps by a group which included the king,
Prince Umberto, Badoglio, Acquarone, Admiral De Courten, three
generals and other officers. The crown prince mentioned that the castle of Crecchio, belonging to the duke and duchess of Bovino, was
nearby. The duchess was lady-in-waiting to the queen. Umberto knew
the castle well, having last visited it during his honeymoon. It would
be better for the king and queen to take refuge there. The king

agreed, and they moved towards the castle while Acquarone went ahead to Pescara to scout the situation. Two comparatively junior officers remained at the crossroads to divert later, lesser arrivals to Chieti, while the others entered the castle.

Here, Antonia Gaetani d'Aragona, the sixty-two-year-old duchess of Bovino, received the fugitives—as they described themselves—and sent servants out to forage for food. In the meantime, she saw to their comfort. When she took towels to Badoglio's room, she asked, "Your Excellency, what's happened with Mussolini?"

"They must have freed him by now," answered Badoglio.

"But did he betray His Majesty? Was it really necessary to arrest him?" persisted the duchess.

Badoglio muttered something and turned away. The duchess, a determined woman, then posed the same questions to the queen, who, with a hint of veiled sorrow, answered, "Il nous a été fidel pendant vingt ans."

The question of loyalty was also bothering Prince Umberto. Still commander in chief of Army Group South, comprising three army corps and a dozen divisions—which he had left without orders—he had long nurtured the desire to be head of the Comando Supremo. It had not been possible under Mussolini. When the dictator's mistress had pushed the proposal, Mussolini had snorted: "Can you see me waking up His Royal Highness at four in the morning and giving him orders?"

But the day before, Under Secretary Baratono had flatly told him, "The King will have to abdicate, only Your Highness can save what there is to save." A friend of the family, Colonel Rossi Passavanti, had reported a Vatican message conveyed by Cardinal Pizzardo, that ". . . the Holy Father is anxiously waiting for him [Umberto] to move." The crown prince had only smiled and said, "What can I do, go against the king?"

Now at Crecchio, just before noon, Umberto agreed with his aide General Gamerra.

"My leaving Rome," he said, "was undoubtedly a mistake. I think it better that I return. The presence of the House of Savoy at this grave moment is, I think, essential. . . ."

Then Umberto went to see the king, who was in the castle courtyard with Badoglio. After the crown prince had stated his case, Badoglio started to answer, but Umberto interrupted him. "This decision," he said, "is up to His Majesty."

"You are wearing a military uniform," snapped Badoglio, hitting a nearby parapet with his hand so sharply that he hurt himself. "You are a soldier and you owe obedience to me."

For the time being, nothing more was said. At noon sharp, the first of three shifts sat down to eat in a salon filled with Capodimonte vases, silver and pewter ornaments and antique furniture.

"To think," said the king at one point, "that all this is happening because of an electoral maneuver."

Noting everyone's surprise, he went on to explain that Roosevelt had had an important electoral meeting and, to make an impression, had decided to announce Italy's surrender. "But it will be all over shortly and we'll go back." As if to confirm this prediction, the king showed that he had only twelve hundred lire in his wallet.

"I am a hard-headed Piedmontese and if I say something it's because I'm sure of it," Badoglio chimed in. "In two weeks, no more, we'll be back."

Acquarone went along with this, even going so far as to reduce the time to three days.

Only the queen seemed to have a clear idea of the situation; she remarked sadly that everyone knew how adventures of this kind began but not how they ended and that they usually ended badly.

Meanwhile, generals were being routed to Chieti, where Ambrosio had set up temporary headquarters at the Hotel Sole.

In a short time, all but two sections of the Supreme Command and just about the entire army staff had arrived. Most of these generals had been advised to transfer their activities to Tivoli or Carsoli, but upon reaching these points they had heard about Chieti.

In response to their questions, Ambrosio said that he did not know where the king and Badoglio were; he did not reveal that he had agreed to meet them later at the Pescara airport. Instead, he let it be known that his command was to be set up in Chieti and that he would stay there until he returned to Rome, which would be very shortly. Roatta took this at face value and started organizing his staff. Zanussi was so convinced that he wrote a note to his wife saying, "Don't worry. I'll see you in eight days."

In order to keep the prearranged airport rendezvous, the royal caravan, consisting of about fifteen cars, left the castle of Crecchio at 4 P.M. At the airport, the unexpected visit caused so much confusion that honors were accorded the queen's maid by soldiers and airmen who mistook her for a lady of the court.

Ambrosio and Roatta had already arrived. A kind of crown council was called which discussed how to leave and where to go. Badoglio proposed Sicily or even Tunisia, but the others held out for a city behind Allied lines still nominally controlled by Italians. Taranto was chosen and then ruled out when word came that the British had occupied it.

At that time there were over a hundred planes at the airport and more than twelve hundred fliers, many of them cadets undergoing training. When Prince Carlo Ruspoli, commander of a fighter squadron and a boyhood friend of the prince, protested to Umberto against the departure of the royal leaders, Umberto, accompanied by Ruspoli and followed by other officers at a respectful distance, again went to the king.

The king's reply, as always, was ambiguous. "I must be obedient to the decision of my government," Vittorio Emanuele said, referring to Badoglio.

Because there had been no sign of the vessels ordered by De Courten, the idea of going south by plane had been proposed. Then, after the aviators' protest, the original plan of going by sea was reaffirmed although the queen's aversion to air travel was given as the reason. To avoid catching people's eyes, the group would leave not from Pescara, where there was too much hostility, but from the port of Ortona, at midnight. Since the ships had not yet been sighted, the groups broke up. Badoglio and De Courten remained at the airport, Ambrosio and Roatta returned to Chieti, and the royal family—with their followers—went back to Crecchio. All the duchess could offer them for dinner was soup, bread, fruit and wine.

Then, for the third time that day, Umberto was asked to return to Rome. "Your Royal Highness, you know the sentiment of our family towards the king and his house," said the duchess of Bovino. "Please forgive me if I urge you to return."

"Thank you," Umberto replied, "I appreciate it. But the king must be convinced."

Once more Umberto went to his father to make his proposal. Acquarone, who was present, pointed out the danger of the Germans capturing Umberto, forcing him to renounce the armistice, and, under the threat of torture or death, making him proclaim himself Umberto II.

At this the king stiffened. He was jealous of his son and wanted no one else to wear the crown, no matter how shaky it might be. "My government," he said, "would never consent to such an adventure."

When the queen added, in French, "You won't go Beppo. They'll kill you," Umberto gave up hope.

At eleven o'clock, the group hurried to their cars and said good-bye for the second time. Then they left Crecchio. Several days later, it was taken by the Germans, sacked and burned; the duke and duchess were deported to a concentration camp.

At 8 P.M., word came that the *Baionetta* had arrived, and De Courten left, supposedly to make a reconnaissance. A half hour later, he sent for Badoglio, instructing the messenger, "Tell Marshal Badoglio I will wait ten minutes for him. After that, I give orders to sail."

As Badoglio was leaving the airfield, officers lined up, stiffly at attention. The head of the government started to shake hands, but the officers, saluting, kept their hands at the visors of their caps. One, Captain Torazzi, came up and asked:

"And for us, Your Excellency, what orders do you wish to leave?"

Badoglio did not even hesitate. "If the Germans come," he said, "you can leave. We'll be back in a week, then you can show up again."

Then Badoglio left. He did not hear Captain Torazzi's indignant comment, nor that of airport commander Colonel Raffaele Martinetti-Bianchi, who called the men about the king "fugitives, worried only about saving their lives."

Despite the presence of Air Minister Sandalli and Badoglio, the planes were left on the ground and eventually lost to the Germans although, as Martinetti-Bianchi wrote, they could have been transferred south, behind Allied lines.

Badoglio made his way to the *Baionetta*, where he joined De Courten, forgetting, however, to notify the king.

At Chieti, Ambrosio finally told a few of his generals that the king would travel south that night. It was a military secret and the news was not to be shared; above all, the unnotified officers were not to be told. As the selected generals prepared to leave, General Zanussi thought of voicing his objections to the strange proceedings. He did not, but later he wrote:

> Even if I say it out loud, what good would it do? I could only think about the impotence to which I am sentenced. A fifty-year-old general of an Army that had a reputation of being one of the best in the world, carried around like a trunk without knowing any destination. . . . Here I am a rebel by nature, but the will to rebel has failed me.

Zanussi's appetite was still good, however, and he joined the other generals at dinner. At about 11 P.M., the select few—who were no longer so few—started for Ortona. To make sure the flight of notables would not be noticed, an air alarm was sounded to get people off the streets.

"The long line of cars," Zanussi wrote, "lights out on the twisted road, moves at moderate speed to what [Ortona] used to be, a nice town, now almost a complete wreck, and enters the narrow road to the small port."

It was a little before midnight, and it was obvious that things had not gone well. Despite all the efforts at secrecy, the quay was full of cars. Major Marchesi saw at least fifty. Traffic piled up in the humid, moonless night. Drivers blew their horns, and generals came out of their cars to order the cars of the subordinate officers pulled back. No one seemed to feel either shame or sorrow. Attracted by the magnet of escape, they had come without hesitation; now they were elbowing for position. The king became nervous and told General Puntoni to find out what had happened.

"Nothing like this had been foreseen," Puntoni wrote in his diary. "Surrounded by generals and high officers, we saw Roatta in civilian clothes, a submachine gun slung over his back. The king looks at him and shakes his head. In the darkness we hear voices and calls; the darkness becomes thicker."

It was not clear whether Roatta and the others who were armed had done so to defend themselves from the Germans or to win a place on the escape ship. For the time being, it did not matter; the *Baionetta* had not yet arrived, even though it had been at Pescara four hours earlier.

By now, there were dozens of cars, over two hundred generals and officers, and at least a score of chauffeurs plus orderlies, attendants and servants. Swarming to the dock, the people of Ortona began peering through the windows of cars that had been halted by the traffic jam. Soon, port officials, fishermen, young boys and women swarmed over the little port. Some, afraid that the presence of so many generals with their limousines and armored cars would cause still another bombing, started to yell, "Let them leave! Go! Go! But hurry up!"

Hearing the hostile shouts, the generals tried to affect nonchalance; when one lit a cigarette, others hissed warnings to put it out.

Finally the *Baionetta* appeared. By now it was twenty minutes

Germans on Via Veneto, September 11, 1943

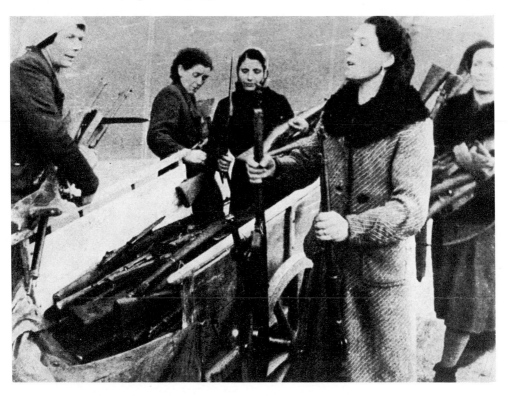

Italian women bringing out arms for the partisans after the disbandment of the army

Mussolini, on September 12, 1943, entering the Fieseler-Storch that took him off Camp Imperatore

Mussolini freed by Germans, Camp Imperatore, September 12, 1943

after midnight, and everybody—invited and uninvited—was there except Badoglio. The king, annoyed, still wanted to wait for him. He could not leave without his "government"; it would look bad to the Allies, to history. The worried king was even heard muttering, "Could it be that Badoglio has betrayed us?"

Finally he decided not to wait any longer, and the royal family, followed, as Puntoni wrote in his diary, "by some of the highest personalities present," prepared to leave.

Two fishing boats were loaded with the "personalities" and their luggage. As they arrived at the *Baionetta*, there, at the top of the lowered gangway stood Badoglio. "No more than thirty can come on board," he shouted.

"We are of the royal house," shouted back Umberto. Then he, the king and the queen went aboard.

Badoglio established his personal control over who should or should not board the *Baionetta*. Regardless of rank, a person was turned back if he did not suit Badoglio. This led to some moments of truth for generals who saw their rank as entitling them to unlimited privileges and precedence. In unconscious irony, General Aliberti, who without orders had brought along two dozen members of his staff, later wrote: "With real regret and deep sorrow I was forced to part with all my officers who, in a fine show of solidarity and attachment to duty had followed me to the pier of Ortona."

Other generals, pushing and shoving, argued with each other over who had the right to go. In their haste, some of them climbed on board a dredge which had no crew and never moved.

By this time, Admiral De Courten had taken over Badoglio's Cerberus-like duties at the gangway. He tried to keep Zanussi off, but Roatta, after an argument, shoved Zanussi and two other officers on board. Major Marchesi and British Lieutenant Mallaby had been pushed aboard by Ambrosio, who had overruled De Courten's objections.

De Courten allowed only three of another group of generals to come on board, telling the others that a second ship would be coming shortly to pick them up. The second ship did not appear until seven o'clock the next morning, by which time the rejected generals, fearful that the Germans might arrive at any moment, had gone inland, searching for refuge.

Fifty-seven people embarked at Ortona, but no complete list of them has ever been found.

The Germans came the next day, devastating homes and burning

P

fishing boats in delayed reprisal. As a bitter reminder of these days, the people of Ortona put a plaque—like an indelible scar—on the dock:

> From this port, the night of September 9th, 1943, the last king of Italy fled with his court and with Badoglio, delivering the martyred country over to German anger. . . . Ortona, from its ruins, from its wounds, shouts eternal damnation to the monarchy of betrayal, of fascism, and, with all Italy, cries out for justice for the people and for history in the holy name of the Republic.

Chapter 38

THE BATTLE FOR ROME

On the morning of September 10, Rome resembled a ship abandoned by its helmsmen. The sky was grey, and it was drizzling; few policemen were to be seen and only an occasional streetcar. The radio continued, mechanically, to broadcast syrupy songs; newspapers had not yet appeared.

Heedless of the rain, Raffaele Persichetti set out on foot for his regimental headquarters. He had decided to rejoin the Grenadiers, not as an act of heroism but as the only way to emerge from the sterile position in which he found himself. He felt compelled to prove that he was capable of fighting more than a paper war.

The evening before he had seen Jeanne Volkoff and told her of his intentions. When she protested, he had gone to the Via Margutta apartment of his brother-in-law, Gunnar Kumlien, the Rome correspondent of the Stockholm *Tidningen,* and spent the night there.

As the sun came out, a wall poster with two communiqués caught Raffaele's eye:

Owing to military inspections that require his presence, Marshal Badoglio is out of Rome. Marshal Caviglia has temporarily . . . assumed powers and coordination of a military character. . . .

The city of Rome is completely calm. Life goes on its usual and normal rhythm. Negotiations with the command of German troops posted in the zone are taking place for the transfer of these units north.

The poster was signed by Marshal Caviglia, in whose mind calm and stability were the goals to be pursued, not honor. Earlier that morning, at the insistent urging of General Sorice, he had sent a telegram to the *Baionetta* asking the king to authorize his assumption of power in Rome. While waiting for an answer—which never came because Caviglia's old enemy Badoglio intercepted the king's favorable reply—Caviglia issued several communiqués, including one announcing the Allied landing at Salerno.

He did not announce that the Italians had fought so hard and well at Monterotondo (despite 156 dead, including 33 civilians), that German paratroopers, reaching the Orsini Castle on the night of the ninth, had remained there not as victors but as prisoners and had been forced to ask for a truce. When the Germans had emerged that morning, Italian soldiers and civilians, with a fine sense of irony, had presented arms.

The night before had seen other developments. Flushed with the success at Monterotondo, General Tabellini wanted to rout the Germans from Rome completely. Earlier, in Carboni's absence, he had had the idea of taking the Motorized Corps in hand and had even sent units available in Rome to help the Grenadiers. When he had started to move the Piave to Cecchignola in order to attack the Germans from the rear, he had been blocked by Calvi, his senior. Now, believing his plan still efficacious and knowing that larger units of the Re and Lupi divisions had arrived, he rushed to Tivoli to tell Carboni. The commander, however, was still asleep; he had given orders not to be awakened for anyone, and Tabellini, crestfallen, returned to his troops.

He did not know that surrender negotiations were by then well under way. Lieutenant Colonel Giaccone had reached Frascati at 9 P.M. the night before and proposed that Rome be considered an open city with Germans keeping their troops outside its limits while General Tabellini's Piave Division and Italian police maintained public order. The Germans agreed, and said that they would occupy only the German Embassy, the German telephone center and the Rome radio. There would be a three-hour armed truce between the Motorized Corps and the Germans to start at seven the next morning, by which time there would be a reply from the Italians.

At 3:30 A.M. on September 10, Giaccone had reported to Calvi, who had sent him on to Carboni. Finding Carboni asleep in a small *pensione*, Giaccone had awakened the general to tell him of the terms for Rome. Then: "I reported to His Excellency General Carboni that, following his request, it had been agreed that the terms proposed for the Centauro would be extended to the Motorized Corps."

"As far as I'm concerned, it's acceptable," the drowsy Carboni had replied. Later, after a brief discussion with his son and Lieutenant Lanza, Carboni told Colonel Salvi—who had shown up, tears dried, at Tivoli—to persuade Calvi di Bergolo to take command of the corps and to prolong the discussion so that Carboni would have time to leave.

By the time Calvi had refused, Carboni had dressed and, according to Monelli, phoned SIM for two false passports; but a call came from War Minister Sorice ordering Carboni to Rome, and he left at 7 A.M.

At exactly that hour, Giaccone was back at Kesselring's headquarters saying that Carboni had accepted.

"Fine," said Kesselring. "Let us put it down in black and white. There are several small modifications to make." One turned out to be quite important, namely, the setting up of a German command in Rome, a modification which was tantamount to violation of the capital's open city status.

When Giaccone objected, he was told that the Italians had no choice, that the Allies had confined their invasion to Salerno and that Italian troops near Rome had been left to stand alone. Giaccone was given until four o'clock that afternoon to secure acceptance from his superiors. If the surrender terms were refused, threatened the Germans, they would blow up Rome's aqueducts and bomb the city with seven hundred planes, which of course they did not really have. Although the ultimatum was a bluff, Giaccone left for Rome with the surrender document, in Italian and German, signed by Westphal.

Kesselring had gotten over his fear that the Allies might appear in the vicinity of Rome; they had failed to exploit the uncertainty and surprise which the armistice announcement had produced. He later said, "The fact that the Allies had missed the chance of an airborne landing had eased the tension; left to themselves the Italian divisions, although outnumbering us by three to one, were no actual danger. It was to be expected that we should not be able to square accounts with our ex-allies without some clashes."

Less important to him was the fact that, as Dollmann wrote, "Little by little we had confirmation . . . of the escape of the royal family and Badoglio . . . the most tragic event in the history of modern Italy." The generals at Frascati, however, agreed that Badoglio had earned a place of honor among the Third Reich's protectors and friends.

It was all too obvious that no plan of action had been left behind and that the Italian divisions lacked a unique command.

Back in Rome, Carboni had undergone a transformation. Now determined to defend Rome, he was dynamic, full of plans, and as strongly anti-German as he had been prior to September 1. Arriving at the War Ministry at 8 A.M., he was immediately taken to Caviglia.

When Carboni showed him Roatta's order to move his troops to Tivoli, the marshal frowned. "This orders you *not* to defend Rome," he said.

Carboni replied that, in Roatta's absence, he had been forced to take over the job. Then, in what must have been a most confusing confrontation, Carboni became convinced that the marshal, although in favor of coming to terms with the Germans, had authorized him to put into effect a plan for defending Rome militarily.

Carboni did not return to his command, which was just across the street at Palazzo Caprara. Instead, saying he feared capture by the Germans, he established himself in the swank section of Parioli, in an apartment at 7 Piazze delle Muse.

The apartment had a splendid view *north* of the city, but most of the fighting was taking place at the other end of the city, miles to the *south*. Even so, Carboni had the apartment fortified with machine guns and proceeded to issue orders which a governmental commission later described as ". . . so little in harmony with the real situation that it raised a sense of deep bitterness and distrust in the troops. He also ordered counterattacking actions, insisting that divisional commanders put themselves at the head of their troops. He wanted them to set examples; but heaven forbid that he do the same and he remained far off and hidden."

This referred to the fact that, at 10:45 A.M., Carboni sent orders for Tabellini to concentrate the Piave in Rome by 4 P.M., while the Ariete was to form two columns and hit the Germans in the flank from the east in order to relieve pressure on the Grenadiers. At the same time, Carboni urged the Grenadiers to hold the line at all costs and if necessary "counterattack with maximum violence."

Paolo Monelli called Carboni's orders "hysterical and late," and General Cadorna, told to lead the Ariete personally, felt the same way. In fact, he thought it might be a German trick and insisted on having the order signed and in writing. In the meantime, he prepared his troops for the return to Rome. One commander, Colonel Rabbi, called in his officers and said that although he could not fight the Germans, he left them free to obey their individual consciences. Then he killed himself.

Carboni, having recovered his aplomb, was now his usual energetic self. At around noon he resumed his dealings with the anti-Fascists, sending Edoardo Stolfi, who owned the apartment above him at Piazza delle Muse, to the committee with a proposal for a popular insurrection. Speaking for Bonomi, Ruini turned him down, saying that Sorice had told Bonomi that he did not want to arm civilians. But Communist leaders Longo and Trombadori managed to locate the Parioli hideout and came to complain that police had taken the weapons Carboni had arranged for them. Carboni phoned Sorice, who claimed he knew nothing about it and referred him to Senise. When Carboni told the chief of police that if the arms were not given back he would send armed troops to get them, the Communists got their weapons. Longo was no novice at warfare; he had been inspector general of the International Brigades in the Spanish Civil War. Now he gathered men and arms and headed for San Paolo.

Other anti-Fascists were already moving towards the sound of battle. At about noon, Raffaele Persichetti reached the Grenadiers' barracks at Piazza Santa Croce in Gerusalemme. A number of soldiers were listlessly lying around while others were leaving their weapons and thinking of how to get home. Raffaele started talking to them and soon was marching with several dozen of them to Porta San Paolo. Just outside, on the Via Ostiense, he found his regimental commander, Colonel Mario di Pierro, and was given command of a platoon.

San Paolo was now the focal point of action. North of Rome, the front was quiet. The 3rd Panzergrenadieren, beaten back by the Ariete and possibly unaware that only units of the Re now faced them, remained in fixed positions. But to the south, things had taken a turn for the worse. At midnight, the Grenadiers, backed up by reinforcements, had moved to retake the Magliana Bridge. Fighting was heavy, and the Italians suffered their most severe losses. Twenty-one-year-old Amerigo Sterpetti, dying from a point-blank gunshot, kept firing till Germans killed him with bayonet stabs, and untrained *Carabinieri* cadets followed their captain, Orlando De Tommaso, who died trying to win back a position.

More reinforcements showed up and the Montebello Lancers came in with their tanks; by dawn of the tenth, the Italians commanded most of the bridge.

Then a German officer proposed to the 1st Grenadiers command that ten thousand men be allowed free passage over the bridge to join troops heading north. If that were all the Germans wanted, why not let them go? After checking with the Territorial Defense Command in Rome, it was decided to accept the proposal, which included the three-hour truce arranged by Giaccone.

At seven thirty the agreement was carried out, and the Grenadiers started to retreat behind the bridge; but as soon as the first sections had started back over the Tiber, German artillery set up antitank guns and mortars and attempted to take Italian prisoners. The Grenadiers fought back and the truce was disregarded.

Now the Italians tried to prevent the Germans from extending their position, but the Montebello's tanks were forced back. At the same time, the Germans were knocking out the Italian artillery posts. The *Carabinieri* cadets proved to be too weak against the veteran Germans. The Grenadiers, who had earlier been proud of their success, began to lose heart; they had already had over a hundred men killed and were still being advised not to aggravate German aggression in any way.

Weakened by losses in men and matériel, with their defense line untenable, the Italians were slowly forced back and a retreat was ordered to the crossroads with Via Ostiense. The wounded were picked up and the troops withdrew while maintaining a solid front. Due to the terrain, however, they were now in an even less favorable position and had to retreat still farther. They started to move towards E. 42, only to discover that during the night German snipers had infiltrated and, perched on the larger buildings, were now in effective control of the area.

On the other side of E. 42, Germans had pushed down Via Laurentina, past Tre Fontane, an abbey run by French Trappists, and finally come up against opposition in the little suburb of La Montagnola.

Here, between a small wood of eucalyptus trees and Fort Ostiense, was an old warehouse which had been transformed into a country church. From it, Father Pier Luigi Occelli watched as, at 8 A.M., the battle began. At first, the five hundred Grenadiers held their ground; then, as they started to give way, civilians joined in the defense but were forced back to the fort and then to a red house which now served as the Grenadiers' command post.

Fifteen-year-old Romolo D'Orinzi was on the street with his mother when he saw a group of Germans going through the priest's house and placing in position a howitzer aimed at the rear of the Grenadiers' defense line. Wrenching himself free from his mother, he ran to warn the soldiers. Hit by a rifle shot in his arm, he kept running, all the time holding his wounded arm with the other hand in an effort to stop the blood. At the command post, he gave the alarm, but it did no good; the Germans' modern arms were too much for the outdated weapons that the Fascist regime had given the Italian army.

At the fort, the nuns became nurses. When resistance collapsed, they put white bands with red crosses around soldiers' sleeves. As time and ink began to run out, the nuns painted crosses on the bands with the blood that had spilled onto the floor.

When the battle was over, the priest buried forty-five soldiers and nine civilians, using wooden planks, originally intended for a new rectory, to fashion temporary coffins.

When the Germans finally took the area, they sacked the houses room by room, snatched gold earrings from women's ears and moved the entire population to a prison camp.

Now the German column left La Montagnola and joined the main paratrooper thrust. Some were already in the working-class district at Garbatella, where local inhabitants, usually members of left-wing parties, formed squads to take the places of retreating soldiers. One group, at Tormarancia, took over two batteries of 72mm's abandoned by the 8th Artillery. The Germans overran them and brought up their own artillery. Italian troops rallied and counterattacked, trying to keep the enemy from reaching the Basilica of San Paolo fuori le mura, St. Paul's Outside the Walls, the largest church in Rome after St. Peter's.

In the piazza before the church, a Grenadier captain told newsman Gino Tomajuoli that his soldiers had been fighting for thirty hours without food rations while contradictory orders continued to pour in. The Grenadiers were being praised for attacking and then told to limit themselves to defensive positions. They even received one message that the Germans had attacked by mistake, while another instructed an artillery commander to keep the invaders out of Rome without using his guns.

Bombs began to rain around the basilica as German artillery found the range. Groups of retreating *Carabinieri* cadets arrived on the run, throwing away their weapons. Civilians went to meet them, picked up their rifles, and joined the soldiers who were still fighting. Slowly, inexorably, they were pushed back beyond the basilica, which, although technically Vatican territory, was then occupied by the Germans.

Leaving a detachment, the paratroopers concentrated their forces at the spot on Via Ostiense where Peter and Paul had taken leave of each other on their last journey. Here, near Via delle Sette Chiese, Captain Romolo Fugazza of the Montebello Lancers, mortally wounded, refused the help of his soldiers. "Don't touch me," he said. "I want to die here. Keep fighting."

On Via Ostiense, the Grenadiers tried to make another stand, but the individual units fighting alongside them—along with the armored cars and tanks of the Montebello—were picked off one by one.

The next goal of the Germans—and the ultimate redoubt of the Grenadiers—was Porta San Paolo, 120 feet high, the city gate within the 1700-year-old Aurelian Wall. With its towers and battlements and its fourteen-foot-thick walls, it provided a perfect defense, but only for battles of a much earlier day.

When the flight of the king and generals began to be known in Rome, there were neither signs of panic nor any attempts to emulate the fugitives. Shops opened, streetcars resumed their runs, and cafés and bars were full of people arguing the merits of the king's flight. Many said that if he had stayed he would have been accused, like Belgium's King Leopold, of collaborating with the Germans. Others said that was nonsense, that the king of Italy had been collaborating with the Germans for years. Other rulers had left their capitals, but Vittorio Emanuele had stolen away like a thief in the night, in a flight without dignity. It was the manner in which it had been done that left such a bad taste. Romans were used to being tricked or robbed or betrayed, but they preferred it be done with style.

Antonio Santovito, listening to Radio London, heard of the flight. He also heard people saying, "The king has left us in a terrible mess." Although thirteen, Antonio became a republican.

He was not alone. Groups of excited young men demonstrated in front of newspaper offices asking that extras be printed denouncing the treasonous flight. SIM tried to keep up morale by spreading rumors that the crown prince was in Rome and that an Allied landing was imminent, but these were lost in the flood of other rumors. At midday, for the first time in the memory of man, St. Peter's was shut. The gates to the Vatican State were also closed and the Swiss guards carried rifles and bayonets instead of medieval pikes.

By afternoon, Friday had become almost a holiday: movie houses filled up and the streets swarmed with people. At the ministries, documents were destroyed and petty cash was distributed to the staff. Gino Savoni even heard one group discussing the attitude to assume depending on who arrived first, the Allies or the Germans!

General Carboni was trying his belated best to invigorate the defense of Rome. Convinced that Caviglia's posters could harm morale, he ordered them torn down. Then he received a phone call from Giaccone, who had gone to Palazzo Caprara to find him. Told of the new demands made by the Germans, Carboni was furious. The Germans could still be beaten, the Allies might yet send aid; he had tried to send them an appeal through the Vatican. When Carboni ordered the negotiations broken off, Giaccone insisted on a written order to that effect. Carboni refused to assume any responsibility and suggested that Giaccone see Sorice.

Sorice refused also, and sent Giaccone on to Caviglia, whom Giaccone finally located at the home of the marshal's ordnance officer, Duke Ferdinando Aldobrandini.

Meanwhile, General Calvi di Bergolo had come to Rome to learn from Giaccone what had happened. He, too, tracked down Caviglia, who refused to assume the responsibility of signing the capitulation because he had not yet heard from the king.

He advised Calvi di Bergolo to have Giaccone return to Frascati with acceptance of the German terms. Calvi, however, did not want to put *his* name on the document either.

The officers were still discussing this when four anti-Fascist leaders, headed by Bonomi and including Piccardi, appeared. Caviglia went to another room, received them, explained the situation, said he had counseled Calvi to accept, and asked, "In my place, what would you have done?"

Possibly intimidated by the marshal's reputation, they unanimously agreed that it was the only course to follow. Nevertheless, none of the anti-Fascists would take upon himself the onus of *signing* a surrender, and it was evident none of the military was willing to sign Rome over to the Germans. After all, they had their reputations to preserve. They, too, were thinking of history and its judgment.

South of the city, the fighting continued. At 1:30 P.M., everyone in the Grenadiers barracks was ordered to Porta San Paolo. Some 116 soldiers and 22 officers, including newly appointed second lieutenants, moved into formation. Many had been wounded. The only arms available were two submachine guns, two hand grenades and some rifles.

Under the command of Captain Count Sigismondo Fago-Golfarelli, the group began moving through the deserted, silent streets. In front of a streetcar depot, drivers and workers came out to applaud. At that moment, a motorcycle policeman skidded to a stop. The Germans were coming into Rome, advancing along Via Sannio. Hastily the young captain placed his men behind some parked streetcars and mounted the two machine guns on motorcycles. As the Germans approached, the Italians fired. The German column spread out and, taking advantage of the numerous streets that converge on Porta San Giovanni, started moving into action. One group came through the gate near Second Lieutenant Alessandro Odescalchi, twenty-two-year-old son of a prince of the Holy Roman Empire. The newly appointed officer waited till the first German armored motorcycle came near, then calmly emerged from his shelter and threw a hand grenade at it. The grenade landed squarely and exploded; the Germans fell to the ground while the motorcycle smashed against the ancient wall.

Inspired by the young lieutenant's action, a Grenadier attacked another German vehicle but was wounded; lying on the ground, he urged his comrades to fight. A German came up to finish him off but the bleeding Grenadier got up, fought back, and returned to safety.

Thinking that reinforcements would soon arrive, Fago-Golfarelli re-formed his men around the bronze statue of St. Francis. There, Lieutenant Argo Pasquazzi, who had already lost an arm, was again wounded, but he dragged himself towards a German hand grenade and threw it back. Slowly the Italians were forced to retreat to Via Carlo Felice, where a World War I veteran, Ennio Brunelli, shouted, "Come on boys, I'm a Grenadier too," and, grabbing the first rifle he could find, started shooting. Fago-Golfarelli, fearing the Germans might execute the mufti-dressed Brunelli on the spot, forced him to leave. The survivors moved back towards the barracks, again passing in front of the streetcar depot. This time the drivers became stretcher bearers, nurses and helpers.

Tom Carini was worried, he had had no word from Raffaele Persichetti since the evening before, and the news was getting worse. Pitched battles were going on in at least a score of localities in and around Rome. Vittorio Gabrieli, while bicycling to Porta San Paolo, saw Italian armored cars leaving there. At Via della Marmorata, he noted others with their guns pointed *towards* the city. At the Fountain of Trevi, he met a group of young men led by the usually easygoing Giaime Pintor. Together they set out in search of arms; at the Territorial Command at Piazza della Pilotta, they loudly demanded guns but, as elsewhere in the city, the military turned them down.

Meanwhile, there were difficulties in getting *L'Italia Libera* published. The proofs had all been ready when the printer refused to put out the paper. While a dozen cyclists waited at Tom Carini's apartment to distribute copies, Carlo Muscetta and Leone Ginzburg, who had just returned from restricted residence in the Abruzzi, took the black, still-damp blocks and went from one printing house to another. Finally, at around noon on September 10, they found one, which, though putting out a Fascist weekly on the ground floor, was willing to print theirs in the cellar. Emerging at around 2 P.M. to get a bite to eat, Ginzburg and Muscetta were almost knocked over when a bomb fell on Piazza Cola di Rienzo, not far from where they were standing.

Other bombs were falling on Rome, some near the university, one on the Hall of Justice bordering the Tiber, others close to Via Cassia, still others around Piazza di Spagna.

When Giaccone's return to Frascati had been delayed, German artillery had started to shell the city. Kesselring was proceeding from strength; he had received an optimistic report from Salerno and at Rome his troops had the Italians on the run.

When the action had reached San Paolo, Raffaele Persichetti had taken a rifle and cartridges from a dead soldier and deployed his men in defensive positions at the corner of the Roman wall. Not far from there, on the Via Ostiense, he recognized a friend, Lieutenant Colonel Enrico Nisco, commanding a group of dragoons of the Genoa Cavalry. About thirty soldiers of the Genoa, commanded by Captain Franco Vannetti Donnini, were positioned next to the Ostiense railway station and along the Via Ostiense as far as the clearing in front of the general markets.

Behind Persichetti was another platoon of the Genoa Cavalry which, together with a group of civilians, defended Via San Saba;

to the right, several dozen Grenadiers and civilians under Captain Giulio Gasparri blocked the opening in the wall that led to the Testaccio area; to the left were light tanks and trucks of the Montebello Lancers under Captain Camillo Sabatini.

Coming down the Ostiense, the Germans attacked in force, loosing a raking fire that swept the broad street and decimated Italian ranks. From the tenements, women and housewives came to carry off the wounded, while others brought pots with boiled water, bound up wounds and comforted the soldiers as much as they could.

At the same time that Grenadiers were fighting on Via Ostiense, fresh soldiers flowed to the city gate. On their own initiative, *Bersaglieri* left their barracks in Trastevere and, gathering civilian volunteers and isolated soldiers who wanted to fight and were looking for their units, went towards the city wall. Elements of the Sassari Division came along.

Other soldiers, however, were *leaving* their posts. They sidled along walls trying not to be seen. When fleeing officers were hailed by civilians who wanted to find out what was happening, the officers hurriedly said that they knew nothing and continued on their way. That afternoon, a group of Socialists—including Bruno Buozzi, Pietro Nenni, Mario Zagari and Oreste Lizzadri—made their way towards San Paolo. On the way, they tried to persuade deserting soldiers to return to the front, but the soldiers were not interested. They had heard that the king and Badoglio had already fled; why shouldn't they do the same? Many had already taken off their army jackets.

For some civilians, the Forty-five Days had been a period of shame and cowardice, of fear and apathy. Now, uncertain and inexperienced, they came forward. With and without weapons, they headed for San Paolo, but they ran into obstacles. Several dozen volunteers with two trucks full of arms were halted at Piazza Venezia by *Carabinieri*. Thinking that the *Carabinieri* wanted to go with them, the drivers stopped, but then the *Carabinieri* surrounded the trucks and took the weapons.

Teams of armed workmen came out of factories, climbed on army trucks, and arrived at San Paolo ready to fight. A small group of Catholic Communists, led by Adriano Ossicini, managed to argue a veteran's organization out of some weapons and took them to San Paolo.

Although the movement to defend Rome had no ideological basis, leftist groups found themselves together with others of similar political persuasion: most, like Cencio Baldazzi (who had returned to

Rome after eighteen years in exile) and Emilio Lussu of the Action party, fought as individuals. Socialists Sandro Pertini, Oreste Lizzadri and Peppino Graccena fought in organized squads. Communists were there also but were acting on their own; party leaders had suddenly issued orders to hide weapons for the future, telling their militants not to take risks in a battle without hope.

From Via della Marmorata came civilians of varying age and social class. Many gathered to one side of San Paolo at Mount Testaccio, a small hill rising above the Tiber consisting entirely of broken ancient Roman crockery. Built in 163 b.c., it had become a working-class district. Now men lined up between the trees while above them teen-age boys perched on branches ready to fire at the Germans.

Other civilians who had been neither organized nor given instructions picked up weapons left behind by soldiers—discouraged or dead—and fired from behind abandoned trucks and cars.

In cases where civilians could not fight they acted as couriers; soldiers of World War I and youngsters carried ammunition, while monks and priests helped the injured. Others dug trenches and pried up paving stones. Sandro Pertini showed how to use the stones to build the first barricades, while shelters for machine-gun crews were constructed out of boxes discarded by the general markets.

The small number of people participating, however, makes it impossible to label it as a popular uprising. As Ugo Moretti, who was there that day, said, "It was only that some people thought they had been locked in a cage and now it looked as if they were going to be locked in another cage."

There was virtually no leadership, and many fought or helped without knowing exactly why. Surprisingly heedless of danger, they took their places and fired their weapons.

Even if only a few thousand Romans decided to resist, this was a great many for a city that had no tradition of middle-class revolution, and for a country that had just emerged from twenty years of dictatorship.

And resist they did, although their casualties mounted as the Germans came closer to the wall. Young Salvatore Lo Rizzo replaced the entire crew of an armored car and kept shooting until he had exhausted the ammunition, after which he was killed. An eighteen-year-old worker named Maurizio Ceccati, hit by a machine gun volley, kept inciting his companions to action as he was carried away to die in the Celio hospital.

A fruit seller named Ricciotti, who had a stall at the general mar-

ket, was on his way home when he saw what was happening. Someone put a rifle in his hand and he turned out to be a sharpshooter.
After he had shot about twenty Germans, he ran out of ammunition,
then promptly took out his false teeth and hurled *them* at the invaders.

There was a lull around 2 P.M., and Raffaele went to the café at
the corner of Viale Aventino to phone Tom Carini and urge him to
come there with armed companions. Raffaele left a map of where they
were to meet with one of the waiters and then rejoined his men at
Viale Giotto.

From where he was, he could look through the opening in the
wall to the large piazza. On the right was the pyramid-sepulchre, to
the left the railway station for Ostia. A lone streetcar was stalled next
to an open-air coffee bar in a green, tree-filled oasis in the center.
Behind it, along the Via Ostiense, dense with smoke and the sound of
battle, Germans were advancing, their backs against the sides of
houses. Suddenly, other Grenadiers who had been forced to retreat
arrived in the piazza. German mortars moved forward and laid down
a concentrated barrage. In front of Raffaele's eyes, Captain Sabatini
and another officer were killed. Shells were falling on Viale Giotto
where thirty Grenadiers and a dozen civilians were hit. Doorways
were full of wounded and dying.

Colonel Nisco moved his men up to take a position near the railway station. Not far off, on Via Ostiense, Captain Vannetti Donnini,
already hit in one knee, continued firing a machine gun until he was
stopped by a volley from German automatic weapons. Five of his men,
one after the other, tried in vain to retrieve Vannetti Donnini's machine gun and died before they could reach it.

Raffaele directed the firing of his men at the German parachutists,
whose advance was finally slowed down. Another lull set in and, at
half past three, Raffaele returned to the café to call his mother. He
told her that he was sorry he had not come home last night, that everything was all right, that she was not to worry, and that he would
be home for dinner. Frequently he covered the receiver so that his
mother would not hear the firing.

He returned to his troops and made one sally after another to
gather up wounded men, carrying them across his shoulder until his
clothes were covered with blood. In the meantime, he kept an eye on
Viale Aventino for his friends.

Near him, three platoons of mechanized cavalry were being

formed to move out into the piazza. Raffaele had a moment to ex-change some words with a friend, Second Lieutenant Guido Bertoni, who commanded six jeeps of one of the platoons. The jeeps left Porta San Paolo to counterattack, but at the corner of Via delle Cave Ardeatine they were hit by German mortars and flame-throwers and Raffaele could see Bertoni, already wounded, lift himself up on his vehicle to spur the other jeeps on, only to be hit again and thrown out of his vehicle to lie lifeless in the street. The company commander, Lieutenant Guido Cordano, also wounded, his left arm hanging use-less, took his place and succeeded in advancing the three jeeps that were left, trying to reach the mortars. His jeep was hit head-on by a howitzer while the others were raked by heavy machine gun fire. More than a dozen dead men lay burning because no one could make their way through the Germans' fire to save them.

All this time Raffaele was going back and forth under fire, en-couraging his men and dragging those who had been hit back to safety. As he saw his friends touched by the chill of death in the warm afternoon, he took more chances. At a little past 4 P.M., Raf-faele Persichetti was hit in the head and throat by bullets from an automatic weapon. Someone dragged his body into the shade and it was carried away, along with those of six others who had fallen that afternoon. Raffaele was twenty-eight.

At the War Ministry at that hour, Calvi di Bergolo and Giac-cone favored surrender, while Carboni—now supported by Sorice and still hopeful that the Allies would arrive—wanted to continue the admittedly haphazard defense of Rome. When Calvi said he trusted the German officers, Carboni snapped that they would not honor even the harsh terms that they had set; if Calvi had such faith in the Germans, let him take the responsibility and assume command of the city.

Suddenly there was a burst of machine-gun fire. The group, told that it came from German troops nearby, hurriedly decided it was time for a second surrender of Italy's armed forces. Since Mar-shal Caviglia, Minister of War Sorice, and Generals Carboni and Calvi di Bergolo had all refused to sign the surrender, it was left to a mere lieutenant colonel, Giaccone, to ratify the document. He did, saying that, in any event, his signature "had no legal value." Then he left for Frascati to tell Kesselring that he was now master of Rome. It was 4 P.M.

Half an hour before, the fugitives on the *Baionetta* had reached the safe haven of Brindisi. The royal family had gone ashore to weak cries of *"Viva il re"* and applause that was described by Marchesi as "the shortest and saddest they ever had in all their lives." Badoglio and the generals had followed. According to all accounts, the lodgings of the country's leaders—and not events in Rome—was their main preoccupation.

When word of the second surrender was brought to San Paolo, the remaining defenders were exhausted and almost out of ammunition; the barricades had been demolished by German artillery and flame-throwers. The Montebello Lancers regiment had disbanded after having almost half its officers killed, wounded, captured or lost. Civilians and soldiers retreated to the Aventino and then were forced to abandon even that as German armored cars passed through the wall at Porta San Paolo waving the white flag of truce. To the left, after a few rapid and desultory clashes, Testaccio was reduced to silence.

Then, in violation of the surrender agreement, new German troops began marching into Rome in force. They met unexpected resistance. A patrol came into Piazza San Giovanni in Laterano, where a group of Grenadiers stood ready to fight. Their commander, however, a major, raised his arms and surrendered. The Germans took the men's weapons, lined up the prisoners, and moved them towards the German Embassy. In the meantime, a young boy with a pushcart approached. Seeing the heap of arms, he stopped and picked up a musket. Suddenly a whole crowd of boys appeared, as if from nowhere, and they too grabbed guns. To everyone's surprise they began shooting at the Germans who, furious, immediately returned the fire. The boys kept shooting until their ammunition was gone and then disappeared as silently as they had come.

At Via Balbo, as German armored cars were passing, a hunchback, armed with a gun and a sackful of bombs, emerged from a door, walked calmly to a corner and threw a bomb, then calmly fired with his rifle. The Germans, still some distance away, fired back; the hunchback threw another bomb and fired again. By this time the Germans were firing with fury but somehow not a single shot touched the man. He kept on shooting and throwing bombs until he had none left, then he too disappeared.

German troops who managed to get inside the Viminale Palace

were immediately attacked by Italian soldiers and civilians. Near the Circus Maximus, some German soldiers, discovering a tunnel being dug for a subway, dove into it and reached the Colosseum only to find Italians standing there, armed with hand grenades and revolvers.

At Piazza Colonna, anti-Fascists, uninformed of the armistice, tried to stage a meeting. Many brandished a newspaper published that afternoon by the committee, hailing "The Victorious Battle of Via Ostiense." A line of demonstrators arrived, led by actor Carlo Ninchi shouting, "Let's get guns and go to Porta San Paolo." A small truck loaded with muskets and bombs, driven by Eugenio Colorni of the Socialist party, stopped nearby and people crowded around it, grabbing the weapons. Just then, an armored car came down Corso Umberto and, at Piazza Colonna, someone in it threw two hand grenades that scattered the crowd.

Untouched by the appeals of the anti-Fascists, Rome's population maintained its imperturbable calm. Even though they heard the cannon, knew about the armed clashes, and saw wounded soldiers, they awaited the end of battle, very likely convinced that it would be lost and certain, in any event, that they could do nothing about it. The center of the city—even where shells had landed—had an absurdly casual air.

North of the city, at Campo Parioli, near Carboni's hideout, Lieutenant Carlo Mazzarella was in an army barracks with troops of the 81st Infantry. Having been told by his captain to teach the men how to salute properly, the young lieutenant lined them up. At that moment, Germans came in the door and took the saluting men prisoners.

The columns of the Ariete and Piave which Carboni had sent against the Germans' right flank barely had time to exchange a few volleys before they were halted near the Via Appia and told of the surender.

Within the city, fighting continued. The German troops who had been held up by Fago-Golfarelli had passed on through Piazza Vittorio and up Via Merulana, heading towards the railway station. While one unit turned at Via Gioberti, another went around the church of Santa Maria Maggiore into Via Cavour.

About one hundred civilians, among them Toti Scialoia and Renato Guttuso, painters and Communists, along with Action party members, local residents and young boys, met the Germans' advance. As the Italians were forced back on Via Cavour, their way was blocked by Germans firing from the Hotel Continentale. Italian soldiers and civilians, armed with machine guns, started firing at the edifice while observers crowded on nearby roofs and terraces.

Up Via Cavour came a truck with a machine gun on top and a man firing it. Suddenly the man looked around helplessly; the gun was stuck. A young Grenadier officer came forward, climbed up, fixed the weapon, and set himself behind it to continue firing. Only a few steps away, people were going about their usual business or coming to a door or window from time to time to watch.

As German squads advanced on Via Gioberti, the Italians were caught between two lines of fire. Standing midway between the two forces, Sergeant Mimmo Spadini, with great calm, kept firing a musket. Behind him were members of his Engineers Company and individual soldiers and officers.

When a white flag appeared from a window of the Hotel Continentale, the Italians stopped firing and an officer went up to deal with the Germans. A minute later a volley was heard and a civilian ran back screaming. "The officer's been killed," he cried, and the battle started again.

By now it was sunset and a small field hospital had been set up in nearby Piazza Esedra. More and more boys took part; some had pistols that had been abandoned by soldiers, while others, unarmed, acted as scouts. Mimmo Spadini saw several hit. Three other boys came forward, one wrapped around with ammunition belts, a slightly taller one holding a machine gun on the back of the third, the smallest. A distinguished gentleman with grey hair loaded a hunting rifle, stood erect, and fired as if he were shooting quail.

An Italian armored car arrived with the machine-gunner dead; the driver asked for help to unload him: "Anyone want to take his place?"

"I'll do it," said a soldier, who climbed in and started firing, only to be killed in turn.

The fighting reached the huge Piazza dei Cinquecento in front of the station. People who found themselves in the middle of the shooting didn't know where to run. Among them were soldiers who had come to find a train home. They all crowded into the station. The fighting here centered around a twenty-two-car army command train which had been moved to the station after Roatta and his staff had left Monterotondo. Only thirteen of the armored train's complement were left, led by train commander Major Carlo Benedetti, but they were joined by railwaymen and soldiers and civilians who had been forced back from the surrounding streets. A 22mm gun was placed at the head of the train and another was placed on the platform. The Germans came forward, took the gun on the tracks and turned it against the Italians. Among the first to be hit were two railwaymen who were given Extreme Unction by a military chaplain. By 8:30 P.M., the Italians were forced to bow to superior force. From then on, no organized Italian unit fought within Rome.

A few isolated German motorcyclists sped across the city. One was killed on Via del Tritone in front of the *Popolo di Roma*. There were some scattered shots, then silence. After about an hour, people started coming into the streets. Not a car was in sight, only bicycles. All laws seemed to be abolished, lights were kept on despite the blackout, no one respected the curfew, and no police were to be seen. But a communiqué was being issued by Berlin: the German army, "without meeting notable resistance," had conquered Rome.

Chapter 39

AN ARMY DISSOLVES

For a few minutes on the morning of September 11, Ruggero Zangrandi and the other political prisoners at Rome's Regina Coeli prison thought that their wildest hopes had been fulfilled. Hundreds of inmates, looking out the barred windows of the fourth wing towards the Gianicolo hill, were shouting and yelling. "The Americans are here!" they cried. They had seen soldiers dressed in khaki coming down the hillside and were convinced the Allies had landed. Minutes later, however, as the figures approached, disillusion set in. The khaki-clad soldiers were Germans.

The first patrols had arrived early that morning, first in groups of three and four, then in squads and finally in formations, crossing the city with submachine guns leveled. Some anti-Fascists had fired at them from windows, while others threw four-pointed nails in front of German vehicles. That afternoon, fighting was still going on between German and Italian soldiers at the Castro Pretorio barracks near the station, and spasmodic firing continued for the next few days.

Newspapers and radio announced that the Germans were remaining at the gates of Rome except for those guarding their embassy, their telephone center and the radio, but they could be seen all over the city, shooting right and left, seizing private cars and bicycles, and rifling banks. Germans moved into public buildings and ministries, placing antitank guns out front. Machine guns were set up at downtown corners, streets were blocked off, and parachutists in yellow-green camouflage uniforms questioned passersby while others sped up and down in armored cars and motorcycles.

There was no denying that the city belonged to them, the streets were empty of buses, streetcars and police. Pools of blood remained on the pavements. No one went to work. The markets had been looted and there was little to eat.

Posters, printed in German and Italian and signed by Kesselring, proclaimed that all Italian territory under his control was subject to martial law. Labor stoppages were *verboten;* strike organizers, saboteurs and snipers would be summarily shot; private correspondence was prohibited; and phone lines would be tapped.

At 1 P.M. on September 11, Luigi Persichetti, who was out of Rome on holiday, tuned in the radio to hear a voice—speaking in Itallian with a heavy Teutonic accent—announce the entry of Germans into the capital. The announcer said that the few "inconsiderate" civilians who had opposed their entry had been "shot immediately."

Now Romans began to realize what had happened. Dazed by the impact of occupation, families passed the next hours in anguish, victims both of contradictory news accounts and of a terrifying reality. Raffaele Persichetti's mother had not seen him since Thursday, and now she recalled hearing what had sounded like gunfire when he had spoken to her on Friday afternoon. The family started phoning friends. Tom Carini said that he had gone to San Paolo Friday afternoon and looked for Raffaele everywhere. Romano Antonelli, phoned by Raffaele's brother Augusto, had also been at San Paolo that day but had not seen his former teacher. He went back; the scene was desolate and forlorn; some burned-out Italian tanks sat in the center of Via della Marmorata, but not a living soul was to be seen.

Army comrades of Raffaele phoned to say they had seen him earlier Friday afternoon, but not after two o'clock. Two officers who knew Raffaele were searching for their sons, both captains, who were missing: Colonel Sabatini, father of Camillo of the Montebello Lancers, and General Vannetti Donnini, father of Franco of the Genoa Cavalry.

Posters appeared, signed by General Calvi di Bergolo, telling of the agreement with the Germans and confirming the 9:30 P.M. curfew. "The population," the proclamation stated, "must pursue normal occupations, conserving perfect order, calm and obedience to the dispositions of military authorities." This included the turning in of arms; soldiers, too, were ordered to report to their barracks within twenty-four hours and give back their weapons.

After a night in their barracks, the Grenadiers came out, each carrying a bundle or a cardboard suitcase tied with string. As they and others left the city, the crack Piave Motorized Division, led by General Tabellini, came in through Via Salaria. Disciplined and well trained, they rode through the streets as Romans applauded and, here and there, a few spectators wept. Was it another illusion? Could it be true that Rome would be left to govern itself, that there would be no reprisals? It was hardly encouraging to note that while some German troops moved south to Salerno, others were still coming into the city, violating agreements. That morning, the 3rd Panzergrenadieren had begun what was to be a victorious march into Rome, but at 10 A.M., the Re Division, stationed on Via Cassia, refused it passage. At 1:30 P.M., following orders from Rome, the Re left the way open for the Panzergrenadieren to pass. But when, at four thirty that afternoon, the Germans came by, they halted, then attacked and disarmed the Italians. The sound of new battle alarmed Romans, and the sight of German armored vehicles moving down Via Veneto caused many of the previously indifferent to shake their heads in apprehension.

Throughout Italy, city after city fell and the disbandment of the army grew. Officers called their men together and told them, "Boys, we've lost the war. Return to your homes but try to avoid railroad stations. The Germans are taking them over."

Frequently, officers embraced their men with tears in their eyes. Others said, "We're out of ammunition, do what you can for yourselves." Some officers, left without headquarters, without directives and even without news of what was going on, took off their uniforms and put on civilian clothes. Noting this, their soldiers saw no reason why they should not do the same. They were seen entering doors in their grey-green uniforms and then cautiously coming out in badly fitted civilian clothes.

Simple soldiers were astonished at the turn of events. The fact that the Germans were shooting at them led some to believe that the Germans had allied themselves with the Americans against Italy. A standard joke observed that "When Badoglio said the war would continue, it stopped; when he said it would stop, it continued."

They were faced with an agonizing dilemma: they could either keep their weapons by swearing allegiance to the German Reich and fighting at its side, or they could give up their arms and risk deportation to labor camps. Those who remained to await orders almost always wound up deported, but thousands abandoned themselves to the desire to escape capture and simply melted away.

Near Rome, twelve-year-old Alfredo Zambelli watched in fascination as soldiers dropped their rifles down wells or into sewers. This wasn't the way he played at soldiers; weren't they supposed to use their rifles for fighting?

Infantry Private Eraldo Meloni, a Roman, felt the same way, but his commanding officer had told his company to stack their guns and remain in the barracks.

"Without a rifle," said Eraldo, "I'm not a soldier," and with that he slipped out of the barracks through the back door.

Another private joined him, muttering, "The Americans are in Calabria and the Germans a half hour away; I'm getting out of here."

The exodus of troops, once a trickle, became a river. That morning in Rome, Bruno Spampanato saw unarmed Italian infantrymen in groups of ten, twenty and more, carrying bundles. Many, he thought, must have left their barracks the night before and slept in the meadows, for they still had grass on their jackets.

Some soldiers had filtered back into Rome in time for mess at their barracks. When food started to run out, they tried to reach their homes. Many had no idea of where they were and stopped people at random to ask for directions.

A navy commander rounded up about fifty of them and tried to find someone in authority who would give him orders, but no one was willing to cooperate. He kept the fifty soldiers with him all day, until finally, in the evening, he let them go.

Outside Rome, the dissolution of the armed forces was even more widespread. Marcello Soleri wrote: "Thursday the 9th at La Spezia, I witnessed the first painful spectacle of the military disbanding. The sailors of the Navy Yard, dismissed by their commanders, crowded the station, loaded with bundles, waiting for trains."

Any trains that halted were filled within minutes as men climbed on the roofs of cars, rode on locomotives, and clung to cowcatchers. The only nationwide organization that continued to function was the railroad, although no one paid for a ticket. As if nothing had happened, railwaymen continued to see that the trains ran, thus enabling tens of thousands of soldiers to avoid capture and reach their homes safely.

General Caracciolo, who had sneaked past German lines into

Florence, heard that all his troops in Pisa had been taken prisoner on the afternoon of the ninth and that, despite resistance at Livorno, his troops there had been forced to surrender on the tenth.

That same day, the Germans had come through the Futa Pass and into Florence. The general watched his men, disarmed and silent, being marched away by a few guards carrying rifles. Crowds were watching, astonished.

Caracciolo looked at the sad procession. "They were my soldiers, my sons," he thought, "now abandoned . . . and I could do nothing for them. The blood rushed to my face. What humiliation for us, an eternal humiliation. An eternal curse on those who led us to this. . .!"

Now, without a platoon left of the thirty divisions he once commanded, he set out for Rome, a trip which took him fourteen hours and involved changing trains fifteen times. Soldiers, sailors and airmen, all animated by one instinct—to get home—climbed aboard without either knowing or caring in what direction the trains were going or how they would eat on the way. Dressed in civilian clothes, the spade-bearded general heard them call it "the damned war" as they cursed their officers. When he finally arrived in Rome, after having been searched, together with other passengers in a bus, by German parachutists, he headed straight for the army command at Piazza della Pilotta.

General Barbieri stood downcast in the midst of a flow of people who, to Caracciolo, seemed like ants after their hill had been destroyed.

"Who's in command?" Caracciolo asked. "What's happening?"

"We don't know," Barbieri answered. "Calvi di Bergolo has assumed a sort of command. Marshal Caviglia at the War Ministry sends out orders. According to agreement, the Germans were to stay outside the city limits but you can see their armed platoons all over the place."

Then Caracciolo went to Caviglia for orders.

"I have none," the marshal said. "I maintain that we aren't enemies of the Germans and we should not be treated as such. For the moment we have to maintain public order."

Caracciolo, seeing that the old marshal still had illusions, shrugged his shoulders and left. The cause of Italy's tragedy, he later wrote, was not betrayal, but rather a policy of grandeur that lacked the means to achieve it.

Generals in the field did not know how to deal with the unparalleled situation. On September 11, General Vercellino, commanding

the Fourth Army, had the Mount Cenis tunnel blown up, along with
a number of trunk roads in Piedmont. He had received OP 44 earlier,
but had judged it to be inapplicable. "It wouldn't have helped anything," he later commented.

Thinking that he still had the Em. Filiberto (2nd) Division at his
disposal, he dispatched one of his officers to have it moved into a
position better adapted for resistance. On his way, at the Dronero
Bridge, the officer met the division's commander, General Giuseppe
Andreoli. Pointing to the few officers with him, Andreoli said, "Here's
my division." The rest of it had disappeared.

That night, Vercellino, caught between the forces of Rommel in
northern Italy and of von Rundstedt in southern France, declared
the Fourth Army disbanded in the hope of preventing the capture of
the few units he had left. Army depots in the area were opened to
prevent their falling into German hands and inhabitants, invited to
pillage them, took whatever they could.

There were innumerable Italian soldiers who, independently and
frequently against orders, kept on fighting long beyond the dictates
of logic, even when surrounded, isolated and hopelessly outnumbered.
Such resistance inevitably evoked a savage response from the Germans, who felt that any reprisal against the traitorous Italians was
justified. The Germans, after all, regarded themselves as having been
betrayed. No one had asked them to leave Italy; they had been told
that the Italians would continue to fight at their side, but suddenly
the Italians were, to all appearances, enemies, having deserted their
ally so as to save their own skins.

The Germans maintained that there was ample legal justification
for their brutal retaliation against the Italians: when they killed Italian soldiers and civilians, they were executing rebels and spies; Italy
was not at war with Germany and her soldiers, when captured, were
therefore not entitled to the protection of the Geneva Convention.

Particularly ferocious was the German reaction in the South.
When a shot fired from a window hit a German officer at Barletta, his
enraged troops executed thirteen men. At Aversa, *Carabinieri* who
had fought the Germans were made to dig their own graves before
being executed. At Nola, a unit of the Hermann Goering Division
captured the 48th Artillery Regiment and executed its commander in
full view of his troops.

Although Gaeta was occupied by the Germans on the evening of
the eighth, Italian sailors still there forced them to retreat to the old
city on the heights. After two days of fighting, the Germans came

back down, and the Italians, seeing that the Germans had strapped captured sailors to their mobile guns, surrendered.

Milan, a city with a long tradition of revolt, took to the barricades as it had three times in the previous century. Civilians fought alongside soldiers. On the night of the tenth, General Ruggiero, who was deprived of transport and unable to communicate with his superiors in Rome, came to an agreement with the Germans. The next morning the SS occupied the city, the Italian soldiers were disarmed and General Ruggiero was deported to Germany, where he died in a concentration camp.

Elsewhere in Lombardy there was prolonged resistance, but Italian troops there stood no chance against the better-equipped Germans. As punishment, the Germans forbade the burying of the corpses which littered the roads between Cremona and Brescia, and the women of the two cities walked among them scattering flowers over the bodies.

Soldiers of the 8th Artillery fought in Verona, and thousands, along with General Orengo, were deported to the prisons of the Reich. Troops still held out in Bolzano, only to be eventually overcome and their officers deported. Elsewhere in the Tyrol, Alpine outfits used their knowledge of the mountains to elude capture.

In Bassano del Grappa, which was occupied on September 9, a group of four hundred Alpine soldiers with artillery and machine guns formed a column and crossed the city while the Germans, surprised by the calm and order with which the movement was carried out, let them leave.

Germans at La Spezia, furious at the escape of the Italian warships, executed Italian naval captains who, unable to move their ships out of port, had scuttled them. Fighting, led by the XVI Corps, went on for three days before armored and motorized German troops completed their possession of the city.

The garrisons of Treviso, Parma, Pavia, Bergamo, Cuneo, Savona, Ascoli Piceno and scores of others surrendered only after they were overcome.

The Italians were more successful where intelligent, energetic chiefs were able to count on outside help. This was shown in Corsica where parts of the island had been occupied by the Germans on the night of September 9. The VII Army Corps, consisting of the Cremona and Friuli Divisions, had retaken most of it with the help of partisans and French units commanded by General Martin, and then met the attack of the German 90th Division after it had been ferried over from Sardinia. The Germans were forced to abandon the island, but the price paid by the Italians—three thousand dead and wounded—was high. Still, at one city alone, Bastia, they killed eight hundred Germans and captured over a thousand.

The story was a little different in Sardinia. The commander of the 180,000 Italians stationed there, General Antonio Basso, at 2 A.M. on September 9, had been ordered by Ambrosio to comply with the German request that their fifteen thousand troops be allowed to leave the island peaceably. For three days Basso tried to obtain further instructions but could reach no one in authority. Suddenly, from Brindisi, Badoglio—in direct contrast to what Basso had been told earlier—ordered him to attack and destroy the German force. By then, of course, it was gone. As a result, Basso was later tried and imprisoned for two years for not having defended Sardinia in the same manner, said Zangrandi, that Ambrosio and Roatta had defended Rome.

There were other places in Italy where superior orders thwarted the armed forces' will to fight. In Naples, on September 10 and 11, soldiers and sailors disarmed and captured Germans and were moving toward control of the city when the arrival of Panzer divisions headed for Salerno enabled the Germans to regain control of the situation, aided by the fact that Italian officers ordered the captured weapons given up and prisoners released.

The real fault lay in the disarray left by the king, Badoglio and the generals. Some commanders were so perplexed that they did not know on whose side they were and suffered accordingly. Most of the XXXI Army Corps, which was in Calabria at the moment of the armistice (five divisions), was wiped out, partly by the English and partly by the Germans. The majority of commanders, taking the easy way out, gave up without a fight. The garrison at Genoa immediately surrendered to the Germans, who promptly deported all American and British prisoners to the Reich. General Adami-Rossi, the commander of Turin who had ordered workers fired upon in July, quickly came to an agreement with the Germans although the Italian garrison, as in many other cities, had been superior in number.

Within the army, Italians betrayed each other. In Novara, garrison commander General Cosentino convened a meeting of officers, ostensibly to give them orders for resistance; but while they were gathered together, the Germans, in agreement with the general, disarmed the soldiers who had been left without commanders. In Sardinia, in one of the rare cases in which most of an Italian unit joined the *Wehrmacht*, Lieutenant Colonel Alberto Bechi-Luserma, chief of staff of the Nembo Parachute Division, was killed by his own men when he tried to keep them from defecting.

As disbanded soldiers traveled south on trains, their captured comrades, shut in sealed cattle cars, were being sent north. Somehow they threw notes out onto the railroad tracks, addressed to families who would never see them again: "We're all right. . . . Everything's fine. . . . Don't worry about me."

Many of these men had neither surrendered nor fought. They had merely awaited orders, which never came. Their understandable indecision was quickly resolved by the Germans, who acted with dispatch and efficiency.

In northern Italy, Marshal Rommel's forces proceeded methodically to execute the occupation plans that had been ready since August 31. By the night of the tenth, two thousand German railway workers had taken over the area's main rail centers and German troops were quickly moved to vital spots. They took Trieste, thus blocking the overland exit for the thirty-two Italian divisions then in the Balkans. These troops, isolated from mainland Italy and receiving either outdated orders or none at all, met varying fates.

Caught by surprise, thousands of soldiers were abandoned south of Trieste, where they had been stationed in ports along the Istrian peninsula and the Croatian littoral. Here the population, some pro-German, some propartisan, hunted down the Italians, who found themselves caught between two lines of fire and in some cases fighting against a third, the *hustacza* of Fascist puppet Ante Pavelic. In other parts of Yugoslavia they were caught between warring partisans, the Chetniks of General Draza Mihailovic, and the Liberation Army of guerilla leader Josip Broz, known as Tito.

In Montenegro, the Venezia and Taurinense divisions fought against the Germans and then formed a new division, the Garibaldi, which became part of Tito's forces.

The Germans gave vent to their fury on the slightest pretext, executing commanders and deporting troops that resisted. In Dalmatia, the Bergamo Division at Split fought for nineteen days and then, after a summary trial, its three top generals were shot. At Zadar, the division of the same name (Zara in Italian) resisted, but its commanders, Generals Francesco Giangreco and Paolo Grimaldi, were captured. Although through a fortunate mistake they escaped execution, they were sent to the Flossenburg concentration camp.

Two other infantry divisions posted in Dalmatia opposed the Germans. General Guglielmo Spicacci, commander of the Messina, was captured after four days' fighting and died in prison. General Giuseppe Amico, commander of the Marche, was also taken. Allowed to address his soldiers, he spoke against the Germans, urging his men to resist. The troops overcame the general's guards and followed him out into the streets of Dubrovnik, where they fought, only to be beaten back by German tanks. Recaptured, General Amico was killed by a shot in the neck because, while being taken to prison by German officers, he *again* encouraged his troops to fight.

The story was the same in Albania, where the Ninth Army chief of staff thought that the armistice applied only to Allied troops and that Germans were not to be considered enemies. Part of the Emilia Division, disobeying his orders, fought their way to the coast and made their way back to Italy by boat. Some Italian units joined Albanian partisans and others fought till overcome by the Germans, but many more, following the orders of superiors, surrendered.

Italian forces in Greece particularly suffered from the ambiguity of the orders from Rome. Here many Italian commands were intermixed and coordinated with Germans. From Athens, the commander of the Eleventh Army, General Carlo Vecchiarelli, ordered his eight divisions not to take armed initiative against the Germans, interpreting literally the last message he had received, ". . . react against attacks. . . ." The Germans for the most part did not attack. Instead they offered the Italians the alternative of following their government's directives by laying down their arms. They even guaranteed the transport of troops to Italy, a promise which was rarely fulfilled. Instead, after long marches or agonizing trips, the Italians wound up in German prisons or concentration camps.

Ruggero Zangrandi's figures indicate that of the approximately 670,000 Italian soldiers east of Italy, 150,000 joined the partisans, 38,000 died, 8,000 were wounded, 21,000 became lost and 450,000 were deported to Germany. These figures included an entire division, the Acqui, which was wiped out on the Ionian islands of Corfu and Cephalonia on orders sent from Berlin by Martin Bormann, Hitler's deputy. The Acqui's commander, Major General Antonio Gandin, had tried to contact Ambrosio—whose deputy he had been at the Feltre meeting—and then Badoglio, but without success. Put before a firing squad, he ripped off the Iron Cross that Hitler had personally given him and threw it at his executioners as they fired.

The bodies of dead soldiers on Cephalonia were either left to rot or soaked with gasoline and set afire. "Italian rebels," said the German commanding officer, "don't deserve burial." In all, eighty-four hundred were killed, and a black cloud covered the island for a week. Even today, in nearby Greek villages, when the sky is dark and the air is heavy, they say, "The Italians are burning."

In Italy, civilians moved to take the place of the military. There were scores of instances of armed reaction to German domination, spontaneous and for the most part little known. The port of Piombino, left without orders, had been abandoned on September 10. Then word came of German troops on their way from the island of Corsica. Workers, along with disbanded soldiers and sailors, hurriedly occupied the port and its facilities, firing the coastal batteries at the approaching ships. The Germans tried to put troops ashore but the landing was repulsed. The results: two corvettes and numerous landing craft sunk, an accompanying destroyer badly damaged, eight hundred Germans dead, and two hundred taken prisoner. Then, using an earlier order of Ambrosio as an excuse, former Fascist hierarch General de Vecchi, as commander of the 215th Coastal Division, ordered the prisoners released. Shortly afterward, Germans arrived by land to take over the city.

At Orbetello, while army units were surrendering, individual soldiers and civilians joined forces against the invader. They, too, were forced to give up, but before they did, they hid their arms. The same thing happened elsewhere in the South. At Teramo, a *Carabinieri* captain formed squads of individual soldiers, farmers, workers and professional men who fought for two weeks, and the citizens of Nola, after the killing of the 48th Artillery officers, organized a popular insurrection under the command of a sergeant and a farmer.

Resistance in northern cities such as Udine, Reggio Emilia, Piacenza, Cremona and Mantova was even more widespread. When they fell, local inhabitants helped imprisoned Italian soldiers to escape, including five thousand at Bologna. At the military academy of Pavullo, near Modena, cadets commanded by Colonel Duca fought and were overcome by Germans; however, a sixteen-year-old girl and a fifteen-year-old boy found their way through a network of sewers to the academy and helped hundreds of cadets escape. Still farther north, people did the same for Allied prisoners, who were then escorted into the mountains or across the frontier into Switzerland.

On September 10, the Allies, with broadcasts and leaflets, had called on the armed forces of Italy to strike back at the Germans. But there was no Italian army. As a German High Command communiqué said that night: "It no longer exists."

From its dissolution, the Germans gathered a fantastic amount of booty: 1,255,660 rifles, 33,383 machine guns, 9,988 pieces of artillery, 970 tanks and mobile guns, 4,553 planes, 15,500 vehicles, 28,600 tons of munitions and more than 32,000,000 gallons of fuel. Jodl sarcastically said that this was ". . . militarily, the greatest service that Italy rendered its ally."

Kesselring was more than pleased to find "enormous depots full of unused equipment," three million garments, uncounted blankets and thousands of automatic weapons which had never been given to the army. Some were sent to Germany, but Italian civilians, in the confusion, managed to get a share.

The Germans disarmed dozens of divisions, fifty-one completely and most of the rest partially. Captured were 547,431 men, including 24,744 officers.

Hitler saw that the catastrophe he had feared had not materialized and that he could hold the territory south of Rome with fewer troops than he would have needed north of the capital. Fortuitously given a chance to catch his breath, he no longer wanted to give up southern Italy. Kesselring's energy and imagination had paid off and after a year of almost continuous retreat German troops were finally able to turn and fight. Hitler recalled Rommel for duty in the West and appointed Kesselring commander of all forces in the Italian theatre.

With Rome occupied, Kesselring sent more reinforcements to Salerno, where Mark Clark was making preparations for evacuation. After fierce fighting, the German counterattacks were beaten back. Yet, although the Allies managed to establish themselves on the mainland, they remained blocked in the South, with the mirage of the Eternal City glimmering in the distance.

At one point, when the Allies had had their way barred by the Germans for months, an anonymous Roman wrote on the wall of a house in Trastevere: "Americans, hold on! We'll come soon to liberate you!"

Militarily, the surrender had little effect in Italy; the Allies were unable to occupy even one of the many positions abandoned by the Italians. Any political advantages were outweighed by the casualties it caused, the destruction and the disruption of Italian life, and the impairment of Allied plans. The precipitate dispersal of the Italian army and the long involvement of Allied forces on the Italian peninsula prevented the Allies from carrying out what Churchill called "a business of great consequences"—invasion of the Balkans. Thus, Eastern Europe was occupied exclusively by the Russians and the postwar possibility of a strong Western position in this area was lost.

Rarely has a campaign been criticized as much. British military

Q

authority Major General J. F. C. Fuller thought it ". . . strategically the most senseless campaign of the whole war. 'Unconditional surrender' transformed the 'soft underbelly' into a crocodile's back; prolonged the war; wrecked Italy; and wasted thousands of American and British lives."

Allied strategy had been intended to draw German divisions into Italy and tie them up there, but it succeeded also in engaging more and more *Allied* troops—sent for reasons of prestige—and in immobilizing them to such an extent that Field Marshal Alexander asked, "Who is containing whom?"

Even Bedell Smith admitted in 1946 that "the whole Anglo-American plan of war in Italy was wrong."

For Hanson Baldwin, the campaign was aimless: ". . . the Allies had no clear-cut, agreed-upon ultimate strategic objective. . . . All roads led to Rome, but Rome led nowhere strategically. That in a nutshell was the tragedy. . . ."

The invasion at Salerno had not led to Italian surrender, nor did it lead immediately to the capture of Rome. The Allies were forced to do just as Guariglia had predicted, ". . . take Italy village by village," and expend their strength in costly and lengthy efforts to reach this irrelevant goal.

Germany was still strong, holding almost all of Europe except Great Britain and part of Russia. Notwithstanding the loss of Italy's eighty-odd divisions, the Axis still had more than three hundred divisions and almost seven thousand first-line aircraft, with giant tanks and more planes coming out of their factories.

In spite of all this, the joint message sent to Badoglio by Churchill and Roosevelt on September 11 said: "The armies of liberation are on the march . . . the German terror will not last much longer," and repeated almost literally one of Churchill's broadcast promises asking Italians to "have faith in your future. Everything will go well."

Not one of these statements proved to be true.

Autumn came, and winter, and more men died to capture a symbol.

Chapter 40

THE SUBMERGED CITY

On Monday, September 13, the Vatican opened its doors, but it was no longer a beacon of hope. German sentinels were stationed in front of St. Peter's, at the border with Italy. Some newspapers hopefully wrote of the free city of Rome, but German censors, now hard at work, realistically deleted the word "free." The black market became the only market, and prices rose continually. Soon bicycles were to be forbidden, along with walking on certain streets, crossing others, bringing food into the city, telegraphing or phoning outside of Rome, entering or leaving the city, and passing the night away from one's home. Curfew was changed from nine thirty in the evening to nine, to seven, to six, and finally to five in the afternoon.

The rake of German reprisal was even felt at Regina Coeli, where the SS started selecting prisoners at random to be shot. Revolts which had started during the Forty-five Days intensified, prisoners were killed and wounded, and many, like Ruggero Zangrandi, were deported to the concentration camps of the Third Reich.

Yet there were still those in Rome who hoped for Allied help, and who saw it even when it did not exist. On the thirteenth, at one of his last meetings at the War Ministry, Marshal Caviglia said that the Allies had landed at Anzio and that he was prepared to go meet them, together with the pope, flying the pontifical flag. Carboni was more circumspect. "It will be at least a month or a month and a half," he said, "before Rome is liberated." No one in Rome, besides Carboni, knew of General Taylor's futile visit and of the turndown of American troops, and even Carboni was beginning to put another interpretation on events.

With the need for strategic reconnaissance over, he had given up the apartment in Parioli and accepted the hospitality of forty-four-year-old Virginia Bourbon del Monte, the half-American widow of Edoardo Agnelli of the Fiat empire. Her house at Porta San Pancrazio was considerably closer to Porta San Paolo than Parioli had been, but the fighting was over there, and a German standard now flew over the city gate.

At some point, Carboni has written, he began to believe that he had been schemed against, that the fall of Rome had been a Machiavellian plot, and that he and Roatta had been chosen to bear the responsibility.

If a scapegoat were needed, General Carboni seemed typecast for the role; as Attilio Tamaro has pointed out, "He was known as a turbulent, undisciplined officer, greedy for luxury, and a specialist in sabotaging projects in which he was supposed to fight."

But it is also true that Carboni had been left in an almost impossible position, entrusted with a mission of whose failure he was convinced, and promised orders which never came.

The possibility that this had been done as part of a larger design was first raised in print by *La Folla*, the organ of the right-wing Everyman's party. On May 24, 1945, it said that the king, for dynastic reasons, had deliberately delivered Rome to the Germans.

Carboni went further. He claimed that General Ambrosio had known the long terms of the armistice and had told Roatta not to mention them. Although Ambrosio, according to Carboni, knew that the Allied landing at Salerno was to take place on the ninth, not on the twelfth, he reached a secret accord with Kesselring to allow the king and the military chiefs to escape in return for their sacrificing Rome and leaving Mussolini where he was.

Carboni obviously subscribed to a conspiratorial theory of history. For years his writings have condemned virtually every protagonist of the period. Eisenhower and Smith were insincere; Eisenhower never intended sending the 82nd Airborne; the armistice had been set for the twelfth but was announced ahead of time, without warning the Italians. Badoglio, Ambrosio, Major Marchesi, Caviglia and Castellano were all engaged in a nefarious plot or plots.

In 1947, Carboni bewailed his position "among a Germanophile Marshal Caviglia, an evanascent and administrative Minister of War, a son-in-law of the king who commanded Fascist troops and was in gang with the Germans, a Committee of National Liberation divided and irresolute, a chief of staff like Colonel Salvi, dismayed, screaming and crying, a Colonel Giaccone at the direct service of the enemy."

Carboni was also suspicious of his new chief of staff, Montezemolo, even though Montezemolo was later tortured and killed by the Germans.

In 1952, Carboni wrote, "The only plausible explanation is that Ambrosio, who had Major Marchesi sustain the acceptance [of the Allied armistice] with such fervor, had some very secret agreements with the Germans for withdrawal. My suspicion was based on people's saying that Ambrosio as well as Kesselring were Freemasons."

In 1964, Zangrandi came to Carboni's support, producing a mass of contiguous, peripheral evidence which, though it was impressive, was not entirely pertinent to Carboni's premise. This included a similar reference to the Freemasons, which in Italy had been a secret but not too powerful organization divided into two rival branches. The supposed Ambrosio-Kesselring agreement is the only plot in recent history to be specifically attributed to it. Could it have provided a bond so strong that Kesselring would risk Hitler's wrath in order to make a fraternal gesture?

Why is it that despite numerous well-publicized books, articles and trials in twenty-seven years not one German has come forward with even a hint of this German–Italian accord? Yet, many Germans would have been involved in carrying out such an agreement. If it existed, German troops, planes, helicopters, submarines and spies would have been busy keeping roads and harbors cleared and airports and cities untouched so that the fugitives could use them.

Of the German generals involved—and it is difficult to see what they would lose by admission of such a coup—not one has admitted that such an accord ever existed. When asked by Dollmann, Kesselring said the rumor had no truth to it. In 1964, Westphal agreed:

Marshal Kesselring would never have assumed the responsibility of consenting to the king's flight. Logic dictated the opposite: it would have been convenient to us to keep the king in Rome. At that moment we had other worries. . . . We were in what could be called a desperate situation with the possibility of a paratroop invasion hanging over our heads. Berlin was torturing us hour by hour requesting continuous reports on the development of events. No one at headquarters in Frascati thought about the king or Badoglio's government.

In a 1968 interview, General Student said:

I exclude with absolute certainty that there had been an agreement between Kesselring and Ambrosio or other personalities to favor the escape of the royal family. . . . What interested us was not the person of the king; we were interested in the Italian armed forces . . . with General Roatta first on the list.

After Roatta escaped to Spain, Carboni was forced to bear the brunt of the guilt. The Commission of Inquiry into the Failure to Defend Rome called Carboni a "typical figure of a man brought by fascism to that very high post [commander of troops defending Rome]" and said of him ". . . in all the military history of our country we have no such example of behavior on the part of a general confronted by the enemy."

Going beyond its mandate, the commission asked not only for the punishment of Carboni, Roatta and generals of lesser rank, but for a more ample and profound political inquest. The commission chairman, Senator Mario Palermo, criticized the king, "who to serve positions, personal and class privileges," betrayed "the supreme interests of the country"; Badoglio, who had given no "precise, political or military orders to those charged with negotiations" with the Allies; and Ambrosio, who had left Rome knowing "of the arrival . . . of Allied representatives" and had refused to apply OP 44.

No political inquest was ever carried out, although Carboni was subjected to further hearings by military commissions which alternately discharged, reinstated, reprimanded and cleared him.

On September 10, Mussolini, who had passed thirteen days confined in the hotel of Campo Imperatore on the Gran Sasso, heard nothing of a speech by Hitler which referred to him as "the greatest son of Italy." He did learn something else that day. In his *Storia d'un anno*, speaking of himself in the third person, he wrote:

The 10th at 8 P.M., Mussolini went downstairs and switched the radio on. By chance he picked up Berlin radio and a news item originating from Algiers: "Allied headquarters officially announce that among the armistice conditions is a clause calling for delivery of Mussolini to the Allies." He was determined not to deliver himself "alive" to the English, and especially not to the Americans.

Following the word "Americans" came several lines which, though never made public, exist in the handwritten manuscript in the Italian government's central archives, as follows:

During the night Mussolini tried and confirmed that the blades of a Gillette razor were sufficient to open one's veins. There was an alarm and an immediate confiscation of all metal objects.

This was done by the *Carabinieri* commander, Lieutenant Faiola, who had gone to Mussolini's room and found his prisoner covered with blood. The flow was stopped by bandages and medicaments while Mussolini kept repeating over and over, "I won't be taken alive by the English."

He did not know that Badoglio's plans for him precluded his being taken alive by anyone. On August 2, the marshal had told Bonomi, "Mussolini is in a safe place, far from here, and he won't leave it alive."

When one of the men responsible for Mussolini, Police Inspector Giuseppe Gueli, was told the same thing by Chief of Police Senise, he had indignantly insisted that he was not a murderer. Senise had calmed him down by assuring him that the *Carabinieri* were charged with carrying out Mussolini's execution. Then, on September 12, a telegram came from Senise recommending "maximum prudence." Gueli received it at 1:30 P.M.

At 2:15 P.M., Otto Skorzeny led twelve gliders to Campo Imperatore, where eight landed. Skorzeny emerged and walked towards the hotel, preceded by General Fernando Soleti, the man considered by many to have been the only hero of July 25. Soleti had been persuaded to cooperate by General Student, who had told him that his uniform would discourage bloodshed. When Lieutenant Faiola ordered the *Carabinieri* to take up positions behind their machine guns, Gueli countermanded the order and told them to give up their arms. He later explained to Faiola that Senise's telegram meant that orders had been changed, and that Mussolini was to be consigned to the Germans if they requested it.

The propaganda-conscious Skorzeny had brought along a photographer who frantically snapped pictures as Italian soldiers stood by and shouted, *"Duce! Duce!"*

Somehow, for a few minutes at least, Mussolini had the idea that he would finally be able to rest. His first words to Skorzeny were to ask to be taken to his home in northern Italy. But Hitler had other plans for him. Mussolini was first taken in a small Fieseler-Storch to Pratica del Mare, where he was transferred to a Heinkel III and flown to Vienna. From there he was taken to Munich, and finally to Hitler's headquarters at Rastenburg.

Later, in *Corriere della Sera*, Mussolini wrote: "I thank the gods for having saved me from the farce of a ridiculous trial in Madison Square Garden—to that I would have preferred being beheaded in the Tower of London."

He was no longer the purposeful leader he had been. The Forty-five Days had taken their toll, accentuating his already uncertain health: his face was emaciated, his frame shrunken, and his will to rule almost gone. But Hitler did not want Mussolini the man, he needed Mussolini the symbol. To accomplish his aim, he very likely used documents the Germans had found in Rome. These were so compromising to Mussolini that he was finally forced to say to Hitler, "I have come for my instructions."

The news of Mussolini's liberation was broken that evening by German radio. In a weak display of symbolic defiance, Rome's newspapers relegated the news to the back pages or played it down with small type.

The Germans, under the direction of SS Colonel Kappler, were busy picking up documents. Kappler found the police files relating to the Forty-five Days, dossiers on anti-Fascist parties and leaders and lists of Jews, which had been kept up to date as if someone knew that the Germans would be coming in to use them.

The haul also included a huge file on Badoglio's dealings during the Forty-five Days, secret military correspondence from the Supreme Command, confidential archives from the Viminale, Mussolini's archives from Palazzo Venezia and part of the personal file of Vittorio Emanuele III. Kappler promptly shipped over forty cases north.

One document which was kept in Rome was the confession which Cavallero had made to Carboni during the Forty-five Days; the fleeing Badoglio had left it in a prominent place on his desk at the Viminale.

On September 11, Cavallero was released—along with other

leading Fascists imprisoned at Fort Boccea and Regina Coeli—and allowed, while under guard, to visit his sick wife. Although he told her not to worry, he was definitely preoccupied. He had heard that the compromising file had been found by the Germans. Then he was taken to see Rahn, who, under Kesselring's aegis, had returned to Rome to reestabish himself in the embassy. As Cavallero was coming up the embassy driveway, he encountered Marshal Caviglia.

According to Caviglia, he was about to drive off when "Cavallero opened the door, got in the car, put an arm around my neck and pressed his mouth to my right ear. With panting voice, in jerks and crying, he said:

'I'm a prisoner, tomorrow they'll take me to Frascati and they'll put a bullet in my head. They'll kill me.'

'But who? Why do they want to kill you?'

'They'll kill me, they'll put a bullet in my head in Frascati.' "

Two days later, Cavallero was found at the Park Hotel in Frascati, with a bullet through his right temple. Suicide was the verdict of German authority, in the person of Marshal Kesselring.

Even so, the Catholic marshal was given a religious funeral. Cavallero, it is worth noting, was left-handed. Mussolini later commented that "Cavallero committed suicide with Kesselring's right hand."

Whether Cavallero's confession had been left behind on purpose or merely overlooked when other documents were burned, the fact remained that Badoglio was now rid of his longtime rival and personal adversary.

With documentary proof of Badoglio's betrayals staring them in the face, the Germans, who during the Forty-five Days had gauged Italian behavior more or less correctly, now marched across the country, crushing it and plundering it. The Italians were at a loss to understand such ferocity coming from an ally who had been among them for years. Italians had never believed that war meant persecution, torture and pointless killing.

Within days of Mussolini's liberation, a Fascist government was set up. In Rome, three hours before its proclamation, General Calvi di Bergolo was asked to swear allegiance to it. When he refused, he was promptly arrested and deported. The Italian police, nominally under Colonial Police Commander General Riccardo Maraffa, were put under the *Sicherheitsdienst*, and General Riccardo Maraffa was taken to Dachau, where he died. General Tabellini watched the Piave Division being disarmed and then was arrested himself.

New security forces were organized which were no better than street gangs. Hoodlums, small-time crooks and bullying youngsters were taken from prisons and reformatories, dressed in militia uniforms, and armed with daggers and guns. A new Fascist army was constituted, attracting such men as General Solinas, who had done more than anyone else to defend Rome.

The Fascist party, with "Republican" added, reestablished itself at Piazza Colonna—with tanks stationed out front. At Palazzo Venezia, Fascist guards stood in front of the sentry boxes. The radio began repeating the clichés of the Fascist years. Newspapers were entrusted to the ambitious, who each day hymned the German occupiers and justified their excesses.

When Fascists first began making their appearance in black shirts, they were beaten up. Then the Germans stepped in and the Fascist "bedbugs" reappeared in buttonholes, black shirts were again generally worn, and groups again sang the Fascist songs. With the Germans protecting them, they installed a new tyranny, extorting money and arresting and consigning innocents to be executed.

More than any other Italian city, Rome felt the fist of the invader and the heel of the collaborator. The German command took over the big hotels on Via Veneto and isolated them from the rest of the city with barriers and armed sentinels. Rome was cut off from the rest of Italy. The Germans even transferred the holdings of the Bank of Italy, three billion lire in gold and currency, to the North.

Soldiers who refused to join the army of Mussolini's new government were rounded up and sent to Nazi concentration camps.

Some Romans fled to the hills around the city the very night of the armistice. Others waited to make sure, even after news of the flight of the king and the generals and the collapse of the army. Friends were arrested, and houses searched; civilians were rounded up, deported, and shot. Men hid in cellars, attics, windowless rooms and closets. There was alarm at the ringing of a bell, tension at a knock on the door, fright at a strange voice or a heavy footstep, and near hysteria when a car door slammed in the middle of the night.

Anti-Fascists looked for new hiding places. The Forty-five Days had given them a false sense of security and their suspicions had been partially diluted. Now, their hopes pulled out from under them, they were forced to return to their former clandestinity. If during that period of comparative freedom they had won some followers, they had also made themselves and their politics better known to their repressers.

Jews were forced to hide, as Christians had been two thousand years before. Aided by lists on file at the Office of Demography and Race, the Germans began a campaign of racial persecution.

For a while, Jews did not think of themselves as being in danger. During the Forty-five Days, they, too, had stopped taking precautions. In the ghetto they had just started observing *Sukkoth*, the Feast of the Tabernacles, when Kappler's SS went through the area, picking up hundreds of men, women and children, even though the community had earlier paid a tribute of 110 pounds of fine gold. They, like other Jews later, were all deported to German concentration camps from which almost none returned.

Ettore della Riccia, who had just resumed work as a reporter, fled to Naples, where he went into hiding. Alberto Moravia went south to Fondi where friends told him to wait for the Allies to arrive. But instead, the Germans came, Mussolini's Social Republic was proclaimed, and its black flag hung from the old Fascist center.

Italy now had four governments: German, Allied, Mussolini's republic and a monarchy in the small enclave of Brindisi. Here, Badoglio and the king, who had left their army and country in chaos, were being backed by the Allies—in the name of law and order.

Despite urging by Allied chiefs, Badoglio issued only a few desultory orders to army units to regard the Germans as enemies. It was a designation Italian soldiers had already made. Although Badoglio maintained that the last phrase of his armistice announcement had been an order to fight, he had done nothing to see to it that it was so interpreted. Now, incredibly, he was telling soldiers to refuse to give up their arms. "Letting oneself be disarmed," he said from his safe haven in Brindisi, "is a crime"; but neither he nor the king would even partially protect Italian soldiers from German reprisal by declaring war.

In a speech from Radio Brindisi, Vittorio Emanuele explained: "For the salvation of the capital and to be able to carry out fully my duties as king, I have gone with the government and military authorities to another point of our sacred and free national soil." In a striking example of royal hypocrisy, he concluded: "I know I can rely on you just as you can count on your king till the extreme sacrifice."

Soon leaflets appeared saying that Italy did not belong to the traitors but to "the sons of those who sacrificed themselves for the country." A clandestine newspaper called Badoglio "that betrayer of the Italian people, disbander of the Army, swindler, profiteer; it's not for him to address the people, he should keep quiet!"

Thus the split between people and state, which had not been closed during the Forty-five Days, now opened wide.

The Communists, who were now placed in a completely revolutionary position, turned out to be the most forceful of the resisters— the best organized, the most active and the most daring. This, added to the fact that they were supplied with equipment and money by the Allied forces, helped to make the party respectable in Italy.

After the Germans had entered Turin, Emanuele Artom wrote in his diary: "Officers escaped first, then the troops and this has of course given an advantage to communism since the bourgeois classes have cut a sorry figure. . . ."

It was only natural that the country's political compass should swing to the left; the doom of the monarchy was sealed when the king made his ignominious flight.

The fall of Rome and the dissolution of the Italian army represented a defeat in which everyone had a share: Fascists, anti-Fascists, the monarchy and the military. There had been no particular group or class to defend Rome; some officers, troops and civilians had tried, but not the overwhelming mass of the population, or the country's leaders or very many of its appointed officials. Once the fighting was over, the structure of the state collapsed and the city which had supported it, Rome, seemed to have been deprived of all importance.

Rome was finally being defended, by the *Wehrmacht*, and the clump of German boots became the sound of the city. All front doors were ordered closed at curfew and anyone out after that was arrested. Streets were deserted, and obscurity and silence fell over what had once been the proud capital of Italy.

BIBLIOGRAPHY

Books in English

ALEXANDER OF TUNIS. *The Alexander Memoirs 1940–1945*. Cassell, London, 1962.

BALDWIN, HANSON W. *Battles Lost and Won*. Harper & Row, New York, 1966.

BARZINI, LUIGI. *The Italians*. Atheneum, New York, 1964.

BOEHMLER, RUDOLF. *Monte Cassino*. Trans. by R. H. Stevens. Cassell, London, 1964.

BRYANT, ARTHUR. *Turn of the Tide. The Diaries of Lord Alanbrooke*. Doubleday & Co., New York, 1957.

BUCKLEY, CHRISTOPHER. *Road to Rome*. Hodder & Stoughton, London, 1945.

BULLOCK, ALAN. *Hitler: A Study in Tyranny*. Odham, London, 1952.

BUTCHER, HARRY C. *My Three Years with Eisenhower*. Simon & Schuster, New York, 1946.

BYRNES, JAMES F. *Speaking Frankly*. Harper & Bros., New York, 1947.

CARTON DE WIART, SIR A. *Happy Odyssey*. Jonathan Cape, London, 1950.

CHURCHILL, WINSTON. *The Second World War*. Cassell, London, 1950.

CLARK, MARK W. *Calculated Risk*. Harper & Bros., New York, 1950.

COLVIN, I. G. *Unknown Courier*. W. Imber, London, 1953.

DAVIS, MELTON S. *All Rome Trembled*. G. P. Putnam, New York, 1957.

DEAKIN, F. W. *The Brutal Friendship*. Harper & Row, New York, 1962.

DE GAULLE, CHARLES. *The War Memoirs*. Vol. II. Simon & Schuster, New York, 1959.

DE GUINGUAND, FRANCIS. *Operation Victory*. Hodder & Stoughton, London, 1953.

DELZELL, CHARLES F. *The Enemies of Mussolini*. Princeton University Press, Princeton, 1961.

DOMBROWSKI, ROMAN. *Mussolini: Twilight and Fall*. Heinemann, London, 1956.

DULLES, ALLEN. *The Craft of Intelligence*. Harper & Row, New York, 1963.

EISENHOWER, DWIGHT D. *Crusade in Europe*. Doubleday & Co., New York, 1948.

FEIS, HERBERT. *Churchill, Roosevelt, Stalin*. Princeton University Press, Princeton, 1957.

FERMI, LAURA. *Mussolini*. University of Chicago Press, Chicago, 1961.

FINER, HERMAN. *Mussolini's Italy*. Grosset, New York, 1935.

FULLER, J. F. C. *Second World War*. Eyre & Spottiswoode, London, 1948.

GILBERT, FELIX. *Hitler Directs His War*. Oxford University Press, New York, 1960.

GOEBBELS, JOSEF. *Diaries 1942–1943*. Doubleday & Co., New York, 1948.

GOERLITZ, WALTER. *History of the German General Staff*. Praeger, New York, 1953.

GINZBURG, NATALIA. *Family Savings*. Hogarth Press, London, 1967.

HEIBER, HELMUT. *Hitler*. Dufour, New York, 1961.

HIBBERT, CHRISTOPHER. *Benito Mussolini*. Longmans, London, 1962.

HIGGINS, TRUMBULL. *Soft Underbelly*. Macmillan, New York, 1968.

HOARE, SIR SAMUEL (Viscount Templewood). *Ambassador on Special Mission*. Collins, London, 1946.

HOLLES, EVERETT. *Unconditional Surrender*. Howell Soskin, New York, 1945.

HUGHES, HENRY STUART. *U.S. and Italy*. Harvard University Press, Cambridge, Mass., 1953.

HULL, CORDELL. *The Memoirs of Cordell Hull*. Vol. II. Macmillan, New York, 1948.

JACKSON, W. G. F. *The Battle for Rome*. Botsford, London, 1969.

KATZ, ROBERT. *Death in Rome*. Macmillan, New York, 1967.

KEITEL, WILHELM. *The Memoirs of Field-Marshal Keitel*. Stein & Day, New York, 1966.

KOGAN, NORMAN. *Italy and the Allies*. Harvard University Press, Cambridge, Mass., 1956.

LEWIS, NORMAN. *The Honored Society*. Collins, London, 1964.

MACGREGOR-HASTIE, ROY. *The Day of the Lion*. Coward-McCann, New York, 1963.

MACK SMITH, DENIS. *Italy: A Modern History*. University of Michigan Press, 1959.

MACMILLAN, HAROLD. *The Blast of War*. Macmillan, London, 1967.

MATTHEWS, HERBERT L. *The Education of a Correspondent.* Harcourt Brace & Co., New York, 1964.

MONTGOMERY, SIR BERNARD. *El Alamein to the Sangro River.* Hutchinson, London, 1949.

MOOREHEAD, ALAN. *Montgomery.* Hamish Hamilton, London, 1946.

MORISON, SAMUEL ELIOT. *Sicily-Salerno-Anzio.* Vol. IX (History of United States Naval Operations in World War II). Little, Brown, Boston, 1954.

MURPHY, ROBERT. *Diplomat Among Warriors.* Doubleday & Co., New York, 1964.

NICOLSON, HAROLD. *Diaries and Letters 1939–1945.* Ed. by Nigel Nicolson. Collins, London, 1967.

NORTH, JOHN. *Memoirs of Earl Alexander.* Cassell, London, 1962.

PANTALEONE, MICHELE. *The Mafia and Politics.* Chatto & Windus, London, 1966.

POND, HUGH. *Salerno.* Kimber, London, 1961.

REID, ED. *Mafia.* Random House, New York, 1952.

RIDGWAY, MATTHEW B. *Soldier.* Memoirs told to Harold A. Martin. Harper & Bros., New York., 1956.

ROMMEL, ERWIN. *Papers.* Collins, London, 1953.

RYAN, CORNELIUS. *The Last Battle.* Simon & Schuster, New York, 1966.

SAPORITI, PIERO. *Empty Balcony.* Gollanoz, London, 1947.

SCHMIDT, PAUL. *Hitler's Interpreter.* Ed. by R. H. C. Steed. Heinemann, London, 1951.

SCRIVENER, JANE. *Inside Rome with the Germans.* Macmillan, New York, 1945.

SHERWOOD, ROBERT. *Roosevelt and Hopkins.* Harper & Bros., New York, 1948.

SHEPHERD, G. A. Lt. Col. *The Italian Campaign,* Baker, London, 1969.

SHIRER, WILLIAM L. *The Rise and Fall of the Third Reich.* Simon & Schuster, New York, 1960.

SKORZENY, OTTO. *Secret Missions.* Dutton, New York, 1950.

SPRIGGE, CECIL J. S. *The Development of Modern Italy.* Duckworth, London, 1943.

STRONG, MAJ. GEN. SIR KENNETH. *Intelligence at the Top.* Cassell, London, 1968.

THOMAS, DAVID. *Europe since Napoleon.* Longmans, London, 1957.

TREGASKIS, RICHARD. *Invasion Diary.* Random House, New York, 1944.

TREVOR-ROPER, HUGH. *Blitzkrieg to Defeat* (Hitler's War Directives). Dufour, New York, 1961.

VILLARI, LUIGI. *The Liberation of Italy.* Nelson, Appleton, Wisc., 1959.

WARLIMONT, WALTER. *Inside Hitler's Headquarters.* Praeger, New York, 1965.

WELLES, SUMNER. *The Time for Decision.* Harper & Bros., New York, 1944.

WESTPHAL, SIEGFRIED. *The Fatal Decisions.* Michael Joseph, London, 1965.

(I)

————. *German Army in the West.* Cassell, London, 1951. (II)

WHEELER-BENNET, JOHN. *Action This Day.* Macmillan, London, 1968.

WILMOT, CHESTER. *The Struggle for Europe.* Collins, London, 1952.

WILSON, HENRY MAITLAND. *Eight Years Overseas 1939–47.* Hutchinson, London, 1950.

YOUNG, DESMOND. *Rommel, The Desert Fox.* Harper & Row, New York, 1951.

American and British Periodicals

Coronet, January 1955. DERI, EMERY. "The Super Spy who Fooled Hitler."

Harper's, October 1944. THRUELSON, RICHARD, AND ARNOLD, ELLIOTT. "Secret Mission to Rome."

History of the Second World War, Vol. 4, No. 7, 1967. BLUMENSON, MARTIN. "The Fight for Southern Italy."

————, Vol. 4, No. 9, 1967. BOEHMLER, RUDOLF. "Retreat to Cassino."

Life, February 26, 1945. "Count Dino Grandi Explains."

Saturday Evening Post, September 16, 1944. BROWN, DAVID. "The Inside Story of Italian Surrender."

————, March 9, 1945. CASTELLANO, GIUSEPPE. Letter.

Sunday Express, June 22, 1969. BARNETT, CORRELLI. "Ice Cool Alex, the Gentle Warlord."

Sunday Times, September 10, 1967. MORTIMER, RAYMOND. "Last of the Whigs."

Sunday Times Magazine, August 4, 1968. LEWIS, NORMAN. "All Honorable Men."

Times, June 17, 1969. "Lord Alexander of Tunis, Brilliant Commander, Governor-General and Minister."

American and British Documents

Foreign Relations of the United States. Diplomatic Papers 1943. Vol. II (Europe). U.S. Government Printing Office, Washington, D.C., 1964.

Fuehrer Conferences on Naval Affairs. Office of Naval Intelligence, British Admiralty, London, 1945.

Garland, Col. Albert N., and Smyth, Howard McGaw, assisted by Martin Blumenson. *Sicily and the Surrender of Italy.* (U.S. Army in World War II: The Mediterranean Theater of Operations.) Office of the Chief of Military History, Department of the Army, Washington, D.C., 1965.

Linklater, Eric. *The Campaign in Italy.* H. M. Stationery Office, London, 1951.

United States and Italy 1936–1946. Documentary Record, Department of State, U.S. Government Printing Office, Washington, D.C., 1946.

Woodward, Llewellyn. *British Foreign Policy in the Second World War.* H. M. Stationery Office, London, 1962.

Books in Italian, French, and German

ABATE, LUIGI. *Pasquino antifascista.* Ferri, Rome, 1944.

ACERBO, GIACOMO. *Fra due plotoni di esecuzione.* Cappelli, Bologna, 1968.

ALFASSIO, GRIMALDI UGOBERTO. *Il re buono.* Feltrinelli, Milan, 1970.

ALFIERI, DINO. *Due dittatori di fronte.* Rizzoli, Milan, 1948.

AMÉ, CESARE. *Guerra segreta in Italia 1940–1943.* Casini, Rome, 1954.

ANFUSO, FILIPPO. *Da Palazzo Venezia al lago di Garda (1936–1945).* Cappelli, Bologna, 1957.

ANGELUCCI, ANNIBALE, and BOTTI, ETTORE. *Il processo dell'oro. La difesa di Azzolini.* La Toga, Naples, 1948.

ARANGIO-RUIZ, VINCENZO. *Schermaglie politiche.* Humus, Naples, 1945.

ARTOM, EMANUELE. *Diari.* Ed. by Paolo de Benedetti and Eloisa Ravenna. La Nuova Italia, Florence, 1966.

ARMELLINI, QUIRINO. *Diario di guerra. Nove mesi al Comando Supremo.* Garzanti, Milan, 1946.

BACINO, EZIO. *Roma prima e dopo.* Atlantica, Rome, 1956.

BADOGLIO, PIETRO. *L'Italia nella seconda guerra mondiale.* Mondadori, Milan, 1946.

BARTOLINI, ALFONSO. *Storia della Resistenza Italiana all'estero.* Rebellato, Padua, 1965.

BARTOLINI, EZIO. *Pietro Nenni.* Partenia, Rome, 1946.

BASTIANINI, GIUSEPPE. *Uomini, cose, fatti. Memorie di un Ambasciatore.* Vitagliano, Milan, 1959.

BANDINI, FRANCO. *Claretta.* Sugar, Milan, 1960.

BASSO, ANTONIO. *L'armistizio del settembre '43 in Sardegna.* Rispoli, Naples, 1947.

BATTAGLIA, ROBERTO. *Storia della Resistenza italiana*. 2nd ed. Einaudi, Turin, 1953. (I)

——. *La seconda guerra mondiale*. Editori Riuniti, Rome, 1960. (II)

BAUER, RICCARDO. *Alla ricerca della liberta'*. Parenti, Florence, 1957.

BENEDETTI, ARRIGO. *L'esplosione*. Mondadori, Milan, 1966.

BELLOMO, BINO. *Sotto il segno di S. Michele Arcangelo*. Ed. Beta, Milan, 1965.

BELLOTTI, FELICE. *La repubblica di Mussolini*. Zagara, Milan, 1947.

BENINI, ZENONE. *Vigilia a Verona*. Garzanti, Milan, 1949.

BERIO, ALBERTO. *Missione segreta*. Dall'Oglio, Milan, 1947.

BERNARDINI, FRANCESCO. *Parlano i morti*. Maglione, Rome, 1945.

BERTOLDI, SILVIO. *La guerra parallela*. Sugar, Milan, 1962. (I)

——. *I tedeschi in Italia*. Rizzoli, Milan, 1964. (II)

——. *Vittorio Emanuele III*. Utet, Milan, 1970. (III)

BEVILACQUA, ALBERTO. *La rivolta di San Vittore*. Screenplay, unpublished, 1968.

BIANCHI, GIANFRANCO. *Il 25 luglio, crollo di un regime*. Mursia, Milan, 1963.

BIONDI, DINO. *La fabbrica del Duce*. Vallecchi, Florence, 1967.

BOCCA, GIORGIO. *Storia dell'Italia Partigiana*. Laterza, Bari, 1966.

BOLIA, NINO. *Colloqui con Umberto II*. Fantera, Rome, 1949. (I)

——. *Il segreto di due re*. Rizzoli, Milan, 1951. (II)

BOLZONI, ADRIANO (under pseudonym Mario Monti). *La guerra questo sporco affare*. De Luigi, Rome, 1946. (I)

——. *Otto settembre*. CEN, Rome, 1954. (II)

BONA, GIUSEPPE. *Martirio ed eroismo di Genserico Fontana*. Pais, Rome, 1954.

BOTTAI, GIUSEPPE. *Vent'anni e un giorno*. Garzanti, Milan, 1949.

BONOMI, IVANOE. *Diario di un anno*. Garzanti, Milan, 1949.

BRAGADIN, MARC'ANTONIO. *Che ha fatto la marina*. Garzanti, Milan, 1949.

CACCIOLA, SALVATORE. *Liriche della Resistenza*. Sediv, Padua, 1957.

CADORNA, RAFFAELE. *La riscossa dal 25 luglio alla liberazione*. Rizzoli, Milan, 1948.

CALVINO, ITALO. *Il sentiero dei nidi di ragno*. Einaudi, Novara, 1954.

CANEVARI, EMILIO. *La guerra italiana. Retroscena della disfatta*. Tosi, Rome, 1948. 2nd ed., 1966.

CAPUTO, GIORGIO. *Problemi e documenti della Resistenza romana*. L'Europa Letteraria, Rome, 1966.

CARACCIOLO DI FEROLETO, Gen. Mario. *E poi*. Corso, Rome, 1946.

CARACCIOLO, ALBERTO. *Teresio Olivelli*. La Scuola, Brescia, 1947.

CARBONI, GIACOMO. *L'armistizio e la difesa di Rome, verita' e menzogne*. De Luigi, Rome, 1945. (I)

——. *L'Italia tradita dall'armistizio alla pace*. EDA, Rome, 1947. (II)

——. *Piu' che il dovere*. Danesi, Rome, 1952. (III)

——. *Memorie segrete 1935–1948*. Parenti, Florence, 1955. (IV)

CARINI, TOMASO. *Il partito d'azione. Note e ricordi*. De Luca, Rome, 1960.

Cassinelli, Guido. *Appunti sul 25 luglio.* SAPPI, Milan, 1944.

Castagno, Gino. *Bruno Buozzi,* Edizioni Avanti, Milan, 1955.

Castellano, Giuseppe. *Come firmai l'armistizio di Cassibile.* Mondadori, Milan, 1945. (I)

———. *La guerra continua.* Rizzoli, Milan, 1963. (II)

———. *Roma Kaputt.* Gherardo Casini, Rome, 1967. (II)

Castelli, Giulio. *Storia segreta di Roma Citta' Aperta.* Quattruci, Rome, 1959.

Caudana, Mino. *Il figlio del fabbro.* CEN, Rome, 1960.

Cavallero, Ugo. *Comando Supremo.* Cappelli, Bologna, 1948.

Caviglia, Ennio. *Diario aprile 1925–marzo 1945.* Casini, Rome, 1952.

Ceva, Bianca. *5 anni di storia italiana 1940–45.* Comunita', Milan, 1964.

Chilanti, Felice. *Il colpevole.* Scheiwiller, Milan, 1967. (I)

———. *Ex.* Scheiwiller, Milan, 1969. (II)

Ciano, Galeazzo. *Diario.* Vol. II. Rizzoli, Milan, 1946.

Cilibrizzi, Saverio. *Badoglio rispetto a Mussolini e di fronte alla storia.* Conte, Naples, 1948.

Cintoli, Giuseppe. *L'italia e' giovane.* Mondadori, Milan, 1961.

Cocchi, Mario. *La Sinistra Cattolica e la Resistenza.* CEI, Rome, 1966.

Collotti, Enzo. *L'amministrazione tedesca nell'Italia occupata.* Lerici, Milan, 1963.

Comandini, Federico. *Breve storia di cinque mesi (dal 21 luglio al 20 dicembre 1943).* Tomar, Rome, 1944.

Consiglio, Alberto. *Vita di Vittorio Emanuele III.* Rizzoli, Milan, 1950.

Conti, Clara. *Servizio segreto (Cronache e documenti dei delitti dello Stato).* De Luigi, Rome, 1945.

Corona, Achille. *La verita' sul nove settembre.* Soc. Ed. Avanti!, Milan, 1946.

Corselli, Rodolfo. *Storia politico-militare della seconda guerra mondiale.* Ediz. Italiane, Rome, 1943.

Cucco, Alfredo. *Non volevano perdere.* Cappelli, Bologna, 1949.

D'Agostini, Lorenzo, and Forti, Roberto. *Il sole e' sorto a Roma.* ANPI, Rome, 1965.

D'Andrea, Ugo. *La fine del regno.* S.E.T., Turin, 1951.

D'Aroma, Nino. *Vent'anni insieme: Vittorio Emanuele III e Mussolini.* Cappelli, Bologna, 1957. (I)

———. *Mussolini segreto.* Cappelli, Bologna, 1958. (II)

———. *Un popolo alla prova: dieci anni di guerra 1935–1945.* Cusimano, Palermo, 1968. (III)

De Begnac, Yvon. *Palazzo Venezia. Storia di un regime.* La Rocca, Rome, 1950.

De Benedetti, Giacomo. *16 ottobre 1943.* Il Saggiatore, Milan, 1960.

De Biase, Carlo. *Badoglio, Duca di Caporetto.* Borghese, Milan, 1965. (I)

———. *L'otto settembre di Badoglio.* Borghese, Milan, 1968. (II)

————. *L'aquila d'oro-Storia dello Stato Maggiore Italiano (1861–1945)*. Borghese, Milan, 1970. (III)

DE FELICI, RENZO. *Storia degli ebrei italiani sotto il fascismo*. Einaudi, Turin, 1961.

DE FEO, ITALO. *L'ultima Italia*. ERI, Turin, 1968.

DE GIORGI, ELSA. *I coetanei*. Einaudi, Turin, 1955.

DE LAUNAY, JACQUES. *Histoire de la diplomatie secrete de 1914 a 1945*. Gerard & Co., Verviers, 1966.

DI BENIGNO, JO. *Occasioni mancate—Roma in un diario segreto 1943–44*. S.E.I., Rome, 1945.

DI BERNART, ENZO. *Nein*, Sciascia, Caltanissetta, 1961.

DI CANTERNO, FIORELLO. *Don Giuseppe Morosini, medaglia d'oro al valor militare*. SELI, Rome, 1945.

DOLFIN, GIOVANNI. *Con Mussolini nella tragedia: diario del capo della segreteria particolare del Duce '43–44*. Garzanti, Milan, 1950.

DOLLMANN, EUGEN. *Roma nazista*. Longanesi, Milan, 1949. (I)

————. *Un libero schiavo*. Cappelli, Bologna, 1968. (II)

EGOLI, EMO. *La gioventu' italiana nella lotta contro il fascismo*. ETI, Rome, 1955.

DEGLI ESPINOSA, AGOSTINO. *Il regno del sud*. Migliaresi, Rome, 1946. (I)

————. *La guerra che nessuno vuole*. Cisalpino, Milan, 1962. (II)

ETNASI, FERNANDO. *Cronache col mitra*. Giordano, Milan, 1965.

FALCONI, CARLO. *La Chiesa e le organizzazioni cattoliche in Italia*. Einaudi, Turin, 1956. (I)

————. *Il silenzio di Pio XII*. Sugar, Milan, 1965. (II)

FALDELLA, EMILIO. *L'Italia nella seconda guerra mondiale*. Cappelli, Bologna, 1959.

FAVAGROSSA, CARLO. *Perche' perdemmo la guerra: Mussolini e la produzione bellica*. Rizzoli, Milan, 1946.

FEDERZONI, LUIGI. *Storia di ieri per la storia di domani*. Mondadori, Milan, 1967.

FIORI, CESIRA. *Una donna nelle carceri fasciste*. Editori Riuniti, Rome, 1966.

FREIDLANDER, SAUL. *Pio XII e il terzo reich*. Feltrinelli, Milan, 1965.

FUMAROLA, ANGELO ANTONIO. *Essi non sono morti*. Poligrafico, Rome, 1945. (I)

————. *La generazione tradita*. Magi Spinetti, Rome, 1946. (II)

GADDA, CARLO EMILIO. *Eros e Priapo*. Garzanti, Milan, 1967.

GALBIATI, ENZO. *Il 25 luglio e la M.V.S.N.* Barnabo, Milan, 1950.

GAROFALO, FRANCO. *Pennello nero. La marina italiana dopo l'8 settembre*. Bussola, Rome, 1945.

GASPAROTTO, LUIGI. *Diario di un deputato*. Dall'Oglio, Milan, 1945.

GESSI, LEONE. *Roma, la guerra, il Papa*. Staderini, Rome, 1945.

GIANNINI, ALBERTO. *Io, spia dell'OVRA*. Vol. II. Soc. Ed. Italiana, Rome, n.d.

GIGLI, EUGENIO. *La seconda guerra mondiale (1939–1945).* Laterza, Bari, 1964.

GIOVANA, MARIO. *Le nuove camicie nere.* Dall'Albero, Turin, 1966.

GIOVANNETTI, MONS. ALBERTO. *Romao, Città aperta.* Ed. Libreria Vaticana, Vatican City, 1960. (I)

———. *Il Vaticano e la guerra.* Ed. Libreria Vaticana, Vatican City, 1960. (II)

GORLA, GIUSEPPE. *L'Italia nella seconda guerra mondiale.* Baldini e Castoldi, Milan, 1959.

GRAZIANI, RODOLFO. *Ho difeso la Patria.* Garzanti, Milan, 1948.

GUARIGLIA, RAFFAELE. *Ricordi 1922–1946.* Edizioni Scientifiche Italiane, Naples, 1950.

HEIBER, HELMUTHI. *Hitler stratega.* Mondadori, Milan, 1965.

HISTORICUS (AMEDEO TOSTI). *Da Versailles a Cassibile. Lo sforzo militare italiano nel venticinquennio 1918–1943.* Cappelli, Bologna, 1954.

ITALICUS (PARMENO BELTOLI). *Il tradimento di Badoglio.* Mondadori, Milan, 1944.

JACOMETTI, ALBERTO. *Uomini e donne al bivio.* Macchia, Novara, 1954.

KESSELRING, ALBERT. *Memorie di guerra.* Garzanti, Milan, 1954.

LA GUIDARA, FRANCO. *25 anni caldi.* Edizioni Internazionali, Rome, 1967.

LANZA D'AJETA, BLASCO. *Documenti prodotti a corredo della memoria presentata al consiglio di Stato.* Ferraiolo, Rome, 1946.

LAPIDE, PINCHAS E. *Roma e gli ebrei.* Mondadori, Milan, 1967.

LEONARDO, RAUL. *Diario di un soldato semplice.* Einaudi, Turin, 1952.

LETO, GUIDO. *Polizia segreta in Italia.* Vito Bianco, Rome, 1961. (I)

———. *OVRA, Fascismo, Antifascismo.* Cappelli, Bologna, 1962. (II)

LIZZADRI, ORESTE. *Quel dannato marzo.* Edizioni Avanti!, Milan, 1962. (I)

———. *Il regno di Badoglio.* Edizioni Avanti!, Milan, 1963. (II)

LODI, ANGELO. *L'aeronautica italiana nella guerra di liberazione.* Ufficio Storico dell'Aeronautica Militare, Rome, 1961.

LODOLINI, ELIO. *L'illegittimità del governo Badoglio.* Castaldi, Milan, 1953.

LOMBARDI, GABRIO. *Italia!* Magi-Spinetti, Rome, 1945. (I)

———. *8 settembre fuori d'Italia.* Mursia, Milan, 1966. (II)

LONGO, LUIGI. *Un popolo alla macchia.* Mondadori, Milan, 1947.

LUSSU, EMILIO. *Diplomazia clandestina.* La Nuova Italia, Florence, 1956.

MAGRI, MARIO. *Una vita per la liberta'.* Puglielli, Rome, 1953.

MALVESTITI, PIERO. *25 luglio alla costituzione.* Bernabo, Milan, 1948.

MARCHESI, LUIGI. *Come siamo arrivati a Brindisi.* Bompiani, Milan, 1969.

MARIN, FALCO. *Una traccia sul mare.* Pesce d'Oro, Milan, 1966.

MANZI, PIETRO. *L'eccidio di Nola (11 settembre 43).* Anselmi, Naples, 1956.

MASSOLA, UMBERTO. *Marzo 1943. Ore dieci.* Editori Riuniti, Rome, 1963.

MENEGHETTI, EGIDIO. *La partigiana nuda.* Ed. Avanti!, Milan, Rome, 1958.

MERCURI, LAMBERTO, and TUZZI, CARLO. *Canti politici italiani, Vol. II, 1793–1945.* Editori Riuniti, Rome, 1962.

MIDA, MASSIMO. *Cinema e resistenza.* Landi, Florence, 1959.

MOELLHAUSEN, EITEL FRIEDRICH. *La carta perdente 25 luglio 43–2 maggio 45.* Sestante, Rome, 1948.

MONELLI, PAOLO. *Roma 1943.* 9th ed. rev. Longanesi, Milan, 1963.

MONTEROSSO, FRANCESCO (Franco Matacotta). *Canzoniere di liberta'.* La Nuova Strada, Tivoli, 1953.

MORPURGO, LUCIANO. *Caccia all'uomo, pagine di diario 1938–1944.* Dalmatia, Rome, 1946.

MUSCO, ETTORE. *Gli avvenimenti dell'8 settembre 1943.* Tipografia Regionale, Rome, 1962. (I)

——. *8 settembre.* Garzanti, Milan, 1965. (II)

MUSMANNO, MICHAEL. *Il generale Mark W. Clark.* Mondadori, Milan, 1946.

MUSSOLINI, BENITO. *Storia di un anno, ottobre 42–settembre 43.* Mondadori, Milan, 1944.

MUSSOLINI, EDVIGE. *Mio fratello Benito.* La Fenice, Florence, 1957.

MUSSOLINI, RACHELE. *La mia vita con Benito.* Mondadori, Milan, 1948. (I)

——. *Benito il mio uomo.* As told to Anita Pensotti. Rizzoli, Milan, 1958. (II)

MUSSOLINI, VITTORIO. *Vita con mio padre.* Mondadori, Milan, 1957.

NAPOLITANO, VITANTONIO. *25 luglio 1943.* Vega, Rome, 1944.

NAVARRA, QUINTO. *Memorie del cameriere di Mussolini.* Longanesi, Milan, 1946.

NENNI, PIETRO. *Sei anni di guerra civile.* Rizzoli, Milan, 1945. (I)

——. *Pagine di diario.* Garzanti, Milan, 1947. (II)

NERI, VIRGILIO. *Il governo dei 45 giorni.* Sestante, Milan, 1945.

NETTI, FAUSTO. *Canti della resistenza italiana.* Vol. I. Collana del Gallo Grande, Milan, 1960.

NIZZA, ENZO. *Autobiografia del fascismo.* Pietra, Rome, 1962.

ORLANDO, FRANCESCO. *Mussolini volle il 25 luglio.* Spes, Milan, 1946.

PAGE, GIORGIO NELSON. *L'americano di Roma.* Longanesi, Milan, 1950.

PAGGI, MARIO. *Addio mia bella addio.* La Voce, Florence, 1954.

PALERMO, IVAN. *Storia di un armistizio.* Mondadori, Milan, 1967.

PANTALEONE, MICHELE. *Mafia e politica.* Einaudi, Turin, 1962.

PARRI, FERRUCCIO. *Il movimento partigiano.* Partito d'Azione, Rome, 1945.

PATTI, ERCOLE. *Cronache romane.* Bompiani, Milan, 1962.

PAVESE, CESARE. *Prima che il gallo canti.* Einaudi, Turin, 1949.

PERRONE-CAPANO, RENATO. *La resistenza in Roma.* Vol. I and II. Macchiaroli, Naples, 1963.

PETACCO, ARRIGO. *L'anarchico che venne dall'America.* Mondadori, Milan, 1969.

PICCARDI, LEOPOLDO. *La storia non aspetta.* Laterza, Bari, 1957.

PILLON, GIORGIO. *Spie per l'Italia.* I libri del No, Rome, 1969.

PINI, GIORGIO. *Filo diretto con Palazzo Venezia.* Cappelli, Bologna, 1950.

PINI, GIORGIO, and SUSMEL, DUILIO. *Mussolini. L'uomo e l'opera, IV (1938–1945).* La Fenice, Florence, 1963.

Pintor, Giaime. *Il sangue d'Europa*. Einaudi, Turin, 1950.

Pisano, Giorgio. *Sangue chiama sangue*. Pidola, Milan, 1963.

Piscitelli, Enzo. *Storia della resistenza romana*. Laterza, Bari, 1965.

Pitigrilli (Dino Segre). *Parla di Pitigrilli*. Sonzogno, Milan, 1950.

Plehwe, Friedrich-Karl von. *Schicksalsstunden in Rom*. Propylaen, Berlin, 1967.

Praz, Mario. *Casa della vita*. Mondadori, Milan, 1958.

Preti, Luigi. *Impero fascista, africani ed ebrei*. Mursia, Milan, 1968.

Puntoni, Paolo. *Parla Vittorio Emanuele III*. Palazzi, Milan, 1958.

Rahn, Rudolf. *Ambasciatore di Hitler a Vichy e a Salo'*. Garzanti, Milan, 1950.

Renzi, Renzo. *Da Starace ad Antonioni*. Marsilio, Padua, 1964.

Revelli, Nuto. *La guerra dei poveri*. Einaudi, Turin, 1962.

Rintelen, Enno von. *Mussolini l'alleato, Ricordi dell'addetto militare tedesco a Roma 1936–1943*. (Trans. of *Mussolini als Bundesgenosse*). Corso, Rome, 1952.

Ripa Di Meana, Fulvia. *Roma clandestina*. O.E.T., Rome, 1945.

Rizzo, Giuseppe. *Buche e croci nel deserto*. Aurora, Verona, 1969.

Roatta, Mario. *Otto milioni di baionette*. Mondadori, Milan, 1946.

Rocca, Massimo. *Come il fascismo divenne una dittatura*. Edizione Librarie Italiane, Milan, 1952.

Rossi, Francesco. *Come arrivammo all'armistizio*. Garzanti, Milan, 1946.

Salvadori, Massimo. *Resistenza ed azione*. Neri Pozza, Venezia, 1955.

Santoro, Giuseppe. *L'aeronautica italiana nella seconda guerra mondiale*. Ed. Esse, Rome, 1955.

Sanzi, Alfredo. *Il generale Carboni e la difesa di Roma*. Vagliotti, Turin, 1946. (I)

———. *Per la verita' (settembre 1943)*. AMI, Milan, 1960. (II)

Savignano, Antonio. *Il processo di Verona*. Cappelli, Bologna, 1963.

Scala, Edoardo. *La riscossa dell'esercito*. Uff. Storico, SME, Rome, 1948.

Scorza, Carlo. *La notte del Gran Consiglio*. Palazzi, Milan, 1968.

Secchia Pietro, Frassati Filippo. *La Resistenza e gli Alleati*. Feltrinelli, Milan, 1962.

Senise, Carmine. *Quando ero capo della polizia, 1940–43*. Ruffolo, Rome, 1946.

Sereni, Marina. *I giorni della vita*. Riunita, Rome, 1955.

Silva, Pietro. *Io difendo la Monarchia*. de Fonseca, Rome, 1946.

Simoni, Leonardo (Michele Lanza). *Berlino, Ambusciula d'Italia 1939–43*. Migliaresi, Rome, 1946.

Soleri, Marcello. *Memorie*. Einaudi, Turin, 1949.

Spampanato, Bruno. *Contromemoriale*. Edizioni di Illustrato, Rome, 1951.

Strazzeria-Perniciani, Amadeo. *Umanita' ed eroismo nella vita segreta di Regina Coeli*. A.I.A., Rome 43–44, 1950.

Susmel, Duilio. *Vita sbagliata di Galeazzo Ciano*. Palazzi, Milan, 1962. (I)

———. *Nenni e Mussolini*. Rizzoli, Milan, 1970. (II)

Talarico, Vincenzo. *Splendore e miserie delle sorelli Petacci.* Conti, Naples, 1944. (I)

———. *8 settembre, letterati in fuga.* Canesi, Rome, 1965. (II)

Tamaro, Attilio. *Due anni di storia 1943–45,* 3 vols. Tosi, Rome, 1949.

Torsiello, Mario. *Settembre 1943.* Cisalpino, Rome, 1963.

Toscano, Mario. *Dal 25 luglio all'8 settembre.* Le Monnier, Florence, 1966.

Tosti, Amedeo (Historicus). *La guerra che non si dovera fare.* Faro, Rome, 1943 (I)

———. *Nove mesi a Roma.* Casa e Lavoro, Rome, 1946. (II)

———. *Storia della seconda guerra mondiale.* Rizzoli, Milan, 1948. (III)

———. *Pietro Badoglio.* Mondadori, Milan, 1956. (IV)

Trabucchi, Alessandro. *I vinti hanno sempre torto.* De Silva, Turin, 1947.

Trabucco, Carlo. *La prigione di Roma.* S.E.L.I., Rome, 1945.

Trizzino, Antonio. *Settembre nero.* Longanesi, Milan, 1956.

Troisio, Armando. *Roma sotto il terrore nazifascista.* Mondini, Rome, 1944.

Trombetti, Ettore. *Ritorno alla libertá.* Alfa, Bologna, 1946.

Vailati, Vanna. *Badoglio racconta.* I.L.T.E., Turin, 1952. (I)

———. *Badoglio risponde.* Rizzoli, Milan, 1958. (II)

Vaina, Michele. *La grande tragedia italiana.* Ed. Tecniche, Rome, 1947.

Valiani, Leo. *Tutte le strade conducono a Roma.* La Nuova Italia, Florence, 1959. (I)

———. *Dall'antifascismo alla resistenza.* Feltrinelli, Milan, 1959. (II)

Vaussard, Maurice. *La Conjuration du Grand Conseil Fasciste contre Mussolini.* Mondiales, Paris, 1965.

Zangrandi, Ruggero. *Il lungo viaggio attraverso il fascismo.* Feltrinelli, Milan, 1962. (I)

———. *1943: 25 luglio–8 settembre.* Feltrinelli, Milan, 1964. (II)

———. *Relazione sui documenti istruttori della Commissione d'inchiesta per la mancata difesa di Roma.* Mimeographed. Rome, 1965. (III)

———. *1943: l'8 settembre.* Feltrinelli, Milan, 1967. (IV)

Zanussi, Giacomo. *Guerra e catastrofe d'Italia.* Vol. II. Corso, Rome, 1945.

Zavatti, Rino. *I 9000 di Cefalonia.* Berben, Modena, 1946.

Zerenghi, Ezio. *Pietro Benedetti.* Mongarelli, Rome, 1950.

Zingarelli, Italo. *Il terzo braccio di Regina Coeli.* Staderini, Rome, 1944.

Ai caduti per la difesa di Roma. Associazione fra i Romani, Rome, 1953.

Antologia poetica della Resistenza italiana. Landi, Florence, 1956.

Ass. Naz. Vitt. Civili di Guerra. *Italia Martire: sacrificio di un popolo 1940–1945.* Mondadori, Milan, 1965.

Atti Commissione d'inchiesta per la mancata difesa di Roma. Ministero della Difesa, Rome.

Atti e documenti relativi alla seconda guerra mondiale. Vol. I–V. Libreria Editrice Vaticana, Rome, 1965–69.

Attivita' delle bande, Sett. 43–luglio 44. C.R.B.P.I.C., Rome, 1945.

Avvenimenti dell'ottobre al dicembre del 1917 (Gli). Ufficio Storico dello Stato Maggiore dell'Esercito (Vol. IV.), Rome, 1967.

I caduti della scuola. Tip. Centenari, Rome, 1945.

I caduti del Partito d'Azione. Tip. Et. Ultra, Rome, 1945.

Cento dei centomila. ANPI, Rome, 1946.

Dal 25 luglio alla Repubblica (1943–1946). ERI, Turin, 1966.

Fascismo e antifascismo—Lezioni e testimonianze (1936–1948). Feltrinelli, Milan, 1963.

Federazione Provinciale Comunista Romana. *Le donne di Roma durante l'occupazione nazista.* Magerelli, Rome.

Istituto Feltrinelli. *La Resistenza in Italia 25 luglio 1943–25 aprile 1945.* Feltrinelli, Milan, 1961.

L'Italia dei quarantacinque giorni. Istituto nazionale per la storia del movimento di liberazione, Milan, 1969.

Lettere di antifascisti dal carcere e dal confino. Editori Riuniti, Rome, 1962.

Mille volte no, voci di donne contro l'oppressione 8 settembre. . . . Unione Donne Italiane, Rome, n.d.

Mussolini, Citazioni, Il manuale delle guardie nere. Ed. by Massimo di Massimo. XX Secolo, Rome, 1969.

Il processo Carboni-Roatta: L'armistizio e la difesa di Roma nella sentenza del Tribunale Militare (Estratto della "Rivista Penale", Maggio-Giugno 1949). Temi, Rome, 1949.

Processo Roatta: I documenti. De Luigi, Rome, 1945.

La Resistenza al fascismo. Feltrinelli, Milan, 1955.

La Resistenza europea. Lerici, Milan, 1962.

La Resistenza italiana. 2nd ed. C.V.L., Milan, 1949.

La Resistenza nella letteratura. Associazione Partigiana, Milan, 1955.

Il secondo Risorgimento. Ist. Poligrafico dello Stato, Rome, 1955.

Il secondo Risorgimento d'Italia. Centro Editoriale d'Iniziativa, Rome, 1955.

Trent'anni di storia italiana. Einaudi, Turin, 1961.

Italian Periodicals

Il Borghese, July 6, 1967. ALESSI, RINO. "Israele e le Destre italiane."

Capitolium, September 1963. CAGIANELLI, GIANNI. "Venti anni or sono Roma insorgeva." PEDERCINI, GIUSEPPE. "La storia minima di 'quei' 45 giorni."

———: June 1964. ALESSANDRINI, FEDERICO. "Pio XII e la difesa di Roma"; Roma"; CAPUTO, GIORGIO. "Bibliografia della resistenza."

Civilta Cattolica, January 3, 1970. GRAHAM, ROBERT A., S.J. "Spionaggio nazista attorno al Vaticano durante la seconda guerra mondiale."

Il Contemporaneo, February 1964. CANALI, LUCA. "Un intellettuale rivoluzionario cattolico."

Corriere della Sera, August 19–21, 1966. MONTANELLI, INDRO. "Gli alleati rivelano la verita' sull'8 settembre" (series).

———, September 6–9, 1966. CASTELLANO, GIUSEPPE. "I drammatici retroscena dell'armistizio" (series).

Documenti del Nostro Tempo, Nos. 1–4, 1965. "Storia della Guerra Civile in Italia 1943–1945" (series).

Domenica del Corriere, March 5, 12, 19, 1968. SUSMEL, DUILIO. "Intervista processo a Carlo Scorza" (series).

———, September 1968. SUSMEL, DUILIO. "Le lame di un rasoio sono sufficienti . . ." (series).

———, July 6, 1969. "Tragico settembre."

Epoca, April 18, 1965. Grandi, Dino. "Ecco Mussolini."

———, October 17, 1965. GRAZZINI, GIUSEPPE. "A Dongo Mussolini aveva un pacchetto in tasca."

———, April 10, 1966. PESCI, LIVIO. "Ecco il dossier del 25 luglio"; "Dino Grandi finalmente rivela il suo piano."

———, January, February, 1968. ARTIERI, GIOVANNI. "Il diario di Vittorio Emanuele III" (series).

———, October 23, 1966. GRAZZINI, GIUSEPPE. "Cefalonia: in coda per morire."

L'Espresso, July 21–July 28, August 4, 1963. BENEDETTI, ARRIGO. "Diario Italiano."

———, July 28, August 4, August 11, 1963. CANCOGNI, MANLIO. "La democrazia nacque di luglio" (series).

———, August 6, 1967. ROSSI, ERNESTO. "Libero in prigione."

———, August 30, 1969. VALIANI, LEO. "I consiglieri del re hanno paura."

L'Europeo, May 20, May 27, June 3, 1956. TRIONFERA, RENZO. "Tutti in ascolto tra casa Petacci e Palazzo Venezia" (series).

———, September 19, 1965. TRIONFERA, RENZO. "Dopo ventidue anni apriamo finalmente l'archivio segreto della Commissione d'inchiesta sul piu' sconcertante episodio della guerra in Italia: Perche' Roma non fu difesa."

———, August 10, 17, 24, 1967. BORGONOVO, ANNAMARIA. "Parlano gli uomini che furono i protagonisti dello spionaggio italiano" (series).

———, July 25, 1968. TRIONFERA, RENZO. "25 anni fa cadeva il fascismo"; DOLLMANN, EUGEN. "Racconta il salvataggio dei fascisti."

———, August 1, 1968. TRIONFERA, RENZO. "Castellano spiega il 25 luglio."

———, August 8, 1968. GALBIATI, ENZO. "Lettere al direttore." TORNABUONI, LIETTA. "La pensionata terribile Rachele Mussolini."

———, September 5, 1968. TRIONFERA, RENZO, e PETACCO, ARRIGO. "Perche' Roma si e' arresa ai nazisti?"

Gente, June–July 1959. MUSSOLINI, VITTORIO, as told to Domenico Campana. "Colloqui con mio padre" (series).

———, May 1962. TORELLI, GIORGIO. "Roma non fu difesa."

———, July 1967. PANCERA, MARIO. "Ecco la veritá sulla difesa di Roma."

———, October–November, 1968. SUSMEL, DUILIO. "La vera storia d'amore del Duce e della Petacci rivelati da documenti segreti" (series).

———, July 1969. SUSMEL, DUILIO. "Dopo 25 anni abbiamo scoperto Frau Beetz, la spia che Hitler mise accanto al genero di Mussolini" (series).

Giornale d'Italia, July 29–September 14, 1943.

———, December 13, 1966. UPI. "Sostiene che la difesa di Roma non era nei suoi compiti."

Il Giornale di Sicilia, September 8, 1968. "Rievocazione dell'8 settembre."

Il Giorno, February 24–March 8, 1968. PAVOLINI, PAOLO. "L'Italia di Claretta Petacci" (series).

Historia, April–June 1969. PADOAN, GIANNI. "L'ultima illusione: un cappotto da tedesco."

L'Italia Libera (clandestine), September 8, 1944. "8 settembre 43."

Il Lavoro Italiano (clandestine), August 22, 1943.

Mercurio, December 1944. ALVARO, CORRADO. "Quaderno." BARACCO, ADRIANO. "La capitale perduta." CONTANI, ERMANNO. "Nostalgia dei nove mesi." DE MATTEI, RODOLFO. "L'interregno ingrato." GABRIELI, VITTORIO. "Settembre 1943." LONGO, GIUSEPPE. "Giorni bolognesi." MUSCETTA, CARLO. "La sfortunata 'Italia libera.'" SCIALOIA, TOTI. "I pittori difendono la citta." TOMAJUOLI, GINO. "La difesa tradita."

Il Messaggero, July 27, 1943. CALCAGNO, DIEGO. "25 luglio." ROSSELLINI, RENZO. "La notte del 25 luglio."

———, July 29–September 14, 1943.

———, July 18–23, 1963. STERPELLONE, ALFONSO. "I tragici avvenimenti del 25 luglio di vent'anni fa" (series).

———, March 7–15, 1967. "Commenti sulla seduta del Gran Consiglio del 25 luglio" (DINO GRANDI, TULLIO CIANETTI, GIOVANNI BALELLA, UMBERTO ALBINI, GIACOMO ACERBO, ALFREDO DE MARSICO, ENZO GALBIATI, ANNIO BIGNARDI, ALBERTO DE STEFANI, CARLO SCORZA).

———, October 31, 1967. DE SANCTIS, GINO. "Addio al Rosati."

———, July 17, 1967. SERRA, ENRICO. "Come e perché Badoglio accettó la resa incondizionata."

———, August 1967. "Il Vaticano si adoperó per salvare ebrei in Polonia." Referring to "NG 4567" dated May 23, 1942.

———, September 7, 1968. MINCHILLI, GUIDO. "L'affondamento della Roma."

———, August 26, 1969. TEDESCHI, BRUNO. "Archiviata un'inchiesta sul massacro di Cefalonia."

———, September 16, 1969. "A Falcone Lucifero il Collare dell' Annunziata."

La Nazione, September 3–8, 1963. PIZZINELLI, CORRADO. "Nel ventennale del settembre 43" (Interviews with Generals Castellano, De Stefanis, Carboni, Roatta, Admiral De Courten, Col. Valenzano and Umberto di Savoia).

Oggi, October 14, 1958. BERTOLDI, SILVIO. "Volevano avvelenare Mussolini."

——— July 11–August 1958. ZAMBONI, MARIO. "Dopo venti anni una testimonianza decisiva." (Series.)

———, March, April 1966. "Le nuove rivelazioni di Rachele Mussolini" (as told to Anita Pensotti; series).

———, February 20–April 3, 1966. BERTOLDI, SILVIO. "Pietro Badoglio, il condottiero sotto processo" (series).

———, August 1968. QUARESCHI, GIOVANNI. "Ti ricordi quando andavi in bicicletta?"

Paese Sera, July 6, 1967. MANZINI, GIORGIO. "Sentenza assolutoria a Milano per la mancata difesa di Roma."

Il Popolo d'Italia, July 26, 1943.

Il Popolo di Roma, July 29–September 14, 1943.

Riforma della Scuola, April 1965. CAPUTO, GIORGIO. "Scuola e antifascismo a Roma (1936–1944)."

Roma Oggi, March–May, 1969.

Quaderni della Federazione Giovanile Ebraica d'Italia, April 1961. "Gli ebrei in Italia durante il fascismo."

Settimo Giorno, February, March 1961. SAINI, EZIO. "Venti anni di battaglie giudiziarie della famiglia Petacci" (series).

Lo Specchio, February 1967. SANZO, DINO. "Roatta 22 anni dopo."

———, September 8, 1968. DOLLMANN, EUGENIO. "La vittoria mancata di Pietro Badoglio."

———, September 15, 1968. DOLLMANN, EUGENIO. "La leggenda del Gran Sasso."

Storia illustrata, August 1960. TABELLINI, UGO. "Gli errori dell'ultima guerra: la mancata difesa di Roma."

———, January, March 1968. ARTIERI, GIOVANNI. "La vita di Vittorio Emanuele III" (series).

———, November 1969. BRAGADIN, MARC'ANTONIO. "Spionaggio: Italia"; MAYDA, GIUSEPPE. "Spionaggio: Germania."

Il Tempo, June–July 1969. PILLON, GIORGIO. "I Savoia nella bufera" (series).

Tempo illustrato, March–June 1958. ARTIERI, GIOVANNI. "Colloqui con Umberto" (series).

———, September–November 1962. DONADIO, PASQUALE. "Una tragica storia d'amore" (series).

———, June–July 1965. SUSMEL, DUILIO. "Il 25 luglio raccontato dai protagonisti" (series).

———, December 20, 1969–January 17, 1970. SUSMEL, DUILIO. "Mussolini e i Savoia."

La Tribuna illustrata, March 31, 1968. "Mussolini era bigamo."

L'Unita, September 9, 1969. CARBONI, GIACOMO. "Consegnai 500 fucili ai patrioti romani."

Vita, July 11–August 29, 1963. "La verità sul 25 luglio" (series).

La Voce della Scuola (clandestine), May 20, 1944. "Raffaele Persichetti."

Sources

BOOK ONE

Chapter 1 THE CRITICS

The Idealists

This account is based, above all, on interviews with relatives, friends, and students of Raffaele Persichetti, particularly Romano Antonelli, Carla Capponi, Laura Formiggini, Ugo Moretti, Luigi Persichetti; on books by Bernardini, Egoli, Fumarola (I), Zangrandi (II, IV), and on *Caduti della scuola* and *Caduti dell Partito d'Azione*; and on the periodicals *Contemporaneo, Voce della scuola, Italia libera.*

Page

9–10 Raffaele's thoughts and writings from notes discovered by his family.

10 Mussolini's remark is from *Mussolini, Citazioni, Il Manuale delle guardie nere.*

The Conspirators

Reconstructing Dino Grandi's plotting has meant putting together bits and pieces from just about everyone: Dombrowski, Hibbert, MacGregor-Hastie, Saporiti. *Sicily and the Surrender of Italy* (hereinafter referred to as *Surrender*).

Acerbo, Anfuso, Bianchi (Grandi's version takes twenty-one pages), Bolla (I, II), Bottai, Canevari, Castellano (II), Ciano, Comandini, D'Aroma (II), Federzoni, Galbiati, Graziani, Leto (I), Monelli, Benito Mussolini, Puntoni, Spampanato, Susmel, Tamaro, Vaussard, Zangrandi (II), *Trent' anni di storia* (Luraghi).

Life. Epoca, April 10, 1966, *"Dino Grandi finalmente rivela il suo piano"* [hereinafter referred to as *Epoca* (Grandi)]; January, February 1968. *Europeo*, August 1, 1968. *Messaggero*, March 7–15, 1967, "*Commenti sulla seduta del Gran Consiglio del 25 Luglio.*" *Tempo illustrato*, June–July 1965. *Vita.*

Page

13 Grandi's praise of Mussolini from Comandini.

14 Grandi's confession, testament, letters from *Vita.*

16 Grandi's version of his meeting with Mussolini rings much truer than Mussolini's. Also see Kesselring.

The Disillusioned

The most authoritative source on Galeazzo Ciano is Susmel, but see also Deakin, Dombrowski, Hibbert, Acerbo, Alfieri, Anfuso, Bastianini, Benini, Bianchi, Bottai, Canevari, Castellano (II), Caudana, Ciano, Comandini, D'Aroma (II), Federzoni, Monelli, B. Mussolini, Puntoni, Savignano, Spampanato, Tamaro, Zangrandi (I, II).

Life. Epoca (Grandi). *Europeo*, July 25, 1968. *Gente*, October, November 1968. *Giorno. Messaggero*, July 18–23, 1963; March 7–15, 1967; October 31, 1967. *Tempo illustrato*, June–July, 1965. *Vita.*

Page

19 "He says he wants a corridor" from Susmel.

19–20 Ciano's intelligence and manners from Alfieri.

21 Description of Edda Ciano as "wild filly" from Susmel.

22 Joseph Kennedy quote from Susmel.

23 Ciano's adhesion from *Epoca* (Grandi).

24 Alfieri-Ciano conversation from Alfieri.

25 Orio Vergani from Susmel.

The Rank and File

Interview with Gino Savoni.

Chapter 2 THE ANTAGONISTS

The Dictator Charisma

A valuable source of information on Mussolini's thoughts, actions and statements is Pini and Susmel.

Page

27 Mussolini's conversation with his mistress from Dombrowski.

27–28 Mussolini's health (spring 1943) and use of glasses to read from Monelli.

28 My authority for saying Mussolini had no ulcer is Professor Franco Stipa, noted Italian surgeon.

28 Kleissheim from Hibbert.

29 'like a servant' told to Ciano.

29 Description of Villa Gaggia from B. Mussolini.

29–30 Feltre: Mussolini's remarks are from Alfieri and Bastianini; background from Schmidt, Warlimont, Comandini, Monelli, Rossi, Rintelen, Tamaro.

31 The king's quote from B. Mussolini.

31 Description of Mussolini—his smile, etc.—from Bottai.

31 Mussolini's description of the hierarchs from *Vita* (head of police was Chierici).

31–32 Conversation with De Cesare from Bianchi.

The Radical Left

This section is mainly based on an interview with Carla Capponi; additional information comes from interviews with Antonelli, Bentivegna, Caputo, Dorazio.

Page

33 Plainclothesmen and Piazza Venezia from Monelli.

35 Christian Communists from Cocchi and *Riforma della scuola*.

35 The Easter incident at St. Peter's from Cocchi.

35–36 The GUF incident from Zangrandi (I).

36 Students without black shirts from Piscitelli.

36 May 1 incident at university from Lizzadri.

36 "liberal" Socialists from *Riforma della scuola*.

The Diplomats

Interview with Count Leonardo Vitetti.

The King

Most of the quotations here come from the diary of General Paolo Puntoni, the king's aide. Also Fermi, Hibbert, Comandini, Monelli, Susmel, Zangrandi (II). *Epoca* (Grandi). *Vita*.

Page

38 Accepted all of Mussolini's actions from *Vita*.

38 King's opinion of politicians from interview with Vitetti.

38 Dissident Fascists from *Espresso*, July 28 1963; August 4, August 11, 1963.

38 "It has to be done carefully" from Puntoni.

38 Assassinated from Petacco.

38 Royal attachés had orders from *Vita*.

38 "I'm blind and deaf" from Fermi.

38–39 King's conversation with Grandi from *Epoca* (Grandi).

39 Description of Grandi from Puntoni.

39 Taciturn king from Monelli.

39–40 Conversation with Ciano and "Hamlet" from Susmel.

40 "My dear Beppo" from Monelli.

40 Umberto's off-color stories, etc. from Susmel.

40 Testaccio from Ciano, Vaussard.

41 Mussolini's remarks about the king from Ciano.

41–42 "a very great mind," King's watching air raid, visit to bombed areas, remark on Claretta Petacci, staff meeting, Grandi letter, meeting with Mussolini from Puntoni.

Chapter 3 THE SCENE-SHIFTERS

The Monarchists

Page

43 "some fresh air" from Susmel.

43–44 Description of Acquarone from Comandini, De Biase (II), Monelli, Spampanato, Vaussard.

44 Acquarone manner from Monelli.

44 OVRA from Leto (I).

44 "a curious Balkan mentality" from Spampanato.

44 King on July 5 from Puntoni.

45 Acquarone to Grandi from Susmel. *Epoca* (Grandi).

The Supreme Command

Page

45 In his pajamas from Monelli.

45 Ambrosio description from Tamaro. *Vita.*

45 "save the salvable" from De Biase (II), Zangrandi (II).

45 Ciano-Ambrosio from interview with Vitetti.

46 Comments on Cavallero from Ciano.

46 As a necessary device from Pintor.

46 Ambrosio talks with king from Puntoni.

46–47 Ambrosio's comments on meetings with king and Acquarone from Monelli.

47 "hopes to take Mussolini's place" from Monelli.

47 The monarch on July 5 from Puntoni.

48 Ambrosio to king on April 16 from Puntoni.

48 Ambrosio and Keitel at Feltre from Alfieri, Bastianini, Monelli, Rossi.

48 Conversation of Mussolini and Ambrosio from Alfieri.

48–49 Ambrosio and Mussolini in 1942 from Alfieri, Monelli.

49 Duty as an officer from Marchesi.

49 Set the plot in motion from Susmel.
50 King's position from Cassinelli.

The Police

Page

51 Like a bank clerk, description from Monelli.

51 Conversations of Castellano and Ambrosio from Ambrosio.

51 Castellano's thoughts and actions from Castellano (I, II).

51–52 "Any further moves" from Zangrandi (II).

52 Castellano and Ciano from Castellano (II).

52–53 Ambrosio to Castellano and developments from Castellano (II), Susmel.

53 Investigations by Castellano and Marchesi from Castellano (II), Marchesi.

53 Sheer daring from interview with Vitetti.

54 Conspiracy underway from Castellano (II).

54 Hazon death from Puntoni.

54 Ambrosio's reaction from Monelli.

54–55 Intrigues leading to naming Cerica from Castellano (II), Tamaro, Zangrandi (II) (particularly Pieche and Farinacci).

55 "legal or illegal" from Vaussard.

55 Description of Senise from Leto (II).

55–56 Senise's background and talks with king, Acquarone, and Castellano from Castellano (II), Vaussard, Zangrandi (II). Quotes from Monelli, Senise.

57 Hiding his face from Castellano (II).

57 A list of Fascists from Castellano (II), Monelli, Senise.

The Secret Service

Description and actions of Carboni from Di Benigno, Castellano (I, II, III), Monelli, Puntoni, Silva.

Page

58 Orders given verbally from Castellano (II).

58 Sorice's description from Silva.

58 "twisting the truth" and general's evaluation from De Biase (II).

58 "First-class intelligence" from Di Benigno.

58 Parents from Carboni (III).

58 "roll on carpets of women" and Mussolini's underwear from *Europeo*, August 10, August 17, August 24, 1967.

59 SIM assassinations, etc. from *Processo Carboni-Roatta; Processo Roatta: I documenti; Specchio*, February 19, 1969.

59 SIM size and complexity from *Storia illustrata*, November 1969, Bragadin.

R

59 Divided into sections from *Specchio*, February 1967.
59–60 Contents of archives from *Epoca*, October 23, 1966.
60 Carboni conversations with Roatta and Mussolini from Carboni (II).
60 Ciano and Suñer from Susmel.
61 Carboni, Castellano, and Ciano from Castellano (II), Monelli.
61 Carboni moving near Kesselring from Carboni (III).
61 Carboni and Ambrosio from Castellano (II).
61 Castellano's moves and instructions from Castellano (II).

Chapter 4 THE SPECTATORS

The Lotus Eaters

Page

62–63 Interview with Mario Masenza.
63 Cost of living from *Trent'anni di storia italiana* (Luraghi).
63 Interview with Luigi Persichetti.
63–64 Ciano lunch from Benini, Susmel. *Vita*.

The Mistresses

The relation of Claretta Petacci and Mussolini based on Hibbert. Bandini, Bottai, Caudana, Ciano, D'Aroma (II), Vittorio Mussolini, Navarra, Pini, Susmel, Talarico (I), Zangrandi (II).

Europeo, May 20, May 27, June 3, 1956; August 8, 1968, Lietta Tornabuoni. *Gente*, March–May 1958; June–July 1959; October 1968; November, 1968. *Giorno*, February 24, March 8, 1968. *Incom*, April–June 1958. *Oggi*, March–April 1966. *Settimo Giorno*, February–March 1961. *Tempo illustrato*, September, November 1962.

Page

64 Claretta Petacci waiting for Mussolini from *Gente*, October, 1968; November 1968. *Tempo illustrato*, September 1962; November 1962.

64 "If you must write" from *Gente*, October 1968; November 1968.

65 Claretta's sense of humor, suggestion of suspenders, jealousy, and women at dinner from *Gente*, October 1968; November 1968.

65 When one of her flimsy films from Piccolo.

65 Description of Petacci family from Monelli.

65 Ugo Montagna and Petaccis from *Giorno*.

66 Art show from Talarico (I); *Messaggero*, July–September 1943.

66 Claretta to her lawyer from *Gente*, October 1968; November 1968.

67 To strangle her from *Europeo*, August 8, 1968, Lietta Tornabuoni.

67 Bigamist from *Tribuna illustrata*.

67 "free as the air" from *Europeo*, August 8, 1968, Lietta Tornabuoni.

67 Possessive mistress and venereal diseases from *Tempo illustrato*, September, November 1962.

67 Mussolini's apartment and Claretta's actions there from Caudana. *Tempo illustrato*, September, November 1962.

67 Italian writer from Gadda.

The Press

Detailed information is from various newspapers of the period.

Page

68 According to their stories from *Oggi*, August 1968.

69 Fellini and the draft from interview with Fellini.

The Jews

This section is based mainly on interviews with Ettore della Riccia, Angelo Caló and Vincenzo Talarico. Also from Fermi, Ginzburg, Hibbert, De Begnac, De Felice, Ciano, Lapide, Preti, Vaussard, Zangrandi (II). *Documenti del Nostro Tempo. Messaggero*, July 18–23, 1963.

Page

70–71 Moishe Mussolin from Monelli.

71 Tough-minded told to Ciano.

72 Story of Enrico Rocca from interview with Zangrandi.

72 "the anti-Semitic battle" from *Messaggero*, July 18–23, 1963.

72 "Neapolitan" or "Tuscan" from Borghese.

The Church

Page

73 "remove the Pope" from *Atti e documenti relativi alla seconda guerra mondiale*, Vol. IV.

73 Vatican no intermediary from interview with Vitetti.

73 Weiszaecker reports from Friedlander.

73–74 German spy network from *Civilta cattolica*, January 3, 1970; interview with Graham.

74 Polish priests from Lapide.

74 Jewish professors from *Messaggero*, August 3, 1967, referring to NG–4567, May 12, 1942.

74 "damage which would have followed" from De Felice.

74 "the man Divine Providence" from Piscitelli.

75 "professional liars" from Fermi.

75 Ida Dasler from *Tribuno illustrato*; "evil eye" from Hibbert.

75 nest of spies and "I replied" from *Foreign Relations of the United*

States (hereinafter referred to as *Foreign Relations*) (Tittmann to secretary of state, June 29, 1943).

75–76 "the government of Italy" from *Foreign Relations* (secretary of state to Tittmann, July 19, 1943).

76 "above any armed conflict" from *Foreign Relations* (Pope Pius XII to President Roosevelt, July 20, 1943).

76 "The responsibility clearly rests" from *Foreign Relations* (secretary of state to the ambassador in Spain (Hayes), July 24, 1943).

76 "did not raise his voice" from *Foreign Relations* (Tittmann to secretary of state, July 23, 1943).

76 "desperately hoping" from *Foreign Relations* (Tittmann to secretary of state, July 26, 1943).

77 Situation dramatic and good will from Castellano (II).

Chapter 5   IN THE WINGS

The Anti-Fascists

Much of this section is based on Bonomi's diary, but the following have also been of value: Comandini, Lizzadri (I), Monelli, Soleri, Tamaro, Zangrandi (II).

Page

79 "95 per cent of the active anti-Fascists. . ." from *La Resistenza al fascismo*.

The Marshals

Page

80–81 Badoglio card game, delegation and proclamation from Castellano (I), Monelli, Tamaro.

81 Caporetto and whitewash from Spampanato.

81 Army report from *Avvenimenti dell'ottobre al dicembre del 1917*.

82 "think it over" and "His telegram" from D'Aroma (III).

82 Badoglio's background and devotion to Mussolini from D'Aroma (III), De Biase (I), B. Mussolini, Spampanato, Tamaro, Zangrandi (II).

82–83 Conversation between Carboni and Badoglio from Zangrandi (I).

83 Farinacci quote on Badoglio from Spampanato.

83 Rivalry between marshals from Comandini, Puntoni (revival of Freemasonry).

84 A following among the masses from Puntoni.

84 The Church approved from Badoglio.

84 "healthy social conservatism" from Comandini.

84 Audience with the king from Puntoni.

84 "a government of ghosts" from Monelli, Soleri.

The Party Hacks

Page

85 "fed up with it" from Navarra.
85 donna Rachele from Dombrowski, Fermi. *Vita*.
85 "something about Ciano, Grandi . . ." from Hibbert.
85 "Have them all arrested" from Bianchi.
85 "He honestly believes" from Rachele Mussolini.
85 Roll on the floor from Navarra.
86 Small piece of paper from *Epoca*, April 10, 1966.
86 "you've killed fascism" from Dombrowski.
86 Card-carrying members from Spampanato.
86 Description of Scorza from Vaussard.
86 Scorza conversation with Mussolini from Scorza, Tamaro.
86–87 Farinacci's warning from *Tempo illustrato*, June–July 1965.

The Germans

Page

88 Kesselring to Mussolini from Kesselring.
88 Descriptions of Westphal, Mackensen, Moellhausen, Dollmann, Kappler from Katz, Dollmann, Moellhausen.
89 "Politics is not my field" from Moellhausen.
89–90 Description of Rintelen from Dollmann.
90 Conversation of Hitler and von Neurath from Warlimont.
90 "pretty good nose" and other Hitler quotes from Warlimont.

The Allies

American and British points of view from Bryant, Buckley, Butcher, Churchill, Feis, Higgins, Howard, Kogan, Macmillan, Murphy, Wilmot. *Foreign Relations*, *Surrender*. Giovanetti, Toscana.

The Hierarchs

Page

98–99 Dino Grandi's actions from Bianchi (Grandi), Federzoni, Monelli. *Oggi*, July–August 1963; *Vita*.
99 Hand grenades from *Vita*.
99 "I await what will happen" from Bottai.
100 Rooms of Palazzo Venezia from Federzoni.
100 Albini from Zangrandi (II).
100 Description of situation from Bianchi (quoting Grandi), Bottai.
101 Description of the hierarchs from Dombrowski. Spampanato.

102 Conversation of Scorza and Mussolini from Scorza.
102 Hand grenades from Federzoni.
102–103 Opening of council from Bottai. *Vita.*

Chapter 6 THE CURTAIN RISES

The Unseen Audience

The description of the atmosphere that evening is based on interviews with Romano Antonelli, Carla Capponi, Ettore della Riccia.

Page

105 Piazza Venezia from *Espresso,* July 21, July 28, August 4, 1963.
105 "*Duce, Duce*" from Abate.
105–106 Meeting at Lizzadri's home from Lizzadri (II).
106 Zamboni's actions from *Epoca,* January, February 1968; *Oggi,* July–August, 1963.
106 Princess Colonna's from interview with Vitetti.
106 Excelsior Hotel from Monelli.

The Grand Council

Details of this highly controversial meeting have been put together from a multitude of sources. The most helpful, because they are written from contrasting points of view, have been Federzoni and Scorza. My reasons for choosing specific conversations are given in the text. Corroborative information comes from Dombrowski. Acerbo, Alfieri, Bastianini, Bianchi, Galbiati, Monelli, Spampanato, Susmel, Vaussard, Zangrandi (II). *Epoca* (Grandi). *Messaggero,* July 18–23, 1963; March 7–15, 1967. *Tempo illustrato,* June–July 1965. *Vita.*

The seating arrangement is from Tamaro. Mussolini's asides, written and verbal, are from Scorza. The dictator's thoughts are from B. Mussolini. Mussolini's words to Alfieri during intermission are from Alfieri. Particularly helpful was the series of statements by hierarchs published in *Il Messaggero* in 1967. After all, they were there.

The Actors Depart

Page

125 "The session is over" from Federzoni.
126 Mussolini's indifference from Alfieri.
126 Federzoni thought from Federzoni.
126 Ever the actor from Federzoni.

126 Was it possible from *Epoca*, April 18, 1965.

126 Ciano's actions from Zangrandi (II). *Tempo illustrato*, June-July 1965.

126–127 The scene in Mussolini's office and the ride home from Scorza.

127 Mussolini's discussions with his wife from *Vita*.

128 At Fascist party headquarters from Cucco.

128 "I would have liked" from *Messaggero*, March 7–15, 1967 (De Stefani).

128–129 Grandi's movements, Zamboni, Talvacchia, and conversation with Acquarone from Bianchi. *Epoca*, April 18, 1965, and January–February 1968; *Espresso*, July 28, August 4, August 11, 1963; *Oggi*, July–August 1963; *Tempo illustrato*, June–July 1965.

Chapter 7 THE BACKSTAGE MANEUVERS

Page

131 Acquarone lost no time from *Europeo*, September 19, 1965 (Acquarone).

131 From that moment on from *Messaggero*, July 18–23, 1963.

131 Conversation of De Stefani and Montini from De Biase (II), Zangrandi (II).

131–132 Mussolini's day from Dombrowski. Federzoni, Scorza. *Tempo illustrato*, June–July 1965.

132 Conversation of Scorza and Mussolini from Scorza.

132 Albini from Federzoni.

132–133 Grandi's activity and meetings from *Epoca* (Grandi).

133 Biggini from *Epoca*, January, February 1968.

133 Grandi sends Talvacchia, worried, from *Epoca* (Grandi).

133 "His Majesty has appointed Badoglio" from *Tempo illustrato*, June–July 1965.

133 Grandi had not been told from *Epoca*, January, February 1968.

133 Phone calls from Puntoni.

133 Goering's visit, Hidaka, "open city," from Bastianini, Zangrandi (II).

134 Meeting with Galbiati and drive to San Lorenzo from Galbiati.

134 Two old women from Cucco.

135 Revised their planning from Castellano (I), Monelli, Spampanato, Vaussard. *Europeo*, September 19, 1965 (Cerica).

135 "The military questions are my concern" from Vaussard.

136 Mackensen at German embassy from *Europeo*, September 19, 1965 (Dollmann, Moellhausen).

136 Report for Ribbentrop from Monelli.

136 "The division must continue" from *Europeo*, September 19, 1965 (Dollmann).

136 But the fact was from *Europeo*, August 8, 1968, Galbiati.

137 King's lunch and instructions from Puntoni.

137 Mussolini's lunch and discussions from Dombrowski. Monelli, R. Mussolini. *Vita*.

137–138 Scorza's phone calls from Colonel Rocca and to Mussolini from Scorza.

138 Mussolini's plans based on notes on back of telegram form from *Epoca*, April 10, 1966, Pesci.

138 Mussolini's moves from *Tempo illustrato*, June–July 1965; *Vita*.

139 Chierici, Cerica, Acquarone from Castellano (I), Senise, *Europeo*, September 10, 1965 (Acquarone).

139 Cerica discussion with Acquarone from Tamaro.

139 "All right" from Puntoni. *Europeo*, September 19, 1965 (Acquarone).

139–140 Mussolini's arrival at royal villa and arrest of Boratto from Dombrowski. Monelli.

140–141 Meeting of king and Mussolini from mainly Puntoni but also Spampanato, Vaussard. *Vita*.

141 "We'll see in six months" from Zangrandi (II).

141–142 Mussolini's arrest from Bianchi, but also Di Benigno, Monelli. *Epoca*, April 10, 1966, Pesci; *Europeo*, September 19, 1965; *Vita*.

142 "We'll wind up hitting someone" from Zangrandi (II).

142 When the ambulance had gone from Puntoni.

142 "but not here" from Montanelli.

142–144 All quotes and actions of takeover from Marchesi and Monelli.

144 Senise's actions from Castellano (I), Senise.

144 "There's no doubt" from Galbiati.

144 A private celebration from Carboni (III), Marchesi, Monelli.

145 Buffarini-Guidi and Rachele Mussolini from Dombrowski. Spampanato. *Vita*.

145 "It was a friend" from *Vita*.

145 The revelation of Mussolini's relationship with Claretta Petacci from *Gente*, June–July, 1959 (Vittorio Mussolini); *Vita*.

145–146 Scorza's actions, conversations and escape from Cucco, Scorza.

146 Efforts by Scorza's assistants from Cucco.

146 Farinacci's escape from Dombrowski. Tamaro. *Europeo*, September 19, 1965 (Dollmann).

146 Hitler at his headquarters from Warlimont.

146–147 Ciano from Anfuso.

147 Armored cars under the trees from Spampanato.

147 Mussolini at Podgora barracks from Dombrowski. Bianchi, Di Benigno, B. Mussolini. *Epoca*, April 10, 1966, Pesci; *Vita*.

BOOK TWO

Chapter 8 THE PEOPLE EXULT

Page

151 The night of July 25 from interview with Antonelli.

152 Raffaele Persichetti sat in his living room from interview with Persichetti relatives, friends, etc.

153 By then from interview with Capponi.

154 Three Socialists from Lizzadri, Piscitelli.

154 "They've arrested him!" hotel doorman and *Il Messaggero* from Monelli. *Espresso*, July 28, 1963, Benedetti.

155 Paola Borboni from Talarico.

156 Press Club from Monelli, Piscitelli, interview with della Riccia.

156 "Fascism is dead" from Hibbert.

156 Opposite the Ministry of War from interview with Schuberth.

156 Die-hard Fascists from Spampanato.

157 Badoglio at Palazzo Vidoni from Marchesi, Tamaro, Zangrandi (II).

157 Arrest of Cavallero from Di Benigno.

158 Carboni asked to be appointed from Monelli.

158 Spontaneous demonstration from Piscitelli. *Vita*.

158 "Today I revoked" from *Storia illustrata*, January, March 1968.

158 "The sensation I feel" from Tamaro.

158 "A great event" from Bonomi.

158 Party badges from Page

158–159 Overnight, flags and description of celebrations July 26 in Rome from *Messaggero*, July 27, 1943, Calcagno.

159 "breathe this free air" from *Mercurio*, December 1944, Alvaro.

159 The habit of years from *Espresso*, July 28, August 4, August 11, 1963.

159 Air of enthusiasm from Piscitelli.

159 At Piazza Montecitorio from *L'Italia dei quarantacinque giorni* (hereinafter referred to as *45 giorni*).

159–160 Vulgarity of Romans—well-dressed gentleman and peddler of white mice from Monelli.

160 Missed confidential documents from Piscitelli.

160 Sent home in their underwear from *Trent'anni di storia italiana* (Luraghi).

160 A pitched battle from *45 giorni*, Senise, Spampanato.

160 A messenger boy from interview with Santovito.
161 "a child any minute" from Cucco.
161 Milan's demonstrations from Gorla, Tamaro.
161 "Toscanini come back" from La Guidara.
161 Turin from *Trent'anni di storia italiana* (Luraghi), *45 giorni*.
161 Bottles of wine from interview with Chilanti.
162 "I won't squash you" from interview with Moretti.
162 Met to discuss from Lizzadri (II).
162 "the corpse of fascism" from Bonomi.
162 Communists collaborate with monarchy from Silva.
162 Anti-Fascists abroad from *Messaggero*, July 18–23, 1963.
162 "Here's to the dictator" from Nenni (II).
162 "pig of a Mussolini" from Tamaro.

Chapter 9 THE ARMIES PREPARE

The Anglo-Americans

Page
163 "no definite knowledge" from Churchill.
163–164 The scene at Chequers from Bryant.
164 An undue liking from Churchill.
164 Macmillan and Eisenhower from Macmillan.
164 Eisenhower to La Marsa from Butcher.
164 "had no very clear picture" from Macmillan.
164–165 Eisenhower said he wanted from Murphy.
165 "a white alley" from Butcher.
165 Generals on the spot from Murphy.
165 Quickly and advantageously from Butcher.
165 "the changes in Italy " "If any overtures come," and Churchill thought from Churchill.
166 "by the necessity" from Eisenhower.
166 "with the resources available" from *Surrender*.
166 British Eighth Army and Patton's Seventh from Baldwin. *Surrender*.
166 Directives from interview with Koffler.
166 "the moronic little king" from Delzell.
166 "increasingly difficult" from Macmillan.
166 "can make the Italians fight" from *Foreign Relations* (Winant to secretary of state, July 26, 1943).

The Germans

Page
167 On the weekend from Dollmann.
167 He did not learn from Rintelen.

167 *"Keine Bierwitze, bitte"* from Moellhausen.

167 "It doesn't seem to me" from Tamaro.

168 When the news came from Moellhausen.

168 Each fought its own war from Shirer, Warlimont.

168 Came away persuaded from Rintelen.

168 "Nothing definite yet" from Warlimont.

169 "jabber" from Shirer.

169 "a shocking and shattering" from Warlimont.

169 "It's simply shocking" from Goebbels.

169–170 Bombings on July 24 and 25 from Bryant.

170–172 This section has been put together from Bullock, Deakin, Heiber, Shirer, Warlimont, Wilmot. *Fuehrer Conferences on Naval Affairs* (hereinafter referred to as *Fuehrer Conferences*), *Surrender*. Collotti. *Europeo*, July 25, 1968, Dollmann.

173 Plans for Italy from Rintelen.

Chapter 10 THE ILLUSION OF FREEDOM

Page

174–175 "The undersigned" and "for his concern" from B. Mussolini.

175 His dilemma from *Trent'anni di storia italiana* (Luraghi), *Vita.*

175 "Yes, but all the anti-Fascists are republicans" from Soleri.

175 Support promised by Communist party from De Biase (II).

176 Acquarone proposed from *Epoca*, January, February 1968.

176 "What's this story" from Monelli.

176 All Fascists from Cassinelli, Tamaro.

176–177 Government ministers and their Fascist backgrounds from Tamaro.

177 At his first cabinet meeting from Susmel.

177 "It seemed" from Piccardi.

177 "since so many" from *Espresso*, July 28, August 4, August 11, 1963.

177 "good government" from Zangrandi (II).

177 lack of change from Piscitelli.

178 A few men from Perrone-Capano, Piscitelli.

178 Threats of a general strike from Lizzadri (I).

178 The trusts from Piscitelli.

178 "a state of things" from Page.

178–179 No move was made and no amnesties, pardons or trial from Zangrandi (II).

179 Changed the name of streets from Monelli.

179 While street cleaners from Lizzadri (I), Morpugo.

179 In Milan, "borne lovingly away " and embraced the tank corpsmen from Ferrata.

180 Walls of Trastevere from Monelli.

180 Rulers were fearful from Pilotti.

Chapter 11 THE REALITY OF REPRESSION

Details on many of the incidents in this chapter come from Zangrandi (II), as I have pointed out in the text.

Page

182 Private and public gatherings, etc. from Canevari, Tamaro. *Messaggero*, July 29–September 14, 1943.

182 "proceed in combat formation" from Battaglia, *Trent'anni di storia italiana* (Luraghi).

183 Five army divisions from *Surrender*.

183 "the foulest of German corporals" from Caviglia.

183 "Never in Italy" from Canevari.

183 "*Viva Badoglio!*" and details from Etnasi.

184 In Milan from *Storia della guerra civile in Italia*.

184 In Reggio Emilia from interview with Franzini, official of ANPI in Reggio Emilia.

184 One of the most serious from Battaglia, *Storia delle guerra civile in Italia*, and of course Zangrandi (II).

185 Zangrandi's figures had been mentioned partially in Tamaro and were confirmed (p. 272) in *45 giorni*.

185 Fascism had gone from Pintor.

Chapter 12 THE EXILES RETURN

Page

187 Beyond his party's orders from Zangràndi (II).

187 Should have resigned from Comandini.

188 Came back from abroad from Lussu.

189 "Thirty years ago" from Nenni.

189 Whenever possible, Raffaele Persichetti and following from interview with Zangrandi.

190 San Vittore prison from Bevilacqua, Vaina, Zangrandi (II).

190 Prison conditions from interview with Zangrandi. Patti.

190 Rossi (arrested) from interview with Zangrandi.

191 "give me the names" from Zangrandi (II) quoting Roveda.

191 Political prisoners not being released from Falconi (hunger strike), Piscitelli, Zangrandi (II). *Messaggero*, July 29, September 14, 1943.

191 "It was enough" from interview with Zangrandi.

192 Italian nobility from *Messaggero*, July–September 1943.

192 What the new arrivals found from Lussu, Piscitelli.

192 Socialist movement and the party was not from Lussu.

192 Party of the elite from Tamaro.

192 "From the palace revolution" from Piscitelli.

192 Communists prone to supporting the monarchy from Silva.

192 Bonomi and Orlando from Giovana.

192 "the war continues" from *Europeo*, July 25, 1968, Trionfera (Acquarone).

193 Carla Capponi also from interview with Capponi.

193 In the tradition of Persichetti from Perrone-Capano.

193 Persichetti had not been feeling well from interview with Persichetti, the rest from interview with Moretti.

194 Enrico Rocca who from interview with Chilanti.

194 Ettore della Riccia's experiences from interview with della Riccia.

194–195 Badoglio and racial laws from De Felice.

Chapter 13 WOLVES BECOME SHEEP

Page

196 Rushed to see the king and "showed the slightest desire" from Senise.

196 "I now take up" from La Guidara.

197 Others, who had been paid from interview with della Riccia.

197 "revolting display" from Croce.

197 Party card a necessity from Monelli.

197 Like other civil servants from interview with Savoni.

197 "rare example" from Page.

197 "a face" from *Mercurio*, Alvaro.

197 Scorza letter from Monelli. *Domenica del corriere*, March 5, March 12, March 19, 1968.

198 Towards most of the Fascists from *Tempo illustrato*, June–July, 1965.

198 "the future Fascist resurrection" from Comandini.

198 Grandi's conversation with king, further actions, meeting with Badoglio, pope from Bianchi. *Epoca* (Grandi).

199 Grandi did not know from Castellano (II).

199 Muti warned Ciano from Susmel.

199 "You have done a great thing" from interview with Vitetti.

200 That same evening from Dombrowski. *Tempo*, June 1965.

200 "the elimination of Fascist Party members" from Spampanato.

201 "any offense or expression of contempt" from *Popolo di Roma*, July–September 1943.

201 "who for twenty years" from Spampanato.

201 Vatican's intervention from Friedlander.

201 Cerica ordered some of his men from Zangrandi (II).

201 "I couldn't" from Senise.

201 Proposals to kill Mussolini from Tamaro, Zangrandi (II). *Oggi*, October 14, 1958.

202 "Forget it" from Monelli.

202 "Mussolini could be useful again" from *Oggi*, October 14, 1958.

202 "Let's not play jokes" from Monelli.

202 "I've worked for Italy for twenty-one years" from Saporiti.

203 His dinner that night from *Vita*.

203 Invisible throng and "you put us" from Monelli.

203 Trick of fate from Spampanato.

203 How Mussolini spent his time from *Vita*.

203 "unspeakable indignities" from Zangrandi (II). Guariglia, Tamaro. *Vita*.

203 "illicit enrichment" from *Messaggero*, July 29, September 14, 1943.

204 Pickpockets and sneak thieves from *Il Lavoro italiano*.

204 Everyone understood this meant from Comandini.

Chapter 14 THE ONSET OF APATHY

Page

205 One of the young Romans from interview with Novelli.

206 "It is difficult" from *Mercurio*, Alvaro.

206 Newspapers generally from *Messaggero*, July 29–September 14, 1943; *Popolo di Roma*.

206 One who tried from Comandini.

206 Neither criticism of fascism from Tamaro.

206 He found his countrymen from *Mercurio*, Alvaro.

207 "If we were to win" from Artom.

207 In spite of all the talk about freedom from Tamaro.

207 Several men of the theatre from *Messaggero*, July 29–September 14, 1943.

208 Other Italians from *Trent'anni di storia italiana*; newspapers of the period.

208 The bread from Benedetti.

208 "But sir, do you think" from Tamaro.

208 Except for the symbols and rationing on food from *Capitolium*, September 1963, Pedercini; newspapers of the period.

208 One family which from interview with De Vitali.

Chapter 15 WAR . . .

Page

210 "nothing but imbeciles" from De Biase (II).

210 "no one had brought up" from *Europeo*, September 19, 1965 (Acquarone).

210 "Opposition with force" from Rossi.

211 "Even after the initial mistake" from Zanussi.

211 Italians could have blown up from Goebbels.

211 "if given a real leader" from Tamaro.

211 "the red-hot rake of war" from Churchill.

211 "done the impossible" from Tamaro, Zangrandi (II).

212 Kesselring and Rintelen conversations with Badoglio and Hitler from Rintelen.

212 The German High Command from Warlimont. *Fuehrer Conferences on Naval Affairs.*

213 "These are things" from Warlimont.

213 The carefully worked-out plans from Deakin, Shirer, Warlimont. *Surrender.* Collotti.

213 Attack on the Kursk salient from Goerlitz.

213 "The change in the Italian government" from Goebbels. *Messaggero,* July 29–September 14, 1943.

214–215 Marras's meeting with Hitler from Simoni.

214 Badoglio had no intention from Badoglio.

215 King's conversations with Carboni, Mackensen and Puntoni from Guariglia, Puntoni.

215–216 "Another night passed" from Carboni (II).

216 Arms were quickly returned from Bartolini, Caracciolo.

216 Minor thefts from Tamaro.

216 Instructions to German soldiers from Zangrandi (II).

216 German troops movements from Collotti. However, the date is not July 26 as given by Collotti but July 30 as confirmed by *45 giorni.*

217–218 Ambrosio's meeting with Kesselring from Moellhausen. *Espresso,* July 28, August 4, August 11, 1963.

218 "The Germans didn't dare" from Zanussi.

218 Fourth Army commanders and "They know Italian very well" from Trabucchi.

219 The German Army Command from Warlimont.

219 Although a special section from Amé.

219 Roatta and Ambrosio from Roatta.

219 "My congratulations" from Amé.

220 "they had started" from Zanussi.

220 "always ready to give in" from Zangrandi (II).

220 "to open dossiers" from Senise.

220–223 The meeting at Tarvisio comes mainly from Guariglia, with sidelights from interview with Vitetti. Canevari, Collotti, Moellhausen, Simoni and *45 giorni.*

223 "At the end" and ordered Mackensen from Dollmann.

223 Italians noted from Gorla.

Chapter 16 ... OR PEACE?

Page

226 Peace feelers before July 25, 1943, from Eisenhower, Macmillan. Monelli, Palermo, Pintor, Plehwe, Toscano. *Espresso,* July 28, August 4, August 11, 1963; *Oggi,* February 20–April 3, 1966.

226 Badoglio's contacts with British intelligence from *Foreign Relations, Surrender*. Badoglio, Toscano.

226 "Our military authorities" from *Foreign Relations* (Eden to Hull, December 18, 1942).

227 "German forces from Russia" from Bryant.

227 Churchill expanded on this from *Surrender*.

227 But with Mussolini gone from Guariglia, Tamaro.

227 Tortuously slow manner from *Oggi*, February 20–April 3, 1966.

228 "The Italians would have found" from *Corriere della sera*, August 20, 1966.

228 Italian secret agents and their prowess from Toscano. *Europeo*, August 10, August 17, August 24, 1967.

229 D'Ajeta's lack of qualifications from Tamaro.

229 But he was only briefed from Castellano (II), D'Ajeta, Guariglia.

229–230 D'Ajeta meeting with Campbell from Churchill. *Surrender*. D'Ajeta, Toscano, Valiani.

231 "Under the influence" from *Foreign Relations* (Apostolic Delegation to secretary of state, August 20, 1943).

231 "may be playing game" from *Foreign Relations* (minister to Switzerland to secretary of state, August 5, 1943).

231 "I understand that the Vatican" from Friedlander.

232 "uncertain and clumsy" from Piscitelli.

232 Mauro Scoccimarro became from Katz, Zangrandi (II).

232 "Mario told me" from Berio.

232–233 Instructions to Berio from Berio, De Biase (II).

233 Berio's mission from Churchill. Berio, Tamaro, Zangrandi (II).

234 "Your agent" from Amé.

235 "political career and future" from Guariglia. *Oggi*, February 20–April 3, 1966.

235 "certain Signor Bussetti" from Macmillan.

Chapter 17 THE BOMBINGS

Page

236 But the two Allies disagreed from Churchill, *Foreign Relations, Surrender*.

237 Churchill also thought from *Foreign Relations* (Churchill to Roosevelt, August 4, 1943).

237 Eisenhower had planned from Butcher.

237 Open city discussions from Castelli, Giovannetti, Piscitelli.

237 Cardinals and bishops never hesitated from Kogan.

237 The Allied bombing of cities from interview with Chilanti, Buckley, Gasparotto, Tamaro. *Vita*.

237 "Search among the dust" from *Antologia poetica della resistenza Italiana.*

238 "It was early in the morning" from Spampanato.

238 Rome anti-Fascists gathered from *Espresso*, July 28, August 4, August 11, 1963.

239 Antiaircraft defense from *Vita.* Page.

239 Bombing of Rome from Benedetti, De Biase (II), Tamaro. *Capitolium*, September 1963, Pedercini.

239 Pope Pius from Giovannetti.

239 "Our best antiaircraft battery" from De Biase (II).

240 But instead of speeding up from Giovannetti.

240 The Italians pointed out from Castelli.

240 In order to feel safer from Piscitelli.

240 Description of Rome on August 15 from *Capitolium*, September 1963, Pedercini; *Messaggero*, July 29–September 14, 1943.

240 "I have learnt" from Spampanato.

241 The Apostolic delegation in Washington from *Foreign Relations* (to the Department of State, August 25, 1943).

241 Supreme Command's trickery concerning open city from Canevari, Zangrandi (II).

Chapter 18 THE LAGGARD EMISSARY

Page

242 Opposing opinions from interview with Vitetti.

243 "I was sure" from Castellano (I).

243 "We shouldn't ask" from interview with Vitetti.

243 "By the way" from Zanussi.

243 Instructions to Castellano from Marchesi, Palermo, Tamaro.

244 "Please, general" from Tamaro.

244 "The Italians are continuing" from *Fuehrer Conferences on Naval Affairs.*

244 Castellano's preparations from Macmillan., Guariglia, Monelli.

244 Reasons for Castellano's choice from interview with Vitetti. Carboni (II, IV), Monelli.

245 Montanari and Casardi from Monelli.

245–247 Castellano's trip and meeting with Sir Samual Hoare from interview with Vitetti. Hoare. *Surrender.* Castellano (II), Monelli, Toscano.

Chapter 19 THE DOUBLE-TRACK

Page

248–249 Hitler's suspicions and German position from Warlimont, *Fuehrer Conferences on Naval Affairs.*

249–250 Background to Bologna meeting from Warlimont, Kesselring, Rintelen, Simoni.

250–251 Quotes and description of meeting from Warlimont. *Surrender.* Canevari, Collotti, Monelli, Rintelen, Roatta ("This is an attitude"), Tamaro, Zanussi ("We are not Saxons!").

252 Vietinghoff was sent down, and established Rommel from Warlimont.

252 Descriptions of Rommel and Kesselring from Strong,· Canevari. *Trent'anni di storia italiana.*

252 "For when the time should come" from Kesselring.

253 The king on August 16 and meeting with Badoglio from Puntoni, Spampanato.

253 "Badoglio is on the wrong track" from Gorla.

253 When he spoke to General Antonio Sorice from Tamaro.

253 "If the Germans refuse" from Di Benigno.

254 Issued its coded telegram "O" from Spampanato.

254 The loss of half a million Italian soldiers from Monelli.

254 Carboni's taking Amé's place from Palermo, Puntoni, Rintelen.

254 "In going through them" and Castellano's "absolute ignorance" from Carboni (I, III).

Chapter 20 THE ALLIED DILEMMA

Page

256–257 "Although it may seem strange" from *Fascismo e antifascismo* (Salvadori).

257 The English did have a network from *Europeo*, August 10, August 17, August 24, 1967.

257 When Tunisia was occupied from *Fascismo e antifascismo* (Salvadori).

257–258 Mafia aid to Americans and its position in Italy from Lewis, Pantaleone.

258 Eisenhower quotes from Eisenhower.

258 "up the garden path" from Baldwin.

258 "large-scale counteractions" from Eisenhower.

258–259 Preparations for Quebec meeting and differences between Allies from Bryant, Strong, Wilmot.

260 "By 10:00 A.M. this morning" from Churchill.

260 "The passport to Italy" from Buckley.

260 "You are no doubt informed" from Churchill.

260 "I certainly don't like" from Sherwood.

261 Eden was against the idea from Woodward.

261–262 "I think the enemy" from Tregaskis.

262 "a pity that we didn't have" from Butcher.

262 "making a deal with Fascists" from Murphy.

262–263 Preparations for mission from Butcher, Macmillan, Murphy, Strong.

263 Actually head of counterespionage from De Launay.

Chapter 21 THE MISSING GENERAL

This chapter is based on accounts from Butcher, Churchill, Kogan, Macmillan, Murphy, Saporiti, Strong, *Surrender*. Interview with Vitetti. Canevari, Castellano (I, II), Di Benigno, De Biase (II), Monelli, Musco, Tamaro, Toscano, Zangrandi (II).

It must be noted that Castellano's version is backed up in the minutes of the conference dated August 18, 1943, and classified "Secret." This is reproduced in Castellano (II).

Page

271–272 Castellano's encounter with the real expert from Saporiti, Monelli.

Chapter 22 REINFORCING POWER

Page

273 The queen asked from *Capitolium*, September 1963, Pedercini.

273 The king complained from Puntoni.

273–274 On August 20, Allied planes from Giovannetti.

274 Shots rang out from De Benedetti.

274 Forty-nine people from *Messaggero*, July 29, September 14 1943.

274 The Rome press continued from Spampanato.

274–275 The strikes from Kogan. Tamaro, Zangrandi (II). *Espresso*, July 28, August 4, August 11, 1963.

275 The situation in Turin from Artom, Tamaro.

275 Badoglio alarmed from Kogan. Di Benigno, Zangrandi (II), *Espresso*, July 28, August 4, August 11, 1963.

276 "Badoglio is getting me" from Puntoni.

276 He sent Princess Maria-José from *Espresso*, July 28, August 4, August 11, 1963.

276 "remain available" and "Yes, but" from Soleri, Zangrandi (II).

276 "I've put fifty mortars" from Bonomi.

276 "Badoglio is scared" from Gorla.

277 The spy plot from Bonomi, Senise. *Espresso*, July 28, August 4, August 11, 1963.

277 "This activity" from Amé.

277 The head of OVRA from Leto (I).

277–278 When Badoglio's office and following from Carboni (III), Senise, Tamaro.

278 Few Fascists of any importance from Vaussard.

278–281 Muti and his death from interview with Paolino, Canevari, Carboni (IV), Monelli, Puntoni, Senise, Spampanato, Tamaro, Zangrandi (II). *Documenti del nostro tempo; Tempo illustrato,* June–July 1965.

Chapter 23 HOUNDS AND HARES

Page

283 In no time at all from Tamaro, Zangrandi (II).

283 Self-styled Marchese from *Giorno.*

284 "Remember, Ben?" from *Gente,* October, November 1968.

284 Three years later from Talarico (I). *Giornale d'Italia,* July 29– September 14, 1943.

284 "illicit accumulation of wealth" from *Messaggero,* July 29, September 14, 1943.

284 "If he does" from Simoni.

284–285 Ciano's escape from Collotti, Dollmann, Susmel. *Gente,* July 1969.

285 Skorzeny and Hitler from Hibbert. *Surrender.* Dollmann, Moellhausen, Zangrandi (II).

286 "Sepp" Dietrich and "that foolishness Adolf" from Warlimont, Monelli.

286–287 Skorzeny's search for Mussolini from Deakin, Dombrowski, Hibbert. *Surrender.* Dollmann, B. Mussolini, Spampanato, (as told by Skorzeny to Barghini).

287 "I have received" and other letters to his wife from interview with Vitali.

287–288 Mussolini's being moved from Deakin, Dombrowski, Hibbert.

Chapter 24 THE NEW NEGOTIATOR

Page

289 He, like everyone else from Zangrandi (II).

289 But the regime had been wary from Tamaro.

290 "the only one of the marshals" from Bianchi. *Messaggero,* July 18– 23, 1963.

290 "Do what you can" and "If your mission" from Bianchi. *Tempo illustrato,* June–July 1965.

290 Without waiting for from Carboni (III).

291 "Do your best" from Carboni (II).

291 "Our troops are badly armed" from Carboni (II).

291 The living credential and both traveling on the same flight from Hoare, De Launay. Zangrandi (II). Interview with Conti.

292 "My heart was wrung" from Bianchi.

292 Ducking behind trees and street corners from De Launay.

292 When the astonished Zanussi from Zanussi.

292 Who really represented Rome from *Surrender*.

292 "The purpose of this latest visitor" from Churchill.

292 Having Zanussi shot as a spy from Castellano (III) quoting Bedell Smith in letter from Pietro Quaroni to Luca Pietromarchi, June 26, 1946.

293 "Why tie his hands" from Feis.

293 Foreign Minister Anthony Eden from Tamaro.

293 "attentuation of unconditional surrender" from Macmillan.

293–294 Sir Ronald and Eisenhower's headquarters from Feis, Macmillan, Murphy, Woodward. *Surrender*.

294 "a crooked deal" from Butcher.

294 "those brutal terms" from Macmillan.

295 Zanussi was in Lisbon from Feis.

295 "I'm a prisoner of war" from Churchill.

295 Under the name of from *Surrender*.

295 Once aboard his plane from Zanussi.

295 "Beetle came to tell Ike" from Butcher.

296 Asking that his bag from Canevari.

296 "give clear proof" from Zanussi.

296 "Why attack from the south" from Murphy. *Surrender*. Zanussi.

Chapter 25 THE RETURN OF THE DOVE

Page

297 Castellano reported from Rossi.

297–298 Details of meeting at the Viminale from Guariglia.

299 On the way out Ambrosio from Tamaro.

299 The means to be used and following from interview with Marchesi.

299 The real reason from Strong.

299 Christmas dinner with him in Rome and "we were only going to Sicily" from Butcher.

300 Bedell Smith had second thoughts from *Surrender*.

300 Eisenhower and Smith still hoped from Castellano (II) quoting letter from Bedell Smith in Quaroni letter.

301 "The long terms" from Macmillan.

301 "It is of vital importance" from *Surrender*. Castellano (II).

301 The message was delivered from Guariglia.

301 "The situation is coming to a head" from Puntoni.

301 "I have always kept my word" from Spampanato.

301 "It's the head of the government" from Tamaro.

301 The king had assumed the role from *Surrender*. Interview with Marchesi, interview with Vitetti.

302 Admitted he could return from Guariglia.

302 "with sufficient contingents" from Guariglia.

302 "precise directives" from Castellano (I).

302 "(1) Refer to" from Castellano (II), reproduced in Badoglio's handwriting.

303 From the small room from interview with Marchesi. Monelli.

303 It had been a day of suspense from Macmillan.

303 Having received the telegram from Castellano (II).

303 On their arrival from Murphy.

303 "No effective help" and "while our Middle East campaign" from Churchill.

304 Montgomery, who had objected from Moorehead.

Chapter 26 THE BLUFFING

Page

305 At nine o'clock from Strong, Castellano (I), Marchesi.

305 "And you!" and following from De Biase (II) and Zanussi.

306 "If we could establish" from Castellano (III), Toscano.

307 "Don't worry about the harshness" from Zanussi.

308 As he later admitted from Castellano (III) quoting Bedell Smith in Quaroni letter.

308–309 Description of lunch from Murphy.

309 The procedure in case from Castellano (II) quoting authenticated minutes of meeting.

310 Zanussi once again attempted from Zanussi.

310 Meeting with Eisenhower from Butcher (Clark's suspicions), Macmillan, Murphy.

311 "I gave them" from Zanussi.

311 At the Viminale meeting from Carboni (II), Castellano (II), Guariglia, Monelli, Zangrandi (II).

311 Then Acquarone spoke up from Carboni (III).

312 Details of flight from interview with Marchesi. Marchesi.

312 Castellano's meeting, his position from interview with Marchesi, Castellano (II), Musco, Tamaro.

313–314 Alexander's encounter with Castellano and nervously pacing from Macmillan, Murphy. Castellano (II), Marchesi.

314–315 Later that afternoon and telegrams from *Surrender*.

314 Castellano's meeting with Eisenhower from Castellano (II), Marchesi.

315 Telegrams and Montgomery attack from Moorehead. *Surrender*. Castellano (II).

Chapter 27 SURRENDER . . .

The details of what happened at Cassibile on September 3 and 4 are from Butcher, Churchill, Strong, *Surrender*. Interview with Marchesi. Castellano (I, II), Marchesi, Monelli, Zangrandi.

Page
317 Eisenhower was the only one the Russians from *Foreign Relations* (Roosevelt and Churchill to Stalin, September 2, 1943).

318 "on the fourth anniversary" from Churchill.

321–322 Ridgway's account of his doubts and subsequent conversations from Ridgway.

322 Macmillan and Murphy to Rome from Murphy and Strong.

Chapter 28 . . . BUT WHEN?

Page
327 The press muzzled from Tamaro.

327 "His Majesty" from *Surrender*.

328 Half soldier, half functionary from Guariglia.

328 "Until now" from Rahn.

328 "Still determined" from Guariglia.

328 "You are negotiating" from Rahn.

329 "I am" from Moellhausen, Rahn.

329 Meeting between Rahn and Ambrosio from Moellhausen.

329 "Count Grandi strictly watched" from De Launay.

329 "will the situation have a solution?" from Bonomi.

330 "Avoid incidents" from Zangrandi (II).

330 "Don't worry about the enemy" from Caracciolo.

330 German position from Collotti.

331 Instructions from and orders to Kesselring from Kesselring.

331 "The landing" from Buckley.

331–332 OP 44 from Di Benigno, Castellano (III), Marchesi, Monelli, Musco, Roatta, Rossi, Tamaro, Zangrandi.

333 Pro-memoria Numbers 1 and 2 from *Surrender*. Musco, Zangrandi (II).

333 "white prisoners can be released" from Zangrandi (IV).

333 On the morning of Sunday, September 5, from Marchesi.

333 Neither did Acquarone or the king from Castellano (III).

333–334 Ambrosio and the three heads of the armed forces from Monelli, Roatta, Trizzino, Zanussi, *Atti Commissione d'inchiesta per la mancata difesa di Roma* (hereinafter referred to as *Atti Commissione*).

334 Roatta, for the army from Roatta.

335 "It's mad" from *Atti Commissione.*

335 From the chief allied command, from *Surrender*.

335 "reserve a room at Palazzo Caprara" from *Atti Commissione*.

335 But Ambrosio did not even mention the possibility from Zangrandi (II).

336 Carboni was getting worried about his role from Carboni (I), Roatta, Rossi, Zanussi.

336 He went to Roatta from Roatta, Zanussi.

336 Roatta had already had from Kogan, *Surrender*. Castellano (I, II, III), Roatta, Tamaro, Zanussi.

336–337 It is generally accepted from *Surrender*.

337 Carboni later maintained from *Atti Commissione*.

337 The Allies should not expect the Italians from *Documento del nostro tempo*.

337 Deny it was sent: in *Surrender*, the authors say, "But Carboni's memorandum was a fabrication."

337 No desire to fight from *Surrender*. Castellano (III) quoting letter from Bedell Smith, December 20, 1955.

Chapter 29 THE SLOW TRAIN TO TURIN

Page

338 On the night of September 6 from Palermo.

338 To save his furniture from Tamaro.

338–339 "You apply your systems" from Marchesi.

339 There must have been a reason from Palermo, Zangrandi (II).

339 The young general had always officially and his chief of staff from Marchesi.

339 Carboni went to army headquarters from De Biase (II), Musco.

340 Carboni could only supply from Musco.

340 Carboni's meeting from Marchesi, Rossi.

340 Rossi knew that most from Rossi.

340 He hurried to army headquarters from Roatta, Rossi, Zanussi.

340 "a communication of fundamental importance" from *Atti commissione*.

341 General Carboni has continually and Castellano, in any event from *Surrender*. Castellano (I), Monelli, Zangrandi (II).

341 "I went immediately" from Palermo.

341 The Allies, at Brigadier Strong's suggestion from Strong.

341 Phone calls to Ambrosio from Marchesi, Rossi.

342 A group of anti-Fascists in Milan from Zangrandi (II).

342 Rome's anti-Fascist leaders from Bonomi, Piscitelli, Tamaro.

342 Not too knowledgeable from Zangrandi (II).

342 Never showed up again from Carboni (II).

342 Carboni's idea from *Documenti del nostro tempo*.

342 Carboni had secured and set aside from Carboni (II), *Unita*.

343 Bonomi partiotically answered from Tamaro.

343 The monarch was visited from Tamaro.

343–344 The king and his men preparing for flight from Angelucci and Botti, De Biase (II), Tamaro, Zangrandi (II), *Tempo*.

344 The telegram to Castellano from Castellano (II), Zangrandi (IV).

344–345 German and Allied preparations from Goerlitz, Higgins, Linklater, Morison, Warlimont. *Surrender*. Musmanno. *History of the Second World War*, Vol. 4, No. 7, 1967, and Vol. 4, No. 9, 1967.

345 The date set for the delivery of the ultimatum from Higgins, Warlimont, *Surrender*.

Chapter 30 CLANDESTINE MISSION

Details of this chapter come from Eisenhower, Kogan, Strong, Tregaskis (Gardiner). *Surrender* (Taylor). Cadorna, Carboni (I),* Castellano (III), Marchesi, Monelli, Musco, Rossi, Tamaro, Torsiello, Trizzino, Zangrandi (II). Interview with Marchesi, interview with Rocchi.

Harper's; Documenti del nostro tempo; Domenica del corriere, July 6, 1969.

Page

348 "A few sandwiches" and details of meal from Trizzino.

350 German troops now dominated from *Atti Commissione*.

351 "in Salerno within the first ten days" from *Domenica del Corriere*, July 6, 1969.

353 "Everything has been straightened out" from Rossi.

BOOK THREE

Chapter 31 CAUGHT IN THE MIDDLE

Page

359–360 Carboni and the telegrams from *Surrender*. Carboni (II), Musco, Trizzino.

360 "Is that how the day" from Moellhausen.

360 Italian leaders, however from Tamaro.

360 Badoglio and Roatta from Musco, Roatta, Rossi.

360–361 Kesselring's preparations from Palermo, Tamaro.

* "Carboni's account (*L'armistizio e la difesa di Roma* . . .) is highly fictitious," say the authors of *Surrender*.

361 In the meantime, Ambrosio from Zangrandi (II).

361 "How is this possible" from Monelli.

361 "Everything's been arranged" from Tamaro.

361 There was panic at Allied staff headquarters from Eisenhower.

361 "to call the whole thing off" from Macmillan.

361 He himself would assume its command from Castellano (II) (quoting Smith to Quaroni, June 26, 1946).

362 Smith and Macmillan from Macmillan.

362 "In case taylor" from *Surrender*.

362 "An old, honorable soldier" and "Tell the Fuehrer" from Moellhausen, Rahn.

362–363 "At the point where we are" from Puntoni.

363 It was a little after noon from *Harper's*.

363 When sirens sounded from Scrivener.

363 Six thousand persons from Canevari, Carboni (III), De Biase (II), Zangrandi (II). *Documenti del nostro tempo*.

363 93 per cent of their houses from Trizzino.

363 In August from Monelli.

363 Kesselring's command and Kesselring was in his office from Carboni (III), Kesselring. *Documenti del nostro tempo*.

363–364 The untouched Monte Cavo radio station from Moellhausen.

364 At *Comando Supremo* from Marchesi.

364 Eisenhower and his reaction from Eisenhower.

364 Since Ike was already in Bizerte from Strong.

364 "act as if they did sign" from Macmillan.

364 "from Eisenhower to the effect" from Bryant.

365 Shocked, Italian general and appearance before Allied officers from Strong. *Surrender*. Castellano (II).

365–366 Eisenhower's telegram from Eisenhower. *Surrender*.

366 "I have just completed" from Churchill.

366 At that moment, the C-47's from *Surrender*. Castellano (III).

366–367 The mixup on the warning message from *Surrender*. *Oggi*, February 20–April 3, 1966.

366 Only years later from *Surrender*. Toscano.

367 They did not believe and the idea of the walk from Trizzino.

367 General Rossi, aware from *Atti Commissione*.

367 "Why don't we leave" from Carboni (III).

367 The Germans were becoming impatient also from *Surrender*.

367 "powerful fleet of about a hundred ships" from Pond.

368 Crown Prince Umberto from *Tempo*.

368 He had not slept much the night before from Pillon.

368–369 The meeting at Grand Hotel from *La Resistenza al fascismo*. (Trombadori).

369 When Carboni finally came from Carboni (III), Marchesi.

Chapter 32 THE COUNCIL OF FEAR

Page

370 Even Carboni claims from Carboni (III).

370 Eisenhower's peremptory telegram from *Surrender*.

371 What Foreign Minister Guariglia from Guariglia.

371 A Crown Council was hurriedly from Carboni (III).

371 General Roatta from Roatta.

371 Foreign Minister Guariglia and his meeting with Puntoni from Guariglia.

371 He had asked the first driver and following dialogue from Pillon.

371 "aged by another twenty years" from Guariglia.

371–372 Scene at German Embassy, "I can hardly believe it," and Ribbentrop's calls from Moellhausen.

372 The Italian Embassy in Berlin from Simoni.

372 The leak, it seemed and American stations from Tamaro.

372 At 5:45 P.M. from Monelli.

372 Someone suggested from Zangrandi (III).

372 "Listen, Zanussi" and rest of conversation from Palermo.

373 "The news is exact" from Carboni (III).

373 *"Nous sommes foutus"* from Zanussi.

373 Roatta's deputy and a kind of inner council from *Atti Commissione*.

373–374 The seating from Carboni (II), Marchesi.

374 "As a matter of fact" and following conversation from Zangrandi (II).

374 "If we don't reject it" from Guariglia.

374 Carboni's position from Carboni (I), *Processo Carboni-Roatta*.

374–375 Marchesi was silently wondering and his further thoughts and moves from interview with Marchesi, Badoglio, Marchesi, Monelli.

376 "There is no doubt now" from Carboni (III).

376 Ambrosio then turned to Carboni from Marchesi.

376 Since time was running short from *Surrender*.

376 By 5 P.M. from *Corriere della Sera*, September 6–9, 1966.

376 Minutes later and "There's been a reprieve" from Tregaskis.

377 Although Ridgway from Ridgway.

377 "for standard military reasons" from Murphy.

377 "As a soldier" from Castellano (III) quoting Westphal.

377–378 In Algiers and description of scene from interview with Koffler.

378 The atmosphere was thick with tension from *Surrender*.

378 Meeting between Rahn and Guariglia from Guariglia, Rahn.

379 "Have you heard the news?" from Monelli.

379 "The truth of the matter" from Strong.

379 "To obtain the postponement" from Rossi.

379–380 Dialogue between Eisenhower and Rossi from Rossi. *Giornale di Sicilia* (from notes taken by Vito Guarrasi).

380 They met with De Gaulle from De Gaulle, *Foreign Relations* (vice-counsel at Algiers to secretary of state, September 9, 1943).

380 At the Rome radio from Marchesi, Tamaro, Zangrandi (II). *Capitolium*, September 1963, Pedercini.

380 In Albania from De Biase (II).

381 "a strange feeling of unrest" from Goebbels.

381 Vietinghoff heard a London broadcast from *History of the Second World War*, Vol. 4, No. 7, 1967.

381 Strongpoints along from Pond.

381 "relaxed their tension" from Churchill.

381 "the mayor of Salerno" from Pond.

Chapter 33 THE ORDER OF BATTLE

Page

382 A little after eight o'clock from interview with Antonelli.

383 "We're going home" from Piscitelli.

383 The going rate and *"Hitler kaputt"* from *Mercurio*, December 1944, Baracco.

383 "Out with the Germans" and "We want bread and peace" from interview with Capponi.

383 In Orte from Caracciolo. Also see De Biase (II).

384 "Dailies will not publish" from Tamaro.

384 "I imagine" from Caviglia.

384 In Rome from *Capitolium*, September 1963, Cagianelli.

384 Emilio Schuberth was amazed from interview with Schuberth.

384 The royal family from Monelli, Zangrandi (II).

384 The king prepared to go to sleep from Pillon.

384 "How was my voice" from Monelli.

384–385 He sent from Canevari, Simoni.

385 As if by magic from Piscitelli.

385 "They're terrorized" from Carboni (II).

385 "If they leave without fighting" from Monelli.

385 "react energetically" from Musco, Zanussi.

385 Kesselring told them from Kesselring.

385–386 His first move from *History of the Second World War*, Vol. 4, No. 9, 1967.

386 "were written off" from Kesselring.

386 "Everyone was expecting" from Dollmann.

386 It would be impossible from Westphal (I).

386 All lines of communication from *History of the Second World War*, Vol. 4, No. 9, 1967.

387 Many military men involved from Musco.

387 German general staff records and Westphal interview from Castellano (III).

387 At 10 P.M. the German radio from Simoni.

387 Kesselring's thoughts and decisions from Kesselring, Rahn, Westphal (II).

388 "It was not easy" from Castellano (III) (quoting Westphal).

Chapter 34 THE DISTANT DRUMS

Page

389 On the night of September 8 from Castellano (III).

389 Components of the [Piacenza] division from Tamaro, Zangrandi (II, IV), *Atti Commissione*.

390 By this time from *Roma oggi*.

390 Colonel D'Auria and Lieutenant Colonel Bianchedi from Comandini.

390–391 The victims of confusion from Westphal (II); Canevari; Monelli; *Mercurio*, Tomajuoli.

391 Cadorna-Carboni dialogue from Cadorna.

392 "It's a false alarm" from Caracciolo.

392 "German units from the largest to the smallest" from Trabucchi.

392 Kesselring, who was surprised from Westphal (II).

392–393 Incidents around La Magliana from Monelli, Musco, Piscitelli. *Mercurio*, Tomajuoli.

393 Not long afterward and his aide from Carboni (II).

393–394 What Carboni did not say from Leto (I), Tamaro.

394 Carboni's meeting with king from Carboni (I, II, III), Puntoni.

394–395 German movements from Tamaro, *Atti Commissione*.

395 "scattered and uncertain" from *Atti Commissione*.

395 "take the initiative" from Roatta, Rossi, *Processo Carboni-Roatta*.

395 Ambrosio maintained from *Atti Commissione*.

395 "give German commands" from Zangrandi (IV).

395 "Destroy the submarines" from Tamaro.

395 Only at nine o'clock and only at 7:30 P.M. from Zangrandi (II).

396 The shooting of General Gonzaga from Pond. Fumarola (I), Tamaro.

396 Following agreement with from *Surrender*.

396–397 Allied invasion fleet and its movement into Salerno from Morison, Pond. Musmanno. *History of the Second World War*, Vol. 4, No. 7, 1967.

397 By now General Roatta from Zangrandi (II).

398 "To acts of force" from Musco.

398 German attacks from Castellano (III), Zanussi, *Processo Carboni-Roatta*.

398 *"Kamerati"* and although their activity from Musco, Palermo. *Capitolium,* September 1963, Cagianelli.

398 "The 2nd Parachute Division" from Roatta, *Processo Carboni-Roatta.*

399 Just then, Air Chief Sandalli from Zangrandi (II).

399 General Cerica, head of the *Carabinieri* from Zanussi.

399 Roatta refused to take the responsibility, Ambrosio said he could not, and Ambrosio said he [Badoglio] could not be found from *Atti Commissione.*

399 Roatta ordered the Ariete to move from Cadorna, Zanussi.

399 Roatta told Colonel Giorgio Salvi from Monelli.

399 At 3 A.M., word arrived from Zanussi, *Processo Carboni-Roatta.*

399 "In the present situation" from Castellano (III), Roatta, Zanussi, *Processo Carboni-Roatta.*

400 Thus there was concentric action from Palermo.

400 Now Roatta allowed himself to believe from Castellano (III).

400 Without checking all the reports and "Missed reception signal" from Castellano (I), Marchesi.

400–401 The landing at Salerno from Linklater, Morison, Musmanno, Pond, *History of the Second World War,* Vol. 4, No. 7, 1967.

401 It was obvious that the Germans from Pillon.

401 Almost immediately from Puntoni.

401 At Ambrosio's request from Roatta, Zanussi, *Processo Carboni-Roatta.*

401 "Gentlemen," said Roatta from *Nazione.*

402 Badoglio said that he, the royal family from *Processo Carboni-Roatta.*

402 When Sorice asked from Di Benigno, Tamaro.

402 Perhaps Badoglio thought from *Surrender.*

402 But when Ricci was found from Tamaro.

402 As yet, no real battles from Castellano (III).

402 Ambrosio called Admiral De Courten from Zangrandi (II).

402 "No orders were left" from Zangrandi (IV).

402 "Perhaps you too, marshal" from *Oggi,* February 20–April 3, 1966.

Chapter 35 THE FLIGHT

Page

403–407 The flight of the king and the generals is pieced together from Carboni (I, II, III), Castelli, Comandini, De Biase (II), Lodi, Marchesi, Monelli, Musco, Palermo, Puntoni, Roatta, Spampanato, Tamaro, Torsiello, Zangrandi (II, IV), Zanussi. *Atti Commissione. Processo Carboni-Roatta. Gente,* July 1967; *Tempo.*

404–405 Conversation between Carboni, Roatta. and Zanussi from Carboni (I), Zanussi.

405 The original hand-written order from Musco. *Gente,* July 1967.

405–406 Now it read from Monelli.

406 "the assumption of General Carboni" from *Processo Carboni-Roatta.*

406 How were they to be supplied from Castellano (III).

407 There he saw Ambrosio about to leave from Zanussi.

407 The convoy and its departure from Zanussi. *Tempo.*

407 "My God, what a figure" from *Tempo.*

407 Furtively roll up the sleeves from Spampanato.

407 Including the only copies from Torsiello.

408 "I'm not such an idiot" and "There's nothing to do" from Zanussi.

408–410 Carboni's flight from Carboni (III), Zanussi, *Atti Commissione.*

409 Reaching Tivoli about 8 A.M. from Carboni (I), Zangrandi (II) (Sandalli), *Atti Commissione.*

409–410 Carboni's actions, Ponti's deposition, Mariella Loti's deposition and the real reason from Carboni (I), *Atti Commissione. Gente,* July 1967.

Chapter 36 WHO DEFENDS ROME?

Page

411 On the morning of September 9 from interview with Schuberth.

412 "a wall" from *Capitolium,* September 1963, Cagianelli.

412 Four doors away from Cadorna, Carboni (I, II), Tamaro, *Processo Carboni-Roatta.*

412–413 When General Tabellini from *Storia illustrata,* August 1960.

413 The battle of Monterotondo from Piscitelli. *Capitolium,* September 1963, Cagianelli.

413 Now Tabellini ordered from *Storia illustrata,* August 1960.

413 At the Monterotondo railway station from Musco.

414 Lieutenant Rosso's action at Monterosi from Cadorna, Monelli, Piscitelli.

414 "I am fighting" from Cadorna.

414 The man left in command and the navy was in the same position from Lodi, Musco, Zangrandi (II).

414 Although individual airmen from Monelli.

415 Towards midnight on September 8 from Zangrandi (II).

415 Fighting on the Magliana from Musco. *Capitolium,* September 1963, Cagianelli.

415 Meanwhile, army and corps commanders and other distress calls from Comandini, Spampanato, Zangrandi (II).

415–416 The night before from *Secondo Risorgimento d'Italia.*

416 Generals Aliberti and Ruggiero from Zangrandi (IV).

416 "Do not attack" from Caracciolo.

417 "a better strategic position" from Zangrandi (IV).

417 At Salerno from Morison. *History of the Second World War*, Vol. 4, No. 9, 1967.

418 The action at Cecchignola from *Capitolium*, September 1963, Cagianelli.

418 "Will the armistice" from Spampanato, Trabucco.

418 Cancellation of the big insurrectional plan from· *La Resistenza al fascismo*. (Trombadori).

419 "I opened the door" from *Espresso*, July 28, August 4, August 11, 1963.

419 "You know what they've done?" and "a strange and grotesque council" from *Trent'anni di storia italiana* (Piccardi).

419 It contained a copy of the armistice from Di Benigno.

419 "to reconquer for Italy" and meeting with Ricci from Bonomi.

420 Still not knowing from Caviglia.

420 His first move from *Atti Commissione*.

420 Civilian members of the cabinet from Tamaro.

420 In an attempt to reconcile from interview with Carini.

421–422 Raffaele Persichetti and his moves from interview with Carini, interview with Moretti, interview with Persichetti, Tamaro, Zangrandi (II).

Chapter 37 THE WITHDRAWAL

Page

423 "the oppressors" from Tamaro.

423 "The Italians have abandoned us" from Plehwe.

423 "Since the fall" from Goebbels.

424 Kesselring could hardly believe from Kesselring.

424 General Student was particularly worried from Dollmann.

424 "Having understood that" and Westphal was so uncertain from Castellano (III) quoting Westphal.

424 "No one" from *Specchio*, September 8, 1968.

424 General Cadorna of the Ariete from Cadorna, Musco.

425 But the once-great division from Tamaro.

425 General Carboni reappeared from *Atti Commissione*.

425 Told of Salvi's hysterical reaction from Carboni (I).

425 Now all the bad news from Comandini.

425 "From the calls" from Carboni (I).

425 Even those commanders from Caracciolo.

426 Fighting to the South of Rome from Musco, Piscitelli, Tamaro, Zangrandi (IV). *Mercurio*, Tomajuoli.

426 "How are things going, Solinas?" from Carboni (II).

427 Schact, Carboni, Calvi and Giaccone from Carboni (II), Musco, Tamaro, *Atti Commissione*, *Processo Carboni-Roatta*.

427 Admiral De Courten from Westphal (II), Trizzino.

427–429 The sinking of the *Roma* from Butcher, Morison. Tamaro, Trizzino. *Corriere della sera,* July 6, 1969; *Messaggero,* September 7, 1968.

429 Admiral Da Zara from Morison. Tamaro.

429–436 The flight of the king and generals from Boehmler, De Biase (II), Marchesi, Palermo, Puntoni, Zangrandi (II, IV), Zanussi. *Tempo; Tempo illustrato,* September, November 1963.

Chapter 38 THE BATTLE FOR ROME

Page

437 Heedless of the rain from interview with Persichetti.

437 He felt compelled to prove from interview with Carini.

437 The evening before from interview with Moretti.

438 Earlier that morning from Puntoni.

438 He did not announce and The night before from Spampanato, Zangrandi (IV). *Storia illustrata,* August 1960.

439 Giaccone, Carboni and Kesselring from Castellano (III); Monelli; *Processo Carboni-Roatta; Gente,* July 1967.

439 When Giaccone objected and seven hundred planes from Spampanato.

439–440 "The fact that the Allies" from Kesselring.

440 "Little by little" from Dollmann.

440 Back in Rome, Carboni from Carboni (I), *Processo Carboni-Roatta. Europeo,* September 19, 1965; *Gente,* July 1967; *Oggi,* February 20–April 3, 1966.

440 ". . . so little in harmony" from *Atti Commissione.*

440 This referred to the fact and following from Cadorna, Carboni (II), Monelli, Musco, Tamaro.

441 One commander Colonel Rabbi from Tamaro.

441 At around noon he resumed from Carboni (II).

441 But Communist leaders from Zangrandi (IV).

441 At about noon, Raffaele Persichetti from interview with Moretti.

441–442 At midnight, the Grenadiers and battle at La Montagnola from Piscitelli. *Capitolium,* September 1963, Cagianelli; *Mercurio,* Tomajuoli.

443 Some were already in from Piscitelli.

443 In the piazza before the church from *Mercurio,* Tomajuoli.

444 "Don't touch me" from Bacino. *Roma oggi.*

444 When the flight of the king from Silva, Tamaro.

444 "The king has left us" from interview with Santovito.

444–445 Groups of excited young men from Monelli.

445 SIM tried to keep up morale from Bellomo.

445 At midday, for the first time from Scrivener. Tamaro.

445 By afternoon, Friday from interview with Savoni.

S

445 General Carboni was trying from Carboni (I).

445 Buck-passing between Carboni, Sorice, Calvi, Caviglia and "In my place" from Bonomi, Caviglia, Tamaro.

446 South of the city from interview with Fago Golfarelli.

447 Tom Carini was worried from interview with Carini.

447 At Via della Marmorata from *Mercurio*, Gabriele.

447 Meanwhile, there were difficulties from *Mercurio*, Muscetta.

447 When Giaccone's return to Frascati from Tamaro.

447 When the action had reached San Paolo from Zangrandi (II).

448 That afternoon, a group of Socialists from Lizzadri.

448 Several dozen volunteers from Zangrandi (IV).

448 A small group of Catholic Communists from Cocchi.

448–449 Although the movement from *Trent'anni di storia italiana* (Baldazzi), *Documenti del nostro tempo*.

449 Socialists Sandro Pertini from Piscitelli.

449 Communists . . . party leaders had suddenly issued orders to hide weapons from *Documenti del nostro tempo*.

449 Information on civilians fighting from interview with Moretti, Comandini, Monelli, Piscitelli, Zangrandi (IV).

449 In cases where civilians could not fight from Lizzadri (II).

449 Even if only a few thousand from Bocca.

449 And resist they did from Piscitelli.

449–450 Fruit seller named Ricciotti from interview with Moretti.

450 There was a lull around 2 P.M. from interview with Carini.

450–451 Description of battle and Persichetti's part from interview with Persichetti. Di Benigno, Fumarola (I), Piscitelli, Zangrandi (IV). *Capitolium*, September 1963, Cagianelli; *Contemporaneo*; *Roma oggi*.

451 At the War Ministry that hour from Carboni (I), Monelli, Tamaro, *Processo Carboni-Roatta*.

452 Half an hour before from Marchesi.

452 The Montebello Lancers regiment from Battaglia, Comandini, Piscitelli.

452 Waving the white flag of truce from Perrone–Capano.

452 They met unexpected resistance from Etnasi, Perrone–Capano.

452 At Via Balbo from Perrone–Capano.

453 Near the Circus Maximus from Scrivener.

453 "Let's get guns" from Trabucco.

453 A small truck from Monelli.

453 Just then from Benedetti, Spampanato. *Mercurio*, De Mattei and Gabrieli.

453 Rome's population and if Parisians from Tamaro.

453 North of the city from interview with Mazzarella.

453 The columns of the Ariete and Piave from Cadorna, Musco. *Storia illustrata*, August 1960.

453–455 The fighting on Via Cavour, Hotel Continentale and at the station from interview with Spadini. Scrivener. Monelli, Piscitelli. *Capitolium,* September 1963, Cagianelli; *Mercurio,* Scialoia.

455 A few isolated German motorcyclists and all laws seemed to be abolished from *La Resistenza al fascismo* (Patti).

Chapter 39 AN ARMY DISSOLVES

Page

456 For a few minutes the morning of September 11 from interview with Zangrandi.

456 Some anti-Fascists had fired from *Trent'anni di storia italiana* (Baldazzi), Tosti (II).

456 Newspapers and radio announced from Gorla, Monelli.

457 At 1 P.M. on September 11 from interview with Persichetti.

457 The family started phoning from interview with Antonelli, interview with Carini.

457 Two officers who knew Raffaele from Di Benigno.

458 "The population" from Tamaro.

458 After a night from Monelli.

459 Near Rome from interview with Zambelli.

459 Infantry private from interview with Meloni.

459 That morning in Rome from Spampanato.

459 A navy commander from De Giorgi.

459 "Thursday the 9th at La Spezia" from Soleri.

459 The only nationwide organization from *Documenti del nostro tempo.*

459–460 General Caracciolo's trip to Rome from Caracciolo.

460 On September 11, General Vercellino and "Here's my division" from Tamaro.

461 The Germans maintained from Tamaro.

461 When a shot fired from *Documenti del nostro tempo.*

461 At Aversa from Scala.

461 At Nola and Although Gaeta from Perrone–Capano, Zangrandi (II).

462 Milan, a city with a long tradition from Tamaro. *Documenti del nostro tempo, 45 giorni.*

462 As punishment from Buckley.

462 In Verona from Tamaro.

462 In Bassano del Grappa from Zangrandi (II).

462 Germans at La Spezia from Rossi.

462 Surrendered only after they were overcome from Monelli.

462–463 This was shown in Corsica and the story was a little different in Sardinia from Battaglia (I), Musco, Tamaro, Zangrandi (II).

463 In Naples on September 10 and 11 from Musco, Tamaro.

463 The garrison at Genoa and General Adami-Rossi from Tamaro, Zangrandi (II).

463 In Novara for instance from Comandini.

463–464 In Sardinia, in one of the rare cases from Musco.

464 Somehow they threw from De Giorgi.

464 In Northern Italy from Collotti, Tamaro.

464 Caught by surprise from Monelli, Tamaro, Zangrandi (II).

464 In Montenegro, In Dalmatia, At Zadar and Giangreco and Grimaldi from *La Resistenza al fascismo.* Musco.

465 General Giuseppe Amico from Musco, Tamaro, Zangrandi (II).

465 Part of the Emilia Division from Monelli.

465 Italian forces in Greece from Lombardi (II), Tamaro.

465 Ruggero Zangrandi's figures from Zangrandi (II).

465 These figures included from Musco, Tamaro, *Trent'anni di storia italiana* (Vaccarino). *Epoca,* September 1966; *Messaggero,* August 26, September 3, 1969.

466 The port of Piombino from Battaglia (I), Musco.

466 At Orbetello and At Teramo from Zangrandi (II).

466 On September 10, the Allies from Higgins.

466 "It no longer exists" from Tamaro.

467 "Enormous depots full" from Kesselring. Also see De Biase (III).

467 Some were sent to Germany from Canevari.

467 Hitler saw that the catastrophe from Westphal (II).

467 After a year of almost continuous retreat from Churchill.

467 "Americans, hold on" from Monelli.

467 The Balkans—Churchill's goal from Baldwin.

468 "strategically the most senseless" from Fuller.

468 "Who is containing whom" from Pond.

468 "the whole Anglo-American plan" from Castellano (III) quoting Bedell Smith in letter from Pietro Quaroni, June 26, 1946.

468 "the Allies had no clear-cut" from Baldwin.

468 "take Italy village by village" from Guariglia.

468 Germany was still strong from Bryant.

468 "The armies of liberation are on the march" from *United States and Italy 1934–1946.*

Chapter 40 THE SUBMERGED CITY

Page

469 Rome on September 13 from Castelli, Monelli. *Capitolium,* June 1964.

469 The rake of German reprisal from interview with Zangrandi.

470 The meeting and "It will be at least a month" from Monelli.

470 Accepted the hospitality from Carboni (II).

470 "He was known as" and the possibility that this had from Tamaro.

470–471 Carboni's charges from: Carboni (I, II, III, IV).

471 "among a Germanophile" from Carboni (II).

471 "The only plausible explanation" from Carboni (III).

471 In 1964 from Zangrandi (II).

472 "Marshall Kesselring would never have" from Castellano (III) quoting Westphal.

472 "I exclude with absolute certainty" from *Europeo*, September 5, 1968, quoting Student.

472 "typical figure of a man" from *Atti Commissione*.

472 "who to serve positions" from Palermo.

472 Carboni was subjected to further hearings from Carboni (III).

473 "The 10th at 8 P.M." from B. Mussolini.

473 Following the word "Americans" from *Domenica del corriere*, September 1968.

473 "Mussolini is in a safe place" from Bonomi.

473 When one of the men from Tamaro.

473 "maximum prudence" from Senise.

473 At 2:15 P.M. Otto Skorzeny from B. Mussolini, Spampanato, Tamaro. *Specchio*, September 15, 1968.

473 Soleti had been persuaded from *Europeo*, September 5, 1968.

473 He later explained to Faiola from Zangrandi (II).

474 *Duce! Duce!* from Fermi.

474 His first words to Skorzeny from Zangrandi (IV).

474 "I thank the gods" from Saporiti.

474 "I have come for my instructions" from Hibbert.

474 The news of Mussolini's liberation from Monelli, Tamaro.

474 The Germans were busy from *Epoca*, October 23, 1966.

474–475 On September 11 from Kesselring.

475 "Cavallero opened the door" from Caviglia.

475 Even so from Gorla.

475 "Cavallero committed suicide" from Tamaro.

475 With documentary proof of Badoglio's betrayals from Matthews.

475 The Italians were at a loss to understand such ferocity from Monelli.

475 Within days from Giovannetti.

475 To Dachau, where he died from Zangrandi (IV).

475 General Tabellini from Giovannetti.

476 New security forces from Monelli.

476 The Fascist party from interview with della Riccia.

476 Newspapers were entrusted to the ambitious and When Fascists first began making their appearance from Monelli.

476 The Germans even transferred the holdings from Angelucci and Botti.

476 Soldiers who refused from *Roma oggi*.

476 Some Romans fled to the hills and Men holed in cellars from *Mercurio*, Contini.

476 If during that period from Hughes.

477 Jews were forced to hide from De Benedetti, De Giorgi.

477 Before they could from Comandini, De Felice.

477 Ettore della Riccia from interview with della Riccia.

477 Alberto Moravia from *Mercurio*, Moravia.

477 Regard the Germans as enemies from Roatta, Zanussi.

477 "Letting oneself be disarmed" and "For the salvation" from Zangrandi (IV).

477 "the sons of those" and "that betrayer of the Italian people" from Tamaro.

478 The Communists from Murphy.

478 "Officers escaped first" from Artom.

Index